Economic inequality has become a focus of prime interest for economic analysts and policy makers. This book provides an integrated approach to the topics of inequality and personal income distribution. It covers the practical and theoretical bases for inequality analysis, applications to real-world problems and the foundations of theoretical approaches to income distribution. It also analyses models of the distribution of labour earnings and of income from wealth. The long-run development of income and wealth distribution over many generations is also examined. Special attention is given to an assessment of the merits and weaknesses of standard economic models, to illustrating the implications of distributional mechanisms using real data and illustrative examples, and to providing graphical interpretation of formal argume…
Examples are drawn from US, UK and international sources.

Economic inequality
and income distribution

Economic inequality and income distribution

D. G. CHAMPERNOWNE
Emeritus Professor, University of Cambridge

AND

F. A. COWELL
London School of Economics

CAMBRIDGE
UNIVERSITY PRESS

PUBLISHED BY THE PRESS SYNDICATE OF THE UNIVERSITY OF CAMBRIDGE
The Pitt Building, Trumpington Street, Cambridge CB2 1RP, United Kingdom

CAMBRIDGE UNIVERSITY PRESS
The Edinburgh Building, Cambridge, CB2 2RU, United Kingdom
40 West 20th Street, New York, NY 10011-4211, USA
10 Stamford Road, Oakleigh, Melbourne 3166, Australia

First published 1998

Printed in the United Kingdom at the University Press, Cambridge

Typeset in 10/12pt Monotype Times New Roman   [SE]

A catalogue record for this book is available from the British Library

Library of Congress Cataloguing in Publication data

Champernowne, D. G.
  Economic inequality and income distributon / by D. G. Champernowne
and F. A. Cowell.
    p. cm.
  Includes bibliographical references and index.
  ISBN 0 521 58055 2 (hc). – ISBN 0 521 58959 2 (pbk).
  1. Income.   2. Income distribution.   3. Equality.   I. Cowell, F. A.
II. Title.
HC110.I5C45   1998
339.2—dc21   96-48221   CIP

ISBN 0 521 58055 2 hardback
ISBN 0 521 58959 2 paperback

Contents

Figures

Tables

Preface

Economics appears to have one great advantage over most other branches of the study of human behaviour: many of the most important economic decisions are made only after a careful weighing of the pros and cons by agents who are relatively expert in calculations concerning the earning and spending of money. Accordingly there are many branches of economics where it is quite helpful to assume that the economic agents involved are well informed and act rationally so as to achieve well-understood objectives as effectively as possible. An extreme form of this assumption is to suppose that everyone behaves as a perfectly informed 'economic man' reminiscent of the super-efficient computerised robots of science fiction. Now that corporate executives are provided with efficient machines, capable of assembling, recording, processing and collating voluminous information, and of composing forecasts of the effects of alternative proposed policies, this assumption of robot-like economic decisions may no longer be quite so absurd as it used to be.

But in the branch of economic study which is the subject of this book, the fictional figure of economic man is, in many respects, useless. For as soon as one turns from the strategy and tactics of finance, trade and production to the struggle to divide up the spoils, rational behaviour is replaced by instinctive animal reactions and the sway of crude primitive passions such as envy, greed and loyalty to the pack, compassion for the weak and the urge to rally round in an emergency. The methods used to change the distribution to one's own advantage include threatening gestures and the extensive use of bluff: economic man is replaced by a group of monkeys grimacing and chattering at a rival group.

There is an obvious reason why efforts to change the distribution of incomes arouse violent and passionate opposition: what is improvement for some almost always seems to others to be detrimental. Even if the change in distribution stimulates the growth of income in total, this is unlikely to be perceived by those who are losing or who are falling behind in the race: and even if it is perceived, they will still feel aggrieved that they are getting less benefit than the others. Decisions about how to share out the cake are, in the nature of things, more contentious than decisions about how big a cake to share.

Since rationally calculated economic behaviour cannot be seen as the general rule where decisions affecting economic distribution are concerned, one should obviously avoid basing any theory of income distribution solely on the normal theories of supply and demand in competitive markets, with well-informed buyers and sellers. The game that one is studying is less like a game of chess than are the other branches of economics, and more like a war game or a game of poker: the key pieces are more concerned with power and prestige and social position than is found in other branches of economics, and the calculations of the players are bedevilled by deep uncertainty, differences of opinion and mutual misunderstanding. No realistic book on this subject can hope to present a simple single theory to account for the whole range of phenomena to be studied.

The fact that decisions which affect income distribution and its modification are so often based on instinctive reactions, rather than on cool calculation, results in people being particularly uncertain what changes in distribution to expect in the future and in different people expecting very different developments. This confusion of expectations is a further cause of incoherent economic and political attempts to engineer or inhibit changes in income distribution.

Readers should note two warnings. Expertise in other branches of economic study is of limited assistance in studying economic inequality and income distribution: it may even be a handicap if it lures the student into making those same simplifying assumptions like those about well-informed rational choice, which may be helpful in studying the economics of finance, trade, production and even consumption, but often hinder the study of income distribution. Secondly, whatever conclusions are reached about this subject of distribution and inequality are certain to provoke strong hostility from one faction or another, if they are at all definite, since the subject matter is concerned with decisions which all appear to damage some parties so as to advance the interests of others.

Yet this study is well worth undertaking, just because all the issues involved are ones about which people do feel strongly and recognise as seriously affecting their own interests at one point or another. By learning to recognise the same patterns of misunderstanding and prejudice repeated over and over again, with variations, under widely differing circumstances and among widely varying types of people quite remote from their own, readers may increase their own ability to make balanced judgements about similar issues which affect them personally.

The book has been in preparation over a number of years spanning the era fom the golf-ball typewriter to WordPerfect for Windows. This and the amount of material involved has inevitably led to some delegation of responsibilities for various components of the finished book. However, although the process of editing and producing the final draft has been the responsibility of Frank Cowell, every chapter and appendix was planned, written, argued about, and rewritten by both authors. In the long time that it has taken to complete this book we have incurred a great many debts. We have received able research assistance from Trudy Ackersveen, Paolo Belli, Julie Litchfield, Lupin Rahman, Kaspar Richter, Elisabeth Steckmest, Robin Sherbourne, and Beverley Wells. Tony Atkinson and Geoff Harcourt read the entire manuscript at various stages, and gave us much encouragement, along with detailed and extremely useful advice, not all of which we have followed. We have also benefited from valuable comments made to us by Yoram Amiel, Arthur Champernowne, James Davies, Paul Menchik, Hashem Pesaran, Virginie Pérotin and Stefano Toso. Our sincere thanks go to them all.

D. G. Champernowne   F. A. Cowell
University of Cambridge   London School of Economics

Symbols

Symbol	Interpretation	Chapter
a/b	Simple inequality measure	3
A	Atkinson index	4, 5, 10, 11
B	Bequest, before tax	9, 10
$c(t)$	Consumption at t	9
C_n	Living standards of generation n	9
$E(t)$	Earnings at t	9
$F(\cdot)$	Distribution function	2, 9, 10
g	Interval fineness parameter	11
I	Inequality statistic	4, 5
k	Number of children	9, 10
K	Maximum number of children	9
n	Generation	9
r	Interest rate	9
R	Lifetime resources	9
s	Savings ratio	9
t	Time (age)	7, 9
U	Reduced-form welfare function	5
w	Wage rate	7, 8
$W(t)$	Wealth at age t	9
W^*	Exemption level of bequests	9, 10
$W_n(t)$	Wealth at t of generation n	10
x_i	'Income' of individual i	4, 5
x	Arithmetic mean 'income'	4, 5
X	Total 'income'	4, 5
$y(t)$	Income at t	9
α	Pareto's constant	3, 10
β	Earnings equation parameter	7
δ	Discount rate	B
ϵ	Inequality aversion	5
θ	Inequality sensitivity parameter	5

1 Why bother about inequality?

1.1 Some preliminary questions

Economic inequality may not be the greatest crisis facing the world today. The danger of nuclear war and pollution of the environment ultimately pose more serious threats. The growing use of terror and torture by oppressive governments and private armies may evoke stronger feelings of moral outrage. But economic inequality is clearly a persistent and pressing problem: one which arouses deep resentment, which can give rise to major social and economic upheavals, and which provokes strongly differing views about the policies that might be adopted to regulate it. It also offers a wide and rewarding field for study.

Before embarking upon such a study of inequality consider some of the preliminary questions that suggest themselves when we look around us:

How much extreme poverty remains in our own and other economies throughout the world, despite the rapid economic progress in recent decades?

What priority should be given to this particular problem?

Is there truth in the claim that the contrasts between the living standards of various economic, social, ethnic and national groups remain grossly unjust and a potential source of damaging conflict?

What side effects might be expected on other objectives – such as a steady rise in general living standards – if vigorous egalitarian policies were implemented?

To tackle these questions adequately requires more than scrutiny of the evidence. It also demands the application of a broad range of economic analysis about the meaning, nature and causes of inequality: there is no one convenient self-contained packet of theory which spans the subject. The analysis extends into peripheral branches of economics such as public finance, economic growth and the interaction of unemployment and inflation.

Later in this chapter we shall take a preliminary glance at the issues raised by our four questions: but at the outset it is important to clarify some more fundamental issues such as the meaning of 'economic inequality', how living standards are to be measured, and the roots of the strong feelings aroused by the whole subject of economic inequality.

1

1.2 What do we mean by economic inequality?

The wording of the first of our introductory questions highlights the conjunction of the extreme poverty of some with the rapid economic progress of others. It is clear that neither extreme poverty nor extreme affluence is a necessary precondition of the problem of inequality. It is also clear that neither of these alone adequately describes economic inequality itself. Rather – at the risk of oversimplification – we may state that economic inequality refers to the contrasts between the economic conditions of different persons or of different groups.

What do we mean by 'economic conditions'? And what sort of groups might be relevant? A brief consideration of each of these helps to clarify what is meant by inequality.

Income

In the opinion of some, 'economic conditions' are summarised by 'income', and so we might usefully begin by looking at the distribution of money income.

Let us look at one of the most easily available – though not necessarily the best – source of income distribution statistics within one country. Table 1.1 gives a first glimpse of this distribution in the United Kingdom during the fiscal year 1993/4. Despite the pitfalls in the interpretation of such statistics – which we discuss below – the table suggests substantial income inequality. To see this, imagine all the 'persons' with incomes as being conceptually arranged in a queue in the order of their incomes; the income (before or after tax) is then assigned to each of these persons in turn.[1] Now divide the 26,900,000 persons in the queue up into tenths: a quick calculation on column (1) reveals that the bottom tenth have incomes of less than £4,500, whereas the top tenth all have incomes of more than £18,000; and from column (2) we can work out that the average income of a person in the top tenth is about ten times the average income of a person in the bottom tenth.[2] The table also suggests that the shape of this income queue does not alter dramatically if we re-examine the situation after tax has been deducted: columns (3) and (4) show that, persons in the top tenth have an average income that is about eight times the average income of the bottom tenth.

The contrast *between* countries in terms of money incomes per head is even more striking, as we can see from a glance at table 1.2. Apparently Sweden has a gross national product per head of more than 100 times that of Somalia. Contrast this with the situation that we have just seen within the UK, where the (before-tax) ratio of income per head in the top group to income per head in the bottom group is just over ten – which is about the same as the ratio of income per head of Australia (eighth in our list) to that of Turkey (fifth in the list). We shall have more to say about these particular ten countries below.

Alternative indicators

However table 1.2 also illustrates the use of other possible indicators of economic conditions. In Somalia, about one baby in every eight died in its first year and there are almost 1,500 people for every medical nurse; but in Australia only one baby in 120 dies

Table 1.1 *Distribution of incomes, UK, 1994/5*

	Before tax*		After tax**	
Income range	No. of incomes (000s) (1)	Total income (£m.) (2)	No. of incomes (000s) (3)	Total income (£m.) (4)
£3,445–£3,999	1,190	4,440	1,330	4,950
£4,000–£4,499	1,010	4,280	1,150	4,910
£4,500–£4,999	1,010	4,800	1,160	5,480
£5,000–£5,499	943	4,950	1,110	5,860
£5,500–£5,999	951	5,480	1,100	6,300
£6,000–£6,999	1,740	11,300	2,190	14,200
£7,000–£7,999	1,680	12,600	2,050	15,400
£8,000–£9,999	3,060	27,500	3,740	33,600
£10,000–£11,999	2,760	30,300	3,080	33,800
£12,000–£14,999	3,350	44,900	3,470	46,600
£15,000–£19,999	3,920	67,800	3,490	60,000
£20,000–£29,999	3,530	84,000	2,140	50,500
£30,000–£49,999	1,220	45,100	627	23,000
£50,000–£99,999	387	25,600	189	12,400
£100,000–£199,999	93	12,400	37	4,840
£200,000 and over	25	9,490	11	3,770

Notes: * By range of income before tax.
** By range of income after tax.
Source: Board of Inland Revenue, *Inland Revenue Statistics*, 1996, HMSO, London, table 3.3, page 35.

in its first year and there are only about a hundred people for each nurse; the prospects for Swedish babies are even better. The contrasts between countries such as Somalia on the one hand and Australia or Sweden on the other, found for these various indicators, will impress many observers as even more striking than those based on income alone. Without any pretence at dealing with the enormous statistical problems involved in making serious detailed comparisons, tables 1.1 and 1.2 illustrate a general tendency: economic inequality between such groups as the developing economies and the market economies in the developed world is more conspicuous than that within a single developed market economy.

The importance of groups

The phenomenon of the inequality of living standards among different nations illustrated in table 1.2 is but one example of contrasts between different groups of people. Throughout this book we shall find that by viewing the population as a collection of groups of individuals, and not merely a collection of individuals, our under-

Table 1.2 *Economic and social conditions in ten nations*

Nation	GNP per capita ($) 1989	Annual energy consumption per capita* 1989	Life expectancy at birth (years) 1989	Infant mortality** 1989	Population per nurse 1984	Population with access water (per cent) 1975
Somalia	170	78	48	128	1,530	33
Niger	290	40	45	130	460	27
Sri Lanka	430	173	71	20	1,290	20
Philippines	710	217	64	42	2,680	43
Turkey	1,370	837	66	61	1,060	75
Algeria	2,235	1,906	65	69	300	77
Iran	3,200	1,019	63	90	1,110	51
Australia	14,360	5,291	77	8	110	n.a.
Germany	20,440	4,383	75	8	230	n.a.
Sweden	21,570	6,228	77	6	n.a.	n.a.

Notes: *Kilograms of oil equivalent.
**Infants under 12 months, per thousand live births.
n.a. not available.
Source: World Bank, *World Development Report*, 1991. For derivations of this table and figures 1.2–1.4 below see section A.2 of appendix A.

standing of the nature of the inequality is enriched. Some important groups, such as those of various nationalities, are immediately apparent and there are many others which deserve consideration. The characteristics of such groups which directs attention and concern to the contrasts between their conditions, is that group membership should convey a common interest with or a feeling of loyalty towards others in the same group. Such groups may be defined by economic function – for example, much of early economic theory was about the distribution between large classes such as landowners, entrepreneurs and workers; they might be demarcated by their members' social function – such as workers in some way specially set apart from others by the special nature of their occupation (doctors, lawyers, miners, sailors . . .); or they might just consist of broader collections – age ranges, ethnic or regional classifications, the fundamental pair of groups, males and females.

The practical importance of the distinction between individual groups lies partly in the insights that it affords upon the underlying economic and social factors contributing to inequality and in the design of policies influencing it. It also lies in the rôle that groups (rather than unorganised individuals) can play in influencing the course of economic inequality: inequality between groups fighting for what they regard as their economic and social rights can lead to damaging conflict.

The very fact that there is such a wide range of economic indicators and so many different types of groups which may be relevant suggests that, in practice, the meaning of economic inequality may be quite complex: and we have not even touched on the difficult question of how the 'contrasts' (between persons or groups) of economic conditions are to be represented in quantitative rather than impressionistic terms.[3] However, we may start by examining those particular aspects which can be found from a study of 'income distribution', the second half of the book's title.

1.3 Why bother about income distribution?

Historically, investigations of economic inequality have largely been based on estimates of the distribution of people's incomes. The reason for this particular focus of interest is partly because income appears to be important in determining people's living standards, and partly because income is so closely associated with other indicators of a person's standing in the community. An additional reason is perhaps that income statistics have been made readily available as by-products of the administration of income tax.

However, there are a number of difficulties in the way of using income data for an examination of economic inequality, and it is worth considering whether we cannot do better. For example, it might be possible to adjust the data in various ways, so that they reveal more about standards of living (we shall review some of the practical steps that could be taken in chapter 2). Alternatively we could try to supplant or supplement the income data with something else. But with what?

What are we trying to do when comparing households' economic conditions? This does not amount to comparing the levels of happiness in the households, since happiness depends on a host of considerations apart from economic conditions. Yet wretched economic conditions can cause great misery and desperate need for goods and services, and it is also believed, although perhaps with less good reason, that better economic conditions do usually bring some more happiness. The essence of a comparison of economic conditions is thus to catch with it a comparison of those elements of happiness that money can buy. Such happiness is a nebulous concept and economists have tried to lend it more substance by naming it 'economic welfare', but nevertheless the relationship between income (which we can observe, at least in principle) and individual economic well being (which we cannot observe) should not be neglected. The supposed relationship is thus of the form:

$$\text{income} \rightarrow \text{consumption} \rightarrow \text{economic welfare}$$

There are theoretical and practical problems with each of the two links, and with the elusive concept of changes in economic welfare itself. One of the most difficult of these is that of the legitimacy of comparing either the levels or the units of measurement of the welfare scales of any two persons. However, if rough comparisons are sufficient and if we are comparing persons of a similar type, then the rule that the person who customarily spends more on his own consumption has the greater economic welfare is probably a reasonable starting point in an attempt at measurement in a study of economic inequality. The point of the comparison is that so long as the prices facing the two persons are roughly the same and the patterns of expenditure similar, this will provide a comparison of the amounts of goods bought.

Suppose that we already have a measure of each individual's consumption suitably corrected for discrepancies in prices. This might have been obtained from a specific

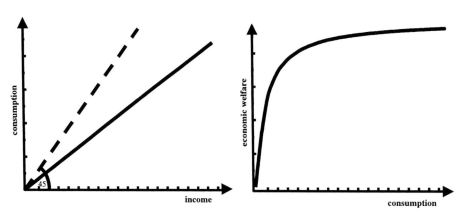

Figure 1.1 Income, consumption and welfare

sample survey, or it might be based on a simple model such as that illustrated in the left-hand part of figure 1.1 where consumption is proportionate to income.[4] Now each unit increase in consumption signifies an increase in economic welfare, but since a person gives priority to satisfying his most urgent economic needs, increases in consumption are presumed to become less and less effective in raising economic welfare, the higher the level of consumption already reached. Thus the dependence of economic welfare on consumption is often indicated by an economic welfare function, such as that illustrated in the right-hand part of figure 1.1: if, as many believe, there is a limit to the level of happiness that mere money can buy, then the curve flattens out, as shown, so that however large one's consumption may be the curve never rises above a fixed ceiling[5] to welfare. The precise shape attributed to this curve can affect the inferences about the overall level of welfare in the community that may be drawn from a particular set of data on income distribution. What this function and its curve mean – or can be made to mean – is a topic that we shall have more to say about in later chapters.

Income data, readily available though they may be, suffer from a number of deficiencies as indicators of living standards: but what about alternative indicators, such as data on consumption or of expenditure on consumption by households? On the one hand, a particular advantage of consumption over income as an indicator of economic welfare is that only under freak circumstances can consumption work out as zero or negative, whereas it is by no means unusual for a person's income over a particular year to come out as zero or negative, even if he is quite wealthy.[6] On the other hand, the quality of any available data on the distribution of consumption or expenditure is likely to be less reliable than that of data on income distribution. However the discrepancies between income and consumption expenditure becomes proportionately smaller if we take periods longer than a single year.

Finally, ownership of wealth as well as real consumption contributes to living standards, so that a thorough treatise on inequality should pay attention to the joint distribution of wealth and consumption: some would argue that economic inequality is far more due to unequal possession of property and power than to inequality of current consumption rates. Accordingly we shall at times shift attention away from income distribution alone to examine the way in which wealth affects the analysis of economic inequality.

1.4 Why does economic inequality rouse strong dissensions?

The most obvious reason why people become indignant about conspicuous economic inequality is that for one reason or another they regard it as unjust. Let us consider why.

Economic injustice

Perhaps the most powerful motive for condemning inequality as unjust is a personal one: the resentful envy aroused by the spectacle of a wealthy few enjoying ease whilst one's own kind have to toil and put up with constant inconvenience and hardship. But the case for condemning the injustice of inequality is more broadly based and does not depend on personal interest. Even the prosperous, so long as they feel secure in their prosperity, feel that there is something unfair about such contrasts as those we noted between the relative survival prospects of Somalian and Swedish babies, or about other stark contrasts in economic conditions between different groups of people, that are not due to the fault or merit of the people themselves. The response to mass-media coverage of particular cases suggests that such feelings of injustice are deep rooted and widespread.

The distinction is often drawn between economic inequality which can in part be attributed to the fault or merit of the affected persons themselves, 'inequality of outcome', and that which cannot, 'inequality of opportunity'. Inequality of opportunity is generally regarded as more unjust than inequality of outcome, but heated argument can still arise over differences of opinion as to which inequality is which in any particular case. It is an issue that affects both one's view of the severity of the problem of inequality, and the measures which might be recommended to alleviate it. For example, the wretched economic conditions to which some innocent babies are subjected may be attributable to the fault of improvident or inadequate parents, and the good conditions enjoyed by other equally innocent babies may well be the outcome for which exceptionally worthy parents made substantial effort and sacrifice.

Dissension also arises over the possible economic advantages that may result from tolerating inequality of outcome and, perhaps, inequality of opportunity also. For example, the propriety of allowing some inequality so as to provide a reward for and inducement to acquire skills, bear risks and take responsibility is widely accepted and deep rooted: it is reflected in the distinctive pattern of earnings dispersion that characterises many economies, and of established earnings differentials between occupations. This approval of certain 'justified' kinds of economic inequality and the resultant opposition to interference with it can at times lead to serious economic problems: in the case of pay, this type of argument justifying some inequality lies at the root of much of the resistance to egalitarian measures, on the grounds that they themselves are unjust.[7] It applies by extension to other types of differential treatment in economic rewards where there are long-established interests, customs or property rights.

The priority of need

The feeling that it is unjust is only one of the reasons why many people object strongly to conspicuous inequality. Consider a second objection: that poverty is particularly objectionable within an economy which is rich enough to afford to alleviate it. Public concern on this point is demonstrated by the flow of gifts from some of the rich to relieve need in their neighbourhoods in normal times; a more powerful demonstration of such concern is the public response when some disaster strikes. In conditions of sudden emergency, it is commonly accepted that the relief of extreme distress – caused by earthquakes, flooding, famine – should be given priority over other uses of economic resources. In practice the response dies away quickly as the disaster is forgotten, but some would argue that the same priority should regularly be given to the alleviation of need by those who can afford it, since such need is always widespread, although less noticeable than in the aftermath of disasters.

The 'priority of need' argument is distinct from the point made earlier about the injustice of inequality. It is based on the idea that if the rich are forced to economise, they can cut down on inessential comforts which they can quite well do without, and that the resources thus released can be used to provide goods and services desperately needed by the very poor. Reinforcing this line of argument is the evidence from studies of consumers' expenditure patterns, that the purchases by the poor consist largely of goods which most of us would regard as ones with which we should find it difficult to do without: and that, considering the expenditure and the possessions of progressively better-off families, we usually find that they can afford in turn each of a hierarchy of more luxurious and less essential goods and services. The availability of essential commodities and services, and their associated prices, may have a strategic importance in determining economic inequality.

In the light of these different motives for concern about inequality we should recognise that different types of policy measures have a part to play in reducing inequality and the relief of need. Both general measures, involving the taxation of the well-to-do and supplementing the incomes of the needy, and more specific direct methods, such as rationing and the explicit allocation of resources, have a rôle to play. The former general measures rely on the workings of the free market, to release the resources from supplying the rich and to divert them to meeting the more urgent needs of the poor; they may also need to be buttressed by safeguards against exploitation, monopolistic restrictions and deprivation of access to public resources. The latter direct measures are appropriate under conditions where free market forces act too slowly and imperfectly to achieve the aim. These points are discussed in chapter 12.

1.5 The scale of the problem of inequality

We began with an assertion that economic inequality is a persistent and pressing problem; this assertion may be regarded by many people as tendentious. Differences in economic status – it might be argued – are a fact of life: they are no more a 'problem' than are biological differences amongst people, or within and amongst other species for that matter. Furthermore, some economists and social philosophers see economic inequality, along with unfettered competition, as essential parts of a mechanism that

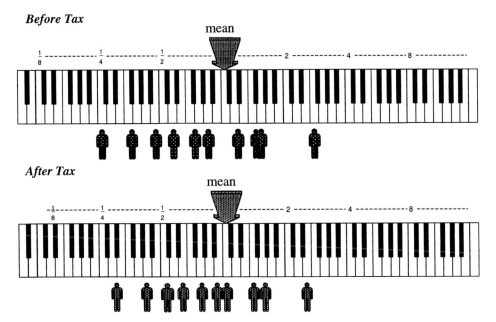

Figure 1.2 UK income distribution 1994/5

provides the best prospects for continuous economic progress and the eventual elimination of poverty throughout the world. These arguments will not do. There are several reasons why they will not do. Some of these reasons are dealt with in our discussion of the topics 'Growth' and 'Upheavals' in the next two sections. However, there is a more basic but powerful reason for rejecting the sort of argument that dismisses economic inequality as part of the natural order of things. This has to do with the scale and structure of inequality. We have already had a glimpse of this when addressing the question 'What do we mean by inequality?' in section 1.2 above: let us use the data introduced there to take a closer look at the scale of inequality between the economies of different nations.

Inequality in one country

To set inequality in perspective, take first the scale of inequality within a single economy, using the data on the distribution of personal incomes before and after tax in the UK during the fiscal year 1994/5 (see table 1.1 above): although these are not the best possible indicators of the distribution of economic prosperity, they are well suited for the present purpose of illustration. To compare the implied inequality within the United Kingdom before and after tax, let us carry out the following experiment: again form the 'income queue' from the information in table 1.1 and divide up the 26,900,000 members of the queue into equal slices of 26,900,000 'persons' (see page 2); let each of these ordered groups be represented by one person who is assigned the average income in his particular slice of the queue. Now make use of the piano keyboard in figure 1.2. The advantage of the piano keyboard is that it forms a natural proportionate scale:

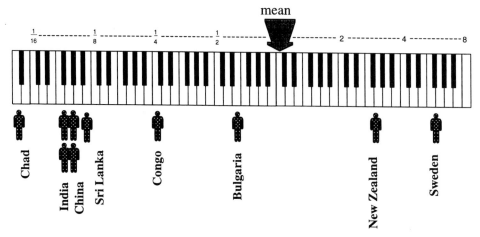

Figure 1.3 World distribution of income

use 'middle C' to correspond to mean income; the note one octave higher has a sound frequency twice that of middle C, and one octave lower has half the sound frequency; so we can use these two notes to correspond to twice mean income, and one half mean income respectively. Scaling the whole keyboard in this fashion (jump two octaves and income rises fourfold, jump three octaves and income rises eightfold . . .) we can display our two pictures of the UK in 1993/4 before tax (top) and after tax (bottom).[8]

The ten little persons representing groups (slices) of the income queue arranged on the keyboard at points corresponding to their group's income. Notice that, before tax, the person lowest on the scale is two octaves below middle C (a quarter of mean income); the highest on the scale is about 1.5 octaves above middle C (2.8 times mean income). The apparent effect of the income tax is fairly slight: the topmost little person (who represents the top 10 per cent slice) is still about one and a half octaves above middle C (he moves down from F to E – 2.5 times mean income); the lowest little person moves up from C to D#; but there is not much movement along the keyboard elsewhere.

Inequality in the world

Now use the same technique to depict inequality between different countries. In principle we could imagine a similar income queue formed for the entire world. Based on the population and dollar GNP per head of the reporting countries in the World Bank's *World Development Report*, 1991 we could find ten representative countries representing ten equal slices of this income queue. This would then give us the piano diagram in figure 1.3. The ten little people now represent the ten equal slices into which the population of reporting countries have been divided after arranging the countries in ascending order of dollar GNP per head.

Of course, drawing such a figure presents a formidable challenge in view of the problems of data comparability: it is not clear what income should correspond to middle C in this case. What is clear is the huge range of keyboard that is required: the ten little

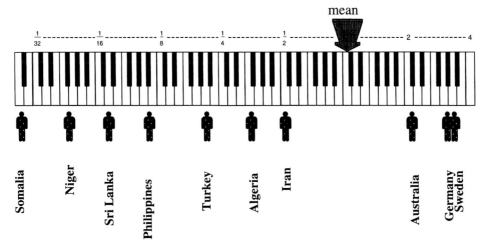

Figure 1.4 World distribution of income omitting China and India

people now cover nearly seven octaves, the full range of a grand piano. Recall that only about three octaves were required to depict the situation within the UK.[9]

One of the obvious problems with this exercise is the apparent arbitrariness of the inclusion of countries in the data: most of the former Eastern bloc countries are in, but the USSR is not; Iran is in, but Iraq is not (no income data). However, the broad conclusions are fairly robust. For example, if we drop the two countries with the biggest populations – China and India – from the data then the revised piano diagram reveals an even starker picture of inequality as we can see in figure 1.4: this picture summarises the situation for the ten countries that we cited in table 1.2. Even if we allow for the possibility that the use of crude dollar GNP per head may exaggerate the contrasts in living standards between countries, the impression of extreme inequality which even this superficial examination of the data conveys is almost staggering.[10]

The structure of inequality

Another striking portrayal of the extreme international inequality is given in table 1.3 comparing the distribution of dollar-GNP, and that of population between six major world sectors covering 120 market economies and much the greater part of the population of all market economies.

Membership of the six sectors is purely on the basis of geographical location, and the sectors are arranged in the table in ascending order of average living standards.[11] The first two groups contain almost a quarter (22.72%) of the population; but – according to the figures of dollar GNP – they receive less than 6 per cent of income in the market economies. By contrast the last (richest) two groups which also contain almost a quarter of the population (24.22%); but these two groups get more than *two thirds* of the dollar GNP in market economies. So if we were just to divide the world map broadly into geographical regions, we would find one quarter of the population ten times better off than another.

Table 1.3 *Distribution of population and gross domestic product amongst world market economies by region, 1985*

	Population		GDP		Adjusted GDP	
	(millions) (1)	per cent (2)	($ billion) (3)	per cent (4)	($billion) (5)	per cent (6)
Africa	554.98	17.03	358.09	3.37	593.00	4.19
Oceania	185.31	5.69	267.43	2.52	464.04	3.28
Asia	1,462.73	44.89	2,256.07	21.25	3,480.30	24.60
South America	266.18	8.17	451.28	4.25	986.75	6.97
Europe	404.74	12.42	2,874.31	27.08	3,955.39	27.96
North & Central America	384.45	11.80	4,408.08	41.53	4,668.00	33.00
World totals	3,258.39	100.00	10,615.27	100.00	14,147.47	100.00

Notes: GDP (columns 3 and 4) is computed at current rate of exchange. Adjusted GDP is computed at purchasing power parity. The table covers 120 market economies: see appendix A for details of coverage of each group.
Source: Summers and Heston (1988).

It could be argued that this simplistic presentation of the structure of inequality worldwide both overstates and understates the scale of the problem. The overstatement arises – as in table 1.2 – because converting from the local currencies to dollars using official exchange-rates exaggerates the contrast in income shares;[12] but, even when we make a crude correction for this and use the adjusted figures in the last column, we still find that the poorest two groups of market economies receive less than 7.5 per cent of income, whilst the richest two (Europe, North and Central America) receive more than 60 per cent. The understatement arises because of the extraordinarily simple grouping adopted in table 1.3: we have made no attempt to distinguish between different types of economy within any one regional group. Developed and developing countries have been lumped together – Japan with Bangladesh, Canada with Haiti – and it is clear that separating out countries by their degree of economic development would further accentuate the extraordinary scale of international economic inequality revealed by this glimpse of the structure of income distribution.

Although the scale of inequality within one country is less dramatic, examination of its structure can again be a useful way of putting into perspective the problem of inequality. As we mentioned in section 1.2 groups are important in understanding inequality: one aspect of this is illustrated in tables 1.4 and 1.5. These tables suggest that within some countries groupings by personal characteristics such as race may be much more important than classification by region in influencing the inequality of income distribution (contrast this with the rôle of geographical region in world inequality).

To a Martian it might seem remarkable that one or two key individual characteristics outside a person's control – his birth place, skin colour or physiognomy – should apparently exercise such an influence upon his prospects of income or economic welfare. To economists and policy makers it suggests a fundamental question: In what sense is one

Table 1.4 *Family income by region, race and Hispanic origin, United States, 1989*

	Number (thousands)				Median family income ($ per year)			
	All families	White	Black	Hispanic	All families	White	Black	Hispanic
Northeast	13,494	11,837	1,279	815	39,484	40,990	25,391	22,627
Midwest	16,059	14,370	1,446	330	34,613	35,789	18,301	26,359
South	23,244	18,746	4,147	1,596	30,499	32,939	19,029	20,520
West	13,293	11,638	598	2,101	35,698	36,144	25,670	25,511
All regions	66,090	56,590	7,470	4,840	34,213	35,975	20,209	23,446

Note: Income receiving unit is the family.
Source: US Bureau of the Census, *Current Population Report* – Series P60 No. 168.

Table 1.5 *Per-capita income by region and race, Malaysia, 1970*

	Number of individuals					Mean income per head (M$ per month)				
	All races	Malay	Chinese	Indian	Other	All races	Malay	Chinese	Indian	Other
South	26,264	13,256	10,449	2,431	128	45	33	57	51	175
Northwest	24,355	10,276	9,841	4,178	60	46	32	62	41	299
North	28,357	15,009	10,262	2,728	358	43	30	57	50	110
East	23,570	20,155	2,523	701	191	36	29	80	74	40
Central	31,631	11,778	13,642	5,972	239	73	50	88	70	391
All regions	134,177	70,474	46,717	16,010	976	50	34	68	56	185

Note: Income receiver is the individual.
Source: Anand (1983).

grouping 'more important' than another?[13] As we shall see, the answer to this question may significantly affect the way in which economic and social factors contribute to inequality and need to be taken into account in the design of policies for redistribution: for example, a widespread source of concern is the almost universal experience that women as a group get worse pay than men, even for the same jobs, and also suffer exclusion from many of the best-paid jobs.

The picture of economic inequality internationally is one major reason for being interested in the subject. The phenomenal scale of the problem is not an artefact of the measuring rod that you choose: tricks with statistics do not make the issue go away. The underlying structure of the problem manifested by the data reinforces the reason for interest in inequality. The data suggest that certain types of social and economic groupings are particularly relevant to an understanding of economic inequality and to the discussion of policy towards inequality. The distinctive pattern of income differences that superficially appears as a mere accident of geography (see the international comparisons depicted in table 1.3) or as a mere accident of skin colour (see the intra-national comparisons depicted in tables 1.4 and 1.5) is evidence of pervasive and persistent forces that generate inequality and that are rightly a focus of concern.

1.6   Inequality and economic growth

One of the most compelling answers to the question 'why bother about inequality?' is that inequality is closely interlinked with important issues of economic policy making. Politicians and others who wish to implement measures to alter the income distribution face some interesting policy choices; economic measures taken for the purposes of macroeconomic regulation or microeconomic adjustment may have important repercussions on economic inequality. For example (as we discuss below), economic inequality can influence, and be influenced by, major upheavals and in turn may influence their development.

It is also argued that there is a connection between inequality and the performance trend of an economy, for example that a fairly high level of economic inequality is required to enable the economy to grow at a healthy rate. This suggestion is part of a more general philosophy which holds that substantial inequality is a necessary ingredient in any healthily functioning economy.

One way of expressing these ideas is as a trade-off frontier between greater equality and greater productivity growth, such as that illustrated in figure 1.5. In this form the diagram is so nebulous as to be little more than a stimulus to think about how to improve on it, since it provides no hint of how to measure the things which are supposed to be measured along the two axes, nor does it explain what is hemmed in by the frontier. We would obviously need to specify numerical measures of economic progress – for example, the growth rate of real GNP per capita – and of the degree of equality – which may be related to the distribution of income in the economy.[14] The position of each of the black spots (marked 'feasible policies') in the diagram would then represent the index of equality and the rate of growth of GNP per head attainable with the corresponding policy. Now it is possible that there is just one *dominant* policy – one that has the property that no other point has both so large an equality index and so large a growth rate. Alternatively there could be several dominant policies having this property – as in the situation depicted in figure 1.5 – in which case the frontier is drawn to pass through all the corresponding dominant points. By definition of the term 'dominant' this frontier must be downward sloping to the right: the implication of this property is that, in choosing between the dominant policies, there is a cost to be paid for faster growth in terms of less equality. The steepness of the frontier will indicate how great is the cost. But why should we suppose that there is more than one dominant policy, that there is an inevitable conflict between growth and equality? Why should we suppose that the implied cost of faster growth is inevitably high? These are old questions, and several standard reasons are commonly given as to why there may be a hard choice between economic equality and economic growth.

Incentives

The operation of the free market in the pursuit of private profit provides strong incentives to work, show enterprise and pursue those lines of production which most benefit

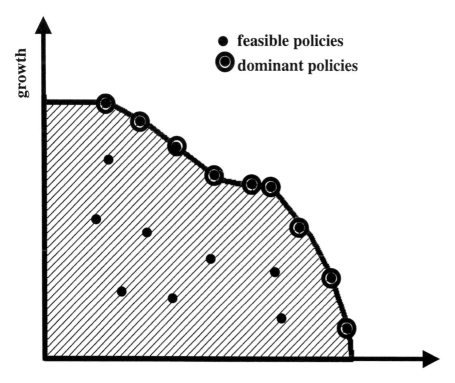

Figure 1.5 The trade-off between equality and growth

the community. The free market may generate economic inequalities as a by-product but, if so, it is a price well worth paying for the generation of the incentives.

The first leg of the argument – dating back at least to Adam Smith – is that growth rates such as those achieved by developed economies over the last few decades owe much to the incentives provided by the chance of raising one's family far above the average standard of living. However, experience suggests that the incentives appear to stimulate preponderantly production of the kinds of goods which the well-to-do can afford to buy, rather than to enable the poor to buy the goods which they most urgently need: though the system may generate 'mountains' of unsold surplus stocks of food, these often do little to alleviate famine.

Savings

A second argument suggests that persistent inequality may foster the growth of a large well-to-do class that voluntarily saves much of its income: such savings release resources for the expansion and modernisation of capital equipment. The poorer strata would have felt unable to afford saving except in the form of amassing durable goods for their own use. However, the rôle of the rich as promoters of growth through saving has sometimes been superseded by the activities of large corporations and of the government sector: the expansion or contraction of the activity of the state in economic production affects an economy's performance not only in terms of overall growth but also the determination of economic inequality: we discuss this further in chapter 6.

Habits

Once people have become accustomed to a degree of comfort they will regard it as a serious hardship to return to an earlier and lower standard of living: if they are compelled to do so, their level of economic welfare is in a sense lower than that which it had been when they were formerly living at that standard. The result is that, if large groups are threatened with the prospect of actually having to lower their living standards as a result of egalitarian measures, they may be prepared to obstruct the change with iron resolution. Attempts to force through energetic egalitarian measures, so rapidly that many of the rich are made less well off in order to enrich the poor, are at the risk of provoking extensive economic chaos during the transition. For this reason, as well as the earlier ones, rapid reduction of inequality is likely to slow down or even halt economic progress. However, this is an argument primarily against certain types of *change* in the economic system rather than against equality itself. Although this type of phenomenon will make the adjustment process difficult, it does not imply that a less unequal distribution of economic rewards, once established, will hamper further economic progress.

Control

The efficient running of large organisations depends on there being a common recognition of the hierarchy of authority for taking decisions and for supervising subordinate staff. Throughout the centuries it has been widely held that those in charge may properly live in a more comfortable and dignified style than those immediately under their charge, and that they should be paid more to enable them to do so. There are good economic reasons for such arrangements in terms of incentives for those within firms to work efficiently.[15] Strong egalitarian policies would hamper the power of exceptionally efficient and successful firms to expand and attract staff with the best talents by offering them the inducement of unusually high pay. Nevertheless, the cynic might reply that these type of arguments are likely to be most popular with the wealthy and the supporters of the *status quo*. Incentives may well be preserved by modifying the pecking order in ways that produce a smaller dispersion of rewards: effective control may be sustainable with a lower degree of inequality.

'Going it alone'

The trade-off frontier for any particular economy cannot be taken in isolation from what happens elsewhere. It is argued that for a single economy egalitarian measures may result in both capital and skilled labour moving to seek higher remuneration abroad unless this is prevented by law. Prevention is difficult to enforce, without so much interference as to hamper the efficient conduct of business, so that once again the egalitarian policies, if pursued vigorously, may retard economic growth. However this argument is predicated on a naturally high mobility of factors: whilst this may be reasonable in the case of capital, very high mobility of labour should not be taken for granted.

So the existence of a clear 'growth-*versus*-equality' trade-off should not just be taken for granted. Even if the trade-off exists, we should not automatically assume that the slope of the frontier – the 'price' of equality in terms of economic progress – is prohibitively steep.

1.7 Inequality and economic upheavals

Economic upheavals are a routine fact of life in economies subject to strong business cycle influences. They also characterise periods of transition that accompany structural change. To many readers the most familiar symptom of this sort of phenomenon will be the violent price movements – in goods markets and on stock exchanges – associated with inflation or deflation. Price movements can have rapid, direct and violent effects upon income and wealth; the effects are likely to be compounded by accompanying movements in the levels and pattern of economic activity and employment: inflation and unemployment can play a major rôle in influencing economic inequality.[16]

This type of economic upheaval appears to have become more severe and widespread as a result of rapid developments in the communication of information and other forms of technical progress. Furthermore there is a two-way connection between macro-economic events and the course of economic inequality; and the potential impact upon inflation – or the prospect of inflation – is a major reason why we should be bothered about inequality.

One example of this interconnection arises where there is an established customary pattern of relative rates of pay. The pattern often becomes widely regarded as tolerably fair: though many would regard it as 'fairer' still if their own group got a rather bigger proportion, every group would regard it as unfair if their own share were reduced in relation to that of their rivals. If inflation is moderate or altogether absent this customary pattern usually persists with little modification, so that the various groups need take little energetic action to maintain their relative positions: provided money rates of pay are not actually reduced many wage earners might put up with a gradual increase in the cost of living for a long time. But substantial inflation upsets the pattern and introduces uncertainty and anxiety about what may happen next. The point may be reached where wage earners shift attention from money wage levels to real wages, and some groups find that ordinary market forces cannot be relied upon to protect real wages from erosion if, through complacency or deference, they refrain from using their muscle in wage negotiations.

Industrial action or the threat of action may be effective in influencing macro-economic policy. However, even if wage negotiators can recover for their group their 'fair' share in the distribution at the time of the settlement, this is likely to be eaten away by the continuation of inflation and by the successful negotiations of rival groups. To secure a fair share on average over the whole period until they again negotiate for more pay, they may try to secure more than their fair share at the outset: how much more depends on their guesses about how fast prices and the pay of rival groups are likely to rise. Resentment and anxiety may cause such guesses to be alarmist, which would further intensify the struggle over income distribution and could result in a set of income distribution targets which add up to more than the economy is capable of producing. Economies with rapid inflation are therefore likely to suffer severe external constraints since they need to import in excess of their exports so as to secure the goods and services that they are incapable of themselves producing; this is likely to intensify both the rate of inflation and the struggles over income distribution.[17] Where the inflationary process is not checked at an early stage there is the further danger of consuming the seed-corn to stave off famine: underinvestment in capital equipment, the loss of control of important sectors of the economy to foreign interests, and, in extreme cases, the violent overthrow of constitutional authority in protest against efforts to regulate income distribution. These further results of persistent rapid inflation are therefore relevant to income distribution and its control, both within and between economies.[18]

The prospect of economic upheavals and the threat of inflation can inhibit policies to modify the income distribution, just as public concern about economic inequality may constrain policies for making the economy more competitive. The design and implementation of programmes of economic management ought not to overlook the issue of economic inequality.

1.8 Arrangement of the book

In the rest of the book we develop the study of the facts and the theory of economic inequality: we discuss the information to be gleaned from the distribution of wealth and income; we examine the way in which broadly based economic theories and specific models can be brought to bear on the subject; and we conclude with an examination of the implications of this analysis when choosing among policies for regulating inequality.

Chapters 2 and 3 lay the groundwork for this. Chapter 2 reviews the intellectual raw materials required for tackling some of the questions which we have already suggested – how can the facts about income distribution be obtained, and how should they be presented? How reliable are the statistics and what precautions may be needed in interpreting them? How are we to account for what the facts show, and what can reasonably be expected of any economic theories to explain them? We also discuss the importance of the climate of opinion concerning inequality, and the basis on which awkward choices are to be made between high economic inequality and other economic ills. In chapter 3 we look at some of these issues in a historical perspective, which may help in arriving at a more dispassionate judgement when regarding contemporary issues.

Whereas the first three chapters deal with the human, social and historical aspects of economic inequality, chapters 4 and 5 adopt a more detached arithmetical approach and are restricted to these narrower problems of measuring and analysing the 'inequality' manifest in a set of statistics, irrespective both of their imperfections and of the human difficulties and resentments underlying them. The purpose of this is to be able to deal precisely with issues such as what is meant when describing one state of the economy as more unequal than another, how overall inequality is related to inequality within constituent parts of the economy. To do this we introduce techniques for measuring inequality numerically, and for analysing it into components. Chapter 6 then links the discussion of the meaning of inequality with the primary concern of the remainder of the book: the way in which economic theory and statistical models can throw light on the causes of inequality.

Chapters 7 and 8 are primarily concerned with income from work in that they concentrate on the facts of the distribution of pay and earnings and theories to explain the available facts. However, there are theoretical links with the following chapters that also deal with wealth and the income from wealth. Chapter 9 reviews theories and evidence on wealth distribution whilst chapters 10 and 11 are mainly concerned with speculative model building: chapter 10 tries out some illustrative deterministic models largely concerned with the effects of inheritance, consumption and earnings behaviour, family structure and taxation; chapter 11 looks at some stochastic models of wealth distribution and ends with an examination of bivariate wealth and income distributions.

The last part of the book, chapter 12, is concerned with national policy in advanced industrial societies and also touches on the problems arising from issues raised in this chapter: the contrasts in living standards of the advanced economies and those in the third world.

Finally we mention two other features of the book. The sets of questions for discussion at the end of each chapter examine further some of the issues raised in the main text, and introduce some of the literature on particular issues raised in the chapters. The three appendices at the end of the book deal mainly with derivation of tables and graphs, mathematical proofs and theoretical points which might interrupt the flow of the main narrative and be off-putting for those who find mathematics tedious, unintelligible or time consuming. Those readers may wish to defer this material until they are familiar with the main issues which are discussed in a more down-to-earth manner. However, we encourage readers who want to understand the methods used in deriving our empirical illustrations and the workings of our formal models to consult appendices A to C.

1.9 Questions for discussion

General Reading: Beach (1981), Blowers and Thompson (1976), Chenery *et al.* (1974), Fields (1980), Frank and Webb (1979), Kravis (1984), Kravis *et al.* (1978a,b), Osberg (1981, 1984), Rainwater (1974), Sen (1987a), Thurow (1983).

1.1   Discuss the problems that may arise in comparing:
- The economic welfare of two or more persons.
- The increase of economic welfare that two specified individuals would obtain from the same gift (of goods and services).
- The increases of economic welfare that a specified individual in a specified situation would gain from two alternative gifts.
- The increases of economic welfare that an individual would gain from the same gift in different sets of circumstances.

(Basu (1994), Becker (1975), Carver (1925), Robbins (1938), Sen (1974, 1987b)).

1.2   (a) 'If a person declares that he would rather win a particular sporting distinction than receive any cash payment however large, then he implies that for him there is a ceiling to his economic welfare function.' Discuss.

(b) Use the relationship illustrated in figure 1.1 and the data in table 1.1 to produce a distribution of economic welfare, assuming that consumption is proportionate to income and that welfare is inversely related to consumption so that $u(x) = 1 - 1/x$ where x is income. Show that in the before-tax case the mean of this distribution is 0.99989 units.

(c) Show that this level of average economic welfare in turn corresponds to an income level of £9,385.36 (this income level is sometimes known as the *equally distributed equivalent* or the *representative income* for the function u – see page 000 in chapter 5) and that this income falls short of the arithmetic mean income by some 36.2 per cent.

(d) Discuss the use of this proportionate shortfall of representative income below mean income as an index of the welfare loss attributable to the inequality of the income distribution.

(e) Show that if we take the after-tax case, representative income for the welfare function u is now £8,519.16, and that the welfare loss attributable to inequality has been reduced to 29.7 per cent.

1.3   Compare the ways in which the following policies might affect economic inequality between national economies:

Provision of facilities and know-how for improving supplies of drinking water.
Provision of fertilisers to raise agricultural productivity.
Financial loans to the governments of underdeveloped economies.
Provision of satellite communications.
Training and equipment to enable rulers to maintain internal stability and repel foreign aggression.
Subsidised supplies of luxury goods to provide incentives for enterprising and productive individuals.

1.4   How would you expect the pictures of inequality captured by figures 1.2–1.4 to alter if, instead of dividing the income queue up into tenths (with ten representative little people), it were divided up into twentieths (with 20 representative people)?

1.5   (a) Show that the average income of the bottom 10 per cent of income receivers in table 1.1 is £4,066 before tax, £3,980 after tax, and that the average income of the top 10 per cent is £40,402 before tax, £31,442 after tax.

(b) Table 1.1 contains no information about those whose incomes are not subject to tax. What might happen to the income queue and to figure 1.2 if these were included (see also questions 2.2 and 2.10 at the end of chapter 2)?

1.6   (a) Explain why dropping the countries with very large populations (China and India) from the data used to construct figure 1.3 will make the inequality of GNP per head in the world appear even greater.

(b) Using the World Bank's *World Development Report 1991* verify the claim made in note 10 that the picture of extreme inequality of income (as represented by the ten little people) is preserved if we use group medians and overall median income rather than the corresponding means.

1.7   Discuss the distinction between economic inequality, economic injustice and inequality of economic opportunity (Broome, 1989; Letwin, 1983; Nozick, 1974; Rawls, 1972; Spengler, 1980; Tawney, 1964).

1.8   In what ways may the prices of strategic consumer goods be taken into account in the design of policy towards economic inequality (Williamson 1976, 1977)?

1.9   (a) Using table A.1 of appendix A, and also the tables in Summers and Heston (1988), explain why Oceania is ranked in terms of living standards between Africa and Asia in table 1.3 (compare Summers and Heston, 1991).

(b) Using table A.1 of appendix A show that the poorest 50 per cent of the population in market economies receive less than 10 per cent of income, and that the richest 10 per cent of the same population receive more than 37 per cent of income, where income is GDP evaluated at international purchasing power parity.

1.10   On what basis may groups be selected for understanding the nature of inequality (Bell and Robinson, 1980; Hanushek, 1978; Thurow, 1979)?

1.11   If you wished to test the suggestion that economic equality in any country has usually been at the expense of economic progress, (a) what facts would you seek and (b) where would you enquire in the hope of obtaining them (see Ahluwalia, 1976a,b; Ahluwalia *et al.*, 1979; Cline, 1972, 1975; Lydall, 1979b, Okun, 1975, Paukert, 1973)?

1.12   'Socialism and equality require a relative transfer of resources from private consumption to public expenditure; economic exigencies may demand a further transfer to higher exports or investment. But under conditions of slow growth efforts to achieve these transfers inevitably provoke inflation. For since they cannot come from the fruits of rapid growth they must come from higher taxation of existing incomes. But higher indirect taxes put up prices; higher direct taxes provoke compensating claims for higher money wages and salaries. In the UK's slow-growth economy the shift of resources away from personal consumption has harshly exacerbated the problem of inflation' Crosland (1964).

   Discuss the ways in which macroeconomic management, and the exploitation of natural resources might provide a way out of such a dilemma.

1.13   What impact will rapid inflation have upon the value of asset holdings? What impact is this likely to have upon income distribution (Cagan, 1956; Minarik, 1979; Stoker, 1986; von Ungern-Sternberg, 1981)?

1.14   What problems would you expect to encounter in trying to estimate a trade-off frontier between equality and growth in practice (Baumol and Fischer, 1979; Browning and Johnson, 1984)?

Notes

1 Care needs to be taken here: the 'persons' in table 1.1 are individuals, but in earlier forms of the data they were tax units many of which consist of more than one person; this gives rise to some problems of analysis and interpretation which we shall face in chapters 2 and 4 (see also Pen's (1971) discussion of the 'parade').
2 See question 1.5.
3 We deal with this exhaustively in chapters 2, 4 and 5 below.
4 In chapters 9–11 – where we take into account the effects of unforeseen shocks and accumulated wealth on consumption – we discuss more sophisticated models of the relationship between consumption and income.
5 This ceiling was given the delightful name 'Bliss' by the philosopher Frank Ramsey: see Ramsey (1928). We discuss the use of such welfare functions in chapter 5.

6 A word of warning: the presence of such zero or negative income in a distribution can play havoc with measuring income inequality by any measures which are sensitive to very low incomes – see chapters 4 and 5.

7 This is developed further in section 1.7: in the meantime readers may care to consider on what basis the relative pay of such performers as judges, rock singers, cabinet ministers, bishops, actresses and domestic cleaners might be justified.

8 Non-musical readers can ignore the notes. Compare figures 1.2–1.4 by considering the distance between any two of the representative little people and remembering that distances on the scale correspond to income *proportions* in reality: see the numeric scale showing multiples or fractions of the mean in each diagram.

9 See also question 1.4 of this chapter. In constructing the data set for the figure we have included all reporting countries in the World Bank tables, except those for which no income data are available (see appendix A). In drawing the figure we have had to place mean income one octave above middle C in order to fit all the little people in.

10 Figures 1.3 and 1.4 have been constructed analogously to figure 1.2 by estimating mean income for each 10 per cent slice and for income overall. However, notice that the conclusions of extreme inequality are robust if we use medians rather than means (within each group and overall): the big arrow is plotted to the left of the point shown, but the little people are just as spread out along the keyboard – see question 1.6.

11 The categorisation is that of Summers and Heston (1988) – see also question 1.9 of this chapter.

12 The method of adjustment is described in appendix A. There is a further important objection to the comparison of economic conditions between nations by using dollar GNP percapita figures: since our main concern is with contrasts between living standards we should ideally be comparing levels of economic welfare. Unfortunately, these levels are rather more difficult to compute from available statistics – see question 1.2, and the extensive discussion in chapter 5.

13 In the case of the USA we investigate this issue in detail in chapters 5 and 6 (pp. 110 and 120) where we investigate the analysis of inequality by other groupings such as age and sex as well as race.

14 In chapters 4 and 5 we consider a number of inequality measures of income distribution and the rules and principles for constructing such measures. The complement of such a measure – equality index – could be plotted along the horizontal axis of figure 1.5.

15 See our discussion in chapter 8 on pp. 181–5.

16 See pages 185–8 in chapter 8.

17 However, there are counterexamples: the experience of Israel has shown that it is possible for an economy to continue functioning efficiently for many years, even when inflation is such that prices may double within a single year.

18 See also pp. 134 and 311 in chapters 6 and 12.

2 Steps in the study of economic inequality

2.1 Obtaining the facts

In chapter 1 we suggested a number of questions about why we should concern ourselves with inequality: a natural next step would be to draw up a list of information which we would like in order to answer those questions, and to compare it with the types of information that could conceivably be available. To make further progress we would set aside those issues about which information is hopelessly inadequate and devise some expedients for consolidating the information about the other issues which is available. This sequence of steps forms a strategy that is common in many fields of economic enquiry.

In the case of economic inequality our questions naturally focus on information about the dispersion of living standards within and across groups. A household's living standard will be partially determined by its purchases of consumption goods, the services of durable assets (such as the house, cooker, TV . . .) it enjoys, and the 'social wage' from which it benefits by having access to publicly provided services. It will also depend on the composition of the household members that share in total consumption. Confining our attention at first to a single nation in a given period, what kind of information is needed to answer questions about the distribution of such standards? The following general indicators for a group may be both relevant and obtainable:

- Statistics of infant mortality and expectation of life at birth.
- The proportion of population with access to public utilities such as safe water supplies.
- The average daily per-capita consumption of foodstuffs measured in calories or grammes of carbohydrates, proteins, fats, etc.
- The dollar value of total consumption per head.
- The dollar value of total disposable income per head.

However, to move on from average living standards of groups to questions about the distribution of households' living standards around those averages usually means having to put up with a more limited coverage of information – perhaps only the value of income or of consumption. Even dollar income per head alone can be useful if the period is sufficiently long since the part of disposable income not spent currently on consumption can be taken as a crude proxy for the omitted money value of the services of consumer durable items.

The data to provide the estimates of both the average standards of living within groups and the dispersion amongst households come essentially from two sources. *Survey data* based on sample enquiries can provide great detail on consumers' expenditure, home consumption and the like. *Official records* are the source of much of the data on personal or household incomes before and after tax, and on the distribution of earnings.

The availability of data naturally varies markedly between countries. In some industrialised countries such as the USA, the UK, Sweden and The Netherlands, a lot of data are available on the distribution of consumers' expenditure, earnings and pre- and post-tax incomes: whereas in many developing countries and in those with authoritarian régimes, the position is much more difficult. Although in recent years sample surveys of consumption and income have been carried out in developing countries, more extensive information extending over longer periods is unavailable. This is partly because of the expense of data collection, the inadequacy of government statistical services and, in some cases, the political inconvenience to which the publication of such data might give rise.

Even in countries well supplied with statistics relating to economic inequality there are areas of profound obscurity: information about the extent and depth of poverty is still scanty compared to that about higher incomes; and although reasonably good 'snapshot' evidence on living standards is usually obtainable, data which track living standards of persons or families over several periods are comparatively rare.[1]

Of course, even if statistics in any country are readily available they may still be unreliable, and the prospective user of any estimates of income distribution or economic inequality should examine carefully the interpretations that may be given to them. It is an area where caution is required.

2.2 Interpreting the statistics

To provide accurate statistical information requires care, time and intelligence. These are only likely to be forthcoming if the informant is anxious to be accurate, and that is only likely to be so under especially favourable circumstances. The presumption is that in the absence of successful precautions most economic statistics are likely to be substantially inaccurate. This presumption is particularly strong with statistics of income distribution where it can often prove expensive in more ways than one to provide accurate information.

Many of the greatest difficulties in the study of inequality arise from the unreliability of much of such information and from the fact that the degree of unreliability may change a lot with the passage of time. Amongst the most common reasons for the poor statistical quality are the following ten sources of error.

• In estimating the distribution of income it is common for some components of income – for example, production for a person's own consumption or investment – to be omitted or seriously understated. Similarly, incomes from work should be calculated net of costs (such as travel expenses) incurred in the course of earning those incomes, but these costs are usually omitted as well.

Table 2.1 *Income rankings and income valuation*

Country	GNP per head 1989	Adjusted GNP per head 1985	GNP per head 1985
Somalia	170	285	499
Niger	290	232	490
Sri Lanka	430	380	1,995
Philippines	710	599	1,710
Turkey	1,370	1,057	3,163
Algeria	2,235	2,587	2,513
Iran	3,200	2,997	4,897
Australia	14,360	10,211	10,953
Germany	20,440	10,261	12,831
Sweden	21,570	11,970	12,118

Notes: GDP per head is evaluated at current rate of exchange. Adjusted GDP per head is evaluated at international prices using purchasing power parity – see appendix A.
Sources: World Bank, *World Development Report*, 1991; Summers and Heston (1988).

- Although it is often appropriate to consider the distribution of incomes after payment of tax, the problems of the incidence of taxation are commonly not adequately dealt with.
- Transfer payments are commonly omitted when estimating income. For example, in developing countries, estimates of income may only cover wage income.
- Even when income has been comprehensively defined, the statistics may be inaccurate just because parts of the income so defined may be virtually impossible to measure since the goods and services represented are not all priced on any relevant observable market. This is particularly true of the services provided free, or at subsidised rates, by government agencies.
- Large incomes are often understated for fear of attracting high taxation.
- Distribution of money income does not provide an adequate picture of the distribution of real income, which is likely to be of more interest to researchers, because of regional variation in consumer prices. This difficulty may be particularly serious in developing economies and in some large countries with poor communications. Similar but more severe problems arise when comparing incomes across national frontiers. Table 2.1 illustrates the importance of this point when comparing the ten representative countries introduced in chapter 1 (see table 1.2 and figures 1.3 and 1.4). Comparing column 1 (copied from table 1.2) with column 2, it is easy to understand why there was a reversal of the relative fortunes of Somalia and Niger during the years 1985–9. But notice the picture that emerges from the

last two columns: moving from valuation at market exchange rates to valuation at purchasing power parities reverses the relative positions of Sri Lanka and the Philippines, and the relative positions of Turkey and Algeria.

- Sufficient detail may not be available about the nature of the income receiving unit. To make sensible comparisons of real income levels or the inequality of living standards it is helpful to know at least how many adults and children are presumed to share in a particular reported income; otherwise we may be unable to distinguish between a large income shared by a large family, each of whose members lives modestly, and a large income accruing to a single, rich person. Better indicators of living standards require that family's total income to be adjusted by a measure of the relative needs of different family types.[2]

- The estimates may be faulty because the sample on which they are based is unrepresentative in some important respect. This is particularly likely to happen where there is no adequate sampling frame, for example, in nomadic populations or where certain regions in the economy are inaccessible. It also occurs quite often where tax data are used as an information source, since a specific segment of the population (usually the poor) may be exempt from the tax. This segment is then excluded from the statistics which thus present a biased overall picture.

- If we compare estimates for different economies – or for the same economy at different dates – we will often find that the various data sources are not fully comparable. Special attention has to be paid to whether 'income' means the same thing in each economy, and whether the definition of an 'income receiver' – as a household, family, married couple, or individual person – is also consistent between economies.

- The flow of personal income may be measured over time periods of different lengths in the economies being compared.

This list highlights the need for caution in accepting and interpreting statistical estimates, and in using them to design policy. Nevertheless, there remain many interesting questions about the outcome of the economic organisation of societies for which such data as are available may be used to throw some light on the answers: it would be over-cautious to abandon such enquiry because of imperfections in the statistics. Our list serves as a reminder that, because of the differing economic structure and social composition among various economies, it is rash to jump to conclusions from simple comparisons based on the published average levels of incomes and of income distributions. Rather, we should try out a number of approaches and become aware, for example, of the contrasting pictures that can emerge once alternative definitions of 'income' and 'income recipients' are taken into consideration: how this is to be tackled in practice is dealt with more fully in chapter 4.

2.3 Presentation of the facts

Having faced the challenge of obtaining, scrutinising and interpreting the raw data, how is the essential information conveyed by such data to be presented?

One approach would be to address the formal problem of defining what is meant by 'inequality' expressed in terms of the income distribution: we shall treat this issue fully in chapters 4 and 5. However, for the moment let us respond to the question at a more

elementary level, by seeing how simple techniques of graphical and statistical presentation can be used to enable us to compare in the mind's eye the different natures of
inequality in different situations. We have already encountered one impressionistic
device for presenting the facts in chapter 1 – the piano diagrams on pages 9–11 – but
our task now is to review the way in which a variety of more standard diagrammatic
techniques can be employed.

First, a word of caution: however the presentation is done, a certain amount of
interpretation or even outright prejudice and bias usually creeps in. Probably the only
occasions in which this does not arise involve artificial examples – such as that of an
economy consisting of just a few persons and a single form of income – in which case
the picture of income distribution is conveniently unambiguous. However, with large
numbers of people, some systematic method of summarising the information is necessary; and there is a danger that the method chosen may colour our reading of the
facts.

The frequency distribution

Let us begin with a straightforward pictorial representation of table 1.1, which shows
– for each of a series of ranges of incomes – the number of persons with incomes in the
range and the amounts of income flowing to those persons. The result is a diagram such
as figure 2.1, the *frequency distribution*, which can be taken as an estimate of the underlying theoretical density function characterising the distribution of income.[3] The
method of exposition can be adapted to show the distribution of other variables such
as consumption expenditure or consumption in physical units.

We might take a step further and summarise the frequency distribution using
conventional statistics. The distributional facts in table 1.1 and figure 2.1 could be
represented by measures of average income and its dispersion – typically the *arithmetic
mean* income (total income divided by number of income receivers; in this case
£14,098.72 before tax) and the *standard deviation* (take the sum of squared deviations
from the mean, divide by the number of income receivers, and then take the square
root; in this case £16,648.50).[4]

By themselves these two statistics can only be expected to yield a crude caricature of
the picture represented by the distribution. We may also be interested in other standard
summary statistics, such as a measure of skewness,[5] but it soon becomes clear that no
single convenient statistic will be uniformly satisfactory for comparing the inequality
of two distributions.

More than that, however, the particular way in which the data are assembled in table
1.1 or figure 2.1 may reveal or conceal important information about the structure of
inequality. This is immediately evident in the choice of boundaries for the income intervals in the first column of the table: which correspond to the vertical lines in the
figure. Finer subdivision of the first and last income intervals would alert us to the presence of any extremely small or extremely large incomes that might be of interest for
policy purposes. It is not unusual to find authors writing persuasively about supposed
trends in inequality, whilst relying on data that are really too coarsely grouped at the
top or bottom end of the distribution to provide adequate support to their argument.[6]

In addition to this problem the apparent extent of inequality revealed by a table

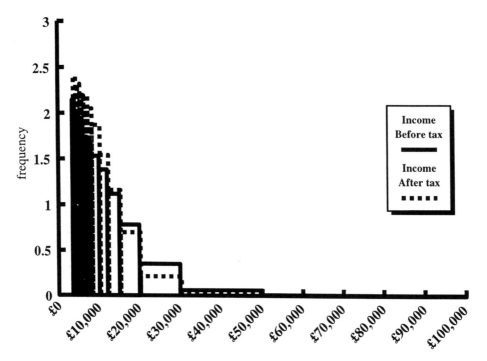

Figure 2.1 Frequency distribution of income, UK, 1994/5, before and after tax
Source: Board of Inland Revenue, *Inland Revenue Statistics*, 1996.

such as table 1.1 (figure 2.1) will depend on the particular choice of income variable – earnings, taxable income, total family income and so on. It also depends on the scale on which such incomes are presented. For example, the same information might be redisplayed using intervals based on the logarithms of incomes – as in figure 2.2 – which generally has the visual effect of producing a much less skewed distribution of income.

The Lorenz curve

The information conveyed by table 1.1 can also be presented using another conventional device: the *Lorenz curve*. Again form the income queue that we described in chapter 1 (recall that the queue is arranged in ascending order of income), and imagine each person being assigned his share of total income as the queue passes along: then plot the graph of the proportion of total income so far assigned against the position in the queue. On doing so for the UK 1993/4 data, figure 2.3 emerges. The Lorenz curve – closely related to the frequency distribution[7] – can be read as follows. Imagine the queue of income receivers divided into ten equal-sized slices; take the point on the horizontal axis marked '10 per cent': the height of the curve at that point gives the proportion of total income (before or after tax, depending on which curve is used) that flows to the people in the poorest slice of the queue; the height of the curve at the '20 per

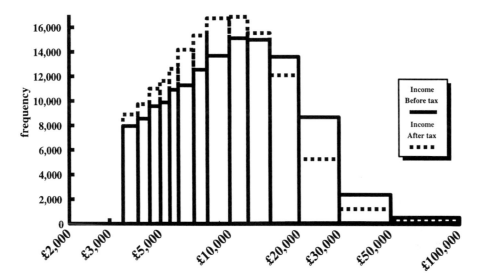

Figure 2.2 Frequency distribution of income, logarithmic transformation, UK, 1994/5, before and after tax
Source: Board of Inland Revenue, *Inland Revenue Statistics*, 1996.

cent' mark gives the proportion of total income that flows to the bottom two slices and so on. In this case the 'after-tax' curve lies everywhere above the 'before-tax' curve: the gap between the two indicates the reduction of inequality in the income distribution after the deduction of tax. In the case of the UK 1993/4 this gap is apparently not very great:[8] whilst the bottom 50 per cent of the population (the five lowest slices) receives 24 per cent of total income before tax, the top 10 per cent (the top-most slice) receives about 29 per cent of the income before tax! If we look at the situation after tax, the two income shares for these two groups become 26 per cent and 27 per cent respectively.

As with the frequency distribution we may again want to go a step further and use a conventional summary statistic to characterise the picture of inequality. In the case of the Lorenz curve this is usually taken to be the area trapped between the curve and the diagonal line expressed as a proportion of the whole area of the triangle – the *Gini coefficient*.[9] As we would expect this confirms the slight reduction in inequality after tax that we noticed, looking at the income shares the Gini coefficient is 0.3860 before tax and 0.3427 after tax.

The Pareto diagram

The third major type of presentation that we shall have occasion to use later, particularly in chapters 9–11, makes good use of information in the upper tail of the distribution in situations where information about low incomes is patchy or non-existent. Plot the proportion of the population receiving at least income x against x itself, on a double logarithmic scale. The result is the *Pareto diagram* – see figure 2.4. The far right-hand

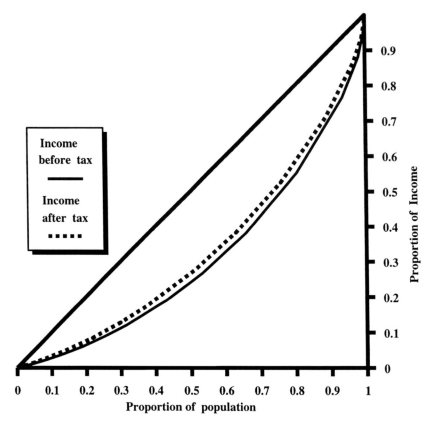

Figure 2.3 Lorenz curve of income, UK, 1993/4

end of the diagram is reasonably approximated by a straight line, and the slope of this line – known as the *Pareto coefficient* – can be taken as an indicator of equality.

To see why this is so, consider the following argument: for any distribution pick some base income b above which the data are taken to be reasonable, reliable and complete; measure a, the arithmetic mean income of those at or above b, and then compute the ratio a/b. This ratio is independent of the income unit and is a rough measure of inequality: if there were to be perfect equality then a/b would be exactly one; if the distribution were highly unequal a/b would be large. It is often found that if the base income b is fairly high the a/b ratio is little affected by the precise choice of b for a given distribution: this is exactly the case where the Pareto diagram (such as figure 2.4) is a straight line. The distribution of income x often approximates to a *Pareto distribution* for which the distribution function is given by $F(x) = 1 - hx^{-\alpha}$, where h is a constant and α is the Pareto coefficient. In such a case the ratio $(a/b)/[(a/b) - 1]$ provides a simple estimator of the coefficient α. High values of (a/b) correspond to high levels of inequality, but to low values of α.[10]

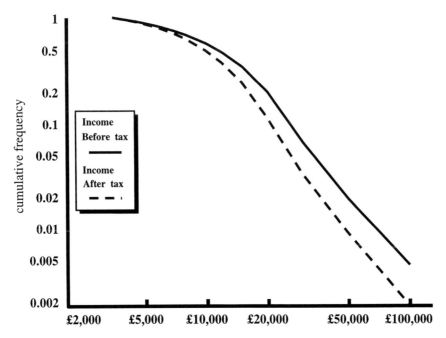

Figure 2.4 Pareto diagram of income, UK, 1993/4, before and after tax
Source: Board of Inland Revenue, *Inland Revenue Statistics*, 1996.

The multivariate approach

Even if authors and readers were in complete agreement about the particular issue of which income variable or variables to present and the method of depicting the distribution (frequency distributions, Lorenz curves, Pareto diagrams or something else), the presentational devices that we have examined up till now may still omit some important descriptive information. How we might depict an extra 'dimension' of economic inequality?

To do this we introduce a data set that permits the representation of a variety of concepts of income and income receiver. Table 2.2 displays total family income for the USA 1986 – expressed in the form of a frequency distribution – as derived from the Panel Study of Income Dynamics (PSID).[11] A panel study is in effect a sample with repeated interviews of the same subjects, yielding a history of data for each interviewee: in this case the interviewees were the heads of 7,061 American families.[12] Table 2.2 is only a very crude picture of the data: from interviews in 1987, information about incomes in 1986 was recorded and we have summarised this for each of nine income ranges; no attempt has been made to adjust the data for possible biases in the sample, to allow for differing needs of different types of family, or to convert a distribution by *families* to a distribution by *persons* – we shall be examining these problems in chapter 4.[13] Setting aside these important issues for the moment let us see how the richness of the data source underlying table 2.2 can illustrate a further step in the study of economic inequality.

Table 2.2 *Frequency distribution of total family income, USA, 1986*

	Range ($)	No. of families in range	Average income in each range
(1)	less than $0	8	−$16,832
(2)	$0	25	$0
(3)	$1–$4,999	631	$3,179
(4)	$5,000–$9,999	883	$7,355
(5)	$10,000–$19,999	1,562	$14,699
(6)	$20,000–$29,999	1,307	$24,680
(7)	$30,000–$49,999	1,589	$38,479
(8)	$50,000–$99,999	926	$64,837
(9)	$100,000 and over	130	$148,727
	All ranges	7,061	$28,905

Source: Own calculations from Panel Study of Income Dynamics (PSID), Wave XX; see appendix A.

There are several ways we could do this. For a start we might look the relationship between total family income and its principal economic components; this can be written as:

Total family income	=	Labour income	+	Asset income	+	Transfer income
$28,905		$21,839		$2,216		$4,850

The figures give the average for each component in 1986.[14] But what of the structure of the distribution of these income components among the families?

Table 2.3, which has been constructed from the same data source as table 2.2, is an example of a *bivariate frequency distribution* for the two variables 'labour income' (earnings) and 'asset income' (income from property). Each cell contains the number of families falling into both a specific labour-income range and a specific range of asset income. The two columns at the extreme right-hand side of the table give the frequency distribution of asset income amongst the families; likewise the two bottom rows of the table give the frequency distribution of labour income.[15] Although table 2.3 omits the last of the three components of total family income (transfer income) this method of presenting the facts can reveal much about the structure of economic inequality. For example, although there are many who do not have any asset income, there is no sharp segregation of families into two distinct groups, 'asset-income receivers' and 'labour-income receivers'. Furthermore, although for the majority of families, labour income is a larger component of income, the inequality of the distribution of asset income appears to be much greater. Notice also that whilst there are, of course, no families with negative labour income (negative earnings), there are families for which negative asset

Table 2.3 *Bivariate distribution of labour income and asset income, USA, 1986*

	Range of labour income									All ranges	Av. asset income in each range
	(1)	(2)	(3)	(4)	(5)	(6)	(7)	(8)	(9)		
(1)	0	7	3	4	6	10	17	11	1	59	−$8,891
(2)	0	874	485	474	969	672	660	197	7	4,338	$0
(3)	0	278	96	116	256	286	521	301	19	1,873	$1,193
Range (4)	0	73	21	19	44	41	60	64	6	328	$6,986
of (5)	0	74	9	6	47	46	39	43	2	266	$13,531
asset (6)	0	24	2	3	2	16	23	12	9	91	$23,838
income (7)	0	13	2	1	2	4	18	20	4	64	$38,082
(8)	0	6	0	0	0	0	9	14	5	34	$65,624
(9)	0	4	0	0	0	1	1	2	0	8	$151,315
All ranges	0	1,353	618	623	1,326	1,076	1,348	664	53	7,061	$2,216*
Av. labour in each range	n.a.	$0	$2,177	$7,412	$14,693	$24,505	$38,254	$63,776	$159,934	$21,839**	

Notes: * Average asset income for all ranges.

** Average labour income for all ranges.

Source: As for table 2.2. Income ranges (1)–(9) are identical to those in table 2.2. The detailed definitions of labour income and asset income are given in appendix A.

income was recorded during 1986: as we shall see in chapters 4 and 5, negative incomes can give rise to awkward problems of interpretation.

As an alternative to analysing the component income sources, we could use the same technique to examine the time dimension of the distribution of income. Is there a substantial amount of mobility of income over time, or do the same families repeatedly appear in the same part of the distribution year after year? A panel study permits this sort of question to be addressed. Table 2.4 illustrates this for the PSID: each cell contains the number of families falling into a specific pair of income ranges in 1985 and 1986. Notice that in contrast to the bivariate distribution of labour income and asset income in a single year (table 2.3), there is much more concentration of observations in the cells on or near the principal diagonal (top left to bottom right). Although there are interesting outliers – for example, the three families who were in range 8 ($50,000–$99,999) in 1985 but dropped back to range 2 and 3 ($0–$4,999) in 1986 – the table suggests a persistence in families' income positions from one year to the next.

As with the univariate methods discussed above, again we can go a step further and summarise the bivariate frequency distribution using conventional statistics. One of the most useful is the *correlation coefficient*, ρ which is the covariance of the two variables divided by the standard deviation of each variable. This statistic confirms the impressionistic story sketched above: in the case of the bivariate distribution of asset income and labour income ρ is positive, but comparatively low (0.1347), but in the case of income in the pair of years 1985, 1986 ρ is fairly high (0.8196).

Without information such as is depicted by tables 2.3 and 2.4 little progress can be made on issues of central importance such as whether recipients of earnings and of asset income fall predominantly into two distinct classes, whether the inequality of income overall is principally due to inequality in the labour market or in the distribution of financial wealth, or whether income inequality is accompanied by substantial mobility of income. Tables yielding only one-variable frequency distributions of each variable – the sort most commonly published by statistical authorities – are only of limited help.

Even if tables 2.3 and 2.4 are not the most apt representation of the structure of income distribution, we may be interested in the bivariate distributions of other pairs of variables, or in multivariate distributions of three or more variables simultaneously (many income components or income over several years for example), although obviously the presentation of this sort of information soon becomes unwieldy. Within the limits imposed by the original data it is a matter for judgement by the individual observer which summaries are presented, and so which relationships between income variables are to be highlighted.

The bivariate frequency distribution is a useful method of presentation not only for an analysis of the composition of income, but also for the composition of the population. In this case the rows of table 2.3 might still represent the appropriate income intervals, but the columns would be labelled according to some other observable characteristic of the population. As an example we might construct a table in which each family had been categorised by income (the rows of the table) and by age group of the family head (where each column represents a specific age range: under 20 years, 20–29 years, 30–39 years and so on). We can thus apply the presentation technique to income distribution amongst groups: the row labelled 'all ranges' would then give the

Table 2.4 *Bivariate distribution of total family income, USA, 1985 and 1986*

	Range of 1985 income									All ranges	Av. income in each range, 1986
	(1)	(2)	(3)	(4)	(5)	(6)	(7)	(8)	(9)		
(1)	0	0	3	1	2	0	2	0	0	8	−$16,832
(2)	0	0	17	4	1	2	0	1	0	25	$0
(3)	0	0	401	134	66	15	13	2	0	631	$3,179
Range (4)	0	0	165	471	171	46	19	9	2	883	$7,355
of (5)	0	2	62	223	909	244	92	25	5	1,562	$14,699
1986 (6)	0	1	16	37	310	673	232	33	5	1,307	$24,680
Income (7)	0	1	7	20	78	349	976	154	4	1,589	$38,479
(8)	0	0	2	0	9	27	274	589	25	926	$64,837
(9)	0	0	1	0	0	0	5	57	67	130	$148,727
All ranges	0	4	674	890	1,546	1,356	1,613	870	108	7,061	$28,905*
Av. income in each range, 1985	n.a.	$0	$2,982	$7,306	$14,627	$14,627	$24,610	$38,309	$65,633	$157,563	$28,382**

Notes: *Average income for all ranges, 1985.
**Average income for all ranges, 1986.
Source: As for table 2.2. Income ranges (1)–(9) are identical to those in table 2.2.

frequency distribution of income between age groups. The same technique could be applied to other interesting social categories such as race, sex or geographical location.

The apparently simple matter of presentation evidently raises a number of demanding theoretical and empirical issues in its own right. But we should perhaps heed the words attributed to Lord Rutherford: 'there are two sorts of science – there is physics and there is stamp collecting'. Although a clear grasp of the scope and the limitations of the available facts about inequality are of central importance to any enquiry, careful presentation and statistical analysis of them by itself may not amount to much more than 'stamp collecting'. The data and their analysis constitute only a few of the steps in providing the answers to the questions which concern us. Let us proceed to the next step.

2.4 Theories and models of income distribution

It is usually not too hard to answer the question of why we might want an economic theory of income distribution – presumably we would like an understanding of the economic processes involved that goes beyond straightforward description. But, what might such an economic theory actually do? That is perhaps not so easily decided, and a number of answers might be suggested:

(a) The theory might explain why certain phenomena would logically follow from certain assumptions about the state of the world under consideration and the way that world works.
(b) It might enable us to infer from observed phenomena the way that world actually works.
(c) On the basis of current and past observations it might enable us to forecast what the income distribution will look like.
(d) It may permit the simulation of the effects of proposed changes in policies.
(e) It may influence support or opposition to such changes in policies.

Let us run through these possibilities in reverse order. Possibility (e) is all too often neglected in serious discussion of economic theories. We think it to be so important that we shall devote an entire section of this chapter to it (section 2.6), and we return to the issue in chapter 12. Evidently (d) and (c) are rather undemanding in their *a priori* restrictions on the type of economic theory that may be admissible. Quite crude mechanical models may serve to illustrate the effects of implementing particular proposed policies, since a reasonably clear picture of the end result might be attainable without a detailed understanding of the economic processes and intermediate steps leading to these results. Moreover, the criterion of suitability of a theoretical framework as a forecasting device may turn on the detail of the statistical specification of the particular model derived from the theory rather than on fundamental issues concerning the theory itself. Many candidates for a theory of income distribution could conceivably fit the requirements of (c) or (d).

By contrast (b) is extremely restrictive. It implies that concealed somewhere in the jungle of economic data there is 'the' unique explanation of the distribution of income – a Lake Victoria lying in wait for explorers from the Royal Geographical Society in quest of the Source of the Nile. Anyone who undertakes a theoretical analysis of income distribution with this view in mind is likely to be disappointed. The most thoroughgoing socialist state and the most unrestrained capitalist economy, along with traditional forms of society, constitute a complex of systems that determine economic rewards, and it is unlikely that a single, intelligible economic theory can simplify or synthesise them all.

Hence answer (a) appears to be particularly intriguing; but we need to be cautious in interpreting it. It may be conceivable to assemble a comprehensive economic theory which would be sufficiently general to incorporate the complex of separate economic influences and their interplay, and which would yield a picture of the world that satisfactorily approximates what is actually observed. But such a theory would involve attributing in precise detail the role of each such influence.

In practice this may mean that a unified theory is just too unwieldy to be represented by a single model. If so, then one possible stratagem is to absorb some of the mass of detail into a simplified version of a 'black box': using this approach, economic processes which could be satisfactorily described in isolation are subsumed into a few well-chosen deterministic and stochastic variables.[16] The principal advantage of this is that it enables us to focus clearly on the process of change in a complex system rather than merely relying on comparison of equilibrium states or on verbal description of the adjustment process. The principal difficulty, of course, lies in the choice of the few variables with which to analyse the process of change within the system.

A more practicable approach is to resort to using a number of theories of different types in order to deal with different questions or different aspects of the same economic process, again like Lord Rutherford who is reputed to have viewed light as particles and as waves on alternate days of the week. This is a natural step since quite different theories of inequality are likely to be applicable to the facts observed in economies which differ dramatically in their institutional structure and code of behaviour. So, for example, in dealing with developed market economies since the second world war one theory might be developed to answer questions concerning only the distribution of earnings, omitting all other forms of income; another might be mainly concerned with the division of gross national product amongst earnings, rents and profits; yet another might be concerned with the distribution between social classes or, instead, between ethnic groups. Moreover, it may be that for each group of questions more than one theory is suitable, so that we end up with a family of still 'credible' suitable theories from which we have eliminated those that have been discredited by the facts.[17] We pursue this line further in chapter 6.

Before adopting any of the ready-made theories relevant to economic inequality one should enquire what these theories take for granted as being fundamental ingredients of the economic system, namely exogenous factors which do not themselves have to be accounted for by the theory. These might be put into the following categories:

- Personal endowments, such as health, intelligence, skills, material and financial property.
- Types of motivation such as desire for status, the profit motive, delight in exercising skill, love of independence or religious principle.
- The 'rules of the game' including the legal system of property rights and contracts.
- The institutional framework, incorporating markets, credit facilities, the government.
- Social divisions such as a caste system.

Two cautionary remarks should be made. Firstly, for some types of enquiry, it is important to explain and predict changes in some of these ingredients and not to take them as fundamental and unchangeable: some of them may be seen as essential parts of the very pattern and process of distribution and inequality that we want to analyse and explain. Secondly, it is important to guard against one's own background and training prejudicing one's judgement as to the suitability of a particular set of ingredients. As an example take two contrasting views of an issue that we shall discuss further in chapter 3. Those who have been accustomed all their lives to the conditions of a highly competitive industrialised market economy may assume a steady social background: they easily forget that, although over the centuries there have been many examples of economic systems where the passport to living at a relatively high standard was the exercising of crude power and influence, supported by a code of customary behaviour, a major disaster or disturbance in available technology may eventually cause a major shift in the power structure and the pattern of economic inequality, despite the stabilising conservative influence of the more powerful classes. By contrast 'catastrophists' – those who are particularly interested in just such major disturbances to the pattern of economic inequality – tend to regard theories which take no account of the mechanism by which the power to alter the rules may be shifted from one ruling group to another as being naive. Yet 'uniformitarian' theories which ignore such shifts and assume a given set of rules and a fairly rigid social and power structure are obviously still of some practical interest: often long periods of calm do follow the upheavals which have resulted in major redistributions of income, wealth, social structure and political power.

Does this difference in stance matter when viewed in a wider context? Economists and policy makers in developed economies have developed theories – usually based on the market mechanism – that are still relevant to the large economic changes arising from upheavals such as natural disasters, war, new inventions or changes in political structure. However, whereas such theories do in many cases account fairly satisfactorily for conspicuous shifts and fluctuations in relative and absolute prices of various services, good and assets, they are usually less satisfactory in explaining the pattern and change of income distribution. How can this be so when so many incomes largely consist of earnings which may be regarded as the prices paid for particular types of services, and of dividends, rents and other profits, which may be regarded as the prices paid for the use or loan of various types of property? There are many possible answers to this question. One explanation is that the working of the market for labour is one for which the orthodox theories of the working of the price system account far less satisfactorily than for the working of commodity and goods markets. In particular, the effects of custom and tradition in preserving relative levels of wages and of salaries in various occupations are stronger than in the case of the relative prices of goods. Another reason is that the influence of uncertainty and speculation is particularly strong in those markets on whose performance the distribution of incomes from profits depends. Although at a general level we may theorise at length about the effects of uncertainty and unforeseen events on markets, such theorising is often not particularly helpful in accounting for actual market behaviour and may be of little use in predicting market behaviour in the absence of detailed knowledge of particular markets.

As we discuss in chapter 6,[18] the problems of ignorance and uncertainty raise difficulties for the explanation of the distribution of income purely in terms of a system of market clearing equilibrium prices of factors. It is only during long intervals of economic calm that the patterns of long-period equilibrium conditions can be approximated so that theories founded on the simplifying assumptions of 'perfect foresight' or 'rational expectations' can avoid being misleading. However, conditions of protracted economic calm are likely to result in these same theories predicting little change in relative prices, and although it may be satisfactory and reassuring it may not be very enlightening. In the case of the distribution of earnings, during such a period of economic calm, relative earnings levels for labour of different kinds would change little, and this type of prediction is well verified by observation. But this gives little grounds for relying on the same theories in times of rapid economic change and disturbance. It has been widely claimed that even then approximate stability in the pattern of relative earnings levels is still observed over lengthy periods covering major upheavals, and it is not clear that such stability would be predicted by orthodox price theory, nor, even if it were, that this would be for the right reasons.

So conventional economic models of market equilibrium will need to be supplemented by other theoretical equipment, which we discuss in detail in chapters 6–11. Some of this equipment may incorporate influences that would normally be deemed to lie outside an economic model. This is hardly surprising since we nearly always have the problem of where to draw the borderline between purely economic forces, and socially or politically determined forces. One simple example can be found in the analysis of the distribution of real income per person. This is determined partly within the labour market and partly within the family. So, are both earnings and family size to be taken as determined entirely through rational economic choice, guided by market forces? Or is one determined by market forces and the other by social custom? Or are both influenced by social custom? At least three different economic models could be constructed, each of which draws a different borderline, and which of these should be used will not be clear until we know the use to which the model is to be put. Furthermore, those issues which are ruled outside the borderline cannot always be safely taken as immutable: the political and social effects of some economic event may eventually have further economic effects themselves. One of the most problematic examples of this is discussed in the next section.

2.5 Opinions and attitudes

If the process of generating and modifying inequality is to be understood we cannot ignore the climate of opinion regarding inequality. The reason for this lies in the behaviour of interest groups within the community: whenever the pattern of distribution begins to change markedly there are bound to be aggrieved groups who will take steps to resist the change. The effectiveness of such resistance is likely to depend on the attitude of the most influential sections of society towards inequality and towards changes in its pattern. To ignore this issue is to render policy evaluation misleading or meaningless.

When the role of attitudes and opinions is allowed for in a study of economic inequality, a fundamental problem arises, which we shall refer to as the PLUM principle: 'People Like Us Matter'. Any group in contemplating and giving its opinions on inequality is likely to underestimate the economic contributions and the sufferings of groups unlike their own, and to pay exaggerated respect to ethical precepts whose widespread observance would support the type of person with whom they themselves mix.[19] Economists and policy makers presumably exhibit the same human tendency.

For the purposes of policy making in general, and for this book in particular, we would like the answer to two essential questions.

• Out of any given national 'cake', which of the distributions are regarded as particularly unequal? On considering the complex of possible distributions amongst many income receiving classes – not just 'rich' and 'poor' – even the ranking of these distributions in some order of 'degree of inequality' is far from self-evident.

• Given such an inequality ranking of distributions for a wide range of total incomes, how much of present total income would we be prepared to have sacrificed for the sake of a specified reduction of inequality from its present level? What other sacrifices would be approved in order to achieve that specified reduction in inequality?

We go into the significance of these questions more fully in chapters 4 and 5, but the astute reader will have noticed a further underlying issue. It is quite likely that the answers to each question will differ radically according to the position of the respondent in the social pecking order. Can such disparate views be reconciled with a single coherent set of objectives for society? If so, how? Either we must adopt a detailed (and rather arrogant) Olympian attitude ignoring conflicts of opinion and imposing our view of correct balanced judgement, or we must assume the existence of a political system in the background that does indeed organise such opinions into consistent social criteria, or we must accept that our own views about the inequality ranking and the inequality/aggregate income trade-off have no more status than any other purely personal viewpoint.

So, before passing on to the next section on the evaluation of policies, it is important to bear in mind that little progress can be made in the analysis of economic policy towards inequality without a clear agreement of what is to be meant by increases and decreases in inequality and at what rate other things are worth giving up to reduce inequality. It is not to be expected that our own views will coincide with 'society's' (the fallacy of the PLUM principle), or that there exists such a thing as a coherent viewpoint of society on these issues at all. Moreover, the attitudes adopted towards inequality by the most influential groups in society will inevitably exert a substantial influence upon the prospects for success or failure of policies to modify income distribution.

2.6 Evaluation of policies

An interest in the way that the distribution of income, economic inequality and changes in them are brought about may be founded on no more than mere curiosity about the economic environment. But for many it arises from strong feelings that the present pattern of relative living standards is highly unsatisfactory and that something practical should certainly be done to improve it; such persons will wish to apply what they can learn about the mechanisms generating economic inequality and changes to it to be better able to compare the merits of alternative policy proposals for regulating it. What is involved in taking this further step?

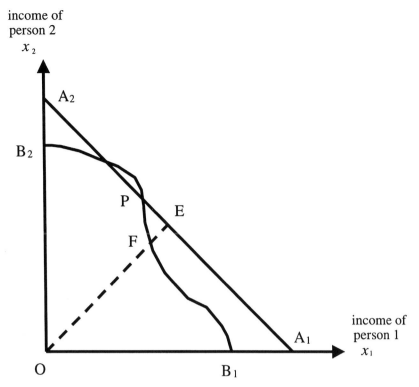

Figure 2.5 Types of income transfer

Most economic policy analysis involves some sort of projection or forecast and it is important to be clear about precisely what we are doing in making such a projection. To do this we must specify the range of policy instruments (taxes, transfers and the like) that are presumed to be available, the way in which they are presumed to operate and the response, if any, that the income generating process is presumed to provide to ensure that the policy instruments are applied. The last, extremely important, assumption can be illustrated by an example using the two-person[20] economy illustrated in figure 2.5, where point P represents a state of the world in which person 2 is rather rich, and person 1 is poor and where people's utility is identical to their incomes. The distance OA_1 (which equals OA_2) represents total income. It is tempting to imagine income redistribution policies that would shift the state of the world along the straight line A_1A_2 in the direction of E – a simple Robin Hood procedure of taking from 2, the rich, and giving to 1, the poor, making no charge for this service. This operation – known as a lump-sum transfer – may be feasible as a practical policy measure, yet it is hard to think of many specific realistic examples. However, imagining hypothetical states along the line A_1A_2 may be helpful for making notional inequality comparisons: this is a device that we shall use extensively in chapters 4 and 5. Clearly the distribution represented by the point P is unequal – how unequal it is may be gauged by reference to E, the notional point of perfect equality of distribution the income total of the two.

However, as we have noted, in a many-person economy measures taken to redistribute income will be resisted by some groups. So when the available policy instruments are applied and the feedback from the income generating processes are allowed for, we may actually find that the best that can be done for two particular persons within it is represented by a frontier such as B_1FPB_2. If we press ahead to consider perfect equality between them, then we may end up not at point E but, say, at point F, with a significant loss of their aggregate income. It might still be argued that points on this frontier at least have a (weakly) desirable property in that they are Pareto efficient – they correspond to states of the economy, and in particular of the two persons 1 and 2, in which it is impossible to increase the income of one of them without reducing the income of the other.[21] Yet in practice it is usually difficult to determine whether the current state of the economy corresponds to a point that is on or inside the frontier; it may even be that there is no well-defined continuous frontier such as B_1FPB_2, but rather a discrete set of points representing a discrete set of options facing the policy maker similar to the case represented in figure 1.5.[22] If so, no point F on the diagonal OE may be available for the two persons even in this simple case.

This exercise reveals two awkward points. Firstly, the desirability of practical moves towards greater equality cannot usually be determined without prior consideration of the sacrifice of overall income which one is prepared to tolerate to secure a particular reduction in inequality. Though many might agree that E is fairer than P – and perhaps that it is more desirable – will F likewise be more approved than P? As we have suggested, this issue becomes even more complicated when the argument is adapted to a many-person economy. Secondly, a heavy burden is thrown back on the model of the income-generating process in order to derive the frontier of possible points B_1FPB_2: without such a model it is difficult to apply the concept of Pareto efficiency to a many-person economy.

Now it might seem to be a straightforward matter to try out the effects of alternative policies within the framework of a theoretical model with all its simplifying assumptions, but there are some major difficulties. The first is that, if a model is to have a useful degree of generality, the numerical values of its parameters cannot be satisfactorily estimated by armchair meditation, but rather by arduous surveys gathering information over a lengthy period followed by the application of statistical techniques which may need to be fairly sophisticated if they are to yield also an adequate indication of the margins of error of the estimates. What is worse, use of sophisticated techniques cannot guard against the possibility that some unsuspected cause may result in a sudden shift in some of the parameters now built into the model and this may prevent the model from providing reasonable forecasts of the likely effects of particular policies. A further difficulty is that from a pint pot of observations we cannot hope to obtain decent estimates of all the parameters in a quart-sized model. So we have to be content with a model employing only a few parameters and resting on some sweeping simplifying assumptions about the irrelevance of a number of economic conditions to many economic variables and on some hopefully inspired guesswork about the values of supposedly uncritical parameters. Alternatively, we might repeat tests for a whole array of alternative sets of parameter values in order to test whether certain parameters are indeed of minor importance in investigating the effects of alternative policies. But the second difficulty remains that a model sufficiently simple to be practically workable will still have to be based on many assumptions known to be false and on ignoring a great many supposedly minor effects and time-lags.[23] So the selection of what to assume as a basis of simplifying assumptions for the model is itself bound to be partly intuitive, and is likely to be subject to preconceptions reflecting a person's cultural and social background.

The danger that these preconceptions may influence the judgements drawn from the chosen model may be lessened by awareness of these tendencies but hardly eliminated. That is one of the main reasons why it is so valuable to give thought to the topic touched on in section 2.5 concerning the influences which one's cultural and social background exert on one's views about economic inequality and income distribution.

2.7 Summary

Systematic study of economic inequality involves the following stages: facts, choices, theories, policies. Each of these steps has its own pitfalls and we hope that readers have heeded our warnings about not expecting to find a ready-made choice of data, economic theories or social criteria that are entirely suitable. The remainder of the book is organised roughly so as to follow these steps: chapters 4 and 5 deal with the complex problem of using the raw data to give a clear picture of inequality; chapters 6–11 consider various theories for explaining the observed income distributions and other indicators of economic inequality and their changes; and chapter 12 discusses choices of policy about economic inequality.

However, although we have argued that economic data and economic theory should be thoroughly studied before choices and policies are advocated, we have also pointed out the pitfall of the PLUM principle: that a person's predisposition about choices and policies may already influence his selection and interpretation of facts and theories. With this in mind, we shall in chapter 3 pay particular attention to the way various historical social backgrounds have coloured thinking about economic inequality and income distribution.

2.8 Questions for discussion

General Reading: Broome (1991), Cowell (1995), Lambert (1993), Sen (1973, 1987a, 1992).

2.1   Discuss the criteria that should be applied in drawing a sample of the population suitable for an enquiry into income distribution and the information you would wish to gather from members of the sample. How might the problem of misleading or incomplete responses be handled – see Kemsley *et al.* (1980)?

2.2   Using either *Inland Revenue Statistics* (UK: Board of Inland Revenue) or *Statistics of Income* (USA: Internal Revenue Service) discuss the limitations of data collected by tax authorities to analyse personal income inequality.

2.3   Consider the problems of representing the information in figures 1.3 and 1.4 in terms of (a) a Lorenz curve, (b) a Pareto diagram.

2.4   Sen (1980) has argued that truth is neither a necessary nor a sufficient condition for a description of an economic phenomenon to be good. Evaluate this assertion with reference to the construction of an economic theory of income distribution.

2.5   Consider possible methods of lump-sum redistribution of wealth or of income. What objections might there be to the implementation of such measures?

2.6   Attempts have been made to define a concept of 'fairness' in a manner similar to that of Pareto efficiency – see pages 41–2 and note 21. An allocation of goods and services amongst persons is said to be 'fair' if no one person would prefer to have the bundle of goods and services that another receives in the allocation. (a) Discuss the relationship of this criterion to that of efficiency. (b) Imagine an economic state in which everyone has the same money income, the same access to markets and perfect information, but where people differ in needs and tastes. Will the resulting allocation be fair? Do you think it to be just (see Baumol, 1986; Hochschild, 1981; Phelps, 1988; Varian, 1974, 1976)?

2.7   (a) A mother has a supply of indistinguishable edible lumps to apportion between identical twins: what further information you would wish to be told before considering how she should do so? Would you expect the same principles to apply to animals and birds?

(b) Why might it be meaningless to speak of 'society's view of inequality' (cf. Solo and Anderson, 1981)?

(c) How might the attitudes of individuals and groups towards inequality be determined (Amiel and Cowell, 1992; Glejser *et al.*, 1977)?

(d) How might attitudes towards income inequality depend on levels of economic development (Amiel and Cowell, 1994a; Hirschman and Rothschild, 1973; Temkin, 1986)?

2.8   Consider the problems that may arise (a) in constructing a general index of economic well being (Beckerman, 1978; Blinder, 1980; Moon and Smolensky, 1977) and (b) in constructing data that permit comparison of income distributions between countries (van Ginneken 1982; Stoikov, 1975; Wiles, 1979).

2.9   Discuss the possibilities of there being income inequality within the same family or household, and how it could be statistically demonstrated.

2.10   The data in table 2.5 show how the relative incomes of the ten slices of the income queue have changed during the 1970s and 1980s. Each 'person' in the queue is in fact a household, and the income received by that household has not been adjusted to allow for the composition of the household. (a) Compare the picture of inequality in 1986 revealed by the above data with that revealed by the Inland Revenue data in figure 2.1. (Hint: use the summary of these latter data presented in note 8.) (b) Did all ten groups benefit from income growth during the period 1971–86? (c) Sketch the corresponding Lorenz curves: do they reveal a consistent picture of rising inequality during the 1980s (see Coulter *et al.* (1994), and question 4.9 of chapter 4)?

2.11   Suppose that individual utility is not proportional to income. (a) How would the frontier in figure 2.5 be altered? (b) In what ways would the Pareto principle (defined in note 21) then differ from the monotonicity principle defined on page 000 of chapter 5 (see Amiel and Cowell, 1994b)?

2.12   It has been suggested by economists that a coherent social view of income distribution could be arrived at either by considering the comparison of income distributions in the same way as a risk-averse person would compare lotteries or by considering

Table 2.5 *Mean income of ten decile groups as a percentage of overall mean income: disposable income per household*

Slice number	1971	1976	1981	1986
1 (poorest)	25	28	28	27
2	39	42	40	39
3	54	55	52	50
4	70	70	66	62
5	84	84	81	76
6	97	98	95	92
7	112	112	111	110
8	129	130	131	130
9	154	154	158	161
10 (richest)	236	228	239	254
Overall mean (£ p.a.)	7,996	8,186	9,040	9,748

Source: Family Expenditure Survey, UK.

the income distribution as a type of 'externality'. Examine the view that these alternative approaches may also suffer from the shortcomings of the PLUM principle (Harsanyi, 1955; Hochman and Rodgers, 1969; Thurow, 1971).

Notes

1 In this book we do make extensive use of such data for the USA: see table 2.3 below, and the description in appendix A.

2 See chapter 4, section 4.5.

3 The underlying frequency distribution is usually assumed to be a smooth curve rather than a jagged line as shown in the figure 2.1. Suppose that income x has a distribution in the population that can be approximated by a continuous function F: $F(x)$ is the proportion of the population with an income less than or equal to x. $F(a+\delta)-F(a)$ is the relative frequency of the population that falls in a particular income interval $[a,a+\delta)]$ (the income range containing people with incomes of a or more but with less than $a+\delta$ (dollars or pounds). If F is differentiable then the limit of $[F(a+\delta)-F(a)]/\delta$ as $\delta \rightarrow 0$, namely $dF(x)/dx$, is the *density* function of x, written $f(x)$.

4 A slightly more useful statistic is found by dividing the standard deviation by the mean so as to yield the *coefficient of variation* (see chapter 4, p. 000) which gives a feel for the disparity in the inequality exhibited by the two curves: its value of κ before tax is 1.1326; after tax it is 0.3427.

5 Some of the standard skewness statistics have unattractive properties as criteria for inequality comparisons – see question 5.19 in chapter 5.

6 Coarse grouping can also introduce substantial error to any summary measure of inequality. The standard deviation is especially sensitive to the choice of income intervals at the top end of the distribution. Most of the inequality measures discussed in chapter 5 are highly sensitive to grouping carried out at the bottom of the distribution: see Cowell and Mehta (1982).

7 The formal relationship with the frequency distribution is as follows. Let income be distributed according to a distribution function F as in note 3: mean income μ is given by $\int x \, dF(x)$ where the integration is performed over the entire range of x; and the proportion of total income received by those who have an income no greater than x is given by $G(x) = [\int^x \chi \, dF(\chi)]/\mu$. The Lorenz curve is then the graph of G plotted against F. The slope of the Lorenz curve at any point is x/μ. Similar results are available in the important, but less tractable, case where F is not everywhere differentiable: see Gastwirth (1971). The Lorenz curve has an important connection with the subject matter of chapter 5: see page 000 below. For further details on this and other presentational devices see Cowell (1995).

8 The principal coordinates of the points in figure 2.3 are:

Population	Income share	
proportion	Before tax	After tax
0.100	0.028	0.033
0.200	0.065	0.076
0.300	0.112	0.129
0.400	0.172	0.194
0.500	0.242	0.268
0.600	0.328	0.356
0.700	0.430	0.461
0.750	0.489	0.516
0.800	0.548	0.585
0.900	0.708	0.733

9 For a formal definition see table 5.1 in chapter 5 below.

10 If least squares were used to fit a straight line to the top six observations of the before-tax data in table 1.1 plotted on the Pareto diagram this would yield a value of $\alpha = 2.358$ – in other words an a/b ratio of about 1.7 (calculated as 2.358/1.358). When we come to examine *wealth* distributions in chapter 9 onwards we shall find much higher values of a/b inequality (*lower* values of α).

11 Notice that the one main difference of presentation between this and table 1.1 is that the last column depicts *average* income in the range (total income in the range)/(number of families in the range).

12 In some cases a person other than the family head was interviewed. Panel studies are inevitably complicated because of the very characteristic that makes them so interesting: the repeated interviewing of subjects. The PSID is especially complicated because it is a panel of *families* rather than of individuals – see appendix A.

13 As an illustration of these problems, consider the fact that these data refer to total family income, and that the income receivers are families. Table 2.2 would have looked quite different if family income had been converted to income per person (somehow defined). Furthermore, the frequency distribution of income could also be radically altered in shape if a family of five were to count five times instead of only once. This type of problem will not go away with further data refinement. Moreover, this reasoning shows that whether families are counted as units or by the numbers in them will also affect cells and the summary columns and rows in the bivariate frequency distributions depicted in tables 2.3 and 2.4 below.

14 Labour income here refers to the sum of labour income of the family head and spouse; likewise for asset income. 'Transfer income' refers to transfers received by the head and spouse,

and *all* the income received by other family members (for other family members there is no breakdown into labour income and asset income).

15 For each row the entry in the last but one column must be the sum of the corresponding entries in columns 1–9; likewise, for each column, the entry in the last but one row must be the sum of the corresponding entries in rows 1–9; readers are invited to check that this is so.

16 We shall examine a particular variant of the latter, the stochastic process approach, in chapter 11. Other 'black box' models are discussed in chapter 10.

17 Some care must obviously be exercised here since some theories can be continued to be sufficiently flexible to be consistent with any facts: an application of the first corollary to Murphy's Law. Murphy's Law, it will be recalled, states: 'Bread never falls buttered side up (BSU)'. The standard empirical test is to hold buttered slices of bread one metre from the floor and release them. If it appears that the experiment freakishly results in the slices falling BSU, the first corollary states: 'Under such circumstances you have probably buttered it on the wrong side.'

18 See section 6.5 below.

19 See in particular the excellent discussion by Pen (1974), chapter 9 in this volume. One of the few attempts at a systematic qualitative analysis of such attitudes is Glejser *et al.* (1977).

20 The assumption of two persons is purely one of convenience. The arguments presented here are valid for as many individuals as you like (and as many dimensions as you can visualise).

21 Strictly speaking, such points would only be regarded as Pareto efficient if incomes correspond to utilities, in that they give a very detailed description of how well off the people are in terms of the goods and services that they can afford. A 'state' of the economy – as described by a catalogue of the bundles of goods and services enjoyed by each person – is said to be Pareto efficient if there is no other feasible state which Pareto dominates it, i.e., no other state in which at least one person would have higher utility and no one would have lower utility.

22 See page 00 above.

23 It is often the case that supposedly minor influences are those that are just too difficult to estimate with sufficient accuracy.

3   Inequality and history

3.1 Introduction

Economic research on inequality often seems to focus on very narrow and localised issues: What accounts for the structure of earnings of qualified engineers? How much has the pattern of wealth ownership been affected by capital taxes? Who benefits from income support provisions? However, economists working in this area also try to address large-scale issues: large scale in terms of the problems of collecting and interpreting data, and in terms of the principles by which contrasting patterns of economic inequality are appraised. For example, the hypothesis that economic development invariably involves a phase of rising inequality or the comparison of economic policies towards income distribution in developed and underdeveloped countries, each raises questions on a manifestly greater scale than are those of the minutiae of the structure of earnings or wealth ownership. When addressing such large-scale empirical and ethical problems it is prudent to consider the context within which comparisons of economic inequality will be made.

This warning applies both to contemporary investigations that span very dissimilar cultures and to those that take in what has happened over long periods. Indeed these two aspects raise rather similar problems: of comparability of data, of differences in economic and social organisation – 'the past is a foreign country, they do things differently there'.

It is not just the facts and the meaning of facts that should be examined in context: the ideas and values by which the facts are interpreted are important too. How the world is and how people perceive it are both shaped by its history. To overlook this in a study of economic inequality would risk misunderstanding the meaning and origins of inequality. The way we go about quantifying and analysing inequality largely depends on our preconceived ideas about justice and the improvement of society, just as the current nature and degree of inequality are due to the history of past economic development.

For reasons such as this we have called this chapter *Inequality and history*. Although we have not attempted to provide a general history of economic inequality (if such a task were possible), we use historical examples to give substance to our discussion: we refer to the available information on the facts and attitudes about inequality in earlier centuries so as to assist in understanding what is meant when we make comparisons of inequality today. We examine how the modern analysis of income distribution has been shaped by historical circumstance and how limited is its applicability to societies with quite different backgrounds and economic systems; we consider how past outlooks have influenced current attitudes towards personal contrasts in living standards.

This approach is relevant not only to sensible interpretation of the evidence about trends in income inequality: it also assists our appreciation of the obstacles to making any useful comparisons of the degree of inequality within one nation with that in another nation whose level of development or whose political and social framework is very different.

3.2 The economic mechanism

Comparing communities in terms of inequality should not be performed in a vacuum: the study of the income distribution and related issues cannot ultimately be divorced from the historical development of the social and economic system. The most obvious reason for this is that this historical development has shaped the economic system of today. Another is that knowledge about the historical development is a valuable guide in choosing policy measures to modify economic inequality.

As an example of this, take the question of what the effective constraints on income redistribution might be: setting aside impractical theoretical constructs such as the lump-sum transfers mentioned in chapter 2 it is clear that answers to this question will be influenced by some theory of income distribution, and that whether the theory is appropriate will depend on the context within which the question is posed. For instance, the classical theory of the level and distribution of a nation's income focused on a tri-partite division of income into wages, profits and rents, but the relevance to practical policy of even this simple subdivision depends on the possibility of distinguishing clearly the three types of income – and the corresponding three types of income recipient – in the nation where economic inequality is under discussion. In Britain in the early nineteenth century it may in principle have been fairly easy to recognise and distinguish the three classes of wage earners, capitalists and landowners and to compare the income levels and economic and social life styles of the three types. But in other parts of the world, in other centuries, and in nations with different types of social organisation, the unambiguous recognition and distinction of the three types are often practically impossible.

Similarly, whatever particular theory of the determination and development of income distribution and economic inequality we might examine, we can only apply the standard tools of that theory if it is first established that certain basic characteristics of the national economy are consistent with the framework of that particular theory. In particular we have to accept some particular account of the nature of the economic mechanism by which resources are allocated and goods and services distributed among the population.

Economists often describe the mechanism in terms of the operation of market forces, and some readers will be content to accept this account as appropriate to the study of income distribution in most countries at most times. However, there are obviously examples of economies today and in the past for which such an account of the mechanism would be of only limited relevance. Whether it is relevant depends on how extensive the market actually is; on whether we are dealing with a well-integrated nation-state or with the type of federated system of semi-isolated markets that characterised medieval Europe; on whether we are dealing with a purely capitalist economy or a mixed economy with substantial intervention by authorities who give higher priority to profit. Where the market mechanism has only limited applicability we should examine what other economic mechanisms determine the pattern and hierarchy of living standards. In addition to the fascinating examples to be drawn from traditional and feudal societies in earlier centuries, there are many modern instances of such alternative mechanisms: the hierarchy of planning committees in the former Soviet Union and the various nationalised boards and public sector bodies found in many other countries in modern times. The warning about the limitations of the market mechanism applies also to the distribution of income between countries: theories which treat national economies as competing freely, subject only to the control of their own authorities, and which attribute the international distribution as the outcome of an economic game with price-taking agents as participants may be less appropriate in the face of the growing political importance of transnational corporations. So the usefulness of distribution theories which assume the predominant influence of free market forces is limited to particular societies at a particular stage of development. Since free market theories are relevant to some important and interesting cases, such as the present and recent past of the USA, and since they have been developed more elaborately and publicised more energetically than others, they are likely to be the most easily accessible and digestible by many readers; so we shall devote considerable attention to them in this book.

Nevertheless the important boundaries to the usefulness of such theories in explaining the actual course of events or the scope for reform should be constantly borne in mind. The location of these boundaries will be influenced by such features of economic organisation as the extent to which money is used, and the extent of social and political administrative control: some distributional changes that would only have been feasible in a feudal society by means of civil war or revolt may come within the range of practical planning in an economy which has a well-developed fiscal system and a common monetary standard. The scope for using the market or other mechanisms to modify economic inequality may be much greater in modern industrialised societies than in previous ones, although even here the pace of such change may be drastically limited by the inclination and power to obstruct of those who will lose by the change.

3.3 The social order

It is not only the economic structure and the scope for redistribution that differ as between traditional and industrial societies, the 'rules of the game' that we mentioned in chapter 2 differ as well and these rules significantly affect judgements about inequality.

Study of the underlying social order can help us identify the questions which are most relevant when seeking to explain distribution and inequality. What does private property include? Which social distinctions confer most economic power? What prospects are there for effective egalitarian policies so long as the social and economic framework remains unchanged? Thinking along these lines may help us to understand what policy objectives are likely to attract wide support in campaigns to secure modifications to economic inequality. Study of the social order should also throw light on the actual processes by which incomes are created and distributed, and on the factual information needed for a significant comparison of inequality between societies.

Changes in the social order affect the type of questions that may usefully be asked about the distribution of the economic prizes within the system, as even a superficial historical enquiry will confirm. The shifts in technology and in administration that take place during the conquest or rapid development of a region cannot be ignored if we are to understand changes in the 'rules of the game' governing economic organisation and the distribution of the prizes. Moreover, it is not only the facts about the system of production and of distribution that alter, but also the view of the social order and the values by which it is widely judged: the range of these views and values may be very wide.

In most comparative studies covering only a brief period of recent history within one economy, some of the deeper questions about the scope of property rights or of other legal rights may naturally be assumed to be of only subordinate interest. In such a brief period the 'uniformitarian'[1] view may be quite appropriate: we might reasonably suppose that during the period there are no overwhelming changes in the social order – such as the introduction or abolition of mass slavery – that could render conventional comparisons of degrees of economic inequality misleading or practically meaningless. For example, provided that we are careful about data definitions, there need be little trouble in comparing income inequality amongst the families covered by table 2.1 with that amongst the same families five years earlier. More caution would be required in examining income inequality in the USA or the UK at the present day in contrast to what it had been in either country five decades earlier. But could we hope to make a simple comparison with the degree of inequality five *centuries* earlier, or even between the degrees of inequality in two economies which were of the type that then existed?

The question seems bizarre because we obviously do not have nearly enough quantitative information about income and standards of living in those earlier societies (although, as we shall see in section 3.4 below, a surprising amount of information is available in some cases). However, even if suitable data were available, perhaps discovered amongst the miraculously preserved records of some ancestral statistician, important issues would still remain. To illustrate this let us take the question seriously and briefly consider the nature of economic inequality in the societies that were then found within the present frontiers of the USA and of the UK.

In English medieval society inequalities were both organised and widely accepted: the functioning of the social system largely depended on the preservation through patronage and inheritance of powerful privileges and responsibilities; and the prevailing moral ethic of people of all ranks (the religion of Christendom) endorsed acceptance of the hierarchy of disparate rôles as being part of a natural order. It is interesting to compare the principal economic bulwark of inequality then – partly social custom and partly legal distinction between classes of individual – with that of today – the unequal ownership of income-yielding assets – and to note the changes in the notion of property ownership and control. In some respects the underlying inequality of social and economic power was much greater then: the pre-industrial medieval lord had much wider powers in his right to tie workers to the land, his control over appointments and through other forms of patronage. Yet there were also features of social organisation that mitigated some of the inequality-generating forces active today: there were laws to prevent merchants from exploiting their customers; usury was forbidden; land nominally owned by the king might effectively be held in common by the ordinary people.

Across the Atlantic the Native Americans organised things very differently. The most striking contrast concerned the nation itself: some were formed into a cohesive state, for example, the Aztecs, others into groups no larger than extended families, and yet others into a variety of intermediate-sized groupings. Here, too, a simplified form of market connected widely dispersed communities, and here too the ownership and distribution of property are seen to have been central to the machinery of social organisation. But property could include slaves, and the ownership of property might involve a kind of trusteeship on behalf of the family or tribe rather than the right of exclusive enjoyment and disposal of it. Again, it was not necessarily the acquisition of property through inheritance or economic enterprise that was the hallmark of power within the community.[2] The society was characterised neither by the crude inegalitarianism of much of the animal kingdom, nor by the materialistic competitiveness of the capitalist economies, nor yet by the disinterested humanitarian concern professed by advocates of a comprehensive welfare state.

These two examples of economic organisation in societies different from our own illustrate how difficult it must be to make comparisons between the degrees of inequality in communities widely separate in time, outlook or background: the interpretation of such comparisons is likely to present even greater difficulties. When in many 'pre-market' economies social, legal and economic inequalities form part of a system for organisation and control upon which persons at all social levels have grown to depend, it is hard to determine whether society is becoming less or more unequal if there are shifts in the distributions of income and wealth. Not only is the coverage of income and wealth data incomplete, but they may not give much idea about many people's economic status. Broader criteria of the standard of living are likely to be crude – for example, we might have to be content with the proportion of the population that existed above some specified subsistence level of consumption.

Indeed, concern about mere income inequality may be of relatively minor importance in societies marked by glaring economic and social inequalities of a more fundamental kind. There will be those who claim that the type of inequality affecting the rights of special groups (the status of the old, the young, the disabled, racial minorities . . .) is particularly objectionable, but the relative degree of urgency of such claims is not the main issue. A much more important point is that our assessment of relative degrees of inequality of living standards may be much affected by other characteristic features of the social order in the contrasted economies. One of the most apparent of these features is the degree of force implicit in the working arrangements by which income is created and distributed. The tying of workers to the land, as under the feudal system, can evidently distort any comparisons that we might make between degrees of inequality in agricultural living standards in two economies. To take a yet more extreme example, even if we had comprehensive data about the material living standards of

Native American tribes, any study of the extent of inequality could be worthless unless it took into account the extent of slavery amongst them.

It is not only the inequality comparisons between economies at widely different dates that is so complicated by the issue of slavery and other such forms of suppression exerted for social control, inequality comparisons within a society remote from our own are also made difficult. For example, in assessing the standard of living and the economic inequality of an economy making use of an enslaved class, how much weight should we give to the degree of poverty and the extent of inequality within the enslaved class?

The issue of slavery is but one example of the great importance of the nature of property rights. These rights affect personal and family consumption in many ways. Apart from the obvious point that the man of property can afford more consumption we find that the extent of property rights can affect living standards indirectly, and may involve more fundamental aspects of inequality peripheral to the scope of this book. For example, wherever property is held in common for all to use, whether among the Native American, or in the pre-industrial English countryside, or in the modern welfare state, this may be an effective agent in reducing inequality. Again, the fact that in some cases the nominal ownership of property is a misleading guide to its effective ownership means that the benefits in consumption that the rich enjoy from it may be less or more than the raw data of such ownership suggest: under certain types of social order the privileges conferred by the ownership of such assets are partly offset by onerous responsibilities.

Addressing such issues can provide lessons which should be borne in mind when making general comparisons of the facts about inequality today and in considering the costs of carrying out any specific redistribution. To compare dissimilar societies we must pay careful attention to the extent of and the power derived from personal property rights, and the degree of compulsion implicit in work arrangements. These observations apply not only to comparisons across a gulf of time, but also to comparisons of different economic states within a particular system that is significantly unlike the one to which we are accustomed, and to comparisons of economies today that exhibit marked differences in their social orders. Moreover, they can give us some guide as to the horizon within which specific comparisons of economic inequality may usefully be made.

3.4 Some examples

Let us turn to the patchy long-range evidence from which economists have sought to draw conclusions about economic inequality. Some of the practical limitations involved in making comparisons of inequality are evident when we address questions such as these:
- Does the statistical evidence indicate that the world of today has a more unequal income distribution than in past eras?
- Does the process of development from pre-industrial to industrialised society have a recognisable impact on inequality?
- How do changes in inequality in response to economic and social events today compare with changes in earlier times?

The first two questions have received a lot of attention by economic historians and development economists. For specific countries and specific features of economic inequality it is often possible to say a great deal. For example, take Williamson and Lindert's (1980a) investigation of wealth inequality in the United States since the eighteenth century:

[There are] apparently episodic shifts in wealth concentration at two points in American history: (1) the marked rise in wealth concentration in the first half of the nineteenth century following what appears to have been two centuries of long-term stability; (2) the pronounced decline in wealth concentration in the second quarter of the twentieth century following what appears to have been six decades of persistent and extensive inequality with no evidence of trend. Furthermore and contrary to the popular view, these episodic shifts in American wealth inequality were not merely the product of changes in the demographic mix.

Although wealth inequality by itself fails to capture several other aspects of economic inequality,[3] such a study has much intrinsic interest, since wealth data are perhaps more readily available and reliable than other indications over such an extensive period, and since the concept of wealth and its significance in the social order did not change drastically, with one major exception, noted below. So the principal findings are of importance to those studying present day economies in the process of development.[4]

Beyond the narrow objective of the analysis of one dimension of economic inequality in one society over comparatively recent periods there are grander issues such as the second and third questions. There are serious pitfalls in studying these – not that they have inhibited some from attempting such ambitious exercises. Naturally data relating to economic inequality in bygone eras are sparse and there is usually a lot more information about the rich than about those who were so poor that their incomes were not deemed to be worth recording. It is thus convenient to have a method of presenting the facts that makes good use of this patchy information. In table 3.1, which concerns income distribution, we use a simple concept that we introduced in chapter 2: the 'average to base' ratio a/b which characterises the Pareto distribution. Table 3.1 is adapted from the classic article on long-range British income inequality by Soltow (1968). Note the variety of sources from which the data have been assembled, and the variety of definition of income, of income receiver and of coverage of the population. On the basis of this collation Soltow concluded:

The argument is thus one that there was a continued widening of opportunity for non-propertied income groups. Statistical evidence indicates that income inequality, particularly in upper-income groups, has decreased for several centuries. This trend has been accelerated in the twentieth century.

British income inequality, like that in the USA, fell throughout the centuries. Obviously, as we have noted, there are problems of comparing data based on different concepts of income and income recipient: but it is unlikely that this alone would dramatically alter the conclusions.

The right-hand column of table 3.1 suggests that income inequality has declined from medieval times until the present, but this conclusion should be qualified. Firstly, whilst the conclusion is perhaps borne out for very long periods, it is less safe over short intervals during times of rapid change. Secondly, over long periods the change in inequality that is apparent from income data may well be insignificant compared with changes in economic inequality on a broader definition, were we able to observe it.

Table 3.1 *British income inequality*

	Year	Region	Coverage	Lower limit of lowest income class(£)	Per cent of total persons covered	*a/b* ratio
1	1436	England and Wales	7,184 men	5	1	6.944
2	1688	England and Wales	1,350,000 families and single persons	2	100	2.604
3	1801–3	England and Wales	2,210,000 families and single persons	10	100	2.564
4	1801	Great Britain	320,759 persons	65	15	5.181
5	1867	GB and Ireland	13,720,000 men women and children with income	15	100	3.650
6	1880	United Kingdom	14,770,000 with occupations and assessments	<160	100	4.386
7	1911–12	United Kingdom	12,399 assessed persons	5,000	0.1	2.299
8	1913–14	United Kingdom	13,231 assessed persons	5,000	0.1	2.299
9	1962–3	United Kingdom	22,242,000 married couples & single persons	180	100	2.012

Notes: Series 1 is estimated as incomes from land; series 2 is Gregory King's survey – see question 3.11; series 3 uses King's framework; series 4 to 9 are estimated from tax returns.
Source: Soltow (1968).

Thirdly, the changes in definition of region covered, the nature of the income recipient, the scope of the income, and the primary source of the data all require great care in any comparison. Fourthly, note that at best we can draw some inferences about what is happening at the very top of the income distribution. Particularly in recent years, a different picture might emerge if a wider income range were to be used.

We should be even more careful of some grander claims that may be based on very limited evidence. The other two examples are drawn from data that have, at various

Table 3.2 a/b *ratio for*
Augsburg, 1471–1526

Year	a/b ratio
1471	3.3
1498	3.1
1512	4.9
1526	8.7
(Germany 1913	2.8)
(Germany 1934	2.0)

Sources: Pareto (1964),
Clark (1950), Hartung
(1895).

Table 3.3 a/b *ratios in three societies*

	a/b ratio
Ancient Rome (28 BC)	3.0
Medieval England (1086)	2.7
Ante Bellum American Southern States (1850)	1.5

Source: Davis (1954).

times, been used to bolster ambitious general conjectures about the shape of the income distribution irrespective of time or place, namely that such distributions have roughly a Pareto shape and that there is a 'natural' range of values of Pareto's α (and so a 'natural' range of the *a/b* ratio) towards which income distributions inexorably tend – a proposition which is almost impossible to test. Each of the examples illustrates several pitfalls. Tables 3.2 and 3.3 illustrate the kind of material that has been used on occasion to draw long-range inferences about inequality; they immediately prompt a number of questions. Was medieval Augsburg really becoming extremely inegalitarian at the beginning of the sixteenth century? Was the American South more egalitarian than William I's England or Ancient Rome?

As we have already seen, the *a/b* statistic takes no account of low incomes, so that we have at best a partial picture: table 3.2 might reveal what was happening amongst the wealthy Bavarian merchants, but it remains silent on the trend in their position relative to the common people; nevertheless, it suggests economic and social change at a truly remarkable rate since the income ratio *a/b* almost trebled in a quarter century (purely by way of illustrating how dramatic this is, we have also reproduced the change in the German *a/b* ratio from Kaiser Wilhelm II to Adolf Hitler). Economic inequality probably was increasing in Augsburg,[5] but it is unlikely that these narrowly based figures in table 3.2 give a true picture: since they are based on the city's wealth tax it is unclear how much of the dramatic change in apparent inequality reflects real phenomena, and how much is due to spurious fiscal manoeuvring.

Table 3.3 presents an even harder puzzle. Taken at face value it suggests that the income distribution in pre-civil war Southern US was more equal than in Norman England, which was in turn more equal than in Ancient Rome. May such conclusions legitimately be drawn? Again there are important problems of the comparability of the data, not least of which is that income data have had to be inferred from information about some component of wealth: the income figures for medieval England were derived from an imputation based on holdings of land and other assets; but the imputation used for the income figures underlying the results for the American South is on the basis of a different asset, slaves (the *a/b* ratio covers the entire population of slaveowners with ten or more slaves). In this case it is hard to make sensible inequality comparisons even if we ignore the welfare of the slaves. Should we compare just the upper strata of society in eleventh-century England and nineteenth-century USA? If so, it is difficult to compare the property rights of the individuals concerned, since the relationship between nominal and effective ownership of income-bearing assets by the nobility in Norman England was sometimes unclear whilst Southern slaveowners had absolute rights of disposal and use of their assets. Should we compare inequality amongst freemen in each case? Again there are problems, because the line between bondage and freedom in medieval England was not clear-cut (nominally unfree villeins could often be much better off than free sokemen, and although in theory villeins had nothing with which to buy their freedom, in practice they often did buy it), and because the inequality comparison appears hollow if the welfare of the slaves themselves is simply ignored. Apart from the tremendous problem of weighing basic civil rights and freedoms against cash income, it is clear that inclusion of the economic welfare of all the people in each society might well reverse the simple inference of a fall in relative inequality that we may be tempted to draw from table 3.3.

Are long-range comparisons of inequality futile then? The above examples suggest that the answer depends on how long is 'long'. The permissible range gets less the more rapid technical and political change become. If the enquiry is restricted to one specific facet of inequality over a period in which the principal features of the social order are reasonably comparable, then sensible statements may be made about trends in inequality: beyond that horizon the danger is obvious, even if good data are available. Yet it is often tempting to make comparisons of economic inequality on a grand scale: for example, to contrast the levels of inequality worldwide within and between countries today. It might be judged that economies with social orders as different as Western Europe, North Korea and the old régime in South Africa are separated by horizons of comparability as effectively as are communities at widely different points in time. Moreover, when evidence on the relationship between inequality and the level of economic and social development is drawn from a cross section of such disparate communities, it merits more sceptical examination than that obtainable from one country with a more or less uniform social order over an extended time period. Finally, when very unlike situations are being contrasted – as in the exercise of table 3.3 – we have to accommodate not only widely differing data about inequality, but possibly also widely different views on how to interpret them. With this in mind we shall now turn to the rôle of history in shaping attitudes on this subject.

3.5 Inequality and social injustice

Social injustice is central to our theme of economic inequality. Some principle of distributive justice, however vague, and of whatever provenance, underlies comparisons of income distributions over time or between countries and influences the recommendations of policies. This applies to the topics that we shall examine later such as the formal methods of analysing income distribution (chapters 4 and 5) and policies aimed at a more egalitarian distribution of income (chapter 12); they presume some sort of consensus about the underlying principles of social justice to be employed. However, these principles do not emerge in a vacuum: the historical development of the social order brings about a corresponding development in the concept of social justice. Let us briefly consider the origins of such principles of social justice and some of the problems in applying them.

In examining the economic history of income distribution it is interesting to know whether equality was widely regarded as intrinsically desirable and, if so, when and by whom, and on what grounds. Since the grounds for desiring inequality could differ according to the historical and social context, it is useful to discuss the following three basic questions.
- By whom and amongst whom is the set of principles to be applied?
- What is the target of desirable distribution towards which policy should aim?
- How are the various deviations from the target to be compared for their degrees of undesirability?

The first question is partly a question of the perspective of the most effective opinion-moulders in the community: the PLUM principle again.[6] It is more pragmatic than might be supposed. This point has already been glimpsed in the discussion of slavery, but, setting aside artificial and institutionalised social barriers such as slavery, apartheid and caste, there is a natural obstacle: in most societies (with a few exceptions such as penal colonies) individuals commonly belong to some family group; they do so for a variety of reasons which include that of economic convenience. This raises the question whether, when observing a community at a particular date, the concept of justice is to be applied to distribution between individuals, between family groups, between dynasties, or some larger groups.

How this is answered drastically affects the view of social processes of income distribution. For example, if distributive justice applies to dynasties then some systems of inheritance might be approved that would be repudiated were distributive justice applied to individuals. Dynastic distributive justice used to be deemed to be perfectly reasonable – witness English hereditary peerages, the system of property rights attached to the Hindu caste system whereby sons would suffer from their father's losing caste, or the hereditary principles of land tenure under the Levitical system of Bible times. Familial distributive justice also has a long tradition in the Western world, as exemplified by the issue of whether a woman may own property in her own name. However in modern industrial societies, whether they have market, mixed or mainly planned economies, an increasing degree of attention is paid to distribution between individuals as well as to distribution between larger groups. This tendency even extends to the applications of the concept of social justice, and the tendency is reinforced by the loosening of the social ties reinforcing the stability of family groups.

On the second question, we do not presume to lay down the law as to what kind of distribution is socially just, or is desirable for some other sound reason. What we can do is examine some of the influences which have moulded prevailing opinions about what kind of distribution is desirable. In particular we may examine why hardly any people claim that justice or some other canon demands that there should be 'equal shares for all'. The arguments against this extreme position are of three kinds: the recognition of special merits, the recognition of special needs, and the recognition of unpleasant side effects that there would be for almost all layers of society if redistribution were to be carried to such extremes. In each case the word 'recognition' has to be stressed since there can be no valid objective test by which particular merits or needs should qualify to identify precisely those persons specially deserving advantages or by which undesirable side effects can be numerically weighed against the presumed desideratum of more equality. No objective test could conclusively establish what kind of distribution would be most worth striving for: these decisions have largely to be matters of judgement.

There are two quite different arguments in favour of special rewards for special merits: one reactionary and one ostensibly egalitarian. The reactionary argument[7] appears in one of its most articulate forms as part of the medieval European ecclesiastical view of society: it draws on the scriptural analogy between the Christian congregation and the human body, to represent a harmonious union of components with widely different talents and functions all working for their mutual glorification. On the basis of this and other notions from Greek philosophy, a theory of 'natural inequality' was formed which confirmed disparities of rank and privilege as morally acceptable and necessary to the functioning of society: a view widely accepted in Europe at least up to the seventeenth century. In modern societies too a certain amount of income inequality is still considered desirable: in both capitalist market economies and planned socialist economies there has been approval of relatively high pay for persons with certain rare skills. One justification for such differentials is that they recompense past sacrifices in acquiring the skills, although this view is unlikely to be uniformly compelling.[8] Alternatively, they might be justified as part of a general argument for the tolerance of some inequality in order to ensure a higher social product in the aggregate: income differences are seen as a necessary inducement to call forth specialised services. Even though such a view has quite a different origin from that of the ecclesiastical confirmation of inequalities as personal rights, it is interesting to note that in each case the privilege granted to merit is defended by appealing to the need to maintain a coherent, efficient economic system. This second version of the case for the preservation of income differences is the essence of the argument that pushing redistribution too far leads to unpleasant side effects.

The purportedly 'egalitarian' case for diversity of incomes is based on quite a different premise, which can be explained by an illustration. Imagine the history of social and economic change as a cinema film, the successive shots of which represent successive social states. One way of pinning down the concept of social justice is to define, independently of the historical epic movie, a picture of society as it ought to be: each shot of the movie can then be compared with that picture. This 'end-state principle'[9] is one that we often employ throughout this book but it must be remembered that the idealised reference picture, whilst a convenient device, is likely to have been recoloured or redrawn at different points in history.

By contrast, an alternative way of regarding the definition of social justice is not as an independent reference state, but as an intrinsic part of the historical process. Instead of being a reference picture outside the movie, justice is defined only within the movie itself. Accordingly we might argue that as long as the economic and political process which determines people's economic welfare is fair (in the sense that a parlour game is fair) then the distributional outcome of the process can be taken as just. This might imply accepting as just whatever distribution of goods and services happens to be thrown up by the competitive market system, on the grounds that there is free entry to the market; or it might be deemed just that those who benefited disproportionately under the *ancien régime* should be relatively disadvantaged at some later time; again, more contentiously, the principle could be applied to the heirs and assigns of those in the *ancien régime*. Thus, social justice shall not necessarily imply equality of outcome for everyone: but shall rather imply that, in good time, the first shall be last and the last shall be first. Revolutions often achieve their driving force with an ill-defined mixture of these quite different approaches to the definition of a concept of distributive justice, the independent reference state principle and the historical principle.

The argument for income differences on the basis of need is not straightforward either: the problem lies in the definition of 'need' itself. An important aspect of this is the time period involved and the degree of urgency of needs. Sudden misfortune claims special provision of resources for the sufferers: this seems to be a simple requirement of social justice, viewed in the short term. In the longer view, if such misfortunes are to some extent seen to be avoidable by the persons concerned, then the case for making special provision for such persons on the grounds of distributive justice may be weakened. How 'need' is defined and what claim it has to special treatment depends on the accepted view of the time scale to be applied, and the control that people are assumed to have over their own affairs.

Likewise it is often accepted in modern industrialised societies that families with many children and persons with physical disabilities have relatively large basic needs and therefore that in a just society they should have a large share of resources; this too is a matter of opinion and judgement, however compelling we may find the argument. What one person might interpret as 'need' might be interpreted by another person in a different social context as the result of free choice. Just as in some earlier societies the responsibility for children's living standards was exclusively that of the parents who chose to beget them, so also in some societies today the disadvantages of disabled people are viewed as the natural consequences of decisions made by their forebears, so that such people are undeserving of exceptional treatment. Even where special disadvantage is recognised, it may be regarded as a reason for social deprivation, as when the Spartans exposed weakling babies on the hillside. Nor, if we do rule out those historical precedents which are repugnant to us, can economic analysis calculate what is the just compensation for each need. For to evaluate how much more income is needed to offset any social disadvantage, we must assume a pattern of consumption requirements specific to the mode of living and price system of the particular society considered.

Now take the third basic question – how to view departures from the 'just' distribution. On what basis might there be a general presumption in favour of more egalitarian distributions?

Our previous example of special reward for high ability illustrates that the goal of extreme equality is not popularly viewed as being either perfectly just or perfectly desirable. If raising the remuneration of the able had such a good effect on aggregate income that even the incomes of the very poor were thereby raised, then any principle of distributive justice based solely on concern to raise the incomes of the poor could reasonably approve measures which would increase both high and low incomes but also increase their inequality. Distributive justice need not imply increased equality in cases where both rich and poor benefit more than they otherwise could hope to do, although measures which increase inequality where it is already very high would almost certainly be regarded as unjust. But what have been the reasons for disapproving of inequality in the first place?

Social philosophers have provided quite different answers to this basic question. Plato's view was that, if society is to avoid fatal disorder, limits on wealth at both extremes should be set; opulence and poverty should thus both be avoided. Aristotle too maintained that for social harmony the state should, as far as it can, consist of equals and peers and in this respect he endorsed the prayer of Phocylides: 'Many things are best for the middling, fain would I be of the state's middle class.' However, such egalitarian sentiments were to be interpreted principally in the context of those viewed as 'naturally equal' (excluding women and slaves) and formed the basis for an egalitarianism tempered by pragmatism and an acceptance of the 'natural order of things', an attitude that had extensive practical force through to the European Middle Ages and beyond.[10]

The change in social attitudes from the seventeenth century onwards, away from acquiescence in inequality on the basis of 'divine right' of authority toward the acknowledgement of equality of political rights, introduced a new framework for arguments about economic inequality: utilitarianism. A popular tag for the principle of utilitarianism is the pursuit of 'the greatest good of the greatest number'; a more precise definition depends crucially on the economic interpretation of the individual 'good' or 'utility', and on the collective representation of those individual utilities.

A case for greater income equality can be based on writings of Bentham and others, but it rests on two key suppositions: that individual utilities are related in a special way to income, and that society's welfare may be represented by the sum of these utilities.[11] The relationship between individual utility and income is supposed to be the following: as income increases, utility increases, but at an ever-diminishing rate (so a dollar of income given to someone rich produces a smaller increment in utility than if given to someone poor – see figure 1.1 on page 6). Since society's presumed objective is to maximise the sum of the individual utilities, measures that raise the incomes with high marginal utilities (those of the poor) but lower those with low marginal utilities (those of the rich) will always be approved so long as they do not lower the total income. Although this approach can still be discerned in writings on economic policy today, it should be distinguished from other recent arguments for egalitarianism which can lead to similar conclusions.

One such approach incorporates a fundamental and explicit desire for economic equality for its own sake – isophilia – and is well exemplified by the work of Rawls (1972):

Social and economic inequalities are to be arranged so that they are both (a) to the greatest benefit of the least advantaged and (b) attached to offices and positions open to all under conditions of fair equality of opportunity.

The extreme interpretation of Rawls – that society should give total priority to the welfare of the least well-off member of society – is a prescription which many would find unacceptable. However, the much weaker assertion that society should regard greater equality as desirable *ceteris paribus* may attract more support. This view may be contrasted with the utilitarian view under which a more equal outcome may (or may not) be desirable, purely on efficiency grounds without any explicit regard (or disregard) for equality in its own right: the sum of utilities being maximised without regard to the distribution of those utilities, except as it affects the whole. The isophiliac regards equality, and in particular a more equal income distribution, as a desirable goal in itself, without any need to appeal to the principle of diminishing returns of income in increasing individual utility, or to any principle of 'nature'.

Finally let us repeat what we have already noted in chapter 1, that whatever the basis for egalitarian arguments, egalitarianism alone is insufficient as a principle for ranking alternative states of society in order of desirability. We shall discuss this again in chapter 5.

3.6 Concluding remarks: contemporary inequality comparisons

The historical development of the economic and social system not only determines the extent of economic inequality, it also influences what we mean by economic inequality within a particular society and delimits the practicable steps that might be taken to mitigate such inequalities. We cannot interpret quantitative comparisons of inequality across widely separated time periods or within a remote era without careful reference to the underlying social order then ruling. These apparently banal conclusions have important implications for the economic analysis of contemporary inequality.

If we attempt to answer such questions as: 'Is economic inequality greater in Russia or in China?', or 'Is there progress towards income equality in India?', or even 'Is there a specific relationship between economic inequality and the level of development of a cross-section of low-income societies?', then we shall encounter fundamental problems quite similar to those discussed in sections 3.2–3.4. Such problems go beyond the technical details of the definition of economic terms and the comparability of data to deeper ones such as the range of opportunities facing individuals within the society and the system of property rights that is in force. Without adequate consideration of these issues it is futile to imagine 'inequality' as a transferable measurable entity that can be applied arbitrarily to radically different societies.

Consequently, when we compare income distribution in different economies and contemplate the scope for a reduction in inequality, we have to be clear about the basis of the comparison. Are changes to be considered only within the confines of the existing social and economic system? Or are we to consider also what might be done by introducing some specified modification to the system?

Just as the basis of the argument for greater equality has changed over the centuries, so it may also differ amongst dissimilar contemporary societies. The grounds for advocating it range from social convenience, through impartial utilitarian optimisation to the fundamentalist egalitarianism of Rawls. If we are to avoid the trap of assuming all societies to have goals basically similar to our own, the grounds for the egalitarian case, as for various claims for distributive justice, must be carefully examined within the relevant historical contexts.

There is unlikely to be universal agreement in selecting the basic units in society between which the various principles of distributive justice are to be applied. Here again, whether we are to take individuals, families or larger groups, must partly depend on the historical context within the country concerned, and this is a matter calling for judgement by the observer. In chapter 4 we shall provide a quantitative discussion of this issue.

3.7 Questions for discussion

General reading: Brenner *et al.* (1991), Phelps Brown (1988).

3.1   You are about to interview two Native American Chiefs whose tribes may differ substantially in their social orders. To what questions would you feel answers to be essential in order to establish which tribe had more economic inequality?

3.2   The 'a/b ratio' for a particular society is often fairly independent of the particular (high) base income b that is selected in a given year; this, and a presumed uniformity of a/b amongst different societies, has been known as Pareto's Law. Consider the status and usefulness of such an empirical 'law' in studying historical trends in economic inequality (Bronfenbrenner, 1971; Cowell, 1995).

3.3   Does analysis of inequality as an 'end state principle' contain an implicit bias in favour of the *status quo* (Nozick, 1974; Hamlin, 1986)?

3.4   Examine the argument that the principles of distributive justice should be applied to individuals rather than households or families if our overriding concern is with the urgency of need.

3.5   'From each according to his ability; to each according to his need' – Karl Marx. Is this principle of distributive justice consistent with the economic rewards of (a) Solzhenitsyn's State Prosecutor; (b) the Prosecutor's daughter in the following quotation?

The Prosecutor was staggered by the insolence, the injustice of [her] attitude. Had she no sense of historical perspective [. . .]?

'But how can you compare the Party of the working class with fascist scum?'

'Oh! Come off it, father! You don't belong to the working class. You were a worker once for two years and you've been a prosecutor for thirty. You – a worker! You live off the fat of the land! You even have a chauffeur to drive your own car! Environment determines consciousness – isn't that what your generation taught us?'

'Social environment, you idiot! And social consciousness! [. . .] You're stupid . . . You don't understand anything and you won't learn . . .'

'Go on then, teach me! Go on! Where does all your salary come from? Why do they pay you thousands of roubles when you don't produce anything?'

'Accumulated labour, you fool! Read Marx! Education, special training – that's accumulated labour, you're paid more for it. Why d'you think they pay you eighteen hundred at your research institute?'

Table 3.4 *Earnings in selected occupations in the USA*

	Urban skilled	Artisans	Engineers	Public school teachers	Methodist ministers
1840	1.498	1.704*	n.a.	0.812*	n.a.
1850	1.736	1.667	1.41**	0.810	n.a.
1860	1.668	1.629	1.73	0.993	4.513
1870	1.754	1.810	1.67	1.250	4.340
1880	1.734	1.906	1.85	1.319	5.163
1890	1.702	1.773	n.a.	1.222	5.163
1900	1.825	n.a.	n.a.	1.421	5.137
1910	1.919	n.a.	n.a.	1.553	4.458
1920	1.806	n.a.	n.a.	0.984	1.903

Notes: *1841, **1851.
Source: Williamson and Lindert, 1980b.

(See Marx, 1938 and Solzhenitsyn, 1968)

3.6   Give examples to illustrate the suggestion that very different kinds of statistics will be required to portray inequality, (a) under different forms of social organisation, (b) at different stages of economic development, (c) in different historical epochs.

3.7   Of what relevance to the choice of policies relating to inequality in your own country are studies of opinion about inequality in societies widely differing from your own in geographical location, historical time, or type of social organisation?

3.8   Table 3.4 gives the earnings for selected occupations in the USA for various years expressed as a ratio of the average wage of unskilled workers in the relevant years. What, if anything, may we deduce about the pattern of inequality in the USA during the period 1840–1920?

3.9   It is commonly supposed that wealth within countries in the modern world is less unequally distributed than in pre-industrial societies. Consider the difficulties involved in establishing the validity of this supposition (Gallman, 1969; Lindert, 1986).

3.10   Gregory King's classic early study of British income inequality published the information on 26 classes of persons in England and Wales in 1688 that is displayed in table 3.5. Discuss the problems involved in drawing inferences about economic inequality from data such as these. Would you expect such problems to be greater or less than in a similar exercise today (Soltow, 1968; Deane, 1955/6)?

3.11   Consider the problems in comparing inequality in the USA in the 1960s with inequality in the USSR in the 1960s. In what respects are these problems similar to those of comparing inequality in each of these countries with their modern-day counterparts (Atkinson and Micklewright, 1992; Bergson, 1984; McAuley, 1979; Wiles and Markowski, 1971; Wiles, 1974)?

3.12   'As an interpretation of the basis of the principles of justice, classical utilitarianism is mistaken [. . .] the conception of justice as fairness when applied to the practice of slavery [allows] the gains accruing to the slave owner [. . .] no weight at all [. . .] Where the conception of justice as fairness applies, slavery is always unjust' – (Rawls, 1972). Discuss.

Table 3.5 *British income inequality in the seventeenth century*

Number of families in class	Class	Yearly income per family (£)
160	Temporal lords	3,200
26	Spiritual lords	1,300
800	Baronets	880
600	Knights	650
3,000	Esquires	450
12,000	Gentlemen	280
5,000	Persons in greater offices and places	240
5,000	Persons in lesser offices and places	120
2,000	Eminent merchants and traders by sea	400
8,000	Lesser merchants and traders by sea	198
10,000	Persons in the law	154
2,000	Eminent clergymen	72
8,000	Lesser clergymen	50
40,000	Freeholders of the better sort	91
120,000	Freeholders of the lesser sort	55
150,000	Farmers	42
15,000	Persons in liberal arts and sciences	60
50,000	Shopkeepers and tradesmen	45
60,000	Artisans and handicrafts	38
5,000	Naval officers	80
4,000	Military officers	60
35,000	Common soldiers	14
50,000	Common seamen	20
364,000	Labouring people and out-servants	15
400,000	Cottagers and paupers	6
30,000 (persons)	Vagrants, beggars, gipsies, thieves, and prostitutes	2(per head)

3.13 'By equality we should understand not that degrees of power and riches are to be absolutely equal for all, but that power shall never be great enough for violence, and shall always be exercised by virtue of rank and law; and that, in respect of riches, no citizen shall ever be wealthy enough to buy another, and none poor enough to be forced to sell himself' (Rousseau). Discuss the possibility of applying this principle (i) to a modern market economy; (ii) to a developing economy.

Notes

1 See page 38 above.
2 In some tribes (such as the Kwakiutl and Tlinglit) there was a ceremonial form of given-away property – 'potlatch'. By performing this ceremony it was possible to claim positions of social prominence and economic influence, and sometimes to ruin financial rivals in competitive potlatches – see Driver (1969).
3 Cf. the discussion on page 2 above.
4 See, for example, Kuznets (1955).
5 As the city attained pre-eminence in Southern Germany, large fortunes were made by mer-

chants and banking houses, and from about 1510 there was a considerable rise in the price of foodstuffs and other commodities which worked to the advantage of merchants and financiers and some peasants, but to the disadvantage of rentiers and day labourers. In 1507 there was a politically expedient reform of the tax system which would seriously affect the conclusions that may be drawn from the data in table 3.2.

6 See page 39 above.

7 Again it can be traced back to Aristotle who accepted fundamental inequalities between certain classes of people, such as slaves and freemen, but argued that extreme inequality was socially undesirable.

8 Even in well-regulated societies such as the USSR of recent times this argument does not always go down well – see question 3.5

9 See Nozick (1974).

10 A brief illustration. The appealing slogan of the English peasants' revolt in 1381 – 'When Adam delved and Eve span, who was then a gentleman?' – met the pragmatic rebuff 'Villeins ye are still and villeins ye shall remain'; but Richard II was as astute as other monarchs in securing social stability by expedient distribution of land and other property rights amongst the ruling classes.

11 See Bentham (1789) and Smart and Williams (1973). To make the simple verision of the utilitarian argument work the relationship between utility and income should be such that utility is measurable and the same function for all persons. These assumptions can be relaxed in some cases.

4 Inequality: meaning and measurement

4.1 Introduction

In earlier chapters we have referred to 'inequality' – either on its own or in connection with concepts such as 'injustice' – as though we knew exactly what we meant by it. The principal aims of this chapter and the next are to examine concepts of income inequality both in the abstract and in specific quantitative senses, so that we can be clear about what it can sensibly be made to mean.

From our preliminary survey in chapter 1 we might superficially conclude that all countries are unequal but some seem more unequal than others. But on what basis may we make clear-cut statements about income inequality – that incomes in the UK are distributed more unequally than in Sweden, or that income inequality in the UK rose more rapidly in the early 1980s than in the late 1980s? We shall suggest principles on which comparisons of this sort can be based and will consider both normative and practical arguments for and against their acceptance; we shall also show how some of these rules can be translated into practical formulae for use with real data.

Although we are concerned here purely with description and measurement of income distributions rather than with the analysis of cause and effect, there are several important and profound issues which must be carefully distinguished and which affect the construction of analytical models of economic inequality. There are three main threads in the argument:
- A clear definition of the basic units in society (labelled 'persons', for shorthand) explaining who are to count: and also of the characteristic (labelled 'income'), whose distribution is to be described.
- A logical base on which to build comparisons of the inequality of distributions of the incomes between persons.
- A recognition of the limitations that the inadequacies of the available data place upon the inferences drawn from that data about comparisons of inequality between income distributions.

All three threads in the argument are essential. No amount of data refinement will get rid of the logical problems and, more importantly, no amount of logical sophistication can extract reliable comparisons of inequality from unreliable data. In chapter 2, we discussed some of the practical aspects of the concepts of 'real income' and of the 'person'; now we focus upon some of the logical aspects of the problem.

4.2 Who is to count?

We start with the meaning of the 'persons' concerned. A person or income receiver indicates a self-contained unit of the population, and the interests of that unit are treated as being indivisible. The population is assumed to be exogenously determined, but what units are to count in the population?

Perhaps the most obvious thing to do is to count as separate each human being in the population, male, female, infant or adult, and to impute to each such unit a real income that may in practice be created by some cooperative unit such as the household of which he is a member. But a reasonable alternative is to count a whole family or household as one unit, provided that in the observation period the family or household is treated as indissoluble, and its members' interest as unanimous. Each approach has something in its favour, but each runs into problems due to comparing unlike units – adults compared with children, or large families with persons living alone.

In providing numerical illustrations for this chapter and chapters 5 and 6 we have usually done the most obvious thing: we have assumed the *individual person* as the income recipent, although the data set – the Michigan Panel Study of Income Dynamics (PSID), from which the summary result for US income distribution in chapter 2 were drawn – focuses upon incomes in families. The data and the procedures we used to derive income distributions are fully described in appendix A.

4.3 Income and personal welfare

When asked how 'well off' somebody is, our thoughts often turn immediately to that person's income measured in dollars, yen, pounds sterling or whatever. However, as we noted in chapter 2, that which is customarily included in income is unlikely to provide a complete and accurate picture of that person's living standard, and there may be problems with using the distribution of income to draw inferences about economic inequality. In this section we examine what can, in principle, be done with the imperfect building materials that we reviewed in chapter 2: what are the underlying principles and practical issues involved in specifying a numerical index of personal welfare?

The formal assumptions required for specifying an income index are apparently straightforward: we assume that it is measurable, comparable and transferable from one person to another. Whether we take as a person's income his annual taxable receipts in dollars or pounds, or some component of his annual consumption in kilograms or litres, the units chosen have to be measurable in the sense that we can usefully talk, for example, about 'a ten per cent increase in the income of person 2'. We cannot assume that an income of x_1 going to 'person' 1 always counts as less than income of x_2 going to 'person' 2 just because x_2 is a larger number than x_1, since 'person' 1 might be a single individual and 'person' 2 a sprawling household of three adults and ten children, but incomes must be defined in such a way that we can always decide for any pair which is the larger or that they are equally large, even when the two 'persons' receiving them are demographically dissimilar: that is what is meant by the incomes being comparable.

We also assume that 'income' is not some nebulous psychological state enjoyed by its recipient, but something observable that one person can gain at the expense of another: we shall go so far as to suppose that it makes sense to think of a fixed total X of incomes which may in principle be distributed among the persons in any one of the arithmetically possible ways consistent with no income being negative.[1] Only a tiny proportion of all these redistributions are even remotely practicable in the light of the economic and political facts of life, but that is not the point. What is essential is that the description and measurement of the distribution of income be examined as a distinct logical issue – as we discuss further in section 4.4.

Once the theoretical points regarding income are resolved, important practical issues remain. In the first place a person's income, as defined for tax purposes, may incorporate items that do not contribute directly to personal welfare such as mandatory or contractual payments, work expenses and the like. More importantly, official income may exclude specific quantifiable receipts that certainly do contribute to his overall living standard. As obvious examples we may cite cash items such as social security benefits, and some non-cash items ('income in kind') such as consumption by self-employed people of part of their own product, special perquisites such as a company car, or the opportunity for employees to purchase at a discount their firm's product or its shares. Whilst the quantities of these items might in principle be readily ascertained, the corresponding adjustment to be made to a person's income is not so straightforward. If some non-cash income is not saleable (such as the use of a company car or subsidised luncheon vouchers), or not officially saleable (such as food stamps in the United States), then a simple market-price valuation of similar items is likely to overestimate their worth to the recipient.

We should also allow for the special advantages of wealth in terms of people's living standards. Under idealised conditions a person's income stream can be converted unambiguously into a single wealth total, and *vice versa*, so we might use either quantity as an indicator for the person's living standards. However, in practice, the observed income from financial assets is likely to be an unreliable guide to a person's wealth and may lead to an underestimate of the true entitlement to economic goods conveyed by his total wealth. We also encounter another valuation problem: it is possible that the wealthy obtain more purchasing power per dollar than the poor. The reasons for this are not only the economies of scale that the rich may be able to exploit through bulk purchases, but the greater availability of credit, on more favourable terms, that may accrue to those with substantial property.

If all taxes and other compulsory payments are deducted from a person's nominal income then all the personal benefits received by the person as of right ought to be included too. This should include a valuation of personal non-cash benefits as well as cash benefits. Furthermore, some publicly provided items such as education and health care can be handled in the same way as direct personal non-cash benefits: in such cases benefits are individually identifiable and quantifiable, and there are marketable close substitutes in the private sector to assist in valuation.

Other items which are by their nature collective consumption goods (as opposed to privately enjoyed goods which happen to be publicly provided) present less tractable problems. Not only is there a problem of measuring the output of activities such as the police perform or the provision of parks and gardens, but also there is some difficulty in obtaining estimates of people's valuation of these things. The idea of a person's 'willing-ness to pay' for a collective consumption good is in practice ill-defined, and a simple imputation of the cost of providing the goods ignores such problems as the variability in quality of public goods and services and the variability in their composition items (would the flow of consumption services be more valuable if more roadways and fewer police riot shields and guns were provided at the same cost?). Furthermore the distrib-ution amongst persons of consumption services arising out of some public good is most unlikely to be equal – some people get more benefit from the services of the CIA than others – so that a simple 'average value' of such services is unlikely to be appropriate. Similar problems arise when we try to take into account other externalities (general amenities or disamenities: publicly produced, privately produced, or naturally present) such as the pleasantness of living in Berkshire rather than the Bronx: such issues play an important part in determining people's level of living standards, but it is difficult to see how we may reliably estimate their impact on the distribution of such living standards.

There are two major difficulties which prevent us from pursuing these issues with the thoroughness they deserve. First, a proper study of the incidence of such expenditures raises theoretical problems that would take us too far from the main themes of this book. Second the available data on this topic usually refer to broad groups and we simply do not have detailed enough individual observations to supplement the information on income distribution in a useful way. So, in common with many other studies of economic inequality, we remain with the uneasy feeling of having set aside important contributions to or alleviations of economic inequality that arise from public goods and public expenditure: we return to a general discussion of this issue in chapter 12.

However, we shall not pass so readily over the effect on living standards of the economies of scale generated by people living in families. Whilst it may not be true that 'two can live as cheaply as one', it may be roughly true that two can live as cheaply as one and a half, so that two persons each with $10,000 income, living separately are not jointly as well off as two persons living together with a combined income of $20,000. As we hinted on page 68 the nominal income of each family should be adjusted by an index that depends, among other things, on the number of persons in the family and their ages. Similar adjustments may be made for persons with special needs, such as the disabled, who require a higher input of resources to provide themselves with the same basket of goods as a healthy person.[2] The main snag is that the adjustments to be made to nominal incomes rest crucially on empirical estimation of households' demand pat-terns; as such the estimates of these adjustments are likely to be sensitive to the method of estimation and the choice of the particular population being investigated.

In the practical examples presented here we take a comprehensive definition of income. Income is 'total family income' as defined in the PSID – including social secur-ity benefits and other transfers, but before deduction of personal taxes. Information about each family's size and composition was available in each year: so in order to make comparisons of incomes accruing to families of different compositions we used this information to construct a conventional index of 'adult equivalents' for each family, based on a standard of food needs. Before we use this data let us make a preliminary examination of the logical issues involved in using the selected ordinal indicators of personal economic welfare to estimate the degree of inequality.

4.4 The logic of inequality comparisons

Start with the simplest distributional problem of all, the division of a given total income between just two persons. Adapting figure 2.5 on page 41 and excluding cases where either person has a negative income, this division may be represented in figure 4.1 where x_1 the income of person 1 and x_2 the income of person 2 are measured along the horizontal and vertical axis respectively. If X denotes the total income then point A_1 represents the case where person 1 gets all the income and person 2 gets none, whereas A_2 represents the opposite case where person 1 gets none. All cases where each get some of the income are represented by points on the line between A_1 and A_2. E, the midpoint of A_1A_2, represents the case where the two persons each get half the total. It seems reasonable to regard a pair of equidistant points such as B_1 and B_2 as representing a pair of distributions which are 'equally unequal' in the absence of any further information relevant to their comparison. It also seems reasonable to regard one point on the line as representing a more unequal distribution than does another if it lies further from E, since in this case the gap between the pair of incomes it represents is larger than for the other point.

We could define an inequality measure for this simple 'cake-sharing' problem – a rule assigning a unique number to each distinct income distribution, such that distributions that exhibit greater inequality receive higher numbers. Adopting the convention that the state of equality is assigned the number zero, then in the case of figure 4.1 the inequality measure is simply some increasing function of the distance from E along EA_1 or EA_2. Any increasing function will do if all we are concerned with is an ordering of states in terms of relative inequality – to say that A_1 is a more unequal state than B_1 which is more unequal than C_1. If we wish to go further and assert that the move from C_1 to B_1 involves a greater *increase* in inequality than the move from B_1 to A_1 then the precise embodiment of the rule connecting the inequality statistic with the distance from E does matter.

This particular embodiment of the inequality statistic – the 'cardinalisation' of the measure – is important also when we compare distributions of different totals. Consider for example comparing points on A_1A_2 with those representing distributions out of some smaller income – say points on a line $A_1'A_2'$. Although the ordering of points within $A_1'A_2'$ is clear there are many ways a correspondence between points on A_1A_2 and points on $A_1'A_2'$ may be established: figure 4.2 shows two of them. We discuss this issue further in chapter 5.

Finally, notice that even if there is agreement on the appropriate cardinalisation of inequality and on the basis of inequality comparisons between distributions with different levels of overall income, nothing has been said about social welfare. Just because the state represented by point B_1 is regarded as equally unequal as that of point B_1' it does not suggest that there is no reason to prefer one over the other. As we have emphasised earlier the distribution of income about its mean is important as well as the level of that mean; so if B_1 and B_1' are to be regarded as each having the same inequality, any decisive superiority of the average income of B_1 say over B_1' would provide a *prima facie* case for preferring B_1 to B_1'. This already suggests that we should try to define inequality in a manner which avoids imputing greater inequality to B_1 than B_1' although mean income was no less in B_1 than in B_1'. It also suggests that the greater

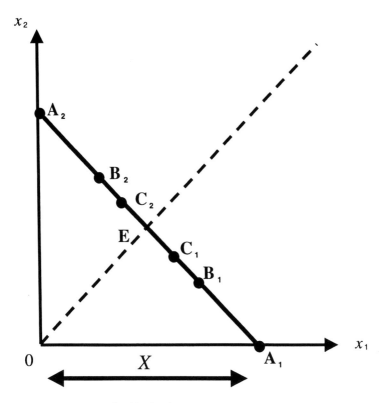

Figure 4.1 Income distribution between two persons

total income available under B_1 might make it preferable even to C'_1, a distribution with less inequality.

4.5 Inequality measures

Although inequality comparisons in a two-person world with a fixed total income are fairly trivial, such comparisons become complex in a multi-person world: an illustration is to be found in questions 4.1 to 4.3 at the end of this chapter. The complexities of the general case provide a strong incentive to simplify the process of comparison by introducing a general-purpose set of alternative inequality measures. Furthermore, in the two-person case we have noted that agreement on a particular numerical measure to deal with questions involving changes in inequality is both possible and useful. In more general cases agreement is unlikely to be possible so that a set of alternative measures should be used to give a range of possible interpretations of the evidence and a range of alternative policies to be considered for improving the situation. What properties should we seek in such measures?

Chapter 5 deals with this issue in detail but two general properties suggest themselves immediately: the measures should indicate the 'spread' of incomes in the frequency dis-

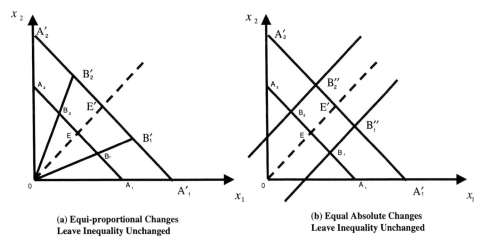

**(a) Equi-proportional Changes
Leave Inequality Unchanged**

**(b) Equal Absolute Changes
Leave Inequality Unchanged**

Figure 4.2 Two methods of relating income distributions with different totals

tribution, and should be easily applied to any population or component population subgroups.

Now in chapter 2 we have already encountered a familiar, ready-made candidate as a generally applicable inequality measure – the standard deviation. Writing $(x_1, x_2, ..., x_n)$ for the list of incomes received by n persons in the population, X for total income $x_1 + x_2 + ... + x_n$ and $\bar{x}$ for the arithmetic mean X/n, the standard deviation is

$$\sigma(\mathbf{x}) := \sqrt{\frac{1}{n} \sum_{i=1}^{n} [x_i - \bar{x}]^2} \tag{1}$$

An increase in spread could simply be interpreted as an increase in σ. For example if, in a two-person world, the income distribution is (2,8), the value of σ is $\sqrt{(\frac{1}{2}[4+64]-25)} = 3$; but if the income distribution is more spread out and becomes (1,9), then σ becomes $\sqrt{(\frac{1}{2}[1+81]-25)} = 4$.

Moreover, σ has a well-known decomposition property, which can be expressed as follows. Let the population consist of two groups of size n_1 and n_2, where $n_1 + n_2 = n$; write $\mathbf{x}_1$ for the n_1 vector of incomes that accrue to the members of group 1, with group-mean $\bar{x}_1$; similarly, define $\mathbf{x}_2$ and $\bar{x}_2$ for group 2; and then write $\mathbf{x}_B$ for an n-vector that has its first n_1 components set equal to $\bar{x}_1$ and the remaining n_2 components set equal to $\bar{x}_2$ – this is the income distribution that would appear if the incomes in each particular group were to be equalised at the group's arithmetic mean. Then we have

$$\sigma^2(\mathbf{x}) = \frac{n_1}{n} \sigma^2(\mathbf{x}_1) + \frac{n_2}{n} \sigma^2(\mathbf{x}_2) + \sigma^2(\mathbf{x}_B) \tag{2}$$

The first two terms on the right-hand side of (2) can be interpreted as a 'within-group' component of inequality, and the third term as the corresponding 'between-group' component. In actual application it is often easier to work with the *coefficient of variation*, $\kappa := \sigma/\bar{x}$, a dimensionless number, rather than with σ which will double when the unit of income is halved: κ will inherit the properties of σ in slightly modified form.

Making the substitution for the coefficient of variation in (2) gives

$$\kappa^2(x) = \frac{n_1}{n} \lambda_1^2 \kappa^2(x_1) + \frac{n_2}{n} \lambda_2^2 \kappa^2(x_2) + \kappa^2(x_B) \tag{3}$$

where

$$\lambda_1 := \frac{x_1}{\bar{x}}, \lambda_2 := \frac{x_2}{\bar{x}} \tag{4}$$

However, the properties of spread measurement and decomposability do not belong exclusively to σ. Quite apart from the fact that they apply in modified form to transformations of σ – such as κ or κ^2 – they apply to many other readily obtainable measures too. For example, take the *geometric mean* x^* of the incomes $(x_1, ..., x_n)$ – found by multiplying the n incomes together and taking the nth root of the product – and the *harmonic mean* x^{**} – found by taking the reciprocal of the arithmetic mean of $(1/x_1, ..., 1/x_n)$; if none of $x_1, ..., x_n$ were negative, we would find $x^{**} \leq x^* \leq \bar{x}$ and we would also find that $x^{**} = x^* = \bar{x}$ if and only if the income distribution were perfectly equal: so we might try using the proportion by which either x^* or x^{**} falls short of $\bar{x}$ as an index of inequality. Doing so, we find the following two statistics that can be employed as inequality measures

$$A_1(\mathbf{x}) := 1 - \frac{x^*}{\bar{x}} \tag{5}$$

$$A_2(\mathbf{x}) := 1 - \frac{x^{**}}{\bar{x}} \tag{6}$$

Given the income distribution (2,8) we would find $A_1 = 1 - [\sqrt{(2 \times 8)}/5] = 0.20$ and $A_2 = 0.36$, for the distribution (1,9) we get $A_1 = 1 - [\sqrt{(1 \times 9)}/5] = 0.40$ and $A_2 = 0.64$. Decomposition rules can also be established for these two measures, so in these respects A_1 and A_2 perform much like the standard measure of spread κ.

$$\log(1 - A_1(\mathbf{x})) = \frac{n_1}{n} \log(1 - A_1(\mathbf{x_1})) + \frac{n_2}{n} \log(1 - A_1(\mathbf{x_2})) + \log(1 - A_1(\mathbf{x_B})) \tag{7}$$

$$\frac{A_2(\mathbf{x})}{1 - A_2(\mathbf{x})} = \frac{n_1 \bar{x}_1^2}{n \bar{x}^2} \frac{A_2(\mathbf{x_1})}{1 - A_2(\mathbf{x_1})} + \frac{n_2 \bar{x}_2^2}{n \bar{x}^2} \frac{A_2(\mathbf{x_2})}{1 - A_2(\mathbf{x_2})} + \frac{A_2(\mathbf{x_B})}{1 - A_2(\mathbf{x_B})} \tag{8}$$

At this point we should make two qualifying remarks. First, the three measures κ, A_1, A_2 are only preliminary suggestions as inequality statistics; when we analyse the formal basis of inequality analysis in chapter 5 we will find that A_1 and A_2 are two members of a whole family of useful inequality measures. Second, the system of disaggregation given in (2), (7) and (8) is not unique: we shall also find in chapter 5 an alternative scheme may be more appropriate for measures such as A_1 and A_2.

4.6 Inequality and the composition of the population

Let us put our three preliminary inequality statistics to work. One of the advantages of ready-made tools is that some of the basic data problems can be appraised in terms of their likely effects on apparent inequality, so that we can obtain some idea of the overall structure of inequality before confronting deeper theoretical and empirical issues.

First examine the data on income distribution amongst American families, introduced in chapter 2. To see the different ways in which we might define income and the income receiving unit in practice, examine table 4.1 where the sample has been sub-

Table 4.1 *Family size, income and inequality*

Family size	Proportions in each family-size group		Group mean income	Group mean income per person	Adjusted group mean income	κ	A_1	A_2
	families	persons	($)	($)	($)			
	(1)	(2)	(3)	(4)	(5)	(6)	(7)	(8)
1	0.234	0.084	18,054.39	18,054.39	17,749.36	0.8040	0.2622	0.5728
2	0.269	0.194	35,440.25	17,720.12	26,614.25	1.0704	0.2641	0.5149
3	0.187	0.202	38,516.46	12,838.82	24,458.06	0.8273	0.2579	0.7320
4	0.179	0.258	43,374.59	10,843.65	22,364.04	0.7982	0.2158	0.4395
5	0.087	0.156	42,063.61	8,412.72	18,323.90	0.9738	0.2370	0.4521
6 or more	0.045	0.106	37,703.56	5,867.94	13,644.37	0.7009	0.2355	0.5839
All families	1.000	1.000	36,854.34	13,135.25	22,155.48	0.9494	0.2589	0.5881

Note: Family is assumed as income-receiving unit for calculation of means and inequality measures. Adjusted total family income is used to compute inequality measures in columns (6)–(8).

Source: Own calculations from PSID, Wave XX. For details see appendix A.

Table 4.2 *Effect on inequality of different definitions of income and income receiving unit*

	Family as unit			Person as unit		
	Total family income (1)	Income per person (2)	Adjusted income (3)	Total family income (4)	Income per person (5)	Adjusted income (6)
κ	1.0011	0.9804	0.9655	0.9392	1.0148	0.9494
A_1	0.3052	0.2916	0.2654	0.2771	0.2932	0.2589
A_2	0.6416	0.6285	0.5913	0.6242	0.6327	0.5881

Source: As for table 4.1.

divided into groups by size of family. For a family of a given size we read across a row as follows: (1) the proportion of families belonging to the group; (2) the proportion of persons belonging to the group; (3) the average family income of the group; (4) the income per person in the group; (5) an 'adjusted income' (discussed below), and (6)–(8) the values of the inequality measures for the group. Whilst income increases with family size, income per head has almost exactly the opposite relationship; also that, with the exception of the last heterogeneous group, inequality within each group usually decreases with family size.

Table 4.2 examines the impact on inequality of various definitions of income and the income receiver. We begin by taking the total recorded income for each family as an index of that family's living standard, and the family as the fundamental unit of population receiving that income (even though we know that this is an unsatisfactory procedure) – see the first column of table 4.2. Because it is inappropriate to regard a recorded income of $50,000 as yielding the same living standard to a family of four as to a person living alone we recompute κ, A_1 and A_2 for income per head as distributed amongst families (column 2). However, as we noted in section 4.3, income per head may not be quite what is required because of possible economies of scale. A better measure of standard of living might be income 'per equivalent adult' or income per person adjusted for economies of scale in subsistence items such as food, housing, etc: column (3) shows the inequality computation for this concept of income. If we are interested in the distribution of living standards of people rather than of 'families' (which may involve some arbitrary groupings), then the weighting attached to each group's contribution to total income and to total inequality may need to be re-examined. For, suppose we have an observation of a family of two persons with a total income that is equivalent to $30,000 each: although there is only one income receiving unit (the family), there are two people whose living standards we are examining; so the $30,000 income ought to be counted twice when we measure inequality. Following this principle would involve replacing the numbers of families n_1, n_2 in equations (2), (7) and (8) by numbers of persons: this will give a heavier weight to groups of large families within which, as we have seen, inequality tends to be lower.

Thus we construct columns (2) to (6) in table 4.2 which show separately the effect of switching from 'income per head' to 'needs-adjusted income' and of switching from inequality amongst *families* to inequality amongst *persons*. The combined effect of these adjustments is a reduction in inequality (by 3.5 per cent in the case of κ and by about 19 per cent in the case of the measures A_1, A_2). It is clear that the appropriate choice of income concept and of income recipient substantially affects our perception of inequality.

4.7 Inequality and the composition of income

Having seen in section 4.5 how total income inequality may be decomposed into inequality within and between groups of the population, we may now consider how it may be decomposed into inequality within and between different components or types of income. Fortunately our ready-made tool, the coefficient of variation κ, despite having some drawbacks as an inequality measure (see page 84 below), is straightforward to decompose by income type: let κ_F, κ_L, κ_P be, respectively, the value of κ for factor income, labour income and property income, let λ be labour income as a proportion of total income, and let ρ be the correlation coefficient between labour and property income; then we have

$$\kappa_F^2 = \lambda^2 \kappa_L^2 + [1-\lambda]^2 \kappa_{P2} + 2\lambda[1-\lambda]\kappa_L \kappa_P \rho \tag{9}$$

which is well defined even in the presence of negative income components.[3] Examine table 4.3: here the sample has again been subdivided by the age and sex of each family head, but we present for each group, and for the sample as a whole, the coefficient of variation κ for earnings and for income from property, and finally for 'factor income', defined as the sum of these two components. We also tabulate the correlation coefficient ρ for labour income and property income within each group so that the decomposition of factor income by components may be carried out.

Note three interesting features that emerge from table 4.3. First, in contrast to the male-headed families, the female-headed families, which form 30 per cent of the sample, are more concentrated in the topmost age groups which we know exhibit relatively high inequality (see column 1); this holds irrespective of whether we look at the proportion of people in, or the proportion of income flowing to, families headed by older women. This phenomenon, the fact that people in male-headed families receive about three times the imputed factor income of people in female-headed families, and the fact that inequality of labour income is higher for female-headed families (column 5) together suggest that sex of head 'accounts for' a substantial proportion of underlying inequality: we will see how this notation of 'accounting for' inequality can be made more precise in chapter 6. Second, for each type of household and each age group except the last, earnings form the overwhelmingly larger component of factor income (column 3), although inequality of property income (column 6) is nearly always much larger than inequality of labour income (column 5). Third, the correlation between property and labour income is usually small and positive (column 7). With the exception of first, fifth and sixth age categories of female headed families where the correlation is very low, the distributions of the two sorts of incomes are certainly not 'independent' in the statistical sense: people do not fall into two distinct groups – those who receive their income from work and those who receive it from the ownership of property. We also find that the high proportion of earnings in factor income and the

Table 4.3 *Inequality of factor income by components*

Age of family head (1)	Number of families (2)	Mean factor income ($) (3)	Labour income as prop. of factor income (4)	Income inequality (κ)			
				Factor income (5)	Labour income (6)	Property income (7)	Corr. coeff (8)
Families headed by men							
0–24	369	17,207.90	0.96143	0.67254	0.67270	3.86356	0.06129
25–34	1,777	30,757.70	0.94950	0.63735	0.61018	3.58964	0.17944
35–44	1,209	44,913.40	0.91986	0.71485	0.69197	2.97883	0.16080
45–54	560	47,243.80	0.87318	1.00272	0.91248	3.80233	0.17973
55–64	527	39,890.87	0.84327	1.31449	1.44757	2.16646	0.14777
65+	512	10,716.27	0.29166	1.85392	2.93764	2.03652	0.25162
All ages	4,954	33,745.56	0.87674	1.05714	1.06943	3.16959	0.11709
Families headed by women							
0–24	220	9,439.59	0.97896	0.91517	0.88052	7.14263	0.27754
25–34	579	13,525.02	0.97244	0.82135	0.82694	4.47395	0.06432
35–44	308	16,014.67	0.93673	0.76338	0.78381	3.29464	0.00074
45–54	235	16,573.89	0.92181	0.81310	0.81731	3.47872	0.04764
55–64	264	10,261.62	0.82525	1.02961	1.19613	1.96438	−0.04741
65+	468	3,892.05	0.17557	2.08205	4.55193	2.39193	−0.06106
All ages	2,074	10,424.17	0.84857	1.10322	1.23084	3.18704	−0.10583
All families							
	7,028	26,471.04	0.87328	1.21454	1.23734	3.38489	0.13329

Source: As for table 4.1.

low correlation between components yields a factor income inequality that is very similar to earnings inequality (columns 4 and 7). The extent of observed income inequality depends not only on the particular concept of income which is used but also on the interrelationships between different types of income that may be flowing to the same income receiving unit. Though we have only considered this for a very special inequality measure, these broad conclusions are quite robust if more sophisticated techniques are employed. We now turn to a further problematic aspect of the income concept in inequality analysis.

4.8 Inequality and time

So far in our discussion we have accepted fairly uncritically the data on income distribution in whatever time units the unseen official statistician happens to find appropriate. Obviously there is nothing particularly meritorious or magic about measuring incomes over a calendar or financial year (the usual time unit), and the apparent amount of income inequality is likely to change if the standard time unit is changed.[4]

The reasons for this can be understood by analogy with the factor component analy-

Table 4.4 *Effect of time interval on measured inequality*

	T	ρ	One-year income Mean	Averaged income Mean	κ	A_1	A_2
1986	1	0	22,250.92	22,250.92	0.9604	0.2600	0.5898
1985–6	2	0.8362	21,345.51	21,798.22	0.9239	0.2431	0.4792
1984–6	3	0.8912	20,498.35	21,364.93	0.9330	0.2327	0.4507
1983–6	4	0.8061	18,674.51	20,692.32	0.8917	0.2238	0.4333
1982–6	5	0.6184	17,544.32	20,062.72	0.8932	0.2185	0.4147

Note: For this table only the basic restricted sample is further restricted to eliminate families that do not have continuous five-year histories ($N=6,973$). See appendix A. For this reason the estimates in row 1 do not match those in table 4.2.

sis of section 4.7. Suppose that person i receives an income $x_i(1)$ in year 1 and $x_i(2)$ in year 2 and that we are interested in the distribution amongst persons of income cumulated over the two years, $Dx_i(1)+x_i(2)$ where D is a discount factor. The inequality analysis of cumulated income can be treated as a problem of decomposition by income components where the two components are the incomes in the two years, weighted by the appropriate discount factor. Inequality of cumulated income will depend on the inequality of each period's income, and the correlation between incomes in different periods. If inequality of one-year incomes remained roughly uniform over time then we would expect inequality of incomes cumulated over two years to be somewhat lower due to the 'averaging effect' of the longer time period; the exact extent to which this happens would depend on the correlation between years:[5] the longer the time interval over which incomes are measured, the lower the measured inequality we would expect to see.

Fortunately the PSID data used to construct the tables in this chapter trace individual families over a 20-year period, so that the transitory inequality effect can be clearly observed. Table 4.4 shows first the correlation coefficient for income between adjacent years, and mean annual income in each of five years (looking 'backwards' from 1987), and then the values of the κ, A_1 and A_2 statistics relating to income measured over periods of 1–5 years. In each case 'income' means income adjusted for need, and 'inequality' refers to the distribution amongst persons of adjusted income, averaged over T periods. The average is unweighted, in other words the discount factor has been set everywhere equal to 1.[6] Note the relatively large proportionate fall in A_2 that occurs when the period is extended from a solitary year to two years. It is evident that examining current year incomes usually reveals quite a high level of inequality compared with the picture from the longer run. But which view gives more information – permanent inequality, or current inequality including the transitory component? Should we be concerned with a period less than a year so that even greater weight is placed on transitory influences?

To address these questions we have to form some view about the fairness or otherwise of the economic 'rules of the game', the openness and impartiality of economic institutions, and the quality of information on which individuals and families may base their plans. If we believe that all people have open access to all markets on fairly equal terms, and that they all have equally good information about the range of economic opportunities, then purely transitory inequality may be dismissed as relatively unimportant.

For, under such idealised conditions, each person would have the same opportunity of smoothing out a fluctuating income stream as between a lump sum now and the prospect of an erratic future income stream with an identical financial present value. However, in practice, we might argue that the poor do not have easy access to the market for loans, that they are regarded as bad risks, that they have scantier information about financial assets, so that they are forced to borrow on much less favourable terms than the well off. The poor may be less well able to bear uninsurable risks. Moreover, their relative disadvantage and ignorance in the capital market may even extend to the labour market[7] so that just through not knowing of any suitable opportunities they miss obtaining the requisite educational qualifications or fail to make suitable occupational choices. Under such circumstances ignorance and uncertainty concerning the future will exacerbate inequality, and the transitory component current income dispersion cannot be casually dismissed.

Although families' incomes vary from year to year, such fluctuations are not purely haphazard. We usually find systematic growth (or decline) in family incomes over the life cycle due to promotion benefits on the job, planned retirement, savings, transfers to other family members and so on. Since many of these systematic effects can be regarded as the outcome of conscious choice it may be argued that some component of the spread of incomes over the various age groups might be regarded as a spurious indicator of economic inequality. This is a reason for regarding the inequality of lifetime consumption expenditure as interesting, were good statistics of its distribution to be available. Let us check how important this spurious element of inequality of might be.

Table 4.5 is constructed on principles very similar to table 4.1 except that the sole criterion for dividing families into groups is now the age of the family head. For the moment let us concentrate on the principal entries in columns (3), (5), (7) and (9) which show how the average pattern of total family income and the inequality of total family income (of a particular age group) change with age. Some important components of an individual's income tend to follow a 'hump-shaped' profile over the person's life (see chapters 7 and 8 for a discussion of this) so it is not surprising to find average total family income following the same sort of path. We note also that, with the exception of the very earliest years, there is a tendency for inequality to increase with age. As a result of these features there is apparently a substantial reduction in inequality if the systematic inter-age group variation in incomes is smoothed out: compare the last two rows of the table, columns (5) to (7).

However, this conclusion does not take into account the accompanying systematic variation in family size over the life cycle. As we have noted an adjusted income concept and correct weighting are important in getting a clear picture of inequality. If we examine the profile of adjusted incomes – column (4) – the hump shape is far less evident. As a consequence, the effect of equalising such adjusted incomes across the age groups becomes far less impressive – see the entries in bold type (columns 6, 7 and 9). If there is an inter-age group component of real income inequality amongst

Table 4.5 *Age and inequality*

Age of family head (1)	Number of families (2)	Mean income ($) (3)	Adjusted group mean income ($) (4)	κ		A_1		A_2	
				(5)	(6)	(7)	(8)	(9)	(10)
0–24	589	16,447.40	**12,318.76**	0.7027	**0.6771**	0.2754	**0.2446**	0.6157	**0.5247**
25–34	2,356	28,358.71	**18,210.91**	0.6624	**0.6845**	0.2333	**0.2355**	0.6788	**0.6674**
35–44	1,517	41,937.35	**23,520.98**	0.7458	**0.7684**	0.2320	**0.2209**	0.5844	**0.5205**
45–54	795	46,615.38	**27,487.18**	0.9630	**0.9223**	0.2693	**0.2546**	0.5696	**0.4819**
55–64	791	40,579.55	**30,418.12**	1.1818	**1.1621**	0.3197	**0.2709**	0.5919	**0.5088**
65 & over	980	19,508.00	**18,350.70**	1.0119	**0.8979**	0.2863	**0.2345**	0.4752	**0.4088**
All ages:	7,028	32,440.18	**22,155.48**	1.0011	**0.9494**	0.3052	**0.2589**	0.6416	**0.5881**
All ages (between-age component excluded):				0.9482	**0.9225**	0.2637	**0.2392**	0.6243	**0.5785**

Note: Columns in plain type (3, 5, 7, 9) are computed using total family income, with family as income receiving unit. Columns in **bold** type (4, 6, 8, 10) are computed using adjusted mean income and the person as income-receiving unit.
Source: As for table 4.1.

persons it is very largely eliminated by allowing for the economies of scale in large families. Of course, even if the systematic 'between age group' inequality component were to be eliminated, most of the transitory inequality, illustrated in table 4.4, would remain.

Finally, let us note a second important issue concerning the choice of time period in inequality measurement. This turns on whether we are primarily concerned about the injustice of inequality or about the alleviation of the economic hardships incidental to inequality. It might be argued that insofar as both rich and poor are subject to life cycles of consumption expenditure, these in themselves do not contribute much to the injustice caused by inequality: accordingly the relevant measures of inequality of consumption would be that of the annual rate over a period comparable with that of a person's working life. In practical terms this implies acceptance of the long-run inequality values given in the last row of table 4.5. But if we are concerned with the alleviation of economic need and with the damage to 'economic welfare' resulting from inequality, then the balance of advantage seems to lie with measuring the inequality of consumption expenditure rate or real income over a short period such as a year. This is because transitory inequality as well as permanent inequality of consumption expenditure – or of any other indicator of living standards – is likely to lower average economic welfare.

4.9 The sensitivity of the inequality index

Although the inequality measures used in this chapter were arbitrarily chosen, they share some essential properties which can be captured in a more general form: κ, A_1 and A_2 can be written

$$\psi\left(\phi(\overline{x})-\frac{1}{n}\sum_{i=1}^{n}\phi(x_i),\overline{x}\right) \tag{10}$$

where ϕ is a function of one variable.[8] In the case of the coefficient of variation, $\phi(x)$ is simply $-x$, and $\psi(z,\overline{x})$ is $\sqrt{(-z/\overline{x})}$; in the case of the measure A_1 the function $\phi(x)$ is $\log(x)$ and the function $\psi(z,\overline{x})$ is $1-e^{-z}$. The functions ϕ and ψ are each important in specifying what we actually mean when we measure inequality.

The function ψ plays a somewhat secondary role: as long as ψ is a strictly increasing function it really does not matter what precise form it takes as far as *ordering* distributions out of a given total X is concerned (although for cardinal purposes, or for comparisons of populations with different n and X, the specification of ψ obviously does have special interest). By contrast the function ϕ always plays a central role in making inequality comparisons, even when n and X are held fixed.

Examine the expression inside the parentheses in (10) which may be read as 'ϕ(average value of x_i) minus average value of $\phi(x_i)$'. To see the significance of this, examine figure 4.3 which depicts a typical ϕ function and take a two-person economy with incomes x_1, x_2, and mean income $\overline{x}$. (A similar procedure works for a multi-person economy.) Draw in the points P_1 and P_2 corresponding to $\phi(x_1)$ and $\phi(x_2)$: C is the midpoint of the line P_1P_2, corresponding to $\frac{1}{2}[\phi(x_1)+\phi(x_2)]$. In each case $\phi(\overline{x})-\frac{1}{2}[\phi(x_1)+\phi(x_2)]$ must be greater than or equal to zero for any x_1, x_2 that are chosen. You are invited to try out values of x_1, x_2, that are more 'spread out' for any

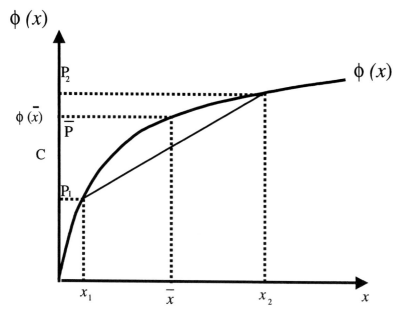

Figure 4.3 Inequality and the φ function

given $\bar{x}$ and to note that, as the spread increases, so $\phi(\bar{x})-\frac{1}{2}[\phi(x_1)+\phi(x_2)]$ increases: in other words, you will find that measured inequality increases.

This property, whereby measured inequality increases whenever the spread around $\bar{x}$ increases, will hold for any function ϕ that is strictly concave when viewed from below (it does not even matter whether ϕ is an increasing or decreasing function). So we appear to have some latitude in the choice of a function ϕ with which to represent inequality: what is there to choose between different ϕ functions? To answer this question properly we need to set out a number of basic principles of inequality measurement, which is the task of chapter 5. However, one central point is that different ϕs exhibit different degrees of sensitivity to income changes at various levels of income (try replacing the present ϕ function with a more sharply curved one as in figure 4.4): the effect on measured inequality of a given increase in the dispersion of x_1 and x_2 around $\bar{x}$ depends on the shape of ϕ in that particular region. A key issue, then, is at which part of the income range we want ϕ to be particularly sharply curved: at which points measured inequality should be especially sensitive to increases in the spread of incomes around $\bar{x}$.

If we examine the three measures defined on pages 73ff. using this diagram it becomes evident that κ will be particularly sensitive towards the right-hand end of figure 4.3, because changes in the income of the rich have a particularly strong impact on this measure swamping the effects of changes in the lower- and middle-income ranges, which might be considered an unattractive property; A_1 is more sensitive to income changes throughout the income range and A_2 is even more sensitive than A_1 to income changes near the bottom of the income range. We can now see the reason for

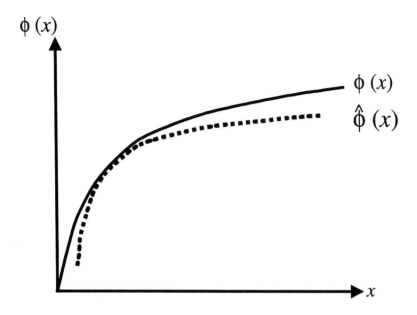

Figure 4.4 ϕ functions reflecting different sensitivity to inequality

the different behaviour of these indices in the applications of sections 4.5 and 4.6. For example, measured inequality using A_1 or A_2 declines rapidly when the time period is extended from one year to two because a large number of temporarily low incomes will be 'averaged away' by taking the two years together. However, high incomes tend to be proportionately less volatile so that the reduction in κ induced by T from one to two years is likely to be much less dramatic.

This sensitivity of κ to high incomes suggests that it may be of limited usefulness as a reliable measure of income inequality in that important distributional changes amongst the lower- and middle-income receivers may be swamped by the aberrations of few large incomes. However, if κ is dropped with what are we to replace it? Can we find companions to A_1 and A_2, with 'suitable' ϕ functions, that are based on something firmer and more satisfying than ready-made convenience and intuition? We shall look at this more carefully in the next chapter.

4.10 Questions for discussion

Further general reading on all questions: Champernowne (1974), Cowell (1995), Jenkins (1988), Lambert (1992), Morgan (1962), Morris and Preston (1986), Nygård and Sandström (1981).

4.1   The following gives four possible distributions of a total income that consists of 36 units amongst four families:

| | Distribution | | | |
	a	b	c	d
x_1	1	1	0	0
x_2	4	2	2	0
x_3	4	8	11	18
x_4	27	25	23	18
total	36	36	36	36

Assuming that the families have identical characteristics other than income, use your own judgement to rank the distribution a to d in order of increasing inequality.

4.2 Calculate the measures κ and A_1 for distributions a and b. Comment on your findings.

4.3 Calculate κ for distributions c and d. What would happen if you calculated A_1 for distributions c and d? Comment on your findings.

4.4 Show that the properties of figure 4.3 still hold if ϕ is a decreasing concave function. Plot the ϕ functions for the inequality measures κ, A_1 and A_2.

4.5 With reference to the data used for tables 4.1 and 4.2 we find the κ computed for *total* family income and using the *family* as unit is less than κ computed for family income *per head* with *each person* as a unit. For the same data and the measure A_1, these two magnitudes are reversed. Discuss the possible reasons for this (Danziger and Taussig, 1979; Cowell, 1984; Lazear and Michael, 1980).

4.6 Suppose all families had perfect foresight. Could (a) systematic income differences between age groups, and (b) transitory income inequality, be dismissed as spurious components of income inequality (Friesen and Miller, 1983; von Weizsäcker, 1978)?

4.7 Discuss the possible use of data on *consumption expenditure* to analyse economic inequality amongst families in a manner similar to the argument of sections 4.5 and 4.6. Would it be possible to distinguish clearly between permanent and transitory economic inequality?

4.8 From the formula for κ write down a formula giving the effect of the immigration to the population of one extra person with income λ times mean income. Compute the increase in κ that would occur if $n=5,000$, $\lambda=100$ and initially $\kappa=1$.

4.9 Table 4.6 gives the change in the incomes of the ten ordered groups (slices of the income queue discussed in chapters 1 and 2. The source is identical to that for question 2.10 of chapter 2. However, the income for each household has been adjusted to convert to 'income per equivalent adult', and each household has been weighted by the number of persons in that household (see the discussion on page 68 above). Do the adjusted figures indicate a clear pattern of change in inequality during the period? Contrast your answer with the picture of inequality that emerges from question 2.10.

4.10 In what ways would changing the definition of income and of the income receiving unit affect inequality comparisons between developed countries (Bishop et al., 1991)?

4.11 What effect on measured income inequality would you expect if the definition of income were to be broadened to include (i) capital gains, (ii) income in kind, (iii) benefits from wealth holding (Bhatia, 1976; Smolensky et al., 1977; Garfinkel and Haveman, 1977, 1978; Weisbrod and Hansen, 1968)?

Table 4.6 *Equivalent household disposable income per person, UK, 1976–1981*

Slice number	1971	1976	1981	1986
1 (poorest)	41	45	41	39
2	56	59	55	52
3	67	68	64	62
4	76	77	73	71
5	85	86	83	81
6	95	95	94	93
7	105	106	106	106
8	119	120	121	122
9	140	140	145	145
10 (richest)	217	202	217	229
Overall mean (£ p.a.)	6,518	6,898	7,588	8,601

4.12   Would you expect the public provision of education and health services to augment or decrease economic inequality (Evandrou *et al.*, 1993; Le Grand 1982; Smeeding *et al.*, 1993)?

Notes

1   In practice the implicit size of X may be affected by the way in which persons are assumed to be grouped into households or families.

2   Note that we are concerned here only with the cost of providing particular collections of consumption services, not the metaphysical issue of whether one person needs, say, twice as much income as another in order to be as 'happy'. Blundell *et al.* (1994) and Coulter *et al.* (1992a) provide overviews of the issues of comparison through 'equivalising' in the context of income distribution, and Coulter *et al.* (1992b) examine the impact of changing the equivalence scale upon measured inequality.

3   For further discussion of the issues involved here see Shorrocks (1982, 1984).

4   See Creedy (1979).

5   This is easily seen in the case of the inequality measure κ. If $\kappa(1)$, $\kappa(2)$ and $\kappa(1,2)$ are the values of κ for income in year 1, income in year 2 and income in the two years together, then, adapting equation (9), the required formula is

$$\kappa^2(1,2)=\lambda^2\kappa^2(1)+[1-\lambda]^2\kappa^2(2)+2\lambda[1-\lambda]\kappa(1)\kappa(2)\rho(1,2)$$

where $\rho(1,2)$ is the correlation coefficient of the two years' incomes and

$$\lambda:=\frac{D\bar{x}(1)}{D\bar{x}(1)+\bar{x}(2)}$$

6   If discount factors in the range (0.9,1.1) were to be used the conclusions would remain unchanged. If the averaging period were to be extended beyond five years up to the theoretical maximum of 20 years the further changes in measured inequality are fairly small – see Cowell and Jenkins (1993).

7   See our discussion in chapter 8, pages 175ff.

8   See equations (1), (5) and (6); a more general representation is discussed in chapter 5.

5   Social welfare and inequality analysis

5.1 Introduction

In the previous chapter we examined income inequality in terms of some basic measures of 'spread' around average income. Although ready-made tools do what they are supposed to do in registering pure increases in dispersion of incomes, there are evidently drawbacks: the mathematical sensitivity of these measures to particular changes in the distribution may not correspond with our own sensitivity to various types of changes in economic inequality and of injustice. In any case we must admit that the specification of candidate measures arose out of an arbitrary generalisation of the simple task of making inequality comparisons in a two-person world. It is time to put this specification on a firmer footing.

If we are looking for a specific index of inequality that accords more closely with accepted ideas of economic injustice, how are we to go about it? Perhaps the obvious answer is by considering which kinds of income inequality are deemed to be most unjust.

There are two basic problems here. One is a self-evident point discussed in chapter 2: there is unlikely to be unanimity in people's attitudes towards inequality, unless we are dealing with a population of clones. The second problem would remain even if the population were to consist of clones; it lies at the heart of the idea of economic inequality between groups: what is the 'society' implied in the specification of a concept of 'social welfare'?

The term suggests a particular reference group, but this concept is unlikely to be unique. In economic matters a person often behaves as though guided by self-interest: by loyalty to the smallest group of which he is a member – himself or his family unit – but he will also have loyalties to larger groups of which he is also a member – clubs, the tribe, the nation – and these loyalties also are likely to be strongly reinforced by self-interest. Again, when one group of which he is a member is a subgroup of some larger organised group, loyalty to the larger may in some circumstances be reinforced by loyalty to the smaller group because of the strength that the smaller hopes to gain from alliance with the rest of the larger group. There are also likely to be conflicts of loyalty to the various groups to which he belongs and these are of particular interest when they involve a conflict between loyalty to a group and loyalty to a subgroup of that group. Although in times of common emergency the different aims of the subgroup may be ignored out of loyalty to the larger group, at other times the individual may have to make a difficult choice as to where his loyalties primarily lie. When there are one or more subgroups commanding loyalty from a high proportion of members who are persuaded that the parent group is characterised by unjust inequality between its subgroups, important repercussions are likely to be felt. So a general discussion of economic inequality should pay attention to the difficult choice posed by such conflicts of an individual's loyalty to a group and to subgroups within it.

5.2 Social welfare functions

Whatever the structure of opinion within a community about the objectives of economic organisation and the degree of success in pursuing them, fruitful discussion about any particular point of view is only possible if it is coherently and consistently expressed. Otherwise, it is impossible to fathom how to rank alternative social states in terms of their desirability and impossible to begin to frame policies to pursue these various objectives due to contradictions between them. The generic term for coherent and consistent ordering of social states in terms of their desirability is a *social-welfare function*. We use the term 'social' because it normally refers to the whole community under consideration, but it does not imply that the ordering was somehow chosen by the whole community: there can be as many social-welfare functions as there are opinions held. The term social-welfare function may occasionally confine attention to orderings applying only to the well-being of specific subgroups of the community.

In order to be taken seriously, an academic writer is expected to be disinterested as to points of view of rival groups. Yet, when each point of view has been presented and treated with detached sympathy, some readers may still welcome a summing-up to suggest a 'best-buy' policy which should somehow draw out and synthesise the best elements from the different points of view expressed in the social-welfare functions of the various subgroups. It may seem that the correct criterion for selecting this best-buy policy is to aim at the greatest value possible for the social-welfare function of the parent group, however that function may have been defined by that group's leaders of opinion, supposing this definition to be coherent and consistent. For example, these leaders of opinion might advocate the policy of maximising real income per head over some specified period, or its annual rate of growth, in which case this might be suggested as the supposedly impartial 'best-buy' social-welfare function.

There are some snags in applying this criterion. First the social welfare criteria of the leaders of opinion may have to pay regard to adjustments felt to be desirable in the pattern of distribution between subgroups – the distribution within the main group. This suggests that coherence in the social-welfare function is unlikely to arise as a matter of course – either because of differing opinions, or because of conflicts of loyalty at different levels of social groups.

The second, more fundamental, difficulty concerns the scope of the social-welfare function. Where, in the pursuit of impartiality, are we to stop in the climb from individuals to sub-subgroups to subgroups to groups to hyper-groups . . . to the universal group containing all others? Is the limit set by state or national frontiers, by continental federations or by the collected market economies of the world? Or have we to maximise some hypothetical social-welfare function for the whole world? But surely, an Englishman might ask, I am to include foreigners such as Greeks and North Americans and yet omit consideration of the welfare of the most noble of creatures, the horse, or include Australians whilst excluding the highly intelligent dolphin's welfare from our calculation? Greeks, North Americans and Australians might feel much the same way about including the English whilst excluding the dignified giraffe. Others might question whether the frontier was to extend in time to doomsday and ask whether the social-welfare function must embrace the interests of all generations to come. To these questions there are no unequivocal answers. Yet simply by posing them we may guard against plumping wholeheartedly for just one particular solution, such as being patriotic and myopic – taking the social-welfare function of our own nation for one life-time ahead and ignoring all other interests. If impartiality really is of such outstanding importance, perhaps we should take the widest group for which it is practicable to frame some social-welfare function that is both credible and capable of being estimated.

In the face of these difficulties, to produce a unique social-welfare function from preconceptions about distributional justice would require a formidably strong set of assumptions that might seem tantamount to a conjuring trick. To do this purely by *a priori* reasoning and to command a wide acceptance of the outcome is almost certainly impossible in general terms. What we can do is to try to throw some light on the necessary structure of a class of inequality measures that is based on preconceptions of social injustice. This enables us to resolve to some degree the issues about the range of choice of 'suitable' measures of spread which were left unfinished from the previous chapter.

The social-welfare function may be constructed by the following procedure: define the set of persons whose welfare is to be numerically indicated; list the numerical indicators of the economic well being (the 'incomes') of each of the set of persons as $x_1, x_2, ..., x_n$; then social welfare ω is given by

$$\omega = \Omega(x_1, x_2, ..., x_n) \tag{1}$$

where Ω is a function whose properties are to be described below. As we saw in chapter 4, a basic difficulty is the accurate interpretation and measurement of x_i for any person i; and as we have seen in this section the further problems that we face in formalising a social welfare function Ω are those of determining who shall be included in the list $\{1, 2, ..., n\}$ of persons appearing as suffixes in (1), and of decisions as to the form of the function Ω in (1).

We might search for a set of ethical and practical principles on which to base the construction of the function Ω in (1); alternatively, we could specify a number of separate objectives which society presumably ought to pursue, and to express overall social welfare in terms of the extent to which these objectives have been achieved. As a suggestion we might take total income X, or average income $\bar{x}$ (equal to X/n) and the degree of inequality I, leaving the exact specification of I unresolved for the moment (it might be, for example, one of the indexes κ, A_1 or A_2) then social welfare would be expressed thus

$$\omega = U(\bar{x}, I, n) \tag{2}$$

where U is some function which is increasing in $\bar{x}$ and decreasing in I. This approach enables us to discuss in a more direct way a key issue concerning social welfare since (2) incorporates a set of views about the trade-off of changes in mean income against changes in inequality.

The function U can be thought of as a reduced form of the function Ω; so, for a given population and for examining states that have the same total income X, ranking states A,B,C, . . . in *ascending* order of I must be equivalent to ranking A,B,C, . . . in *descending* order by Ω. The inequality index is to be seen as one aspect of the social-welfare function: this interpretation is discussed below. We proceed by examining the twin problems of defining a social-welfare function and a measure of inequality in four stages.

- First we need a detailed examination of the ranking of income distributions out of a fixed income X in a multi-person society of fixed size n so as to extend the work of figures 4.1, 4.2 to more interesting cases.
- We extend this to the cases where n is variable.
- We extend the problem of inequality comparisons out of a given income X to cases where X is variable.
- We examine the effect on social welfare of changes in aggregate income X and of inequality.

5.3 Inequality measurement: further logical rules

In chapter 4 we examined three convenient measures of spread, κ, A_1 and A_2, and noted how differently their ranking of economic equality was affected by various changes in the definitions of the data. Each of the three was consistent with the limitations set by the rules adopted in section 4.4. Evidently each measure captured somewhat different nuances of the inequality changes, and these differences in nuance could not be adequately represented in our elementary discussion of a two-person world. To advance to more significant questions we analyse, from first principles, the comparison of distributions between three persons out of a given total income. We shall find this apparently minor complication reveals a number of issues that are central to the whole concept of inequality and its measurement and to the analysis of a social-welfare function.

We illustrate this for three persons in figures 5.1 and 5.2. Figure 5.1 corresponds to figure 4.1 but contains a third axis along which to measure the income x_3 of person 3. All possible distributions of the total X which contain no negative income must lie on or within the triangle $A_1A_2A_3$; figure 5.2 shows this in plan form; A_3 is the distribution $(0,0,1)$ in which persons 1 and 2 each get nothing and person 3 gets all; points A_1 and A_2 correspond to the cases where all income goes to person 1 and to person 2 respectively, just as they did in figure 4.1. The point E at the exact middle (the centroid) of the equilateral triangle again represents the distribution where each person gets exactly the same ($\frac{1}{3}X$, $\frac{1}{3}X$, $\frac{1}{3}X$).

Let us see how to represent any three-person distribution (x_1,x_2,x_3) within a diagram such as in figure 5.2. First, a distribution in which person 3 gets no income and persons 1 and 2 get all, can be represented by a point plotted on the line between A_1 and A_2 such that $A_1P_3/P_3A_2=x_2/x_1$: so, in figure 5.3 P_3 represents the distribution where 16 units

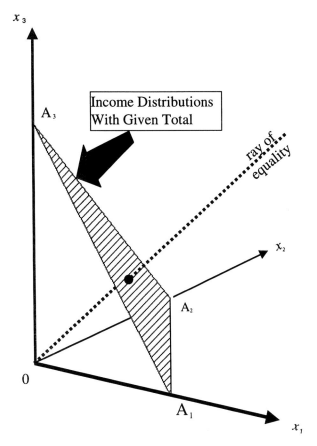

Figure 5.1 Income distribution amongst three persons

are divided such that person 1 receives 5/9 (about 8.9 units), person 2 receives 4/9 (about 7.1 units) and person 3 receives nothing, so that $x_2/x_1=4/5$. Now, noting that any point on the line A_3P_3 represents a distribution in which the ratio of x_2 to x_1 is the same as at P_3, we can see that figure 5.4 illustrates the case where person 3 has an income $x_3=7$, whereas the other two incomes are $x_1=5$ and $x_2=4$ so that $x_3/[x_1+x_2]=7/9$: this distribution is represented by the point B_3 on the line between A_3 and P_3 placed so that $P_3B_3/B_3A_3=7/9$.

Within this framework some inequality comparisons can be easily made. For example, draw a line from the point of equality E through B_3 and extend it to Q, as shown in figure 5.5. It seems clear that distribution Q is more unequal than distribution B_3 because Q is further away from E. Given some fairly mild assumptions (see page 71 and question 5.3) Q must represent a more unequal distribution than B_3. But there is no reason to suppose that this will always happen when the distance EQ exceeds EB_3 but the points E, B_3 and Q do *not* lie on a straight line.

With three or more persons it is no longer possible to decide just by common sense how to rank in terms of inequality all the possible distributions of a given total income,

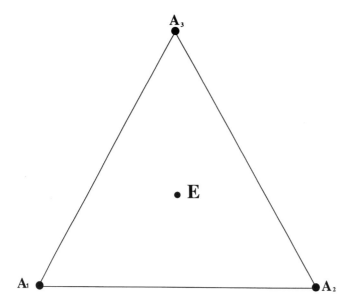

Figure 5.2 Distributions of a given total amongst three persons

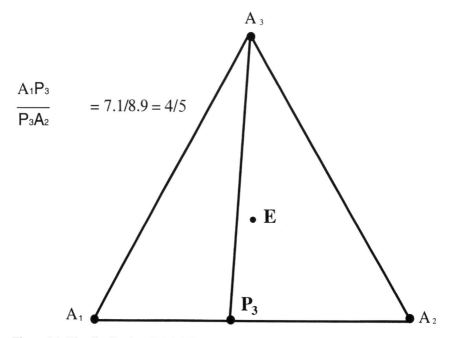

Figure 5.3 The distribution (8.9,7.1,0)

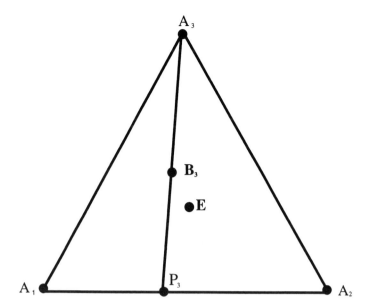

Figure 5.4 The distribution (5,4,7)

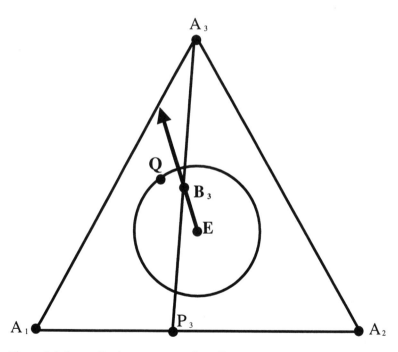

Figure 5.5 Inequality increases away from E

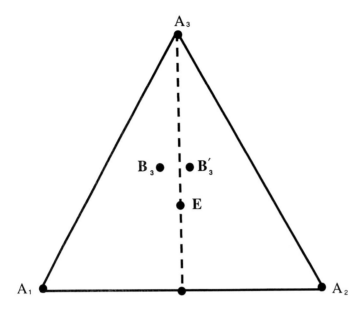

Figure 5.6 The anonymity principle applied to B_3

as it was with only two persons. However it may be possible to agree on a set of rules which both provides some such ranking of all distributions represented by points inside the triangle $A_1A_2A_3$ and is consistent with our common sense and our stronger pre-conceptions about inequality. The fact that such a ranking may not be unique illustrates that the inequality of a set of positive numbers is a tricky concept which has more than one aspect. Let us examine one such set of rules for deciding how to rank by inequality the possible distributions among a fixed number of persons of a fixed total income; we will do this in detail for three-person distributions, but the principles generalise to the *n*-person case.

The first rule carries over simply from our observation in figure 4.1 that the symmetry of the diagram allowed the labels '1' and '2' to be interchanged without altering any conclusions about inequality ranking. It generalises to:

Anonymity principle If one income distribution can be derived from an another simply by a permutation of the individual incomes, inequality remains unchanged. Apply this to the three-person diagram: by the anonymity principle if two people swap incomes the inequality of the distribution is unaffected: so if we start with B_3 – the distribution (4,5,7) – we may obtain the distribution B (5,4,7) by reflection in EA_3: see figure 5.6. In like manner we can construct the four other similar points[1] shown in figure 5.7 and by the anonymity principle each of the distributions B_1, B_1', B_2, B_2' and B_3, B_3' may be ranked equally in terms of inequality with the other five: given any distribution of three positive incomes we can plot a symmetric hexagon like $B_1B_1'B_2B_2'B_3B_3'$ in figure 5.7 whose vertices are distributions all having the same inequality. For convenience call this a *B* hexagon. Now for the second rule.

Principle of transfers If an income distribution B can be reached from an income distribution C by a series of income transfers between pairs of persons, none of which

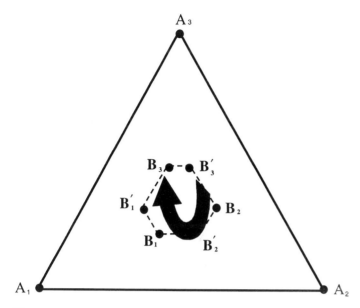

Figure 5.7 The *B*-hexagon

decreases the gap between the pair of incomes and at least one of which increases the gap, then distribution B is more unequal than C.

The principle requires that during each transfer the sum of the pair of incomes remains the same and so does every other income remain the same. In terms of the three-person diagram the principle of transfers says that any distribution C which is inside the *B* hexagon may be regarded as less unequal than B – see figure 5.8. To see this, draw a line from E through C to cut the hexagon at a point F: distribution F must be more unequal than C (because ECF form a straight line – see question 5.3) and any intermediate point on the side of the hexagon B'_1B_2 represents a distribution that can be attained either by rich to poor transfers starting from B'_1 or B_2 (see figure 5.7); and of course distributions B_1 and B'_2 are ranked just as unequal as B_3. But suppose we try to compare the distribution B_3 with a point such as D in figure 5.9. Which of the two distributions is the more unequal? No vertex of the *D* hexagon lies within the *B* hexagon, nor does any vertex of the *B* hexagon lie inside the *D* hexagon: neither distribution can be derived by a sequence of rich to poor transfers from the other. This situation is quite common and illustrates that the principles we have as yet enlisted will often be inadequate to decide which of two distributions of the same total income is the more unequal.

There is an important link between the principle of transfers and the Lorenz curve discussed in chapter 2; let B and C be two distributions with the same numbers of persons and the same total income; then the Lorenz curve for C lies partially or wholly inside (and nowhere outside) the Lorenz curve for B if and only if B can be reached from C by a sequence of gap-increasing pairwise transfers, as described above. In cases such as that depicted in figure 5.9 the Lorenz curves for B and D would intersect.

The problem of comparing distributions such as B and D would be resolved if we

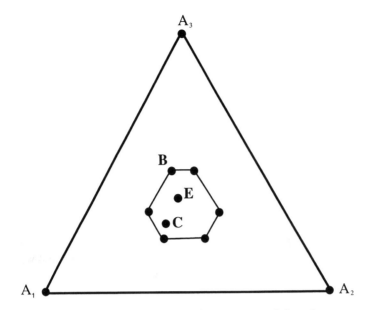

Figure 5.8 Principle of transfers – B is more unequal than C

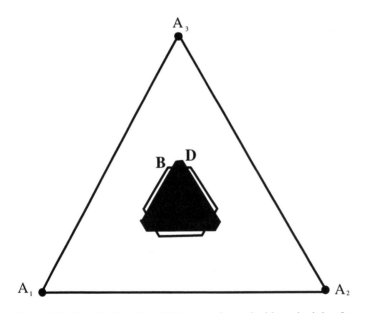

Figure 5.9 Distributions B and D cannot be ranked by principle of transfers alone

had rules which would superimpose on our diagram some system of contours such as those used in geographical maps. The rule would mean, for example, that if the contour through B_3 say lay between E and the contour through D_3 then distribution D_3 would be regarded as more unequal than B_3. To be consistent with the principles stated above contours must be consistent with the hexagon rule and symmetrical about each of the lines EA_1, EA_2 and EA_3, and no two contours must ever cross one another. But these restrictions still leave open an extremely wide choice of systems of contours, even with only three persons and the fixed total of incomes, and with more persons the scope for choice is even greater. Let us look for further acceptable rules to limit the choice of contour systems.

5.4 Inequality contours

A clue to the problems of narrowing the choice among possible contour maps appears if we allow a fourth person into our population and relax the condition that the total of the incomes is fixed. In following this clue it is important to keep in mind a basic distinction: between a rule that imposes merely a restriction on the form of the contours (irrespective of the labels attached to these contours) and a rule that imposes a restriction on the form *and* the labelling of the contours.

Let us suppose that in addition to the persons 1, 2 and 3 whose possible income distribution we have so far been discussing there is a hitherto overlooked person 4 with income x_4. Our new rule asserts that provided we keep x_4 fixed during the ranking of distributions of the total income $X + x_4$ amongst the four people, we may take the same ranking for the corresponding distribution of the residual income of X between persons 1, 2 and 3; moreover – and this is the essence of the rule – this ranking for the distributions between 1,2 and 3 should be the same whatever 4's income x_4 may happen to be. The argument is that 4 is not part of the set $\{1, 2, 3\}$ whose income distribution we are concerned with, so his income x_4 is irrelevant to the *shape* of the contours or the inequality ranking of distributions among the other three.

Once the rule has been accepted as reasonable it can obviously be extended to apply to distributions among more than three or four people. In its extended form it is:

> *Weak independence principle* In a population of n persons the ordering (by inequality) of alternative income distributions out of a given total amongst a subgroup of m persons shall remain independent of the incomes of the remaining $n–m$ persons in the population.

Now for our fourth principle: this is concerned with the effect of a change in X, the total distributed among the fixed number, 3 say, of persons on the inequality contours. Take the special case where X changes solely because we choose to measure incomes in dollars at the ruling exchange rate with the pound, and although the total to be distributed is exactly the same as we had supposed when measured in pounds, yet we find that our information about the exchange rate between pounds and dollars has become out of date so that the total X in terms of dollars has to be revised. Need this alter the form of the contours? In this particular case it seems innocuous to agree that the contours can remain the same since in the triangular diagram the position of a point denoting a distribution depends only on the proportions between the three incomes and not on what the fixed total is. Let us therefore introduce the fourth rule:

> *Scale-irrelevance principle* The inequality ranking of possible distributions of a fixed total X of income among a fixed number n of people shall be the same, so far as proportions between the incomes is concerned, whatever the (strictly positive) value of X.

This is a powerful rule with economic and social implications that could in special

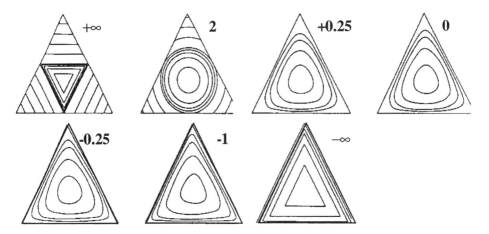

Figure 5.10 Contours for seven values of θ

circumstances be unacceptable (see questions 5.5–5.7). But let us provisionally investigate what simplification can be obtained in drawing up the contour map if we adopt all four of our suggested principles, those of (i) anonymity, (ii) transfers, (iii) independence and (iv) scale irrelevance.

Let the fixed number of incomes be n and the fixed total income be X. A natural way to define a set of contours for the possible distribution $(x_1, x_2, ..., x_n)$ would be to set them out in the form $f(x_1, x_2, ..., x_n)=\lambda$, where $x_1+x_2+...+x_n=X$, the number λ is just the label which distinguishes the different contours, and f is the particular function which describes the shape of the contours.

Our four principles are so powerful that they limit the available contour systems to those for which f can be expressed in one of the following three ways

$$f(x_1, x_2, ..., x_n)=x_1^\theta+x_2^\theta+...x_n^\theta, \text{ if } \theta\neq0,1, \tag{3}$$

$$f(x_1, x_2, ..., x_n)=x_1x_2x_3,...,x_n \tag{4}$$

$$f(x_1, x_2, ..., x_n)=x_1^{x_1}x_2^{x_2}x_3^{x_3},...,x_n^{x_n} \tag{5}$$

where θ is a parameter that may be assigned any value from $-\infty$ to $+\infty$, and where (4) corresponds to the case $\theta=0$, and (5) to the case $\theta=1$. A fairly good idea of the whole family of contour maps in the cases where there are only three persons can be gained by looking at the contour maps depicted in figure 5.10. These show the contour maps for the cases $\theta=+\infty$, $+2$, $+0.25$, 0, -0.25, -1 and $-\infty$.

Notice that the contours for $\theta=+\infty$ and $-\infty$ are all straight lines. These two extreme cases implement two particularly simple criteria for ranking the distributions by inequality. Bearing in mind that X is supposed to be the same in the two distributions being compared, the criteria focus exclusively on extreme incomes: with $\theta=+\infty$ the greater the top income, the higher the inequality; with $\theta=-\infty$ the less the bottom income, the greater the inequality.[2]

Notice also that in the case $\theta=2$ the contours consist of those parts of a set of concentric circles which lie within the triangular frame. The case $\theta=0$ yields a contour map which is intermediate between those for $\theta=+0.25$ and -0.25 although superficially the formula, $f(x_1, x_2, ..., x_n)=\lambda$, for mapping it bears little relation for those obtained in the cases $\theta=+0.25$ and -0.25. Had we compared it with these for much smaller values, such as 0.001 and -0.001 it would have been impossible to distinguish it from either of them by eye. In the map for $\theta=-1$ the transition towards the triangular form of the map for $\theta=-\infty$ has already become fairly strong and this would become more and more marked with larger negative values of θ.

The parameter θ may be interpreted as a measure of the sensitivity of the ranking rule to two kinds of inequality. High positive values of θ, particularly those greater than 2, result in rules sensitive to incomes of a small proportion of persons at the top: we are here supposing that the number of persons, n, runs into thousands, but if n is quite small the rule would be particularly sensitive to the ratio of the top income to the arithmetic mean. Conversely, with θ large but negative, the rule would be sensitive to the incomes of a small proportion of persons who were the worst off, or if n were small, to that of the poorest person.

Even if agreement has been secured as to the desirability of principles (i)–(iv), further important and possibly politically sensitive decisions must be made. Which value of θ should be used to fix the specific family of inequality contours? There can be no simple *a priori* answer to this question so that we may have to employ a variety of values of θ and to accept the fact that the resulting inequality contour maps may at times conflict in significant respects. However, we suggest that there is little point in choosing large positive values of θ, so that the inequality criterion is very sensitive to the detail of what happens to the rich. One reason for concern about inequality is the injustice of extremely low incomes, in which case it is important that our measuring tool be calibrated so as to be particularly sensitive to such incomes.

5.5 Inequality measures yet again

Now let us move on from the form of the inequality contours to the labels attached to them. How this is done crucially affects the cardinal properties of the resulting inequality measures, and here we are on much less firm ground. Having already imposed the condition that the *form* of the contours shall for any given n be independent of X, then an attractive next step is to insist that the inequality measure be so calibrated that the *labels* are independent of n and X. So we tentatively introduce a fifth principle:

Inequality normalisation Let $I(\mathbf{x})$ be the inequality index for the distribution $\mathbf{x}=(x_1, x_2, ..., x_n)$, where contours of I are given by (3), (4) or (5). Then
   (a) $I(\beta\mathbf{x})=I(\mathbf{x})$ for any scalar β,
   (b) $I(\mathbf{x})=I(\mathbf{x},\mathbf{x})=I(\mathbf{x},\mathbf{x},\mathbf{x})=I(\mathbf{x},\mathbf{x},...,\mathbf{x})$ for any replication of the vector $\mathbf{x}$,
   (c) $I(\bar{x}, \bar{x}, ..., \bar{x})=0$.

What this says in plain language is that (a) rescaling (halving, doubling, trebling) each of the n incomes leaves measured inequality unaltered, (b) if r clone-like copies of the distribution are run off then inequality in the combined population is identical to inequality in each of the r identical clones, and (c) when all incomes are equal then inequality is zero, its minimum value. This combined restriction means that the inequality measure must adopt one of the forms[3]

$$I(x)=g\left(\frac{1}{\theta^2-\theta}\left[\sum_{i=1}^{n}\frac{1}{n}\left[\frac{x_i}{x}\right]^{\theta}-1\right]\right), \text{ if } \theta\neq 0,1, \tag{6}$$

$$I(x)=g\left(-\sum_{i=1}^{n}\frac{1}{n}\log\left(\frac{x_i}{\bar{x}}\right)-1\right) \tag{7}$$

$$I(x)=g\left(\sum_{i=1}^{n}\frac{x_i}{xn}\log\left(\frac{x_i}{x}\right)\right) \tag{8}$$

where g is some increasing function. The cardinalisation of the inequality measure is not determined until g has been agreed upon. One perfectly reasonable suggestion would be simply to drop $g(.)$ and to take the expression in the large parentheses in (6)–(8) as the cardinalisation in each case. However, other cardinalisations have also become widely accepted, and some of these are shown in table 5.1 which summarises several commonly used inequality measures.[4]

All but the last entry in table 5.1 satisfy all the principles that have been provisionally suggested so far in this chapter. The questions immediately arising are – what would happen if one or more of these principles were relaxed? Is there any point in doing so? Let us examine two of the principles that may be regarded as being the most questionable.

Take first the principle of independence (rule (iii)). Clearly it is convenient to know that the inequality contours for an arbitrary trio extracted from the population retain their shape whatever happens to incomes in the rest of the population and regardless of additions to or subtractions from the members of the population. Indeed, without this principle it is generally impossible to express overall inequality as a simple mathematical function of the inequality in component subgroups of the population and of the inequality between those groups. However, some might feel that changes elsewhere in the population ought to affect the inequality contours for the chosen trio. Perhaps the most obvious is the following. Suppose that in the trio $\{1,2,3\}$ we have $x_3 > x_2 > x_1$ (this is purely for convenience – they could be in any order). Now introduce a person x_4: if his income is either above x_3 or below x_1 then maybe the contours for $\{1,2,3\}$ could remain unchanged since the newcomer might still be considered irrelevant to orderings within the subgroup $\{1,2,3\}$; if he or she does fall in the income bracket (x_1,x_3) then maybe the inequality contours ought to be affected because, after all, the relative positions of persons 1, 2 and 3 in the 'pecking order' of the whole population will unavoidably have been affected. If we admit this notion as a replacement for the principle of independence then we shall end up with the Gini coefficient (given in the last row of table 5.1) or some transform of it.

Now consider the principle of scale irrelevance (rule (iv)). There are both theoretical and practical grounds for objecting to this. We do not want the inequality index to change just because nominal income is measured in dollars rather than pounds; but suppose everyone's real income increases to the same proportionate extent, it is possible then that we might wish measured inequality to alter. It has been argued that as national income grows, *ceteris paribus*, the inequality contours should change shape in such a fashion that they now exhibit greater sensitivity toward the incomes well below the average – in other words, as X increases we should adopt contour maps that resem-

Table 5.1 *Measures of inequality*

Atkinson's index	$1-\left[\dfrac{1}{n}\sum\limits_{i=1}^{n}\left[\dfrac{x_i}{\bar{x}}\right]^{1-\epsilon}\right]^{\frac{1}{1-\epsilon}}$ $\quad\theta<1,\theta=1-\epsilon,\epsilon\neq1$
	$1-e^{\frac{1}{n}\sum\limits_{i=1}^{n}\log\left(\frac{x_i}{\bar{x}}\right)}$ $\quad\theta=0\;(\epsilon=1)$
Theil's index	$\dfrac{1}{n}\sum\limits_{i=1}^{n}\dfrac{x_i}{\bar{x}}\log\left(\dfrac{x_i}{\bar{x}}\right)$ $\quad\theta=1$
Coefficient of variation	$\sqrt{\dfrac{1}{n}\sum\limits_{i=1}^{n}\left[\dfrac{x_i}{\bar{x}}\right]^{2}-1}$ $\quad\theta=2$
Gini coefficient	$\dfrac{1}{2n^2\bar{x}}\sum\limits_{i=1}^{n}\sum\limits_{j=1}^{n}\lvert x_i-x_j\rvert$

ble those curves relating to progressively decreasing values of θ. The practical objection can be most easily seen by examining equations (6)–(8), the inequality measures satisfying principles (i)–(v). Suppose for some person i we find that x_i goes to zero: then for any member of the family of inequality measures for which $\theta\leq0$ the inequality measure assumes its maximum value. The measure becomes enormously sensitive to any one income that is recorded as being very small, a property which may limit its usefulness: for example, if inequality has already reached a maximum when just one person approaches zero then it cannot get any worse if two, three, four or a hundred people approach zero. Both the theoretical and practical difficulties could be overcome by a neat stratagem: instead of measuring each income x_i starting from zero dollars as an origin we might measure it from some shifted origin, say $-a$, where we know that all incomes are substantially greater than $-a$. Now, if we impose a modified form of scale irrelevance, with reference to this shifted origin, we find that expressions (6)–(8) would be simply modified by replacing each term x_i by x_i+a, and both the theoretical and practical problems would have been solved.[5] The objection to this procedure is that shifting the origin and using modified scale irrelevance will have arbitrary results which may be crucially affected by the precise choice of the shift a.

To summarise, the four principles discussed in the previous sections plus the principle of normalisation introduced here yield a specific family of inequality measures, or criteria for ranking income distributions. Although the functional form is fairly narrowly defined – being limited to the formula (6) and its two special variants (7) and (8) – the range of distributional judgements encompassed by the range of the parameter θ is large. Nevertheless, one or other of the principles used in deriving this family might seem unacceptably strong to some readers, in which case they are invited to replace them with suitable alternatives, perhaps in the manner suggested in the previous paragraphs. Whatever course is adopted we should then immediately proceed to the

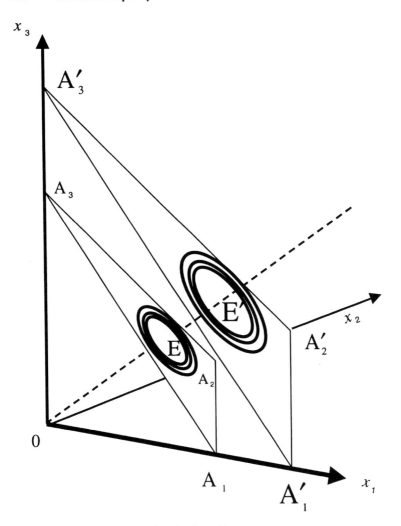

Figure 5.11 Contours at two levels of total income

implications for social welfare judgements of the ranking of possible income distributions.

5.6 Social welfare functions again

So far we have achieved two things: we have discussed a fairly plausible set of principles concerning the ordering of social states that could in principle be achieved by redistribution out of a given total; we have also shown how this ordering may be suitably calibrated and normalised for the purposes of constructing a specific inequality measure. What we have not yet done is provide complete characterisation of the function Ω representing social welfare.

There is an important gap, as we can see from figure 5.11 which shows schematically the contours of Ω at two different levels of total income X, for $n=3$; the set of income distributions at each level is given by the triangle $A_1A_2A_3$ and $A'_1A'_2A'_3$ respectively. E and E' are, respectively, the centroids of the two triangles. Let us see how much we can say about social welfare. Two relatively uncontroversial statements may at once be made: (i) points lying farther away from O along the 'equality' ray will represent states of higher (or at least no lower) social welfare; (ii) within a triangle such as $A_1A_2A_3$ or $A'_1A'_2A'_1$ points lying on contours successively further away from the centroid represent states of successively lower social welfare. But we cannot at the moment say anything about the way in which a point other than E in $A_1A_2A_3$ is ranked relative to a point other than E' in $A'_1A'_2A'_1$. Though we may have agreed on a system of contours at any level of X – like the pattern of rings that is revealed when a tree trunk is cut at any point – we have as yet no agreed system for connecting these contours to form indifference surfaces of the function Ω. As a result of this we cannot yet draw, say, the indifference curves for x_1 and x_2 keeping x_3 constant, nor can we pronounce on the rate at which overall income X ought to be sacrificed in the interests of greater equality. To do this we must introduce some further principles. The first of these should command wide support:

> *Principle of uniform income growth* If *every* person in the population receives exactly $1 more real income, then social welfare increases.

This principle states that wherever you start from in figure 5.12 a movement in the same direction as the ray of equality represents an improved state of affairs. As such it is rather a weak requirement and is consistent with a number of starkly contrasting views on social welfare when X changes. If we keep x_3 constant and draw social indifference curves that correspond to the uniform income growth principle in (x_1, x_2) space we find, for example, that either of the systems sketched in figure 5.13 or figure 5.14 is consistent with the uniform income growth principle. Moreover, each of these is consistent with any of the cross-sectional contours presented in Section 5.4.

A much stronger, but very widely accepted criterion is the following.

> *The monotonicity principle* If anyone in the population receives more real income but no one receives less, then social welfare increases.

This implies that whenever you unambiguously move away from the origin in *any* direction then social welfare increases – see figure 5.15. Many social scientists would take this as axiomatic. Nevertheless, it is also apparent that it goes against the grain of some people's social consciences. It implies that even though society might consist of a million paupers and a single disgustingly rich person we would nevertheless count as a welfare increase an income change that left the paupers exactly where they were whilst further increasing the highest income: in pictorial terms, contours of the form of figure 5.14 are ruled out. It also rules out some social welfare judgements based on income differences.[6]

Despite these reservations we may be forced into accepting the monotonicity principle if we place a great importance on simplifying the structure of the function Ω. To see this, examine the following extension of the independence principle.

> *Strong independence principle* In a population of three or more persons the ordering (by social welfare) of all possible income distributions of persons within a given subgroup shall remain independent of the incomes of the remaining persons in the population.

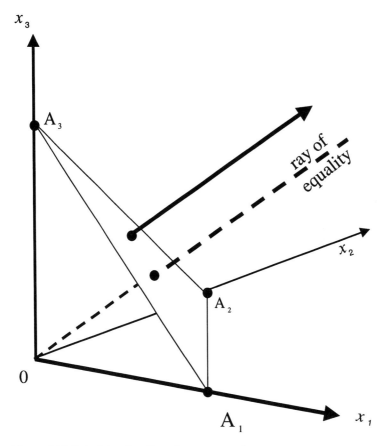

Figure 5.12 Principle of uniform income growth

The strong independence principle in conjunction with the anonymity principle implies that the function Ω must be expressible in the form

$$\Omega(x) = \sum_{i=1}^{n} \phi(x_i) \tag{9}$$

If we require that the principle of uniform income growth hold, then ϕ', the first derivative of ϕ, must be positive; if we require the principle of transfers to hold then the second derivative must be negative. But clearly the requirement that $\phi'(x) > 0$ for all incomes x would mean that the monotonicity principle is also satisfied by (9).

The social-welfare function (9) is a representation of a utilitarian social welfare function that underlies many economists' thinking (see the discussion on page 61). We now have a very simple interpretation of the function ϕ introduced in chapter 4 – it is the 'utility' function by which each individual's income is transformed before being aggregated additively. Since ϕ' is a positive decreasing function we see that in the aggregation high weight is thus given to people with low incomes and relatively low weight to

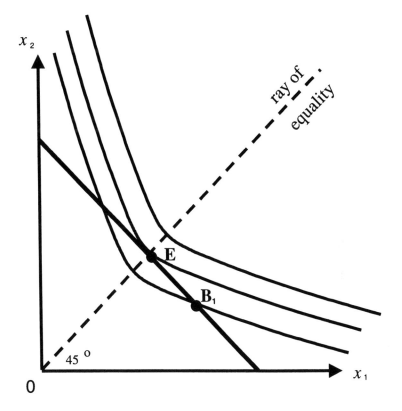

Figure 5.13 Contours of the welfare function in (x_1, x_2) space

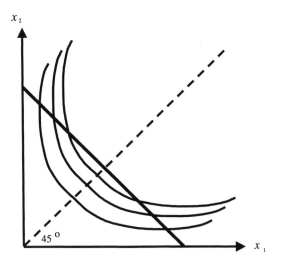

Figure 5.14 Alternative welfare contours in (x_1, x_2) space

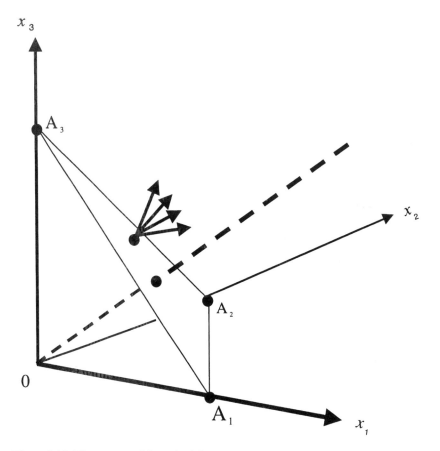

Figure 5.15 The monotonicity principle

those with high incomes. Thus our attitudes towards inequality are simply expressed in the specification of the curvature of this 'utility' function.

Moreover, an inequality normalisation suggests itself. We saw in section 4.6 that one possible way of writing the inequality measure was the cardinalisation given by

$$\hat{I}(x) := \phi(x) - \frac{1}{n}\sum_{i=1}^{n}\phi(x_i) \tag{10}$$

This corresponds to the distance PC in figure 4.3 and has the possible objection that $\hat{I}$ will depend on the units in which ϕ happens to be measured, although if the scale-irrelevance rule is also invoked, we found a way of avoiding this problem by normalising as in (6)–(8).

However, in some cases, an alternative cardinalisation of inequality is often more useful. Consider the following

$$\tilde{I}(x) := 1 - \frac{1}{\bar{x}}\phi^{-1}\left(\frac{1}{n}\sum_{i=1}^{n}\phi(x_i)\right). \tag{11}$$

where ϕ^{-1} denotes the inverse function corresponding to ϕ.

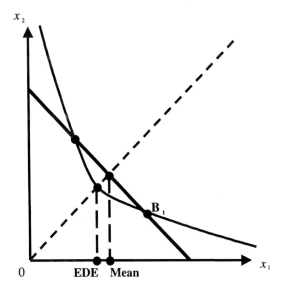

Figure 5.16 The representative of equally distributed equivalent income

Clearly $\hat{I}$ has the same inequality contours as $\tilde{I}$, and the usefulness of this cardinal-isation becomes apparent if we introduce one more concept in the analysis of social welfare. Define the *representative income* or *equally distributed equivalent income* for a particular income distribution vector **x** as a number ξ such that

$$\phi(\xi)=\frac{1}{n}\sum_{i=1}^{n}\phi(x_i) \tag{12}$$

ξ is simply that income which, if given to everyone uniformly, would yield the same level of social welfare as is actually observed – see figure 5.16. Using representative income, inequality $\tilde{I}$ given in (11) may be rewritten as

$$\tilde{I}(x)=1-\frac{\xi}{x} \tag{13}$$

On the right-hand side of (13) we have a ratio of two (dollar) incomes. If the scale irrel-evance rule is applied then (13) becomes the *Atkinson inequality measure*

$$A_\epsilon(x):=1-\left[\frac{1}{n}\sum_{i=1}^{n}\left[\frac{x_i}{x}\right]^{1-\epsilon}\right]^{\frac{1}{1-\epsilon}}=1-\frac{\xi}{x} \tag{14}$$

where the parameter ϵ is a positive number.[7] This ϵ is closely related to the parameter θ which we have used to characterise the shape of inequality contours: the contours in figure 5.10 are also the contours of A_ϵ where $\epsilon=1-\theta$: the larger is ϵ the more sensitive is the measure of transfers in the lower tail of the distribution. The family (14) includes the specific measures A_1 and A_2 which we introduced in chapter 4.

The 'representative income' approach to the cardinalisation of an inequality measure is certainly an extremely attractive procedure, but to obtain a specific form (13) or (14) does require a specific assumption – such as the strong independence prin-ciple – about the function Ω. There will in general be other functions like Ω having the same inequality contours but violating the strong independence principle. Take, for example, the function

$$\Omega(x) = \psi\left(\sum_{i=1}^{n}\phi(x_i), X\right)\phi \tag{15}$$

where ϕ is as in Equation (4.10). This new specification produces exactly the same inequality contours as in (9), but generally represents a different set of social preferences, so that there will be a different equally distributed equivalent income, depending on the specific form of ψ. In (15) we find that anonymity, the principle of transfers and weak independence hold, but not strong independence. Obviously, there is flexibility in a specification such as (15) – we could have a ψ that was extremely sensitive to its first argument and insensitive to its second argument, or the other way about. Each such specification would indicate a specific willingness to forgo X for possible reductions in the level of inequality, whatever inequality criterion – whatever function ϕ – happens to have been agreed upon.

The assumption of the strong independence principle and the selection of a particular function ϕ jointly specify a particular rate at which we are prepared to trade overall income for any reduction in inequality as measured by the index $\hat{I}$. It may be a good idea to check whether relaxing the strong independence principle and so abandoning the link with the utilitarian approach would enable us to represent our views about the trade-off between total income and various aspects of income inequality more accurately. If not, the principle is worth adopting on grounds of simplicity, even if for no other reason.

5.7 The structure of inequality

One of the most valuable steps in turning the inequality measure from a theoretical toy into a practical tool is to use it to decompose inequality into specific contributions. As we have noted in chapter 4 there are two ways of doing this, by population subgroups, and by sources of income.[8] Pursuing subgroup decomposition further we can ask the questions: what contribution to overall inequality is made by the inequality within each of a number of social groups and by the inequality between those groups? How is overall social welfare related to the welfare of each group? Which groupings or classifications are particularly important in accounting for the overall level of inequality?

To fix ideas, examine figure 5.17. Imagine that we are looking down on the entire population grouped together in a large field. Assume that although the income of each person has been standardised (so that we may compare the incomes of people in unlike circumstances) the population is noticeably heterogeneous: the members differ in characteristics such as age, sex, race and so on. Moreover, we suspect that certain characteristics are particularly important in understanding the overall structure of inequality. For example, we might guess that a particular racial group not only suffers a markedly lower average income than other racial groups but also, perhaps, has a markedly higher degree of inequality amongst its own members. If this is so then the distribution of population amongst such groups is particularly interesting: there is a temptation to enquire whether we can represent the overall level of inequality as some

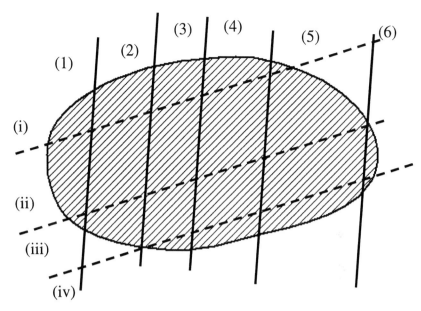

Figure 5.17 A two-way division into groups

function of inequality within each group and of inequality between the groups. We can, as we shall see. But first notice that the procedure of partitioning the population into a collection of groups can be done in many ways that may be of interest. Two such partitions are illustrated in figure 5.17: one classification – indicated by the solid lines – gives us groups $\{1, 2, ..., 6\}$; the other – given by the dotted lines – gives us groups $\{(i), ..., (iv)\}$. Moreover, the combination of these two classifications may itself be an interesting partition: this would give us, in principle 24 groups $\{1(i), 1(ii), ..., 6(iv)\}$. Clearly there is no reason why further subclassification should not take place; the principal constraint is one of practicality since with a multi-way classification we may generate such a large number of groups – many of which, like group $1(iv)$ contain zero or few members – that we contribute little to practical understanding of inequality in the society under consideration.

There are two annoying but unavoidable problems when we try to assign overall inequality to between-group and within-group components. First, although inequality within a given population or group is a purely ordinal concept, assigning specific values to components of inequality requires a specific cardinalisation of the inequality measure. Clearly, we will have a different decomposition formula for each different cardinalisation. The situation is not quite as bad as it might seem because there are usually only very few cardinalisations that are likely to be at all interesting. Second, two different meanings can be given to 'between-group inequality'. To see this, suppose a particular *partition* – a mutually exclusive and exhaustive collection of groups of all the members of the population – has been specified. Note that we can define mean income, x_s and representative income ξ_s for any given group s in the partition: if s consists of the group of persons $\{1, 2, ..., k\},^9$ then ξ_s has the property that

$\Omega(\xi_s, \xi_s, ..., \xi_s) = \Omega(x_1, x_2, ..., x_k)$. For any given partition we can then interpret the between-group component as inequality amongst the group-means – the inequality of the income distribution vector

$$\mathbf{\overline{x}_B} := (\underset{(n_1)}{\overline{x}_1, \overline{x}_1, ..., \overline{x}_1}, \quad \underset{(n_2)}{\overline{x}_2, \overline{x}_2, ..., \overline{x}_2}, ..., \quad \underset{(n_S)}{\overline{x}_S, \overline{x}_S, ..., \overline{x}_S}) \tag{16}$$

or we can take the between-group component to mean the inequality amongst the group representative-incomes – the inequality of the income distribution vector[10]

$$\mathbf{\xi_B} := (\underset{(n_1)}{\xi_1, \xi_1, ..., \xi_1}, \quad \underset{(n_2)}{\xi_2, \xi_2, ..., \xi_2}, \quad \underset{(n_S)}{\xi_S, \xi_S, ..., \xi_S}) \tag{17}$$

Whilst the former interpretation involves merely the arithmetic mean, the second interpretation requires complete specification of a social welfare function which, as we have seen, is more demanding than specification of just a suitable inequality index.

Let us now look at specific decomposition formulae. Out of the many possible versions of such formulae we shall present just two, which happen to be particularly easy to interpret. It so happens that decomposition of inequality in the cardinalisation $\hat{I}$ – equation (10) – is most easily interpreted using $\mathbf{\overline{x}_B}$ whereas the decomposition of $\tilde{I}$ – equation (13) – is most easily interpreted using $\mathbf{\xi_B}$. The two systems of decomposition can then be written as follows.

The decomposition into 'within-group' and 'between-group' components of $\hat{I}$– equation (10) – using *group mean incomes*, is given by

$$\hat{I}(\mathbf{x}) = \hat{I}_W + \hat{I}_B \tag{18}$$

$$\hat{I}_W := \sum_{s=1}^{S} v_s^\theta u_s^{1-\theta} \hat{I}_s \tag{19}$$

where u_s is the population share, and v_s the income share of group s,[11] and $\hat{I}_s$ is the inequality

$$\hat{I}_B := \hat{I}(\mathbf{\overline{x}_B}) \tag{20}$$

in group s. On the other hand, decomposition into 'within-group' and 'between-group' components of $\tilde{I}$ in (11) using *group representative incomes* can be written as[12]

$$1 - \tilde{I}(\mathbf{x}_B) = [1 - \tilde{I}_W][1 - \tilde{I}_B] \tag{21}$$

$$\tilde{I}_W := \sum_{s=1}^{S} v_s \tilde{I}_s \tag{22}$$

$$\tilde{I}_B := \tilde{I}(\mathbf{\xi_B}). \tag{23}$$

Let us now look at an application of this decomposition analysis which also serves as an introduction to the subject matter of chapter 6. To make comparison with chapter 4 easier we shall discuss the indices A_1 and A_2 introduced in chapter 4, expression (14) for the parameter values $\epsilon = 1$ and $\epsilon = 2$ respectively.[13]

Table 5.2 extends the information presented in table 4.5 where the group classification was by age of family head, but we have now merged the data into six age groups and added columns 3 and 4 showing representative income. Table 5.2 also gives a

Table 5.2 *Inequality by age and race groups*

	Total weight	Mean income	Representative income $\varepsilon=1$	Representative income $\varepsilon=2$	Atkinson A1	Atkinson A2
White family heads						
<25	333	13,751 13,336	10,327	6,728	0.2257	0.4955
25–34	1,313	70,423 19,859	16,109	11,661	0.1888	0.4128
35–44	981	71,747 25,112	20,319	13,157	0.1909	0.4761
45–54	486	36,613 29,132	22,114	16,402	0.2409	0.4370
55–64	517	34,218 32,348	23,722	16,277	0.2666	0.4968
65+	673	36,540 19,246	14,952	11,810	0.2231	0.3864
All ages	*4,303*	*263,292 23,777.16*	*18,237.06*	*12,558.94*	*0.2330*	*0.4718*
Non-white family heads						
<25	256	3,536 8,361	6,206	4,094	0.2578	0.5103
25–34	1,043	15,403 10,678	7,144	1,894	0.3309	0.8226
35–44	537	11,616 13,663	9,653	5,974	0.2935	0.5628
45–54	308	6,439 18,184	13,338	8,205	0.2665	0.5488
55–64	274	4,834 19,433	14,037	9,470	0.2777	0.5127
65+	307	4,855 11,614	8,784	6,728	0.2437	0.4207
All ages	*2,725*	*46,683 13,284.36*	*9,097.94*	*3,602.91*	*0.3151*	*0.7288*
White and non-white family heads						
<25	589	17,287 12,319	9,305	5,946	0.2446	0.5174
25–34	2,356	85,826 18,211	13,922	6,056	0.2355	0.6674
35–44	1,518	83,363 23,517	18,318	11,269	0.2211	0.5208
45–54	794	43,052 27,494	20,504	14,270	0.2543	0.4810
55–64	791	39,052 30,749	22,230	14,947	0.2770	0.5139
65+	980	41,395 18,351	14,048	10,849	0.2345	0.4088
All families	*7,028*	*309,975 22,196.92*	*16,423.71*	*9,138.00*	*0.2601*	*0.5883*

Source: As for table 4.1

second break-down by two race categories, giving altogether 12 age-cum-race sub-categories. Notice that, almost without exception, incomes are higher and inequality is lower for whites than for non-whites and that whilst the age–income relationship is clearly marked for whites it is much less for non-whites. Inequality for all age and race groups merged together is given in the bottom row of the table.

Now, what portion of that total should be attributed to the income differences between races and amongst age groups? As we have noted there are two ways of answering this question, according to whether we use arithmetic means or representative incomes for the between-group inequality concept. Table 5.3 displays the results for the age, race and age-cum-race classifications: clearly the two methods yield very similar results for the measure A_1; race by itself accounts for a larger proportion (about 8–12 per cent) of total inequality than does age (about 6½–8 per cent); together, both effects account for 14–20

Table 5.3 *Inequality between groups for table 5.2*

	Number of groups	A_1		A_2	
		Method 1	Method 2	Method 1	Method 2
Age alone	6	0.0264	0.0238	0.0534	0.1173
Race alone	2	0.0187	0.0259	0.0427	0.1848
Race and age	12	0.0435	0.0471	0.0923	0.2326
Total inequality		*0.2601*	*0.2601*	*0.5883*	*0.5883*

Note: 'Method 1' assumes that between-group inequality is computed on the basis of group *mean incomes* (equations 18–20); 'Method 2' assumes that between-group inequality is computed on the basis of group *representative incomes* (equations 21–3).

per cent of total inequality. The method – which is analogous to the traditional analysis of variance – can be extended to further levels of subcategorisation and is applicable to any decomposable inequality measure: we examine this further in chapter 6.

The illustrative example reveals a number of things. It suggests the relative importance of particular social characteristics in accounting for the between-group components of inequality. It shows that some characteristics may also affect overall inequality through the within-group component – the more non-whites, the higher is the level of inequality we would have observed even if inequality between non-whites were eliminated (see the first two parts of table 5.2). We find that even after two major personal characteristics have been 'controlled for', substantial inequality remains – we discuss this point further in chapter 6.

If the data on individual and family income gave sufficient detail on personal and other characteristics we might in this fashion try to account for a substantial proportion of observed income inequality. However, this statistical procedure should not be mistaken for a thorough economic analysis of the factors which determine inequality. We also take up this point in the next chapter.

5.8 Summary

In this chapter we have been able to provide only an introductory overview to two important issues: the relationship between abstract principles for comparing income distributions and specific formulae for inequality indices, and the relationship between inequality judgements and broader concepts of social welfare based on income distribution. However, the analytical equipment we have encountered in this chapter will prove to be very useful in addressing the issues that arise in subsequent chapters.

5.9 Questions for discussion

Further general reading for all questions: Atkinson (1970), Cowell (1995), Lambert (1992), Marshall and Olkin (1979, chapter 1), Meade (1973), Sen (1973, 1978).

5.1 Consider the three possible income distributions A,B,C amongst three persons:

	A	B	C
person 1	3	2	4
person 2	6	8	4
person 3	9	8	10

(a) Rank them (according to your view) in ascending order of inequality (see also: Amiel and Cowell, 1992; Cowell, 1985).

(b) Hughie, Dewey and Louie are three persons who will make up this society, though they do *not* know which of the identities $\{1, 2, 3\}$ they will adopt. They hold the following opinions about the ranking of inequality (in ascending order)

Hughie: A, B, C
Dewey: B, C, A
Louie: C, A, B

Discuss whether a consensus view of inequality is likely to emerge. (The problem illustrated here is known as the Arrow problem – see Arrow, 1963; Cowell, 1986, chapter 13; Sen, 1970.)

(c) Consider the validity of possible political mechanisms which might be used to determine a 'social ranking' of A, B, C.

(d) Discuss the usefulness of examining social judgements about fairness in income distribution as though there were a veil of ignorance as to one's identity, as in part (b) (see Harsanyi, 1955).

5.2 Redraw figure 5.4 and verify that the same point B_3 is finally selected to represent the distribution if one approaches it via P_1, the point representing the distribution where person 1 gets no income and $x_3/x_2 = 7/5$, or again via P_2, the point representing the distribution where person 1 gets no income and $x_1/x_3 = 4/7$.

5.3 (a) Why may we say that, if EB_3Q lie on a straight line as in figure 5.5, then Q must be a distribution that is more unequal than B_3? Explain any assumptions you make. (Hint: show that the movement from B_3 to Q can be represented as a sequence of rich-to-poor transfers.)

(b) In the same figure show that the distribution (10,3,3) lies further from E than does (7,7,2): why can we not say that it represents a more unequal distribution?

(c) Draw the hexagon for the distribution (3.2,6.3,6.5) and compare it with the B-hexagon in figure 5.7. Can the two distributions be ranked by the transfer principle?

5.4 Show that the Gini index generally violates the independence rule. Does this rule appear to be reasonable (Cowell, 1988)?

5.5 Kolm (1976a,b) proposed an alternative to rule (iv), the scale irrelevance rule. His suggestion was that the form of inequality contours remains unchanged not when each income is increased by a given proportion but when a uniform absolute amount is added to each income. Discuss the relative merits of his principle and the scale-irrelevance principle.

5.6 Consider the contours given by

$$f(x_1, x_2, \ldots, x_n) = e^{\beta x_1} + e^{\beta x_2} + \ldots + e^{\beta x_n}$$

Show that they satisfy principles (i) to (iii) but not the scale irrelevance principle (iv). Show that they satisfy Kolm's principle (see question 5.5).

5.7   Show that the contours given by

$$f(x_1, x_2,..., x_n)=x_1^2+x_2^2+...+x_n^2$$

satisfy both the scale irrelevance principle and Kolm's principle. Does this provide a good argument for selecting this set of contours in favour of other possible candidate contour maps?

5.8   Using the contour map of question 5.7 produce two normalisations of the resulting inequality measure such that: (a) the correspondence between distributions of different X-levels is as in figure 4.2a; (b) the correspondence is as in figure 4.2b.

5.9   (a) Discuss the shape of the contours

$$f(x_1, x_2,..., x_n)=[x_1+a]^\theta+[x_2+a]^\theta+...+[x_n+a]^\theta$$

where $a>0$, paying particular attention to what happens when all the x_is are changed by the same proportionate amount.

(b) Assuming that for every i, $x_i>a$, and that $\theta\leq0$, discuss the behaviour of the inequality measure yielded by (a) as x_i goes to zero or as x_i becomes indefinitely large. What happens if θ approaches $-\infty$?

(c) This formulation is equivalent to measuring incomes from the origin $-a$ mentioned in section 5.5: consider the practical problems of specifying a when inequality comparisons between countries, or over long periods of time are to be made.

(d) Using the result that

$$\lim_{\beta\to0}\frac{1}{\beta}[y^\beta-1]=\log(y)$$

show that the limiting form of the contours in (a), as the parameter $a\to\infty$ is that of question 5.6 – see Blackorby and Donaldson (1978, 1980).

5.10   Consider the possible argument for relaxing the requirements that inequality measures are independent of (a) scale transformations of income, (b) replications of the population, given that principles (i)–(iv) are satisfied.

5.11   Group A contains the four incomes 1, 6, 6 and 6. Group B contains the four incomes 2, 4, 4 and 9.

(a) Which has the higher Gini coefficient of inequality? Can the distribution with the lower Gini coefficient be reached from the other by a sequence of rich-to-poor transfers as in question 5.3?

(b) Compare the inequality of distributions A and B by using the indices κ, $A_{1/2}$, A_1, A_2, and the Theil index.

5.12   (a) Using the Atkinson (1970) inequality index with parameter ϵ (equation 14) prove that the value of the index must be greater for Group A than for Group B in question 5.11 if and only if

$$\frac{1-2^{1-\epsilon}-2\times4^{1-\epsilon}+3\times6^{1-\epsilon}-9^{1-\epsilon}}{1-\epsilon}<0$$

(b) Use the facts that the left-hand side of the above expression can be written

$$[1+2^{1-\epsilon}+3^{1-\epsilon}]\frac{1-2^{2-\epsilon}+3^{1-\epsilon}}{1-\epsilon}$$

and that $x^{1-\epsilon}/[1-\epsilon]$ is a concave function for all $\epsilon>0$, to prove that the condition in (a) is satisfied.

(c) Discuss the implications of the fact (which can be deduced from the correct answer to part (a) and questions 5.11) that the comparison of inequality of distribution A and B using the Gini coefficient contradicts that obtained by every member of the Atkinson family of inequality measures.

5.13   Use figure 4.3 in chapter 4 to depict representative income and the inequality index $\tilde{I}$.

5.14   Consider the following three income distributions
   A : (2,10,8) B : (3,11,6) C : (2,10,7)

(a) Draw Lorenz curves for each of them. Show that if the social welfare function takes the form (9) then the ranking of these distributions (in increasing order of desirability) must be C, A, B. Show that if the social welfare function satisfies the principle of uniform income growth, but not the monotonicity principle, then it is possible to have the ranking A, C, B.

(b) Shorrocks (1983b) has suggested the use of a *generalised Lorenz curve* to analyse problems such as those of part (a) where total income differs between distributions. A generalised Lorenz curve can be derived from the ordinary Lorenz curves by rescaling the vertical axis in proportion to the total income being distributed. Draw generalised Lorenz curves for the above example: in which order do they rank the three distributions?

5.15   Write a report on the income redistribution brought about by the new fiscal measures in Mordecatia, designed to promote economic growth and equalise incomes amongst the bulk of the members of the population, incorporating alternative measures of the change in inequality revealed by the accompanying table 5.4 taken from the Mordecatian Statistical Yearbook for 1999. Compare the redistributive effects of taxation in the UK shown in table 1.1 in section 1.5 of chapter 1 with those achieved in Mordecatia in 1999.

5.16   (a) Comment on the system of social values implicit in figure 5.14. Are they consistent with the principle of anonymity?

(b) If a system of inequality contours satisfies the principles of anonymity, and transfers, does this mean that the system must consist of convex curves?

5.17   In a population consisting of two persons consider the social welfare function

$$\Omega(\mathbf{x})=[x_1+x_2]^\beta-\beta|x_1-x_2|$$

where $\beta>0$.
   (i) Show how this can be written as a function of $\bar{x}$ and κ.
   (ii) Discuss the shape of the contours of the social welfare function for different values of the parameter β.
   (iii) Is the monotonicity principle satisfied?

Table 5.4 *Distribution of incomes before and after tax, Mordecatia, 1999*

Range of incomes before tax (thousand crowns)	Number of incomes (millions)	Amount of income before tax (thousand million crowns)	Range of incomes after tax (thousand crowns)	Number of incomes (millions)	Amount of income after tax (thousand million crowns)
<3	0	0	<1	0	0
3–5	6	24	1–2	2	3
5–7	14	84	2–4	0	0
7–10	14	112	4–5	18	81
10–15	6	72	5–7	18	108
>15	0	0	7–10	0	0
			>10	2	27
All ranges	40	292	All ranges	40	219

5.18   It is sometimes argued that the skewness of a frequency distribution is in itself an indication of inequality. Discuss this view using a conventional measure of skewness.

5.19   Discuss the way in which a decomposable inequality measure may be used to analyse world income inequality (Berry *et al.*, 1981, 1983; Theil, 1979, 1989; Summers *et al.*, 1984; Whalley, 1979).

Notes

1 The distribution B'_1 (7,5,4) is found by reflecting B_3 in A_1E produced and the distribution B'_2 (4,7,5) by reflecting B_3 in A_1E produced. The distributions B_1 (7,4,5) and B_2 (5,7,4) may then be obtained by reflecting B'_3 in A_2E produced and A_1E produced.

2 See Hammond (1975) and Rawls (1974).

3 See Bourguignon (1979), Cowell (1980), Shorrocks (1980, 1984).

4 As a simple exercise, try to identify the cardinalisation function g(.) in the case of Atkinson and Theil indices and the coefficient of variation, κ. Further, note that the Atkinson index with $\epsilon=1$ and $\epsilon=2$ (for which $\theta\geq0,1$ respectively) are identical to the indices A_1, A_2 introduced in chapter 4 – see Atkinson (1970), Theil (1967). The cardinal representation of inequality measures was discussed in chapter 4, page 81.

5 See question 5.9

6 See Amiel and Cowell (1994c).

7 The measure A_ϵ is undefined for $\epsilon\leq0$ (i.e., for $\theta\leq1$). The limiting form of (14) in the special case where $\epsilon=1$ is given by $1-x^*/\bar{x}$ in this case representative income ξ is just the geometric mean x^*. See table 5.1.

8 For an introduction to the issues on decomposition by income components, see section 4.7 (page 77); for discussion of the decomposition issue by population subgroups, see Shorrocks (1988).

9 Recall that the labelling of individuals is arbitrary, so the first k individuals have no special significance.

10 The vectors $\bar{\mathbf{x}}_B$ and $\boldsymbol{\xi}_B$ are, respectively, the income distributions that would arise if each member of group s were to receive exactly $\bar{x}_s$ and if each member of group s were to receive exactly ξ_s.

11 These are, respectively, the proportion of population in group s, and the proportion of income flowing to group s.

12 See Blackorby *et al.* (1981).

13 Or, equivalently, the measure $\tilde{I}$ in equation (13) for the particular values $\theta = 0$, $\theta = -1$ respectively.

6 Determinants of economic inequality

6.1 Introduction

Chapters 3 to 5 cover the first of the stages mapped out in chapter 2 for an investigation of economic inequality: the historical and philosphical underpinnings of inequality comparisons and the statistical apparatus for comparing communities' living standards, or social welfare in terms of income distribution.

But as explained in chapter 2, methods for describing and comparing income distributions and other aspects of economic inequality are no more than useful tools for an investigation concerned with inequality. Now that we are equipped with these tools, we proceed to the task of trying to explain and understand the processes that generate the growth and the inequalities of incomes and of other indicators of living standards which have been observed. It is useful to distinguish four stages in this task:

- From a study of data on income distribution and other relevant information on economic inequality we can use the tools of chapters 4 and 5 to examine the *structure* of inequality. This enables us to form an idea of the personal or social characteristics that principally determine the economic conditions of an individual, household or other particular group.
- At a more ambitious level we may try to provide an economic *theory* of the principal determinants of average income out of the inequality of the income distribution in which we are interested.
- To complement the presentation of such theories, some account ought to be provided of the *processes* by which the determinants are supposed to exert their influence.
- One ambitious form of such an account would be a specific theoretical *model* of the process of the generation and evolution of the income distribution. The 'determinants of inequality' could then be interpreted in terms of the relationship between the values of the model parameters and the position and shape of the income distribution generated by the model.

Each stage is progressively more analytically demanding, and the last stage – detailed parametric model building – is particularly challenging. Where possible models should be evaluated by presenting data on actual income distributions, and then verifying, by use of the available statistical tools, that the actual evolution of the income distribution corresponds well with what the theory predicts. If the fit is unsatisfactory, then the theories and models ought to be reworked and improved in the hope of achieving a better explanation of the actual developments.

However, the procedure obviously has limitations. Because of limitations of comprehensibility, the number of parameters in the model has to be kept fairly small. Because of limitations of data on the distribution of income, wealth and other indicators of living standards – such as those we discussed in chapter 2 – satisfactory verification of a distribution model is likely to be achieved only for a few, perhaps minor, aspects of the distribution. Nevertheless, even verification of hypotheses about comparatively minor aspects of inequality can be useful: for providing tentative support for a particular approach to modelling, for illustrating the techniques of model verification, and for ruling out manifestly inappropriate versions of economic models of the determinants of inequality.

Later in this chapter we discuss several general types of economic theory that have been applied to income distribution problems; in chapters 6–9 we shall examine how the economic processes associated with these theories act to generate inequality of income and wealth; and in chapters 10 and 11 we examine a family of purpose-built income and wealth distribution models. But we begin – in section 6.2 – with the first of these four stages, an examination of the structure of inequality using tools and income distribution data introduced in previous chapters.

6.2 Inequality analysis

In chapter 1 we took a first look at the structure of inequality in terms of apparently important groupings within the population. We can now use the analysis of inequality structure (chapter 5) to obtain insights on the determinants of economic inequality. As in chapter 1, we examine the issue both in terms of inequality within a single country, and on the world scale. The method is as follows: select a particular group-defining characteristic that might be supposed to be a determinant of inequality in some sense, and partition the population into groups according to the values of this characteristic (for example, the characteristic 'sex' obviously gives us a very simple partition consisting of exactly two groups): call this partition Π. Also select an appropriate definition of income, 'income receiver', and of the inequality index. Then, use the decomposition analysis presented in section 5.7 of chapter 5 to compute:
• overall inequality, I for the whole population,
• between-group inequality $I_B(\Pi)$ for the specified partition Π,
• within-group inequality $I_W(\Pi)$ for the partition Π.
We could then look at the proportion of inequality 'accounted for' by between-group inequality with reference to the partition Π, and thus the amount of inequality 'explained' by the population characteristic defining Π; this is the normalised residual:[1]

$$R(\Pi):=1-\frac{I_W(\Pi)}{I} \tag{1}$$

The component $I_W(\Pi)$ tells us the amount of inequality that is left unaccounted for by the particular partition Π. Given two alternative partitions Π_a, Π_b corresponding to two population characteristics a and b, if we find that $R(\Pi_a)$ is much greater than $R(\Pi_b)$, then it is reasonable to say that the population characteristic a is more important as a determinant of inequality than is characteristic b. The same technique can be used to analyse more than one determinant of inequality at a time: this extension simply requires specification of a subpartition of the original partition. For any characteristics a and b

$$\left.\begin{array}{l} R(\Pi_{a\ \mathrm{and}\ b}) \geq R(\Pi_b) \\ R(\Pi_{a\ \mathrm{and}\ b}) \geq R(\Pi_a) \end{array}\right\} \tag{2}$$

Applying this to a succession of subpartitions we can get a consistent representation of the importance of any specified group-defining characteristic as a determinant of inequality. Of course, we still have to resolve the problems of the appropriate cardinalisation of the inequality index and of the method of decomposition (see the discussion in chapter 5 concerning equations 18 to 23 in that chapter 5), and of the order in which we choose to bring in successive characteristics so as to generate ever finer partitions but, as we shall see in the examples which follow, these issues can usually be handled pragmatically.

Inequality in one country

We have already glimpsed this technique in our discussion of the PSID: table 6.1 is an extension of table 5.3 which addresses the question of the degree to which three principal demographic factors – age, sex and race of the family head – can be seen as determinants of income inequality. Income is total family income per annum, adjusted for family needs (the same concept that we used in chapter 5, and in most of chapter 4), and the data are weighted so as to give a distribution amongst persons rather than among families. 'Inequality' here is measured by two of the tools that we introduced in chapter 4, the indices A_1 and A_2 that have a straightforward interpretation in terms of social welfare.[2]

Three levels of partition of the population are presented in table 6.1, corresponding to the situations in which one, two or all three supposed determinants of income inequality are brought into the analysis. The first nine rows of the table are arranged in groups of three: each of these illustrates the effect of one particular experiment taking one characteristic as a primary partition and then bringing in either of the other two characteristics to create a two-level subpartition; the tenth row shows what happens when all three characteristics are brought in to make a fine mesh. (Incidentally we can see that relationship (2) is satisfied as the between-group component increases in each of the three experiments of making the mesh of subgroups progressively finer.) Four columns are required to show the details of the decomposition for each of the two inequality measures according to each of the two decomposition schemes.

One of the remarkable things that immediately emerges is the comparatively small amount of inequality that is explained by even the finest of these partitions – some 20 per cent of total inequality – irrespective of the inequality measure, and irrespective of the decomposition method. Within one country we find that attempting to invoke social or personal characteristics as potential determinants of inequality has only a modest success in accounting for inequality.

Table 6.1 *Accounting for components of inequality amongst American families*

	Number of groups	A_1		A_2	
		Method 1	Method 2	Method 1	Method 2
Age	6	0.0264	0.0238	0.0534	0.1173
Age and race	12	0.0435	0.0471	0.0923	0.2326
Age and sex	12	0.0474	0.0525	0.0961	0.2290
Race	2	0.0187	0.0259	0.0427	0.1848
Race and age	12	0.0435	0.0471	0.0923	0.2326
Race and sex	4	0.0406	0.0470	0.0964	0.2357
Sex	2	0.0187	0.0259	0.0427	0.1848
Sex and age	12	0.0474	0.0525	0.0961	0.2290
Sex and race	4	0.0406	0.0470	0.0964	0.2357
Age, sex and race	24	0.0610	0.0643	0.1332	0.2692
Minimum within-group inequality		0.2120	0.2092	0.5605	0.4367
Total inequality		0.2601	0.2601	0.5883	0.5883
Maximum inequality explained R		18.47%	19.56%	4.73%	25.77%

Notes: 'Method 1' assumes that between-group inequality is computed on the basis of group *mean incomes*; 'method 2' assumes that between-group inequality is computed on the basis of group *representative or equally distributed equivalent incomes*. The 'Maximum inequality explained' row is computed using expression (1).
Source: As for table 4.1.

Inequality in the world

What of the determinants of inequality on a transnational scale? In chapter 1 we said that inequality between the rich and the poor market economies is even more spectac-ular than the inequality between the rich and the poor within any typical market economy in either the rich or poor sector of the world. It should be possible to use the same tools of inequality decomposition to verify this bald assertion.

Although the available statistics are not sufficiently comprehensive to allow a detailed decomposition comparable to table 6.1, we may use the techniques for break-ing down overall inequality into components associated with inequality within and inequality between nations, by generating a 'synthetic' world distribution[3] based on data for five representative countries. The five countries – Ghana, India, the Philippines, Brazil, West Germany – have been chosen as coming one each from the five quintile slices (by population) into which the world market economies have been divided after arrangement in order of dollar-per-capita income. For each of these coun-tries table 6.2 shows the per capita income in 1985 in dollars of equal purchasing power,

Table 6.2 *GDP per head and group-mean income ratios for five countries (percentages)*

	GDP/head ($)	(1)	(2)	(3)	(4)	(5)
Ghana	411	32.5	54.5	78.5	111.5	223.0
India	955	40.5	61.5	81.5	110.5	207.0
Philippines	1,710	27.5	48.5	74.0	110.0	240.0
Brazil	3,979	12.0	28.5	53.5	93.0	313.0
Germany	12,831	34.0	63.5	89.0	120.5	193.5
Average	3,977					

Note: See appendix A for details of derivation.
Source: Summers and Heston (1988).

and the estimated distribution of income about the mean. This distribution is shown by displaying the mean income for each of five key subgroups for each economy: the five equal slices of the 'income queue' that we introduced in chapter 1. The mean for each within-country subgroup is presented as a percentage of the overall mean.[4]

Since the five countries, despite their very unequal populations, represent in our synthetic world distribution five slices whose populations are equal in the world's market economies, we need to use a reweighted combination of the data. This adjustment gives the five countries equal weight in order to obtain estimates of the distribution for the market economies as a whole.[5] Similarly, since each of the five slices within any one of the five economies represents equal numbers of persons, we regard the combined population as consisting of 25 groups of equal size, with the 25 incomes indicated by the 25 percentages in the above table applied to the appropriate mean incomes.

The results are displayed in table 6.3 which has the same basic layout as table 6.1 except that we take only one partition – by the component countries of the synthetic distribution. The table reveals that there is indeed substantial inequality on a world scale. Not only that, however, but we find a substantial amount of overall inequality is explained by the country partition: on the basis of method 2 decomposition we find that some 60 per cent of the total is accounted for in this way.[6]

As these examples suggest, simply setting out an 'accounting framework' for observed income inequality reveals some interesting glimpses of some of the social and personal characteristics which may determine inequality between groups. Applied within one country it suggests that even after controlling for important factors such as age, race and sex there still remains a substantial proportion of total inequality that is left unaccounted for by the group analysis. In the case of international inequality elementary decomposition analysis can 'explain' a lot of the measured income inequality. However, this latter finding pushes the question one stage further back, since it clearly highlights the importance of differing economic régimes amongst specific market economies, and of what might grandly be called the 'world economic order'.

Furthermore, it is clear that this type of framework, no matter how sophisticated and comprehensive, can only provide suggestive hypotheses about inequality either within

Table 6.3 *Inequality within and between countries*

	A_1		A_2	
	Method 1	Method 2	Method 1	Method 2
Between countries	0.4902	0.5071	0.7139	0.7110
Within countries	0.2416	0.2156	0.6676	0.3712
Total	0.6134	0.6133	0.8183	0.8183
Percentage inequality explained	0.6061	0.6485	0.1842	0.5464

Source: As for table 6.2.

or between nations. Let us consider how we might approach a theory of economic inequality.

6.3 The theory of factor rewards

In this and the three following sections we shall look at five alternative approaches towards explaining the various aspects of economic inequality. First, we examine the traditional theory of distribution in market economies: the theory which considers the rewards to factors used in production. This approach provides useful insights but inevitably involves drastic simplifying assumptions, which often play a crucial rôle in the interpretation of the income distribution process. We shall be questioning these assumptions and their implications, both in this chapter and in chapters 7–9.

The two-factor model

In developed economies the two principal types of factor of production by means of which people obtain their incomes, are the ability to work in production and the various kinds of productive equipment with which they work: labour and capital. One view of economic inequality is of the contrast between the 'haves' – who own the means of production – and the 'have-nots' – who have nothing other than their ability to work in whatever job they may be able to get for whatever pay they may be offered. Like all intelligible views of economic inequality, this relies on simplifying assumptions: but in this case it is perhaps an oversimplification. It would be convenient if 'workers' and 'capitalists' formed two distinct groups; however in practice there is a substantial overlap of the group of workers and the group of owners of capital equipment and other property. So even if we arrive at a coherent theory of the distribution between two types of income, this is not going to tell us much about what determines the distribution between any two particular groups of persons.

Despite this, theorists have devoted much attention to models of imaginary economies with just two factors of production, labour and capital, to suggest conclusions about the proportions of total income that will be channelled to each of the two factors and their owners: this would be relevant to the real world if most people derived their income either *predominantly* from their labour or else *predominantly* from their capital (a rough guide to the suitability of this assumption is provided by the analysis of the joint distribution of labour income and asset income presented in tables 2.3 and 4.3). Because there are many other influences affecting income distribution besides those taken account of by such models, the insights they provide might seem to be of limited value. But broadly defined factor shares do have an important impact on personal inequality[7] and no serious student of income distribution should ignore the traditional economic theories about the employment and rates of reward of the factors of production in such simplified economic models.

The supply and demand mechanism

What is the mechanism that determines the division of income and wealth between the factors of production? Economic textbooks sometimes convey the impression that all important economic developments, including the evolution of the distribution of income, can be accounted for by the working out of the market forces of supply and demand. There is a widespread disposition to regard the determination of the rewards for the services of the factors of production and of the pattern of employment of these services as being just one particular case of the determination of prices and of amounts being produced and sold in all kinds of markets. This is one reason why income distribution theory has come to occupy a relatively minor place in economic studies as a whole. Were this all that could be said, our discussion of models could be extremely brief: however, we shall argue that models of market equilibria alone are insufficient for providing useful insights into the process of determining income distribution, and that income distribution theory has to advance beyond a discussion of the rates of reward to factors of production.

Let us briefly look at the textbook approach: take the familiar 'scissors diagram' of intersecting supply and demand curves and use it to illustrate the workings of the market in determining the proportionate division of the total product in rewarding the services of labour and of capital, as in figure 6.1. Along the axes are measured K/L, the ratio of the amount of capital services employed to that of labour services, and w_K/w_L, the ratio of the rate paid as profits rewarding the services of capital to the rate of earnings rewarding the services of labour. The upward slope of the supply curve suggests that in order to persuade owners to hire out more capital equipment for use, it will be necessary to pay more highly for its services: the downward slope of the demand curve suggests that industry will only find it worthwhile to employ more capital equipment if the interest which they have to forgo or to pay out in order to secure its services is lowered; the point of intersection P indicates the only values of the ratios K/L and w_K/w_L which clears the market under the given conditions of supply and demand. Consider the effects of changes in the economic environment on the curves in this diagram in the case of a fixed employable population.

• If the population becomes more thrifty, making savings available for financing an expansion of the amount of capital equipment, the supply curve shifts to the right: provided conditions of demand for equipment are not affected, the point of intersection simply moves to the right and downwards along the (fixed) demand curve. The amount of capital used per worker rises, but the ratio w_K/w_L falls: these two effects act in opposite directions on the ratio of total profits to total earnings,

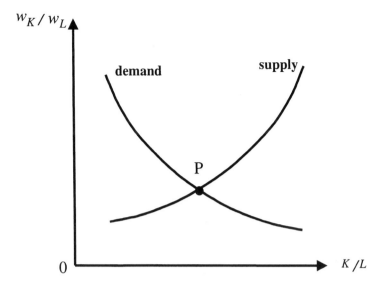

Figure 6.1 Supply of and demand for factors of production

and which of them predominates depends on whether the demand curve or the line OP is steeper at P.

- Technical progress will shift the demand curve: to the right if progress is labour saving, to the left if it is capital saving. Assuming no change in supply conditions, the point of intersection of the two curves would simply move along the supply curve in the appropriate direction. So labour-saving technical progress would raise both the ratio w_K/w_L and K/L which implies an increase in the ratio of total profits to total earnings, suggesting an increase in inequality: capital-saving technical progress would have the converse effect.

The standard account of the shape of the demand curve figure 6.1 in rests upon a market-based theory in which the fundamental assumption is that firms adjust output and the amount of capital per worker so as to maximise profit. Sweeping aside problems of aggregation over firms and commodities, let us see how this works by supposing that there are just two factors of production, used in amounts K, L, to produce an amount of output Q by a single representative firm characterised by the differentiable linearly homogeneous production function Φ, thus

$$Q = \Phi(K,L) \tag{3}$$

We use (3) to define a key concept that characterises the production function Φ: the *elasticity of substitution* of the two factors in production is

$$\sigma := \frac{\Phi_K(K,L)\Phi_L(K,L)}{Q\Phi_{KL}(K,L)} \tag{4}$$

where subscripts denote the relevant partial derivatives. The *marginal productivities* of the two factors – the first partial derivatives of the function Φ – play a central role in the distribution theory (and for this reason it is often described as the marginalist theory). If w_K and w_L are the corresponding rates of pay for the factors, then a necessary condition for minimising total cost of this particular output is

$$\frac{w_K}{w_L} = \frac{\Phi_K(K,L)}{\Phi_L(K,L)} \tag{5}$$

This condition implies that the supply and demand diagram in figure 6.1 can be interpreted very simply in terms of the elasticity of substitution: σ is (minus) the ratio of the slope of the line OP to the slope of the demand curve at P.

To see how the key parameter σ works in the marginalist model, let Θ denote the ratio (share of income going to capital) / (share of income going to labour) and k the ratio K/L. Then we find

$$\frac{k}{\Theta} \frac{\partial \Theta}{\partial k} = \frac{\sigma-1}{\sigma} \tag{6}$$

The implication of this is that, given cost-minimising behaviour by the representative firm, the relative shares of factors in total output are determined purely by the particular value of the technological parameter σ. So, if the demand curve remains fixed, (6) shows that an increase in the supply of capital will lead to an increase in the proportion of its total reward if $\sigma > 1$ and to a corresponding decrease if $\sigma < 1$.[8] The effect of this mechanism upon the distribution of income between classes of persons is easily seen if we adopt the conventional assumption that additional capital is financed principally by the capitalists' savings: the rate of profit on capital falls as more capital per worker comes into use which offsets the redistribution of income in favour of the property-owning class, which would otherwise have resulted from the rise in the capital owned per worker employed: the balance of these two effects is determined simply by σ, the ease with which capital can be substituted for labour in production.

Modifications to the standard model

As we noted above, simplified models of production, although useful for illustrating a simplified mechanism of income distribution, inevitably omit several matters which could be relevant as determinants of income distribution and inequality. Some of these omissions can be rectified just by multiplying the number of factors (skilled and unskilled labour, different types of capital goods and so on): with more than two inputs the interpretation of the model becomes more cumbersome, but the same basic analysis applies. However, there are other influences on the distribution of income by factor shares which cannot be handled so straightforwardly.[9]

One of these other influences is *technical progress*, the discovery of more effective methods for producing and selling. In the supply and demand analysis of figure 6.1 we interpreted this just as exogenous shifts in the demand curve; but although technical progress may enhance the marginal product of factors of production, it does not make sense to treat it as a factor in its own right with its own marginal product. As we shall see in our discussion of earnings models in chapters 7 and 8, the distinction between returns to accumulated capital (which must have required some 'sacrifice' in order to accumulate it) and the returns to pure technical progress (which could be regarded purely as a windfall) is important to the interpretation of the different rates of reward to different skill levels of labour.

Secondly, there are important resources which do not fit in well with the standard analysis of capital. One of the most interesting of these is *land*. In sharp contrast with capital, land is regarded as being inelastic in supply. It may be thought of as acres of real estate, whose use is controlled by an easily recognised land-owning class (although land can be improved by the services of labour and capital, it is difficult to increase the total acreage). But the characteristics of land apply to a wide range of productive factors. For example, one of the most important and interesting features of land is that the results about the share of the product going to landowners are analogous with those about the shares going to the owners of natural resources which are in highly inelastic supply, such as minerals, fishing rights and rare inborn personal abilities – naturally gifted sportsmen, politicians and other entertainers. Where it is difficult to substitute labour and capital for land, the growth of population and the amassing of capital would drive up the proportionate share of landowners in the total reward, but where either can easily be substituted – by investing capital in fertilisers to boost yields per acre, for example – then the proportionate share of landowners rises more slowly or may even fall. Analogous arguments apply to the demand for other scarce resources: large fluctuations in the demand for oil are likely to cause violent swings in the price of these natural assets, just as unregulated fluctuations in the supply and demand conditions for agricultural produce cause big swings in the rewards of owning agricultural property; and if the inborn spellbinding skills of a politician can be amplified and substituted for by public-relations techniques, rival politicians will bid up the prices charged for these services (and the financiers who enable them to pay for the PR services may as a consequence benefit more than the politicians themselves).

Thirdly, the apparently neat result about the distributional consequences of the parameter σ – that the relationship between the relative share received by a factor and the supply of the factor depends purely on whether the size of the elasticity of substitution with other factors is greater than one – is difficult to interpret in any operationally useful sense when we relax some of the crucial assumptions which had to be made in order to derive conclusions from the deceptively simple figure 6.1. Take the assumption that the amounts employed of the factors are so chosen as to minimise the cost of the output produced at given factor prices: under certain circumstances this seems innocuous when applied to the policy of an isolated firm, but there are problems in extending it to the whole economy in order to draw conclusions about the distribution of income between two factors such as labour and capital; one technical obstacle is the difficulty of estimating and interpreting an aggregate production function using aggregate indices of labour and capital. More problematical is the implicit assumption that every firm acts as a profit maximiser under conditions of perfect certainty about the levels of market prices. Apart from the more blatant examples of interference with the competitive mechanism (such as monopoly) there is a more subtle, pervasive and fundamental problem: given uncertainty about future market conditions, the *expectations* formed by key economic decision makers become of paramount importance, and this can affect the analysis of distribution between factors when it is extended to the whole economy.

The Keynesian model

In the alternative Keynesian approach to the theory of factor rewards expectations about the future play an important role in the determination of aggregate income. By contrast savings behaviour plays a minor, passive role in the expansion of the capital stock and primarily affects the nature and extent of the consequent redistribution of income. Whereas the marginalist equilibrium model underlying the scissors diagram assumes that supply conditions or demand conditions can alter independently, in practice supply conditions often do respond to changed demand conditions and *vice versa*. The most important determinants of the movements in the conditions of demand are often business expectations, the actions of the monetary authorities and government fiscal policy. The Keynesian model focuses on such interactions, and recognises that an increased demand for capital will call forth the necessary savings, by stimulating higher production, employment and incomes: this recognition has formed a basis for justifying fiscal and monetary policies for stimulating production and employment during a depression.[10]

The Keynesian approach also suggests conclusions about income distribution under the circumstances of near-full employment. In this situation increases in the demand for capital can still call forth the extra savings required by increasing the proportion of total profits to total earnings, provided that a higher proportion is saved out of increases in profits than out of increases in earnings. This type of theory and its assumptions leads to a set of conclusions quite different from those based on the marginalist supply and demand theory. They suggest that under conditions of near-full employment, the effect of a stimulus to economic activity, such as improved export prospects, domestic government expenditure, or simply business optimism, is unambiguous – and does not depend on the economy's production conditions. The stimulus will increase the inequality of income distribution by swelling profits enough to provide the further savings needed to make room for the extra capital investment without causing 'over-full employment'. This may be complicated by international trade and by the possibility of price inflation resulting from the struggle of the 'earning' class against the shift of income distribution away from themselves to the 'capital-owning' class. If a country imports a large proportion of its consumer goods, the effects of the stimulus to economic activity will be lessened, since a part will be diverted to other countries; the effects will remain in the direction of increasing inequality by boosting the profits to earnings ratio, but this will come about through driving up goods prices faster than money wage rates.

These brief sketches of two theories of factor shares show that the dynamic response of the macroeconomy can strongly influence the determination of economic inequality. They also suggest a couple of notes of caution.

First, two-factor models of income distribution (and three- or four-factor models for that matter) are only going to afford rather limited insights into the problem of economic inequality. This is because they really are too blunt as instruments with which to address the more interesting issues of income distribution. This is principally due to the level of aggregation involved: 'earnings' include such different items as the wages of unskilled workers and farm labourers, along with the salaries of company directors, surgeons and higher civil servants, and part or all of the incomes of the self-employed;

'profits' may cover dividends, the incomes of landowners, companies' retained profits and part of the profits of transnational corporations. It is unlikely that any model whose workings can be described in terms of elementary diagrams, such as figure 6.1, can give an adequate account of the division of the total income between two such complex sets of payments.

Second, even if we confine our attention to problems where the two-factor type of theory is relevant, the traditional theory is of limited applicability perhaps to the point of being misleading. It requires acceptance of behavioural assumptions that may simply miss out on important processes that actually operate upon the distribution of the rewards to factors of production. This broad conclusion also applies to theories concerning the detailed structure of the income distribution between persons.[11]

Superimposed on the basic mechanisms of free market competition highlighted by standard economic theory, are a variety of other forces and structures which may have an important part to play in determining economic inequality. In the remainder of this chapter we shall focus on the following issues in particular:

Pecking orders Various economic and social rigidities arise from monopoly power and social stratification and from the division of the community into various demographic and social groups. The manner in which these rigidities modify the free play of market competition and thereby affect the degree and pattern of economic inequality is considered in section 6.4.

Accidents will happen People base important economic decisions on incomplete information about the current situation and the choices available to them, and on even greater ignorance of future economic prospects. This can invalidate theoretical conclusions about distribution and inequality which are based on the postulate of pure competition in free markets with perfect foresight. Instances of this are discussed in section 6.5.

Rough and tumble Many of the decisions which crucially affect distribution and inequality are the outcome of struggles in which threats, bluff and violence are often near to the surface. In section 6.6 we discuss whether such departures from the assumptions of free competition seriously undermine the conclusions drawn from free market distribution theories.

Governments and other very big fish A particular example that brings in elements of all three of the subjects outlined above is that the policies of government agencies and international agencies, including large international companies, do not fit neatly into theories relying on free market postulates. The implications of this will be pursued in section 6.7.

6.4 Economic and social rigidities

The scissors diagram approach of section 6.3 presupposes a tidy world of pure price competition in which complications associated with other social institutions or non-competitive forces are absent – or at least are too insignificant to matter alongside big questions such as the division of national income between the factors of production. What if we were to relax the assumption of universal pure competition? In this section we shall take a brief look at three issues which seem to require a fresh approach to the theory of income distribution, and which will play important rôles in later chapters.

Monopoly power

The economic analysis of the influence of monopoly and monopsony on income distribution has a long and respectable ancestry. Traditionally this approach has concentrated on income distribution interpreted as a theory of factor rewards: many nineteenth-century economists believed that the pressure of increasing population would keep wages down to the level of subsistence, and some argued that wealth-owners would consequently derive high profits which they would use to accumulate capital equipment for amassing yet more profits with no larger a labour force. Whilst today it would be unreasonable to suggest that wages in the advanced market economies are held at subsistence levels, this might still be argued in parts of the developing world.[12]

A related theory attempts to explain the distribution of income between wages and profits in terms of the *degree of monopoly*, the degree of divergence of the state of the market from that of free competition. The maintenance of a high ratio of total profits to total earnings was attributed to the survival of a substantial degree of monopoly. The difficulty in accepting this as a general theory of income distribution – as with other two-factor distribution theories – lies principally in the heterogeneity of factor payments, as we explained at the end of section 6.3.

However, monopoly power often plays an important part within particular markets and in the determination of the incomes of particular groups of people, as we shall see in the discussion of earnings in chapters 7 and 8.

Social rigidities

There appear to be many glaring instances of rigidities embedded in the social structure. For example, what underlies the observed income differences that appear to be attributable to personal characteristics in table 6.1?

The story that is illustrated by the results of table 6.1 is fairly typical of developed economies. Although income inequality between the sexes accounts for only a small proportion of the total inequality, in most advanced industrial societies the earnings of males are substantially and persistently higher than those of females. Furthermore, for both males and females, there is a characteristic life-cycle pattern of real earnings, and a characteristic life-cycle pattern for total incomes; as we noted in chapter 4 these effects can have an important impact on the distribution of family incomes. The apparent influence of social rigidities is further reinforced by the systematic and persistent differences between the average incomes and patterns of distribution for different racial groups. However, are such phenomena to be considered as 'determinants' of inequality in any sense deeper than the basic accounting framework that we discussed in section 6.2? There are two issues here: whether the systematic income differences genuinely represent economic inequality, and whether there is at work some determinant of inequality that is sufficiently strong to override the effects of pure competition.

On the first issue, the argument in terms of inequality as priority of need is clear: in inter- or intra-national comparisons of income levels, poverty remains as poverty whether it is due to being at an age at which average earnings are low, being a woman, or belonging to a particular race. In terms of the fairness or economic justice of economic inequality the argument is less clear. In the case of income differences attributable to age (as we discussed in chapter 4) it can be argued that the young can look forward to reaching the peak of the age cycle in earnings eventually, and accordingly suffer no unfairness from the currently low income. In the case of income differences between the two sexes some might try a similar argument (females who want high earnings have as good opportunities as males, but that really most females prefer various non-economic satisfactions which they are better able to enjoy than males) but it is more plausible to suppose that the lower average income of females is rather due to their being disadvantaged in their economic opportunities.

This is where the second issue becomes particularly relevant. If women really are disadvantaged, then this is presumably due to either a quirk of their characteristics as valued in the market, or a quirk in the working of the market. For example, the immediate cause of their low earnings might be diagnosed as their having obtained inferior training: this might be because women are inherently less able, or because they fail to acquire these skills before entering the labour market because they are hindered from doing so. Either way gender acts as a determinant of inequality; but in the second case we have to consider a theory of inequality that explains why the free market does not work as it 'should' do.

Similar thoughts apply also to the inequality between members of different races. The economic mechanisms which underlie these social rigidities and act as determinants of inequality are discussed further in chapters 7 and 8.

Class behaviour

There is a further important way in which social and economic rigidities may act as determinants of inequality. We have already noted (in section 6.3) the rôle of class-based economic theories of the distribution of national income by factor shares. Although individuals do not usually fall into neat distinct classes of idle property owners and propertyless workers, nevertheless, if the economy consists of classes distinguished by the extent of property ownership of their members, and if the economic behaviour of those who fall into each of the classes is significantly different, then interesting conclusions follow about the division of income between the classes. For example, in a simple two-class model, the savings ratio of the predominantly wealth-owning class, in conjunction with the technically determined capital–output ratio, play an overwhelming role in determining the division of income between the predominantly wealth-owning class and the predominantly earning class.[13]

Class behaviour also has an a important part to play in models of distribution of wealth and income between persons as opposed to broad-defined factors of production. But why should a person's behaviour differ according to the 'class' of which he is a member? If people really were segregated into the various classes of pure capitalists, workers, landowners, and so on it might be reasonable to suppose that this differential behaviour was entirely attributable to habits, tastes or some kind of class conditioning. An alternative explanation that is perhaps more appropriate to an economic theory of inequality, is that what appears as 'class' behaviour really has more to do with the economic circumstances of individuals, and the type of income involved. Poor people might rationally choose to save a smaller proportion of their income than rich people with the same tastes and social background; the proportionate composition of a poor person's 'income package' (in terms of labour earnings, asset income and so on) is likely to be quite different from that received by an otherwise similar rich person – see for example table 2.3 on page 33.

On top of this, apparent behaviour according to class may also be influenced by decisions made in the face of uncertainty or risks associated with the type of 'income package' that they receive, and with their economic prospects more generally.

6.5 Ignorance, uncertainty and inequality

The effects of ignorance and uncertainty on the mechanisms determining economic inequality are widespread. Despite this many simplified economic models assume that every individual in the model has perfect knowledge of the economic present and foresight of the economic future. The assumption of perfect certainty is made in order to focus attention on aspects of the economic system which are believed not to be seriously affected by the actually prevalent uncertainty and ignorance about economic upheavals that may already have taken place elsewhere, let alone those that are yet to occur. But in trying to build models concerned with economic inequality, this approach misses one of the main features of the economic system that can reasonably be identified as a determinant of inequality.

The ability to peer rather further through this fog of uncertainty than can the next person will often be more useful for bettering the lot of the persons concerned than almost any other skill, and could eventually be worth more than the whole of their current wealth. How much such prophetic skill is worth can largely depend on the other advantages that accompany it, such as powers of persuasion, good credit facilities and access to those with money to spend on wise forecasts. A simple and adequate theory of the effects of the spread of access to good forecasts of economic events on economic inequality is not likely to be practicable, but common sense can suggest a few broad conclusions.

• Exceptional foresight about the near future is more useful than such foresight about the more distant future. For only tentative or minor conclusions can normally be drawn about the remote future, unless it is the unhelpful vision of inevitable doom. Apart from that, expectations of the far future have continually to be revised due to events that upset expectations about the intermediate future.

• The expectations held by economic agents themselves significantly affect economic events and thereby later expectations, so that it is important to be well-informed about current opinion and expectations, and about the astuteness or obtuseness of influential agents in forming their expectations.

• Economic models which assume a high degree of economic foresight on the part of all persons are particularly ill-fitted to diagnose the economic and social reasons for the survival of widespread intense poverty in the world today.

As we shall see in chapters 8 and 11, uncertainty and imperfect foresight play a significant role in strengthening the impact of particular social and political factors on the formation of income distribution. So the theory of factor rewards must pay close attention not only to property rights and people's endowments, but more especially to the mechanisms by which these endowments result in the flow of incomes.

6.6 Conflicts of interest and struggle

Several theories of distribution regard cost-push, trade-union muscle or outright class struggle as key elements in the dynamics of adjustment to the inequality of the income distribution. 'Struggle' is often associated with Marxist theory, which regards the determination of the distribution of income between the wages of labour and the profits of capitalists as the economic front of the general class struggle between labour and capital. In addition, there are other theories which regard the use of crude force as exerting a powerful effect on the distribution of income and on the degree of economic inequality. Let us look at the possibility of modifying economic inequality by such methods.

At first sight it seems that the belief that the working class as a whole can gain by industrial action to raise wage levels is just an error. The argument against it is that unless prices can be raised sufficiently to offset the increase in labour costs, firms will find their profit rates lowered and be driven out of business or operate below capacity; this would result in increased unemployment, and reduce both the current real income going to the working class, and their power to continue the struggle for higher wages; however, if prices do rise sufficiently to match the nominal wage increases, then the hope of real gains by the working class will be illusory. This sort of refutation of the effectiveness of struggle as a means of modifying income distribution appeals both to laissez-faire economists, who place their main reliance for progress on the smooth working of free market forces, and mildly interventionist economists, such as those of the Keynesian school. Nevertheless, there are powerful arguments available in reply to the effect that wages can be pushed up ahead of prices in a manner which need not result in higher unemployment.

One such argument is that full employment and growth may persist together at any one of a range of possible distributions between wages and profits. The ceiling to this range is set by the condition that there must remain sufficient profits to make it worth the while of industrialists to avoid any actual fall in average real output per employed worker.[14] This argument concedes that the gains which struggle may win for the proportionate share of labour are likely to be partly at the expense of the growth rate of output. It thus becomes difficult to predict the long-run prospects of economic gain for the working class as a whole from any such struggle: opponents of the theory would go so far as to claim that, in the long run, the working class as a whole are likely to damage their own interests by adopting the tactics of struggle.

A more moderate argument for the partial effectiveness of 'struggle' is based on the idea that by struggle they can always keep just ahead of the employers in the race for more. The wage earners start the race by a successful skirmish for a wage increase; the employers react (after a delay) by pushing up prices in proportion; the wage earners then thwart the counter-move by a prompt further struggle to raise wages. Even if employers can adjust prices more expeditiously than wage earners can secure wage increases and thus get ahead in the race, the working class need to put up a struggle if they are to avoid being left ever further behind. Either way, the race continues in the same fashion, round after round.

Theories attributing a role to struggle in the determination of income distribution can also be used to justify tough policies by employers and the authorities acting in their support to make industry more profitable and to promote economic growth. For example, the availability of extra profits for ploughing back to modernise and improve the industrial plant coupled with the opportunity to employ cheap labour and pay high managerial salaries may attract investment and skilled management from international companies and from other countries.

The strong feelings aroused in such struggles for better incomes has sometimes led to more violent conflict: civil unrest and even an increased risk of war. Although these forces are sometimes assumed to be outside the conventional 'rules of the economic game' they should not be ignored in any attempt to understand the actual extent of economic inequality. Being outside the conventional 'rules of the economic game' does not mean to say that these forces are economically irrelevant: in some societies one of the most valuable resources is the ability to set the rules.

Although it would be difficult to cite convincing examples of civil or international wars where the sole motive was demonstrably that of altering the income distribution, some of the most dramatic alterations in income distribution have been the result of conflict. The complex economic effects of violence should not be ignored either: the heavy costs involved in demonstrations of violence – war, revolutions and other civil conflict – and in steps taken to frustrate violence and to maintain law and order.

The immediate effects of violence and of the expenditure involved in countering violence are likely to be to increase economic inequality, since the poor and the weak are those most likely to be caught in the crossfire between the rebels and the authorities' counter-measures (although there are conspicuous exceptions to this, such as losses to the wealthy victims of kidnaps and to the well-to-do owners of property destroyed by civil conflict). The medium- and long-term effects of violence are less clear: although the opportunity of a change in administration by democratic processes may reduce the causes of violence so that it no longer affects inequality; the authorities may be violently overthrown by forces intent on an egalitarian redistribution policy, or possibly by forces with the opposite intention.

What of the effect on international inequality? It is far from clear that heavy investment in military power pays off economically, whatever may be its political value in terms of prestige. Minor economies often incur economic disaster through grandiose attempts to gain military prestige; autocratic régimes sometimes face ruin as a result of relying too heavily on a corrupt unpopular police apparatus whose cost and intransigence get out of hand. So expenditure on violence could distribute income away from the more violent to the less violent régimes, but it is doubtful whether this would be a significant factor restraining international inequality. History suggests that the overwhelming effect of the escalation of violence is the overall retardation or reversal of economic progress. International inequality is increased so long as inefficient governments continue to impoverish backward economies further by excessive expenditure on force; and even when they eventually provoke their own overthrow, the opportunity of reversing the process is often missed: the conflict often continues with the economy sinking yet deeper into disorder and poverty.

6.7 The public sector

The mention of violence and conflict directs our attention to the major influence which governments can exert on economic inequality in their role of maintaining law and order and national defence. But political authorities also influence income distribution through more commonplace channels: their general social and economic policies. This influence on living standards is considerable, both internationally and domestically, and merits a prominent place in the list of 'determinants of inequality': we devote the final chapter of this book to a discussion of the issues that it raises.

The subject of the influence of governmental actions upon economic inequality is especially challenging because of a point that does not arise with the other determinants of inequality that we have considered: there is a distinction to be made between the issue of how a government *does* act in this regard and how it *should* act. The subject is also controversial because of the deep disagreement about whether the intervention by authorities in economic matters is mainly beneficial or harmful. Much analysis of public policy regarding inequality presumes that all those affected by it accept that its aims are right and – although this presumption seems rash – let us suppose that there is this complete acceptance, and examine the effects that government action might exert under such ideal conditions.

The problem of establishing how a government acts to affect economic inequality is illustrated by the provision of transfer incomes, such as subsidies to certain groups, financed by taxing the incomes of others. The intended effect of the tax-cum-transfer policy is often only partially achieved: the actual incidence of taxes diverges from the ideal because of incomplete information and ineffective tax collection. As for the beneficial effects from the transfer incomes, it may be relatively easy to estimate the effects on the distribution between the particular groups which are subsidised and those which are not, but much less easy to assess the overall impact on economic inequality. In the case of educational subsidies, for example, an estimate could be made of the effect on the distribution between those households with children of school age and those without them, but not only are there difficulties with incomplete information and ineffective administration of the transfer schemes, as with the taxation side of the operation, but we also have to overcome the difficulty of valuation of the subsidised services, as we discussed in chapter 4. A further complication is that public expenditure in general, or on specific items such as health or education, may have important 'spillover effects' – on workers' market power, on location of industry and on firms' hiring policies.[15] This is one example of the distinction between the private effects of economic decisions and their total social effects, taking account of indirect channels of influence on distribution: other important examples of such spillover effects can be found in public expenditure on items which are largely consumed collectively rather than individually.

Practical difficulties also affect the issue of how governments should act. Governments often pay at least lip service to principles of social justice, and so some of the measures used by the authorities to raise revenue and to modify income distribution, such as progressive income taxes, avoid concentrating their effects on particular groups, particularly in cases where there are no obvious distributional advantages from doing so. But often the impact of tax policy on inequality is less clear cut. There can be practical advantages from discarding such high principles and applying taxes to various easily defined groups such as car owners, drinkers and smokers: this can be a useful, although perhaps mildly inequitable, means of reducing the problem of poor information. Moreover, where groups are perceived as particularly important to the government in attaining its chosen goals, overt or covert fiscal discrimination is often expedient: lowering taxes on those groups whose support is critical or who most deserve encouragement, and levying taxes on those of less immediate consequence or apparent worth.

Shortage of information can also cause problems when targeting government expenditures. Concern for inequality in terms of 'priority of need' should arguably focus attention upon particular individuals or households rather than on broadly defined groups such as we have mentioned in this chapter. To some extent this can be achieved by subsidising readily identifiable groups such as the unemployed, the disabled, the aged poor, or inhabitants of disaster areas; but a more straightforward method is to supplement all household incomes which fall below some statutory minimum, which may be defined so as to depend on the constitution of the household. Whilst these methods all suffer to various degrees from the fact that the groups benefitting may include households or individuals not suffering from any such particular hardship or emergency, they do go some way to directing help towards those most likely to benefit from it.

Finally, note that the issues discussed in this section have an important application beyond national boundaries. Some of the remarks that apply to the influence of national governments on income distribution intra-nationally apply also in principle to the actions of international bodies such as the United Nations or the European Union. In chapter 1 we pointed out also that the most glaring instances of economic inequality in the market economies are found between the living standards in Africa, Asia and South America on the one hand and the developed economies in North America, Europe and Australasia on the other. The operations of international agencies – intentional or otherwise – can have a significant impact on this form of inequality. We shall treat such issues briefly at the end of chapter 12.

6.8 Tasks yet to be tackled

This is an appropriate point at which to take stock.

As we have seen, the 'determinants of inequality' can be interpreted in a way that does not really invoke much economic theory at all. We can just specify an appropriate partition of the population in question in order to examine the composition of inequality. However, the results of this approach typically leave 'unexplained' a substantial component of inequality: where the data are available we usually find that income differences between groups account only for a small part of the total observed inequality within any one national economy. Moreover, the results always require careful interpretation: for example, although the results shown in table 6.1 suggest that the contribution of ethnic inequality is less than that of inequality between the sexes, this does not mean that in some deeper sense racial discrimination is a less important economic problem than discrimination by sex; nor does it provide the basis for a *theory* of what determines economic inequality.

As we have seen there is a number of candidate theories that could be advanced to do this job of explaining the determination of income distribution and economic inequality This raises the question of which amongst these is nearest to being the 'right' approach. That is a problem we shall not tackle – at least not in that simplistic form.

One reason for not trying to do this is that the apparently simple economic answers – based on naïve models of pure competition – often leave out issues which are of particular relevance to the development of inequality in practice. Barriers to and restraints on the competitive mechanism – inconvenient though they may be for the economic theorist – form an important part of the determinants of economic inequality. They substantially affect both the structure of rewards within various occupations and segments of the market and the divisions of income among the owners of broadly defined factors.

Furthermore, as we discussed in chapter 2, it is unlikely that any one theory would stand out clearly as better than all the alternative explanations, even if much more detailed evidence became available. Empirical evidence and critical reasoning may show that some versions of theories are so extreme or oversimplified as to be virtually useless for better understanding actual distribution processes: but such evidence and reasoning are unlikely to pick out a convincing and consistent winning theory. No single simplified economic model is likely to succeed entirely in dealing with even the most important questions about economic inequality.

As we pointed out in chapter 3, very dissimilar systems of social and economic organisation may require different theories for explaining the development of inequality, and even in a single country, because of the complicated nature of the subject, different types of questions about income distributions may often be better tackled by different types of theories. Accordingly, the fact that no consistently best theory can be identified is no reason for ignoring the alternative theories which have been outlined: rather, this variety provides us with useful alternative approaches most suitable for application to specific issues that we wish to study.

This last point will become evident in considering the questions about earnings, wealth and income which we discuss in the rest of this book. Let us briefly consider some of the more important of these.

The form of frequency distribution

A primary task is to find an explanation for the distinctive shape of distributions of wealth and income which are commonly observed, as well as their implied inequality. So we shall take a close look (in chapters 7 and 8) at what may explain the distribution of earnings, since these account for a high proportion of total personal incomes in advanced industrial societies. Then (in chapter 9) we tackle the theoretical study of the distribution of wealth.

Wealth and income interactions

A second task is to explain the ways in which the accumulation of personal wealth and a person's economic success in terms of labour earnings may be interlinked; in particular, we should study how both effects of this positive feed-back system may have been protected and strengthened by the institution of the inheritances of property, and how this interaction affects economic inequality. This will be tackled in chapters 10 and 11, using models to provide some insight into the effects which particular changes in economic circumstances or policy may exert on these distributions. This introduces the strong effects on the shapes of these distributions which may be produced by the fortuitous elements affecting the wealth of particular families and in their more general economic circumstances.

Modelling the unexplained component

Since only a small proportion of actual inequality can be accounted for by those suggested factors about which there is good statistical evidence, our third task is to indicate some method by which all other factors (both those known but lacking good statistics and the unknown ones) which affect the distribution of incomes may yet be represented in a theoretical model. One such method is to represent them using a *stochastic variable* – one which may take any one value out of a set of possible values extending over a whole range. Which of these values is taken is decided by some chance process: that is, by some experimental procedure such as spinning a roulette wheel, throwing a die or generating a pseudo-random number in a calculator. The effect of including such a stochastic component in each income in a model is, in an important class of cases, to spread the distribution more unequally by adding different contributions to the different incomes. This must, for instance, be the effect when the stochastic variable is independent of, or just uncorrelated with, the level of the income with which it is to be compounded. By choosing a suitable variance for the stochastic variable the amount of additional inequality that it generates can be adjusted to match the inequality which has been left unexplained by the observables in the model. In chapter 11 the discussion will be extended to using stochastic variables to represent changes from year to year in incomes or changes from generation to generation in wealth in a line of descendants. These models are quite powerful in that they permit predictions of future income and wealth distributions to be made relatively easy given the current distribution and given assumptions about changes in observables during the forecast period.

World inequality

Finally, we have still to address what for many is the big issue in economic inequality: the persistence to the present day of such massive poverty widespread over the world, despite the flow of new inventions and high standards of living and extravagant rate of consumption of natural resources by the residents of most of the developed economies. We also have yet to consider the implications of the conflicts of interest over growth and inequality which provoke struggle and violence which both endanger growth and exacerbate inequality. These issues will be partially addressed in chapter 12.

6.9 Questions for discussion

General reading: Bronfenbrenner (1971), Ferguson (1969), Howard, (1979), Johnson (1973), Sattinger (1980).

Table 6.4 *Analysis of inequality $A_{1/2}$*

	Method 1	Method 2
Between countries	0.27288	0.28290
Within countries	0.10719	0.11286
Total	0.36384	0.36384

Table 6.5 *GDP per head and group-mean income ratios for Venezuela and Sweden (per cent)*

	GDP/head ($)	(1)	(2)	(3)	(4)	(5)
Venezuela	4,071	23.5	46.0	70.0	107.5	253.0
Sweden	12,118	40.0	66.0	87.0	127.5	184.5

Table 6.6 *Replacing Brazil by Venezuela in tables 6.2, 6.3*

	A_1		A_2	
	Method 1	Method 2	Method 1	Method 2
Between countries	0.49022	0.50144	0.71486	0.71786
Within countries	0.19948	0.18147	0.63971	0.32904
Total inequality	0.59192	0.59192	0.81070	0.81070
Inequality explained R	66.30%	69.34%	21.09%	59.42%

Note and source: As for table 6.2.

6.1   Using table 6.2 carry out the 'world decomposition' analysis of inequality for the inequality index $A_{1/2}$ (the Atkinson index with $\epsilon = \frac{1}{2}$: see chapter 5, page 101); show that breakdown corresponding to table 6.3 is that given in table 6.4.

What is the amount of total inequality 'explained' by the between-country differences in the case of this inequality measure? Comment on your results in the light of table 6.3 and the associated text (see also question 5.19 on page 116).

6.2   Examine the possibility of replacing some of the representative countries used in table 6.2 and its accompanying discussion. Table 6.5 shows the data for two further countries, set out in the same format as table 6.2.

(a) Suppose the representative country for group 2 (used in the within- and between-countries discussion) is switched from Brazil to Venezuela; show that we now obtain the decomposition of inequality shown in table 6.6.

Table 6.7 *Replacing Germany by Sweden in tables 6.2, 6.3*

	A_1		A_2	
	Method 1	Method 2	Method 1	Method 2
Between countries	0.47726	0.50224	0.70358	0.71443
Within countries	0.23592	0.19757	0.65883	0.33988
Total	0.60058	0.60058	0.81149	0.81149
Inequality explained R	60.72%	67.10%	18.81%	58.12%

Note and source: As for table 6.2.

(b) Now suppose that the representative country for group 5 is switched from Germany to Sweden; show that we now obtain the decomposition of inequality shown in table 6.7.

6.3   Use the analysis of income inequality in Canada given in Blackorby *et al.* (1981) to discuss the decomposition of income inequality in Canada by regions and by the sex of income recipient. Show how inequality can be decomposed in two stages by each of these two characteristics. Does inequality between sexes account for more inequality than does inequality between regions? Contrast the total amount of inequality explained with the results for the USA presented in table 6.1 on page 121.

6.4   Show that definition (4) and the cost-minimising condition (5) imply (a) that σ is (minus) the ratio of the slope of the demand curve at P to the slope of the line OP in figure 6.1, (b) the result in equation (6) (Cowell, 1986, chapter 2).

6.5   Distinguish between the claim that the distribution of income mainly depends on luck or chance and the view that the best way to model or represent the process which determines income distribution is to include stochastic (random) variables as well as deterministic variables. If individuals in an economy have enough information to be able to estimate correctly the distribution of random variables appropriate to the model of income distribution in their economy would it be appropriate to use a 'rational expectations' approach to model their behaviour? (see question 2.12 and Friedman, 1953; Sheffrin, 1983)?

6.6   In an international comparative study, Winegarden (1979) found that income inequality country by country was negatively associated with mean educational attainment and positively associated with the dispersion of educational attainment. Consider the possible significance of this finding, with particular reference to the economic processes and the data problems that might be involved.

6.6   Long *et al.* (1977) found greater income inequality in large cities than in small. Suggest possible economic reasons why this might be (see also Adams and Nestel, 1976; Datcher, 1982).

6.7   Consider the likely impact on economic inequality of the following social trends:
• a slowing down of the birth rate,
• a reduction in mean age of first marriage,
• an increase in the divorce rate,
• an increase in longevity.

Table 6.8 *Percentage shares of gross national product, UK, 1860–1984*

	Wages and forces' pay	Salaries	Self-employment income	Profits	Rent and property income from abroad	Adjusted share of labour*
1860–9	39	6	37	18	n.a.	
1880–9	39	8	34	19	n.a.	
1900–9	38	10	33	19	n.a.	
1921–9	41	18	16	13	12	67
1930–8	40	19	14	14	13	68
1946–9	45	20	12	17	6	73
1950–9	44	22	10	18	6	73
1960–9	67	8	18	7		73
1970–9	68	9	15	8		75
1980–4	67	9	16	8		73

Note: *Including estimated labour component of self-employment income.
Source: Atkinson (1983) table 9.1, and 1980–4 from *National Income and Expenditure.*

To what extent would you expect each of these phenomena to respond to economic incentives (Duncan, 1983; Duncan and Morgan, 1981; Kuznets, 1974, 1976, 1982; Treas and Walther, 1978; Wolf, 1984)?

6.8   It has been argued that there is a long-run tendency for the relative shares of national income going to labour and capital to remain relatively constant over time. How would this be accounted for by the theories discussed in section 6.3? Examine the validity of this proposition in the light of the information for the UK in table 6.8.

6.9   What influence can macroeconomic policy exert on factor shares and economic inequality in the context of (a) the standard model of factor shares, (b) the Keynesian model (Mitra, 1980; Schultze and Weiner, 1964; Soltow, 1959; Weintraub, 1981)?

Notes

1 See Cowell and Jenkins (1995) for a detailed discussion of this concept.

2 See the definitions given in (5) and (6) in chapter 4, page 74 and the summary table 5.1 on page 101. To use these tools with weighted data we use the equivalent forms specified in appendix A, page 335.

3 The data are derived from Summers and Heston (1988) and World Bank reports – see the sources described in section A.2 of appendix A. We have used data for the year 1985 in view of the lack of comprehensive data on intra-country distribution and the problems of achieving commensurability of the income distribution statistics for several different economies. Satisfactory estimates of the distribution of income within market economies are extremely rare amongst the less developed economies.

4 The selection of these five countries underestimates the implied mean of GDP/head. The arithmetic mean of GDP/head (adjusted for purchasing power parity) for all of the 120

countries in the Summers–Heston sample detailed in appendix A is $3,181.90: Cf. the bottom row of table 6.2, and the results obtained in question 6.2 at the end of the chapter.

5 The inequality for each of the five countries according to these two inequality statistics is as follows:

	A_1	A_2
Ghana	0.1914	0.3361
India	0.1430	0.2553
Philippines	0.2358	0.4030
Brazil	0.4437	0.6690
Germany	0.1484	0.2843

6 This conclusion is not an artefact of the particular inequality measures A_1 and A_2 that we have used, nor of the countries we have chosen. The broad conclusions would stand even if we used other Atkinson-type inequality indices, and changed the countries used as representative of each of the five quintile groups: see questions 6.1 and 6.2.

7 See Nolan (1987).

8 See, for example, Bronfenbrenner (1971), Ferguson (1969) and Johnson (1973).

9 See for example Lester (1946), Machlup (1967).

10 Keynes (1936).

11 See in particular pages 181ff. in chapter 8.

12 Where monopoly power is confronted by 'countervailing power' in the form of unionism, or the threat of unionism, wages may well be higher than otherwise – see Weiss (1966)

13 For example, Pasinetti (1962) argues that the more spendthrift are the wealth-owning class, the higher will be their proportionate share of total income, but the decision of the members of the earning class on how much of their income to save will, on his simplifying assumptions, exert no influence on their proportionate share of the total income.

14 Cf. Harrod (1948)

15 See, for example, Courant *et al.* (1979).

7 The distribution of income from employment

7.1 Introduction

Many people see earnings disparities as the central topic of income distribution analysis. It is not hard to see why in view of the importance of labour earnings in determining people's living standards, the prominence given to rates of pay in public discussion of questions of social status, and the glaring differences in personal earnings in most industrialised countries. A glance at the evidence prompts some tough questions.

- The evidence of the bivariate distribution of income components derived from the PSID in chapter 2 (page 31) suggested that not only is total family income skewed to the right but so also is family labour income or earnings (see figures 7.1 and 7.2). Why is this so? It is a property that also applies to earnings of *individuals* – see figures 7.3 and 7.4. This phenomenon is apparent in other countries' earnings distributions too – see figures 7.5 and 7.6. The *shape* of the earnings distribution is an important question in its own right.
- What is the relationship between the distribution of earnings (labour income) amongst families such as that illustrated for the US data in figure 7.2 and the distribution of earnings amongst individual workers?
- Why do women earn so much less than men? This is also evident from figures 7.3–7.6 and its impact on family earnings is clear from figure 7.2. Is this state of affairs just something to be expected in an efficiently organised economy or could it be changed without causing serious damage? Do such disparities represent 'genuine' inequalities or can a large part of them be dismissed as the outcome of personal choice to work less and to earn less?
- Why is there such a regular 'hump shaped' pattern of earnings when plotted against age in each profession and amongst wage earners as a whole (figures 7.7–7.11)?
- Also why does the earnings distribution amongst non-manual workers generally and within professions appear to 'fan out' with age (figures 7.10 and 7.11)?

If we are interested in the structure of inequality and not just in miscellaneous issues such as why the heads of some large companies earn 50 times as much as their workers – the reasons for the distinctive shape of the distribution and the processes by which an

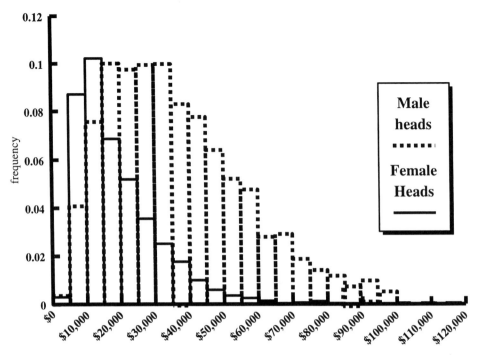

Figure 7.1 Total family income for male- and female-headed families, USA, 1986
Source: PSID, Wave XX.

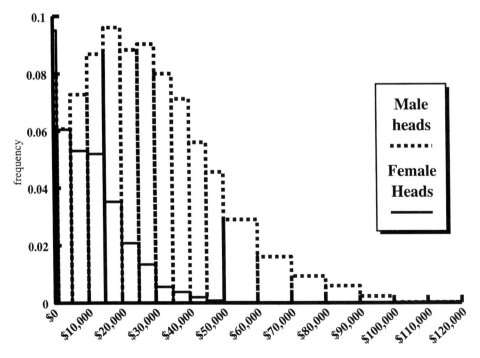

Figure 7.2 Earnings (labour income) for male- and female-headed families, USA, 1986
Source: PSID, Wave XX.

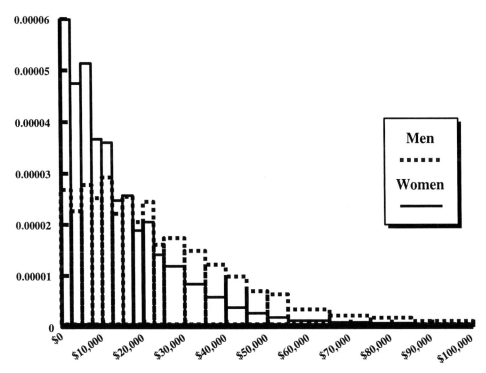

Figure 7.3 Distribution of earnings by individuals, USA, 1991
Source: Current Population Reports, 1992.

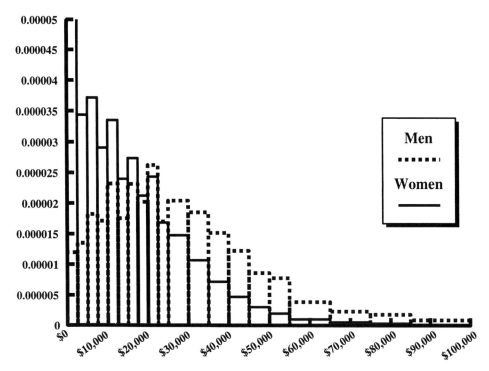

Figure 7.4 Earnings of individuals aged 25–64, USA 1991
Source: Current Population Reports, 1992.

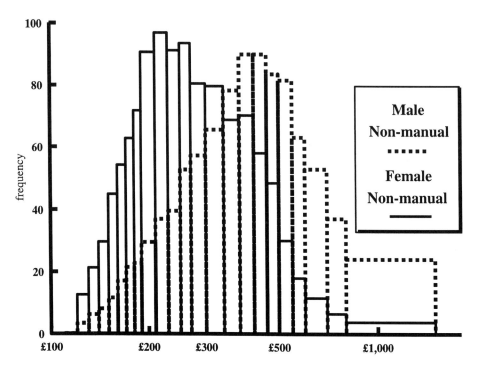

Figure 7.5 Distribution of manual earnings, UK, 1994 (adult workers on full-time rates)
Source: New Earnings Survey, 1994.

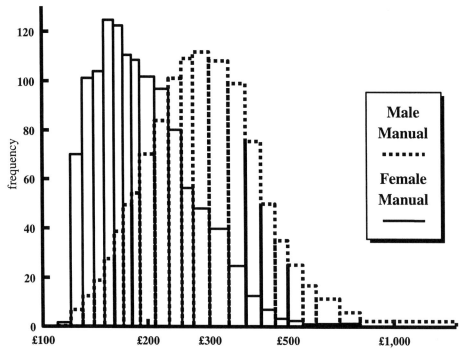

Figure 7.6 Distribution of non-manual earnings, UK, 1994 (adult workers on full-time rates)
Source: New Earnings Survey, 1994.

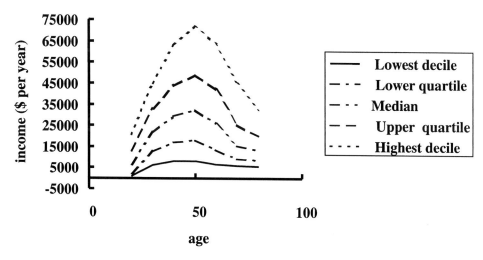

Figure 7.7 Dispersion of men's earnings by age, USA, 1991
Source: Current Population Survey, series P60, no. 180.

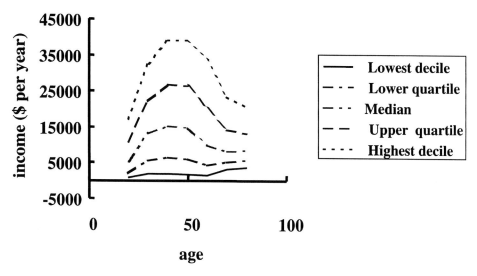

Figure 7.8 Dispersions of women's earnings by age, USA, 1991
Source: Current Population Survey, series P60, no. 180.

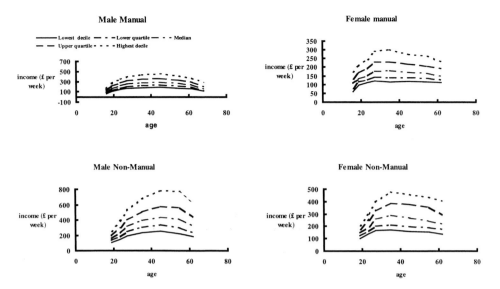

Figure 7.9 Earnings and age, UK, 1994

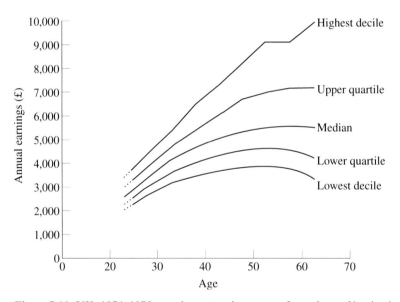

Figure 7.10 UK, 1974–1975: earnings at various ages of members of institutions which were constituent members of the Council of Engineering Institutions
Source: The 1975 Survey of Professional Engineers, Council of Engineering Institutions

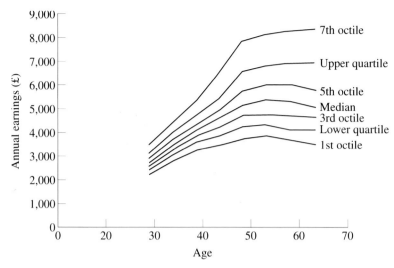

Figure 7.11 UK, 1973–1974: earnings at various ages of fellows and associates of the Royal Institute of Chemistry
Source: Royal Institute of Chemistry

earnings distribution changes over time are of central importance. These issues should be addressed before discussing what could or should be done by way of interpersonal redistribution.

In chapters 7 and 8 we examine the economic issues raised by these questions: the present chapter looks at alternative explanations of why earnings distributions – such as those depicted in figures 7.2–7.10 – display these characteristics in so many developed economies; Chapter 8 considers in detail the dynamics of wages and how economic changes will alter the distribution of earnings.

We shall examine a number of analytical approaches to the answers to these empirical questions. First, sections 7.2 and 7.3 focus on the free-market, perfect-information approach to the workings of the labour market. This does not mean that we believe that such theories – prevalent though they may be in the literature – should be given primacy in explaining why the earnings distribution is the way it is. On the contrary, we also reveal some serious objections to the premises of this type of theory and, as we shall see in sections 7.4 and 7.5, other models of a different nature appear to be a more satisfactory in terms of an explanation of the 'snapshot' cross-sectional evidence on the structure of earnings.

As we argued in chapter 6 with respect to theories of the overall income distribution, it is futile to suppose that there is one theory of the earnings distribution that can be satisfactory in all respects. However, the particular type of theory that is used to address particular questions in this area matters a great deal. A theory that appears to tell the right story purely in terms of the cross-sectional evidence – that is coincident with the pictures in figures 7.2–7.10 – may be quite misleading on other counts. It may give quite a wrong account of the mechanism by which earnings are generated – a point we take up in chapter 8; or it may suggest hopelessly inadequate or wrongheaded

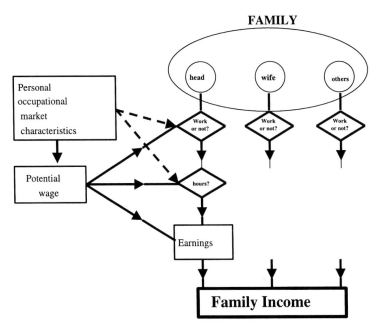

Figure 7.12 Family work decisions and labour earnings

policies – a point taken up again in chapter 12; or it may mislead us about the relation-ship between the structure of earnings and the wider issue of inequality amongst fam-ilies' living standards.

7.2 Earnings and income inequality

Most people's standards of living depend on their own labour or that of someone in their household, family or extended family. For the majority of families in advanced economies, the money earnings from some regular employment largely determine how well off its members are, and thus the extent of observed inequality of living standards between families.[1] The relative importance of labour income merits the special consideration given in this chapter to the inequality of money earnings from regular employment.

The process of turning labour power into earnings and thence into the family's consumption prompts a number of interesting questions. How much does the inequal-ity of the (relatively easily observable) distribution of earnings reveal about the (more obscure) inequality of living standards? What role do personal choices about jobs, on the one hand, and external forces from social institutions, such as the market, on the other hand, play in determining individual money earnings and consumption stan-dards? Figure 7.12 gives a sketch of the complex of issues involved. Each family member can potentially contribute to total family income, and thus to the living stan-dards of all family members, although sometimes social conventions or lack of job opportunities may preclude some from working: the 'decision tree' shown for the head ought to be set up also for the spouse and for other possible earners such as teenage children. We must also recognise that a family member who is not earning may still be contributing to the family living standards by working in the home.

To avoid crowding the diagram, only the determinants of the family head's earnings have been sketched, and it should be remembered that the influences determining any earnings by other members of the family may differ from those shown in their precise nature and importance, and that there will be substantial interaction between the activities of the various members of the family: the earnings of the family head usually have a significant effect on the amount of work of the spouse away from home: the lower the head's earnings the more likely the spouse is to go out to work.

Although some people work for fun, for charity or to keep fit, the most obvious reason why people go out to work is to get money income: this motive focuses our attention first on the 'potential wage' occupying the lower left-hand box. This means the amount which the person can expect to earn in the relevant period if they take a job. Leaving aside, for the moment, the possibility that this expectation may be vague the more immediate question is the effect of this expectation on work decisions (see the solid arrows): do higher expected earnings encourage more persons to take jobs and to work for longer hours per week if they do take them? If they do have these effects, does this provide a satisfactory explanation of the lopsided character of the distribution of earnings discovered in such diagrams as those of figures 7.3–7.6?

So far as the principal earner of the family is concerned, there is only a weak tendency for those with higher rates of pay to work more hours.[2] However, the effect is much more pronounced in the case of other earners in the family, for whom a supply elasticity of as much as 1.5 may be observed: for example, a 2 per cent excess in hourly wage rates could correspond to a 3 per cent excess in their average hours, and thus a 5 per cent excess in weekly earnings.

What does this signify for the analysis of inequality? If, as a general rule, there were a very high response of hours worked per week to hourly wage rates, it could be argued that the lopsided earnings distribution need not imply any such lopsidedness in the capacity for earnings. For if earnings capacity, w, were distributed among people symmetrically, like height, body weight, IQ or various other physiological attributes are, and if hours worked, h, were highly responsive to earnings capacity, w, then the distribution of earnings, $E=wh$, might still exhibit the lopsided shape found in figure 7.3. Since, for heads of families, this is not so, such a mechanism cannot be the explanation for the lopsided pattern of male earnings which consist predominantly of the earnings of heads of families.

But could the mechanism account for the lopsided nature of family earnings if other earners were to be included? Even for secondary workers in the family strong reservations apply. Whilst the price of labour – the wage rate – is of central importance to economists who regard market forces as overwhelmingly powerful in every aspect of decision making, many other factors have to be taken into account. For example take the items marked 'personal characteristics' and 'occupational characteristics' in the box on the left of figure 7.12. A characteristic such as age has an indirect influence on earnings via the potential wage through both the medium of work experience and the effect of senility, but age has a direct influence also: retirement plans, or plans to postpone starting work when young. Age also influences a person's willingness to work at any given wage. The combined effects of these influences could be subsumed under the general heading of the 'opportunity cost of working time' – high for women with young children and low for young unemployed men with no independent source of income – but this approach may in practice conceal more than it reveals. What is clear is that even though the responsiveness of 'additional' earners in the family to wage-rate changes may be higher than for the primary earner, this in many cases is likely to be swamped by the effects of other non-market facts of life, such as the arrival of young children.

It is wrong to think of figure 7.12 as representing a unique static picture, for personal and occupational characteristics and market conditions keep changing. More importantly, in the long run individuals and families usually have more control over these characteristics or over the way in which they influence potential earnings and the decisions about working. For example, those at a given moment who are in part-time education, in an occupation working part time due to slack product demand, unemployed, suffering from a physical disability or caring for their children, are all disadvantaged or discouraged in their efforts to earn. But in the long run, many of these disadvantages leave some scope for personal choice: there may be the option of taking further education, giving up full-time work to have children, changing occupation, moving to where there are better job prospects, or of finding a job with longer or shorter hours per week. It is important to distinguish between earnings distribution in the short and in the long run, and between societies where there are different social conventions about who may properly participate in various sections of the workforce.

This makes the analysis of inequality more complex: whilst the major determinant of earnings inequality amongst single-worker households must be that of market wage rates and not the workers' short-run responses to them, in families with more earners, this relationship is obscured by the wage-sensitive working behaviour of these other members and by the complex of factors other than wages which do or do not permit spouses and children to take jobs. Interpreting trends in the earnings distribution over a period when there are changes taking place in social conventions, in the general level of job opportunities, in legal rules governing the workforce, or in the structure of the family, is an exercise that requires special care.

However, given the very low or even negative elasticities of labour supply found among principal earners, we obviously cannot explain away the lopsided shape of their earnings as being merely the result of skilled and other highly paid persons choosing to work longer hours. The distribution of earnings capacity – indicated by hourly earnings – itself has this lopsided character, and it is of interest to enquire why.

7.3 The worker as price taker

As we have seen, an understanding of the structure of wage rates is an important key to understanding the inequality of personal earnings which itself accounts for a significant part of the economic inequality within a modern market economy. The detail of wage bargaining actually involves a complex of different factors in most cases, but an obvious first step is to consider the simpler case where each individual job applicant is faced with a choice between a range of take-it-or-leave-it offers of contracts by firms. The wage rate may then be regarded as the best offer, if any, available to him for hiring out his bundle of skills: but what determines this demand price for a person's labour?

The theory which might first spring to mind is that of marginal productivity analysis. We might perhaps relabel the axes of figure 6.1 (page 125) and then apply the discussion of section 6.4. The crudest interpretation of this theory implies that in equilibrium the real wage paid to labour is proportional to the marginal revenue from employing the labour, an apparently elementary proposition which may be deduced from the axioms of the model of the profit-maximising firm operating in a competitive factor market. If we are to apply this conclusion realistically to the problem under discussion, there is a complication. 'Labour' is not a homogeneous entity, since different workers have different skills, several of which may be required by the employer for use within the firm. In principle, each skill or attribute may be thought of as having its own marginal product; and because of the heterogeneity of the bundle of skills associated with each person, the match between the various wage rates and the marginal products of the earners may be far from perfect, even though the demand price for any person's labour is partly dependent on his skills. Although we shall have cause to question the practical relevance of some aspects of marginal productivity analysis, the importance attached to the prices paid for different skills may still be justified, since they may be significant and observable determinants of the demand price for the services of persons having these skills.

But why should the relationship between jobs and skills produce such a lopsided pattern of demand prices such as is apparent in figure 7.4? It is conceivable – but in practice unlikely – that this phenomenon is due to the chance that the distribution amongst humankind in general of one particular innate attribute, or group of attributes just happens to be skew. This is unlikely because the distribution of many other measurable personal attributes – such as IQ and height – are not skewed in this way. A less fanciful explanation lies in the possible interaction of particular skills with each other and with market opportunities. For instance, secretaries who excel both at shorthand and at foreign languages may secure posts in an international organisation that are a lot more lucrative than posts available to those with just one of these skills. Such an interaction in conjunction with the scarcity value of the rare 'superstar' performer in a particular field suggests that this approach may help to explain the skewness of earnings distributions that we noted in section 7.1.

However, this sort of mechanism does not seem to account for some of the other features of the earnings distribution that we noted. Moreover these, such as those illustrated in figures 7.10 and 7.11, put a great burden of explanation on the special type of skill interaction which firms happen to reward very highly, and the luck of the draw of individuals in the multi-variate skill distribution. In view of these shortcomings we pursue two further lines of enquiry: the possibility that people consciously acquire skills over time in the pre-knowledge of their market value, and the possibility that the evaluation of a person's skills may change systematically over time. These issues are discussed in the next section.

7.4 Investing in yourself

One obvious line of enquiry as to why the distribution of marketable talents appear to be so markedly skewed is the possibility that there may be an endogenous selection mechanism which ensures that the talented gain further talents. If those born with skills commanding a relatively high demand price also have a relatively strong incentive to acquire further skills then we can see that an interpersonal distribution of natural abilities with quite a low dispersion may become more unequal and be translated into a distribution with very high inequality of earnings. Moreover, if these skills are progressively acquired over the person's lifetime then we have here a natural explanation of the rising profile of some people's earnings and of the 'fanning out' of the wages of a cohort (see figure 7.10 and figure 7.11). Whilst suspending judgement on this process as a primary explanation of the inequality in the world about us, let us see how the story goes.

Every young man or woman on starting out to make a living faces three crucial bits of decision making in the labour market that have long-term consequences:
• Which occupation?
• What level of formal training and education?
• Which sequence of jobs?
Although each of these may be linked with the others, it is convenient to distinguish them as separate issues. Then, we may suppose that if a prospective employee behaves 'rationally,' he will choose that occupation which he considers likely to give him the greatest potential return over his lifetime, suitably aggregated. In some societies this choice may be restricted by law, or by a custom such as the tendency among wealthy families in Victorian England to send their younger sons into the Church.[3] There then remain the two further issues of how much to pursue formal education and of what sequence of jobs to pursue.

These issues amount to a whole complex of decisions that a person faces about how to spend his time – and possibly also his own or his parents' money – to his best advantage. There is a difficulty here because, even if the person is totally self-interested, his 'best advantage' may not mean getting the most money, in the above sense of behaving 'rationally', to those who place a higher intrinsic value on leisure time than on the consumption goods for which they devote time at work. However, persons can be imagined to be going round and round the loops in figure 7.13, following the decision sequence illustrated there. At any stage the person can decide to take life easy and live off his pension, his savings out of pay or off his parents (the 'leisure' route); or he can look for a job. Furthermore, applying for a job has two aspects: (α) 'cashing in' on the marketable skills he already has; (β) improving his skills by gaining experience at the job. In some cases it may be possible for the worker to control those two aspects by selecting a suitable job – which is why there are the two branches 'job α' and 'job β'; furthermore, this may involve selection from not just two but a whole range of jobs.

First, what would be the logical order of events over a person's lifetime if he were persistently dedicated to a rational plan? Whatever he chooses at each moment, he is getting older, and this by itself has an adverse effect on his value to an employer after a certain stage of his life. So, if he decides to retire when he is 60 years old, he becomes less employable after this and is accordingly less likely to find a job if he wishes to reverse his decision. To simplify the discussion we shall suppose that the retirement date has been irrevocably determined by his own choice or by outside circumstances.

Here in brief is the marginalist optimisation story – which some extreme critics dismiss as myth. Our person's attitude towards his working life may be viewed as analogous to that of a manager towards the running of his business. He is supposed to be

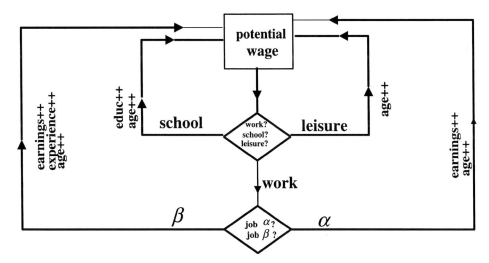

Figure 7.13 A dynamic decision sequence

well informed about market opportunities, about his own original endowment of abilities and about the possibilities for improving them by education. His 'firm's' theoretical objective in this case is to maximise the present value of earnings obtainable during a working lifetime; this objective is to be pursued by a 'rational' selection of the appropriate branch in figure 7.13 during each working year (neglecting the 'leisure' branch). To simplify further assume that job α can be represented as working full time throughout the year with the abilities the person already has, and that job β involves devoting some amount of his time during the year to further training – in other words going without a part of his potential earnings in order to increase his stock of *human capital*, the stock of future earning ability. The effect is analogous to that of an increase savings on relative factor prices as discussed on page 000. We may imagine the person deciding how much time in each working year to 'save' – how much to divert to investment in further human capital instead of earning money with the human capital he already has.

  The decisions are governed by three things: the person's own capacity to improve his ability by more education, constraints such as the physical upper and lower limits on the time available for investment in skills during one year, and the requirement that at each stage in his working life the opportunity cost of an additional dose of skills should equal the shadow value of such an additional dose – i.e., the value in terms of its increments to the discounted total value of earnings to be expected in all remaining years. It is this last marginalist requirement which ensures that all training is not crammed into one block at the beginning of his working life. But, what is this opportunity cost? In a world of perfectly efficient markets it would be earnings forgone during the year – regarded as inputs used for building further human capital. Under orthodox marginalist assumptions, the shadow value of a dose of skills gets less as the person ages, as he becomes slower to learn and draws closer to retirement: further education and training become more expensive to acquire and there is less time in which to make

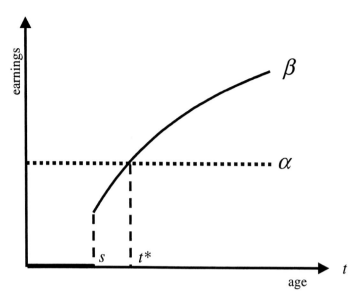

Figure 7.14 Earnings profile β overtakes α

them pay off. Human capital – the capacity to earn – and earnings themselves there-fore typically increase over the working life but do so at a diminishing rate.[4]

This theory is also consistent with the observations that (a) those with a high stock of inborn human capital follow, *ceteris paribus*, rather flat income–age profiles (not needing to invest so much near the start of their careers) and that (b) those with a high aptitude for profiting financially from further training and education will have rather steep income–age profiles (being encouraged to invest more time and cash in further education and training). A stylised picture of each of these two cases is illustrated in figure 7.14, where earnings stream β is at first zero (during the schooling period *s*) con-tinues for a time below earnings stream α, 'overtakes' α at age *t** and thereafter lies above α. So in a large cohort of workers, if each makes different decisions about train-ing after school, and if the overtaking ages are fairly similar we would expect observed earnings to bunch together in the early years from *s* to *t** and then fan out thereafter, so that, eventually, earnings inequality increases monotonically with age.

Finally, notice a very important further postulate about the distribution of income amongst persons. According to the above human capital model the variability in people's earning capacities arises from variations in their inherited personal endow-ments of human capital, variations in personal rates of return to investment in educa-tion and variations in self-investment strategies induced by the first two factors. Now if inherited personal human capital and rates of return to investment are independent of personal wealth (plausible, perhaps) and of parental wealth (less plausible) then the interpersonal distribution of earnings capacity is independent of the distribution of financial wealth, as long as there are perfect markets everywhere. The reason for this remarkable result is that in comparing or evaluating prospective earnings streams, only their present value at the market rate of interest need be considered; so a sum of

$100,000 (discounted) additional potential earnings is regarded as equivalent to an additional $100,000 in the bank now; so as long as further education makes commercial sense for an individual he could borrow on the strength of those future earnings, and lack of current assets need not prevent anyone from acquiring further earning capacity through the educational process.

Does the human capital theory appear to be supported by the facts? Four important predictions claim our attention:

- Since those who are more 'able' in the sense of having lower marginal costs of producing earning capacity also invest more in themselves we may have an explanation for the way in which a symmetrical distribution of innate abilities leads to a skewed distribution of earnings.•
- The human capital approach can also be used to account for the low earnings of women.[5] For, if we recognise that the learning/earning decision loop of figure 7.13 is only one aspect of household decision making, we must also allow for the decision sequence in figure 7.12 and decisions spent on work that is not done for a cash payment – housekeeping, child care and so on. Now if it turns out that (for whatever reason) women spend a higher proportion of their time in such home activities then they cannot spend so much time either earning or acquiring human capital. So they invest less and they earn less.
- The hump-shaped earnings profile is predicted by the rational investment programme that emerges from the model.
- And, as has been noted above, there is also an account of why earnings fan out over time. If the dispersion of earnings is measured by the variance of the logarithm of earnings, then the schooling plus experience model described above appears to account for about one third to one half of the earnings variability.[6]

So the human capital model appears to account for most of the features of the earnings distribution that were highlighted in section 7.1 and thus, perhaps, to 'explain' a substantial proportion of earnings inequality. However, to suppose that we now have an entirely satisfactory explanation of inequality in the labour market would be misleading. First, it is difficult to see how the theory would stand up to having just one or two of the tremendously strong assumptions relaxed or modified: What if people do not have good foresight about labour market conditions? What if prices do not adjust competitively in labour markets? What if educational loans are not readily obtainable? We return to some of these points in chapter 8. Second, it is not hard to find economic and social systems that are radically different from what is described above and yet provide rather similar earnings profiles. We shall examine these issues next.

7.5 Without marginal products

As a rather dramatic example of a system that differs from the elementary competitive model, examine figure 7.15. This shows two of many possible officers' career paths in the British Army. The procedures for following either path are straightforward. There is a given pay scale commensurate with rank and length of service which is determined by a review board and is readily available (we looked it up in *Whitaker's Almanac*). How rapidly you progress up the pay ladder is determined by a series of aptitude tests. Though there is competition at the point of entry (the bottom of the ladder – you

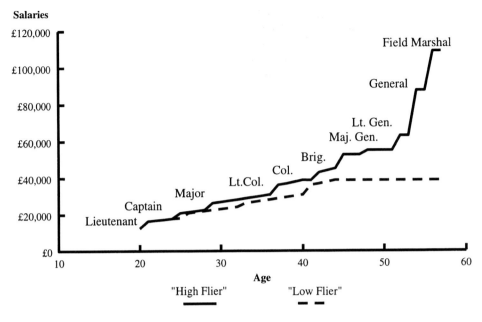

Figure 7.15 Career profiles in the British Army
Source: Whitaker's Almanac, 1993.

cannot just go and apply to be a colonel, even if you are very clever), there is initially no external competition further up the ladder, except for the loss by attrition of serving officers who do not 'make the grade'. Earnings of a cohort necessarily 'fan out' (there are not that many vacancies for colonels), and women tend to earn less than men (there are even fewer women colonels). It is interesting to see whether this kind of social and economic structure can also help us understand why the earnings distribution looks the way it does.

The first point is that if the 'firm' is taken in a very wide sense it is obvious that certain types of firm's productive activity by its very nature cannot be carried on competitively.[7] The most obvious examples of this are to be found within the public sector – the administrative departments of government, the armed forces and the like. In the case of the armed forces. there is no clearly identifiable marketable output so that the 'value of the marginal product of labour' may be ambiguous or meaningless. Indeed marginal productivity would almost defy definition in this case, although there are personal attributes – such as leadership, initiative, courage – which will naturally enhance the rate of promotion and thus raise pay (the 'demand-price') throughout the person's career. The extent of this non-marketed sector is potentially quite wide, and it is notable that the majority of advanced industrialised economies have a non-marketed public sector that is much wider than that required by a 'minimal state'. Moreover, superimposed on this, in many such countries there is a substantial sector of publicly operated firms whose output is marketed although not usually under competitive conditions, and which relies heavily on specialist skills (telephone engineers, railway staff, etc.).[8]

Obviously, a simple competitive model is not going to be adequate to account for the pay structure within such organisations which enjoy some sort of publicly sanctioned monopoly. But a similar point may also be made in connection with large private corporations that either enjoy some degree of monopoly *de facto*, or at least, because of the structure of their product market, do not behave as passive price takers. Under such circumstances firms that do not continuously adjust their employment mix and pay scales so that each grade of labour is rewarded exactly according to its marginal product can and do survive. Why firms should want to act that way is considered in more detail below, but a reason can be found within the complex structure of the large corporation itself. Particularly in the case of managerial staff individual marginal productivities can be extremely hard to determine, even in an informal fashion, because tasks are carried out as part of a team operation.

So the marginal productivity model will commonly be misleading in both public and private enterprise either because the concept is ill-defined (for example, because of a lack of measurable output), or because of complex team organisation, or because firms are able to pursue some other policy because of limited competition in the product market.

The second point concerns income determination in such cases. Usually some sort of fairness rule emerges, and to understand the earnings distribution we have to understand the fairness rule. In the case of some team organisations – football teams, orchestras and the like – where the absence of one person may mean a zero output from the firm, the fairness rule may give weight to seniority principles and to the output that might be achieved if alternative teams were formed by replacing individual members. It is easy to see that seniority rules themselves may yield the kind of picture that emerges in figures 7.10 and 7.11. In other cases, where outputs or inputs are difficult to quantify, fairness usually involves 'comparability' with some other reference group, whether formally or informally established. Although the reference group may be in a part of the private sector it would be stretching the point too far to suggest that marginal productivity theory, combined with the process of human capital accumulation, solely determines the rewards in that part of the private sector which by extension through the fairness rules then determines the pay structure elsewhere.

The principal reason for this is that even in the private sector the labour market is to some extent segmented so that, although the conventional forces of competition may be intense in some unskilled jobs, they may attenuated in some specialised areas. Why this arises is discussed in more detail in chapter 8. For the purposes of the discussion here, let us note two main types of obstacle to competition: 'vertical' segmentation, where the recruitment to senior positions within a firm is primarily from the lower ranks of the firm itself, with less effective competition from outside, and 'horizontal' segmentation, where workers are 'labelled' as belonging to different skill classes, and these labels play a dominant role in firms' selection of workers for particular tasks.

The next two sections examine earnings inequality in the light of this segmentation. They do this by reference to medieval England.

7.6 The manor

The 'manor' was a form of rural property ownership and a feudal system of social organisation. Within it those with power and their underlings were arranged in a type of hierarchical structure; mobility into and out of the manor was restricted. In this sense it provides a neat paradigm for the vertical segmentation that is observed in some labour markets today.

Labour skills, like capital, may be specific to a particular occupation or even a particular job, a phenomenon that may be fostered by trade unions and also by employers who wish to recoup training costs internally. The rewards to experience within the firm can be enhanced by arranging a suitable internal promotion structure and offering relatively lower inducements to workers of equivalent standing who wish to transfer from other enterprises. Competition among firms can be effectively suppressed either if experience is genuinely nontransferable, or if sufficiently many firms operate a restrictive practice in hiring that is collusively enforced. The resulting 'manorial' structure will allocate jobs and rewards according to the internal requirements of the firm given the technology currently in use. There may be competition within each 'manor', a phenomenon known as the internal labour market, and there is a strong incentive for firms to use some kind of preselection methods when recruiting employees. A 'vertically segmented' market emerges.[9]

The extreme case of a manorial structure is one where entry to a firm is possible only at the lowest, unskilled, level so that all skills are then acquired within the firm. Let us examine the distribution of earnings within the organisation by assuming that the organisation maximises profit, individual workers' marginal productivities are measurable, and the technology is given. The wage of unskilled workers on entrance may be taken as exogenously given, so too may the wage of skilled workers if labour unions have the power to enforce uniformity of skill differentials as between organisations. The numbers employed of each type of worker will be determined by the firm such that the marginal product of an unskilled worker exactly equals w, and that the marginal product of a skilled worker exactly equals w', which is w plus the unit training costs borne by the firm. Then – apart from the inclusion of internally borne labour costs – the determination of the within-firm distribution of earnings, of the elasticity of demand for the two grades of labour, and hence the changes in the earnings distribution in response to external forces, will be as in the competitive model with the elasticity of supply of unskilled workers being infinite. The essential difference lies in the process of adjustment. Because of the vertically segmented structure, skilled workers cannot easily move to find skilled jobs in other firms and so, even in a period of excess supply of workers, the established w'/w differential may not be eroded and firms will make adjustments by changing the numbers of employees who are situated on different 'rungs' of the internal ladder of economic opportunity.[10]

The approach has two serious weaknesses. First, it assumes that the unions of the skilled workers are able to ensure a kind of comparability between 'manors'. This is unlikely if there is a large number of grades of labour within each firm, and if the trade union structure is fragmented. Secondly, marginal productivity analysis may not be particularly appropriate for such manorial structures: because the skills acquired at different levels within the organisational structure are likely to be diffuse and the contributions of marginal workers at different levels will be difficult to evaluate. So what may be said in this case?

Salary is very often commensurate with status within an economic organisation (though whether status begat salary or salary begat status is not always clear in the eco-

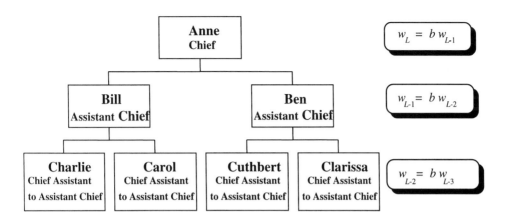

Figure 7.16 A hierarchical wages structure

nomic genealogy). So where the conventional wage determination rules provided by economic theory seem fuzzy, we may enquire what type of wage structure status theory might yield – whether in an authoritarian structure like the army, or in a large corporation.

Take the example of a single enterprise organised entirely as a 'status tree' – a person's reward being determined by how far up the tree he is located – see figure 7.16.[11] To avoid complication suppose that each position in the tree entails authority over just two subordinates, each of whom in turn has authority over two further subordinates, and so on. With some exceptions status may roughly be indicated by the total number (direct and indirect) of subordinates that a person has: if people are rewarded according to status, we assume that each person receives a reward of b times that of each of his two direct subordinates. The total number of persons in the top two levels will be 3, and in the top three will be 7; in general if each person has oversight of m others then the number of persons in the top l levels will be m^l-1. If the total number of levels is L, and the bottom people are paid $\underline{w}$, those in the top two levels will each get $\underline{w}b^{L-2}$ or more, those in the top three, $\underline{w}b^{L-3}$ or more and in general those in the top l levels will get $\underline{w}b^{L-l}$ or more. Hence, for $l = 1, 2, ..., L$, the number of persons with wage $\underline{w}b^{L-l}$ or more is m^l-1 and this number equals $m^L A[\underline{w}b^{L-l}]^{-\alpha}-1$ where

$$\alpha = \frac{\log m}{\log b} \tag{1}$$

and

$$A = \underline{w}^{\alpha+1}. \tag{2}$$

Within an error of one person all these L observations of the wage distribution satisfy Pareto's conjecture that the proportion of earners with wages less than or equal to w is given by the formula

$$F(w) = 1 - Aw^{-\alpha} \tag{3}$$

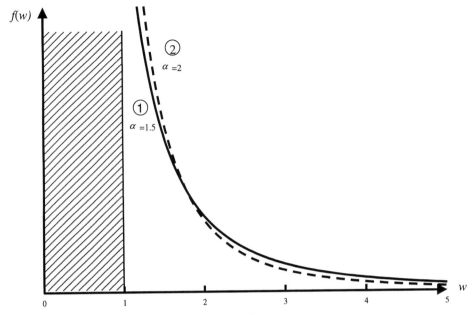

Figure 7.17 The Pareto distribution $f(w)=\alpha A w^{-\alpha-1}$

and this formula yields a curve which appears to approximate the shape of the upper tail of earnings distributions quite well: figure 7.17 illustrates two cases which closely approximate the distributions derived from the examples on page 000 in appendix B.[12]

However, the assumptions used in this model of one firm are strong, and in order to extend the analysis to the whole economy we need yet further strong assumptions. Relaxing any of these may result in a distribution which diverges from a Pareto distribution. It is clear that the model can only account for a part of the shape of the overall earnings distribution, since it produces a one-tailed curve. Also, it leaves open the issue of mobility between manors or trees. Obviously this is no problem if we accept an extreme form of the internal labour market whereby entry only occurs at the bottom of each tree, but otherwise we need to account for the persistence of the uniformity of the reward ratio b in the face of competition at all levels from those outside.

In spite of these warnings, this model nevertheless provides a useful parable concerning the administrative and executive segment of the earnings distribution. In particular, it is easy to see that the salary of top executives will bear a close relationship to the size of the firm, which may in turn be proxied by the firm's sales: there is a link between industrial structure and the structure of top salaries.

The theory also explains the phenomenon of increasing earnings dispersion with age. A formal demonstration requires precise specification of the dynamics of the promotion structure within the firm, but an intuitive argument runs as follows. The cohort of new labour market entrants must perforce enter on level 1 so that there is little earnings dispersion amongst them. Although the rate of promotion is going to differ according to ability, access to higher levels in the tree requires time to elapse, and it is reasonable to suppose that the highest rung attainable by a high-flyer of any given age will in general increase with age. As the age-cohort moves on through the firm the most able move to progressively higher levels with proportionately higher salaries, the mediocre make modest progress up the levels, whilst the inept remain on level 1 where they may be joined by later entrants of unknown ability. Thus within each age cohort there is a progressive 'fanning out' of salaries in a fashion similar to that predicted by the human capital approach, but arising from a model incorporating a very different view of the world.

Why such structures emerge and, having emerged, stay in place is a question that we examine further in chapter 8. For the moment let us turn to the other dimension of segmentation.

7.7 The guild

The social organisation of medieval Europe into groups with specialised economic functions, provides the convenient label for the contents of this section. Guilds were formed to control the membership and working practices of specialised crafts, such as the goldsmiths and the silversmiths. The modern-day guild appears in a number of guises: the trade union, the professional association, and other less specific, but very powerful, forms. The horizontal segmentation of the labour market into strata of multifarious skills and grades is perhaps even more striking than the vertical or 'manorial' segmentation discussed in section 7.6. and is reminiscent of Marshall's discussion of non-competing groups. Let us adapt the elementary supply-and-demand diagram of figure 6.1 to investigate how the phenomenon may manifest itself.

The scope of the subject matter of trades unions and individual earnings, which forms only a part of the general topic, is enormous, and it is only possible to touch on those features which are directly relevant to the discussion of this chapter. What are the functions of a 'guild' such as a trade union? The obvious primary aim is to secure the best remuneration for its members. It can achieve this by a number of strategies which restrict competition, three of which are caricatured in figures 7.18–7.20. In the first strategy (figure 7.18) the guild merely attaches a skill-specific premium p to its competitive supply price, shifting the effective supply curve from S_0 to S_1 and increasing wages for guild members at the expense of some employment (the equilibrium point is shifted from Z_0 to Z_1). This strategy is not necessarily a restraint on competition: in practice it will often promote the effects of the competitive mechanism by providing an information function that secures geographical and interfirm equalisation of specific wage rates. It broadly corresponds to the behaviour of 'industrial' unions that seek to ensure that all card-carrying members get at least the union rate for their particular skill.

By contrast the second and third strategies are manifest obstacles to competition and require effective market power such as may be possessed by some craft unions and professional bodies. Strategy two (figure 7.19) effectively alters the shape of the supply curve to S_2 and deliberately seeks to restrict employment of its particular grade of labour to N_2. There are losses to potential labour market participants of the sort that are incurred when distortionary excise taxes are imposed within the markets for their commodities. Strategy three (figure 7.20) is for the guild to exploit the monopolistic power it may have in the supply of its particular type of skill. Then S_0 again ceases to

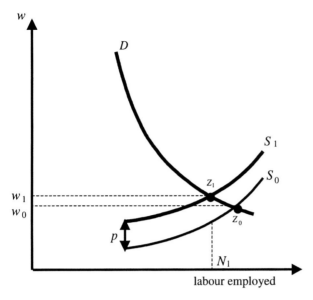

Figure 7.18 Supply-side restrictive practice, union gets a premium

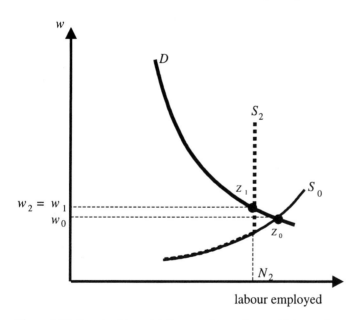

Figure 7.19 Supply-side restrictive practice, union restricts employment

be a competitive supply curve, but can now be seen as an average-cost-of-labour curve: the guild, in its role as a monopolistic supplier, determines equilibrium at the point where the associated marginal-cost-of-labour curve cuts marginal revenue curve: and the wage is set as w_3. Other variants of these two may easily be conducted to cover cases wherein no conscious attempt is made to pursue the surplus maximising behaviour of

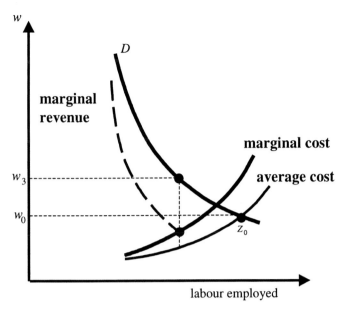

Figure 7.20 Supply-side restrictive practice, union acts as a monopolist

the monopolist – perhaps through lack of information – but the market power is used merely to buttress traditional differentials.

The static equilibrium effects of each strategy appear to be in the same direction: in each case the restrictive practice raises wages and cuts employment. However, the second and third type of practice represent a significantly different type of market form which may have special implications for the dynamics of earnings. Moreover, whilst the market power required for strategies two and three may be eliminated by legislative action or technological change, the factors underlying the earnings differentials emerging from strategy one will be far more resilient.

The reason for this lies in the second, but very important function of the 'guild'. It acts in a fashion rather like that of firms producing brand-named goods. A brand name serves to differentiate the product and enhance monopoly power; but it also provides a potentially useful signal about product quality in a market characterised by consumer ignorance (why else would it be worth the trouble of unscrupulous traders in various parts of the world to produce forgeries of Parker pens or Chanel perfumes?). In like manner the guild organisation attaches labels to groups of workers – skilled fitters, social workers or surgeons – which provide useful information for employers. The premium p in figure 7.18 may be then taken as the price of providing the service of certification. We shall return to this point in chapter 8 but there is a further aspect of guild-like segmentation which needs to be examined here.

Some types of stratifying restrictive practice appear to derive entirely from the demand side of the labour market. Many of these are lumped together under the general heading of discrimination. Figure 7.21 represents a simple discrimination model, where an employer distinguishes two groups of workers: the Americans (A) and the British (B), let us say. The employer is only prepared to take on British workers at

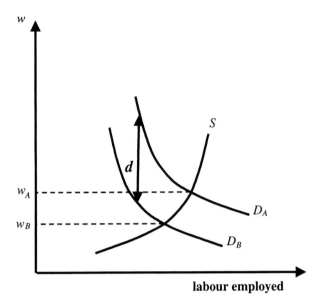

Figure 7.21 Demand-side restrictive practice

a discount d, either because he genuinely believes their marginal productivities to be lower, or because he is just stars-and-stripes biased. The effect is that, given the same supply function S, fewer Britons get employed, and at a lower wage.

There is a deliberate vagueness about what is being measured on the horizontal axis in figure 7.21. It could be labour in efficiency units or labour measured in straight man hours. If it is the former then we have a pure market-discrimination model: either A or B workers can provide work of uniform quality and the discount d represents a taste for discrimination. This type of horizontal segmentation may then be eliminated by equal opportunity legislation. However, if labour is being measured in man hours we have to take into account another phenomenon, pre-market discrimination. Here the labour productivities of As and Bs at the time of hiring may be genuinely different, and thus wage differences (per man hour not per efficiency unit) will not be removed by equal opportunity legislation within the labour market. The pre-market discrimination may be due to a number of possible causes – unequal access to educational facilities, differential home upbringing and other background conditions, and genetic effects.

This type of segmentation may be self-perpetuating across generations since disadvantaged parents will have less resources to provide education and other facilities in order to augment their offspring's market productivity. Its effects on rates of pay may also be exacerbated by differences in the supply conditions of the two sorts of workers: the supply of B workers – married women, immigrants? – is often much more elastic than the supply of A workers. These additional features can make the interpretation of such models quite tricky.

Discrimination – to the disadvantage of women, some racial groups and others – has been evident in both advanced and developing economies, and its effects are fairly pre-dictable. Yet how much pre-market and market discrimination affects earnings is remarkably hard to determine because discrimination can be difficult to identify either in principle or in practice. For example, a glance at figure 7.2 or figure 7.6 is not sufficient to establish the existence of either sort of discrimination since the relatively low earnings of women may be due to:

- the social orientation of women as wives and mothers (for which roles the economic returns are not accounted in money earnings);
- employers' preference in jobs where a high on-the-job training component makes long service desirable;
- restricted entry to some occupations by employers or co-workers; or
- differential pay within occupations for identical work.

Clearly the third and fourth items in this list represent pre-market discrimination and market discrimination respectively. Whether the first two represent discrimination is largely a matter of interpretation since an important element of choice by the female worker may exist. Similar issues of principle can arise in analysing racial discrimina-tion. On top of this, in each area of discrimination there is the problem of quantifying the components of the wage differential. The orthodox approach involves a statistical analysis of the pay differential between, say, American black male workers and white male workers, and having noted that about 30 per cent of this is due to family back-ground and other personal characteristics and 30 per cent due to attainment in occupa-tion, education and other observable job-related characteristics it then attributes the unexplained residual of 40 per cent to discrimination.[13] This imposes a burden on the correctness of the specification of the model linking earnings and characteristics. For example, with groupings across occupations, pre-market discrimination would be mis-takenly attributed to market discrimination and it is quite possible that further subdivi-sion or reclassification of occupations might significantly alter the apparent amount of discrimination.

It is here that the concept of the 'guild' again has a subtle role to play. If we abstract from differences in education, training and all other apparent forms of pre-market education why on earth would firms pay blacks less than whites? It is understandable if everywhere employers have a quasi-monopsonistic market advantage in employing blacks and if what employers are doing is exploiting that advantage; but such condi-tions may not be applicable: it is hard to imagine that this can be the sole explanation in any economy with a degree of competition amongst employers and free entry amongst firms. After all, if the differential is just the result of a 'taste for discrimina-tion', then discriminating firms are operating inefficiently, thus forgoing profits and possibly laying themselves open to being undercut by other firms. Can plain bigotry be stronger than the profit motive? The answer seems to be in many cases that women because they are women, and blacks because they are blacks form a 'guild' in the eyes of potential employers.

This 'guild' – from which a worker cannot opt out – again transmits signals about the probable ability or suitability of a member of the group. Thus 'statistical discrimi-nation' against women and blacks, and in favour of white males, forces the same results as the perfectly respectable organisations that explicitly certify skills.

7.8 Summary and some unsettled questions

We began with some observations to be explained: the distinctive shape of earnings distributions, age–earnings profiles and the persistent earnings differential between men and women. One approach to the analysis of such puzzles might be via the specification of a theoretical model of individual choice in competitive labour markets, coupled with an econometric model of individual earnings in which measures of schooling attainment, ability and experience along with other personal characteristics appear as independent variables: there are two general comments to be made on this.

First, even with fairly rich data sets that permit the inclusion of a large number of such variables, the 'explanatory' power of such models seems limited since about one half to two thirds of the dispersion of individual incomes is left 'unexplained' in most studies.[14] This is not in itself alarming: it merely indicates that although education, training and so on may play an important role in earnings inequality, so may a lot of other things that are not so readily observed.

Second, such empirical observations are also consistent with a number of quite different theoretical foundations. This reopens the question of why earnings distributions have this characteristic shape, and it raises a new question of what the role of education, and experience actually is.

The conflicting 'stories' told by different schools can be labelled crudely as on the one hand simple free market theories; on the other theories that attribute much to the influence of institutions and customs.

The best thing about the free market theory is that it readily provides an account that appears consistent with the overall view of the earnings distribution illustrated in figures 7.2–7.10. The device that produces this is the theory of human capital accumulation, but there are grounds for being less than satisfied with this account as an explanation of the inequality of pay. The specific versions of this theory that produce particularly strong conclusions can be challenged on both theoretical and empirical grounds. More serious though is the question of whether the supposed underlying mechanism of the model – 'rational' planning of self-investment with accurate foresight – is itself realistic and verified in practice, and not just the broad pattern of outcomes in terms of earnings. Do conditions approximating those of perfect competition, information, foresight and 'rationality' pervade in all sections of the labour market?

Those who answer this question with a clear 'no', will probably turn to the heterogeneous body of analysis that attributes a substantial role to the independent influence of institutions such as firms, government agencies, trade unions and professional associations that appear to play an executive role in determining relative rates of pay. Seeing them all around us leads to the suspicion that they do have an important function in modifying or even over-ruling free market outcomes: we ought to enquire what is the process by which such institutions determine relative rewards – whether it be on the grounds of fairness, supervisory status or incentive. But perhaps a more fundamental, unresolved question is why should such institutions have such an important influence on pay in the first place? Why do the rigid structures they may impose not automatically break down in the face of competition?

It is important to get further insight on these questions because in many ways it would be unsatisfactory even to take the competitive model as an 'as if' device. If there is equal access to education regardless of wealth, if people have good foresight, and if monopolistic restrictive practices are absent, then perhaps observed earnings inequality is not much to worry about. It is merely the competitive outcome resulting from a perhaps unfortunate, but much smaller, dispersion of productive talents. But if the world does not really work like that there may be cause for concern at the extreme inequality of earnings. Moreover, if non-market institutions do have an important part to play, then the way in which we might seek to go about modifying that distribution so as to reduce earnings inequality will be very different from what we might suggest if the outcome were an equilibrium distribution resulting from rational choice in free and frictionless markets.

We have more to say about these unresolved issues in the next chapter.

7.9 Questions for discussion

General reading: Hirsch and Addison (1985), Atkinson *et al.* (1992), Becker (1962, 1964), Blinder (1974), Creedy and Whitfield (1988), Disney (1983), Hartog (1981), Hornstein *et al.* (1981), Jencks *et al.* (1979), Lundahl and Wadensjö (1984), Lydall (1979a), Martin and Roberts (1984), Mincer (1970), Osterman (1984), Tinbergen (1975), Wood (1978).

7.1 'The whole of the advantages and disadvantages of the different employments of labour and stock must, in the same neighbourhood, be either perfectly equal or continually tending to equality' – Smith (1976, page 111). Discuss the theoretical and empirical problems encountered in investigating the substance of this proposition (Brown, 1980; Duncan and Holmlund, 1983; Killingsworth, 1987; Rosen, 1974).

7.2 (a) How would you attempt to assess the influence of other family members' economic opportunities on an individual's earnings (Ashenfelter and Heckman, 1974; Becker, 1985; Brown, 1983; Mincer and Polachek, 1974)?

(b) In a study of family incomes in the United Kingdom, Layard and Zabalza (1979) found that the inequality of total family income approximately equalled the inequality of head's earnings but was much less than the inequality of wives' earnings. Does marriage reduce overall income inequality, and if so, why (see also Greenhalgh, 1980)?

(c) Dex *et al.* (1995) claim that the presence of other earners in a family probably accentuate income inequalties rather than reduce them. Why would this be so?

7.3 (a) Suppose you are involved in a project that is investigating the determinants of salary differences between workers within a firm or group of firms. Discuss the ways in which such evidence might confirm or refute the hypotheses of human capital theory (Alexander, 1974; Blaug, 1972, 1976; Blinder, 1976; Eckaus, 1963, 1973; Frank and Hutchens, 1993; Lucas, 1977; Medoff and Abraham, 1980, 1981; Mincer, 1974; Suzuki, 1976; Wise, 1975).

(b) Does human capital theory provide a satisfactory explanation of why some industries 'traditionally' pay low wages (Craig *et al.* 1982; Krueger and Summers, 1986; Metcalf and Nickell, 1980; Mincer, 1974)?

7.4 (a) What are the limitations on the use of statistical evidence to establish the existence or otherwise of discrimination in the labour market (Aigner and Cain, 1977; Kuhn, 1987)?

(b) How would you expect male/female pay differentials and black/white pay differentials to be affected by: (i) a switch from economic recession to boom; (ii) an expansion of government-subsidised education and training programmes (Arrow, 1972; Ashenfelter, 1970; Bergmann, 1971; Borjas, 1983; Buchele, 1981; Butler, 1983; Chiplin and Sloane, 1976; Dex, 1986; Duncan and Hoffman, 1979; Hoffman, 1979; Lazear, 1979; Malkiel and Malkiel, 1973; Shorey, 1984; Schwarz, 1986; Stewart, 1983; Welch, 1973)?

7.5   In a team organisation what sort of fairness rules regarding remuneration would you expect to emerge (Ullman-Margalit, 1977)?

7.6   Why do superstars earn lots of money (Houthakker, 1974; Mayer, 1960; Rosen, 1981; Roy, 1951)?

7.7   (a) Consider the possible reasons for the observed long-term stability of occupational and skill pay differentials in many countries until recent times (Kalachek and Raines, 1976; Klevmarken, 1982; Phelps Brown, 1978; Routh, 1965).

(b) Consider the possible reasons for marked increase in the occupational and skill pay differentials during the 1980s (Gosling *et al.*, 1994).

7.8   Using an earnings equation of the type specified in appendix B (see page 000) consider the practical problem of distinguishing between (a) the impact of ability and of schooling on earnings, (b) the impact of age and of experience on earnings growth (Griliches, 1977; Hause, 1980; Heckman and Polachek, 1974; Johnson and Stafford, 1974; Klevmarken, 1972, 1982; Wachtel, 1976; Weiss and Lillard, 1978).

7.9   (a) Why might there be a close relationship between the size of firms and the earnings of their chief executives (Beckmann, 1977; Cosh, 1975; Lewellen and Hunstman, 1970; Lydall, 1968; Roberts, 1956; Rosen, 1982; Simon, 1957)?

(b) Using the second example in appendix B show how table B.2 needs to be modified if the hierarchical structure is truncated.

7.10   Discuss the problems that might arise in attempting to assess the impact of trade unions on the inequality of earnings (Craig *et al.*, 1982; Freeman, 1984, 1986; Freeman and Medoff, 1984; Oswald, 1985; Robinson and Tomes, 1984; Shah, 1984).

7.11   How might you establish empirically whether the labour market is effectively segmented (Gordon *et al.*, 1982; Loveridge and Mok, 1979; Magnac, 1991; Mayhew and Rosewell, 1979; McNabb and Psacharopoulos, 1981; Reich, 1984; Reich *et al.*, 1973)?

7.12   To what extent are the conventional market theories of wages useful in explaining the earnings of professional people (Friedman and Kuznets, 1954; Shah, 1983)?

7.13   (a) Comment on the pattern of earnings inequality in table 7.1 and its implications for the UK.

(b) Green *et al.* (1992) show that earnings inequality in several market economies follow a pattern similar to that of the UK in table 7.1. Consider (i) the reduction in trade union influence, (ii) the shift from public to private sector employment, (iii) the effect of educational attainment as possible explanations for this development (see also Dooley and Gottschalk, 1984).

Table 7.1 *Structure of earnings in UK, 1968–1994 (per cent of median)*

	MALES				FEMALES				
	Lowest decile	Lower quartile	Upper quartile	Highest decile	Lowest decile	Lower quartile	Upper quartile	Highest decile	Female/ male median
1968	65.7	80.0	126.7	161.4	67.0	80.0	129.7	171.2	53.0
1970	65.4	79.7	126.7	160.6	66.4	79.8	129.3	170.4	53.7
1972	65.5	79.7	126.4	160.9	65.6	79.6	128.6	167.1	55.7
1974	66.8	80.7	124.6	157.0	67.7	81.0	126.4	159.1	56.4
1976	67.6	81.3	125.6	159.5	66.1	80.2	125.9	165.9	64.4
1978	66.8	80.6	125.1	157.9	69.1	82.2	125.3	161.4	63.2
1979	66.0	80.3	125.1	156.9	69.4	82.1	124.7	158.6	62.2
1980	65.9	80.1	126.5	161.6	68.4	81.3	126.1	161.3	63.9
1981	65.6	79.8	129.5	167.7	68.0	80.6	129.8	172.6	65.0
1982	64.5	79.0	129.8	168.1	66.9	79.7	129.4	169.0	64.7
1983	62.7	78.2	130.2	170.4	66.5	79.9	129.9	167.4	67.2
1984	61.6	77.2	130.6	171.5	66.2	79.2	130.2	166.3	66.5
1985	60.8	76.9	131.0	171.5	65.8	78.7	130.9	164.5	66.7
1986	60.2	76.6	131.3	173.3	65.1	78.6	132.7	170.0	66.7
1987	59.4	75.7	132.5	176.2	64.2	78.1	133.5	171.7	67.0
1988	59.0	75.5	134.0	178.3	63.4	77.2	136.6	177.5	67.4
1989	58.5	75.1	134.0	179.9	63.1	77.1	138.0	180.5	68.0
1990	58.3	74.9	134.6	181.1	62.5	76.7	137.9	178.6	68.7
1991	57.9	74.6	135.7	183.0	61.7	77.0	138.8	180.5	70.5
1992	57.5	74.1	135.8	183.9	61.1	76.4	140.0	183.2	71.4
1993	57.4	74.2	137.0	186.2	60.5	75.9	139.5	181.5	72.8
1994	57.5	73.9	136.6	186.0	60.6	76.1	139.5	182.1	73.3

Sources: Royal Commission on the Distribution of Income and Wealth, *New Earnings Survey*, 1990, Part A, various years

Notes

1 Although there is usually a substantial group of families whose standard of living is principally determined by monetary transfers and these, along with non-cash benefits, must also be taken into account in examining the overall extent of economic inequality. See page 32 in chapter 2 and page 69 in chapter 4.

2 Typically a 1 per cent increase in the wage calls forth only a 0.05 per cent increase in hours worked (an elasticity of 0.05). At the upper end of the scale a wage increase may even reduce average hours worked by principal earners. See Zabalza *et al.* (1980), Cain and Watts (1973), Metcalf *et al.* (1976). The 1 per cent increase in the wage may have a stronger effect on participation (arrow 3) – see Greenhalgh and Mayhew (1981). For married women see Greenhalgh (1977), Hausman (1981), Layard *et al.* (1980). For general surveys see Killingsworth (1983), Killingsworth and Heckman (1986) and Pencavel (1986).

3 Older sons were groomed for inheriting the family estate (see page 000 below), or went into the army. Younger sons also entered the universities, or other respectable, but less lucrative posts.

 4 See section B.1 of appendix B for a formalisation of this model.
 5 It has also been used to explain the sexual division of labour – see Becker (1981, 1985), Rosen (1983).
 6 See section B.2 of appendix B for details of the empirical model and its estimation. Whilst the variance of log earnings is a convenient device for measuring earnings variability it is not a satisfactory measure of inequality as such since it violates the principle of transfers – see Cowell (1995).
 7 See, for example, the arguments on information and organisational costs in Coase (1932).
 8 For example, in the UK in 1979 one third of all employees and 40 per cent of non-manual employees worked in the public sector – Trinder (1981). See also Gregory and Thomson (1990) pp. 172–206. Hall (1982) drew attention to the remarkable extent of 'lifetime jobs' in the USA.
 9 This type of structure may actually enhance the firm's efficiency – see Williamson *et al.* (1975), Williamson (1985) and chapter 8 below.
10 This phenomenon will also emerge if there is a substantial component of firm-specific investment in the human capital acquisition process – Oi (1983). Such investment costs are likely to be shared by employer and employee – Hashimoto (1981).
11 This model is originally due to Lydall (1968) and Simon (1957): examples illustrating its advantages and weaknesses are given in appendix B. See also question 7.9 at the end of the chapter.
12 See Cowell (1995) for further discussion of this distribution.
13 See Blinder (1973a), Corcoran and Duncan (1979).
14 See aection B.2 of appendix B.

8   The dynamics of earnings

8.1 Introduction

In chapter 7 we concentrated on the outcome of the process of earnings determination – the observed pay distributions. The present chapter directly addresses that process itself. Why is this useful?

The discussion of chapter 7 concentrated on equilibrium analysis, but an obsession with equilibrium may obscure important points about the way the system actually works. Different economic processes may yield apparently similar looking outcomes, and although a particular simplified equilibrium story might be suitable for certain descriptive purposes it could fail to give a satisfactory answer to other interesting questions. For example, it is interesting to know what happens when the economy is disturbed: by what means is a new equilibrium established, if at all? How this takes place can have substantial repercussions on people's incomes. In addition some structural peculiarities of the system can only be understood by examining the process of earnings determination: for example, why is it that vertical and horizontal segmentation takes place? Are such features aberrations which an appropriately directed policy might remove, or are they inherent in the system? It would be dangerous to undertake any policy measures on incomes solely on the basis of equilibrium distributions without understanding what happens out of equilibrium.

In our brief treatment on these topics we distinguish between *short-run dynamic problems* – what happens within a particular cohort of workers when various external changes are imposed – and *long-run problems* – how the distribution of earnings may change from one generation to another. Different types of decisions and institutions are involved in short- and long-run problems. These issues are dealt with in sections 8.5 and 8.6 respectively: the main body of the chapter (sections 8.2–8.4) is concerned with how to take proper account of the fact that individuals, firms, families and unions all have to make decisions over time in the face of uncertainty. The importance of this should not be underestimated. If everyone had perfect foreknowledge, the future would be as simple to analyse as the present and there would be little point in devoting much time to anything other than equilibrium models. But, as we have noted, equilibrium models by themselves do not tell all we would wish to know about the sources of earnings inequality or the impact on people's earnings of events in the real world. So we begin with an examination of uncertainty in the labour market.

8.2 Ignorance and uncertainty

The basic economic models used in the discussion of sections 7.2–7.4 of chapter 7 assumed that rational economic agents – workers – make decisions affecting the quantity and type of labour that they supply under idealised market conditions of perfect certainty. While such a story may be useful in explaining certain economic principles, it can be misleading as a basis for a theory of income distribution between persons. To see why, let us think about the rôle of risk in the labour market.

The nature of uncertainty

Uncertainty proper is to be distinguished from risk. When the outcome of a particular event is not perfectly foreknown, a person may be able to attach (in his own mind) a certain specific probability to the event's occurrence. For example, if he applies for a specific job for which he supposes that there are nine other equally well-qualified applicants he might reasonably consider the probability of being offered the job to be 10 per cent. Such a situation may be described as one of *risk*. The supposition of just ten equally well-qualified applicants enables us to assess the relative probability of different possible occurrences; additional information may lead to a modification of the supposition and the probabilities. By contrast there are many cases – for example, where a person considers his prospects of success or failure within a particular occupation – where this attaching of probabilities to various alternative possible events in advance cannot reasonably be done: the outcome is strongly influenced by special factors about which we have little or no prior information. However, whilst the conventional economic theory of the household can readily be extended to cover decision making in the face of pure risk, it cannot easily be extended to do so in the face of uncertainty proper.

We also need to distinguish between *exogenous* and *endogenous* forms of uncertainty. In some areas of decision making under uncertainty a person is really 'playing against nature': however careful he is about transatlantic flying or investing in the stock market there is, ultimately, very little he can do to influence the *ex ante* probability of there being a crash (in either case). In other areas the reactions of other people to our own decisions and actions may modify the risks, or may actually generate the uncertainty which confronts us: the way in which a particular contract of sale is drawn up could encourage one party to lie to the other about essential points which will only become evident after the contract is fulfilled. This uncertainty – generated within the system rather than being imposed by the random influences of the outside world – may discourage participation in certain labour contracts or stimulate the participants in the labour market to devise contractual safeguards to reduce the risk of such fraud being effective.

Modifying the human capital approach

Even where only pure risks are involved in the labour market, often they cannot be insured against – as can the risk of financial loss from a person's house burning down, for example. The problem of planning working lives in the real world cannot simply be reduced to an 'equivalent' problem to planning them under perfect certainty. Knowing *who* bears the risk is central to an understanding of how earnings dynamics impinge on economic inequality.

The standard investment approach to the determination of people's earnings power needs to be reworked once it is recognised that each worker anticipates, not a determinate return to his investment in education or training, but a set of fairly nebulous possible payoffs. Two questions are central to understanding the effect that exogenous uncertainty may have on income distribution:
- How is the riskiness of a person's potential wage affected by his level of education?
- Which groups bear what risks?

The answer to the first question is ambiguous: specific training may increase the risk associated with the potential wage by narrowing the specialisation for which a person is competent; but a higher general level of education increases a person's chances of attaining a stratum of jobs where the risk of becoming unemployed is rather low, and it may also improve the ability to evaluate job prospects well. The answer to the second question is much clearer. If there is uncertainty, a person's best choice of education policy will generally depend on his family's financial wealth; whereas in the case of perfect certainty it would have been independent of wealth.[1] Just as wealthier persons usually have a greater propensity to devote a proportion of their wealth to the acquisition of risky assets – so also with a worker's (or his parents') propensity to invest in human capital. The relatively rich, being in a sense better equipped to bear the risks associated with skilled work, are those who undertake greater investment in skill and will be likely to earn more in the actual conditions of uncertainty.

Moreover, we have so far made unrealistic simplifying assumptions – that there are perfect credit facilities, that everyone has the same information about the probability distributions of the potential wage, and that all persons try to act in a rational way when making economic decisions – which may distort one's conclusions. People's creditworthiness can differ dramatically according to their own or their parents' station in life; relatively wealthy people can afford to obtain rather better information about the uncertain future, directly and through informal contacts; and it is quite common to make impulsive economic choices. Allowing for each of these would clearly exacerbate the inequality-generating effect of the rather simple notion of risk in the human investment model which we have just considered.

The problem of rationality

This prompts an important question about workers and potential workers namely: how rational are they? It all depends on what you mean by 'rational'. If education or training is pursued only for the sake of the additional financial rewards which it is expected to yield, and if a person really could easily and correctly foresee the financial consequences of any decision he might make, it is reasonable to suppose that he would select some strategy with effects quite like those of the maximising strategy described in section 7.4 of chapter 7. But if the future cannot be foreseen in this way, the possibilities become much more complex. Each person may possibly continue to be 'rational' in that he pursues that training programme which offers the most attractive financial prospects according to his perception of the future;[2] but the conclusions he may draw about the probability of his own success or failure in any sector of the labour market may differ from those held by others concerning his prospects.[3] Moreover, his estimates of the relevant probabilities may change abruptly as the foggy future unfolds into the present. So we must not expect such 'rational' behaviour from each individual to provide a set of consistent choices of policy which will lead to a unique optimum. It is not hard to see why apparently inconsistent judgements arise, particularly in choices concerning the labour market, since so many of the factors which prospectively determine a person's success or failure at work are highly specific to the person himself and since so much of the information needed to form a view about the future demand prices of different grades of labour is going to be either out of date or inaccurate.

Furthermore, unlike competitive firms that may eventually go bankrupt if they make bad investment decisions, there is no effective natural selection process to 'weed out' individuals who make irrational or ill-informed decisions about investing in themselves. The results of mistaken expectations – in particular the consequences for the inequality of earnings – may persist for a long time after the mistakes were made. It is a particularly dangerous simplification to suppose that all in the labour market form similar expectations about the uncertain future and act uniformly in a mutually consistent fashion.

In sum, exogenous uncertainty concerning payoffs to career plans is itself an important source of inequality. Because people are confronted not by diversifiable and insurable risks but by more fundamental uncertainty about their income prospects, their economic decisions cannot be assumed to be 'equivalent' to those that would be made in the face of mere risk or under perfect certainty. The rich are better able to cope with uncertainty and thus more likely to invest in any form of risky asset – including skills. They are also better placed to help their children overcome the tiresome restrictions that an imperfect credit market may impose. As rationality becomes fuzzy edged in the face of the unknown, so access to good information becomes more advantageous and that advantage usually goes to the wealthy. So when we come to examine the actual path of individual earnings, projected into an imperfectly foreseen future, the human capital 'explanation' of earnings inequality must be very heavily qualified. Even in a world untrammelled by artificial restrictions to competition – to be rich helps in coping with uncertainty.

A final question: even if the well-informed worker does try to act 'rationally' in pursuit of his economic self-interest, what is he being rational about? Is it really about socially productive investment decisions – as the human capital model would have us believe – or could there be an alternative explanation? The next section shows that there is such an alternative view, which leads to a different view of education in the process of generating personal incomes.

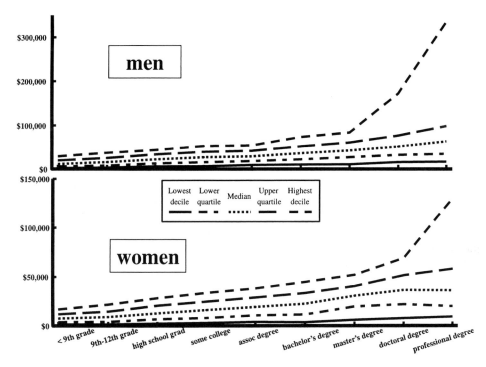

Figure 8.1 Earnings structure and education attainment

8.3 Education as a label

As we have seen in the previous section ignorance and uncertainty about the future raise problems for the 'rational investment' view of human capital formation. However, there is a more important difficulty to be raised concerning ignorance in the context of education and earnings. May it perhaps be the case that education does not directly improve marginal productivity in some jobs at all, but rather serves as a device for identifying relatively gifted workers who would otherwise have gone unrecognised?

Of course we are not suggesting that education or training never raises a person's productivity, but merely that formal education may often be seen not so much as a means of instilling or enhancing skills, but rather as an elaborate device for detecting and labelling those who have skills, and other potential personal qualities available for use and improvement. In chapter 7 we have seen straightforward productivity-based arguments for the kind of relationship between educational qualifactions and the pattern of earnings as depicted in figure 8.1; can a coherent explanation be found in terms of a 'labelling argument'?

To clarify the issue, let us greatly simplify the story of the hiring process. Assume that firms offer applicants wages that correspond to the apparent marginal productivity of each worker, and that a person's marginal productivity is determined only by his ability, which cannot be observed by a potential employer, and (possibly) by his education which is known to all from the diplomas and other pieces of paper which he can display. The return to ability is like the rent on 'land' in the elementary production model discussed in chapter 6 (page 123). If all markets are competitive and if schooling really does make workers more productive (as in the human capital model), then of course firms will make wage offers in accordance with the educational evidence presented. But if the employer has no independent check on ability he may still offer the highly educated worker more pay even if education itself is known to have no effect on a worker's productivity: educational attainment acts as a 'screening device' by identifying for the employer those workers with high innate ability and providing the credentials for people to claim rents on their abilities. The educational certificate is a device used by the employer to reduce the endogenous uncertainty. The source of the endogenous uncertainty in this case is the possible unwillingness or inability of an applicant to reveal all about his personal characteristics which affect his aptitude for the job – no one likes to highlight his weak points.

The argument is appealing because we probably all have at least indirect knowledge of an employer who was unduly swayed by an applicant's glowing certificates, but what assumptions about market processes are required for this signalling procedure to be generally applicable and useful?
- Schooling must be unambiguously certified.
- Ability at passing academic examinations must be related to ability at tasks on the job.
- It must be too costly for the employer to acquire information about ability from other sources.

Under these circumstances we have to be careful about describing education as 'unproductive', since it provides a useful service to employers, but there is a distinction between the private rate of return on schooling (which is positive since without the paper qualification the worker does not get the higher reward) and the social rate of return which will be smaller – perhaps even zero. One implication is that if education only provides ability certificates but does not enhance a worker's economic efficiency, then there may be some other procedure which will eliminate the endogenous uncertainty by providing the same information without the costly charade of going through college or university. In practice, there may be procedures which can do this to some extent, and which are thus used alongside educational certificates to provide information to employers. We shall examine these more closely in section 8.4 below; first we examine the economic consequences of the screening mechanism.

The theory of screening provides an insight into the market determination of the distribution of earnings and inequality that is rather different from the conventional, certainty models. Firstly, the system may yield a number of quite different equilibrium outcomes, so two apparently similar economies might have drastically different distributions of earnings.[4] Secondly, we find an interesting interaction between ability groups: in the two-group example just discussed it is only the presence of the low-ability people that compels the high-ability people to spend some of their income in acquiring an educational certificate. More generally, we may find that in economies with large numbers of different ability groups and different grades of certificates, any increment in the educational attainment by low-ability groups may prompt higher-ability people to acquire yet further educational qualifications in order to differentiate themselves from the rest. Thirdly, the process automatically leads to the 'guild' type horizontal segmentation in the labour market, based on educational or other certificates, as discussed in section 7.7.

To assess the importance of the screening mechanism, let us examine the plausibility of its three main assumptions:

- Presumably skills can be certified – although there is in practice some latitude introduced by well-known differences in quality between colleges.
- Successful performance in school may be a signal of perseverance and drive, of susceptibility to industrial discipline and of suitability for specific training, and thus an indicator of 'ability' at work. However, if ability can take many forms, then the education system may only provide an imperfect screen.
- Whether information about each candidate's potential is available from an alternative source depends crucially on the institutional framework which we envisage.

On this last point the vital rôle played again by experience as a complement to education (although this time on the demand side) may be illustrated with two extreme examples. One is the odd situation of enforceable lifetime labour contracts. Employers would find the information provided by the screening mechanism vital in order to avoid taking on 'dud' workers. On the employee's side there would be a substantial private return from education, but it would be unclear how much of the dispersion of wages at any age was due to variation in ability. However, if lifetime contracts were *not* enforceable, time spent on the job would provide an opportunity for employers to learn from experience and act on it. So, in the second extreme example, if the contract period were very short and learning by employers very rapid, there would be no point in potential workers 'paying for screening' by getting educational qualifications, because the firms would sort them out by promoting the able and immediately firing the inept. Wage dispersion in a competitive system would then be entirely attributable to differential ability.

The truth probably lies between these two extremes so that there is a gradual sorting-out process of matching workers to jobs as each cohort ages, the speed of which will be governed by the rate of acquisition of learning by employers, the transferability of 'ability' between jobs and the degree of job mobility. This then produces a dispersion of wages that increases with age: each cohort starts out imperfectly sorted with a low dispersion roughly corresponding to the observed education level; as time rolls by, workers get sorted out and the dispersion of wages increases accordingly, although there is a natural upper limit to this once the cohort is completely sorted according to ability. Note in particular that this 'fanning out' will also occur within any one group consisting of workers with identical educational certificates.

It has been argued that because time on the job allows employers to learn about the quality of their workers and because the differential returns to formal education persist throughout a worker's career, the screening hypothesis cannot be taken as a serious explanation of the wage structure. Whether this is so depends on the amount of job mobility and the opportunities for learning by the employee as well. Suppose experience on the job in the early years within any one occupation is important in determining future earnings prospects. Then the distribution of job opportunities to each cohort of new entrants will be vital since, in the subsequent rat race, it pays to be at the front of the starting grid. If job mobility is not extremely high then in a few years a person of low innate ability may acquire sufficient talent through on-the-job learning to out-shine later potential entrants with high innate ability. Able people will use the educational self-selection system to get a head start by identifying themselves early. Also, if learning on the job persists, then the differential returns on education will persist over the age groups.

So far we have used the simplifying assumption that education is intrinsically unproductive, whereas in practice the 'screening' process may increase the social product in a number of ways. It can increase cognitive skills, in which case the conventional human capital argument is then overlaid with this selection mechanism. It can improve skill matching – if ability is multi-dimensional there is a clear potential gain in matching workers to those jobs in which they have a comparative advantage. It can improve the allocation of productive factors: if labour supply is elastic and a uniform wage equilibrium is enforced, then the relatively low wage that is being paid to the more able can be viewed as a distortionary tax on skilled labour, the effects of which may be eliminated by allowing a selection process. In each of these three cases market equilibrium may even provide too little screening rather than too much, especially if ability is unknown to potential workers as well as to firms, since risk-averse people may not provide the costly time and resources to acquire certificates.

Clearly education as a label could play an important role in the determination of earnings, but how important is it in practice? One of the difficulties in appraising the validity of the screening hypothesis is simply that in order to contrast it effectively with the simple human capital hypothesis of directly productive education, we really need to adduce evidence about an economic process and not just the observed consequences of that process. Each theory predicts that it is worthwhile (from an individual's point of view) to take a degree; each, as we have seen in this section, is consistent with the typical profile of individual professional earnings, and with the typical fanning out of profiles as in figures 7.9–7.11. The overall static features of the structure of earnings are not of much use in discriminating between the two hypotheses. Can we, then, shed some light on the subject by looking at different specific groups of workers?

Several studies[5] have attempted this by estimating earnings functions that explicitly incorporate years of schooling, educational certificates and ability measures as explanatory variables. The intention is to establish whether the observed earnings differentials can be accounted for entirely by experience, measured ability and years of schooling (as in the standard human capital story) or whether there is an independent explanatory role for the educational certificates themselves. This approach is fraught with difficulties of interpretation. How do we standardise and compare educational certificates of different levels and of different qualities? How do we correctly incorporate data on ability, given that ability is supposed to be unknown to employers (who may be using educational proxies) and yet known to the researchers estimating the earnings equations?

These issues, on top of other imperfections that abound in the labour market in practice, make a definitive general test of the 'screening' hypothesis against its 'education as capital' alternative extremely difficult. Some light can be thrown on the issue by case-study analysis of pay setting and hiring practices of individual firms and government agencies, and these suggest that certification does play a role independent of that of the direct productivity enhancement of education. An alternative approach is to attempt to distinguish certain groups of occupations which may be classified as 'screened' or 'unscreened' and then compare the earnings profiles of the 'screened' and 'unscreened' categories and examine whether these verify the theoretical predictions about certification. If a representative worker A from the 'screened' sector is compared with worker A' (who has the same earnings as A) from the 'unscreened' sector, A should have, on the average, a higher education level than A'; conversely, if worker B from the 'screened' sector is compared with worker B' (who has the same education as B) from the 'unscreened' sector then B' should have a higher earnings level than B. So we may tentatively distinguish 'screened' occupations as those having high mean education and whose members get low earnings if their education is low, and the 'unscreened' occupations as those with low mean education and whose members' earnings are not especially low if their education is low.[6] Although the method obviously depends critically on the way in which the occupations are sorted – so that it should not be taken as a definitive test – it is interesting to note that it often appears to place occupations in the categories we might expect, and that, in the screened sector, educational qualifications are better predictors of individual earnings, and earnings profiles fan out more rapidly with experience.

We may summarise thus. Because all aspects of ability cannot be easily checked, potential employees have an incentive to be less than honest about their true capabilities. This creates uncertainty for potential employers who seek to reduce that uncertainty; the problem may be further compounded by an exogenous element of uncertainty if the applicants themselves are genuinely unsure of their own abilities. To this end the educational credential becomes a useful tool to the employer – but perhaps not to society as a whole, since the education system is costly to run and may increase earnings inequality. Thus education is used to 'pick the winners' in this uncertain environment, and enables them to be rewarded. Because of the nature of the selection mechanism earnings dispersion in any one cohort is likely to go on increasing as that cohort ages. And, as a note for policy makers, earnings inequality will not generally decline as the levels of (certified) education of the lowest strata are raised: all that happens is that everyone revises upwards the educational credentials expected of the more able, leaving earnings dispersion just as it was.

8.4 Job competition

So far you, the reader, have been invited from time to time to put yourself in the position of someone offering his or her services in the labour market. Now change places and imagine yourself as the personnel officer in an expanding firm. Imagine what happens when you are confronted with job applicants. Because you cannot know for certain each applicant's ability at the job, you pay attention to the credentials each can produce and also look for potential trainability of each applicant in the specific skills of your firm; you might use a standard device for reducing the risk to the company, such as a probationary period of employment on low wages. However, it is unlikely that you will be able to vary freely either the wage or the contracted work hours, especially if yours is a large company; instead you rank the candidates in your perceived order of desirability so that the job offer is on a take-it-or-leave-it basis for the most suitably qualified. Unsuccessful candidates look elsewhere, possibly revising downwards their wage aspirations, and totally unsuccessful candidates join the dole queue. If this sort of procedure is customary then, instead of finding continuous shifts in rates of relative remuneration to ensure simultaneous and continuous clearing of markets for all grades of labour (wage competition), we find a process of sorting people into given wage slots: job competition. Let us consider why this process is likely to occur, and its implication for economic inequality.

One of the main reasons for this process is that workers do not view their employment contracts in isolation, that not only their own particular wage but the structure of wages is important to them, and that wage differentials within a firm or an occupation incorporate principles of comparability and fairness as perceived by the workforce. This applies both to workers who are perceived as being on the same level, and to 'vertical' discrepancies between workers on different levels. Since the views of individuals and groups about distributional justice are likely to change only very slowly, this factor reinforces the short-term rigidity of wage and salary differentials. This bias towards rigidity may be established by the wage-fixing activities of trades unions but is likely to persist in an industrialised economy without such explicit direction. We have already noted that the wages of skilled workers may contain a substantial component attributable to experience, but in large firms experience does not take place in a vacuum. Workers need to perceive clearly the rewards of experience for this to act as an incentive; and in any structure involving supervisory authority it helps if the rewards and responsibilities are clear to all. So there is good reason not to disturb unduly the delicate web of relative remuneration in the course of adjustment to changing market conditions. People are often easier to shift than pay structures.

Apart from the issues of distributional justice there is also a 'teamwork-training' argument: the specialised circumstances of particular firms and the complexity of many jobs in an industrialised economy mean that worker-to-worker contact on the job is usually the most cost-effective form of acquiring useful training, even if this involves little more than learning how to get on with the boss. The 'marginal productivity' concept applies to the job rather than to the worker in isolation, and firms actually offer jobs-cum-training opportunities rather than plain jobs. Then these reasons of stability become important to the firm, so that job security is fostered within the firm and the firing of workers, should it become necessary, is focused where it does the least damage – on the newest, and therefore least trained, workers. Unemployed workers are prevented from competing freely with experienced employed workers so that wage competition is largely suppressed, and a job ladder such as that described in section 7.5 of chapter 7 is established.

Both the fairness and the teamwork-training arguments are strengthened once we allow for the effects of uncertainty. Clearly straightforward inertia, a general desire for control and the attractive simplicity of established pay scales would themselves be powerful reasons for firms to suppress pure wage competition in favour of the more structured process of job competition in an uncertain world. However, in the light of our discussion about endogenous uncertainty we can identify more specific reasons for firms adopting a job-competition approach: from the point of view of the firm's evaluation and exploitation of the unknown qualities of a new recruit, it makes sense to confront him with a wage ladder which deliberately underpays him during a probationary period and then overpays him thereafter – if he is successful and lasts the course.[7] Not only would this result in a well-established promotion ladder, but also the firm would be disinclined to respond to an overall excess supply of applicants by reducing the wage offers; to do so might simply lose the firm its best, and as yet unidentified, workers. Of course, if the firm cannot observe a worker's abilities with 100 per cent accuracy, neither can his fellow workers. Therefore, there is good reason for firms not to 'rock the boat' by overtly discriminating amongst workers of apparently similar qualifications since the overall profitability of the firm will usually depend on the cooperation of its labour force as a team and not on isolated, individually rewarded work contributions. Finally, the worker himself, though perhaps knowing better than others his own strengths and weaknesses, may nevertheless not know his performance potential within a particular firm. This may be because his 'marginal productivity' is in reality part of a team product which depends critically on the composition of that team, and because there are other data about the firm – such as the demand for its products – about which the worker has only sketchy information. Under those circumstances a risk-averse worker may himself prefer to face a relatively rigid wage structure to an auction carried out in every period ensuring that market-clearing wages are continuously enforced for every grade of labour.[8]

The most striking feature of job competition is perhaps the stickiness of wage structures in the face of changes in the firm's environment. In place of instantaneous wage adjustment associated with conventional models of market dynamics we find a system reminiscent of the child's game of 'snakes and ladders'. The 'ladders' are there to assess and train the favoured employees; the 'snakes' are the queues for jobs. This is not to assert that wage competition is never present: under certain circumstances this still plays an important market-clearing role, particularly where there is excess demand for particular specialised types of skilled worker. Alongside the snakes and ladders phenomenon, however, we also note the central importance under job competition of 'fairness' rules with reference to hiring and firing decisions and to levels of and changes in relative rates of pay. Whether or not education and experience play a direct role in enhancing the productive ability and thus each worker's earnings, under job competition they also play an important more subtle role in determining people's earnings expectations. Particularly within bureaucratic institutions, such as those found in the public sector, paper qualifications and length of service can strongly influence the fairness rules concerning who keeps his job when times are hard, and who, from a pool of otherwise apparently similar candidate employees, is advanced to more senior positions in the job ladder. Because of these rules, each worker does not stand in an isolated relationship with his employer under job competition, but instead relative positions on the ladder become important. We would expect there to be resistance on the part of apparently unrelated workers to 'unfair' wage changes that substantially upset established pay differentials. Such resistance need not be dismissed as irrationality or envy, but may be a perfectly reasonable response in a complex and uncertain environment where teamwork is important.

The snakes and ladders mechanism can be seen as sorting workers roughly into two groups. Group one, the highly attractive and highly employable workers, will usually be well educated and occupy places at the front of labour queues at all levels. Almost all of them will have relatively secure jobs and almost all of the top echelon posts will be filled from their ranks. At the back of the labour queues we find the members of the second group. They tend to be unskilled and quite prone to spells of unemployment which in a job-competition model become self-reinforcing, since such workers will have had less opportunity to build up the experience that places them more favourably in the queue. As Nickell (1980) notes:

At any point in time, some people in Britain are far more likely to find themselves unemployed than the average. Such individuals probably have at least one of the following characteristics. They are either young or old or unskilled, with a large family or living in a council house in the northern half of Britain. There is little evidence that being prone to unemployment is very much a matter of personal choice. Of course, it may be argued that people choose to be highly paid building workers rather than poorly paid park-keepers in spite of the insecurity of the former job. The fact remains, however, that members of both these occupations are more likely to become unemployed than solicitors, and few bricklayers ever had much in the way of a choice to be a solicitor.

It is an oversimplification to imagine that there is a rigid segregation into two classes of 'employables' and 'unemployables', but the way in which job competition perpetuates inequality, even where labour mobility is quite high, is clear enough. The dynamics of the income distribution amongst a particular age cohort of workers is also clear where job competition prevails. 'Group two' workers are constrained on a relatively low-income profile and erratic movements in their earnings correspond to spells of unemployment. 'Group one' workers gradually ascend job ladders in both the private and the public sector. The pecking order in the labour queue for progressively more senior and well-paid jobs is progressively adjusted as more information becomes available, but pay dispersion amongst them must also increase over their working life as the favoured few at the front make it to the very top of the pyramid in figure 7.16 whilst the bulk achieve only more modest advancement. Job competition does not collapse the pyramid but ensures that workers' earnings profiles must 'fan out' over time.

In summary, it can be seen that the job competition process reinforces many of the points made in section 8.3 about the screening phenomenon. Whereas the screening mechanism leads to horizontal segmentation in a labour market with incomplete information, and so to a suppression of some forms of competition, the forces behind job competition lead to vertical segmentation. The screening mechanism and job competition play complementary roles in the earnings dynamics of an industrialised economy. Notice that in such an economy, with complex production and administrative processes, barriers to competition should not really be seen as 'aberrations' – to be assumed away for convenience or legislated away by laws against restrictive practices – but are an almost inevitable outcome of a 'rational' process of organising the workforce. Moreover, vertical or horizontal segmentation, whether attributable to firms or workers, will help to perpetuate earnings inequality.

It is interesting to note too that schooling under job competition has a similar effect to schooling in the screening model. It picks out the winners and so it makes sense to ensure that you or your offspring are ripe for the picking, even if formal education adds nothing to your productive abilities. Increasing the general level of education in the population will not change matters much: once again the labels on the 'winners' will be upgraded. Yet the available cross-sectional evidence on earnings, age, education and experience could well be used to support either this account of heavily modified competition or the conventional human capital story with unrestricted and universal wage competition. The important differences between the two approaches is that screening-cum-job-competition provides an account of why there are institutional constraints within the labour market and queues of unemployed or underemployed; the conventional model does not. Further differences between the two approaches emerge in their treatment of economic change within the system, to which we turn in the next section.

8.5 The short run: shocks

Whilst equilibrium models are an aid to understanding some important features concerning the structure of earnings, they do not say much about what happens if that structure is disturbed. This matters for several reasons. Firstly, such shocks usually involve unanticipated changes in real income for many people and, as we argued in chapter 4, the resulting changes in observed inequality, even if transitory, may be of concern to a social policy maker. Secondly, the impact on economic inequality and social welfare over any length of time cannot usually be dismissed as transient: even if the income distribution process can be shown to be stable in some appropriate sense, it is unlikely that the time required to restore equilibrium will be negligible. Thirdly, an apparently temporary shock to the economy may have a permanent effect on some people's incomes even though there might be little effect on the income distribution in the long run: for example, older workers could be made redundant by some such apparently minor economic perturbation. Finally, an understanding of the way in which the system responds to such shocks may affect the particular choice of policy instruments.

To focus the discussion let us consider two particular types of exogenous economic shock: shifts in aggregate demand and technological change. Objections could be raised to treating either of these phenomena as exogenous to the income distribution system, since a change in the distribution of income itself is likely to affect the level of demand through both the aggregate consumption function and the incentive to invest: it may affect not only firms' particular choices of production technique but also the direction of their research and innovative activities. It might be argued that these economic changes could be anticipated by workers and employers so that, instead of regarding such perturbations as 'shocks', the process of income creation and distribution may be viewed as one of dynamic equilibrium, steadily adapting to such exogenous shifts. This argument is unconvincing, for whilst it is true that some macroeconomic events could be pretty well foreseen by a diligent student of the financial press it would be remarkably difficult to square such a view with the facts as a general account of how particular workers' earnings are determined. As we argued in section 8.2, uncertainty proper is important for individual workers' and firms' decisions; we do have to examine how the system is likely to respond to events which are genuinely unforeseen.

As we have noted in previous sections, there are two principal mechanisms which affect income changes in response to economic shocks. The first mechanism is that of quantity adjustment. The obvious manifestation of this is that of people being thrown out of work when aggregate demand falls. Under this same category we may consider shifts of workers from one region to another, or one industry to another, moving as a result of changes in the relative prospects of obtaining a job rather than because of changes in wage differentials. Furthermore, within industries and within firms, a falling off in product demand may result in slower upgrading and less overtime pay. These various forms of responses to changes in demand will be accompanied by the second mechanism – price adjustment. A shift of product demand in the direction of the computer industry should improve wage rates there and thus attract more workers to that industry. It should also enhance the returns to the particular forms of human capital that are specific to that industry (degrees and diplomas in computer science) and thereby stimulate the flow of workers equipped with them. In these ways the price or wage mechanism will help to adjust the interindustrial, interoccupational and interskill mix of the labour force in response to product demand changes.

The idea that this price–wage mechanism is so speedy and all pervasive that quantity adjustment can be blandly ignored as irrelevant or insignificant should be treated with scepticism. It rather appears that generally neither mechanism operates exclusively in an industrialised economy, that the relative importance of each depends on the particular circumstances of each industry. Moreover, the system's responses to 'upward' and 'downward' shocks are likely to be asymmetric. Competition, as we have seen, is often job competition, and so the implications for the behaviour of the income distribution and inequality are going to be far more complex than an equilibrium, flexible-price model would suggest. We would need to take account of the particular detail of the adjustment mechanism acting upon individual incomes in order to be able to say much about the practical issues which affect year-to-year earnings inequality. Let us examine this further in the context of aggregate demand shocks.

Take first the principal features of the business cycle which are likely to affect the inequality of personal earnings in the short run. Consider in particular two phenomena that have been suggested as particularly important in industrialised economies:
 (i)   Skill differentials in pay tend to contract in the upswing and widen in the downswing.[9]
 (ii) Unemployment is not like flu which everyone gets from time to time; but hits certain industries, certain occupational groups and certain groups of low paid workers particularly hard.[10]

The first interesting thing about these phenomena is that the price system does not work quickly enough to smooth out the effects of such demand shifts upon workers' income, nor to anticipate and so to 'discount' them before they happen. The second point worth noting is that both price and quantity adjustments in the labour market result from these shocks. The third point of interest is that the impact on the inequality of earnings is likely to be of a quite complex nature. Let us examine this more closely.

At a first glance the two points above appear to have effects on earnings inequality that are roughly in the same direction: inequality is higher in the slump. However, the story is found not to be so simple when we look at the possible reasons for the first phenomenon. As we noted in section 8.4, competition in the labour market of industrialised economies with large-scale firms and bureaucratic structures resembles a struggle by workers for positions on a job ladder where the rungs correspond to particular salary levels. So in the upswing, as some firms expand in sales and in size, promotion on the ladder will be more readily sanctioned, and may even occur to the point where dilution of skills occurs. Labour shortages in upper echelons are met by more rapid advancement from below – but of course this mechanism cannot operate properly at the lowest skill levels because there is no lower level of recruits on which to draw once the reserve army of the unemployed has been called up. In periods of excess demand for labour additional units of lower grades of labour can only be attracted by bidding up the wage to attract overtime workers and part-time casual and temporary workers such as many married women who simply withdraw from the active labour force rather than joining the ranks of the registered unemployed when times are hard. The result is that in the upswing the observed pay scales in the middle and upper echelons may remain relatively stable (though people are moving more rapidly up them), but the lower wages are drawn up by the pressure of excess demand and so the observed skill differentials narrow.[11]

Now, whilst the job-competition system apparently contracts the wage structure during the boom, this does not mean that earnings inequality then necessarily falls. Imagine a hierarchical model of managerial salaries[12] and suppose that anyone who is not a manager must be an unskilled worker receiving a uniform wage w. If the demand for labour increases people move more rapidly up the pyramid-like structure and w is forced up. Obviously, the gap between unskilled workers' wages and the wages of any given grade of managerial appointee must contract; but at the same time the boom has shifted the 'centre of gravity' of the pyramid to the right due to rapid promotion and expansion stretching the upper tail of the distribution of earnings to the right. So, overall, the inequality amongst persons could actually have increased during the period of generally rising wages.[13]

In the subsequent downswing, promotion up the ladder is slowed down so that many individuals' salaries do not immediately move up very much, yet as far as possible firms will try to retain their skilled staff, because they will have made a substantial special-ised investment in their workers in the form of education and on-the-job training.[14] So, as we have seen, it is typically on lower-paid workers that the burden of cyclical unemployment falls most heavily. But maybe we ought to be a little cautious about interpreting this differential incidence of unemployment as a contributory cause of inequality during the slump. Apart from the official cushioning of the effects of unemployment through social insurance schemes, it is conceivable that, in the long run, wage differentials between occupations and workers' freedom of choice to switch jobs mean that the risk of income loss through being laid off is compensated for by the hope of higher wages eventually. And – who knows? – maybe in the fullness of time the young unemployed will find that judged by lifetime earnings the incidence of unemployment was not so inegalitarian after all.[15]

Let us now turn attention from changes in aggregate demand to shocks that take the form of changes in the composition of the demand for labour. Obviously, such shifts come about for a variety of reasons – intersectoral shifts in consumer demand, a change in the supply conditions of some other factors of production, the introduction of new technological possibilities such as micro-chip technology. However, in each case the issues are broadly similar: which groups of workers will experience substantial changes in the demand price of their labour; which group will experience further income changes because of losing their jobs; what will be the overall effect on the inequality of income. As with the case of aggregate demand changes it is quite misleading to see the adjustments in the labour market taking place as a reallocation of homogeneous efficiency units of input.

Whatever the reason for the intersectoral shift in the demand for labour, the impact on workers' economic prospects depends crucially on their skill level and skill type. As with cyclical unemployment many older workers are likely to be particularly vulnerable to 'structural' or 'technological' unemployment. There are a complex of reasons for this. Old workers are not only more likely to be fairly immobile for social reasons, but are also likely to be relatively 'economically immobile' because to some extent they resemble old machines in that they embody a relatively large proportion of specific human capital; firms tend to place people in job queues in reverse order to their training or retraining costs. Furthermore, from the workers' point of view, in terms of life-time earnings there are smaller returns to persistence in searching for employment in a new field if a person is near the end of his or her working life. These factors are particularly important for the unskilled, skilled manual employees and other technical staff, but are much less so for managerial or administrative staff:[16] for unskilled workers the story is much the same as for aggregate demand shocks; for skilled workers the problem is obviously the specialised nature of their skill.

By contrast, managerial and administrative staff will have acquired fairly general skills during their careers and are thus more adaptable to demand shifts. The nature of their employment contracts often renders them less easily sackable, and so amongst such staff adjustments have to be made elsewhere, usually in the wages and employment of the young. The reason for this is to be found in the vertically segmented structure of the labour market (discussed in section 7.6) and its associated job ladder. Because this ladder incorporates an incentive scheme for workers, a system of fair seniority differentials and a sorting mechanism, altering the relative positions of the 'rungs' on such an integral component of organisational structure of business organisations and public authorities can be a costly exercise. The main burden of adjustment to technological change or product demand switches is unlikely to fall principally on internal pay structures. If a firm is forced to contract, it will be least willing to lose those employees who embody large amounts of human capital that is specific to that particular firm. So quantity adjustments will again involve slower rates of advancement of those already in employment and also the curtailment of new recruitment.

There is a further factor which reinforces this effect on the young. Those already in a firm's 'manor' may to some extent be shielded from competition by aspirant new entrants even in times of significant excess supply of labour to that industry or occupation – the chances are that their firm is not going to sack them and replace them with untried and untested novices. But competition amongst new entrants may well be intense so that if there is excess supply of workers with some particular kind of skill the effect of such active competition will be most marked amongst the young – potential new entrants. For this reason relative wage adjustments are likely to be most noticeable within that group.[17]

8.6 The long run: families

As we noted in the introduction to this chapter, in addition to the issues discussed in the last section there is also a major long-run question to be answered. How do earn-

Table 8.1 *Percentage probabilities of being in each quarter of the log earnings distribution, USA, National Longitudinal Survey*

Log earnings class of fathers	Log earnings class of sons			
	Top quarter	Second quarter	Third quarter	Bottom quarter
Top quarter	41	33	17	9
Second quarter	25	27	27	21
Third quarter	17	22	31	30
Bottom quarter	12	19	29	40

Table 8.2 *Percentage probabilities of being in each quarter of the income distribution, UK, Rowntree Follow-up Survey*

Earnings class of fathers	Earnings class of sons			
	Top quarter	Second quarter	Third quarter	Bottom quarter
Top quarter	50	29	15	6
Second quarter	19	27	36	18
Third quarter	17	25	26	32
Bottom quarter	14	19	23	44

ings of individuals behave over time periods measured in generations? Notice that we are not talking here about occupational or skill differentials on earnings, but rather about whether high earnings capacity will be passed from parents to children and if so, how.

To see the issue more clearly, refer back to the discussion of the determination of family income in chapter 7. There certain characteristics of the family head and other earners in the family were taken as given: innate skills, early education, etc. The distribution of these characteristics amongst persons and families influences the distribution of earnings via people's choices about further education, training, occupation, labour force participation and so on. But the distribution of characteristics is itself, in the long run, affected by people's choices and is susceptible to change. People do not line up at their 'birth' in the labour market, to collect a randomly drawn tombola ticket with their skills, abilities and other attributes written on it: there is usually a striking resemblance between each person's ticket and that of his parents. That this is so is strongly suggested by tables 8.1 and 8.2. Of the top 10 per cent of income receivers in the USA more than a quarter had parents who were in the top 10 per cent on the scale of social and economic background; the same is true at the bottom end in table 8.1.[18] The British data also reveal that a disproportionate number of sons with high earnings also had fathers with high earnings. Something more than blind chance appears to have been at work in both countries. It is interesting to see what this might be.

Financial wealth is an obvious connection: even where the state taxes away a substantial proportion of personal estates, straightforward bequests are a powerful mechanism for transmitting and augmenting inequality from one generation to the next, as we shall see in the next chapter. Parental wealth may affect not only their children's property incomes, but also their incomes from employment by making it easier for them to acquire the educational qualifications to set foot on the right job ladder. However, parents may also provide 'bequests' in more subtle ways than through cash sums since there appears to be a clear connection between the measured IQs of parents and offspring. Let us examine each of these links.

The IQ connection is contentious. If able people breed able people like stud race-horses then surely earnings inequality is almost bound to be self-perpetuating from generation to generation. Whether this is so depends on two things: how effective some particular measure of ability is as an indicator of people's earnings and whether IQ – or any other ability measure – reflects anything actually inherited genetically to a significant extent. On the first point it is obviously foolish to attribute some large part of the 'unexplained' variance in the observed earnings–schooling relationship to individual ability effects without further direct information. One major problem is that ability has so many different manifestations, not all of which could be measured. However, measured IQ, both in its direct association with a person's earnings and in its indirect association through the person's education, accounts for only a small part of the correlation between the parents socio-economic position and the child's subsequent income: other direct influences in the home, school and workplace appear to be much more important.[19] Nevertheless, the IQ correlation is there, and it may be that the relationship between ability and earnings has been incorrectly modelled so that the importance of IQ for earnings prospects is grossly understated. So let us turn to the second issue – is IQ inherited? The common view that indeed a very high proportion of observed IQ variance is accounted for by genetic variance was put into doubt by the work of Jencks et al. (1972). More recent research has concentrated on the analysis of data on identical and fraternal twins in an attempt to statistically control for the genetic component in IQ: this appears to support Jencks' conclusion that slightly less than half of the individual variation in IQ is attributable to the genes; but the whole approach is extremely sensitive to the precise specification of the statistical model and it would be unwise to place heavy reliance on these results.[20]

So there is no strong automatic mechanism by which high earnings capacity is passed down through the members of a dynasty. Rather than biological transmission of earnings inequality across generations we need to look once again at the social and economic linkages: design rather than genetic chance. For the sake of brevity we may summarise the principal features of economic interest in this complex process thus: nepotism and nurture.

Nepotism sounds nasty, but it may not be all bad. Indeed, in an uncertain world there could actually be much to recommend it purely in terms of efficiency,[21] though of course it is usually extremely inegalitarian in its effects. Personal acquaintance or a trusted recommendation may be more useful to a potential employer as a 'screen' than a whole battery of applicant's credentials although, if carried to an extreme, this nepotistic process must lead to an ossified, caste-ridden and unproductive labour force. If nepotism is abolished in favour of pure meritocracy, although the dynamics of transmission of earnings inequality may alter, the fact of the perpetuation of such inequality may not. Meritocratic selection for well-paid jobs may involve greater mobility from generation to generation than would exist if the distasteful phenomenon of nepotism were to prevail; but it would not necessarily promote equality of opportunity. For unless family preferences and freedom of action towards their own offspring were completely removed, there would still remain ample scope for the transmission of inequality via 'nurture' within families.

Under the broad heading of 'nurture' come both the formal provision of primary and secondary education by parents for their children and the informal education, or cultural and social training, given within the home. In a meritocracy these types of intangible 'bequests' are clearly important if we wish our children to be at the front of the starting grid in the earnings race, and are likely to be complementary to other forms of tangible bequest in influencing the prospective living standards of the next generation. Furthermore, irrespective of whether market forces, pure wage competition and the acquisition of human capital are the dominant forces influencing the subsequent development of the earnings of the members of a new cohort, it is evident that in determining the starting point of each person it is the institution of the family rather than the market which is dominant.

The generation-to-generation transmission of earnings inequality is likely to be most insensitive to change that involves purely market forces. Far more important will be simple yet powerful alterations in the social structure, such as the number of children per family and the extent of marriage between certain social groups. In addition the pattern of ownership of wealth itself will also strongly influence families' decisions on the provision they make for their children. These issues are taken up in chapter 9.

8.7 Conclusions

Rather than attempt a short summary of the answers suggested to the many questions raised in chapters 7 and 8, we select two themes which have been developed here.

Mechanisms matter

As we have noted in both chapters 7 and 8 there is a variety of stories that we can tell that are consistent with the summary facts of earnings inequality. But, largely because of uncertainty, different stories can have drastically different implications for individuals' income prospects in the short and the long run and for the impact of policy. The distinction between education as human capital and education as a screen matters not only because of its effect on the relative prospects of the able and the dull, but also because of the likely long-term impact of public educational policy on economic inequality. The distinction between job and wage competition matters crucially for those so unfortunate as to be thrown out of work during recession.

Bias is built-in

There are rigidities in the system which competition does not completely eliminate. Once again uncertainty is very largely responsible for this: the better-off are often better informed and have better educated children; better educated people are likely to become better off even if they are not demonstrably more able; and again both short-run and long-run issues are involved. Because of the job competition mechanism relatively poorly endowed workers are likely to find it particularly burdensome to cope with economic shocks, especially if they are old and their skills are obsolete. And, even in a relatively open society, high earnings capacity is quite likely to be 'bequeathed' from one generation to the next. The implications of this are drawn out in more detail in the next two chapters which introduce wealth and its effect on income inequality.

8.8 Questions for discussion

General Reading: Brittain (1977), Cain (1976), Levy and Murnane (1992), Sewell and Hauser (1986), Taylor (1987), Thurow (1975), Weiss (1991).

8.1   Discuss the view that the conventional economic assumptions of 'rational' decision making by individuals is a misleading guide to the way choices about work, effort, career and training are made in practice (Leibenstein, 1976; Scitovsky, 1976; Akerlof and Dickens, 1982).

8.2   Consider the effect that different degrees of uncertainty in the labour market may have on choice of career and the amount of time and resources searching for a better job, with particular reference to the resulting impact on the distribution of earnings (Johnson, 1977; Metcalf, 1973).

8.3   Evaluate the use of 'tournaments' as work incentives in internal labour markets (Calvo and Wellisz, 1979; Green and Stokey, 1983; Lazear and Rosen, 1981; Malcolmson, 1984).

8.4   One way in which firms can reduce the uncertainty which they face concerning the qualities of their new recruits is to offer wage contracts such that only the 'right' sort of workers will bother to apply. Discuss what forms such contracts might take (see Guasch and Weiss, 1981; Salop and Salop, 1976; Spence, 1973, 1981; Starrett, 1976).

8.5   One feature of many screening models is that an equilibrium with screening involves greater income inequality and lower aggregate income than an equilibrium without screening (Arrow, 1973; Stiglitz, 1975b). May we thus infer that screening is inefficient and undesirable? Is there a case for restricting the use of screening devices such as educational certificates (Weiss, 1983)?

8.6   Because people are usually better informed about their own marketable skills than those who collect data on the labour market, it is argued that to interpret the distribution we should take into account the self-selection of people into groups. Consider the effect of this self-selection process on the inequality of earnings (Heckman and Sedlacek, 1985; Willis and Rosen, 1979).

8.7   It is often observed that when there is an excess supply of workers wishing to work in industrial firms wages for new recruits do not immediately fall. Why (Salop, 1973; Stiglitz, 1975a; Weiss, 1980)?

8.8   The accompanying table (table 8.3) and comment are from Beck's (1951) study of unemployment in Britain between the world wars:

'Why was age a more serious handicap in 1937 than it had been ten years before? Elderly men were not harder hit by the slump than the young – the table shows that the increase in unemployment between 1927 and 1932 was proportionately much the same

Table 8.3 *Male unemployment rates by age-groups in Great Britain*

Ages	1927	1932	1937
18–24	8.8	20.2	8.8
25–34	10.2	22.3	9.4
35–44	9.4	21.9	11.4
45–54	11.0	24.8	14.1
55–64	13.9	29.1	20.3
18–64	10.2	22.9	11.8

in all age-groups. Mass unemployment, like area-bombing, is not selective of its victims; young and old, good workers and bad, suffer together when a pit or factory is shut down. Re-employment, on the contrary, is selective. When trade revived the younger men were in general the first to get back to work.' – What long-term impact would you expect the economic phenomenon described above to have upon income inequality?

8.9   What practical problems would you expect to encounter in trying to determine whether a 'dual' labour market was in operation in an economy (Bosanquet and Doeringer, 1973; Dickens and Lang, 1985; Dickens and Summers, 1985; Neiman and Ziderman, 1986; Wachter, 1974; White, 1983)?

8.10   Consider the ways in which education affects
 (i) the probability and duration of unemployment,
(ii) access to jobs with a high degree of security of tenure.
What effect on economic inequality would you expect from an increase in the overall level of education attainment (see question 6.6 and also Ashenfelter and Ham, 1979; Bhagwati and Srinivasan, 1977; Card and Krueger, 1992; Knight, 1979; Marin and Psacharopoulos, 1976; Psacharopoulos, 1985; Rosen 1968)?

8.11   In what way would you expect fiscal and monetary policies to affect the structure of individual earnings and the overall inequality of incomes (Beach, 1977; Blinder and Esaki, 1978; Gramlich, 1974; Haslag *et al.*, 1989; Nolan, 1986, 1987; Russell *et al.*, 1986)?

8.12   Some researchers have suggested the following empirical propositions about the relationship between family background and earnings:
• having more brothers or sisters reduces lifetime earnings prospects;
• higher parental status is associated with higher earnings prospects but a lower rate of return to schooling;
• there is a strong association between the earnings of fathers and sons-in-law.
Discuss the economic and social conditions which might give rise to such phenomena, and the implications for the transmission of economic inequality in the long run (Atkinson *et al.*, 1983; Behrman *et al.*, 1994, 1995; Cohn and Kiker, 1986; Corcoran *et al.*, 1976; Datcher, 1982; Hauser and Sewell, 1986; Kearl and Pope, 1986; Leibowitz, 1977; Papanicolau and Psacharopoulos, 1979).

8.13   It has been argued that the substantial increase in wage inequality that has been experienced in the USA, the UK and elsewhere is largely attributable to a rapid increase in the premium for skill. Discuss the mechanisms through which this may have occurred (Bound and Johnson, 1992; Gosling *et al.*, 1994, 1996; Juhn *et al.*, 1993; Raisian, 1983; van Reenen, 1993).

Notes

 1 See, for example, the model in appendix B. Simple versions of the model under uncertainty are given in Levhari and Weiss (1974) and in Olson *et al.* (1979); the dependence on wealth in this case holds even where everyone has access to a 'perfect capital market'.

 2 A number of studies have attempted to examine whether individuals do behave in this fashion of limited rationality under uncertainty. For example, Freeman (1971) uses a 'cobweb' model to examine the market for highly educated manpower: (1) supply in any period is determined on the basis of expectations formed in the previous period, (2) at any instant the wage rate adjusts to clear the market given the current demand and the predetermined supply and (3) expectations about pay in future periods are based on the pay in the current period. The more responsive are pay changes to present supply and the more responsive is the forthcoming supply to changes in anticipated pay, the more rapidly the system adjusts in response to any disturbance. Freeman found that for new Bachelor of Science graduates in engineering the system would converge to a stable equilibrium within about five years, but that the market for those with doctoral qualifications was much more sluggish. On interviewing students still at college about their career plans and choice of their course he found 'a realistic formation of expectations and a well-informed body of decision makers'. Although they tended to be rather too optimistic about their own personal prospects they were on the whole correct in their ranking of careers in terms of market payoffs and in their estimation of the prospective salaries of college-trained manpower generally. However, the USA is in some respects a special case: in countries where there are substantial educational subsidies, rationing of college and university places, or substantial influence by parents or others over the individual's choices in higher education, different results are likely to emerge; the interviewees are also special since they belong to a narrowly defined and well-informed sector of the upper echelons of the labour market.

 3 There are at least four problems, as follows. Let all possible states of the world be indexed by $s = 1, 2, 3, \ldots$, let the financial payoff to a particular person in state of the world s be y_s, let the utility which he attaches to such a payoff be $u(y_s)$ and let him perceive the probability of state s occurring be p_s. Then, (1) except in a model of pure risk, different persons may have completely different views about the values of $p_1, p_2, p_3, \ldots$; (2) people may differ in their u-functions; (3) if the probabilities $p_1, p_2, p_3, \ldots$ cannot be objectively and confidently determined there are several strategies each of which might be described as 'rational' behaviour: for example 'choose a policy that will maximise $\Sigma_s p_s u(y_s)$', or 'choose a policy that will maximise $\min_s \{u(y_s)\}$'. The second and third points raise issues which go beyond the scope of this text – see Arrow (1951), Cowell (1986, chapter 10), Hey (1979), Schoemaker (1982); (4) people may manipulate each other's u functions and yet be ignorant about each other's u-functions.

 4 As a simple example of this take an economy that contains just two sorts of people – 'high-ability' and 'low-ability' – and one grade of educational certificate. Suppose everyone is paid according to their presumed ability, but that unless able people possess a certificate to prove they are able they just get paid the same as everyone else. There may be one equilibrium with everyone getting exactly average earnings – if the high-ability–average-ability differential is less than the private cost of education then there is no incentive for anyone in the high-ability group to acquire the educational certificate and thus the label that would entitle him to above-

average earnings, so everyone gets paid a wage corresponding to the average ability of the workforce. However, there may be another equilibrium with all the able people holding certificates entitling them to high earnings and the rest getting low earnings – if the high-ability–low-ability earnings differential exceeds the cost of education all the high-ability people have a material incentive to avoid being categorised as low ability by default. See Stiglitz (1975b).

5 See Taubman and Wales (1973, 1974), Layard and Psacharopoulos (1974), Wolpin (1977), Liu and Wong (1982).

6 This is the approach of Riley (1976, 1979). Using this classification criterion he found that teachers, librarians, sociologists and social workers fell into the 'screened' category whilst authors, designers, computer programmers and computer analysts fell into the 'unscreened' category. Other combinations of education and earnings characteristics were categorised as 'indeterminate'.

7 See questions 8.3 and 8.4 at the end of this chapter. The evidence of this type of effect has recently been challenged by Abraham and Farber (1987) and Altonji and Shakotko (1987) using panel data methods; but see Topel (1991).

8 The argument is similar to the 'implicit contract' theory of unemployment – see Azariadis (1981), Grossman and Hart (1981). The problem of rewarding members of a complex team is discussed in Lazear and Rosen (1981) and the use of the promotion ladder to discourage shirking is discussed in Lazear (1981), Lazear and Moore (1984). The rôle of the seniority system and unionisation in determining layoffs is discussed in Grossman (1983): see also Elbaum (1983), Reich et al. (1973).

9 This was noted by Reder (1955), although Phelps Brown (1978) queries the extent to which this occurs in practice.

10 Nolan (1986, 1987) pointed out that total weeks of unemployment concentrated among a very small proportion of the labour force. However, the impact of unemployment on the size distribution when we take into account family or household structure is rather more complex. Increased unemployment causes a significant shift in the distribution: the shares of the top increase, but the reductions in share are not uniformly concentrated at the bottom of the distribution (35 per cent of the families affected by unemployment were not in the bottom half of the distribution). The reason for this is the dispersal of low-paid workers throughout many parts of the income distribution by family or household.

11 Some interesting evidence for this is presented by Nissim (1984), who found the employment of skilled labour varies less than for lower-skilled grades; that the hours per worker of skilled workers vary more than for unskilled grades; and that the cyclical wage-rate variation is greater for unskilled workers. Bils (1985) noted that the wages of those who stay at the same job vary little over the cycle in contrast to those who switch jobs.

12 See page 161 above.

13 Beach's (1977) model of the postwar US income distribution throws light on the complex interaction of wage adjustments and employment changes involved in points (i) and (ii) above. The effect of the unemployment rate, taken by itself, was found to be inegalitarian in that an increase in the level of unemployment had a much greater impact on the incomes of those in the bottom 30 per cent of the income distribution than elsewhere; but at the same time an increase in wage rates had a much greater impact on the upper echelons of the income distribution. Taken together, these two influences operate in a counteracting fashion in terms of their effect on aggregate earnings inequality and income inequality over the business cycle. Blinder and Esaki (1978) carried out a somewhat similar exercise, for the USA but divided the income distribution into 20 per cent income slices. Their basic model is

$$s_{it} = \alpha_i + \beta_i U_t + \gamma_i \pi_t + \delta_i T_t + \epsilon_{it}$$

where s_{it} is the share of the ith group in total income in the USA in year t, U_t is the overall unemployment rate, π_t is the rate of inflation and T_t is a linear time trend. Comparing Blinder and Esaki's results for the US with those obtained by Nolan (1987) using the *Family Expenditure Survey* for the UK we find:

	Unemployment		Inflation	
	UK	USA	UK	USA
Bottom 20%	−0.21	−0.13	+0.02	+0.03
Second 20%		−0.14		−0.03
Third 20%				
Fourth 20%	+0.32			−0.03
Top 20%		+0.27		
Top 5%	−0.41			

Unemployment clearly has a major impact on the bottom of the distribution – see also the work of Buse (1982) for Canada. The effect of inflation is, however, less clear cut.

More direct evidence is provided by Blank (1989) using the Panel Study of Income Dynamics (see appendix A). She found that income distribution becomes less unequal during times of economic expansion, even though the share of the poor in labour income is small. Both wages and hours of the household head vary strongly with the cycle (although women's earnings are much less responsive) illustrating the importance of both price and quantity adjustments. Both income differences between groups, and income differences within groups narrow during expansion. See also Schwartz (1986).

14 See Blakemore and Hoffman (1989).

15 The irony is intentional. There is little evidence of such lifetime equalisation and, as Nickell (1980) shows, there is also little evidence that people actually 'choose' unemployment at certain stages of their career – see page 000 above. Furthermore, the long-run view of inequality may just simply miss the point. An interesting insight on this is provided by Nolan (1986) who simulated the effect of unemployment benefit on income inequality in the UK: in terms of annual income he found that the effect was spread throughout the distribution; but in terms of weekly (current) income the effect was much more narrowly focused at the bottom of the distribution.

16 It is this difference according to skill type that would lead to a difference in feedback effect on the demand for human capital under uncertainty.

17 These conclusions are confirmed by Freeman's (1977) analysis of the collapse of the graduate job market in the USA, a phenomenon not attributable to the usual cyclical forces. The market adjustments corroborated the 'vertically segmented' model with a mixture of job and wage competition. In view of the 'production lag' in turning out educated people a drop in the demand for such manpower inevitably meant a substantial period of job scarcity for new graduates which led (predictably) to a fall in the reward for this group relative to others in their age group. If the various forms of human capital are close substitutes for each other and wage competition prevails everywhere then the forces which depressed the earnings of the educated young should also depress the earnings of more senior workers. But this was not what happened: the cross-section profiles for college graduates 'twisted' in favour of older workers in the 1970s. Those who held relatively secure positions on the job ladder were somewhat insulated from the impact of wage competition – just as the job-competition model predicts.

18 The US data are from Zimmerman (1992) based on a sample of 876 father–son pairs from the National Longitudinal Survey through to 1981. See also Bowles (1972, 1973) and Solon (1992). The British data are based on a special follow-up survey of sons whose fathers had been included in the Rowntree survey reported in Rowntree and Lavers (1951) and is documented in Atkinson *et al.* (1983); see also Atkinson (1981, 1983).

19 See Bowles (1973).

20 See in particular Goldberger (1979). The main difficulties arise concerning what one assumes about the genetic similarity of fraternal twins and the similarity of upbringing of twins. Small changes in these assumptions can drastically alter the results. An interesting speculative exercise of the influence of 'inherited IQ' in determining earnings inequality is also to be found in Bowles and Nelson (1974).

21 See Saloner (1985).

9   The distribution of wealth

9.1 Introduction

Some of the most conspicuous aspects of economic inequality are associated with the display of great wealth. Moreover, the source of a large proportion of some of the high income appears to be the ownership of wealth. So the distribution of wealth is a subject that merits extensive treatment in its own right.

However, this chapter – along with chapters 10 and 11 – can provide no more than an introduction to some of the issues. We make no claim to provide a comprehensive discussion of the nature and extent of the observed inequality of wealth, let alone a theory of wealth distribution. In a comparatively short book dealing with many other aspects of inequality of living standards it is impossible to do justice to a topic that is so vast, that presents so many peculiar obstacles, and that is still in the process of intellectual development.

Let us begin with four key questions which introduce some of the most important difficulties in the analysis of wealth distribution.

What counts as wealth?

Presuming that we have some rough idea of what we mean by wealth in principle, how is it to be measured in practice? The specification of the stock of wealth owned by any individual presents several major problems.

Firstly, there is the heterogeneity of the types of asset as is illustrated in table 9.1, which shows the composition of household wealth in the UK. The items in this list differ enormously in the extent to which they are marketable and therefore in the degree of economic power that they confer upon their possessor: about one sixth of household net wealth as defined there, consisting of £467,000 m. funded pensions, is not marketable at all, even though it represents contingent income rights analogous to other forms of wealth. Whether we use a very narrow definition of wealth (readily marketable assets only) or a more comprehensive specification depends on the type of questions we wish to ask about economic inequality and the distribution of wealth.

However we must take into account the general point on economic data raised in

Table 9.1 *Household wealth by type of asset, UK, 1992*

	Amounts (£ thousand million)	Proportions of total net wealth
Dwellings	1,105	48.7%
Buildings, trade assets and land	94	4.1%
Consumer durables	193	8.5%
Bank deposits and liquid assets	339	14.9%
Government and municipal securities	50	2.2%
Company shares	155	6.8%
Life policies	279	12.3%
Other assets	458	20.2%
Total assets	*2,673*	*117.8%*
Mortgages	325	−14.3%
Other debts	79	−3.5%
Total debts	*404*	*−17.8%*
Net wealth	2,270	100.0%

Source: Board of Inland Revenue, *Inland Revenue Statistics*, 1996, tables 13.2, p. 130.

chapter 2: a balance sheet of wealth such as table 9.1 will only cover that which the official statistical authorities choose to define as personal or household wealth. Table 9.1 – based on the Office of National Statistics national and sector balance sheets – excludes more nebulous forms of 'wealth' such as human capital (which is not perhaps very worrying); but includes non-negotiable items such as the value of occupational pension rights, which are sometimes excluded in other estimates of total wealth. So we have to be careful of definitions when examining wealth distributions. For some purposes we might wish to include much of material wealth of the community that is not directly attributable to particular personal holdings, since it is held by public or private corporations, which in some cases transcend national boundaries. Such corporately held wealth may nevertheless contribute substantially to the power of particular individuals, but it is not at present practicable to include this when considering the inequality of the distribution of wealth.

What limitations are imposed by the data?

These are in some ways much more severe than in the case of earned income. The problem is partly due to the heterogeneity of wealth – with the added complication that the rich and the relatively poor tend to hold their wealth in different forms – and partly due to the arbitrary demarcation imposed by the tax authorities. Although there is quite a lot of information about the ownership of the type of personal asset that is likely to be subject to probate, comparatively little detail is available about the possession of other assets or about the net worth of individuals of moderate means whose assets may consist primarily of housing and consumer durables, even though some ingenious estimates or guesses can be attempted to fill in the gaps. Usually we are forced, by the

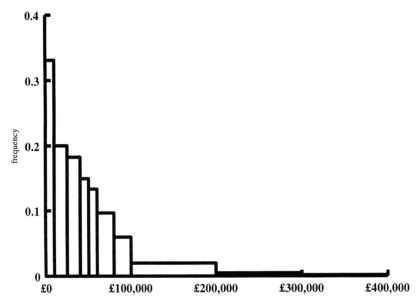

Figure 9.1 Frequency distribution of identified personal wealth, UK 1993
Source: Board of Inland Revenue, *Inland Revenue Statistics*, 1996. Year of death basis.

limitations of what can be observed and measured, to examine the distribution of wealth amongst the fairly well off, to the comparative neglect of the quantitative analysis of the wealth – or lack of it – of the poor. These data limitations suggest that a health warning be put on empirical tests of the validity of wealth distribution models and on estimates of the parameters included in such models.

What does the distribution of wealth look like?

It is commonly supposed that wealth ownership is concentrated amongst a relative few. This is unarguable in the case of *identified personal wealth* by contrast to that for income (figure 2.1 on page 28) – in the wealth identified by the tax authorities' conventional methods from inheritance tax statistics, for example the frequency distribution (see figure 9.1),[1] is single tailed – and there appears to be substantial weight in the tail. That this indicates greater inequality of wealth holdings than inequality of income is borne out by comparison of the Lorenz curves for wealth and for income as depicted in figure 9.2. The point is further reinforced if we compare the distribution of wealth with the distribution of income before tax using the Pareto diagram (see figure 9.3) and compute Pareto's coefficient α: the α value then gives us the 'average/base' income-ratio measure of inequality which we discussed in chapters 2 and 3. Contrast the α value of about 1.8 for wealth on the basis of the data used in figure 9.3 (an a/b ratio of 2.2)[2] with an α value of about 2.3 for income (an a/b ratio of 1.7).

However a sensible answer to the question of the shape of the wealth distribution inherits the difficulties imposed by the data limitations to which we have just

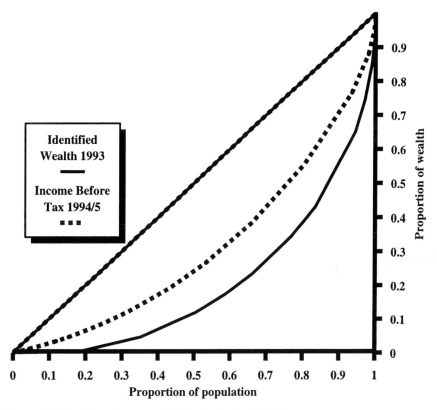

Figure 9.2 Wealth and income distribution in the UK, Lorenz curves
Source: Board of Inland Revenue, *Inland Revenue Statistics*, 1996, tables 3.3, 13.3, pp. 35, 131, 132

alluded. We should make two important distinctions: between the section of the population that is effectively represented by standard methods using inheritance tax statistics and the population in general, and between the narrowly defined concept of marketable wealth and broader concepts of resources. An estimate of the distribution of marketable wealth covering the otherwise 'excluded' population is given in column (1) of table 9.2. Even if the concept of wealth were to include valuations of occupational and state pension rights we can see from columns (2) and (3) of table 9.2 that the distribution of wealth is clearly more unequal than the distribution of income before tax.

How can high concentration of wealth survive in market economies?

Several types of explanation for the much greater inequality of wealth might be suggested. The simplest explanation would be that those who have inherited or otherwise already acquired great wealth may be well placed to defend it from passing out of their own or their close relations' ownership and control. A second distinct line of argument is that although a large proportion of the very wealthy lose much of their wealth, another large proportion of the wealthy succeed in accumulating substantial additions

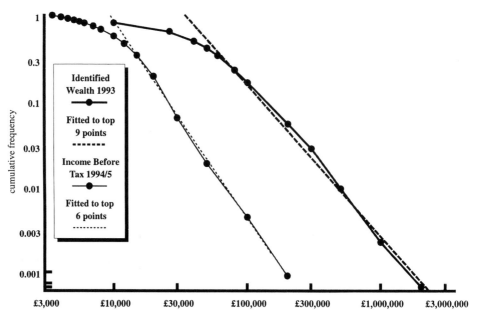

Figure 9.3 Wealth and income distribution in the UK, Pareto diagram
Source: Board of Inland Revenue, *Inland Revenue Statistics*, 1996, tables 3.3, 13.3, pp. 35, 131, 132

to their wealth. A third very different line of explanation is that much of the inequality of wealth holdings may be a statistical illusion due to the definitions of both the wealth holdings and the wealth owners. For example, if the wealth owners are households, part of the inequality will be due to the characteristic fluctuation of the typical wealth holding over the life cycle of the head of the household; reaching a peak a few years before his retirement and falling back thereafter. Other explanations may be derived from the observation that there is a two-way relationship between wealth and income: not only does wealth provide an income yield – or may be consumed directly – but wealth may be accumulated by saving part of income.

Having reconnoitred these obstacles we proceed as follows. In section 9.2 we examine in a rudimentary way the processes by which personal wealth is accumulated and the ways in which the enquiring economist may analyse these processes. Section 9.3 briefly considers the conventional wisdom on the theoretical analysis and modelling of the wealth distribution and section 9.4 considers the impact of social forces within such models. In chapter 10 we then illustrate these accumulation processes in piecemeal fashion by a series of oversimplified models that nevertheless suggest the power of certain economic and social forces in shaping the inequality of wealth and income.

9.2 How to become wealthy

• Three methods for honestly becoming wealthy stand out clearly:
   by earning sufficient to enable us to set part of the earnings aside to put into
      property,

Table 9.2 *Wealth and income shares of the rich, UK*

	Wealth			Income	
Top	Series C (1)	Series D (2)	Series E (3)	Before tax (4)	After tax (5)
1%	17%	13%	10%	8%	7%
2%	24%	18%	14%	12%	10%
5%	36%	29%	23%	20%	17%
10%	48%	41%	34%	29%	27%
25%	72%	65%	57%	51%	48%
50%	93%	89%	82%	76%	73%

Notes: Series C covers marketable wealth only; series D includes a valuation of occupational pension rights as well; series E includes a valuation of state pension rights. See section A.3 of appendix A for further details.
Source: Board of Inland Revenue, *Inland Revenue Statistics*, 1996, tables 13.3 and 13.5–13.7, pp. 35 and 134–6.

- by owning some property already and by allowing income from it to accumulate,
- by having the conspicuous skill or good luck to obtain capital gains from property already acquired, and then retaining these gains.

In addition, there are a number of ways in which a judicious mixture of dishonesty and unpleasantness may assist the process of enrichment, but there are some risks involved in applying them.

Without appeal to detailed empirical arguments or formal economic theories or statistics we may sense that wealth is likely to gravitate towards certain types of persons, such as those with well-paid jobs, who value security more than the enjoyment of leisure or who are naturally conscientious and thrifty, those who are already wealthy and at least mildly frugal, those who are skilful speculators or who have exceptional initiative and luck and, of course, the more fortunate of the unscrupulous.

Although there are important parent-to-child continuities in earnings – as we saw in chapter 8 – it is difficult to avoid the conclusion that in many societies inheritance plays a larger part in the determination of wealth distribution than in that of income distribution, for the possession of wealth already confers such overriding advantages for accumulating more of it. This conclusion suggests two difficulties in the way of developing a self-contained theory of the personal distribution of wealth.

In the first place, there is a problem with the time scale of such a theory. Since the distribution of wealth in any one generation often depends largely on the distribution in the previous generation, no theory of wealth distribution can be self-contained, unless it covers a span of history over many generations. To be realistic, it must take some account of the more important changes in the opportunities for amassing wealth during that span of history.

Secondly, there is a problem about what happens in the long run. A satisfactory theory of wealth distribution has to face the argument that since wealth does confer

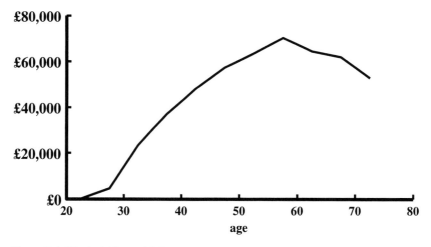

Figure 9.4 Marketable wealth by age
Source: Banks, Dilnot and Low (1994), tables 3.6 and 3.7.

such great advantages in the race to acquire more wealth, no halt to the process of increasing the degree of inequality of wealth distribution is possible, and that wealth is bound to become concentrated in fewer and fewer hands. Either it must be shown that this indeed is happening, or the theory must suggest what countervailing influences keep this tendency in check, and it must illustrate the working of the mechanism by which they do so.

It has been argued that one such countervailing influence is the way people arrange their financial affairs over their lifetimes. In chapters 4 and 7 we noted a tendency of incomes to vary systematically with age and, whilst the direct effect of this on the measured inequality of incomes may be quite small, such a process might nevertheless affect the concentration of wealth significantly. For we might suppose that the tendency for a person's wealth to vary systematically over his lifetime – rising until near retirement, and then possibly slipping back a little – would be far stronger than for income. If all persons were reasonable and knew most of what their economic future held in store for them, they would perhaps so manage their affairs that they built up a tidy pile of assets during their early years to provide for likely needs later, for supporting a family, or to supplement low income after retirement, or as a provision against possible risks concerning needs, resources or exceptional longevity. In later years, they might be expected to run down this hoard of wealth, both to meet such needs and because the time remaining for nasty surprises diminishes. In the aggregate this effect is evident in the pattern of wealth holding by age – see figure 9.4. So it is conceivable that the phenomenon of becoming wealthy – and of dissipating wealth – might be confined within one generation, and that even though inheritance plays a more important role in causing wealth inequality than in causing income inequality, that contribution to wealth inequality might not be particularly large in comparison to the inequality arising from the cycles of wealth accumulation and decumulation within each generation. This confronts the builder of any self-contained theory of wealth accumulation and distribution with a further conundrum: how may we systematically sort out the inequality contributed by the age-cycle fluctuations in wealth ownership from the long-lasting effects of wealth inheritance that transmits inequality down through the generations?

The next section sets out the elements of the standard approach to these problems.

9.3 Theories of wealth distribution

A theory of wealth distribution has to take account of the two-way relationship between wealth and income that we have noted. Whereas income is a flow, wealth is a stock, and the mutual effects of the two on each other involve time lags which may differ for different kinds of wealth: any adequate theory should therefore be dynamic, which is likely to entail the use of either fairly sophisticated mathematical modelling or computer simulations. The complexity of the process of the accumulation and transmission of wealth has resulted in great variety in the bases of theories designed to explain the process. The theories differ not only in their ideological or philosophical positions but also in the particular aspects of the process on which they choose to focus and in the level of aggregation at which they are developed.

When we discussed the structure of income inequality in chapter 6 we noted that there were significant income differences between readily identifiable groups in the population but that, however these groups were specified, substantial income inequality within each group would remain. The same is true when trying to account for wealth distribution. The 'unexplained' inequality within groups is so large that any theory which turns a blind eye to it will be highly misleading: yet a fully detailed explanation of it is not practicable, since its causes are presumably very numerous and largely unmeasurable.

To take account of the presence and persistence of this large degree of inequality due to unidentified causes we can represent these causes by one or more random variables and develop a stochastic theory of income and wealth distribution. This kind of theory attributes each individual's income and wealth partly to what type of person he is and to which groups he belongs, but partly also to his 'luck' in the draw for random variables. A stochastic theory of income and wealth distribution tells us no more than do the determinist theories about which persons are so much better or worse off than others; but it can give a more realistic account of the overall shape of the frequency distribution of wealth and income between persons, since it makes allowance for the aggregate effects of the unidentified causes on the overall frequency distribution. Chapter 11 will be concerned with stochastic theories of income and wealth distribution, in the present chapter and chapter 10 we concentrate on determinist theories to explain how a person's wealth and income depend on his identifiable economic and social characteristics and on his economic decisions.

A theory of wealth and income distribution should allow that many persons can influence the growth or decline of their wealth and income by their own deliberate or casual choices. This is especially true of certain types of persons but largely untrue for others: however, as a starting point for a crude theory, it is reasonable to suppose that a person will make some attempt to estimate the probable effects of his economic choices and take these effects into account before deciding on those choices. The extreme instance of this would be *homo economicus* achieving a vision of definite economic goals and a ruthless efficient pursuit of them with all the means at his disposal.

This vision of *homo economicus* may be extended: a person's economic goals are often supposed to include not only his own economic well being but that of his descendants as well, so that if he is fairly wealthy he may plan to retain much of his wealth to pass on at death, rather than invest it all in an annuity to look after his own comfort in his declining years. Such theories thus have two aspects, one concerning wealth and income changes during a person's lifetime which are carried out in his own interest and the other concerned with the wealth then created for the advantage of his descendants. Some theories concentrate on one of these aspects only and ignore the other, so as to study specific questions in greater depth. Much of the literature on the subject concentrates either on the question 'how will the wealth holding be likely to change over the lifetime of a typical individual who aspires to live comfortably and yet make some provision both for his own retirement and for his heirs?', or else on the question 'taking the lifetime earnings as given, how will the financial provision by parents for their children and the demographic trends within the community determine the patterns of wealth holding in successive generations?'. Of course, a unified theory to answer both questions can be developed, but it demands less mental effort to start by considering each of them separately.

The conventional introductory theory of wealth accumulation during one generation runs as follows.[3] A person anticipates satisfaction from consumption at every stage of his life (and possibly from the bequest he will leave at his death – a point which we defer for the moment). A certain regularity in the pattern of his preferences over his lifetime is postulated so there need be no special concern over how well he will be faring over some particular short interval. Suppose also that, as well as being able to accumulate some wealth he has access to an efficient market for loans. On this basis it is argued that the appropriate foundation for lifetime decisions about the pattern of consumption is an estimate of the person's 'resources' (defined as his inherited wealth, if any, plus the discounted sum of all further amounts he expects to receive during his lifetime, apart from payments of interest) and these resources will be so handled over the lifetime as to even out any fluctuations in his standard of living. The maximising theory suggests the following kind of story: the person's 'lifetime resources', R, are given by

$$R = W(0) + \int_0^{t_D} E(t)e^{-rt}dt \tag{1}$$

where $W(0)$ is the initial wealth he inherits (if any), $E(t)$ is his earnings at age t (taken to include all forms of income other than interest on wealth), r is the rate of interest, and t_D is the date of death. Consumption at any age t, $c(t)$, is given as a function of these resources

$$c(t) = \phi(R,t). \tag{2}$$

The time pattern of current wealth holding at time t, $W(t)$, then follows immediately. The rate of change of the person's wealth (his net savings) at any moment simply equals the difference between current income and consumption

$$\frac{dW(t)}{dt} = rW(t) + E(t) - c(t) \tag{3}$$

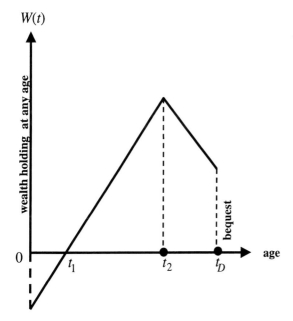

Figure 9.5 Wealth-holding over the life cycle

where $rW(t)$ is the interest income accruing from the wealth holdings. From (3) we may plot the outcome of the person's wealth holding over time. This fundamental equation, or some variant of it, is central to the specific models that we develop in chapter 10 (see for example equation 10.4 and footnote 3 on pages 220–1).

The exact nature of the outcome predicted from (3) must depend on the particular pattern of preferences of the household and on the way their earnings change, but a simplified typical pattern is suggested in figure 9.5. Current net wealth holding (measured as the excess of the financial value of current asset holdings over liabilities) is plotted vertically as a function of age plotted horizontally. According to the story represented in figure 9.5 the person becomes an independent agent at time 0; up until t_1 he has negative wealth since outstanding liabilities (mortgage debt on the house and hire purchase debt on the car) exceed assets; from t_1 until retirement from work at t_2, his currently held wealth is positive and still growing; from t_2 until his death at t_D his wealth is steadily run down to finance his years of retirement but some remains at t_D for his heirs.

Two unanswered questions stand out. If this sort of humped graph of current wealth holding according to age is fairly typical, does such a phenomenon contribute substantially to the overall inequality of the frequency distribution of wealth holdings observed at any one time? And is it fruitful to regard such a pattern of wealth holding as the outcome of a rational series of decisions designed to maximise a determinate objective function subject to the constraint set by the level of a person's lifetime resources?

The answer to the first question depends on the range of assets which are included when estimating the wealth holdings and on how the value of these assets is to be estimated.[4] For, except in the case of very wealthy persons, most of the holdings are likely to be either non-marketable (such as rights to occupational pension schemes) or substantially illiquid (owner-occupied houses) or liable, if sold, to fetch a price well below the discounted value their expected future yields would suggest (life insurance policies, owner-managed small businesses).[5] Furthermore, the value of assets such as pension rights will be contingent on events very specific to the person doing the saving. It is known that the inclusion of non-marketable, imperfectly marketable or non-transferable forms of wealth substantially reduces the extent of inequality of current wealth holdings,[6] and increases the importance of within-life-cycle savings patterns in determining that inequality. But when considering the development of inequality in the long run over many generations, it can be argued that the detail of within-life-cycle savings patterns is largely irrelevant. Consideration of the long run concentrates attention on rather a different set of assets and on rather different criteria in developing the accumulation of wealth.

The second question is important for the macroeconomic analysis of the aggregate rate of savings in an economy as well as for the effect on wealth and income distribution. But is the simple version of the maximising theory outlined above a good aid to understanding what is going on? The predictions of that theory would have to be substantially modified to take account of the actual uncertainty that prevails about such things as the future course of interest rates, share prices, future earnings and employment prospects and a person's length of life.[7] Credit markets are far more complex than is allowed for in simple versions of the theory such as presented above. As a result poor people are often constrained in their choices by their current income, and cannot prudently draw much on their prospects of wealth later. So as an alternative to the elementary model specification (2) where consumption is determined by R, it is interesting to consider the possibility that consumption is strongly influenced by current or recent income: this is something that we pursue in detail in the next chapter (see for example the model on page 226). We might go as far as to suggest that the two sorts of model are appropriate oversimplifications for the behaviour of two groups of people – on the one hand the minority of affluent and well-informed persons with access to efficient credit and insurance markets, and on the other hand the majority who lack these advantages; although it is interesting to note that much of the personal savings of even quite well off people accrue through income-linked superannuation schemes over which the individual has little immediate control.

Now let us turn to the transmission of the patterns of wealth and income distribution from generation to generation. Readers who are familiar with theories which attribute the day-to-day decisions of consumers and the life-cycle patterns of their savings to a series of rational choices may have found the situation apropos the very long-term shifts in the wealth distribution unsatisfactory. Even if crude marginalist theories of consumption patterns and of self-investment are readily available for analysing short- and medium-range problems, it is difficult to translate these theories to give a plausible account of the ways individuals plan the transmission of wealth to subsequent generations. There are some formidable philosophical problems here – for example, just who or what are we mainly concerned about when planning for the hopefully numerous generations yet unborn?

One approach is to abandon the quest for a general solution to this intractable problem and to substitute a simpler exercise which retains some of its features. By considering the solution of the exercise and comparing its predictions with what is found in the real world, we may be guided to modify the exercise, making it more similar to the real problems, without rendering it insoluble; by a succession of such steps one might hope to gain insight into what actually goes on.

Several authors have used this approach.[8] As an oversimplified synthesis consider the following story. Taking the unit of time to be the representative interval between one generation and the next, let W_n be the wealth (of all types) available to a representative family in generation n. The parents may choose to divide it between financing their own consumption and bequeathing it to their offspring in the form of cash, educational investment, real property and the like. Each couple has exactly k offspring, so that the ratio of the numbers of children to parents is $\frac{1}{2}k$. Let C_n be the part of W_n devoted to their own consumption and let the total value of the bequest received by the offspring be B_{n+1} (we are abstracting here from wealth or inheritance taxes).

We would then have the budget constraint

$$C_n + \frac{B_{n+1}}{1+r_n} = W_n \qquad (4)$$

where r_n is the discount rate over one time unit. The total wealth of the next generation consists not only of the parental bequest but also of an independent endowment E_{n+1} that derives from the person's inborn talents, abilities and good fortune. The simplest interpretaton of E_{n+1} is as the independent earnings of the child generation, but we could extend the concept to incorporate other components over which the family has no direct control some of which will be systematic, such as genetically transmitted human capital, and some dependent on pure luck. We then have the basic wealth accumulation equation

$$\tfrac{1}{2}k W_{n+1} = B_{n+1} + E_{n+1} \qquad (5)$$

Once again this is a fundamental relationship in the intergenerational mechanism that transmits wealth and income iequalities. If we were given some information about
(i) the determination of E_{n+1} over the generations and
(ii) rule by which the division between C_n and B_{n+1} in (4) may be determined,
then we would apparently have a complete theory of the process of intergenerational wealth transmission. The first of these topics is discussed in more detail in chapter 11. The second topic is of more immediate interest: put crudely, what is lifetime consumption a function of, and what is the specific function?

The conventional approach to this topic is to model consumption as a function of aggregated resources available to the generation, irrespective of the timing of the availability of those resources or the uncertainty that may attach to some of the component assets or returns to assets. On this interpretation the parental generation would base its consumption/bequest decision on the quantity

$$W_n = \frac{E_{n+1}}{1+r_n}, \qquad (6)$$

the sum of their own wealth and the discounted value of their children's endowments including their 'luck' – compare equation (1) above. As for the type of function ϕ in (2), it is common to find this is assumed to be one of proportionality.[9] Take these assumptions on board for a moment: suppose a proportion $1-s$ of lifetime resources, as defined in (6), is consumed, then manipulation of (4) and (5) yields

$$\tfrac{1}{2}kW_{n+1}=s[1+r_n]W_n+sE_{n+1} \tag{7}$$

or equivalently

$$W_{n+1}=\gamma[1+r_n]W_n+\gamma E_{n+1} \tag{8}$$

as the difference equation describing the future course of wealth accumulation, where $\gamma:=2s/k$ is the savings to the population growth factor. Given these simplifying assumptions, a constant discount rate and a suitable stochastic specification of E_{n+1}, then an equilibrium distribution of wealth can be determined – i.e., a frequency distribution of W_n that is invariant with n. The solution of this is very similar to that described in chapter 11. Obviously this long-run distribution of wealth is going to depend on the assumed savings (consumption) behaviour, family size and the distribution of earnings and luck. We might worry about the exact values of the relevant parameters which determine this equilibrium distribution and indeed query the conditions under which the wealth-generating process will converge to an equilibrium distribution, but these quibbles should not obscure the main message of those who adopt this sort of model: long-run inequality is rooted in relatively simple economic mechanisms.

But there are two more substantial difficulties with the specification of the consumption function. The more immediate of these concerns the simple proportionality of the function. If the marginal propensity to consume out of lifetime wealth differs markedly amongst different types of family, or if the consumption function, although uniform across families, is not simply proportional to family resources, this in itself will powerfully influence inequality in the long term.[10] For example, if bequests are a luxury item which can be afforded only by the wealthy then it is not hard to see that the already rich families are thereby helped to become richer over the generations whilst those who have inherited nothing are handicapped from bequeathing anything.

The other difficulty with the consumption function is to determine the quantity which is to be taken as its argument. On the basis of the previous discussion about what happens during a person's lifetime, we might reasonably expect the proportion saved and bequeathed out of different types of asset to vary considerably. It is a case of the 'bird in the hand': unless perfect markets for risk are available to every individual, yielding for him or her the actuarially fair value of any risky income stream, then currently held, marketable wealth will have a more decisive impact upon savings and bequest decisions than such a prospective stream with identical expected present value. Since this reasoning applies to a person's own earnings over his own lifetime, it must apply with even greater force to the prospective earnings of his offspring. Furthermore, consumption patterns are often conditioned by habit; and habits are transmitted systematically from generation to generation within a dynasty.[11] This, as we shall see in chapter 10, has a dramatic impact on the wealth accumulation process.

9.4 Social forces

Apart from the obvious economic factors which influence wealth accumulation – the determinants of the lifetime consumption function, the possible interrelationship between wealth and earnings – economists have also shown great interest in wider social issues which have a direct bearing on the pattern of bequests and on the propagation or attenuation of wealth inequality over the generations. The selection of partners in marriage, the structure of families and the principles on which gifts are made within families all seem to be important real-world influences in the process of wealth accumulation and transmission. The question naturally arises: what rôle will these play in an economic model of wealth distribution?

Mainstream microeconomics, which concentrates on the satisfaction of individual wants, finds itself on shakier ground when it tackles the subject of gifts and mutual help. This remark applies to the planning of bequests in particular, and in the context of the theory sketched above throws doubt on the assumptions about the scope of each family's rational maximisation of anything. If every parental pair rationally calculate how to divide the family fortune between financing their own consumption and leaving wealth to their offspring, even taking into account their offspring's expected but as yet unrealised earnings potential, should we not expect them to apply the same degree of economic sophistication to other decisions?

Economic motives have undoubtedly been known to enter into decisions whether to have more children and even into the selection of a marriage partner,[12] and in societies where such influences remain important, they may overwhelm the effect of any simple savings-rule such as that described above. For if children are an 'inferior good',[13] and if marriage is a highly selective process between pairs of similar wealth and income backgrounds, then each of these phenomena is likely to preserve or even to augment inequality of wealth and income distribution from one generation to the next despite the egalitarian effects of progressive taxation and of some aspects of savings behaviour. Further complications are introduced if we allow for the possibility that some people may use their bequeathable wealth strategically to 'buy' the affections of their offspring,[14] and for the possibility that some people benefit in their wills persons and groups other than their own descendants.

Moreover, having admitted that the nice computations and strict conformity of practice suggested in the above account seem far-fetched, it then turns out that even fairly minor relaxations of the rigid assumptions which entail the bequest patterns determined by a theory may have dramatic effects on the results to which the theory leads.[15]

Here is a dramatic instance of this. Let us think more carefully about the rule for distributing the total bequest B_{n+1} among the heirs. It has been argued that given certain specifications of family preferences it would be rational to divide the bequests in such a fashion that the net advantages should be the same for each heir to the family fortune. This seems to beg the question of who is to count as an heir – all children, or sons only, or own children and nephews and nieces?[16] Moreover, the choice of these particular specifications of preferences may amount to little more than a device for arriving at the rule for equalising the net advantages. Whether or not rationality enters into the planning of bequests, assuming axioms which entail such an equalisation of net advantages may be seriously misleading in a study of the transfer of wealth by members of wealthy elites. On the contrary it can quite reasonably be argued that in the case of some societies a rule of favouring the already favoured would fit the facts better:

Unlike the male codfish which, suddenly finding itself the parent of 3,500,000 little codfish, cheerfully resolves to love them all, the British aristocracy is apt to look with a somewhat jaundiced eye on its younger sons.[17]

We would expect that a theory based on assumptions entailing making the eldest son, if any, the sole heir would lead to the conclusion that wealth distribution would become more unequally distributed in later generations than would the theory which we considered earlier in this section. This expectation is indeed in accord with the results of various theoretical investigations of the contrasting effects of systems of primogeniture and systems involving more equal divisions of estates among beneficiaries.[18]

The discussion about division amongst our heirs naturally raises related questions about the formation of families through marriage and bearing children. At the individual level, are such events best viewed as rationally planned and responsive to economic incentives? At the community level is there a systematic relationship between the wealth of individuals who pair up in marriage, and between the wealth of couples and the size of their families? It is possible to conceive of a specific microeconomic model which caricatures the decision process by which each of these family events is determined;[19] but it is unrealistic to suppose that all of these can be satisfactorily incorporated in a single simple model of wealth accumulation. Accordingly, these social characteristics are perhaps best incorporated in a piecemeal fashion as exogenously imposed assumptions concerning the behaviour of families within the community under consideration.

9.5 Wealth and income distribution

Although we have so far arranged the discussion of the inequality of wealth and income into separate, distinct chapters, it is clear that earnings inequality and wealth inequality should not be treated indefinitely as watertight compartments of economic inequality: earnings and wealth inequality react on one another in more ways than one. For example one important mechanism is evident in the wealth accumulation equation (8) above. Furthermore there is the straightforward demarcation difficulty that if your financial status or your parents' financial status is used in the job market as an indicator of social background – and therefore of your potential value to an employer – or if your wealth or your parents' wealth is used to 'purchase' human capital, then there is a sense in which a component of the earnings of the well-to-do should be regarded as a return to financial assets rather than to earnings potential.

Apart from that, there is this deeper issue. In both this chapter and chapter 8 we have glimpsed from two points of view, income distribution and wealth distribution, the elements of a joint theory of income and wealth distribution. This theory would regard the ownership of wealth as the key both to an income stream for yourself and for securing well-paid employment opportunities for the children. From the point of view of income distribution, the well-paid can afford to save enough of their income to build up a secure stock of wealth: the other side of the coin is that those with little or no wealth can ill afford the expenses involved in securing really remunerative employment opportunities and those with low incomes cannot save enough to provide much property or really good job prospects for their heirs.

This resonance effect, by which high income stimulates growing wealth and wealth stimulates higher income, whilst the ill-paid run out of wealth and those without wealth get low-paid jobs, provides a basis for a combined theory of wealth and income distribution. Without any pretence of the detail needed for realism, we shall explore this avenue of approach using some purpose-built models of our own in the next chapter.

9.6 Questions for discussion

General reading: Atkinson (1972b), Atkinson and Harrison (1978), Field (1983), Harrison (1977), Kessler and Masson (1988), Jenkins (1990), Lebergott (1976), Meade (1973, 1976), Smith (1980), Projector and Weiss (1966), Wedgwood (1929a), Wolff (1987).

9.1   How would you account for the reluctance of many elderly people to liquidate fixed assets (such as their house) to purchase an annuity that would ensure them a guaranteed income stream over their remaining life span (Brittain, 1978, chapter 3; Hamermesh, 1984; Pissarides, 1980)?

9.2   Critically examine the view that an imputation of the value of (a) occupational pensions and (b) state pensions ought to be made in any empirical investigation of the inequality of wealth distribution. What effect would you expect to find that these broader definitions of wealth would have upon trends in the inequality of wealth in market economies in recent years (Royal Commission, 1975b; Feldstein, 1976; Good, 1990, Rowntree Commission, 1995; Stewart 1991)?

9.3   (a) Discuss the claim that a more informative measure of inequality of the personal distribution of wealth holdings could be obtained if *human wealth* were imputed and added to financial wealth. (b) What practical difficulties would you expect to encounter in such an empirical investigation?

9.4   In the light of tables 9.3 and table 9.4 for the United Kingdom, discuss the possible links between the prices of shares and the concentration of personal wealth (see Atkinson *et al.* 1989).

9.5   Many people suppose that inherited wealth contributes substantially to observed wealth inequality. What problems are involved in investigating the validity of this supposition empirically (Atkinson, 1971, 1980; Bevan, 1979; Brittain, 1978; Davies, 1982; Davies and Shorrocks, 1978; Harbury, 1962; Harbury and Hitchens, 1979; Harbury and McMahon, 1973; Kotlikoff and Summers, 1981, 1988; Kurz, 1984; Loury, 1981; Menchik, 1979, 1980b; Modigliani, 1988; Wedgwood, 1929b)?

9.6   Griliches (1979) suggests that families tend to act as income equalisers amongst their children. Discuss why this might be so, and the channels through which such equalisation might take place. Will this behaviour imply equal division of estates? (See also Menchik (1980a, 1988), Kotlikoff and Spivak (1981), Sheshinski and Weiss (1982), Tomes (1981).)

9.7   In the text we assumed that the number of children per family was exogenously fixed. What are the implications for the observed distribution of wealth of family planning decisions that are highly sensitive to a family's financial resources?

9.8   In some communities it is common for people to live in households that consist of extended families rather than nuclear families. Consider the possible impact of this

Table 9.3 *Stock market prices and the distribution of marketable wealth*

	Stock market price (April 1962=100)	Percentage wealth share of top			
		1%	5%	10%	25%
1966	100.46	33	56	69	87
1971	164.49	31	52	65	86
1972	212.66	n.a.	n.a.	n.a.	n.a.
1976	153.04	21	38	50	71
1977	191.91	22	39	50	71
1978	216.68	20	37	49	71
1979	245.52	20	37	50	72
1980	271.32	19	36	50	73
1981	307.96	18	36	50	73
1982	342.24	18	36	49	72
1983	434.70	20	37	50	73
1984	516.67	18	35	48	71
1985	631.95	18	36	49	73
1986	782.10	18	36	50	73
1987	1,025.07	18	38	52	75
1988	931.67	17	38	53	76
1989	1,110.29	18	38	53	75

Sources: Board of Inland Revenue, *Inland Revenue Statistics,* 1991, CSO, *Financial Statistics.*

type of social arrangement upon wealth accumulation and inequality (Desai and Shah, 1983).

9.9   Consider the following three proposals: (a) An annual wealth tax of 1½ per cent per annum. (b) A 50 per cent tax on all substantial transfers of wealth. (c) A once-for-all 10 per cent levy on wealth. Assuming that the difficulties of choosing a practicable definition of wealth for these purposes, and of collecting the taxes have been dealt with, discuss the likely relative impact of each of these on long-run wealth inequality (see Atkinson 1980, Davies, 1986; Tait, 1967).

9.10   'Over the period 1976–1988, there has been little change in the distribution of marketable wealth of individuals measured by the Gini coefficient, although the share of the top 1 per cent has reduced slightly, while that of the upper quartile has increased a little' – Good (1990, p. 137). Discuss in the light of table 9.5.

9.11   How would the analysis of equations (1)–(3) be affected by the presence of credit constraints (Shah, 1992)?

Table 9.4 *Composition of identified marketable wealth, 1993 (percentage composition of gross wealth)*

Lower limit	% of wealth holders in range	Cash plus interest-bearing assets	Household goods, etc.	Insurance	Residential property	Shares	Land, etc.	Net as % gross
£0	18	26.9	18.7	21.4	34.8	−1.3	−0.5	1.7
£10,000	17	33.0	7.8	18.4	38.3	1.9	0.6	75.8
£25,000	15	22.3	3.9	16.7	54.7	2.0	0.5	88.0
£40,000	16	17.2	4.3	18.7	56.2	2.2	1.4	85.4
£60,000	18	20.0	4.9	20.1	50.2	3.1	1.6	89.8
£100,000	15	21.0	6.9	19.3	37.9	11.3	3.7	91.4
£500,000	1	16.6	14.2	10.1	18.2	34.7	6.2	95.4
All	100	20.7	7.1	18.2	41.9	9.4	2.7	87.3

Source: Board of Inland Revenue, *Inland Revenue Statistics* (1996).

Table 9.5 *Distribution of marketable wealth among the adult population, UK*

Wealth owned by top	1976	1977	1978	1979	1980	1981	1982	1983	1984	1985	1986	1987	1988	1989	1990	1991	1992	1993
1%	21	22	20	20	19	18	18	20	18	18	18	18	17	17	18	17	18	17
2%	27	28	26	26	25	24	24	26	24	24	24	25	23	24	24	23	25	24
5%	38	39	37	37	36	36	36	37	35	36	36	37	36	35	35	34	37	36
10%	50	50	49	50	50	50	49	50	48	49	50	51	49	48	47	46	49	48
25%	71	71	71	72	73	73	72	73	71	73	73	74	71	70	71	70	72	72
50%	92	92	92	92	91	92	91	91	91	91	90	91	92	92	93	92	92	92
Gini	0.66	0.66	0.64	0.65	0.65	0.65	0.64	0.65	0.64	0.65	0.64	0.66	0.65	0.65	0.64	0.64	0.66	0.66

Note: 1993 provisional.
Source: Board of Inland Revenue, *Inland Revenue Statistics*, 1995.

Notes

 1 For the data on which this and related figures are based see page 322 in appendix A.
 2 The least-squares estimates of α (found by fitting a straight line to the truncated data in a Pareto diagram) were 1.7680 in the case of wealth and 2.388 for income – see appendix A for details.
 3 See Blinder (1974), King (1985) for comprehensive surveys. A succinct formal statement of the basic theory is given in Yaari (1964); the distributional implications are examined formally in Vaughan (1988).
 4 See Atkinson (1971), Flemming (1979).
 5 See Hills (1995) and table 9.4.
 6 See for example table 9.2, and also Royal Commission (1977), Atkinson and Harrison (1978).
 7 For example, only in the case of perfect markets for life insurance is uncertainty about a person's length of life irrelevant to the 'hump' model of lifetime asset accumulation – see Pissarides (1980).
 8 This is, for example, the approach of Becker and Tomes (1979) whose work has the twin advantages of being a succinct statement of the most conservative neoclassical approach and of being very wide in scope. They seek to incorporate all forms of 'wealth', both financial and human. Thus their treatment covers the issues that were discussed in chapter 8, section 8.5 and provides a useful benchmark for comparison with other theoretical approaches.
 9 The proportionality rule can be supported by the special assumption that parents are supposed to be maximising a Cobb–Douglas utility function under certainty subject to a lifetime budget constraint.
10 See, for example, Meade (1973), Schlicht (1975), Stiglitz (1969).
11 Kurz (1984) shows that for certain population groups there is a marked difference between the effect on bequests of private marketable wealth and non-marketable wealth (in the form of rights to social security), and that the planned divisions between bequests and a person's own consumption differs strongly between social groups.
12 See Becker (1973).
13 Or in plainer language, if in the absence of the efficient capital markets the rich have less need than the poor to have children for support in their old age.
14 See Bernheim *et al.* (1985).
15 On this point and on the selection of marriage partners see Blinder (1973b) and Menchik (1980a).
16 Sometimes all these issues are conveniently resolved by the law. For example, in France a law dating from Napoleonic times makes equal division among heirs mandatory (Kessler and Masson, 1988, page 117).
17 Wodehouse (1935). An economic rationale for this behaviour has been offered by Chu (1991). See also question 9.6.
18 See Blinder (1973b) and Wolfson (1980).
19 See, for example, Becker (1973, 1974, 1981).

10 Fantastic models of wealth and income distribution

10.1 Introduction

It would be very convenient to have to hand a single straightforward explanation of the complex forces governing the structure of wealth ownership. But trying to develop one is a pretty hopeless task, for the reasons explained in chapter 9. The search for a unified general theory of personal wealth distribution, which could be quantitatively illustrated and tested for validity, is much like hunting a Snark.[1]

In this chapter we adopt an alternative strategy which highlights some of the many forces generating the inequality of wealth discussed in chapter 9. We shall examine a few artificial simplified models, concentrating on one or two features of the wealth accumulation process which apply to an idealised world, like a Robinson Crusoe economy. By constructing separate models highlighting different aspects of the process, and trying them out on a number of different initial underlying conditions, we shall gain some insight into how we might explain what is – imperfectly – observed in the real world.

The purpose of these fanciful models is not primarily that of explaining facts. The main purpose is to draw attention to the drastic effects on the conclusions that may be drawn from apparently innocuous simplifying assumptions that are sometimes adopted in models of wealth and income distribution, in order to make their operation less tedious, or their conclusions more readily available and clear cut. In view of the continuities that are to be expected from generation to generation, these effects are likely to be much more disturbing than those that might arise in simplified models of earnings such as those that we have discussed in chapters 7 and 8, where we concentrated mainly upon what happens within a generation.[2] The simplified models set out in sections 10.2–10.6 illustrate this point by focusing on a number of key features of individual behaviour and social structure: we defer until chapter 11 attempts at introducing further complexity.

Section 10.2 introduces our most primitive model in which individuals act like unresponsive automata. The following four sections introduce, respectively, more plausible savings behaviour, two types of earnings variability, differing family structures and different marriage patterns. The main features of each of the six models are summarised in table 10.9 on page 247.

10.2 Mutt island

We set the scene in an imaginary island somewhere far out in the Atlantic Ocean, with a large and quite well-educated native population, earning their living and attempting to live comfortably and amass personal wealth, under certain handicaps, which we shall outline before setting out formally all the assumptions built into the model.

The industries on the island of Mutt have fallen entirely into the hands of foreign industrialists, following a period of heavy unemployment and inflation. These foreign industrialists employ the Mutts at standard wage rates. The Mutts now have such a horror of inflation that in terms of their unit of currency, the cutt (¢), both wage rates and the index of retail prices remain fixed.

The government of Mutt is happy to encourage the operation of the foreign companies on their island, by levying a stiff progressive tax on all wealth inherited by native Mutts, which has no loopholes, and by spending the proceeds on law and order, and the military. Any residual is spent on good communications and public services for the benefit of the firms and their employees. On their side, the foreign industrialists are well satisfied, since they have ample scope for investing the savings of such Mutt employees, in expanding their own operation either on the island or in other factories outside it: in exchange the Mutt employees are sold preference shares in the island factories where they work.

For the moment we abstract from all differences between individual native Mutts. They all behave according to the rules laid down in assumptions 1 to 8 for our *model 1*:

Assumption 1 All employed Mutts get the same earnings, E^*, measured in thousand cutts per annum. We set this at

$$E^* = 10 \tag{1}$$

Assumption 2 The only other income a Mutt may have is interest at the rate of r per annum on any preference shares in which he has invested his savings: the price of these shares in cutts is guaranteed and immutable. We take $r = 2\frac{1}{2}$ per cent. Owing to the distressing economic history of Mutt in recent years, no Mutt owns any wealth apart from his preference shares. All durable goods are rented from foreigners and, because of the somewhat hazardous conditions on Mutt island, the foreign managers spend as little time there as possible, relying on modern communications systems to enable them to run the Mutt factories from offices overseas: so nobody on Mutt owns any wealth apart from their preference shares.

Assumption 3 All employed Mutts continue to work until near death, and then get a pension from their firm equal to the earnings rate E^* to tide them over their few remaining weeks of life. Each draws up a will leaving all his wealth and oddments to one individual employed Mutt – to be described as the next Mutt in his line.

Assumption 4 Any wealth left in excess of W^* (thousand cutts) is subjected to an inheritance tax at rate τ. We shall assume $W^* = 120$ and $\tau = \frac{2}{3}$.

Assumption 5 No Mutt is left wealth in more than one will.

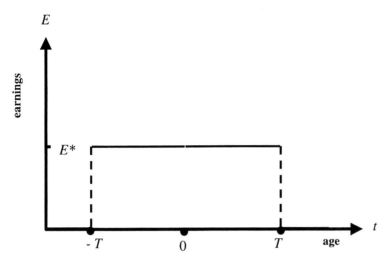

Figure 10.1 A Mutt's life

Assumption 6 Any Mutt devoid of wealth spends all his earnings, E^*, on current consumption. He saves nothing.

Assumption 7 Those Mutts who do own some wealth adopt a very simple consumption rule in the face of the uncertainties of life: they spend at the rate C^*, which exceeds E^*, on current consumption, so long as their wealth lasts. For the numerical example we set this at

$$C^*=12 \qquad (2)$$

Assumption 8 Every Mutt inherits T years after attaining adulthood and dies T years after that; we take adulthood to be achieved at age 15 and set $T=25$.

The earnings history of any Mutt – whatever the wealth he might inherit – is thus as depicted in figure 10.1. Now consider the wealth, income and consumption of a typical Mutt who inherits some wealth. For convenience the generations of Mutts have been indexed $n=0, 1, 2, 3, \dots$: see figure 10.2 for a sketch of the sequential time overlap of the generations. Our specimen belongs to generation 1: from the time that he first takes a job until he first inherits wealth, his income consists of his earnings, E^*, and his consumption will also be at this level due to assumption 6 since he is as yet devoid of wealth. What happens when he inherits depends on how much he inherits.

Let the amount a Mutt inherits net of tax be $W(0)$. His current wealth holding may rise or fall during the T years left to him by assumption 8: write the amount of this after t years as $W(t)$. It then follows that his total income must be

$$y(t)=E^*+rW(t) \qquad (3)$$

whilst his expenditure on consumption is C^* (so long as he still has some wealth). His rate of saving – the rate of accumulation of his wealth – must therefore be

$$\frac{dW(t)}{dt}=\begin{cases} y(t)-C^* & \text{if } W(t)>0 \\ 0 & \text{otherwise} \end{cases} \qquad (4)$$

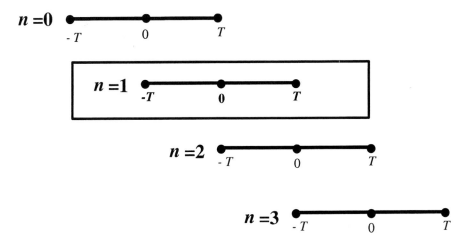

Figure 10.2 Generations of Mutts

If we let $\hat{B}:=[C^*-E^*]/r$ (the economic significance of $\hat{B}$ will become clear in a moment) then equations (3) and (4) imply that

$$W(t)=W(0)e^{rt}-\hat{B}[e^{rt}-1] \tag{5}$$

so long as this remains positive, and that $W(t)=0$ thereafter.[3]

Let us examine the outcome of this at the Mutt's death, where $t=T$, for our particular case $T=25$, $r=2\frac{1}{2}\%$, $C^*=12$ and $E^*=10$; substituting these values in (5), we find that the amount B_1 that he leaves in his will is given by

$$W(25)=1.8683\,W(0)-69.4597 \tag{6}$$

if this is positive, but if not, $B_1=0$. We may note that $W(25)$ will be positive as long as

$$W(0)>37.1791 \tag{7}$$

Denote the amount (before tax) bequeathed to the Mutt under consideration by B_0. Then, by assumption 4

$$W(0)=\min\{B_0,[1-\tau]B_0+\tau W^*\} \tag{8}$$

Substituting for $W(0)$ from (8) into (6) and (7), we find for our particular numerical example

$$\Delta B_0=\begin{cases} 80-0.37725B_0 & \text{if} & 120\le B_0 \\ 0.8683B_0-69.4597 & \text{if} & 37.1791\le B<120 \\ -B_0 & \text{if} & B_0<37.1791 \end{cases} \tag{9}$$

where $\Delta B_0:=B_1-B_0$.

We can trace in the same way the history of the Mutt who benefits from the legacy of $B_1=B_0+\Delta B_0$: this heir will eventually leave in his will $B_2=B_1+\Delta B_1$, and the value of ΔB_1 conditional on B_1 is given by an expression exactly analogous to (9). Extending the argument to the nth and $[n+1]$th wills in the line of Mutts

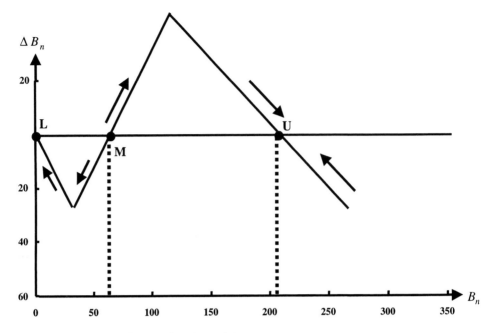

Figure 10.3 Paths to ruin and glory in model 1

$$\Delta B_n = \begin{cases} 80-0.37725B_n & \text{if} & 120 \le B_n \\ 0.8683B_n-69.4597 & \text{if} & 37.1791 \le B_n < 120 \\ -B_n & \text{if} & B_n < 37.1791 \end{cases} \tag{10}$$

where likewise $\Delta B_{n'} := B_{n+1} - B_n$. The general form of the solution may be obtained in like manner by setting $t = T$ in (5) so as to obtain

$$\Delta B_n = \begin{cases} [1-e^{rT}][\hat{B}-B_n]+e^{rT}\tau[W^*-B_n] & \text{if} & W^* \le B_n \\ [1-e^{rT}][\hat{B}-B_n] & \text{if} & H < B_n \le W^* \\ -B_n & \text{if} & B_n < H \end{cases} \tag{11}$$

where $H := \hat{B}[1-e^{rT}]$.

This behaviour is illustrated in figure 10.3. Along the horizontal axis the size of bequest B_n is measured, and along the vertical axis the change in bequest $\Delta B_{n'}$: above the horizontal axis the bequests are increasing from generation to generation, and below they are decreasing. The graph on which the points $(B_n, \Delta B_n)$ lie consists of the three straight lines corresponding to the equations (10). It is clear that movement of bequests through a dynasty will be to the right along the segments above the horizontal axis and to the left along the segments below it and consequently there will be exactly two locally stable equilibria in this system: one at 0 where the line of Mutts bequeath nothing for ever and ever, and the other at where each Mutt bequeaths 212,060¢ to his heir. There is also one unstable equilibrium at point M, where each Mutt bequeaths exactly 80,000¢ to his heir: for any bequest slightly greater or less than this sum the system will eventually converge towards point U (equilibrium $\hat{B}$) or point L (equilibrium 0) respectively.[4]

We may therefore expect that in the long run there will be the following state of affairs in Mutt island:

- There will be a class of employed Mutts who have not yet benefited from a will, and have therefore no wealth, and an income of 10,000¢, all of which they will be spending on consumption; some of these have expectations of eventually inheriting wealth amounting to about 212,060¢ gross, which will leave them with 150,686¢ after tax.
- There will be a smaller class of employed Mutts, who have already inherited 212,060¢, but are only consuming at the very modest rate of 12,000¢ per annum, because of assumption 7, and are saving all the rest of their income, which will be between 1,767¢ and 3,302¢ per annum. This will enable them to leave 212,060¢ when they die.

Let us now examine the long-run equilibrium wealth distribution. In order to do this we have to make some assumption about the age distribution. The obvious simplifying assumption is that it is rectangular, since we have already assumed that death takes place at T and not earlier. This implies that at any particular moment a fraction t/T of the Mutts have lived t years or less since their inheritance. In a stable equilibrium there are only two classes of people: those with no inheritance ($W(0)=0$), and those with a uniform, positive inheritance ($\tilde{B}=150,686¢$ after tax in our example). Now for those with positive wealth the specific relationship between wealth and t is given by equation (5). Given that age is distributed rectangularly, if F is the distribution function for W we have

$$F(W(t))=\frac{t}{T} \tag{12}$$

with $W(t)$ given by (5). Using (5) to give t in terms of $W(t)$ we thus find

$$F(W)=\frac{1}{rT}\log\left(\frac{W-\hat{B}}{\tilde{B}-\hat{B}}\right) \tag{13}$$

which, upon differentiation, yields a frequency distribution

$$f(W)=\frac{1}{rT[W-\hat{B}]} \tag{14}$$

In our particular numerical example, with $T=25$, $r=2\frac{1}{2}\%$, $C^*=12$, $E^*=10$ we have $\hat{B}=80$ and $\tilde{B}=212.06$ we thus obtain the long-run wealth distribution in the left-hand side of figure 10.4. In view of the linear relationship in we can also easily obtain the long-run equilibrium distribution of income amongst wealthy persons – those with incomes exceeding 10,000¢ per year as shown.

At the other end of the scale are the mass of Mutts who have no wealth and subsist on their meagre earnings of 10,000 cutts per annum. Some of these are young persons with expectations of inheriting over 212,000¢ later in their lives. We may imagine that they already enjoy economic and social advantages as 'poor relations' of wealthy Mutts: but in view of the fanatical savings and spartan consumption standards of even the most wealthy Mutts (with over 212,000¢ in wealth) these advantages cannot be overwhelming. To describe the whole distribution we need to take account of those

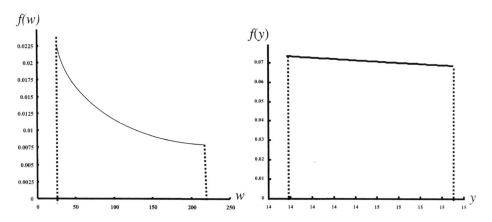

Figure 10.4 Wealth and income distribution of wealth amongst the wealthy (model 1)

Mutts who in the long run are concentrated at the lower equilibrium with zero wealth: these have an income of just 10 units, so the overall distribution must look like figure 10.5.

Judged by the resulting long-run distribution, we must admit that our first model gives results which are very unlike those found for any actual economy. The only semblance of realism is the emergence of plenty in the midst of pervasive poverty: there is a privileged wealthy class with a proportionate share in total wealth close to 100 per cent in the long run, but with incomes ranging from only about 37 per cent to about 53 per cent above the income of each worker who owns no property. In fact there are essentially two sources of inequality in long-run inequality within model 1:

• Wealth (and hence income) differences amongst those Mutts who belong to the propertied class but who are at different stages of their economic life cycle.
• A gap between the propertied class – those at the upper equilibrium U in figure 10.3 – and those who inherit nothing, who are at the lower equilibrium for ever.

However, model 1 contrasts very sharply with the real world in that wealth and income are perfectly correlated, and in that anyone who does have any wealth at all must fall into an extremely narrow range: he must have at least 150,000¢, but he cannot have any more than just over 212,000¢. Of course, these features are due to the depressingly restrictive social and economic conditions that we have imposed on the Mutt citizens. These were chosen merely to enable us to present a reasonably simple model which incorporates the following features:

• Wealth inequality, quite apart from earnings inequality, contributes to income inequality – although earnings inequality was eliminated by assumption, and there is substantial income inequality amongst propertied Mutts.
• Higher income can be used to provide savings which increase the wealth holding of the Mutt and his heir.
• The first two effects can lead to a positive feedback effect so that for a long time the

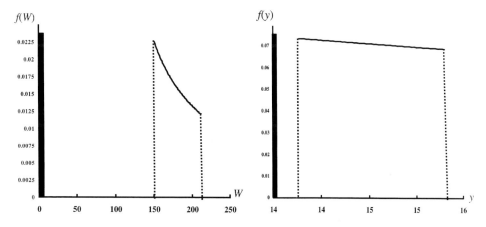

Figure 10.5 Distribution of wealth and income amongst all Mutts (model 1)

wealthy and their heirs grow more wealthy, whilst those with no wealth and their heirs remain in that state.

• These inegalitarian tendencies can be regulated to some extent by the imposition of an inheritance tax on wealth above a specified exemption level.

To illustrate this last point by using our very crude first model, let us consider the effect of lowering the tax τ on large bequests from two thirds to one half, leaving the exemption level W^* unchanged. Then the upper branch of equation (10) would become

$$\Delta B_n = 42.6383 - 0.065877 \, B_n \qquad (15)$$

so that the long-run equilibrium level of wealth would now be given by

$$\tilde{B} = \frac{42.6383}{0.065877} = 647.507 \qquad (16)$$

If we had lowered the tax rate still further to 0.45 then the upper branch equation would have become

$$\Delta B_n = 31.4285 + 0.027535 \, B_n \qquad (17)$$

Since the coefficient of B_n in (17) is positive, the upper branch would now slope *upwards* so that, there would no longer be any limit to the gap between the wealth and income of the rich and of the poor. However, such apparently drastic conclusions about inequality in long-run equilibrium must always be considered in the light of some estimate of the time it will take to get anywhere near that equilibrium.[5] Fortunately, the approach to equilibrium in many of the examples we shall encounter in this chapter and the next will be fairly rapid; but it will always be necessary to supplement a study of long-run equilibrium distribution with some consideration of the short-term approach towards it.

In the light of modifications to our models in later sections of this and the following chapter we shall reconsider the sensitivity of the shape of the upper tails of the wealth and income distributions to changes in the tax rate and the rate of return on assets, and also to changes in the specification of the Mutts' consumption behaviour.

10.3 Revised consumption behaviour

One particularly drastic feature of the Mutt economy was assumption 7 restricting all those Mutts who still own any wealth to spend on consumption at the same rate C^*, regardless of age, income or wealth. It is obviously more realistic to suppose that a Mutt's expenditure will be affected by how much he can afford. From chapters 8 and 9 there are two features that we might wish to capture: ignorance about the future may restrict a person to adjust his consumption to some rate close to that of his current income; and there are likely to be distinct continuities in consumption patterns across generations within a dynasty, arising out of the process of material bequest and the conditioning of habits and preferences.

In *model 2* we incorporate these two features by modifying assumption 7 so as to introduce two consumption parameters ξ and v. The modified behavioural rule is accordingly in two parts:

Assumption 7a (pursuit path) Those Mutts who have some wealth adjust their rate of consumption expenditure, $c(t)$, towards their current income, $y(t)$, according to

$$\frac{dc(t)}{dt} = \xi[y(t) - c(t)] \tag{18}$$

unless their consumption would then fall below C^*, in which case they consume C^*, as in model 1. If a Mutt has no wealth he just consumes his earnings, as in model 1.

Assumption 7b (lifestyle inheritance) When a Mutt receives a legacy providing some wealth, he immediately increases his consumption to

$$c(0) = \max\{[1-v]C_n, C^*\} \tag{19}$$

where C_n was the terminal consumption rate of the testator.

The effects of these changes in assumption 7 are to break down the previous spartan consumption habits of wealthy Mutts, and thereby to retard their accumulation of more wealth for their descendants. We retain the other behavioural rules, including assumption 1 which ensures that all Mutts get the same earnings E^* throughout their working lives.

As in model 1 we may examine the wealth and consumption expenditure of a single Mutt who inherits post-tax wealth $W(0)$ in year $t=0$; he will have been living since taking a job on his earnings E^* up to the moment when he inherited wealth. Equation (3) giving income at time t is unchanged from model 1. However, we find that equation (4) is now slightly modified to

$$\frac{dW(t)}{dt} = \begin{cases} y(t) - c(t) & \text{if } W(t) > 0 \\ 0 & \text{if } W(t) = 0 \end{cases} \tag{20}$$

This and assumption 7a immediately reveal that

$$\frac{dc(t)}{dt}=\begin{cases}\xi\dfrac{dW(t)}{dt} & \text{if } W(t)>0 \text{ and } c(t)>C^*\\[2mm]0 & \text{if } c(t)=C^* \text{ and } \dfrac{dW(t)}{dt}\leq0\end{cases} \tag{21}$$

so that in model 2 consumption changes at a rate ξ times that at which wealth changes; except that $c(t)$ must not fall below C^* until wealth is exhausted, but if wealth is exhausted, consumption $c(t)$ then collapses to the level E^*. Accordingly

$$c(t)=\begin{cases}\max\{C^*,c(0)+\xi[W(t)-W(0)]\} & \text{if } W(t)>0\\[2mm]E^* & \text{if } W(t)=0\end{cases} \tag{22}$$

From equations (4) and (22) we may substitute in (20) to yield the equation of motion of wealth during a Mutt's lifetime:

$$\frac{dW(t)}{dt}=\begin{cases}[r-\xi]W(t)+E^*+\xi W(0) & \text{if } E^*+\xi W(t)>c(0)\\[2mm]rW(t)+E^*-C^* & \text{if } E^*+\xi W(0)\leq0 \ \& \ W(t)>0\\[2mm]0 & \text{if } W(t)=0\end{cases} \tag{23}$$

The two lower lines of (23) show that in the region where $E^*+\xi W(0)<c(0)$, model 2 behaves like model 1.[6]

At the end of the Mutt's life we find that the size of bequest and consumption are, respectively

$$B=W(T)=\begin{cases}W(0)+A[rW(0)-c(0)+E^*], \text{ or}\\[2mm]0\end{cases} \tag{24}$$

$$c(T)=\begin{cases}c(0)+\xi A[rW(0)-c(0)+E^*] & \text{if } B>0\\[2mm]E & \text{if } B=0\end{cases} \tag{25}$$

where

$$A:=\frac{e^{[r-\xi]T}-1}{r-\xi} \tag{26}$$

Contrast equation (24) with equation (5) when $t=T$ in (5) and compare (25) with assumption 7. We see that model 2 allows far more variety between the histories of different lines of Mutts. For the terminal wealth $B=W(T)$ and terminal consumption $c(T)$ of a typical Mutt each depend on initial wealth $W(0)$ and initial consumption $c(0)$, and these in turn each depend on the financial inheritance and the standard of living acquired from the previous Mutt in line. In cases where there remains some terminal wealth the change in consumption over the last T years of the life cycle will be a

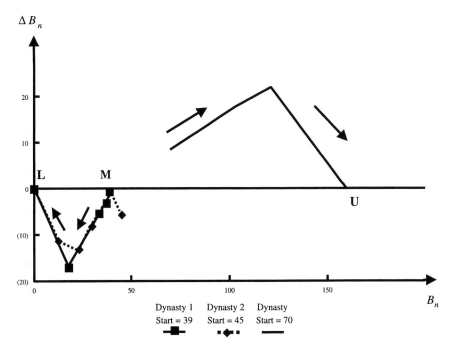

Figure 10.6 Paths to ruin and glory in model 2

multiple ξ of the change of wealth. Let us see how this affects the development of consumption and wealth, in the course of a dynasty.

Using (24)–(26) we may write down the expressions which govern the succession of bequests $(B_0, B_1, B_2, ...)$ and succession of terminal living standards $(C_0, C_1, C_2, ...)$ in any Mutt dynasty. In the case of bequests there are, as in model 1, three possibilities:

Substantial wealth: $B_n \geq W^*$. The change in bequests is then given by the formula

$$\Delta B_n = [Ar - Ar\tau - \tau]B_n + [1 + Ar]\tau W^* + A[E^* - c(0)] \tag{27}$$

where $c(0)$ is given by (19).

Moderate wealth: $0 \leq B_n \leq W^*$. The change in bequests between generations is given by

$$\Delta B_n = \max\{A[rB_n - c(0) + E^*], -B_n\} \tag{28}$$

Abject poverty: $B_n = 0$ so that $B_{n+1} = 0$ in all subsequent generations and each Mutt's consumption is constrained to equal E^*.

The possibilities regarding consumption are as follows. If the Mutt is not in abject poverty, then either consumption is stationary at C^* or it changes over the $n+1$th generation in the dynasty according to the relevant bequest régime, as follows:

Substantial wealth

$$\Delta C_n = -\nu C_n + \xi \Delta B_n + \xi \tau [B_n - W^*] \tag{29}$$

Moderate wealth

$$\Delta C_n = -\nu C_n + \xi \Delta B_n \tag{30}$$

The mechanism of model 2 in generating lines of bequests B_0, B_1, B_2, ... can again be illustrated by a diagram like figure 10.3, plotting B_n horizontally and ΔB_n vertically. However, although with model 1 the points $(B_n, \Delta B_n)$ all lie exactly on two straight lines through the equilibrium points M and U as in figure 10.3, some may not fit exactly to them in model 2 if the retirement wealth for the first testator (the Mutt in generation 0) deviates substantially from the equilibrium value, or if the coefficient v is small.[7]

Let us examine three of such routes in detail. To obtain specific results we again impose specific parameter values which – as with model 1 – will be found to affect the routes significantly: for example, once again the existence of a positive equilibrium level of bequests depends crucially on the tax system. For ease of comparison let us use most of the same parameter values as before ($T=25$, $E^*=10$, $r=2\frac{1}{2}\%$, $\tau=\frac{2}{3}$ and $W^*=120$); however, it will facilitate the comparison if we lower the value of C^* from 12 to 11 to offset roughly the stimulus to consumption from the two new consumption adjustment parameters which we will take to be $v=0.2$, $\xi=0.1$.

These parameter values ensure the existence of an equilibrium with $c(0)=C^*$ and with positive bequests. This can be checked by calculating from (26) that $A=11.288$ and putting (27) and (30) equal to zero from which we find the equilibrium bequest and consumption at retirement to be 159,429.6¢ and 12,314.32¢ respectively.[8] Similarly, the neutral equilibrium can be found by setting $\Delta B_n=0$ in (28) as $B_n = [C^*-E^*]/r=40$ – a bequest of 40,000¢.

A dynasty that starts with an inheritance of less than 40,000¢ is heading for ruin: ponder the fate of the first line of Mutts in columns 1, 2 and 3 of table 10.1 – starting from an inheritance of 39,000¢, they lose it all within six generations. The fate (columns 4 to 6) of the second line of Mutts should act as a warning to all aspiring young Mutts who inherit wealth! The first heir in the line was misled by his father's squandering much of his modest fortune at 17,000¢ a year and leaving just 45,000¢, having reduced his income to only 11,025¢. Accustomed to his parent's lifestyle, the son on inheriting the 45,000¢ raised his spending from 10,000¢, his earnings level, to 13,600¢ a year (having applied the 20 per cent cut to 17,000¢ since $v=0.2$). This resulted in his 45,000¢ falling below the critical level (40,000¢) to 39,638¢ by the time of his own death, thus bringing his line to utter destitution within eight more generations. This is shown in columns (4)–(6) of table 10.1. We may end this paragraph on a more cheerful note when we consider (columns 7 to 9) a line that starts by leaving 70,000¢ when consuming at less than 11,750¢ per annum. They progress steadily: within three generations they join the wealth tax paying class; and within six further generations pass on a fortune (before tax) within a mere 250¢ of the top equilibrium level.

Now consider the wealth distribution in model 2. As in the case of model 1, we may expect that on Mutt island in the long run there will be a large class of impoverished Mutts with no wealth and with an income of 10,000¢ per annum, all of which they spend on consumption. Some of these have expectations of eventually inheriting 133,143.2¢, after tax (representing 159,429.6¢ before tax). There will also be a class of Mutts who have already inherited this sum, and their amounts of wealth will each lie somewhere in the range (133,143.2¢, 159,429.6¢) depending on how old they are and therefore on how long ago they inherited. If we assume these times t are uniformly distributed over the interval, 0–25 years (as in model 1), we can substitute the parameter values into our equation (24) to obtain

Table 10.1 *Bequests in three dynasties*

	Ruin			Ruin			Glory		
n	(1) B_n	(2) ΔB_n	(3) C_n	(4) B_n	(5) ΔB_n	(6) C_n	(7) B_n	(8) ΔB_n	(9) C_n
0	39.000	−0.868	11	45.000	−5.362	14.5	70.000	8.466	11.000
1	38.132	−1.622	11	39.638	−0.314	11	78.466	10.856	11.847
2	36.510	−3.031	11	39.324	−0.587	11	89.322	13.919	12.086
3	33.479	−5.662	11	38.736	−1.097	11	103.242	17.848	12.392
4	27.818	−10.557	11	37.639	−2.050	11	121.090	21.953	12.785
5	17.240	−17.240	11	35.589	−3.830	11	143.043	9.383	13.268
6	0.000	0.000	10	31.759	−7.155	11	152.426	4.010	13.474
7				24.604	−13.368	11	156.150	1.714	13.563
8				11.236	−11.236	11	158.150	0.733	13.600
9				0	0	10	158.883	0.313	13.617
10							159.196	0.134	13.623
12							159.387	0.057	13.628
14							159.422	0.024	13.628
16							159.420	0.008	13.629
18							159.429	0.001	13.629
20							159.430	0.000	13.629
24							159.430	0.000	13.629
…							…	…	…
∞	0	0	10	0	0	10	159.430	0	13.629

Note: Bequests and consumption are in '000¢.

$$W(t)=W(0)+[1-e^{-0.075t}]\frac{0.025\ W(0)+10-c(0)}{0.075} \tag{31}$$

From the equilibrium described above we have $W(0)=133.143$ and $c(0)=C^*=11$ (initial consumption of 11,000¢); and so we obtain the equations

$$W(t)=164.1909-31.0477e^{-0.075t} \tag{32}$$

$$F(W(t))=0.04t \tag{33}$$

where $F(W)$ is the proportion of those who have inherited some wealth whose wealth does not exceed W. Hence, solving (32) to find t as a function of W and then using (32)[9] we obtain

$$\left.\begin{array}{l} F(W)=-13.3333 \log\left(\dfrac{164.1909-W}{31.0477}\right) \\[3mm] f(W)=\dfrac{13.3333}{164.1909-W} \end{array}\right\} \tag{34}$$

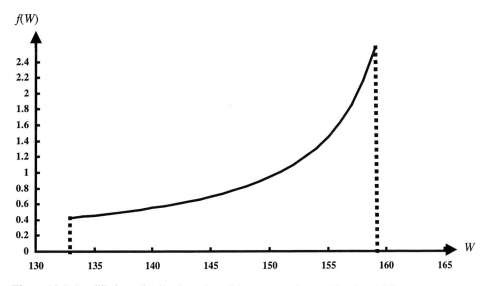

Figure 10.7 Equilibrium distribution of wealth amongst the wealthy (model 2)

From (34) we may construct figure 10.7 which shows the equilibrium wealth distribution generated by model 2.

The main improvement of model 2 over model 1 is that it displays some wide variations in living standards, since long-run equilibrium consumption, rather than being uniform, is linked to long-run wealth. In our particular numerical example this took the form of the linear equation $C=0.1W - 13.314$ (approximately), over the range of wealth covered by the holdings of members of the wealthy class. In model 2 of Mutt island we again find examples of wealth inequality soaring to high levels for long-run equilibrium, despite our assumption of complete equality of earnings: but this is only possible when ξ is kept very small and the approach is slow. Because, in model 2, consumption has to be a simple linear function of wealth, the shape and properties of the distribution of consumption expenditure, C, will be the same, apart from the change of scale and shift of the lower limit, as those of the distribution of wealth.

However, the shape figure 10.7 of appears to be very unrealistic: not only is the wealth distribution truncated above and below, but it is also heavily skewed in the 'wrong' direction, rising to a sharp peak at the upper truncation level. Since income – like consumption – is also a linear function of wealth in model 2, this shape depicted in figure 10.7 also characterises the long-run distribution of income: this seems to be at variance with the evidence about actual income distribution noted in earlier chapters.

However, in this version of Mutt island we still have only the two inequality-generating factors that were present in model 1 (see page 219 above), and figure 10.7 only depicts the result of one component of this inequality – that within the class of propertied Mutts – and not that between the propertied and propertyless. This component is due solely to the within-lifecycle story of wealth accumulation of wealthy Mutts, and so it is perhaps not surprising that figure 10.7 reveals an unconventional picture.

In the hope of enriching the picture of inequality generation within Mutt island and of introducing further realism we will now modify our assumptions to allow earnings inequality.

10.4 Variable earnings

Up till now we have retained the assumption of the complete equality and constancy of the earnings of all employed Mutts. In this section we shall relax this in two different ways:

- In *model 3* we consider the possibility that all Mutts have identical prospects of earnings over their working lives but that these earnings vary *during* them. Clearly this change in the rules may affect the path of wealth accumulation: but will it significantly affect the distribution of wealth and income?
- In *model 4* we suppose that Mutts differ as to their endowments of earnings capacity. What is then the link between dispersion of earnings and the concentration of wealth? We shall enquire whether either change in the model results in the distributions on Mutt island appearing more like those observed in the world about us.

By letting earnings vary over a Mutt's lifetime we can make some allowance for the fact that the pattern of earnings and saving for retirement during a person's lifetime may significantly affect the observed distribution of wealth at any moment. A chance visitor to Mutt island might wonder to what extent the inequality of wealth holding is attributable to worthy Mutts engaged in saving for the lean years of old age – rearranging their earnings to a pattern of consumption more in tune with a Mutt's lifetime needs[10] – and to what extent it reflects the outcome of the cumulative economic and social inheritance process that forces further apart well-funded and ill-funded dynasties.

To allow for a sharp early rise and later flattening out or drop in a Mutt's earnings during his life, we replace the constant-earnings assumption 1 by the following rule:

> *Assumption 1a* Each Mutt receives earnings $E(t)$ at age t (measured from the time of the Mutt's receiving his inheritance) where

$$E(t)=E_0+E_1t+E_2t^2 \tag{35}$$

Write the coefficients of the earnings equation as the vector $\mathbf{E}:=(E_0, E_1, E_2)$ and, as illustrative values, let us take $\mathbf{E}=(11,0.1,-0.002)$ which means that a Mutt starts adult life ($t=-25$) with earnings of 7,250¢, has earnings of 11,000¢ by the time he is due to inherit ($t=0$), and reaches maximum earnings of 12,250¢ by the end of his life ($t=25$).

Assumption 1a introduces far more variety into the range of possible 'economic lifecycle stories' that a Mutt experiences. At any stage of his life a Mutt may be in one of three phases:

- following a 'pursuit path' of consumption given by (18);
- consuming at rate C^*, possibly running down his stock of marketable wealth in order to do so;
- subsisting on his low earnings below the conventional consumption rate C^*.

Also, the Mutt may switch from phase to phase during his life in a manner dependent

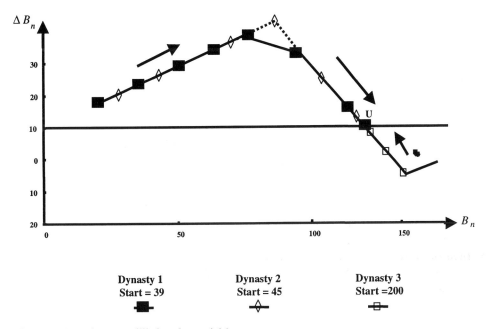

Figure 10.8 Paths to equilibrium in model 3

upon the initial consumption and wealth $c(0)$ and $W(0)$ and the time shape of the profile $E(t)$. Limitations of space and of readers' patience prevent us discussing all types of such possible sequences that might emerge in the long run. But insofar as model 3 is concerned, in cases where v is large enough to ensure that the heir does not raise his consumption rate, $c(0)$, at inheritance above C^*, the conventional level,[11] the slopes of the lines in the diagram for model 2 (figure 10.7), will be unaffected by replacing the constant earnings coefficient E^* by the quadratic earnings profile $E(t)$. At the same time the two sloping lines will continue to intersect on the ordinate through W^*: however, their point of intersection will be shifted vertically. Figure 10.8 shows – in a manner similar to figure 10.7 for model 2[12] – the dynamics of approach to equilibrium in this model from the starting points $B_0=0$, $B_0=39$, $B_0=45$ and $B_0=200$. Note that those who inherit nothing (point 0) will bequeath nothing, so that such a dynasty stays at 0 for ever.

In the long-run equilibrium of model 3 there are three sources of inequality. The first two of these were present in models 1 and 2

• Amongst the propertied Mutts (all of whom will incur the wealth tax), there is a moderate inequality of wealth arising from their savings as they grow older. The nature of this age dependence and hence of the moderate wealth inequality within the propertied class will depend on the shape of the earnings profile $E(t)$.
• Again, two types of Mutt will eventually emerge: ordinary Mutts with very small or zero bequests[13] and propertied Mutts with large bequests: in each of these two cases a constant amount would be passed on at death generation after generation.
• For propertied and ordinary Mutts alike earnings are non-constant over time, so that

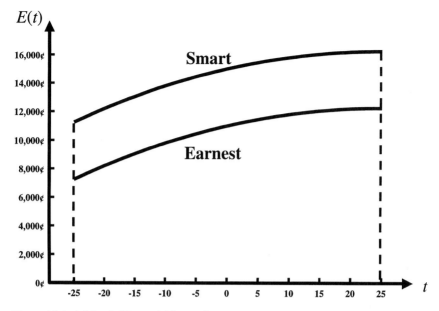

Figure 10.9 A Mutt's life: variable earnings

in any population of Mutts with representatives of different cohorts alive at the same moment there will be an additional proximate reason for *income* inequality deriving directly from the curved profile of the Mutt's earnings, since income is now given by

$$y(t) = E(t) = r W(t) \tag{36}$$

It is instructive to use standard inequality measures to summarise the resulting long-run equilibrium both for model 3 and for model 4 (see pages 236–9. below). We argued in chapter 4 that the between age group component of income inequality is in practice likely to contribute very little to total inequality, and a similar point emerges in the characteristics of equilibrium wealth and income distribution models. Using the same Atkinson inequality indices as we used to characterise real-world data in chapters 4–6 we find (see figures 10.9–10.11) that the inclusion of earnings variability with age *by itself* has an almost negligible impact upon long-run inequality; our simulations show that inequality within any class of Mutts – which was small in the constant earnings case – remains moderate in the variable earnings case.

However, this point comes out more clearly once we have introduced model 4 of Mutt island. We now allow the variation in earnings to be amongst different Mutts, and so we qualify the earnings assumption 1a by the following:

Assumption 1b The base-line earnings E_0 may be different for different lines of Mutts, although constant across the generations within each line.

Assumption 1b allows for inherited personal qualities which enable some types of Mutt to earn more than others; as we shall see this modification can cause quite a dramatic increase in inequality by comparison with model 3.

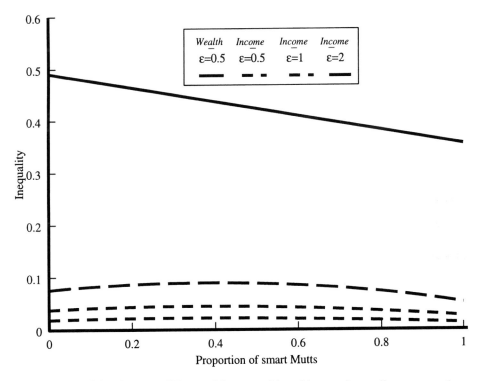

Figure 10.10 Mixing Smart and Earnest Mutts: wealth and income inequality amongst the wealthy

Let us illustrate this for the case where there are just two groups of Mutts, Earnest Mutts for whom $\mathbf{E}=(11,0.1,-0.002)$, and Smart Mutts who start life with a greater endowment of earning capacity, but whose earnings grow thereafter at the same rate: $\mathbf{E}=(15,0.1,-0.002)$. The other parameters are all exactly the same for both groups and have the same values as in model 2: ($T=25$, $C^*=12$, $r=2\frac{1}{2}\%$, $\tau=\frac{2}{3}$, $W^*=120$, $\xi=0.1$, $\nu=0.2$). The earnings histories for the two types are illustrated in figure 10.9.

The equilibrium distribution of wealth and income can be separately found for each type of Mutt, and the results are displayed in rows 3e ('Earnest') and 3s ('Smart') of the two parts of table 10.2 using the inequality measures $A_{1/2}$, A_1 and A_2. It should be emphasised that table 10.2 deals only with those Mutts who are at a U-equilibrium in the long run – we will come to the poor propertyless Mutts later – but even with this restricted coverage some interesting features emerge:

- In presenting the inequality of the equilibrium wealth distribution in table 10.2 some of the entries are deliberately left blank because the inequality indices A_1 and A_2 automatically assume their maximum value of 1 given the presence of any zero wealth holdings in the distribution[14] and Earnest Mutts have no wealth when young, even though they will inherit later.
- Taking old and young Mutts together there appears to be a substantial wealth inequality as measured by the index $A_{1/2}$ – see the *All ages* columns for models 2,

3e or 3s in the top part of table 10.2. This phenomenon is entirely attributable to the fact that young Mutts have yet to inherit. If we check equilibrium wealth inequality amongst those who have inherited ($t \geq 0$) we find that it is very low – see the *Old* columns.

• There is some inequality amongst young Smart Mutts which arises from their earnings being sufficiently great to permit them to acquire wealth before inheriting at $t = 0$ (this will occur as soon as $E(t) > C^*$).

• In terms of the timing of bequests ageing does contribute to wealth inequality in models 2 and 3, since young Mutts have either zero wealth or – in the case of Smart Mutts – much less wealth than those who are old enough to have inherited.

• However, the impact on equilibrium wealth inequality of model-3 type earnings variability is relatively slight, whether we look at inequality amongst Mutts of all ages, or inequality amongst old Mutts alone. This is seen to be so by comparing the constant-earnings model (row 2) to the quadratic earnings case with the same present value (row 3e). Of course, by definition – compare equation (36) – the impact on *income* is greater.

Now let us put the Smart and Earnest Mutts together so as to examine inequality in model 4. There are two distinct important issues to be resolved: the proportions of the ability types (Smart and Earnest) that are present in the upper wealth equilibrium, and the proportions of propertied and propertyless Mutts (i.e., the proportions at the U and 0 equilibria).

Although the proportionate numbers in the two groups will remain constant throughout the approach to equilibrium, their differing rates of enrichment may be expected to alter the relative proportions of those owning any wealth. The impact on wealth and income inequality amongst the class of propertied Mutts of varying the ability types is illustrated in figure 10.10; we shall assume that the initial conditions are such that by the time equilibrium has been closely approached, the proportion of Smart Mutts amongst all Mutts who own wealth has risen to 1 in 5, the remaining 4 being Earnest Mutts.

The impact on wealth and income inequality of varying the proportion of those at the U-equilibrium (the propertied Mutts) in the population is illustrated in figure 10.11. Moving from one curve to another within any of these figures picks up the effect of changing the model assumptions concerning earnings; moving from left to right along any one curve illustrates the impact of the 'poverty in the midst of plenty' effect of the multiple wealth equilibria: in the case of wealth, increasing the proportion of Mutts at the upper equilibrium cuts inequality, as property is spread more diffusely in the population; in the case of income the propertyless equilibrium (left-hand end of the figures) has a relatively low inequality base that is generated just by earnings and the propertied equilibrium (right-hand end of the figures) has a substantial component of inequality that arises because of the income differences between those who have already inherited and those who have not. Table 10.3 illustrates the breakdown of income inequality if exactly half of the Mutts of each type are located at the lower and the upper equilibria; notice that since there are by construction only two ability types, the amount of inequality 'explained' by the between-group component appears to be quite high compared with real-world decompositions of inequality (cf. table 6.1 on page 121).

Table 10.2 *Wealth and income inequality amongst (eventually) wealthy Mutts*

	All ages				Young ($t<0$)				Old ($t\geq0$)			
Model	Mean	$A_{1/2}$	A_1	A_2	Mean	$A_{1/2}$	A_1	A_2	Mean	$A_{1/2}$	A_1	A_2
Wealth inequality												
2	76,479¢	0.4905	—	—	0¢	0.0000	—	—	150,016¢	0.0007	0.0014	0.0028
3e	78,394¢	0.4907	—	—	0¢	0.0000	—	—	153,773¢	0.0010	0.0020	0.0040
3s	103,935¢	0.3559	—	—	12,244¢	0.0256	—	—	197,432¢	0.0010	0.0020	0.0040
Income inequality												
2	11,912¢	0.0063	0.0126	0.0250	10,000¢	0	0	0	13,750¢	0.0000	0.0001	0.0002
3e	12,527¢	0.0185	0.0374	0.0752	9,258¢	0.0036	0.0073	0.0147	15,669¢	0.0004	0.0008	0.0016
3s	17,165¢	0.0127	0.0256	0.0516	13,425¢	0.0022	0.0044	0.0089	20,761¢	0.0003	0.0006	0.0012

Note: '3e' means model 3, Earnest Mutts; '3s' means model 3, Smart Mutts

Table 10.3 *Equilibrium income inequality in model 4: 50 per cent propertied, 50 per cent propertyless Mutts*

	Mean	$A_{1/2}$	A_1	A_2
Young Earnest	9,258¢	0.0036	0.0073	0.0147
Old Earnest	13,747¢	0.0053	0.0105	0.0209
All Earnest	11,547¢	0.0141	0.0279	0.0546
Young Smart	13,342¢	0.0020	0.0040	0.0080
Old Smart	18,293¢	0.0048	0.0096	0.0190
All Smart	15,866¢	0.0096	0.0191	0.0370
All Mutts	12,410¢	0.0174	0.0345	0.0672
	number of groups	$A_{1/2}$	A_1	A_2
Inequality between groups				
Age alone	2	0.0086	0.0173	0.0343
Type alone	2	0.0044	0.0086	0.0160
Age and type	4	0.0132	0.0262	0.0515

Clearly this version of model 4 is somewhat restrictive in that there are only two ability types which persist throughout the dynasty. By generating a variety of persistent ability types we can get more within-group income variation and it is interesting to see whether this yields income and wealth distributions that accord more closely with what we find in reality. If we take a large number of Mutt types distributed with the 'Smart' and 'Earnest' types as extreme cases,[15] then the resulting wealth and income distributions are as illustrated in and figure 10.12. Notice the greater dispersion that arises in comparison to models 1 and 2, and the bimodality that arises from the inclusion of the young Mutts alongside those who have inherited.

The principal conclusion which emerges from the simulations of model 4 is that whereas the variation in earnings over the lifetime has a minor effect on long-run wealth inequality, any substantial variation of earnings between the Mutt lines which persists from generation to generation, eventually boosts substantially the dispersion of wealth and hence also income inequality. However, none of this makes any reference to possible mobility of earnings between generations within a particular dynasty of Mutts: in the models we examine in this chapter, earnings differences between dynasties are maintained from father to son in perpetuity. The question of shifts in earnings as well as the fortunes of individual lines of Mutts between generations will be considered in chapter 11.

10.5 Family size and wealth distribution

So far all the models of Mutt island have focused on the process of accumulation and preservation of wealth. Our *model 5* examines the effect of variations in family size on the long-run distribution of wealth, and in so doing emphasises the rôle of the *disper-*

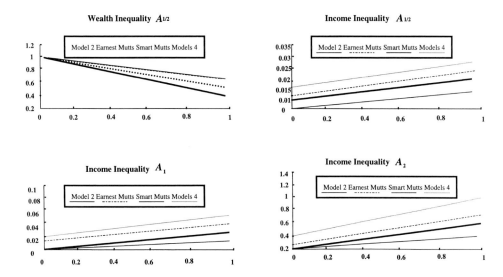

Figure 10.11 Wealth and income inequality: varying the proportion of the propertied class

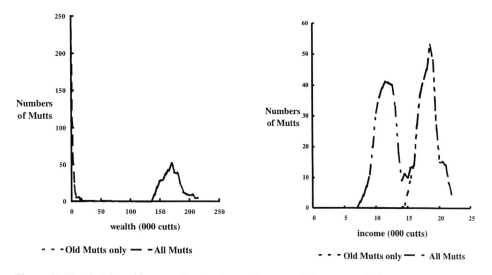

Figure 10.12 Wealth and income distribution with many ability types of Mutts

sion of wealth amongst heirs. In order to avoid complicating the exposition unduly, we shall confine model 5 to the study of the effects of inheritance on wealth distribution and ignore in it all saving and dissaving so that we may also ignore the distributions of income and of consumption expenditure, which are the results and not the causes of the wealth distribution in this model. We retain the assumption of a simple inheritance tax.

In models 1 to 4 only one person benefited from any one will: but the distinguishing feature of model 5 is that more than one person may do so. Indeed, we shall make the further assumption that people arrange themselves in pairs (Mum and Dad), coordinate their bequests, and divide their joint wealth equally between a given number of heirs. The heirs consist of k kids where k is an integer between 1 and K (a finite maximum) inclusive: this means that there are no childless couples.[16] In this model we also require:

> *Assumption 9* There is a strict caste system for marriage in that the pairs always consist of people with equal wealth.

For example, under these assumptions, if the wealth inheritance tax did not apply to the will, and if the division was among three heirs, each would get wealth equal to just two thirds of the wealth owned by one parent.

In this model we make the following further simplifying assumption. At every level of wealth the average number of persons who benefit from a person's bequest is one (or from the bequest of a pair, it is two), and no person benefits from more than one such coordinated bequest. This is to ensure that the number of bequests remains constant from generation to generation. As in previous models, there is a uniform proportional rate of inheritance tax τ on all bequests where the wealth of the testator (or of each of a pair of them) exceeds a specified limit W^*.

At any wealth level W in excess of W^*, the proportion of testators with exactly k kids is p_k, where p_k is independent of W, and obviously $p_k \geq 0$ and $\Sigma_{k=1}^{K} p_k = 1$. At levels of wealth below W^*, the rates of wealth tax may be lower and they may be varied so as to favour those who have had to share with many others, and, at very low levels of inheritance, the tax may be negative; the whole system is such that everyone is assured of inheriting at least W_{min}, a specified strictly positive level of wealth. We also impose the restriction that the bequest is divided equally amongst a given number of beneficiaries from a will: this will enable us to derive simpler and more powerful conclusions about the long-run wealth distribution.

Now it can be shown[17] that for large wealth holdings (i.e., $W(0)$ in excess of W^*) the equilibrium distribution of wealth is well approximated by the Paretian formula

$$F(W) = 1 - AW^{-\alpha} \tag{37}$$

where F is the distribution function, A is a constant and α is the largest root of:

$$\sum_{k=1}^{K} p_k \left[\frac{k}{2}\right]^{1-\alpha} = [1-\tau]^{-\alpha} \tag{38}$$

In order to see the implications of this for wealth inequality let us examine two special cases, given by table 10.4.

For our first example we take $W^* = 100$ (an exemption limit of 100,000¢), the proportional rate of estate tax τ as 10 per cent (for convenience we assume that where tax is payable, it is levied on the whole of the bequest), and case (i) of the family proportions in table 10.4.

In this case it may be helpful to think of this in terms of 100 married couples, 30 of whom each have an only child who inherits $2W$, 45 of whom have two children each of whom inherits W, 20 have three children each of whom gets ⅔W and 5 have four children each of whom get ½W. Altogether the 200 parents would leave wealth to

Table 10.4 *Two family structures*

	p_1	p_2	p_3	p_4	p_5	p_6
(i)	0.30	0.45	0.20	0.05	0.00	0.00
(ii)	0.35	0.45	0.10	0.06	0.03	0.01

$30+90+60+20=200$ children, so they are exactly reproducing their numbers. However, because of the 10 per cent wealth tax the average wealth of the descendants is only 90 per cent of that of the parents.

Then (38) becomes

$$0.3\times2^{\alpha-1}+0.45+0.2\times\left[\tfrac{2}{3}\right]^{\alpha-1}+0.05\times\left[\tfrac{1}{2}\right]^{\alpha-1}=0.9^{-\alpha} \tag{39}$$

We may solve to yield the value of the Pareto coefficient $\alpha=2.113$. The equilibrium wealth distribution is illustrated in figure 10.13.

Examination of this diagram of the long-run wealth distribution generated by model 5, with the particular parameter values we have selected for illustration, yields a picture that seems closer to reality than those we found when running previous models of Mutt island. This model can be used to explore possible insights about the long-run effects of varying the conditions represented by the various parameters of the model, for example, the steepness of the inheritance tax and the pattern of family sizes. We return to this below.

Here we have discovered one way of possibly explaining the skewed wealth distributions of the real world, without making them dependent on the skew nature of the distribution of earnings. An obvious further step is to consider some combination of the assumptions of models 3 and 4, to see if the Pareto-type long-run distribution of wealth is still found when we allow for the mutual interaction of income, wealth and savings. In this chapter we shall merely foreshadow some of the results presented in chapter 11's analysis of stochastic models of income distribution and wealth distribution.

Now we shall examine the effect on distribution of a further small change in the structure of the model. Take the following example using the more dispersed distribution of family sizes given in case (ii) of table 10.4. Notice that in comparison with our previous example there are a few more families with one child, fewer fairly large families, but a significant number of very large families. Once again we can use formula to find the Pareto coefficient of the long-run wealth distribution. Doing so for an inheritance tax at the rate $\tau=10$ per cent we find $\alpha=1.9002$ which is lower than the α obtained for the previous example: the increased spread of family sizes has increased the inequality of the wealth distribution.

This effect is an illustration of a more general result: in this sort of wealth distribution model, unless there is substantial counteracting 'overcompensation' of bequest behaviour by individual members of the population, *greater variety of personal circumstances leads to greater wealth inequality*. We shall develop this point more fully in chapter 11.

Obviously in either of the above examples, the exact long-run distribution of wealth depends critically on the rate of inheritance tax that is imposed, a feature that we have

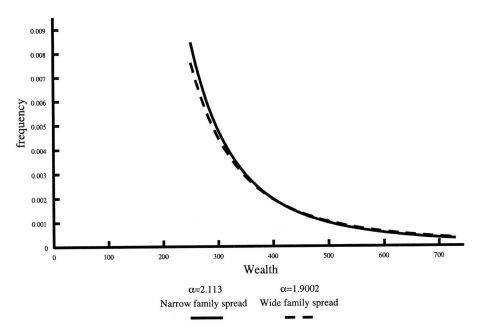

Figure 10.13 Equilibrium wealth distribution in model 5

noted in previous models. Let us examine the relationship between the tax rate τ and the Pareto coefficient α in model 5. Inspection of equation (38) suggests that α increases with τ (long-run inequality *decreases* as the rise in the rate of inheritance tax increases) which is what we might expect. We may draw up table 10.5 for the two different cases of family structure.

In computing the inequality measure A_1 we consider only the subpopulation of wealth holdings which exceed some level well above the tax exemption level W^*. It is a property of distributions which approximate Pareto's law closely at high levels that A_1 calculated this way is almost independent of the lower boundary of the subpopulation.

By comparing the second and fourth columns of entries in table 10.6 we can see also how much higher are the rates of tax required with the wider spread of family size than with the smaller spread of the first example to attain various levels of α, the index of equality. Note that roughly 2 per cent has to be added to the tax to balance the inegalitarian effects of the increase in the spread of family size. Instead of considering the effects of tax and family structures on wealth distribution, the controllers of the Mutt economy might be interested in the following question: 'What rate of taxation would be required to ensure any given degree of inequality of wealth distribution?' The answer to this may be found by evaluating τ using for specified values of α and cases of family structure. Take for example our two structures given in table 10.5. Repeated application of (38) provides the results displayed in table 10.6 which also tabulates equilibrium inequality A1.

We are now ready to take account of one further feature of many societies, namely

Table 10.5 *Rates of taxation needed to produce various values of* α

	τ: rate of wealth taxation (%)	
	Case (i) Narrow spread	Case (ii) Wider spread
α	of family size	of family size
1.5	4.6	5.9
2.0	9.0	11.0
2.5	13.2	15.5
3.0	17.0	19.5
3.5	20.5	22.9
4.0	23.5	25.8

Table 10.6 *Effect of family structure on wealth inequality*

	Case (i) narrow spread of family size		Case (ii) wider spread of family size	
Tax τ (%)	α	A_1	α	A_1
2	1.22	0.909	—	—
5	1.55	0.768	1.42	0.821
10	2.11	0.579	1.90	0.641
15	2.73	0.446	2.44	0.502
20	3.43	0.349	3.07	0.393
25	4.28	0.274	3.86	0.307

that it is common for the partners in a marriage to differ appreciably in regard to the wealth of their parental backgrounds.

10.6 Marriage and wealth distribution

One of the simplifying features of model 5 was assumption 9 – that people only could marry if both had the same amount of wealth. In *model 6*, we allow them to marry beneath (or above) their station. This will enable us to investigate some of the effects on wealth distribution of the extent to which marriages tend to be between persons with similar amounts of wealth.

In most of the world the ratio ρ, of the greater to the lesser wealth holding in the marriage, takes values spread over a substantial range, and the shape of the distribution of the ratio amongst couples is likely to vary systematically with the pooled wealth level of the couple. But in the model 6 version of Mutt island, we assume that for all Mutts with ρW_{min} or more:

Assumption 9a The wealth ratio is independent of the pooled wealth level.

Assumption 9b The ratio is a particular positive number ρ.

Assumption 9b will be relaxed in an extension of this model at the end of this section, but at present we retain it, since it makes it easier to follow the argument establishing the effects on the long-run distribution, which result from the strength of the tendency to marry a person ρ times ($1/\rho$ times) as wealthy as oneself.

To fix ideas, we take an example in which the pattern of families with any substantial wealth is the same again as it was in case (i) of table 10.4 above; but now, instead of the two partners having equal wealth before marriage, we insist that one is just twice as wealthy as the other ($\rho=2$), and we enquire what effect that would have on the degree of inequality of the long-run equilibrium wealth distribution in the model. We would expect it to change the wealth distribution that would result from any particular initial distribution after many generations.

To see how this may come about, consider the bequests made to children of families with a combined wealth level of two million cuts (M¢). In the case of model 5 above, 15 per cent of their descendants leave $2[1-\tau]$ M¢, 45 per cent leave $[1-\tau]$ M¢, 30 per cent leave $\frac{2}{3}[1-\tau]$ M¢ and 10 per cent leave $\frac{1}{2}[1-\tau]$ M¢. But now, in each of these four groups of descendants, some (a proportion λ let us say) will marry partners twice as wealthy, and so the average wealth will be 1.5 M¢ – one-and-a-half times the climber's pre-marriage wealth: the remaining proportion, $1-\lambda$, will marry beneath them partners only half as wealthy, so for them the average wealth after marriage will be only $\frac{3}{4}$M¢ – and thus only three quarters of their own pre-marital wealth.[18]

With these rules, the value of λ which will allow equilibrium such that every wealthy person can find a partner of suitable affluence will depend on the distribution of wealth. If wealth has a Pareto distribution with parameter α, the satisfaction of both assumptions 9a and 9b is only possible if[19]

$$\lambda = \frac{1}{1+\rho^{\alpha}} \qquad (40)$$

So to allow a Pareto distribution with $\alpha=2$ and $\rho=2$ and with the above pattern of family size, we should need $\lambda=0.2$. The above formula for λ enables us to deal similarly with the general case where the richer partner must always have the same multiple ρ of the other partner's wealth before marriage.

We should expect the new assumptions of model 6 to modify the relationship found in model 5 between the rate of inheritance tax τ and the long-run inequality of wealth distribution (which is inversely related to the Pareto coefficient α). Recall that when marriages were between equally wealthy partners as in model 5, the equation (38) for the tax rate which would allow the Pareto coefficient α to be 2 in long-run equilibrium implied a 9 per cent value of the tax rate τ. Now we find that – with marriages between partners of whom one is twice as wealthy as the other ($\rho=2$), the tax rate τ which will allow $\alpha=2$, is given by

$$\tau = \left[\frac{\frac{5}{9}}{p_1 + \frac{1}{2}p_2 + \frac{1}{3}p_3 + \frac{1}{4}p_4} \right]^{\frac{1}{2}} \qquad (41)$$

which, on substituting from table 10.5 for the *p*-values in case (i) gives $\tau=0.04107$. In other words, an inheritance tax of about 4.1 per cent is required to restrain inequality at the specified level as against 9 per cent in the 'class-loyalty' case, model 5.

Table 10.7 *Pareto's α for wealth distribution: uniform class disloyalty*

τ:	0.02	0.05	0.10	0.15	0.20	0.25
ρ			Value of α			
1.0	1.17	1.43	1.90	2.44	3.07	3.86
1.2	1.17	1.44	1.93	2.50	3.17	4.03
1.5	1.20	1.51	2.10	2.78	3.65	4.89
2.0	1.31	1.80	2.71	3.87	5.57	8.88
2.5	1.66	2.51	3.93	5.79	9.22	21.50
3.0	2.67	3.66	5.44	8.32	16.25	—

Given the assumptions of model 6, and given that the family size distribution parameters p_k satisfy the population stationarity condition

$$\sum_{k=1}^{K} k p_k = 2 \tag{42}$$

then the general equation for the inheritance tax level required to secure any given level α of the Pareto coefficient, when all marriages are such that the wealth ratio between the two partners is ρ ($\rho \geq 1$), may be written[20]

$$1 - \tau = \frac{1}{1+\rho} \left[\frac{\sum_{k=1}^{K} p_k k^{1-\alpha}}{1+\rho^{\alpha}} \right]^{-\frac{1}{\alpha}} \tag{43}$$

Table 10.7 gives the relationship between the inheritance tax τ and the equilibrium value of Pareto's α in the special case where the class disloyalty parameter ρ is the same for all marriages, and where the wider spread of family size – case (ii) in table 10.5 – is assumed.

The second simplifying assumption that we adopted in model 6 was that there was one particular ratio ρ between the two marriage partners. Now let us relax this assumption and assume that a distribution of wealth ratios $\rho_1, \rho_2, \rho_3, \dots$ with relative frequencies be $f_1, f_2, f_3, \dots$ We continue to maintain assumption 9a, that the pairs (ρ_1, f_1), (ρ_2, f_2), $(\rho_3, f_3), \dots$ are independent of the joint wealth level. Then we find

$$[1-\tau]^{-\alpha} = \left[\sum_{k=1}^{K} p_k k^{1-\alpha} \right] \left[\sum_{k=1}^{K} f_k \frac{[1+\rho_k]^{\alpha}}{1+\rho_k^{\alpha}} \right] \tag{44}$$

The application of (44) is illustrated by the set of values given in table 10.8 which allows for heterogeneity in class disloyalty as follows. Let $\bar{\rho}$ be some given value of mean class disloyalty. Then let $\rho_1 = 0.5\bar{\rho}$, $\rho_2 = 0.75\bar{\rho}$, $\rho_3 = \bar{\rho}$, $\rho_4 = 1.25\bar{\rho}$, $\rho_5 = 1.5\bar{\rho}$, $\rho_6 = 1.75\bar{\rho}$, with $f_1 = 0.2, f_2 = 0.2, f_3 = 0.3, f_4 = 0.1, f_5 = 0.1, f_6 = 0.1$. Table 10.8 then tabulates the relationship between τ and equilibrium α for different values of $\bar{\rho}$.

Comparing table 10.7 and table 10.8 we can see that the effect of spreading out class disloyalty depends on the level of average class disloyalty $\bar{\rho}$ and the tax rate τ at which

Table 10.8 *Pareto's α for wealth distribution:*
heterogeneous class disloyalty

τ:	0.02	0.05	0.10	0.15	0.20	0.25
$\bar{\rho}$			Value of α			
2.0	2.08	2.42	3.09	3.89	4.90	6.29
2.5	2.41	2.84	3.65	4.62	5.90	7.74
3.0	2.87	3.39	4.37	5.64	7.48	10.51
3.5	3.42	4.03	5.26	6.98	9.76	14.96

the comparison is made: for low values of $\bar{\rho}$ and τ increasing the spread of class disloyalty reduces inequality: for high values of $\bar{\rho}$ and τ the opposite is true.

10.7 Conclusion

The fables that have been developed in sections 10.2–10.6 and whose principal features
are summarised in table 10.9 by no means exhaust the interesting possibilities for Mutt
island. However, their purpose is not the proliferation of examples but the demonstration in simplified form of the impact that social forces and a variety of patterns of economic behaviour may have on the development of wealth distribution: naturally there
are further possibilities that we might explore.

For example, when we consider the impact of social forces, we might introduce other
social or economic rules about the selection of spouses, or other rules about bequests,
such as primogeniture. The modelling of economic behaviour might be extended to
incorporate more sophisticated relationships between planned bequests and lifetime
resources, or to allow for the possibility of voluntary retirement of the more wealthy
Mutts from the labour force in advance of the normal retirement age.

But, in our view, such modifications would largely miss the point.[21] The various
fables about different situations on Mutt island reveal that simplistic explanations of
the observed properties of actual wealth distributions are very sensitive to the choice
of assumptions about the economic mechanisms involved. Neither a particular feature
of the social structure, nor a special quirk of economic behaviour will *by itself* provide
a suitable account of the actual data about wealth distribution, briefly discussed in
chapter 9. Indeed, some of the forces that we have investigated induce effects that run
counter to features that are commonly observed. So it would be useful to investigate
the simultaneous interaction of the several different social and economic phenomena
that affect distribution. This is pursued in chapter 11.

10.8 Questions for discussion

10.1   Using equations (27) to (30): discuss the development over six generations given
the parameter values ($T=25$, $E^*=10$, $C^*=12$, $r=2\frac{1}{2}\%$, $\tau=0.5$, $W^*=120$, $\xi=0.2$), starting from initial pre-tax bequests of (i) 75,000¢, (ii) 115,000¢ and (iii) 660,000¢.
10.2   From inspection of your results in question 10.1 make a rough guess of the

Table 10.9 *Mutt island: six exploratory models*

Model 1	Model 2	Models 3 & 4	Model 5	Model 6
Fixed consumption	Adaptive consumption	Adaptive consumption	All income consumed	All income consumed
Those with no means cannot get into debt	Those with no means cannot get into debt	Those with no means cannot get into debt	...	...
Fixed earnings	Fixed earnings	Earnings vary with age	...	...
	All working Mutts have same earnings	Earnings vary amongst Mutts (model 4 only)	...	...
One beneficiary, one inheritance	One beneficiary, one inheritance	One beneficiary, one inheritance	Many children, caste marriage	Many children, non-caste

equilibrium level $\bar{B}$ which is being approached and then check this by means of algorithm 1 in appendix C.

10.3 Using algorithm 1 (see question 10.2) devise sets of parameter values which would result in the equilibrium bequest being very large in relation to W^*, but without B_n tending to infinity. Check whether starting with a bequest equal to the exemption level W^* any appreciable proportion of the distance between W^* and can be covered within a few generations.

10.4 Appendix C (page 000) provides numerical examples illustrating the applications of algorithms 2a and 2b: compare the equilibrium distributions arising from these and apply the suitable algorithm in the case where v takes the value 0.09 (half way between 0.1 and 0.08 in the two examples) but keeping all the other parameters the same ($T=25$, $E^*=10$, $C^*=12$, $r=2\frac{1}{2}\%$, $\tau=\frac{2}{3}$, $W^*=120$, $\xi=0.2$).

10.5 What is the economic rationale for individuals adapting their expenditure towards the levels of (a) their own incomes (b) incomes of preceding generations?

10.6 In model 3 what would be the implications for income and wealth inequality of a more sharply curved parabolic path of earnings?

10.7 Discuss the claim that a major explanation of wealth inequality is that certain family lines retain a superior capacity for high earnings generation after generation.

10.8 Alfred Marshall suggested that although families might through inherited ability and exertion rise quickly from poverty to riches, the ascent would only be likely to last for three or four generations before a fall back towards poverty because the heirs would indulge in ease and luxury and would entrust their infants to upbringing by second-rate domestic staff. Would such a process prevent the wealth distribution from approaching an equilibrium?

10.9 Will the rapid development of means of communication result in a concentration of wealth into the hands of a small group?

Notes

1 Neither the building of wealth models nor the Snark hunt has been short of imaginative pursuers:

> They sought it with thimbles, they sought it with care;
>   They pursued it with forks and hope;
> They threatened its life with a railway-share;
>   They charmed it with smiles and soap.

2 For expository purposes we concentrate on a statement of the assumptions of each model and on making its workings clearly seen without developing in detail the necessarily tedious algebraic arguments involved in a rigorous demonstration. For more on these models see appendix C.

3 Suppose $\Omega(t):=W(0)e^{rt} - [e^{rt}-1]\hat{B}$. Then $\Omega(0)=W(0)$ and $d\Omega/dt = r[\Omega(t)-\Omega(0)]+r[W(0)-\hat{B}]$. Therefore, by (4)

$$\frac{dW}{dt}=E^*+rW(t)-C^*=\frac{d\Omega}{dt}$$

if $W(t)=\Omega(t)$; but this condition holds whenever $\Omega(t)\geq 0$, which establishes (5).

4 M may be thought of as the 'Micawber point'. A quick check, using (1) to (4), reveals that at $\hat{B}$ we have $y(0)=C^*$: 'income equals expenditure'. For lower bequests, income falls short of expenditure. Result: misery.

5 To illustrate: instead of lowering the tax from $\tfrac{2}{3}$, suppose we raise the rate of return on assets from $2\tfrac{1}{2}$ per cent to $4\tfrac{3}{8}$ per cent, leaving all other parameters at their standard values. The long-run equilibrium level of bequests before tax will then rise to over 30 million ¢: and that of the incomes of the wealthy to between 458,690 ¢ and 1,345,572¢ – i.e., between 38 and 112 times that of the poor! But when we study the pace of approach we find that for the gap to reach one half of this size would take over 3,500 years.

6 Compare (3) and (4) on page 220 above.

7 In appendix C we distinguish two cases of model 2: in the normal case (2a) the value of v is large enough, and that of ξ small enough, to ensure that if a bequest B_n has the value W^* and $[1-v]C_n<C^*$ then $[1-v]C_{n'}<C^*$ for all $n'>n$ also. Figure 10.3 illustrates this case, in which the $(B_n,\Delta B_n)$ values are independent of C_n: once the left-hand branch has been reached, all subsequent points $(B_n,\Delta B_n)$ lie precisely on the same branch as in case 1 of figure 10.3. In the other case (2b) the left-hand branch may split into two, because before W^* is reached $[1-v]C_n$ exceeds C^*. The first branch will be the same as in model 1; however some points may not lie very close to the second upward-sloping branch, and again some points near the top of the third downward-sloping branch may lie not very close to it. Nevertheless, apart from the first two or three bequests, and for observations near the two switch points, the divergences from the line are unlikely to be visually conspicuous.

8 See question 10.4 for the solution when v is lowered to 0.08, in which case $c(0)>C^*$ and $\tilde{C}-\tilde{c}(0)=\xi[B-W(0)]$ in long-run equilibrium.

9 From (32) $-0.075t+\log(31.0477)=\log(164.1909-W)$. So $t=(40/3)$ $\log(31.0477/[164.1909-W])$ and hence, using (32), $F(W(t))=0.04t$, we obtain (34).

10 See, for example, Atkinson (1971) and the discussion on page 000 above.

11 A sufficient condition for this is that $1-v<C^*/c(T)$, where $c(T)$ is the testator's rate of consumption at T, his retirement date.

12 The basis of comparison was that the present value

$$\int_{-T}^{+T} E(t)e^{-rT}\,dt$$

should be approximately equal (to within ½ per cent) in the constant earnings case and in equation (35) above.

13 We took the case where the proportion of Mutts in the propertied class is 0.593; their share in total income is 0.75.

14 This problem will arise for any Atkinson index A_ϵ for which $\epsilon \geq 1$.

15 Specifically we simulated fourteen equal-sized ability groups with E_0 set as follows: 11, 11.5, 12, 12.5, 12.7, 12.9, 13, 13, 13.1, 13.3, 13.5, 14, 14.5, 15.

16 Alternatively we may simply assume that childless couples do not leave bequests.

17 For details see appendix C.

18 These rules would lead to constantly declining wealth unless we prescribed some minimum level of wealth W_{min} and relaxed the rules for those marrying with less than twice W_{min} so as to avoid situations in which marriage partners were unavailable at the prescribed levels for some in this band. We shall suppose that these difficulties have been overcome: the simplest amendment to make is that all those in that predicament take spouses with twice their wealth.

19 There must be ρ^α times as many marriages of spouses in the range $[1\pm\epsilon]$ M¢ with spouses in the range $[1\pm\epsilon]/\rho$ M¢ as with spouses in the range $[1\pm\epsilon]\rho$ M¢; this yields the formula for λ.

20 See appendix C.

21 In fact other remote and fanciful locations similar to Mutt island have been toured before. Blinder (1973b) examines the implications of different types of marriage patterns and bequest rules in a community of two-adult, two-child families. Atkinson (1980) extends the Blinder model to more interesting examples of family composition; he also investigates the case where preferences in each generation are such that consumption and bequests for each person are proportional to that person's lifetime wealth – contrast equations (19), (22), (24). In the model of Stiglitz (1969), both the rate of return on capital, and labour earnings are endogenously determined by a production function; these features are also present in Pryor (1973), who further simulates the impact of different marriage and inheritance rules.

11 Stochastic models of wealth and income distribution

11.1 Some preliminary questions

The various stories of Mutt island in chapter 10 make the case for simplified modelling of income and wealth distributions: the role of commonly made, but questionable, assumptions is clarified and the operation of forces generating long-run inequality are brought out one by one. No one should pretend that Mutt island is the UK or the USA, but the fate of the poor Mutts in the long run provides a lesson for those interested in why extreme inequalities establish themselves and persist. This chapter takes our primitive models of income and wealth distribution one important stage further: we graft on to the deterministic models of chapter 10 a stochastic component that captures some of the influences that had hitherto been assumed away.

Although the use of stochastic models is familiar in many branches of applied science such as biology, agricultural research, industrial chemistry and engineering, and although they are commonly employed for econometric modelling in macroeconomics, their use as models of the distribution of wealth and income is less familiar and sometimes misunderstood. As a quick method of guarding against some of the more common misunderstandings, we set out a preliminary catechism about such stochastic models.

Q. What is meant by a stochastic theory or stochastic model of a process?

A. A theory or model which includes one or more variates.

Q. What is a variate?

A. A variate is a variable whose value may take one out of a range of alternative values, with probabilities which depend not only on the value of that variate, but possibly on the values of the other known variables as well.

Q. What is the point of including a variate in a model?

A. It is useful because in fields of study such as biology, meteorology, astronomy and economics it is often impossible to identify all the determining variables; some may represent the influences of the unknown variables by the probabilities attributed to the different possible values of each included variate.

Q. But can such nebulous stochastic theories or models be of any practical or theoretical assistance?

A. Yes. They have been found useful in life insurance, Darwinian models, experimental design in agricultural field trials, social surveys, epidemic and queuing problems, to name a few examples.

Whenever there is a problem of analysing the variation of a variable about a central or expected value, arising from the disturbances caused by the changes in other variables which cannot be exactly predicted, it is often helpful to represent that variable by a variate. In particular, if we wish to investigate the complete frequency distribution of any measurable social variable – income, wealth, sizes of firms – as distinct from just studying its average value, then the use of variates is one of the most promising approaches.

Does this amount to claiming that changes in the variable concerned are simply a matter of chance? No: whilst the approach allows for chance variability (in the sense of changes whose size and direction cannot be precisely foreseen) in the other influential variables, the relative importance of this chance element may be small or large, depending on the type of model and the quality of the available information. Stochastic models allow for both systematic influences and chance elements – with variates representing the disturbances caused by these various chance elements – and there are few if any alternative approaches to a distribution theory of such economic variables that can offer such detailed predictions of changes in their frequency distributions.

We shall see how stochastic models may be treated as generalisations of deterministic models. In section 11.2 we shall use the simplest wealth distribution model of chapter 10 to illustrate a determinist model of development over time: the model has an easily computable equilibrium, and change from one generation to the next can be expressed in terms of a set of simple *bequest multipliers*. In section 11.3 we show how such multipliers may be adapted for use in stochastic models: the multipliers are represented there as variates whose distributions are determined partly by the parameters that we used in the determinist models, and partly by the rules governing an endlessly extended game of chance.

11.2 Mutt island revisited

To model the development of distributions of bequests in conditions of uncertainty we retain most of the drastic simplifying assumptions made in chapter 10, model 1. This makes manipulation of our stochastic model practicable, and facilitates comparisons with the deterministic models of Mutt island. However, in setting out the framework for our analytical examples and numerical exercises, simplicity in modelling economic behaviour and clarity of exposition are not the only criteria. As we shall see, the interaction of several simplifying assumptions that individually may seem quite reasonable can produce results which are implausible, so that special care must be taken both with the set of basic assumptions that are to form the structure of the stochastic model, and with the combination of parameter values which are then used when running the model.

Let us recapitulate the essential features of Mutt island model 1 to be carried forward into our stochastic model of wealth and income distribution. Some of these involve important implications for the ranges of parameter values which may be reasonably assumed in numerical exercises when running the model.

The technology Income consists of labour earnings and the return on financial assets (property income). The Mutts own no equity capital and there is no perceived risk of inflation, so the interest rate may be assumed to be low.

The population Heirs are provided as though by spontaneous reproduction: we can interpret this as being the result of perfectly matched couples marrying, and then having just two children who inherit equally the bequests jointly left by their parents. In order to concentrate on the stochastic model components we brush aside the many complications – including those we made some allowance for in the later models of chapter 10 – such as differential fertility, marriage between partners of unequal wealth, and alternative schemes of allotting wealth between two or more heirs. One important feature of these simplifications taken over from model 1 is that we confine attention to a stationary population of Mutts, which further justifies the assumption of a low rate of interest.

Economic institutions Like the Mutts in model 1, those in the stochastic model will usually adopt an absolutely rigid pattern of expenditure, as long as they have the means of doing so. This is given by the parameter C^*, normally set at 12,000¢, which exceeds annual earnings E^*, set at 10,000¢. We also assume there to be some social mechanism to prevent the mass of indebtedness or the starvation that would otherwise result from the gap between the earnings and the expenditure of heirs getting small or zero bequests: we postulate a social mechanism to ensure at least a minimum wealth level P at age $t=0$ which we may regard as the level of bequest after subsidy.[1] If this assumption were to be relaxed, then either such support might be afforded to some extent through the family or extended family, which could involve more complicated and less intelligible modelling, or in many versions of the model we would evolve progressively towards a situation in which a very large population of destitute Mutts confronted a very small set of Mutts who had inherited all the personal wealth. Such an unequal structure would only be likely to survive by means of external support.

Table 11.1 contains the principal notation that we use, including the list of parameters of the bequest mechanism $\pi := (T,E^*,C^*,r,\tau,W^*,P,g,N)$; most of this carries over from chapter 10. The first numerical example of chapter 10 also provides the benchmark parameter values (π_0) for the work of this chapter: these values are listed in the first row of table 11.2; the rest of table 11.2 summarises the parameter values for other cases treated in our stochastic simulation model.

To introduce the main apparatus for the wealth and income model consider the equilibrium to which a sequence of bequests $B_0, B_1, B_2, \ldots$ in a line of Mutts will converge. Assuming the benchmark values π_0 in table 11.2, we can use the result for Mutt island model 1 (see pages 000, 000 and figure 10.3) that there are two (stable) equilibrium bequest levels, zero and 212,000¢. In general the lower equilibrium will be zero for all parameter values, and the upper equilibrium, where it exists, will be given by

$$\tilde{B} = \frac{\tau W^* + A}{e^{-rT} - 1 + \tau},$$

Table 11.1 *Notation*

Symbol	Description	Comments
$\tilde{B}$	Equilibrium bequest	Upper value (lower value is 0)
B_n	Line of bequests	Sequence is $B_0, B_1, B_2, \ldots$
m	Multiplier	Ratio B_{n+1}/B_n
T	Generation length	Interval between bequests
E^*	Earnings p.a.	Same constant for all
C^*	Consumption p.a.	Same for all able to afford it
r	Interest rate p.a.	Yield on wealth
τ	Bequest-tax rate	Applies only above W^*
W^*	Tax-exemption level	Relevant only above W^*
P	Poverty level	Level to which lower bequests are subsidised
g	Interval width	
N	Number of the game	

Note:
For further discussion of the parameters see appendix C.

$$\text{where } A := [E^* - C^*] \frac{1 - e^{-rT}}{r} \tag{1}$$

the discounted value of lifetime accumulations. Substituting the standard parameter values into we verify that $B = 212.06$ (a bequest of 212,060¢). The manner of approach to equilibrium from any initial value B_0 may be found by repeated application of equation (10.11). For comparison with stochastic models it is more convenient to rewrite the equations (10.10) and (10.11) so as to give the values of the *multiplier*, $m(B_n, n, \pi) := B_{n+1}/B_n$, instead of the *difference* $\Delta B_n := B_{n+1} - B_n$. In the particular case of the parameter values in line 3 of table 11.2, the multiplier is given by

$$m = \begin{cases} 0.6228 + \dfrac{80}{B_n} & \text{if } 120 \leq B_n \\[2mm] 1.868 - \dfrac{69.46}{B_n} & \text{if } 37.18 \leq B_n < 120 \\[2mm] 0 & \text{if } B\hat{n} < 37.18 \end{cases} \tag{2}$$

and in general we have

$$m = \begin{cases} \left[1 - \tau + \dfrac{\tau W^* + A}{B_n} \right] e^{rT} & \text{if } W^* \leq B_n \\[2mm] \left[1 + \dfrac{A}{B_n} \right] e^{rT} & \text{if } -A \leq B_n < W^* \\[2mm] 0 & \text{if } B_n < -A \end{cases} \tag{3}$$

Table 11.2 *Parameter values for numerical examples*

	T	E^*	C^*	r	τ	W^*	P	g	N
Standard case π_0	25	10	12	$2\frac{1}{2}\%$	$66\frac{2}{3}\%$	120	60	—	—
(Tables 11.5–11.8)	25	10	12	$2\frac{1}{2}\%$	90%	120	60	2	0
(Tables 11.9, 11.11)	25	10	12	$2\frac{1}{2}\%$	90%	120	60	2	2
(Figure 11.6)	25	10	12	$2\frac{1}{2}\%$	90%	120	60	$2^{1/3}$	7
(Figure 11.6)	25	10	12	$2\frac{1}{2}\%$	$66\frac{2}{3}\%$	120	60	$2^{1/3}$	7
(Tables 11.12, 11.13)	25	10	12	$2\frac{1}{2}\%$	$66\frac{2}{3}\%$	120	60	$2^{1/5}$	25
(Tables 11.15, 11.16)	25	10	12	$2\frac{1}{2}\%$	60%	120	60	$2^{1/2}$	2
(Figure 11.9) π_1	25	10	12	$2\frac{1}{2}\%$	$66\frac{2}{3}\%$	120	60	$2^{1/3}$	25
(Figure 11.9) π_2	25	10	12.3	$2\frac{1}{2}\%$	80%	240	60	$2^{1/3}$	19

Note that the multiplier is a function of B_n, the pre-tax bequest left in generation n, and of the parameters of the system π.

Now let us take the idea of the bequest multiplier and develop it.

11.3 Mutt island: the stochastic version

To allow for the many other influences which may affect bequests, we introduce one or more random variables into the system's equations of motion. The determinist multiplier m in will be replaced by a *stochastic multiplier* $\mu(B_n, n, \pi)$. Like m, μ represents a ratio of B_{n+1} to B_n, but, unlike m, it may take any one of a set of values with associated prescribed probabilities. In this section we shall view the effects of such a stochastic multiplier under further simplifying assumptions, to be relaxed later in the chapter; appendix C reviews the general properties of models of this class.

Suppose that there is a finite number M of sizes, S_1 to S_M, which a bequest may have; suppose also that for any particular bequest size (S_4, for example) the next bequest in line can only have one of a particular triplet of values (a subset of the M sizes). The triplet which follows some other particular size (S_5 or S_{10} say) may of course be different from that which follows S_4: however, we suppose that the rules governing the triplets remain fixed generation after generation, so that for each size the three possible values for the next bequest in the line, together with their three probabilities, remain the same throughout the generations. Let us further simplify the problem by supposing that, for any bequest level S_i, the three available sizes for the next bequest in the line are the same size (S_i) and the sizes immediately above (S_{i+1}) and below (S_{i-1}) – see figure 11.1.[2]

As an illustration take a variant of the game of double or quits, where the generations are represented by the turns in the game. The player purchases an initial stake of one unit in the game and then there is a sequence of turns: in each turn a fair six-sided die is thrown and if the result is 5 or 6, the stake is doubled, subject to an upper limit of 8 units; otherwise the stake is halved, subject to a lower limit of 1 unit. How much on average may we expect the player's stake to be in the long run? In any turn the probabilities of increasing the stake from the levels 1, 2 and 4 are each $33\frac{1}{3}$ per cent and the probabilities of lowering the stake from the levels 2, 4 and 8 are each $66\frac{2}{3}$ per cent: in

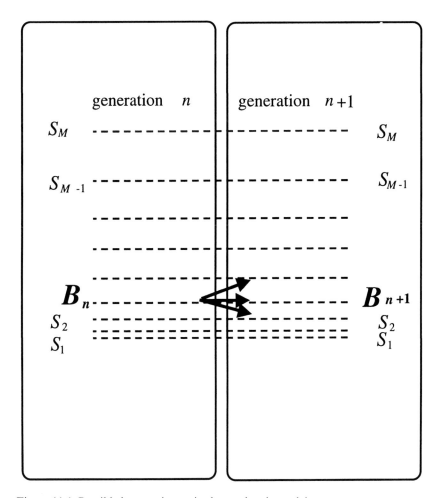

Figure 11.1 Possible bequest jumps in the stochastic model

equilibrium, the net movement between each pair of consecutive levels is zero. If there are many players, and if equilibrium proportions p_1, p_2, p_3 and p_4 of them hold stakes at the four levels, it follows that

$$p_1=2p_2,\ p_2=2p_3,\ p_3=2p_4 \tag{4}$$

Since the four proportions must add up to one we get

$$p_1=\frac{8}{15},\ p_2=\frac{4}{15},\ p_3=\frac{2}{15},\ p_4=\frac{1}{15} \tag{5}$$

So the average value of the stakes in equilibrium is $p_1+2p_2+4p_3+8p_4=32/15$. Assuming that the equilibrium proportions will be closely approached in a long series of turns by a large number of players using fair dice, the average value of their stakes will be close to the equilibrium level 32/15, the actuarially fair price for the stake of one unit.

Table 11.3 *Long-run equilibrium distribution of bequests*

Level of bequests	45,000¢	90,000¢	180,000¢	360,000¢
Number of bequests	100,000	400,000	500,000	100,000

Table 11.4 *Short-term development of bequest distribution*

	Bequest interval			
Generation	60,000¢ or less	60,000¢– 120,000¢	120,000¢– 240,000¢	Over 240,000¢
	Numbers of bequests			
0	500,000	600,000	0	0
1	220,000	580,000	300,000	0
2	160,000	470,000	416,000	54,000
3	126,000	435,000	458,320	80,280
4	112,280	414,748	482,446	90,526
5	105,406	407,227	491,475	95,893
	...	...	...	...
(Long run) ∞	100,000	400,000	500,000	100,000

The method used in this example will calculate the equilibrium frequency distribution of bequests in the long run whenever the movements are limited to one step up or down and the probabilities of each movement at any given bequest level remain constant. For example, suppose the four possible levels of bequest are (45,000¢, 60,000¢, 120,000¢, 240,000¢), that the probabilities of the next bequest in the line being one higher are (0.8, 0.5, 0.18, 0), the probabilities of it being one lower are (0, 0.2, 0.4, 0.9) and the probabilities of the next bequest being the same as at present are (0.2, 0.3, 0.42, 0.1): then, by the same argument as in the above example, the equilibrium proportions f_1, f_2, f_3 and f_4 at the four levels must satisfy the equation

$$8f_1 = 2f_2,\; 5f_2 = 4f_3,\; 18f_3 = 90f_4 \tag{6}$$

so that, since they must add up to one

$$f_1 = \frac{1}{11}, f_2 = \frac{4}{11}, f_3 = \frac{5}{11}, f_4 = \frac{1}{11} \tag{7}$$

So with 1.1 million lines of bequests, the equilibrium distribution would be as in table 11.3.

We have discussed probabilities of a discrete set of bequest levels, but the same method can be used for a discrete set of bequests *intervals*. For instance, the above example could be adjusted so that now the probabilities related to bequests in any four intervals such as (less than 60,000¢), (60,000¢ to 120,000¢), (120,000¢ to 240,000¢), (240,000¢ and over); we could calculate a table of the equilibrium distribution of bequests over the four intervals with the same lower line as that in table 11.3. We shall work with such distributions over bequest intervals throughout the remainder of the

Table 11.5 *Bequests in the determinist model*

bequest B_n (after-tax)	<60,000¢ 60,000¢	90,000¢ 90,000¢	180,000¢ 126,000¢	360,000¢ 144,000¢
B_{n+1}	42,635¢	98,682¢	165,939¢	199,567¢
Multiplier m	0.9474	1.0965	0.9219	0.5544
$p=(4/3)m-1$	0.2633	0.4620	0.2292	*

Note:
Unless otherwise stated bequests are before tax or subsidy; *means $(4/3)m-1$.

chapter, but we usually take more than four intervals and allow movement by more than one interval in each generation.

The same example illustrates the way any given initial distribution of bequests between intervals will approach the long-run equilibrium during the first few generations. Suppose the distribution over the four intervals is

$$\begin{bmatrix} 500,000 \\ 600,000 \\ 0 \\ 0 \end{bmatrix} \tag{8}$$

From (6) and (7) we can then find the distribution over the four intervals in generation 1

$$\begin{bmatrix} 0.2\times500,000+0.2\times600,000 \\ 0.8\times500,000+0.3\times600,000 \\ 0.5\times600,000 \\ 0 \end{bmatrix} = \begin{bmatrix} 220,000 \\ 580,000 \\ 300,000 \\ 0 \end{bmatrix} \tag{9}$$

Using the same methods the distribution of bequests in generation 2 is

$$\begin{bmatrix} 0.2\times220,000+0.2\times580,000 \\ 0.8\times220,000+0.3\times580,000+0.4\times300,000 \\ 0.5\times580,000+0.42\times300,000 \\ 0.18\times300,000 \end{bmatrix} = \begin{bmatrix} 160,000 \\ 470,000 \\ 416,000 \\ 54,000 \end{bmatrix} \tag{10}$$

and continuing in this way we can construct table 11.5, showing the approach to the long-run equilibrium of table 11.3. Notice that it is quite rapid in this simple model; in models with a finer interval structure (narrower intervals and more of them) and a larger number of possible values for the stochastic multiplier, we usually find that the approach is much slower.

In section 11.4 we introduce a 'logbinomial variate' in a simple form whereby – as in the models of this section – the stochastic multiplier has only three possible values, $1/g$, 1 and g, where g is a constant greater than one. As a preliminary to that, take a bequest model which introduces a small amount of stochastic variation into the previous determinist model: we use the standard parameter values (π_0), as shown in table 11.2, except that we set $\tau=90$ per cent and $g=2$.

Table 11.6 *Probabilities of values of the bequest multiplier* μ

Bequest level before tax or subsidy	(45,000¢) <60,000¢	90,000¢	180,000¢	360,000¢
Values of μ	Probability			
¼	0.0000	0.0000	0.0000	0.2609
½	0.3684	0.2690	0.3854	0.5000
1	0.5000	0.5000	0.5000	0.2391
2	0.1316	0.2310	0.1146	0.0000
Σ probabilities	1.0000	1.0000	1.0000	1.0000
m (mean value of μ)	0.9474	1.0965	0.9219	0.5544

From equation (1) we find that the upper equilibrium value for the bequest value before deduction of tax is 162,710¢ and the equilibrium value after tax is therefore 124,270¢. The lower equilibrium after subsidy is 60,000¢ (before subsidy it would have been $[80,000 - 20,000e^{0.625}]¢=42,635¢$). Given a set of bequests such as the four values shown in table 11.5 (values before tax or subsidy in the top row, after tax in the second row), the method of section 11.2 can be used to find values of the next bequest in line and the value of the multiplier in each of these four cases: rows 3 and 4 of table 11.5. For the corresponding stochastic model we need four stochastic multipliers μ, each satisfying

$$\mathscr{E}(\mu)=m \tag{11}$$

where m is the corresponding value of each deterministic multiplier in each of the four columns of table 11.5. In each case we try to do this, allowing the multiplier μ to take the three values ½, 1 and 2 with non-negative probabilities summing to one, and with the second of them (i.e., the probability that $\mu=1$) being ½. The solution is in each case the triplet $\frac{1}{2}[1-p]$, ½ and $\frac{1}{2}p$ where $p=(4/3)m-1$, where $0\le p\le 1$. However, we allow exceptions in the first and last columns: in the first column we may if necessary allow $\mu=1, 2$ with probabilities $1-p$ and p and in the last column $\mu=$ ¼, ½ and 1 with probabilities $\frac{1}{2}[1-p]$, ½ and $\frac{1}{2}p$. In this example we need to do this for the last column: the value of m must then be $(8/3)m-1=0.4783$. The probabilities of values of μ can now be written out as in table 11.6.

The information in table 11.6 is sufficient to determine the equilibrium distribution between the four specified values of the bequest levels. Write the proportions of bequests taking the four values as f_1 to f_4. To find the equilibrium ratio of f_2 to f_1 write down the condition that the number of bequests moving out of the bottom class (those less than 60,000¢) must equal the number moving in, thus

$$0.1316 f_1=0.2690 f_2 \tag{12}$$

Likewise the condition that the inflow to the top class (360,000¢) must equal the outflow

$$0.1146 f_3=(0.5000+0.2609) f_4 \tag{13}$$

By the same method we obtain a third equation, namely

$$0.2310 f_2=">0.3854 f_3+0.2609 f_4 \tag{14}$$

Table 11.7 *Equilibrium distribution of 1,000,000 bequests*

Level of bequests	<60,000¢	90,000¢	180,000¢	360,000¢
Number of bequests	556,949	272,515	148,214	22,322

expressing the condition that the numbers of bequests crossing the boundary between 90,000¢ and 180,000¢ are the same going up and going down. From (12)–(14):

$$f_3 = 6.6398 f_4$$
$$f_2 = 12.2085 f_4 \qquad\qquad (15)$$
$$f_1 = 24.9509 f_4$$

If there were, say, a total of one million bequests, then – from (15) and the condition that the four numbers f_1 to f_4 must sum to 1 – the equilibrium numbers in each class will be as set out in table 11.7.

Finally, note that the level of 90 per cent chosen for τ kept the solution simple by limiting the number of levels which could be occupied to just four. If we lower τ to $66\frac{2}{3}$ per cent we still get a simple solution but with more than four bequest levels,[3] but if we lower τ further to 50 per cent, we find that there is no limit to the mean level of bequest and no equilibrium is approachable.

To summarise: the stochastic multipliers $\mu(B_n, n, \pi)$ are powerful tools for describing the development of the distribution of wealth over time. They differ from the multipliers $m(B_n, n, \pi)$ used for the deterministic model in two important ways:
- there is a set of 'rules of the game' describing the probabilities of jumping from one wealth position to another, given one's present position;
- the set of values of B_n to which they can be applied is finite: the collection of sizes $\{S_1, \ldots, S_M\}$.

We now turn to an important development of this technique.

11.4 Introducing the logbinomial variate

Take another look at table 11.6 which gives the probabilities of movements between bequest levels from one generation to the next, and consider how these could represent the rules of a simple game of chance involving the movement of counters. Table 11.8 sets this information out in a more general form and can be used for a wide class of other models by choosing different values for the parameters p_1 to p_4.

Imagine a game in which players are provided with the following equipment: a counter and a board with four adjacent columns numbered 1–4 (from left to right), and four packs, also numbered 1–4, each containing large numbers of black and red cards only, the proportions of red cards being respectively p_1, p_2, p_3, p_4. The game starts with a counter placed in any of columns 1–3, and consists of a series of turns, each of which may move the counter into another column. A turn consists of two steps: (1) spin a fair coin and (2) draw a card from the large pack numbered the same as the column at present containing the counter. These steps jointly determine the movement of the counter in that turn as follows:

Table 11.8 *Probabilities of* μ *values: a generalisation of table 11.6*

Bequest level *j*:	1	2	3	4
Move 2 to left	0	0	0	$\frac{1}{2}-p_4$
Move 1 to left	$\frac{1}{2}-p_1$	$\frac{1}{2}-p_2$	$\frac{1}{2}-p_3$	$\frac{1}{2}$
Stay put	$\frac{1}{2}$	$\frac{1}{2}$	$\frac{1}{2}$	$\frac{1}{2}-p_4$
Move 1 to right	p_1	p_2	p_3	0
Values of p_j	0.1316	0.2310	0.1146	0.2391

Table 11.9 *Values of* m *and* p *in model based on game 2*

	(45,000¢)			
Pre-tax bequest	<60,000¢	90,000¢	180,000¢	360,000¢
(after-tax)	60,000¢	90,000¢	126,000¢	144,000¢
m	0.9474	1.0965	0.9219	0.5544
$p=(8/9)m-1$	**	**	**	0.9710
$p=(16/9)m-1$	0.6844	0.9493	0.6389	*
$p=(32/9)m-1$	*	*	*	*

Notes:
(1) 'Pre-tax' means before tax or subsidy.
(2) Values of *m* are taken from table 11.5.
(3) * denotes cases where the computed *p* would be negative, and ** where it would be greater than 1.

heads and a red card: move counter one to the right (unless it is already in column 4 and so does not move)
tails and a black card: move counter one to left (unless it is already in column 1 and so does not move, or is in column 4 in which case it moves to column 2)
heads-and-black or *tails-and-red*: the counter stays put unless in column 4 in which case it moves one to the left.

The probabilities of moving the counter in this game will coincide exactly with the probabilities of the movements between the four possible levels of bequest in successive generations for any line of bequests in the model discussed above. The reason that this game has been so painstakingly described is that it is merely the most elementary version of a whole sequence of such games: the main change in the rules being that in each turn the coin has to be spun some other specific number of times. Refer to the game already described as game 1 and number each other game in the sequence by *N*, the number of times the coin has to be tossed in each turn of that game, and we will use the term 'logbinomial' to describe variates whose probability distributions are established by the rules for any game of this type.

Game 2 is sufficiently adaptable to illustrate the wide range of types of bequest distributions which may develop out of different sets of circumstances as represented

Table 11.10 *Probabilities of values of bequest multiplier* **μ**

Bequest B_n	<60,000¢	90,000¢	180,000¢	360,000¢
Level of **μ**	Probability			
$\frac{1}{8}$	0.0000	0.0000	0.0000	0.0072
$\frac{1}{4}$	0.0789	0.0127	0.0903	0.2572
$\frac{1}{2}$	0.3289	0.2627	0.3403	0.4928
1	0.4211	0.4873	0.4097	0.2427
2	0.1711	0.2373	0.1597	0.0000
Σ probs	1.0000	1.0000	1.0000	1.0000
m (mean of **μ**)	0.9475	1.0965	0.9219	0.5544

by the values of the parameters. It also illustrates the wider choice of which set of four consecutive columns to make available for entry from a given column. As an illustration let us use game 2 to build a stochastic version of the same determinist model which formed the basis of our experiment with game 1 on page 259: this comprises the drawing of a card and *two* spins of a coin ($N=2$) instead of one. In each turn there will now be four consecutive columns available for the counter to enter from any one column instead of the three in game 1. Counting one for each head thrown and for drawing a red card (zero otherwise) the possible scores are 0, 1, 2 and 3; these values dictate which of the four columns the counter is to move to (0 indicates the left and 3 indicates the right). If p_j is the proportion of red cards in the pack for column j then the probabilities of each of the four scores are $\frac{1}{4}[1-p_j]$, $\frac{1}{4}p_j+\frac{1}{2}[1-p_j]$, $\frac{1}{2}p_j+\frac{1}{4}[1-p_j]$ and $\frac{1}{4}p_j$, which simplifies to $\frac{1}{4}[1-p_j]$, $\frac{1}{4}[2-p_j]$, $\frac{1}{4}[1+p_j]$ and $\frac{1}{4}p_j$.

In setting up the corresponding stochastic model of the inheritance of bequests, let us start by trying the four possible movements in each generation: two to the left, one to the left, no move and one to the right. The relation between p and m will now have to be different if (11) is still to hold. Remembering that the four scores 0, 1, 2, and 3 involve multiplier values $\frac{1}{4}$, $\frac{1}{2}$, 1 and 2, we may recalculate the mean value of the stochastic multiplier **μ**

$$\mathscr{E}(\boldsymbol{\mu})=\frac{[1-p]+2[2-p]+4[1+p]+8p}{16}=\frac{9[1+p]}{16} \tag{16}$$

so that to satisfy (11) we must put $p=(4/3)^2m-1$ in place of the formula $p=(4/3)m-1$ used in table 11.5. This yields table 11.9.

As we have noted above, the normal rule is that there are four permitted shifts, 'two left', 'one left', 'stay put' and 'one right' and this led to the formula $p=(16/9)m-1$: however, in the right-hand column, this would result in a negative value for p. To avoid this we permit the four shifts 'three left', 'two left', 'one left' and 'stay put' from this column, which requires the formula $p = (32/9)m-1$. The probabilities of the various values of **μ** can now be written out as in table 11.10 – compare this with table 11.6. We obtain the equilibrium conditions from table 11.10 by the same methods as used in the earlier example for finding them from table 11.6. They are[4]

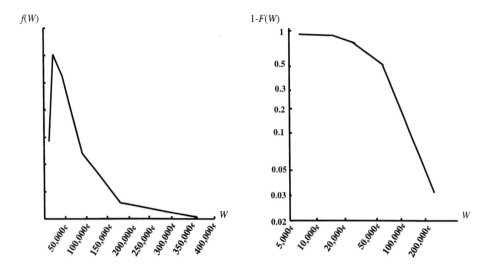

Figure 11.2 Equilibrium bequests in the elementary stochastic model: the frequency distribution and the Pareto diagram

$$\left.\begin{array}{rl}f_3 & = 4.7408f_4, \\ f_2 & = 9.7153f_4, \\ f_1 & = 18.1803f_4, \\ \dfrac{f_4}{f_1+f_2+f_3+f_4} & = 0.0297\end{array}\right\} \tag{17}$$

So, if there were to be a million bequests in total then, according to this model, they would be distributed as follows

$$\left.\begin{array}{llll}\text{at} & 360: & f_4= & 29{,}730 \\ \text{at} & 180: & f_3= & 140{,}944 \\ \text{at} & 90: & f_2= & 288{,}833 \\ \text{Total} >60 & & f_2+f_3+f_4= & 459{,}507 \\ \text{Total} <60 & f_1=1{,}000{,}000-f_2-f_3-f_4= & 540{,}493 \\ \text{at} & 11.25: & q_1= \quad 0.078913f_1= & 42{,}652 \\ \text{at} & 22.5: & q_2=0.328913f_1+0.012679f_2=181{,}437 \\ \text{at} & 45: & q_3= \quad f_1-q_1-q_2= & 316{,}404\end{array}\right\} \tag{18}$$

Given the interval means we could use equation (18) to calculate the values of bequests in each of the six intervals, and then set out the equilibrium distribution of bequests. Taking the interval midpoints as estimates of their means the results are as shown in figure 11.2: even though this is a very simple version of the stochastic model, it produces a distribution of wealth and of income that is similar to to the real-world distributions.

In the rest of this chapter we develop models of wealth and income distributions using stochastic multipliers of the logbinomial type. We do this in the following five steps:

• First we rectify some of the deficiences of the simple version displayed in figure

11.2. For example in models with intervals whose upper boundary is at twice the level of the lower, the divergence of their means from their centres may be large: for more reliable estimates we work with narrower intervals of bequests, adjusting other parameters where necessary. We shall also find it important to work with stochastic multipliers which have more than four values. This is done in section 11.5.

- In section 11.5 we also examine the sensitivity of the equilibrium distributions to changes in the key components of the parameter list π. For example we ask whether a higher tax rate on bequests really will lead to lower inequality in the long run.
- We examine the short-run behaviour of the logbinomial model out of equilibrium (section 11.6).
- We extend the logbinomial idea to encompass bivariate distributions and the endogenous determination of consumption and earnings for individual Mutts in the distribution (section 11.7).

11.5 A million Mutts in equilibrium

The next step is to examine the equilibrium bequest distributions obtainable from the stochastic model using a variety of parameter values; this step transforms the toy exercise of section 11.4 into one that conforms more closely to the type of income and wealth distributions that can be observed in the real world. This will also allow us to look at a number of variants on the model that incorporate different assumptions about the mesh of income intervals, or different assumptions about fundamental economic parameters such as the tax rate, the exemption level or the rate of return on capital.

We take a Mutt population of one million, but we group bequests into a finer mesh (a larger number of narrower intervals), so that the stochastic multiplier μ takes a larger number of values set closer together. Doing this reveals more about the equilibrium, and is more helpful in examining the sensitivity of the distributions to parameter changes. We can also relax some of the more extreme assumptions – such as exogenously fixed consumption and the high rate of taxation – without introducing excessive inequality into the equilibrium distribution or making the analysis too complex. As a first step let us keep the wide income intervals ($g=2$) and just make N larger (from 2 to 7) while decreasing τ from 90 per cent to 66⅔ per cent. The resulting equilibrium distributions (see figure 11.3) suggest that the combined effect of this change would be to increase inequality. We can say more: figure 11.4 shows the effect of lowering the wealth tax τ from 90 per cent to 66⅔ per cent in the two subcases of the logbinomial model ($N=2$ and $N=7$) treated separately. The conjecture that the cut in τ will increase equilibrium inequality is confirmed. For example, in game 7 with $\tau=90$ per cent the bottom 20 per cent of bequests constitute over 2.4 per cent of the total value, but when $\tau=66⅔$ per cent, the bottom 20 per cent accounts for only 1.73 per cent of total value: lowering the tax increases the inequality of the equilibrium distribution at the lower end. Likewise at the top of the distribution: when $\tau=66⅔$ per cent the top 2 per cent of bequests contain over 26 per cent of the value, but when $\tau=90$ per cent even the top 2 per cent of the bequests only contain 16.3 per cent of the total value of bequests. Notice that increasing N while keeping g constant also increases inequality.

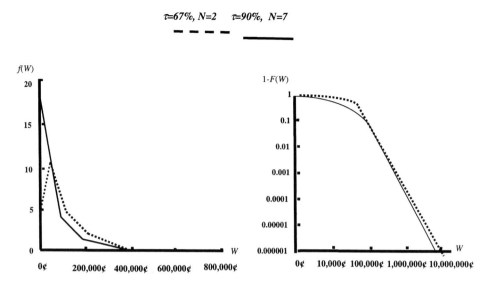

Figure 11.3 Equilibrium wealth distribution: two cases where $g=2$

Figure 11.5 shows the equilibrium distributions when the interval width g is reduced from 2 to $2^{1/3}$. This means that we have a finer mesh of wealth intervals: three of the new intervals fit into one of the intervals in the previous model illustrated in figure 11.3.[5] Again we find that lowering the tax increases inequality throughout the distribution – as in figure 11.4 – although the effect at the top of the distribution is less pronounced.

But how does the finer mesh version model compare with the original simulations? In principle there is a large number of comparisons that could be made between this case ($g=2^{1/3},N=7$) and the earlier models, but a comparison of the Lorenz curves in figure 11.6 with figure 11.4 suggests – correctly – that all of these can be ordered simply in terms of inequality.[6]

These comparisons illustrate the advantage of using a fine interval mesh in estimating the equilibrium distribution, and suggest that it may be desirable to experiment with the fineness structure to discover the impact on the equilibrium distribution. Figure 11.6 and table 11.11 report such a fineness experiment on the the logbinomial model, with (g,N) pairs given by (2,2), ($2^{1/2}$,5), ($2^{1/3}$,11), ($2^{1/4}$,15) and ($2^{1/5}$,25) (the tax rate is $\tau=66\frac{2}{3}$ per cent and the values of all other parameters are the same as in the last example). The results confirm that the finer interval mesh results in a less unequal distribution: in the implementation of a stochastic model of income and wealth distribution the choice of a discrete approximation to the underlying continuous distributional process is an important matter. One of the reasons for this phenomenon lies in the simplified consumption behaviour within our model.

Experimentation with the (g,N) parameters might be regarded as primarily a technical matter of special interest to model builders. Not so with the other model parameters. It is of particular interest to see how this type of stochastic model responds to variations in the values of parameters corresponding to public policy

Table 11.11 *Shares in the bequest distribution of top 10 per cent and bottom 20 per cent*

g	2	$2^{1/2}$	$2^{1/3}$	$2^{1/4}$	$2^{1/5}$
N	2	5	11	15	25
Before tax/subsidy					
Share of top 10%	37.4	33.4	32.3	29.8	30.4
Share of bottom 20%	3.79	5.04	2.11	5.07	5.09
After tax/subsidy					
Share of top 10%	22.6	21.1	22.1	19.6	20.0
Share of bottom 20%	11.8	12.5	12.1	12.0	12.0

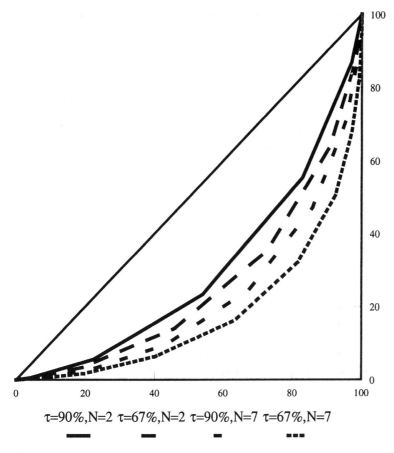

τ=90%,N=2   τ=67%,N=2   τ=90%,N=7   τ=67%,N=7

Figure 11.4 Inequality before and after tax cut: two values of *N*

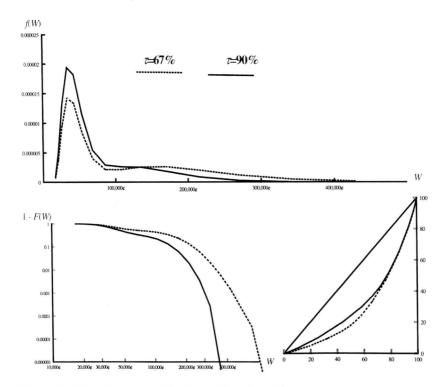

Figure 11.5 Equilibrium distributions with different fineness parameter *g*

instruments. Taking the (*g*=2$^{1/5}$,*N*=25,*τ*=66⅔ per cent) model as a reference case we compute the long-run (equilibrium) effect of the following:

- raising the tax rate *τ* from 66⅔ per cent to 75 per cent;
- lowering *P* (the level to which all lower bequests are subsidised) by one interval from 60,000¢ to 52,233¢;
- lowering the tax threshold *W** from 120,000¢ to 100,000¢;
- raising the return on assets *r* from 2½ per cent to 3 per cent.

Figure 11.7 shows the impact of these one-by-one changes upon the equilibrium bequest distributions. The long-run effect of increasing the bequest tax from 66⅔ per cent to 75 per cent would be to cut high bequests drastically (those over 960,000¢ would drop from 155 to 4 per million), and at the other end of the scale the number of bequests falling below the poverty level 60,000¢ increases from about 46 per cent to about 52 per cent. Similar (but smaller) effects would have resulted from lowering the wealth tax threshold from 120,000¢ to 100,000¢.

In contrast to these two revenue-raising measures which soak the rich, the third measure is at the expense of the poor by lowering the poverty threshold *P* from 60,000¢ to 52,233¢. This reduction of only 13 per cent in the subsidy threshold has devastating long-run effects on the poor but – because of the mobility implicit in the stochastic model – to some extent it also damages the rich in the equilibrium distribution. On the other hand, raising the rate of return on assets (from 2½ per cent to 3 per cent per

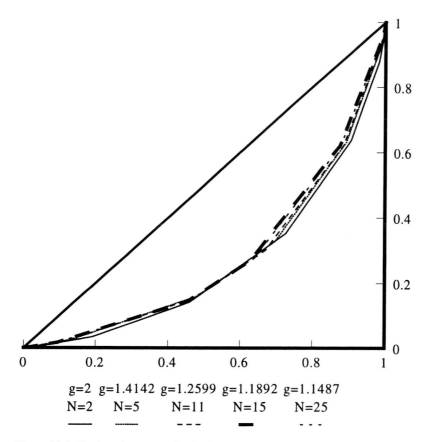

g=2 g=1.4142 g=1.2599 g=1.1892 g=1.1487
N=2   N=5   N=11   N=15   N=25
―――   ·········   ― ― ―   ▬▬   · · ·

Figure 11.6 Cutting the tax rate in the finer-mesh model

annum) enriches the poor as well as the rich, since all those with bequests start out with property income of at least rP. This lowers the proportion in poverty from 46.5 per cent to 1.5 per cent and the proportion with bequests over 480,000¢ before tax (or 240,000¢ after tax) rises to 13 per cent from less than 1 per cent, which indicates a typically very high sensitivity of the long-run equilibrium distribution to changes in r.

For an overview of the policy changes examine the impact on measured inequality in table 11.12: columns 1–4 give the values of the standard measures (introduced in chapters 4 and 5); columns 6 and 7 those of a pragmatic index γ, the proportion of bequests which exceed the poverty threshold, and of α, the Pareto coefficient (although Pareto's α has some shortcomings in general comparisons of economic inequality, it does have advantages when we are concerned with distributions of bequests of wealth, since the Pareto index focuses on large bequests or fortunes). Notice that, although the various inequality indexes agree fairly well on the direction and relative magnitude of the effects of the eight policy changes, there are some notable exceptions, as we can see from table 11.13 which gives the rank order by inequality of the nine distributions in table 11.12.

The three Atkinson indices agree closely in the ways in which they rank the inequalities of the nine distributions. But Pareto's α ranks the high τ as the strongest

Table 11.12 *Effects of policy changes on inequality indexes*

	κ	$A_{1/2}$	A_1	A_2	γ	α
τ=60%	0.9062	0.1481	0.2689	0.4260	61.09	6.0
τ=67%	0.8057	0.1178	0.2126	0.3377	53.64	9.2
τ=75%	0.7205	0.0929	0.1669	0.2658	47.57	15.5
P=52,530¢	0.6863	0.0448	0.0706	0.0959	7.52	9.2
P=60,000¢	0.8057	0.1178	0.2126	0.3377	53.64	9.2
P=68,920¢	0.6149	0.0807	0.1552	0.2800	82.39	9.2
W*=100,000¢	0.6410	0.0630	0.1099	0.1704	36.25	9.2
W*=120,000¢	0.8057	0.1178	0.2126	0.3377	53.64	9.2
W*=150,000¢	0.6819	0.1128	0.2277	0.4304	80.96	9.2
r=2%	0.2520	0.0079	0.0133	0.0200	6.21	11.9
r=2½%	0.8057	0.1178	0.2126	0.3377	53.64	9.2
r=3%	0.5646	0.0672	0.1314	0.2548	98.48	6.8

Table 11.13 *Rank order of inequality in table 11.12*

	κ	$A_{1/2}$	A_1	A_2	γ	α
Distribution with...						
Low τ (60%)	1	1	1	2	4	1
High W* (150)	5	2	3	1	3	7
Standard values	**2**	**3**	**2**	**3**	**5**	**6**
High τ (75%)	3	4	4	5	6	9
High P	7	5	5	4	2	8
High r (3%)	8	6	6	6	1	3
Low W* (100)	6	7	7	7	7	5
Low P	4	8	8	8	8	2
Low r (2%)	9	9	9	9	9	4

egalitarian policy, whereas all other indices suggest that the strongest measure is to lower the rate of return r. The effect of lowering the poverty level is ranked as highly inegalitarian by the Pareto coefficient and only weakly egalitarian (compared to the standard policy) by the coefficient of variation whereas all the other three indices rank it as the second most egalitarian measure. The index γ is not a reliable criterion of high inequality. The high values given for Pareto's α in table 11.12 indicate a very low level of inequality compared with what would be found for the distributions of bequests tabulated in publications describing actual wealth distributions. The explanation of the high values of α found in our modelled distributions is that we deliberately assumed high levels of taxation so as to ensure that almost all the bequests would be included in a small number of intervals.

In our models α is – as seems reasonable – sensitive to the level of the tax rate on bequests τ and the rate of return on wealth r. The impact of varying the tax rate in the

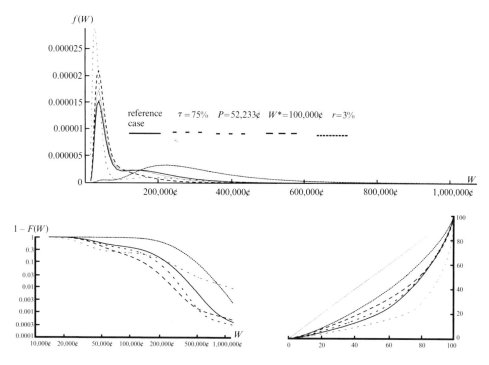

Figure 11.7 Sensitivity to parameters

fine-mesh model (where $g=2^{1/5}$, $N=25$) is illustrated in figure 11.8: as τ falls from 55 per cent to 50 per cent α falls from about 3.12 to 2.36; if τ falls as far as 47.5 per cent then Pareto's α falls to 1.88. As with the models of chapter 10 the simple message is that tax cuts drive long-run inequality, in this case because of the progressive cumulation of wealth through the increased spread of the bequest multiplier.

11.6 Short-run dynamics

Let us see how the logbinomial model will adjust from an arbitrary initial distribution to the theoretical equilibrium distribution and examine the changes of the distribution to be expected in the short term. Iterating the bequest model to calculate the short-run dynamics is actually easier than finding the equilibrium distribution directly.

Take as an example the story depicted in figure 11.8 (top and bottom left panels). The initial distribution (the curve labelled generation 0) is an equilibrium relative to the parameter values π_2, given in table 11.2 on page 254. Suppose the parameter values are suddenly shifted to those of π_1: the other curves in figure 11.9 show the approach over three generations towards the new equilibrium distribution relative to π_1: to translate this into a real-time process remember that a generation of 25 years has to elapse between each bequest and the next in the same line. The essential differences between the two parameter systems are that π_2 has a more progressive tax and a higher consumption rate than π_1, and that the spread of the bequest multiplier in π_2 ($N=19$)

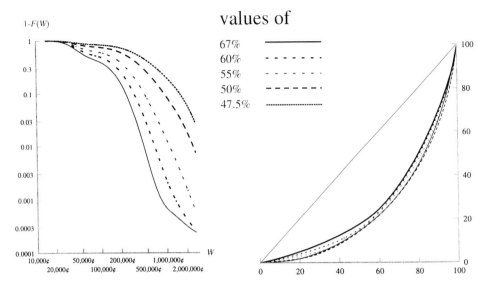

Figure 11.8 The tax-rate experiment

is narrower than in π_1 ($N=25$). One of the consequences of these different values are that the π_1 equilibrium is single peaked, but the π_2 equilibrium (the starting point) is bimodal: apart from the principal mode in distribution 0 in the top part of figure 11.9 the relatively high values of W^* and C^* produce a secondary mode near 300,000¢.

We can see that the bimodality is smoothed out by the π_1 process after only one generation; after two generations three quarters or more of the transition to the equilibrium number of bequests has been achieved in most intervals (see table 11.14): this is largely due to the extensive spread of the stochastic multiplier ($N=25$) in the π_1 process. This can be confirmed by running the exercise in the opposite direction: starting generation 0 at parameter values π_1 and applying the π_2 process. The path of the reverse process to the π_2 equilibrium – depicted in the bottom right-hand panel of figure 11.9 and the right half of table 11.14 – reveals that the reduced spread of the bequest multiplier ($N=19$) slows the adjustment process a lot: the discrepancies between the generation 3 densities and the equilibrium densities in the π_2 process are about twice as large as the corresponding discrepancies in the π_1 process. This suggests that it is likely to take about twice as long for equilibrium to be reached, within a specified level of accuracy, in the latter exercise as in the former. Calculations over 300 and more generations confirm this expectation – see table C.3 in appendix C.

The spread of the stochastic multiplier, captured in the parameter N, is crucial to the out-of-equilibrium behaviour of stochastic income and wealth distribution models. In our version of the logbinomial model a restricted spread of the multiplier makes it unlikely that a high proportion of those with bequests below P in any one generation will make bequests well above P. If the stochastic process is closer to that represented by π_2 rather than by π_1 then, as we have just seen, the approach to equilibrium is likely to be very slow.

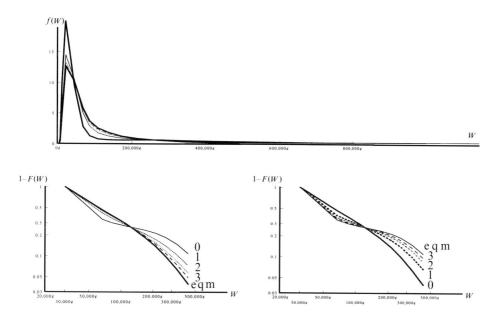

Figure 11.9 Short-run dynamics

11.7 Extending the basic model

The idea behind the elementary logbinomial model can readily be extended to richer specifications. Some of these can be obtained from the basic model by modification of the values or interpretation of the parameters, some by generalising the stochastic process.

For example the basic story ignored taxes on property income and of the responsiveness of the expenditure of households to current income. It is straightforward to adjust the model parameters to allow for an income tax at constant marginal rate and a constant marginal propensity to consume. For example suppose income tax is charged at a marginal rate τ' on incomes above normal earnings E^*. Then income taxes are

$$\tau'[y-E^*] \tag{19}$$

where

$$y=E+rW \tag{20}$$

If individuals consume a constant proportion σ of disposable income in excess of E^* then total consumption is

$$[1-\tau']\sigma[y-E^*]+C^* \tag{21}$$

Table 11.14 *Frequency density of bequest distribution in each generation: detail of figure 11.9*

Wealth values	Generations in π_1-process					Generations in π_2-process				
	0	1	1	2	equi.	0	1	1	2	equi.
67,500¢	2.7565	5.0303	5.5000	5.6681	5.8171	5.8171	3.8345	3.2295	2.9823	2.7565
85,000¢	1.2600	2.8168	3.3333	3.5371	3.7057	3.7057	2.2908	1.7419	1.4974	1.2600
107,500¢	0.7431	1.7353	2.1894	2.3808	2.5367	2.5367	1.6190	1.1767	0.9628	0.7431
135,000¢	0.6247	1.2446	1.5767	1.7255	1.8467	1.8467	1.2981	0.9783	0.8095	0.6247
170,000¢	0.5780	0.8952	1.0634	1.1447	1.2108	1.2108	0.9698	0.7987	0.6979	0.5780
215,000¢	0.5921	0.7099	0.7637	0.7948	0.8190	0.8190	0.7673	0.7031	0.6564	0.5921
270,000¢	0.5954	0.5661	0.5491	0.5472	0.5430	0.5430	0.6078	0.6178	0.6128	0.5954
340,000¢	0.4833	0.3787	0.3344	0.3176	0.3003	0.3003	0.4038	0.4494	0.4688	0.4833
430,000¢	0.3658	0.2485	0.2028	0.1835	0.1636	0.1636	0.2593	0.3113	0.3382	0.3658

The effects of the income taxation and the marginal expenditure on the long-run equilibrium distribution of wealth are equivalent to reducing the annual rate of interest from its level R to the level r given by

$$r=[1-\tau'][1-\sigma]R \qquad (22)$$

So we need only reduce the parameter r to accommodate the reduced propensity to accumulate wealth in this type of model. Suppose, for example, that all property income is taxed at a rate of $33\frac{1}{3}$ per cent and that those with property income spend one half of their after-tax income on consumption. As a result there will be left only a third (i.e., half the value net of tax) of the gross yield for accumulating wealth. So if the gross yield R were $7\frac{1}{2}$ per cent, then the effective yield for the equilibrium distribution of bequests r would be $2\frac{1}{2}$ per cent.

Another complication that can be similarly dealt with by modification of the basic model is the possibility – highlighted in chapters 8 and 9 – that the wealthy may provide human capital for their dependants by investing in training and education for them to enhance their earnings prospects, and that this investment is sometimes encouraged by taxation policy. Suppose that people are allowed to set up trust funds for the benefit of their heirs which are exempt from wealth tax. The effect of this depends on how much advantage is taken of this opportunity: assume that each owner of wealth beyond the exemption limit W^* puts a fixed proportion of his subsequent flow of savings into such a trust fund. Then, if $\hat{\tau}$ is the nominal marginal rate of tax on wealth (including the fund) above W^*, the effective marginal tax rate is $\tau=[1-\lambda]\hat{\tau}$: the equilibrium distribution of total wealth (including the fund) can be calculated by using the effective tax rate. Also assume that investment in the fund provides the heir with an increase in earnings over his lifetime just equal to the income he could have expected from the fund had it been used solely for investments but had not been taxed; given that earnings remain fixed throughout the life span we may then calculate the earnings level obtainable from any given size of fund. This means that full earnings are given as

$$E=E^*+\lambda\,\frac{B-W^*}{1-e^{-rT}} \qquad (23)$$

over the T years of his remaining working life. Note that the additional earnings have present discounted value $\lambda[B-W^*]$.

To illustrate the discussion take the elementary case $N=2$ and set a high nominal rate of tax $\hat{\tau}=90$ per cent in order to keep the number of intervals low, and to make the equilibrium distribution compact. As in earlier examples set basic earnings and consumption at $E^*=10$; $C^*=12$; the poverty level at $P=60$; the interval width at $g=2^{1/2}$, and the exemption limit at $W^*=120$ and the effective rate of interest as usual at the low level $2\frac{1}{2}$ per cent per annum. Take $\lambda=33\frac{1}{3}$ per cent so that, if total wealth exceeds W^*, a third of further savings are put into the trust fund: the effective rate of tax τ is 60 per cent. (These were the levels which resulted from the assumptions that $\hat{\tau}=90$ per cent and $\tau'=33\frac{1}{3}$ per cent and that half of the income after tax in excess of 10,000¢ was spent on consumption in excess of 12,000¢.) To avoid introducing too many complications at once, suppose $\tau'=0$ (no income tax).

We can then calculate the equilibrium distribution of bequests by our usual methods, and from this the distribution of property income at retirement age (for each person it is $2\frac{1}{2}$ per cent of the value of his bequest). From this we can deduce the corresponding equilibrium distribution of earnings, and construct table 11.15 showing the bivariate distribution of property income and labour earnings; table 11.16 gives the corresponding means and coefficient of variation for property income, earnings and total incomes in this bivariate distribution and the correlation coefficient for the two income components.

Appendix C (page 000) uses another simpler example to explain how tables like these are derived; they require the assumption that the earnings which have been augmented by the fund are held constant over the working life of the heir, and also that these are immune from stochastic disturbances, all of which are assumed to be inflicted upon wealth (and so upon income derived from it). This unrealistic assumption largely accounts for the low variance of earnings and the very high correlation between property income and earnings in table 11.16. Common sense suggests that, by concentrating the stochastic disturbances more on earnings instead of all on property income, we would find high variance of earnings, low variance of property income and high correlation of incomes and earnings.

Generalisation of the story to incorporate this sort of stochastic process would be difficult to model and present lucidly in sufficient detail; it certainly goes beyond the technique of reinterpreting the basic parameters of the logbinomial model that we have been able to employ thus far. However, the basic methodology of deriving equilibrium distributions and computing short-run changes in distributions in the univariate logbinomial model can indeed be applied to multivariate distribution models. This extension of the basic approach could be used to model the joint distribution of wealth and income, or of earnings and property income, though we should warn that computational complexity increases rapidly with the number of variables used. To show what may be done let us use a simplified arithmetical example. To make it compact, we work with a discrete bivariate model whose stochastic variates $\mathbf{u}:=(u_1,u_2)$ are restricted to only three and six values respectively (for example three wealth levels and six income levels).

Suppose that initially there is a population of 960,000 with the bivariate distribution given by the following array

$$\begin{bmatrix} 24{,}000 & 40{,}000 & 80{,}000 & 80{,}000 & 0 & 0 \\ 0 & 96{,}000 & 160{,}000 & 160{,}000 & 96{,}000 & 0 \\ 0 & 0 & 80{,}000 & 80{,}000 & 40{,}000 & 24{,}000 \end{bmatrix} \tag{24}$$

for example there are 96,000 persons with $\mathbf{u}=(2,5)$. Let the transition probabilities of moving from the 12 non-zero cells of to each of the 18 cells in one generation be those shown in table 11.17: applying these probabilities to the data in we can calculate the bivariate distribution of $\mathbf{u}$ one generation later; working this out for each cell we obtain[7]

$$\begin{bmatrix} 26{,}667 & 83{,}333 & 100{,}666 & 34{,}667 & 0 & 0 \\ 0 & 58{,}667 & 176{,}000 & 176{,}000 & 58{,}667 & 0 \\ 0 & 0 & 34{,}667 & 100{,}666 & 83{,}333 & 26{,}667 \end{bmatrix} \tag{25}$$

By repeating this method we could obtain the dynamic approach to equilibrium of the bivariate distribution. The equilibrium distribution may be found by methods similar to those used in the univariate models earlier and is[8]

$$\begin{bmatrix} 30{,}000 & 90{,}000 & 90{,}000 & 30{,}000 & 0 & 0 \\ 0 & 60{,}000 & 180{,}000 & 180{,}000 & 60{,}000 & 0 \\ 0 & 0 & 30{,}000 & 90{,}000 & 90{,}000 & 30{,}000 \end{bmatrix} \tag{26}$$

Table 11.15 *Equilibrium distribution of earnings and property income at retirement age*

Property income	Labour income												Total
	10,000¢	10,000¢	10,000¢	10,446¢	11,521¢	13,043¢	15,195¢	18,288¢	22,541¢	28,627¢	37,234¢	49,407¢	
640¢	39,944												39,944
905¢	100,875	4,673											105,548
1,280¢	81,919	16,316											98,235
1,811¢	20,989	18,612	6,970										46,571
2,561¢		6,970	18,110	19,481									44,561
3,621¢			15,311	51,373	51,366	9,515							127,564
5,121¢			4,170	44,301	107,257	58,616	9,213						223,557
7,243¢				12,410	60,411	88,687	31,588	3,308					196,404
10,243¢					4,522	39,586	35,538	9,154	701				89,501
14,485¢							13,163	8,384	1,739	99			23,385
20,485¢								2,538	1,376	229	10		4,153
28,971¢									338	163	22	1	524
40,971¢										33	14	2	49
57,941¢											3	1	4
Total	243,727	46,571	44,561	127,565	223,556	196,404	89,502	23,384	4,154	524	49	4	1,000,000

Table 11.16 *The principal statistics for the bivariate distribution (see table 11.15)*

	Earnings	Property income	Total income
	E	rW	y
Mean	11,717¢	4,833¢	16,549¢
Coeff. of var.	0.1773	0.7099	0.3191
Correlation coefficient $\rho(E,rW)$: 0.8280			

large numbers of possible values for each variate, or a large number of variates of the equilibrium – and even of short-term dynamics – the method becomes tedious. However, it is possible to approximate the equilibrium and the short-term development of stochastic models involving several variates in special cases. An example of this is where the simplifying assumptions ensure that in every period the distribution remains multi-variate lognormal, and that the values of the parameters of that distribution can be derived from the parameters of earlier distributions. This topic is discussed in appendix C where the bivariate case is illustrated in more detail.

Univariate stochastic models of income and wealth distribution have much to offer in terms of the insights that they offer on the long-term impact on inequality of changes in strategic parameters such as the tax on bequests and the interest rate; and, as we have shown, 'tweaking' the basic model can be used to incorporate other factors in the generation of inequality such as alternative assumptions on income tax and consumption behaviour. Furthermore, although the univariate approach to stochastic models has been adopted primarily for convenience of exposition, it is clear that the techniques we have developed in this chapter can in principle be extended to much richer specifications.

11.8 The bridge between theory and policy

Stochastic models of wealth and income distribution are powerful examples of the fourth stage of 'explaining' economic inequality and income distribution that we identified in chapter 6 (page 119). They demonstrate the potential of analytical methods combined with simple computations in generating and presenting concisely a range of conclusions from precisely formulated initial conditions and a detailed set of rules governing the development of the income distribution.

Although the version presented here is a very special model, it is by no means isolated from the approaches to inequality and income distribution adopted in preceding chapters. Chapters 7–11 have all been concerned with understanding the theoretical underpinnings and analytical models of the principal features of economic inequality – such as those described in chapters 1–6 – and the models of Mutt island have inherited some of the main theoretical features of the earlier chapters. For example the analysis of chapters 8 and 9 stressed the two-stage process – within and between generations – through which income and wealth inequalities are created and perpetuated: continuities of economic status across generations arise from the rich being able to afford enough out of their high incomes to build up their own wealth and potential bequests, and their use of wealth and position to secure better education, training and social contacts to gain better-paid jobs for themselves and their offspring; the variants of the model presented in this chapter have used this idea in the specification of the stochastic multipliers and the interpretation of the model parameters. What is to be learned from a specific stochastic model of distribution over and above discursive accounts of the generation of economic inequality?

One lesson suggested by the Mutt island experiments is that simplified models of income and wealth distribution have clearly defined limitations in describing complex economic processes. For example the time scale of adjustment means that concentrating exclusively on equilibrium distributions is of little practical use in understanding many real-world shifts in income distribution and the costs associated with them. For the same reasons we should not expect much from simple income distribution models in terms of forecasting. Much as policy makers in the private and the public sector devote expenditure and attention to forecasts of economic indicators based on theoretical models – and continue to do so even when the forecasts are wide of the mark and are repeatedly revised – the usefulness of the model depends on the reliability of parameter estimates and the need to modify the parameters over time. As in most social and economic fields long-term forecasting will be more hazardous than short-term. In the context of the theoretical models presented here the short-term step-by-step forecasts are certainly easier to carry out; and, as with more serious forecasting, the unreality introduced by ignoring the probable need to vary the parameter values is less over the short period than in considering the long-run equilibrium distribution.

There is also a lesson to be learned in terms of the empirical foundation of income distribution models. Although Mutt island provides an instructive story of the generation of inequality we should not pretend that it is constructed out of anything more substantial than thin air. So on what could or should the components of a comprehensive model – the economic and social data, the behavioural responses and the mobility mechanisms – be based?

Some parts of the model can be founded on straightforward practical observation. For example parameters T, r and E^* in the basic model (the generation length, the rate of return on wealth and earnings) might be based upon published demographic, financial and earnings data. Choosing other parameters would require more information; for example C^* (normal consumption expenditure in the basic model) would be determined, not as an arbitrarily selected constant, but through some explicit behavioural assumption or model. Despite the abstract nature of the discussion, we have tried to use down-to-earth considerations to guide the choice of this sort of assumption, but in applications of modelling technique that have greater pretensions to reality the choice would be guided by some econometric study, based on sample survey data. However we should not suppose that these estimates are easily obtained in practice, nor that they will provide sharp, unambiguous answers on the appropriate values for parameters – the discussion in chapter 7 about labour supply repsonse illustrates this point.

Other features of the model are not so easily handled even in principle. These have principally to do with the treatment of uncertainty in the model. Parameters such as g and N governing the assumed nature of the stochastic disturbance are particularly difficult to select. Econometric studies of bequests over a number of generations are unlikely to be of much help: in this matter both the links between the past and the future and the information available are so weak that the advantage of the econometric study over results obtainable by trial and error and sensible guesswork are likely to be slender. Nevertheless trial and error can be used to give some idea of the robustness of the model to alternative ways of representing uncertainty – as our treatment of the implications of the fineness structure in the logbinomial model has shown (see the discussion about figure 11.6 above).

In sum, a practical comprehensive model of income and wealth distribution would be much more complex than the one whose variants have been considered in this chapter; as far as short-term developments are concerned, the procedures for predicting changes over time from an initial distribution would probably be little more complex in principle; but, the difficulty of deriving the long-term equilibrium distribution would probably be enormously increased.

Finally, the models in this chapter have not included parameters to allow for expected changes in political or legal institutions or macroeconomic conditions, although such changes may affect the behaviour of individuals in the ways in which they amass and bequeath wealth. In practice judgements have to be made by those designing and implementing policies for regulating inequality, as to what indirect effects on inequality they may have through modifying expectations. Politicians, managers of firms and others try to influence expectations and to manipulate events through propaganda and advertising. Above all the State will take a direct rôle in the formation of expectations and in the explicit manipulation of income distribution. All of this should be incorporated in an approach to economic inequality and income distribution that goes beyond simple-minded mechanical modelling.

In short we need to provide a rudimentary bridge between the academic approach of most of the chapters in this book and the confused conditions of the world outside as it appears through the media or through the window. That is a matter for chapter 12.

11.9 Questions for discussion

Further reading: Aitchison and Brown (1957), Aghion and Bolton (1997), Champernowne (1952, 1953, 1973), Creedy (1985), Pestieau and Possen (1979).
11.1   Tables 11.5–11.7 were based on the assumption that the rate τ of tax on bequests was 90 per cent. The effects of lowering the tax to 66⅔ per cent in table 11.5 are:
(i) to alter the entries in the columns headed 180,000¢ and 360,000¢,
(ii) to introduce a further column headed 720,000¢.
   Make these adjustments to table 11.5.
11.2   The changes made to table 11.5 in question 11.1 also involve changes to table 11.6 in the columns headed 180,000¢ and 360,000¢, and in the additional column headed 720,000¢. Make these adjustments to table 11.6.
11.3   The changes made to table 11.6 in question 11.2 modify the long-run distribution set out in table 11.7. Show that the modified solution is

<60,000¢	90,000¢	180,000¢	360,000¢	720,000¢
477,913	233,842	187,196	90,109	10,940

11.4   Show that equations (46)–(51) in appendix C (page 356) imply that for any integer values N and i such that $0 \le i \le N+1$, the value of p_i may be found from those of N, g and m_i by using the following formulae

$V=[N \log(1+\frac{1}{2}g)-\log(m_i)]/\log(g)$,

$k=1+\text{int}(V)$,

$p_i=[g^{V-k}-1]/[g-1]$.

Hence obtain the value of p_i when $m_i=0.8$, $g=1.25$ and $N=7$.

11.5   Given the parameter values $N=7$, $g=1.25$, $m=0.75$ show that the formulae given in question 11.4 yield $p=0.01424304$; check that the first three possible values of the stochastic multiplier have probabilities: 0.0001113, 0.00084801, 0.056062 and give the other six.

11.6   At a constant rate of interest r the present value of an annuity for T years of one unit per annum is $[1-e^{-rT}]/r$. What is the greatest constant stream of consumption that a person with constant earnings E per annum can maintain for T years (without getting into debt) if initial wealth is W and there is no further income? What are the constant earnings of an heir with basic earnings E^* of 10,000¢, at interest $r=2\frac{1}{2}$ per cent, over a generation $T=25$, if his parents have invested 100,000¢ in enhancing his skills under the régime of section 11.7?

11.7   The information in table 11.10 may be rewritten as the transition matrix

$$\begin{bmatrix} 0.82891 & 0.27536 & 0.09027 & 0.00724 \\ 0.17109 & 0.48732 & 0.34027 & 0.25724 \\ 0 & 0.23732 & 0.40973 & 0.49276 \\ 0 & 0 & 0.15973 & 0.24276 \end{bmatrix}$$

where the (i,j)th element gives the probability of moving from wealth interval j to wealth interval i for the four wealth intervals (under 60,000¢), (60,000¢–120,000¢), (120,000¢–240,000¢), (240,000¢–480,000¢). Verify this and use the matrix to trace the changes in distribution over two generations of an initial distribution

[500,000, 300,000, 140,000, 60,000]

Check that the number of bequests under 60,000¢ in the two generations would be 510,137 and 518,579. Find the distribution after one generation if the present distribution were

[540,493 288,833 140,944 29,730]

11.8   Check that if the probability of moving from interval j to interval i is given by the (i,j)th element of the matrix

$$\begin{bmatrix} 0.8717 & 0.4963 & 0.0442 & 0 & 0 & 0 & 0 \\ 0.1119 & 0.3137 & 0.1952 & 0.05701 & 0.04601 & 0.03045 & 0.00845 \\ 0.0165 & 0.1581 & 0.3385 & 0.23351 & 0.20052 & 0.15385 & 0.08787 \\ 0 & 0.0319 & 0.2865 & 0.36401 & 0.34201 & 0.31090 & 0.26690 \\ 0 & 0 & 0.1173 & 0.26099 & 0.28299 & 0.31410 & 0.35819 \\ 0 & 0 & 0.0183 & 0.07898 & 0.11198 & 0.15865 & 0.22464 \\ 0 & 0 & 0 & 0.00550 & 0.01649 & 0.03205 & 0.05405 \end{bmatrix}$$

then the following estimate (to the nearest bequest) of the equilibrium distribution of one million bequests remains constant between one generation and the next

[565,202, 136,539, 107,633, 101,784, 65,175, 21,220, 2,447]

11.9   In an example using wealth intervals each of proportionate width $g=2$, preliminary calculations suggest that, above a certain wealth level <u>W</u>, every wealth interval contains about a third as many bequests as the interval next below it. Assuming the frequency curve of bequests to be smooth, would you consider some revision of the estimate 1.5 for the ratio of the arithmetic mean to the minimum for bequests in such intervals? If so which would you prefer of say 1.35, 1.45, 1.55 and 1.65? Explain why.

11.10   Show how a bivariate frequency distribution

$$\begin{bmatrix} 40{,}000 & 90{,}000 & 90{,}000 & 30{,}000 & 0 & 0 \\ 0 & 60{,}000 & 180{,}000 & 180{,}000 & 60{,}000 & 0 \\ 0 & 0 & 30{,}000 & 90{,}000 & 90{,}000 & 20{,}000 \end{bmatrix}$$

develops over four generations given the transition probabilities in table 11.17.

11.11   The probabilities of the $N+2$ values of the stochastic multiplier in the logbinomial model: are the coefficients of 1, and the first $N+1$ powers of g in the expansion of $2^{-N}[1-p+pg][1+g]^N$ (see equation (47) on page 000). Verify that when $N=7$ the nine probabilities are: $[1-p]/128$, $[7-6p]/128$, $[21-14p]/128$, $[35-14p]/128$, $35/128$, $[21+14p]/128$, $[7+14p]/128$, $[1+6p]/128$ and $p/128$.

11.12   What problems would you expect to find in examining empirically continuities of wealth and income from one generation to the next (Pearson, 1914)?

Notes

1 The level of bequest (before subsidy) T years later will be less than P since the excess of the gap C^*-E^* over the initial investment income rP would have to be financed by running down the stock of wealth. The excess of the tax receipts over the payment of this subsidy is disposed of in the manner explained on page 219 of chapter 10.

2 With exceptions at each end: S_1 may be followed by S_1 or S_2 only, and S_M by S_{M-1} S_{M-2} or S_M only.

3 See questions 11.1–11.3.

4 These equations are derived from table 11.10 thus
$0.1710 f_1=0.2754 f_2+0.0903 f_3+0.0072 f_4$
$0.2373 f_2=0.4305 f_3+0.2645 f_4$
$0.1597 f_3=0.7572 f_4$.

5 If we were to try the logbinomial model with $g=2^{1/3}$ and $N=2$ we would find that there is no possible equilibrium distribution, whether the tax is 90 per cent or 66⅔ per cent, except in the trivial case where all bequests are less than P. For this reason we focus solely on the two cases $(g=2^{1/3}, N=7, \tau=90$ per cent) and $(g=2^{1/3}, N=7, \tau=66$⅔ per cent).

6 We have $(g^{1/3},N=7,\tau=90$ per cent) $\prec (g^{1/3},N=7,\tau=66$⅔ per cent) $\prec (g=2,N=2,\tau=90$ per cent) $\prec (g=2,N=2,\tau=66$⅔ per cent) $\prec (g=2,N=7, \tau=90$ per cent) $\prec (g=2,N=7,\tau=66$⅔ per cent), where $\prec$ denotes Lorenz dominance.

7 For example the number with $\mathbf{u}=(2,2)$ is found as follows:
$[0.1667\times24+0.1667\times40+0.0833\times96+0.0833\times160+0.1667\times80+0.1667\times80]\times1{,}000=$
58,667.

8 Applying the transition probabilities of table 11.17 to the entries in (26) we can confirm that these are the equilibrium values: for example, the entry for cell $\mathbf{u}=(3,6)$ may be confirmed as:
$[0.0833\times180+0.0833\times60+0.0833\times90+0.0833\times30]\times1{,}000=30{,}000$ (unchanged).

Table 11.17 *Transition probabilities for* (u_1, u_2) *cells in the bivariate model*

		To cells (u_1, u_2)											
		(1,1)	(1,2)	(1,3)	(1,4)	(2,2)	(2,3)	(2,4)	(2,5)	(3,3)	(3,4)	(3,5)	(3,6)
	(1,1)	0.0833	0.2500	0	0	0.1667	0.5000	0	0	0	0	0	0
	(1,2)	0.0833	0.1667	0.0833	0	0.1667	0.3333	0.1667	0	0	0	0	0
	(1,3)	0	0.0833	0.1667	0.0833	0	0.1667	0.3333	0.1667	0	0	0	0
	(1,4)	0	0	0.2500	0.0833	0	0	0.5000	0.1667	0	0	0	0
From cells	(2,2)	0.0833	0.2500	0	0	0.0833	0.2500	0	0	0.0833	0.2500	0	0
(u_1, u_2)	(2,3)	0.0833	0.1667	0.0833	0	0.0833	0.1667	0.0833	0	0.0833	0.1667	0.0833	0
	(2,4)	0	0.0833	0.1667	0.0833	0	0.0833	0.1667	0.0833	0	0.0833	0.1667	0.0833
	(2,5)	0	0	0.2500	0.0833	0	0	0.2500	0.0833	0	0	0.2500	0.0833
	(3,3)	0	0	0	0	0.1667	0.5000	0	0	0.0833	0.2500	0	0
	(3,4)	0	0	0	0	0.1667	0.3333	0.1667	0	0.0833	0.1667	0.0833	0
	(3,5)	0	0	0	0	0	0.1667	0.3333	0.1667	0	0.0833	0.1667	0.0833
	(3,6)	0	0	0	0	0	0	0.5000	0.1667	0	0	0.2500	0.0833

12 Policy

12.1 Introduction

A chapter on economic policies to affect inequality could easily expand into an entire book by itself. But our limited discussion has only a modest purpose. In chapter 1 we pointed out that a reduction in inequality would have a price: now that we have looked at issues concerning what inequality means and what economic forces generate inequality can we say more about that price? What determines it? Through what means is it paid?

The principal aim of this chapter is to suggest ways to move forward from inequality analysis and the modelling of income distribution toward a practical approach to the sort of problems that will arise when setting out to manipulate the forces that determine income distribution and economic inequality. We do not attempt a comprehensive programme for revolution, nor even proposals for a reform of little bits of the system.

Chapters 6–11 illustrated the multitude of forces which generate economic inequality and the complexity of their interaction. As we have seen, some of the models could be used to suggest specific policy proposals within the context of particular parts of the system; but here we take a fresh look at a number of general policy questions that are likely to be important irrespective of the specific community under consideration.

What subject matter ought to be included in a chapter on policy towards economic inequality and income distribution? To address this question sensibly requires some general consideration of how broad the range of issues ought to be. Let us look at four directions in which the discussion of this chapter will be developed:
- the purpose of egalitarian policy,
- scope of the policy,
- time span,
- targets of the policy.

The purpose of egalitarian policy

The basic objective can be described as income adjustment. Through fiscal or other means the government tries to ensure that, in any given situation, low incomes or low

consumption levels are raised at the expense of high ones. Although this is the principal goal of progressive taxation, wealth levies and poor relief, it cannot be the only
goal, since it ignores many aspects of inequality which cannot be measured in terms of
money, as we noted in chapter 1. Apart from this, the importance of uncertainty attaching to income prospects also makes income adjustment by itself too limited an aim. In
developed market economies, because of the risks to jobs and incomes (of the sort discussed in chapter 8) social insurance often plays an important role in restraining
inequality: it has usually been regarded as a responsibility of government to design
such schemes to benefit those who are most at risk and least capable of coping with
emergencies. There is, however, an alternative view of the responsibility and of the
appropriate purpose of government action in view of the uncertainty and of human
reactions to it. Rather than try for redistribution of actual consumption (through taxes
and transfers) and of prospects of consumption (through insurance) the government
ought to aim at a fairer structure of opportunities of earning enough income to secure
a decent standard of living. Such an objective could involve a more diverse programme
including, for example, educational reforms, intervention in capital markets and
effective employment policy.

Scope of the policy

The fundamental choice is between the 'root-and-branch' and the 'piecemeal'
approach to policy. The root-and-branch approach requires many aspects of income
distribution and economic inequality to be tackled simultaneously: the distribution of
labour earnings through education programmes and intervention in the labour market;
the distribution of profits, interest and rent, through a reform of the system of ownership or the transfer of wealth; also of the material aspects of economic inequality and
poverty such as overcrowding and slums. Like all vigorous schemes of government
intervention – egalitarian or otherwise – such a programme is likely to provoke serious
concern about the scope and legality of government interference with the decisions and
liberties of private individuals and associations. Moreover, the informational requirements – concerning the way the economic system works, the objectives and the moni-
toring of the policy itself – are clearly formidable and so effective implementation
might take a long time. Politicians and the electorate usually demand quick results,
which is one reason why the piecemeal approach is so often preferred. Piecemeal
methods, such as adjustments to the structure of income tax rates, increases in the levels
of welfare payments for particular groups and changes in unemployment benefit,
appear to need less information and to be easier to design, since in each piece of the
economic system the main things to be considered are the general direction in which
to steer the policy and how that piece of the system actually works. Such an appearance can be quite deceptive, often for well-known reasons; yet the everyday circumstances of policy making – the country's constitution, lack of administrative
coordination, defective information – may entice politicians towards the piecemeal and
away from the root-and-branch approach.

Time span

Although a lot of thinking about policies to affect income distribution and other aspects of economic inequality tends to be piecemeal and mainly concerned with short-term results there is no logical reason why this has to be so, and occasions arise which give opportunities to plan major changes in the economic and social structure that will affect the long-run mechanisms transmitting inequality. The time span relevant to governments and public policy making may be influenced by the resources available to the community, and in this respect there is a parallel with the issue of time span in the process that determines individual incomes (see sections 8.6 and 9.4 of chapters 8 and 9). Just as those with a secure and wealthy family background are best able and likely to devote many years in training for a highly paid career, so also institutions and authorities are most likely to provide for long-term needs when they are prosperous and well established, whereas in times of crisis they concentrate on quick gains and disaster-management and will cut down on or defer long-term investment.[1]

Targets of the policy

In chapter 1 we stressed the distinction between inequality among individuals and inequality among groups. The same distinction is also important for policy decisions for regulating inequality. Even when the primary concern is with the well being of and the inequality amongst persons, policy is often more effectively administered by using specific groups as a basis: families, households, ethnic groups or particular occupations. But the use of groups in targeting poses problems. The way in which the groups are specified and the distribution of the population among the groups will affect the apparent pattern of inequality – since a good deal more information is usually available about inequality between groups than within them. Deeper issues may be involved with group targeting: eventually the membership of the groups may itself be altered by the policy measures – families may decide to have more children if it becomes financially advantageous, the unemployed may seek work less assiduously if the burden of unemployment is relieved by state aid. So targeting may force the choice between alleviating cases of hardship now and investing in a more efficient resource allocation for production in the future. The way in which the immediate claims of disadvantaged groups are balanced against the costs resulting from the risk that people may 'select themselves' into such groups will depend on the type of economic need being considered and the extent of information and control available.

   Although it is neither practical nor interesting to discuss every policy issue at length in each of these four directions, we have tried to avoid dogmatism in our discussion of the choice of approach in each case. The particular circumstances of individual economies and the aims and prejudices of those who shape policy in them are bound to influence the choice between a broad or narrow approach when considering the purpose, scope and time span of a policy affecting inequality, as well as other economic objectives. Readers are invited to generalise some of those points which we discuss through specific examples, to consider the long-term consequences of measures that we introduce only in a short-term framework, and to provide specific examples for some of the issues that we discuss only in terms of general principles.

In the light of earlier chapters it is evident that several complementary approaches to policy for regulating inequality can be distinguished. Recall that chapters 4 and 5 dealt with the subject of inequality in a direct fashion – characterising the analysis of income distribution as an extension of the cake division problem. This direct approach to the topic of inequality yields a focus on the gains or losses resulting from the policies through economic growth or decline and through decreases or increases in economic inequality. By contrast chapters 7–11 approached the subject by means of theories and models of the mechanisms underlying the inequality and the processes which preserve it. In the rest of this chapter we shall pursue both lines of argument: we discuss policy questions which, on the one hand, directly relate to redistribution of resources between the rich and the poor – taking as given the pattern of inequality that has been established in the past by the social and economic system – and, on the other hand, questions about policies that aim to adjust these mechanisms which determine the distribution of goods available for consumption and their prices.

We begin with an issue which affects all kinds of distributional policies, and which crops up repeatedly in later sections.

12.2 Efficiency and equity

Chapter 1 introduced a beguilingly simple diagram[2] that purported to represent the outcome of policies in terms of efficiency and equity. It is beguiling because in depicting the 'price' of a reduction in inequality it seems to set out the issue of policy choice in stark, direct terms; actually it diverts attention away from some key questions of economic policy. The focus of attention is manifestly the frontier consisting of the dominant points representing policies which could not be surpassed by any other policy, both on grounds of efficiency and on grounds of equity. Along this frontier the choice between any pair of options affecting the distribution of output to consumers as well as the production of that output may be regarded as involving a 'trade-off' to be resolved by the implicit price that it is judged appropriate to pay for efficiency at the expense of equity. Clearly, there are usually several other desirable entities at stake – freedom, dignity, pride, peace of mind, to mention some of those which are particularly difficult to measure objectively, and this in turn makes all but the most sophisticated versions of the efficiency-versus-equity line of argument inappropriate. But, even if we set aside that problem, the issue of this notional trade-off – which arises in several of the subsequent sections of the chapter – conceals other major problems.

In our discussion of the conflicting demands for economic growth and for more equity (chapter 1), and again in our examination of alternative indices of income inequality (chapters 4 and 5), we have examined some of the difficulties involved in giving a clear meaning to the notion of efficiency and the terms of its exchange with equity (or equality). In this chapter we shall resume this discussion and focus on the issues raised by the following questions:

- Can an appropriate efficiency criterion be specified?
- If so, to what can it apply?
- Is the criterion adequate to rank alternative policies in order of efficiency?
- C:n efficiency be clearly distinguished from equity in order to be able to specify the trade-off between them?

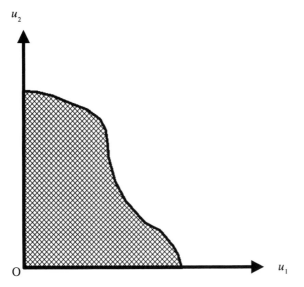

Figure 12.1 Utility possibilities

Can Pareto efficiency be an operational concept of any practicable economic policy? As we discussed in chapter 2 the fundamental idea underlying Pareto efficiency can be represented in a simple diagram. Figure 12.1 is the first step in constructing a figure such as figure 2.5 on page 41. For a two-person economy – the idea can easily be extended to the n-person case – the shaded area shows the notional set of utility pairs that are attainable given the resources and the technology in the economy. In the various guises that diagrams such as this may take, the shape of the frontier will depend not only on the pattern of endowments of income-yielding assets and of abilities, but also on individual preferences and on the set of alternative policies, whose conse-quences for the two individuals (or groups) have supposedly been divined. As it stands figure 12.1 is not very informative, except that the highlighted frontier corresponds to Pareto-efficient allocations in the economy – cases where no dominant utility pair is feasible – and that the concept of Pareto efficiency in turn is conditional upon the resources and technology which determine the shaded set. To make the issue of efficiency-versus-equity sharper it is common to impose some stronger assumptions upon the apparatus depicted in figure 12.1.

Were all output or all consumption to consist of a single homogeneous good, then the questions in our list could be very much simplified; if, in addition, each person's utility is proportional to income (possibly incorporating the equivalising procedures mentioned in chapter 4) then figure 12.1 can be simply transformed into figure 12.2. *Income* is now measured along the axes, and the shaded area now represents the set of all possible distributions of *income* (or consumption) between the two persons: the concept of Pareto efficiency is now reinterpreted in terms of the boundary of this income set. In this simplified framework we may represent the terms of the trade-off between equity and efficiency in income terms. Aggregate income is measured in the direction of the 45° ray through the origin; income differences are measured along each

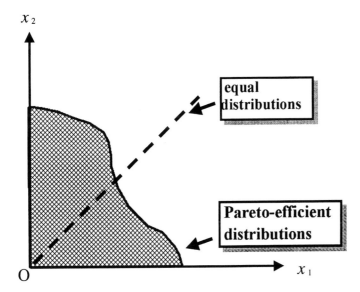

Figure 12.2 Efficiency and equity in income distribution

normal to that ray. Given a suitable system of inequality measurement, the frontier in figure 12.2 may then be used to derive the 'equity–efficiency trade-off', where efficiency is interpreted as the total of the two incomes and equity as the opposite of inequality, and where inequality means just the difference between the two incomes.

As in the utility-based diagram there is more than one Pareto-efficient income distribution. Were we to agree on a social-welfare function to order all these possible distributions, we could then superimpose its contours on to figure 12.2 which would then indicate the best available pair of incomes. Figure 12.3 shows a particular example using contours of the sort introduced in chapter 5. An appropriate transform would enable these contours to be mapped into the efficiency–equity diagram. Use of the SWF makes a particular selection from the frontier in figure 12.3 or from the efficiency–equity trade-off.

However it is arguable that the situation of some economies in practice is better represented by a point *inside* rather than on the frontier. This might seem odd since apparently there must be a feasible alternative which would give both parties more income and which is no less egalitarian; but such an objection presupposes that the consequences of the policy achieving such a solution really are accurately known. Typically, the position of the frontier will be known only vaguely. In a two-person single-commodity world the practical complications of imperfect knowledge do not detract seriously from the theoretical simplicity of the equity–efficiency trade-off. But if the diversity of goods and of people's tastes and endowments are taken into account then fundamental questions about the meaning of efficiency, and of the terms of trade between efficiency and equity, become difficult to resolve. We often have to allow for this diversity when examining the impact of particular policy measures on inequality. Measures such as commodity taxes, subsidies, price controls, programmes of public works and public investment may affect the composition of and demand for

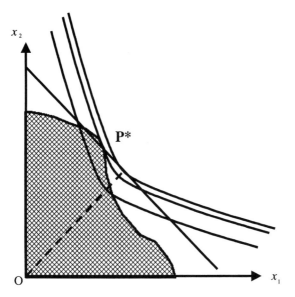

Figure 12.3 Social choice of a distribution

the output of the community and the composition of the flow of available inputs, including specific types of human and material capital.

Within a market economy the relative prices of goods and services – the valuation of the volume of output – will depend (amongst other things) on the distribution of income. The interdependence between the measure of volume of national income and its distribution makes it difficult to speak unambiguously of any movement 'towards the frontier' in the sense of an improvement in efficiency, and even more difficult to define any unambiguous terms of trade between equity and efficiency along the supposed frontier. Furthermore, whilst there may be good arguments for policies that would enhance 'technical efficiency' – in that they would economise resources under all possible arrangements for production and distribution – uncritical advocacy of Pareto efficiency as an objective in itself is unwarranted. Pareto-efficient situations may have to be obtained at the cost of a system of prices and of income distribution that many people would regard as truly appalling.

These points are important because of the way in which the notion of economic efficiency is so often presented. It slips into the discussion of alternative policies in an apparently unloaded form. After all, no one, of whatever economic school or political affiliation, is likely to advocate waste in so many words. Yet the entry of Pareto efficiency into the discussion may significantly influence the choice of policy in a particularly loaded manner. Since this can have important distributional implications we should be quite clear about what 'efficiency' is defined to mean and scrutinise what relevance this definition has to the choice between policies for regulating economic inequality.

The point is especially relevant to the subject matter of most of the rest of this chapter. In the next five sections we shall be addressing the following interrelated topics:

- Whether redistribution should be in terms of money, or of the things that money will buy (section 12.3).
- Traps to be avoided in framing redistributive mechanisms (section 12.4).
- The rôle of the 'social product' and 'social control' in inequality regulation (section 12.5)
- Arguments about whether to choose private or public provision of goods and services (section 12.6).

Regulation of wages and prices to support living standards (section 12.7).

Where the issue of economic efficiency appears to be significant for the discussion of these topics we shall try to supply some guide to the sense in which efficiency is to be taken, and to what extent it should influence judgements between policies affecting economic inequality and total income.

12.3 Cash versus goods

One of the fundamental questions of redistribution policy is how best to benefit the very poor, both in terms of their present living standards and in terms of their protection against exploitation of their weak bargaining position in the future. From this fundamental question devolves an important issue concerning short-run redistributional policy: whether the needy should be provided with money or with goods. There are good economic arguments for each sort of provision; there are also some bogus arguments which need to be exposed.

The argument for the view that instead of setting up soup kitchens it would be better to provide money for the purchase of soup seems straightforward: unless there is a good reason for the authorities to adopt a paternalistic attitude to the citizens, it is likely to be more efficient if they provide any given level of support in cash rather than in kind; and whatever the objectives may be in terms of distributional justice, they might as well be achieved efficiently wherever possible. The argument that the cash solution is more efficient stands on two legs. The first is in terms of informational and administrative efficiency: if people can recognise where their own interests lie and can implement the actions to secure those interests by their purchases out of a given budget, then it would be simpler to allot them the cash than to arrange for government agents to enquire about and appraise appropriate patterns of expenditure and then to organise the provision of corresponding amounts of the various goods on their behalf. The second leg is based on the belief that people will be willing to substitute amongst purchased goods in response to shifts in relative supply prices and to shifts in their own relative needs for different goods.

The point can be illustrated by the problem of how best to support poor families during bouts of inflation. Suppose potatoes increase in price rapidly and that the authorities aim to offset the damage that this does to their living standards: should they do so by controlling prices, by withdrawing potatoes from being supplied elsewhere and distributing them to the poor, or by allowing the potato prices to rise unchecked but subsidising the money incomes of the poor? This last option is the one suggested by orthodox free market theory, on the grounds that if poor people substitute rice or pasta for potatoes, even to a small extent, then it is likely to cost less in terms of real resources to provide them with the money than to allow them to buy potatoes at below the market price.

Of course we have already seen – in chapter 1 – at least one theoretical argument on the other side: money income by itself is not a sufficient indicator of living standards for a thorough examination of economic inequality. Income as conventionally measured does not include fringe benefits, beneficial externalities, or 'positional goods', whereby people derive benefit directly from a favourable position in the pecking order for some goods. More importantly, income flows can affect the standard of living through 'stock shortages' of housing, sanitation and the like. However, this argument is not of itself overwhelming since in some cases it is quite possible that the most effective way of offsetting such components of economic inequality is to supplement people's incomes so that they can find and obtain better housing or otherwise rectify stock shortages and offset their lack of adequate 'positional' goods. Although the economic inequality may reveal itself in terms other than income, the prescription may still be cash.

Yet there are still three prescriptive arguments for direct action to supply goods rather than cash for the impoverished group in order to alleviate inequality. Of these the simplest is what is politely termed the 'merit goods' argument or, less politely, 'father knows best'. If social objectives are not strictly individualistic, it is reasonable to try to persuade some population groups to consume a different pattern of goods to what they would do if left to themselves. The authorities may decide that if they dole out cash, much of it may be foolishly squandered instead of being gradually expended on things that are 'really needed' and 'healthy'. This sort of paternalism is not especially ridiculous or offensive: the very young, the very old, the mentally handicapped and the ill-informed can all be greatly helped by it if it is expertly carried out.

The second argument allows that cash transfers may be the more efficient under ideal conditions but objects that in substantial and relevant respects conditions are not ideal. Efficient well-ordered markets where everyone can buy and sell freely at a common price may be absent: capital markets, for instance, are often imperfect in ways which discriminate against the poor; poor people may have to pay more for food because of handicaps to shopping effectively; markets for housing, education and medical care may already be substantially distorted by institutional restrictions that are politically awkward to remove. In such instances the unrestricted reliance on the free market will not ensure an efficient use of resources and there may be a case for providing resources and goods directly, or through voucher schemes, or through some form of discriminatory subsidy. Particularly in cases of calamities or other urgent need, time may be far too short for market forces to operate efficiently. Thus, in a very deprived community starvation and other serious diseases may have to be quickly alleviated, water supplies and transport services provided as a matter of urgency. In such situations the approach may have to be one of blunt directness: teams of experts in medicine, water supply and road construction must draw up immediate plans for fulfilling these tasks, for directing labour to the various operations, and for financing the hire of needed equipment and the provision of medical supplies.

Thirdly, some services such as public sanitation may by their nature always be supplied more efficiently through the authorities directly. This and some other arguments will be dealt with more thoroughly in section 12.5.

Finally, here is an example of a bogus argument based on the concept of 'stigma' or personal embarrassment at receiving handouts. The reason for regarding this argument as bogus is that transfers of either cash or goods can be made unpleasant or embarrassing to recipients: the issue is primarily an administrative more than an economic one, although this does not reduce its importance in many welfare programmes in existence at the time of writing.

To summarise: simple arguments based on the concept of efficiency usually claim that cash should be transferred rather than that the authorities should replan the pattern of production, or supply particular needed goods directly to the needy; but there are important exceptions in both developed and underdeveloped economies where arguments to the contrary deserve careful attention. Finally, two caveats must be supplied. Even where cash transfers are not the most effective method, several problems often arise when alternative solutions are attempted – we shall examine these in sections 12.6–12.8. Also, even where cash payments seem superficially attractive, it is often difficult to ensure the award of these just to those who will most gain from them – as we shall see in section 12.4 which will consider examples of such administrative difficulties.

12.4 Traps for armchair administrators

We now turn to an examination of the economic mechanisms for transferring income between individuals or groups by focusing upon income-adjustment schemes that are the responsibility of the taxation and social security authorities. Transfer schemes involving payments or levies in kind (free school meals for certain families, special orange juice for expectant mothers, financial assistance for university fees for low-income families, for example) can be examined in a rather similar fashion, if there are perfect markets for all relevant goods, in which all can buy and sell at the same prices freely; but as we have remarked, these are idealised conditions that are seldom likely to be satisfied, even approximately.

Transfer mechanisms that focus on *income* rather than some other asset or commodity have a special interest. As we saw in chapter 2 (page 00) transfer incomes are an important component of family incomes, and they play a particularly important part in determining the living standards of the poor. In addition income is a useful guide for identifying the rich or moderately well off who have the taxable capacity to fund the transfers to the poor. For present purposes the effects of income-transfer mechanims may be modelled thus

$$c = x - T \qquad (1)$$

where c is disposable income for direct consumption, x is original income and T is the net tax liability. Net taxes for any one family or household in the population are defined as

> T = [personal taxes paid by the family] + [other forms of obligatory payment, e.g., National Insurance payments] – [cash benefits] – [estimated cash value of goods and services received in kind].

Because T includes both receipts and payments of cash it can be positive for some families and negative for others: indeed for many families the value of x in may be effectively zero so that theoretically all their income consists of $-T$, where T the tax

$c(x)$

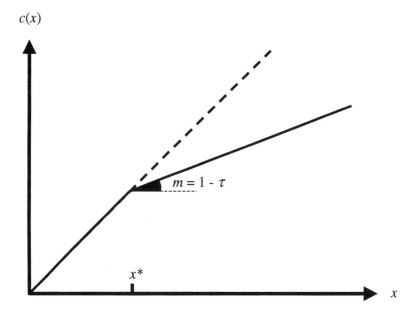

Figure 12.4 A constant marginal-tax rate scheme

liability is negative. The authorities can choose how T is to be determined for each family of the population by laying down a rule by which to obtain the level of tax payment (or benefit receipt) as a direct function of each family's original income x and of other attributes of the family, such as the number and ages of children in it, the health of the family head and so forth: to avoid complication we shall not distinguish such other attributes affecting the tax by a separate notation. The main problem facing the authorities is to select a suitable formula $T(x)$ or instead an appropriate function $c(x)$ – which is equivalent to x–$T(x)$ – to give the disposable income of a family with original income x. It is a problem beset with pitfalls and dilemmas.

As we have noted in chapters 1 and 2, the definition of both c and x presents practical difficulties, in particular the time period over which income is to be measured and the prices at which benefits in kind should be evaluated. Again, the definition of the population who are to be eligible for any income maintenance schemes will often involve awkward choices. The particular family attributes which the government chooses to take into account when defining $T(x)$ are vulnerable to arbitrary change at a later date; also the attributes of the family may adapt themselves to the eligibility requirements for benefit – an important point to which we return.

The authorities have a wide field from which to choose the formula relating disposable income c to original income x. One of the simplest is the form depicted in figure 12.4 which is analogous to the form of tax function introduced in chapters 10 and 11. The tax leaves untouched the incomes of those below a threshold income level x^*, and impinges upon incomes above that level at a uniform rate τ; the proceeds of the tax may, for example, be spent on public goods. A slight modification of this is illustrated in figure 12.5, which allows for the proceeds of the tax to be used to finance direct

$c(x)$

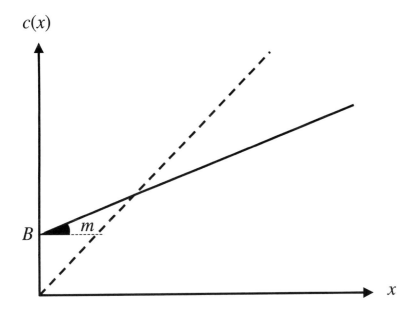

Figure 12.5 Extension of figure 12.4 to a negative income tax

income transfers. Here a minimum income of B dollars is guaranteed to any family eligible for the scheme, and for every dollar that the family then earns it receives only a fraction m dollars ($m<1$). The trivial case where there is no adjustment is given by the 45° line through the origin in each case. The slope m of the dotted line – the marginal benefit rate – equals $1-\tau$, where $\tau=T'$ is the marginal tax rate. The authorities could – as in Germany – choose a tax formula with a continuously variable m (see figure 12.6) but it is more common to find schemes of a further type combining simplicity and flexibility, where m stays constant over a range of original income but then jumps to a higher slope over the next income range, and so on for further income ranges.

The scheme depicted in figure 12.5 can be used to illustrate a number of the main issues to be discussed. Take the question of incentives arising from the ability of some families to influence their original income by their attitude to obtaining and doing jobs. Persons in such families may take the details of the tax scheme into account when deciding where and how strenuously to work, how much of their earnings to spend or save and so forth. Similarly, these decisions about work and savings might alter the scale of spending and the forecast of tax receipts on which the authorities were basing their own plans.

Suppose, for example, that a family's original income x consists just of the earnings of a single member paid by the hour, free to vary hours of work to any extent, and that its total disposable income is of the form

$$-B+mwh \tag{2}$$

where h is the number of hours worked and w is the constant hourly wage rate. Any change of m or B can alter the relative attractions of more leisure from shorter hours and more to spend from longer work – a choice which we have assumed to be freely

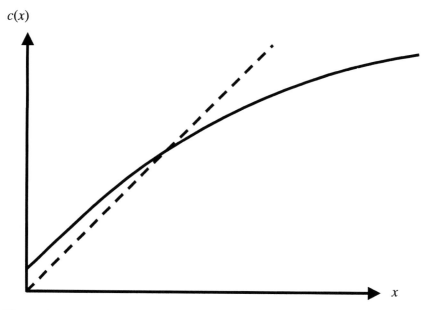

Figure 12.6 A continuously varying *m*

available. A cut in *m* would tip the scales towards leisure whereas a cut in *B* would tip them towards obtaining more income. It is easy to picture stupid tax/benefit schemes which would make at least some people want to give up work altogether: this might not mean that less work would get done in total, but if there were no queues of unemployed persons, it could result in less work in total and perhaps even cause a fall in the total national product. As a consequence it could reduce the total cake to be distributed between personal consumption and the various other ways in which goods and services get used up, including such regrettable necessities as medical services, defence, policing, repair of buildings and communications and entertaining important clients. One of the minor arts of civil servants is to design the schedules for *c*(*x*) so as to give some appearance of being just, without causing any substantial disincentive to work. We briefly discuss one or two distinct issues that may arise.[3]

First, there is the problem of misrepresentation caused by the inability of the authorities to discover all they need to know about the citizens in order to tax them efficiently. Imagine for a moment an authority which miraculously can obtain all this information: they not only know what each person actually earns and actually obtains as income from assets, but can divine how much each person might get in these ways if he wanted to. In effect they have complete information on each person's human, physical and financial asset holdings. They could then use this as a base for levying taxes from which escape would be impossible. Even in the 1990s such omniscience is not yet practicable, and so the authorities rely instead on fairly unreliable indicators of taxable capacity: for example, a high reported income may be assumed to be some indication of a high ability to pay tax, and a justification for a stiff tax on the recipient. But even if everyone could be forced to tell the truth the pitfalls would remain: a person with a low nominal income may really be well off; perhaps he or she has just decided to retire from work, or to deploy his financial assets carefully so as to yield little taxable income. For whenever the officials define 'income' – or any other such quantity – as a basis for taxation, or for eligibility for a state subsidy or other perk, they thereby may create an incentive for the nimble-witted to clothe themselves as deserving poor or anyhow as unlike the tax-worthy rich.

Perhaps an answer to this problem is to concoct a rather broad definition of income and so reduce the opportunities for crafty tax avoidance and manipulations of benefit: for instance, capital gains can be lumped in as part of taxable income. But the broader the base of the tax/benefit scheme – the more comprehensive are the indicator of ability to pay and the indicator of need for support – the more the government must spend on the costs of collection and interpretation of the statistics needed. How to strike a balance between inefficiency arising from misrepresentation and extravagant expenditure on collection and sifting of information will depend on a host of circumstances that will vary between one type of community and another: general principles are accordingly hard to come by.

However, there is a footnote to this point about misrepresentation which applies in some degree to many industrialised economies with a fairly free labour market, and so merits a separate discussion. As noted in the introduction, it is widely regarded as a proper function of the authorities in an economy to provide social insurance: this shares several of the problems encountered in private insurance schemes, although differing from them in many important respects. One of the problems common to both kinds of scheme is 'moral hazard': the income schemes which provide unemployment benefits so as to mitigate the ill effects of lengthy unemployment have to consider this hazard, since although most unemployed persons have strong reasons apart from financial pressure to get back into employment, there may be some who will be more prepared to give up the attempt or to turn down reasonable opportunities to work, if they are receiving fairly generous unemployment benefit. It is worth considering whether this does or does not matter.

The problem goes deeper than newspaper references to 'scroungers' might suggest. In figure 12.7 the two dotted lines labelled u and u' represent two possibilities for the level of consumption in the event of unemployment. Take a person whose income when in work is x_0 and suppose for the moment that income support scheme (the solid line) does not exist; for administrative or political reasons the authorities will not support the incomes of those in work. Consumption under each level of unemployment benefit, u or u', is greater than x_0 and there may be a disincentive to seek re-employment in the manner discussed above; this need not be a bad thing, because income u might be so very low that prevailing opinion held it undesirable that anyone, whether in work or not, should have to subsist on it; one effect of providing the unemployment insurance in this case could be eventually to turn off the supply of labour willing to take jobs at such very low wages and this might secure better rates being paid for them. Now introduce the income maintenance scheme, so that the person would get $c(x_0)$ if in work. If the unemployment benefit is set at u, fine; but setting it at u' would be an administrative nonsense since the authorities would be automatically discouraging people from taking jobs by the manner in which the relative levels of consumption in the two schemes had been set. It is still quite common for

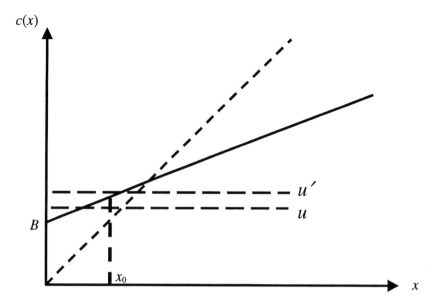

Figure 12.7 The redistribution scheme and unemployment insurance

authorities unwittingly to set such an employment trap, but it really is a blunder for which no reasonable case can be made out on grounds of distributional justice. If $c(x_0)$ is too low, then the c schedule should be adjusted rather than providing backdoor income support by allowing a relatively high level of unemployment benefit.

The issue of the employment trap focuses attention on the relative setting of the benefit schedules for employed and unemployed persons. Another similar issue concerns the shape of the benefit schedules – the particular form of the disposable income function $c(x)$ illustrated in figure 12.4. Consider for example the family cited above with disposable income $B+mwh$, where \$$w$ per hour is the wage rate and h the hours of work, and suppose that h can be altered, either by adjusting the amount of overtime or by other members of the same family taking or leaving jobs. Suppose the authorities wish to boost the income of this family, they will have to do so at the expense of the incomes of other families unless they can increase the total at the same time: presumably they will seek for this to be at the expense of those better off than the family in question. This could be done by increasing the minimum income B while reducing the marginal benefit rate m, flattening the entire $c(x)$ schedule and so raising the incomes of the poorer and lowering those of the richer. But we should also consider the effect of a tilting $c(x)$ schedule on how many hours of work (h) will be done. Each extra hour is now less rewarding to a rich family, since it is mw, where m has decreased. There appears to be a work disincentive; but the reduction of the overall disposable income of the rich family may on the other hand goad it to work more so as to maintain its accustomed standard of life. In contrast, the poor family faces a stark disincentive, since m has fallen lowering the marginal yield of working, whilst the authorities have raised B, thus bettering the poor family and so relieving the urgency of the need to obtain more work. This further suggests that for any $c(x)$ schedule decreasing the mar-

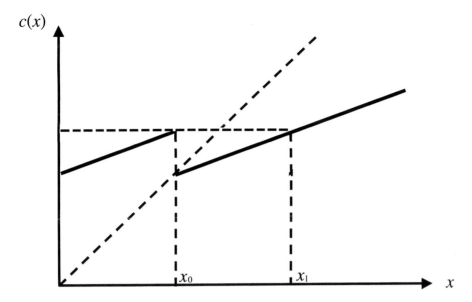

$c(x)$

x_0

x_1

x

Figure 12.8 The notch problem

ginal benefit rate at any point whilst increasing disposable income will discourage all families at that point from working longer, that altering one section of the $c(x)$ schedule will usually affect not only the families whose original incomes x fall in that section but others as well, and that if a proposed $c(x)$ schedule has a section where the marginal benefit rate is zero or negative, there is a disincentive within that sector. These issues are illustrated in real life by what in the USA is known as 'the notch problem' and in the UK as 'the poverty trap'. One version of this runs as follows. Suppose the authorities define all families with original income less than x_0 as 'poor' and assume that they deserve special help in the form of an enlarged benefit payment B; suppose for simplicity that all forms of income are taxed at a uniform rate. This well-intentioned scheme has a peculiar result, illustrated in figure 12.8: if a family with original income just under x_0 earns a dollar or two more, it suddenly suffers a significant *drop* in its disposable income c as it steps over the threshold x_0. As the diagram is drawn it would be in the interest of a family member to refuse better-paid jobs unless they enabled him to earn x_1 or more at his given hours of work. What goes wrong? Over the range of income around x_0 the $c(x)$ schedule shows a sudden dip – the marginal benefit rate is actually negative. This 'notch' in the schedule clearly affects families just to the left of the notch and indeed all families in the interval from x_0 to x_1, since they could become better off by letting the family head work part-time so that they became officially regarded as 'poor'. They are trapped into poverty.

The general conclusions to be drawn from this view of the poverty trap and the notch problem are simply stated: well-meant piecemeal income adjustment proposals can have unjust inefficient side effects unless they form part of a carefully planned overall scheme of taxes and benefits and other measures; these side effects can be so large as to offset the intended impact of the policy. No legislator is likely to arrange matters intentionally so that many unemployed would find it a financial disaster to be awarded a job, or that poor families would actually lose out if the family head worked longer or harder or secured promotion, but such things can arise from the interaction of separate schemes of cash handouts, rebates and benefits in kind, designed to assist specific segments of the community. If the fiscal system is to be used as an effective tool of redistribution, the entire $c(x)$ schedule – covering all incomes and all socially insured contingencies – should be planned as an integrated whole.

The disincentive effect of the poverty trap on tax schemes may also be regarded as due to the arbitrary characteristics of the choice of the boundary marking off those who are to be subject to the tax from those exempt. It is one example of an arbitrary demarcation trap, to cover all cases where the setting of such a boundary creates strong incentives for those just on the disadvantageous side of it to move inside it and imposes severe penalties on those who through no fault of their own are unable to do so.

Examples of this type of trap are familiar in many contexts – in the support of students in higher education, in the framing of regional policy (help to firms situated in designated depressed areas will draw complaints from firms just outside the areas' boundaries), or even in the case of the selection of suitably 'needy' persons for receiving aid from religious and other charities. In sections 12.6 and 12.7 we shall meet further examples to do with the classification of commodities for taxation or subsidies.

12.5 The social wage and social ownership

Public expenditure has made a shadowy appearance in previous chapters, for example in the wealth distribution models of chapters 10 and 11. Public ownership and control of the means of producing goods or, less drastically, an increase in the scale of provision of goods and services by the government agencies are often advocated as powerful methods of restraining inequality of living standards. But such methods are also often hotly contested by advocates of the free market system on the grounds that the restraint of inequality by such methods will involve an inordinate cost in terms of efficient economic growth and possibly also of certain personal liberties. Personal tastes, beliefs and prejudices will play an important part in selecting just where to choose the balance between these two attitudes: it is desirable to perceive these subjective judgements clearly as just what they are and to avoid confusing them with more objective reasoning about equity and efficiency.

The discussion in the present section will assume merely that both private and public ownership and management of the means of providing goods and services of various kinds are worth examining as methods of fostering both equity and efficiency: it will not be so ambitious as to claim to result in any clear precise answer as to where the balance between public and market solutions should be struck in each instance. We deal with the following three topics:
• truly public goods and services,
• the public provision of goods which really are private goods,
• the public ownership and control of factories, land or other assets.
The first two topics concern what has been referred to as the 'social wage' and it will be convenient to discuss them together and incidentally to point out some essential differences between them. The term 'public goods' has the following connotation in

economic theory. As opposed to providing a clear-cut private good such as bread, the provision of a pure public good or service involves *non-rivalness*; this term means that further consumers could be allowed the benefits of its provision without this costing the provider anything substantially more: although it costs extra labour, fuel and other resources to increase the supply of bread, granting more persons access to fresh air or the enjoyment of the sight of flowers need involve no significant extra cost, provided the nearest park is not overcrowded. In addition a pure public good has the distinct property of 'non-excludability' meaning that there is no sure way to prevent people from consuming the good even when they have not in any way paid for it: unlike fresh bread, fresh air and the enjoyment from seeing fresh flowers are often difficult to collect charges for; similarly, it would in a number of countries be difficult to levy charges for the use of supplies of fresh water. There are few public goods in such a pure form, although a variety of public goods and services – tap-water, sanitation, broadcasting, various forms of transport, national defence, police, fire services – exhibit non-rivalness and non-excludability to some extent. The case of pure public goods deserves consideration.

These highly public goods introduce economic problems of their own and for this reason their supply should be treated separately from the topic of publicly providing private goods. The authorities may decide to nationalise firms producing private goods for a variety of reasons, but from our viewpoint this may be seen as another form of market regulation and as raising the same kind of questions as are raised by a scheme of state regulation of private firms through taxation and quantitative controls such as import quotas or rationing of supplies of materials to them: we shall accordingly postpone discussion of this second topic until section 12.6.

The classic economic problem arising in the provision of public goods in the strict sense is this: what quantities of such goods should there be supplied if this has to be at the expense of the supply of privately consumed goods? Again there are the related problems of the quality and variety that should be allowed in the supply of public goods. Whereas with private goods free competition should ensure an efficient allocation of resources, in the sense that the price of each good would reflect the willingness of each purchaser to buy what he did buy and at the same time the marginal costs of the various producers of producing the amounts they did provide, there is no comparable mechanism for setting such a neat matching in the case of goods exhibiting 'public' characteristics. First, 'non-rivalness' implies that there would have to be some collective 'willingness of the community to pay' in place of that of each individual, to be reflected in the marginal production costs relevant to whatever might be the amounts actually produced: any such 'community willingness' would be a metaphysical concept and it is difficult to suppose it would have practical content. For, second, 'non-excludability' makes it very hard to design an effective scheme to persuade people to reveal how willing they are that the public goods should be charged for when they themselves must pay: the temptation to conceal their keenness to acquire more goods when there is no effective sanction against 'free-riders' is well attested. How far the 'public goods' sector should be expanded and the private sector restrained, or *vice versa*, is therefore a matter for dispute. There is no automatic economic mechanism to resolve this dispute, but rather political decisions and political theories. Much more to the point, the answer that will be suggested may be strongly affected by the degree of economic inequality currently existing: cash transfers can help people to accept a restricted private supply of goods in order to get improved standards and supplies of public services and publicly provided goods.

Suppose that the tasks of planning and programming the provision of a range of public goods were completed; the claims that greater equality can be found from greater provision of public goods without damaging the efficiency of the private sector needs to be treated with caution. It would be hard to demonstrate that the benefits of a public good or service are usually likely to be distributed equally between households. Of course no precise answers can be found to the question of whether some will benefit much more and others much less than the average: for if we try to identify exactly who benefits from the services of a public utility and to what extent, this would run into the problem of people's tendency to conceal their true preferences. Nevertheless, a lot can be said by distinguishing between various categories of public expenditure and between various groups of consumers, and the evidence suggests that for those expenditure categories where direct beneficiaries can be identified, such as education or health, consumers with above-average incomes actually gain proportionately more than others from publicly provided goods and services.

As we suggested in section 6.7 of chapter 6, the distribution of the benefits of some categories of expenditure is nebulous – amongst other things it will depend on the social competence and political attitudes of the civil authorities and on the instructions and funds issued to them. As for expenditure on such things as law and order or the armed forces, common sense suggests that those with property worth protection are likely to benefit more from the policeman than will the destitute, and with rather less assurance the same might be surmised about military expenditure, although if the contracts for policing work were bid for by private enterprise the distribution of benefit might quite possibly be even more unequally distributed. The general conclusion still appears to be that the benefits from an expansion of the public sector of the economy cannot safely be assumed to be one-sidedly egalitarian in their effects, regardless of how any taxes needed to finance part of it may be allocated over the population.

The third topic on page 000 – the public ownership and control of public assets – seems to offer a more straightforward means of reducing inequality. The next section examines this more closely.

12.6 Public or private?

The 'public versus private' debate contains several distinct issues that have a bearing upon inequality. In this section we shall attempt to give a flavour of each of these and to set them in context alongside the topics of sections 12.5, 12.7 and 12.8 which also deal with ways in which the authorities may attempt to influence the workings of the economic system.

In some respects the different issues are a result of a choice of language. In speaking of public versus private *ownership* we have in mind the entitlement to the income generated by these assets. Expropriating private landlords, buying out mine-owners or, in the reverse direction, 'selling off the nation's silver' to speculators and dividend drawers obviously has a direct impact on economic inequality, the nature of which depends on the exact terms of the buy-out or the sell-off. However, in a sense this issue of itself raises little that is new, since proposals for the public ownership of assets can be seen as an extension of proposals for wealth redistribution. The short- and long-term effects of such proposals could, in principle, be analysed using the body of theory surveyed in chapter 9; more specific, if speculative, answers could be obtained by using the type of dynamic models of wealth and income distribution that we considered in chapters 10 and 11.[4] The debate is usually perceived to be not only about ownership but primarily about private versus public management and control which raises deeper questions that have a bearing upon economic inequality. When considering the régime of management and control, it is convenient to refer to 'regulation or liberalisation?'[5] rather than 'nationalisation or privatisation?' so as to avoid overemphasis on questions more properly concerning how wealth should be distributed.

The issue of management and control draws attention to the discussion of equity and efficiency as potentially rival goals for policy makers. We have already stressed that assuming away the diversity of commodities and of individuals desperately oversimplifies the analysis. But, assuming that some meaning can be given to the equity–efficiency frontier discussed in section 12.2, we can use the idea of the frontier to illustrate two strands of argument in the debate. The first of these concerns the issue of whether a change in the way productive enterprises are managed – for example, a switch from firms run by profit-grubbing capitalists to public corporations run by selfless civil servants – would result in a shift along the frontier in the direction of equality. The second strand of argument concerns the point that we may not even be on the frontier in the first place, and that a switch of régime (from public to private, or *vice versa*) may actually push the economy towards it. The story might be even more complicated than that, since a root-and-branch programme of nationalisation or privatisation in an advanced industrialised economy would presumably shift the frontier – still assuming that we know (a) how to define it and (b) where it is.

As an example take the proposal that an extensive switch from the private to the public sector might substantially alleviate economic inequality. Such a step might be expected to provide a partial alleviation of the extremely unequal distribution of benefits from wealth ownership 'at a stroke', whatever the effect upon the efficiency of the allocation of resources within the economy. Whether it is likely to be particularly successful, and how widely it is likely to be welcomed, depend largely on the scope of the action undertaken. Whilst a thorough conversion to state ownership would presumably have a profound and long-lasting effect on inequality in most market economies, such sweeping measures would have to involve so many further political and social issues that it is barely possible to comment concisely and impartially on the desirability or otherwise of such measures. But one formidable problem should be emphasised here: state purchase of industrial enterprises and of equity shares in them, even if reinforced by levies on financial capital, will only be fully effective if followed up by steps to ensure the continued growth of the infrastructure and productive capacity and, except possibly in large self-sufficient economies, thriving export trade as well. Continued expansion might have to be partly at the expense of immediate living standards, and so the authorities might attempt to plan in detail the relative shares and structure of consumer industries and investment industries on the one hand, and of privately owned and state owned undertakings on the other. Wholehearted changes would probably provoke widespread objection, especially if any well-established sections of the population stand to lose by them. Half-hearted measures risk having little equalising effect upon the distribution of wealth;[6] furthermore the vital control over the industrial capacity and other assets absorbed into the public sector might after all remain firmly in the hands of the same prosperous types who managed them before the changeover, since those with the most suitable skill and experience for management of state enterprises may be judged by the politicians to be those who were from the same prosperous circle as were the managers of most private firms.

Despite these qualifications, it is hard to deny that public control and ownership of assets and the provision of public goods may substantially alleviate economic inequality, especially in conditions where it has been particularly glaring. But half measures will still leave half unsolved the inequality stemming from the unequal financial distributions of personal incomes and personal wealth ownership for use in maintaining private consumption standards. This has sometimes led to vociferous demands for an extension of public enterprise. But where these demands have been met, the results have not in all cases been particularly satisfactory: partly for this reason, there have also emerged equally vociferous demands for a curtailment of the public sector and greater reliance on an expanding private sector free to derive the most benefit from the operation of market forces. What are the economic arguments which would enable a policy maker to form a sensible judgement of the balance between the two systems?

The conventional argument for the private enterprise free market system of using resources is that by using prices as signposts, firms can respond appropriately to public demand and thus produce a pattern of output which is Pareto efficient. The relative price of any pair of goods (as seen by the consumer) should ideally be guided under this régime to exact equality with the ratio of their marginal costs. But there are well-known problems where this mechanism 'fails', in that prices are distorted or simply provide ambiguous information;[7] for example, in the production of infrastructure capital or in the field of education and training. Now take a public sector enterprise operating on the basis of directives from the authorities. Assume that the authorities have sufficiently experienced and well-trained and disciplined officers to be able to plan the inputs and outputs so as to secure outcomes reasonably close to or on the technically efficient frontier and at the 'correct' point on the frontier, that appropriately takes account of the income distribution which has governed the purchasing power of the various consumers. As we have seen, the private sector free market enterprise would not be likely to select this particular composition of output: but is there any good reason to suppose that the specialists whom the authorities will employ will follow their guidelines with better success?

Many have argued that the absence of commercial pressures will result instead in a waste of productive resources, so that although the composition of output may perhaps be better provided proportionately with the essential ingredients required for a simple healthy life at a modest level of comfort, the total volume of output will be less than it would have been if the competitive spur had been fully operative. Without the hustle of the chase for profits administrative lethargy may prevail and result in waste and technical inefficiency. Against this it can be argued that free market competition can result in overproduction of the 'wrong' goods which, although immediately profitable to their producers, may cause serious damage to others; by exhausting non-renewable resources, by pollution, or even by interfering with the ecological balance in whole continents.

Such opposing viewpoints lead to heated and emotive language and take one well outside the boundaries within which a pedantic economist is likely to wish to contain his subject. The important point to keep hold of is that since the motivating forces behind economic choices and activities do range far beyond the boundaries usually attributed to the arts and science of economics, power, resentment, superstition, maternal instincts – to name just a few – no 'optimum' calculated in terms of simple economic concepts alone will likely be attained by leaving all citizens to pursue their own aims freely. But neither is such as optimum likely to be attained by entrusting all important decisions to one person, and whilst there is a good case for entrusting such decisions to select bodies of intelligent unharassed specialists in the various aspects of administration, the manner of their selection, promotion and retirement is critically important to the success of the method, but it is also liable to abuse. These matters can only be mentioned briefly in a book written by theoretical economists or statisticians. But they have to be mentioned if a false impression that there are simple foolproof remedies for injustice and waste is to be avoided.

So it seems that neither free enterprise nor full-blooded state ownership and control can claim an overwhelming case on grounds of greater efficiency or equity. What, though may be said about piecemeal moves involving quite localised switches between public control and the free market? To deal with this issue we now pass on to a more direct examination of the distributional arguments involved in the debate for and against 'deregulation'.

One quite powerful argument for deregulation on such grounds is that it is likely to reduce, or even eliminate, 'rent'. A useful example of this is that of transport industries – airlines in the USA, bus services in the UK – where it may be claimed that the switch to private competition has led to reductions in fares, and in the case of the US airlines to cuts in the incomes of pilots. What impact this has on economic inequality will naturally depend on which groups' incomes are cut, on which group of consumers benefits most from price reductions (see section 12.7) and on who owns the assets which yielded the high rent. In the case of the airlines and bus services the direction of the effect of deregulation on economic inequality may well be finely balanced, so that if a clear case could be established for (or against) deregulation on pure efficiency grounds it might seem that the question were settled. However, as we have just pointed out, underlying economic policy decisions there are likely to be a number of considerations which are not purely economic which have also to be taken into account, so that simplistic economic criteria are unlikely to settle the issue in this straightforward manner. Unless statutory penalties are rigorously enforced so as to prevent undesirable side effects, the more vigorous contest for profits arising from transport deregulation might harm the interests of disadvantaged third parties such as children with long journeys to school, harassed pedestrians or those who suffer from excessive aircraft noise.

A clearer case for deregulation and liberalisation might be made on the grounds which we discussed in chapters 7 and 8 relating to the professional bodies such as institutes and councils of legal or medical practitioners, and other large bureaucratic organisations which ensure established lifetime careers and safe incomes for the senior personnel which may be regarded as a lucrative form of rent. But it is arguable that the advantages available to senior executives in large private enterprises – the company car, generous expense allowances, share options, occasional *ex gratia* payments, private insurance schemes, lump-sum payments on retirement – are even greater than those enjoyed by the senior personnel in the professions such as teaching, the health services and other civil services within the public sector. There are a number of further reasons why an argument for deregulation as a general panacea for improving both efficiency and equity is likely to be misleading. We have stressed the risk that less regard will be paid to the interests of disadvantaged third parties and the distorting effects of fixed costs: apart from these, the segmentation of the labour market, as we saw in chapters 7 and 8, far from being an artificially imposed monopoly may actually be reinforced by the competitive mechanism. In this case, rent-like components of income – which mainly accrue to the rich – being endemic to the competitive system, are unlikely to be successfully countered by diminishing regulation.

Indeed, one motive for regulation in the form of controls on private monopoly or of thorough nationalisation is that of providing some 'countervailing power' against that of private monopolies. We have cited the case of the professions, but more important is that of large international corporations which are very strongly placed, however, to evade such controls to some extent by switching their operations away from those economies which attempt such regulation and control and in favour of those economies relying on the free market.

Finally, there are the important problems arising from uncertainty which also under-lay much of the theoretical discussion of chapters 8 and 11. These often strengthen the case for regulation on grounds of equity. Amongst the many ways in which uncertainty can cause special difficulties for the very poor, is its effect upon prices and employment. We shall discuss price uncertainty in the next section; but the employment question (which, as we noted in chapter 8, is often crucial to the income prospects of the poor) is of immediate relevance to the 'public or private' issue. Unregulated competition is certainly likely to make loss of employment more sudden than a system of public enterprise. More importantly, public management and control enables the authorities to protect the economy from the worst effects on overall unemployment of sudden shocks external to the economy. Even if the effectiveness of such intervention is often overstated, it is still the case that since uncertainty is an unavoidable constituent of the economic and political situation, there are good reasons for a Keynesian admixture of competitive free enterprise and sensible carefully planned regulation by a disinterested and expert corps of public servants. The prevalence of uncertainty also reinforces our earlier conclusion that no simple body of economic theory can concoct valid rules for deciding just where the balance should be set between regulation and private enterprise. Like so many disciplines relating to human behaviour, economics is more an art than a science.

12.7 Market intervention

There are two main types of policy for regulating inequality through the market mechanism: the redistribution of property and the control of prices. Property in land might be transferred to the landless; house rents might be controlled. Principles applying to these two types of policy may be extended to those redistributing benefits from other assets and to price control of a variety of consumer goods both durable and non-durable. But as so often when considering redistribution, the application of a general theory based on such considerations proves to be more complex than in many other fields of economic theory. Intervention in each particular market is likely to have its own peculiar features and must be examined on its own merits.

To assist the poor, the goods they need may be lowered in price and the prices they get for the services and goods that they supply may be raised or supplemented. In this context the prices of certain 'key' goods and services appear to be especially important: for example, the wage rates of unskilled labour, and the prices of basic constituents in poor people's cost of living, including food, clothing, shelter, water supplies, heating, transport and medical services. That administrators do pay particular attention to these is shown by the frequent discussion of minimum-wage legislation, rent rebates, tax exemption and subsidies for the purchase of gas and electricity and clothes by certain groups of consumers. But it is important not to be persuaded solely by the immediate appeal of price-interventionist measures: we should examine the way in which economic reasoning can contribute towards such discussions.

As we noted in section 12.3 it may often be efficient just to hand over cash to those who need it for buying what they need, without operating at all on prices. The apparent inefficiencies of price control of consumer goods may not only make redistribution policy blunt and ineffective, it may also make it seem unjust: well-off households may choose to alter their diet to take advantage of the opportunities of cheaper eating afforded by food subsidies and thereby cause shortage of the very goods whose supply to the poorer families the rationing scheme was designed to ensure. Moreover, the arbitrary demarcation trap may itself introduce new sources of personal injustice as some, apparently 'key' prices are controlled whilst others remain unregulated.[8] Conventional arguments thus suggest that consumer prices should be free from any controls. Yet there are clear objections to such reliance on cash transfers. The administrative difficulties of identifying which persons are in real need, and of ensuring that the money is efficiently and punctually made available personally to them, can give rise to problems of injustice greater than those from the demarcation trap of consumer price regulation. And for goods exhibiting the property of non-rivalness discussed in section 12.4 it may be actually both easier and more efficient to adjust prices for selected groups of individuals as, in the case of allowing cheaper train and bus fares for the elderly at off-peak times and seasons, than to dole out cash to them.

Now let us turn to subsidies and other props to selling prices of what the poor may be able to sell, including their labour. Unfortunately, the effective and comprehensive control of wage rates and the selling prices of other income-yielding assets can prove to be even less tractable than the case of regulation of buying prices. Items of transferable property – such as real estate or shares in firms – could be redistributed by means of cash-and-coupon rationing schemes to a certain extent, but it is very hard to see how this could be arranged in the case of human capital or, more broadly, *labour power*, taken to mean the potential, in the form of marketable skills and abilities, to earn income in the labour market. Limited possibilities of redistributing these inputs, such as schooling, which influence labour power are not quite the equivalent of the redistribution possible in the application of cash-and-coupon rationing schemes for foods. So, despite the difficulties of implementation, in the case of labour the adjustment of market prices – the wage rates – becomes very important.

The two main methods of income adjustment in this case have already been touched on in section 12.5. There is income taxation in some form, which may be designed so as to reduce the marginal earnings of the rich whilst not affecting that of the poor; in principle, some of the economic effects would be similar to those of commodity taxes, and raise the same wider issues as were involved with taxation for redistribution. Of more immediate relevance are the designs of the authorities for various schemes setting minimum rates of pay.

Minimum-wage legislation often appears attractive as a means of supporting disadvantaged workers, but its effectiveness as a practical policy tool is typically called into question by orthodox economic analysis.[9] The obvious argument in favour of a minimum wage is one of equity: it is unfair that any group of employers should be paying substantially below what is customary for labour of similar grades to be paid elsewhere in the economy. The principal argument commonly advanced against minimum-wage schemes is that such measures merely cause unemployment.[10]

This unemployment argument is often made by using a simplistic analogy to the supply and demand argument examined in chapter 6; if the price of labour were held above the level at which the supply curve cuts the demand curve, then fewer people would be employed than actually wanted to work even at the unaltered wage rate. A variant of this line is that by insisting that nobody may be employed at a wage below the statutory minimum, the authorities may make it impossible for the disadvantaged to find any employer prepared to take them on apart from charitable persons or institutions, although this objection can be countered either by legislation to require employers to include in their workforces a percentage of disabled, on those in disadvantaged groups,[11] or by subsidising their employment by firms and charitable organisations. A rather more sophisticated argument focuses upon possible unintended side effects of minimum wage enforcement. The minimum wage may prevent certain young workers from acquiring human capital – for employers find that it is not worthwhile assigning such workers to activities where they have substantial opportunities to acquire on-the-job training but currently produce little.[12] So, in the face of a minimum wage, the employment strategy may be to make such youthful workers earn their keep by assigning them to tasks giving a higher immediate return, but little training value.

Under idealised conditions of perfect competition in a free market with perfect information all this seems logical. But evidence that these conditions generally apply in labour markets, or that the forced unemployment must inevitably result, is far from overwhelming.[13] As we have discussed in chapters 7 and 8 labour market adjustments are more complicated than a naive application of supply and demand analysis might suggest.[14] One reason for this is the quasi-monopsonistic position which many employers of specific skills enjoy in the labour market, a point discussed within the topic of segmentation in section 7.7; the inherent uncertainty associated with many job contracts and the lack of market power of the disadvantaged means that this quasi-monopsony is not transitory. The 'countervailing power' argument – mentioned in connection with the regulation of monopoly – is relevant here: it implies that a carefully chosen minimum wage can support the poor without loss of employment by cutting into the monpsony rents;[15] in doing so it will also improve economic efficiency. There is a further efficiency argument in a world of imperfect information: minimum wage laws may foster efficiency by forcing firms to pay the same for labour of the same quality; otherwise inefficient firms can get away with passing some of their losses on to their workforce by underpayment, then the process of replacement of the unfit and expansion of the fit firms will be inhibited.

The points about efficiency and employment can be extended from particular labour markets to the economy in general. Simple arguments on the supposed cost of minimum wages based on strong assumptions of perfect competition may be inappropriate.[16] Even though the real wages of affected workers will increase, there is no reason to expect an automatic adverse effect on aggregate unemployment if markets are not everywhere perfect and prices are not fully flexible: the outcome will also depend on demand conditions in the economy, and even if foreign competitors apparently gain a competitive advantage because of not being subject to the minimum-wage legislation this can be offset by conventional exchange-rate mechanisms.

Although wage intervention is tricky because of the segmented and diverse nature of the labour market and the potential for investment implicit in the job discussed in chapters 7 and 8, and although incautious or overambitious wage-support programmes may be self-defeating in terms of their effect on the economic circumstances of the poor, they should not be dismissed as inappropriate or impractical. In a world with market imperfections sensible intervention in the prices of strategic commodities may be the best that can be done.[17]

12.8 Rationing

Direct government control of quantities of goods and services is a particularly emotive subject. To some people it is the last refuge of inept politicians in a mismanaged economy; to others rationing is an invaluable policy tool that can prevent an emergency turning into a disaster.[18] However, as with the discussion of market intervention, we want to see how economic arguments can be brought to bear in order to reveal the value of rationing as a policy measure to mitigate economic inequality.

Consider a rationing scheme like those which were operated during the second world war in Britain whereby goods such as fuel and food could be obtained at reduced money prices by purchasing them with a combination of coupons and cash to cover both 'coupon prices' and 'cash prices' (a packet of powdered eggs might have cost two shillings and required the surrender of ten coupons). Perhaps every household gets coupons of the same amount per head; or perhaps the awards reflect some estimate of need, with women (at that time) judged to need less than men and children even less than women; or needs and coupon awards might be reckoned with even greater sophistication. The belief was that the poor could thus be enabled to purchase essential goods without substantially influencing market prices, and this belief was justified by the results.

How should rationing be reconciled with free choice and the market mechanism though? For example, suppose that fuel coupons have been issued and that they must be handed over in order to obtain gas, petrol or other fuels at their controlled prices, and that that a similar scheme applies for certain foods. Imagine that Toad[19] in his sports car has used up all his fuel coupons but has cheese coupons to burn, whereas Rat has exhausted his cheese ration but has a pile of unwanted petrol coupons: what objection can there be to allowing them to trade in the two kinds of coupons? No objection to this benevolent proposal? Then how about encouraging trading amongst all classes of coupon and publishing all the latest prices in the *Wall Street Journal, Private Eye* and *Exchange and Mart*? British readers with historical prejudices might instinctively oppose this, suspecting links between such operations and the notorious black markets of the 1940s, and there are indeed good reasons to fear inequitable results from such dealings as we shall shortly see. First, consider the purely economic consequences.

Where the coupons market is well organised the effective prices of any two wanted goods will partially reflect the ratio of a buyer's marginal evaluations of them: thus Toad clearly must pay a premium on each litre of petrol equal to the extra fuel coupons he has to buy for it: but the true price of petrol is made higher for Rat as well, even though he has a pile of fuel coupons to sell, since he needs some fuel for heating his hole, and marginally each kilogram of fuel used for that costs him not only the controlled money price of that kilogram but the forgone trading gain that he might have obtained by selling that coupon to the likes of Toad. It appears superficially that a happy solution has emerged, in that it is efficient – in the narrow Paretian sense discussed above – aggregate consumption is still limited by the scale of the coupon issue and the distribution of purchasing power is still in the hands of the coupon-issuing authority.

The most basic objection may be that in a national emergency like war, where it is most likely that rationing will be accepted, 'father knows best' may well be true, and be seen to be true. But even though the maxim may be true for some goods, it is unlikely that the government is really omniscient to the required degree over the whole range of household goods. However there is a more serious point concerning the likely workings of such secondary markets in coupons, given the circumstances under which rationing systems of this kind are introduced: imperfections in these markets will often work systematically to the disadvantage of the poorest. Because of inadequate information, urgent needs and lack of bargaining skill, the poor may get bilked in the market even when nominal prices are controlled: neither can this be rectified by the authorities taking steps to spread more information about the state of supply and demand. There is also a third argument: in times of pressing social need – such as arise in wartime – the criteria of equity, fairness and equality of sacrifice become far more acceptable, so that many aspects of welfare are so recognised as though for the first time. Then the public will no longer feel tolerant of the wasteful Toad gadding about in his sports car swallowing up scarce fuel which could otherwise have been diverted to urgent uses (by lowering the total fuel ration) had not Rat traded them to him for food coupons.

Let us examine the problems which may stand in the way of implementing such a scheme to override the free market in consumer goods.

Even where black markets are disallowed, market intervention schemes can have their administrative difficulties. The most persistent of these is the arbitrary demarcation trap discussed in section 12.7. Consumer goods which have the same name often are marketed in very different qualities for the rich than for the poor, so that setting a maximum price per unit in terms of coupons and money may well award a higher subsidy to the rich than the poor. Again, take an example from Britain in the second world war. To buttress food rationing elsewhere a maximum price of five shillings was set for a meal in a restaurant: to ensure distributional equity it might be thought this sort of scheme could be elaborated by subdividing the kinds of meal finely enough and allowing different prices for each kind, and that the same process of fine subdivision of goods into qualities could be extended to all such rationing schemes. But if this is done two further problems are likely to emerge: there may be unfortunate unforeseen inequities in the scheme itself, and the scheme may then create economic incentives specifically to thwart its own aims.

These rationing schemes were undoubtedly successful in reducing the inequality in living standards. But clumsy rationing schemes can slide into the trap of arbitrary demarcation: for example, if everybody is tied to the same ration of butter, and of cooking fat, and of cigarettes and of sugar, making no allowance for their differences in tastes and relative needs for these various goodies, much inconvenience and time-wasting haggling could result. The second world war solution to this difficulty lay in a points rationing scheme mentioned in the last paragraph, which awarded each person the same total points value of coupons for a whole category of goods – for example clothing and footwear – at standard points prices set by the authorities for different articles within that category, at levels chosen so as to adjust the pattern of demand to the pattern of supply immediately available. This is a good instance of the fact that many arbitrary demarcation traps can be avoided by exercising ingenuity, on the part of the alert policy maker.

Is rationing no more than a historical curiosity as a policy instrument for modifying economic inequality? To dismiss market intervention and rationing schemes as curiosities relevant only to rare emergencies is to fall into the intellectual trap of uniformitarianism that was mentioned in chapter 2. Practical policy making has to take into account the fact that economic shocks and the process of change and economic transformation generate some of the most acute inequalities. The relevant time scale is not so generous as to permit the comfortable ubiquitous assumption of long-run market equilibrium. 'Catastrophism' is relevant. Furthermore where the market mechanism fails, even in the short run, mechanisms that act directly on perceived inequities may appropriately take priority over those that would have been prescribed solely on the basis of a simplistic interpretation of efficiency criteria. Interference in the price structure and the non-market allocation of goods have a proper place in the policy maker's toolkit; but they are tools that must be used with skill.

12.9 Global inequality

A theoretical treatment of economic inequality need impose no difference of principle between the analysis of inequality within a small economy and the analysis of inequality over most of the world. In each case we can analyse inequality between persons and inequality between large representative groups, such as those working in particular industries or those residing in particular regions. Nevertheless, the theories which it is sensible to apply may be different when dealing with large parts of Africa, Asia and South America from what they would be when considering the USA and the UK.

In this final section, we pay attention to this necessary variety of approach. We do not attempt to offer a set of new prescriptions or to reinterpret each of the issues that we have discussed in the previous sections of this chapter. In chapter 1 we took a nibble at the problems of world inequality by examining statistical summaries of some of the numerical information about inequality and economic development. We now focus on the choice of theoretical approach that is appropriate in such an extended study and in particular on the shortcomings of the market mechanism as the driving force behind inequality and as the main explanation of inequality or as the best means for income redistribution. Three issues which we have already stressed in this chapter increase in importance when we move to the global comparisons: the handicaps imposed by ignorance and uncertainty, the deleterious side effects of productive activities on other groups, and the important role played by the threat and exercise of power and force. Each of these three issues reinforces the importance of the others.

Ignorance and uncertainty

These difficult twins have, as we have seen, played an important role in the generation of economic inequality within developed countries. It comes as little surprise that they aggravate the generation of inequality within individual developing economies and of inequality between different economies.

In early encounters between Europeans and the African communities lack of information placed the latter at an immense trading disadvantage, quite apart from any use of force by the traders. Even today the contrast in the information available to the two kinds of economy is such as to make it seem fatuous to apply economic models based on perfectly informed and free market competition for studying processes and policies affecting international economic inequality: improved education and supply of information are two of the resources of which the impoverished economies stand in the greatest need.

It is well recognised that the economic organisation of developing countries can make them especially prone to external shocks such as fluctuations in commodity prices or vagaries of the climate: the dependence on the sugar crop, or the predominance of low-lying land liable to flooding are bound to accentuate their vulnerability to inequality-generating unforeseen events. On top of this other recent trends – arguably inherited in intensified form from the developed world – have increased the effects of uncertainty and imperfect information in poor countries. One is that the increasing concentration of political influence in some economies has resulted in more abrupt swings in policy, which make it difficult for the many other policy makers to anticipate; this can in turn cause the postponement of parts of development plans and from this to a slowdown in overall economic growth as well as both intended and unintended shifts in the distribution of income. An impulsive leader with idiosyncratic opinions may indulge in declarations of political and economic policies which, to the more conventional, seem very risky. A second example concerns the uncertainty resulting from changing consumer technology. The profit motive may prompt intensive marketing of unfamiliar products (baby formula food to African mothers?) or the promotion of new technology that requires complementary purchases by consumers with an erstwhile traditional lifestyle (the refrigerator?). The result can be a dramatic impact on the living standards that people can attain from given resources. It becomes increasingly difficult for ordinary people of modest means to continue to live their traditional lifestyle without the aid of new-fangled apparatus which they are ill able to afford: firms supplying traditional products go out of business; eventually the former luxuries become necessities for the supply of basic needs of the poor; the refrigerator

once unnecessary becomes difficult to do without for those who live in a remote location without adequate transport. The market mechanism acts to reinforce the inequality-generating effects of imperfect information.

External effects

There is a further important dimension of ignorance: the motivation and aspirations
of people in developing lands are so different as to be almost incomprehensible to many
of the citizens of the highly developed economies, another example of the PLUM
assumption which we discussed in chapter 2. One consequence of this is that the large-
scale industrial, mining, agricultural or military activities by the industrialised world
on developing lands may inadvertently do immense damage to what their inhabitants
hold to be most essential. To the well-meaning developers from the prosperous
economies it may appear that the needs of the inhabitants of the impoverished lands
are on the one hand a release from the terrors and cruelties incidental to tribal super-
stitions and 'false gods' and on the other the materialist improvements that can result
from modern medicines, fertilisers and technical facilities. But, as we noted in chapter
3, the economic and social circumstances relevant to one community do not invariably
apply to another, and the inhabitants of developing economies often have firm convic-
tions, based on many centuries' experience of their environment, that their own way of
life has comparable advantages and their own methods of living preserve the material
basis of their economy for their offspring, whereas the wealthy invaders recklessly both
squander the local natural resources and violate the structural stability of their community. Mutual incomprehension increases the importance of the risk that the activities of one community may inadvertently do serious damage to the other, and this
damage often falls disproportionately upon the poor, so worsening the distribution of
economic welfare. Externalities which – as we have discussed in chapter 4 – can have a
significant impact upon living standards and economic inequality in developed
economies can be overwhelmingly important in the relationship between the developed
and developing world.[20]

Power and force

When considering the main topics of debate about global inequality in all but the most
parochial of ivory towers, it is difficult to avoid the impression that the way change is
attempted is often through the exercise of raw power. Thirty years ago it might have
been argued that influence and persuasion were the most effective means of change;
and this may still be true even now in some advanced economies. But the tendency to
back up influence and persuasion by the threat and exercise of power has become far
more evident: circumstantial evidence reinforces the strong suspicion that power is the
key to radical changes in the distribution of income and control of wealth, and not the
calculus of efficient allocation and Pareto optimisation.

   If this conclusion is correct then the market will prove to be an awkward, ineffective
and possibly perverse mechanism through which to attempt measures that might alleviate the most glaring inequalities on a world scale. It would also explain why there are
many people, especially in less-developed economies, who believe that the key issues in

redistribution are about ensuring adequate satisfaction of a small number of basic needs for everyone; or at least everyone in the group to which they feel they belong. Such views have wide appeal: the reaction of the public to sensational disasters is evidence of sympathy with individuals who through no fault of their own are faced with sudden horrific economic hardship, although the same public opinion, because of the strength of group loyalties, will often support intolerant and damaging attacks on rival groups. This scope for and public interest in counteracting the effects of non-market causes of inequality is one good reason for extending the study of economic inequality and its regulation from the parochial study of its workings within one country such as the USA or the UK to its operation all over the globe.

Our discussion in this area has been necessarily limited to a few suggestive remarks. But in our view it is important to pursue the subject of economic inequality in that direction and in particular to use the lessons of such a study to recognise the validity of points of view common in groups far different from our own and to grasp the opportunities to modify our own prejudices in the light of the evidence. We urge the reader to do so.

12.10 Questions for discussion

General Reading: Barr (1993), Deacon and Bradshaw (1983), Field (1981), Le Grand (1982), Le Grand and Robinson (1984), McClements (1978), Piachaud (1982).

12.1   Can redistribution in kind be efficient (Foldes, 1969; Garfinkel, 1973; Weitzman, 1977)?

12.2   Construct an economic argument for the use of (a) food stamps, (b) education vouchers as devices for earning a more equitable distribution of goods and services. How would you quantify the benefits of these provisions to those families who qualify for them (Paglin, 1980; Smeeding, 1977; Moon and Smolensky, 1977)?

12.3   It is sometimes argued that public expenditure is actually regressive in its redistributional impact. Should public spending therefore be reduced? What effect will the democratic voting on the allocation of these goods have on inequality in the long run (Arrow, 1971; Aaron and McGuire, 1970; Maital, 1973; Merrett and Monk, 1966; Perotti, 1993)?

12.4   Discuss the case for the use of a negative income tax or basic income scheme as a device for reducing the inequality of consumption (Atkinson, 1973, 1995; Brittan and Webb, 1990; Piachaud, 1982, chapter 8).

12.5   'Old age, ill health, the bringing up of children, interruption of earnings, provision of housing for the family, these are contingencies of life to be paid for out of one's income. If the value of money is reasonably stable, responsible people, even if poor, can normally provide for the contingencies of life by saving and insurance. State provision, all too often expensive, as well as inadequate, as it cannot be adjusted to the widely different circumstances of families and individuals, is necessarily financed by taxation. As a result many people's post-tax income becomes like pocket money, not required for major necessities and hazards of life because these are paid for by taxes largely levied on themselves. This policy treats adults as if they were children. Adults manage incomes; children receive pocket money. The redistribution of responsibility means the reduction of the status of adults to that of children. The policy also under-

mines the cohesion of the family' (P. T. Bauer – *The Times*, 7 October 1982). Discuss.
12.6   '... with the methods of redistribution currently used, complete equalisation of income would, at least in theory, bring the entire productive mechanism to a halt. One is led to surmise on a continuity assumption from this extreme case that very large output losses are also likely to accompany any attempt to get anywhere very close to equality' (Baumol and Fischer, 1979).
'To get a grip on the problems of poverty, one should also forget the idea of overcoming inequality by redistribution. Inequality may even grow at first as poverty declines. To lift the incomes of the poor, it will be necessary to increase the rates of investment, which in turn will tend to enlarge the wealth, if not the consumption, of the rich. The poor, as they move into the work force and acquire promotions, will raise their incomes by a greater percentage than the rich; but the upper classes will gain by greater absolute amounts, and the gap between the rich and the poor may grow. All such analyses are deceptive in the long run, however, because they imply a static economy in which the numbers of the rich and the middle class are not growing' (Gilder, 1982).
Is it possible to reconcile these views with the argument that measures which diminish inequality can often stimulate demand and thereby raise living standards in the short and long term?
12.7   In what ways may geographical mobility affect the possibilities for redistribution (Epple and Romer, 1991)?
12.8   What long-run effects on income inequality would you expect to find from a government programme to shift the balance between publicly and privately provided education (see question 8.10 and Glomm and Ravikumar, 1992; Peltzmann, 1973)?
12.9   The following is a list of entry charges to Shrewsbury School in the 1570s.

Son of a lord	10s.
Son of a knight	6s. 8d.
Eldest son of a gentleman	2s. 6d.
Youngest son of a gentleman	2s. 4d.
Those of lower degree born outside the county of Salop	2s.
Those of low degree born in Salop	1s.
Inhabitants of Shrewsbury	8d.
Sons of Shrewsbury burgesses	4d.

(O'Day, 1982). Consider the impact on inequality of the widespread adoption of a similar system of charges in a modern industrialised economy.
12.10   Examine the view that the choice of theory of income redistribution when considering the United Kingdom might reasonably be quite different from that which would be appropriate when considering the United States (O'Higgins and Ruggles, 1981; Ruggles and O'Higgins, 1981).
12.11   In what ways might the 'cash versus goods' argument of section 12.2 need to be modified if we consider redistribution between rich and poor countries rather than between persons (see Singer *et al.*, 1987)?

Notes

1 This point comes close to home: the investment constraints affect not only the railways and drains, but also fundamental research and the production of economic and social statistics on which constructive discussion about policy towards economic inequality relies.

2   See page 15 above.

3   The issues of tax design are discussed in Sandmo (1976), Seade (1977), Tuomala (1990) and the formal limits on armchair administrators in a world of imperfect information are discussed in Roberts (1984). All of these models require some estimate of the way individuals' behaviour will react to changes in the tax system; attention is usually focused upon the supposed labour-supply response – see the discussion on page 000 above and Keeley (1981), Rosen and Welch (1971) – although other reponses such as savings are important too – see Danziger *et al.* (1981). For an application to the UK see Atkinson *et al.* (1983) and Cowell (1979).

4   Proportional and progressive wealth taxation has already been examined in the Mutt island models: these can be manipulated to examine the impact of across-the-board wealth increments, so that we may analyse the immediate and long-run effects of a redistribution of the entitlements to shares in the productive capacity of the economy.

5   Cf. Redwood and Hatch (1982).

6   Opposition might be widespread even if only piecemeal movements in the direction of state ownership were undertaken, and might not come predominantly from the very wealthy; this is because partial measures are likely to enable the very wealthy to avoid severe financial loss by skilful management of the composition of their financial assets, thereby switching the main burdens on to the fairly wealthy instead.

7   The causes of market failure may be summarised thus: (i) Because of poor information, taxes or subsidies on the consumption of some goods, the prices facing consumers may differ from those considered by producers. (ii) It may pay the producer to distort the prices in order to exploit some monopolistic power. (iii) Prices may mislead due to there being a marginal social benefit from extending production of one good and less of another, not represented by the (private) willingness of each consumer to pay for the two goods. This is another aspect of the 'externalities' discussed in 12.5. These three problems can arise whatever the technology of production may happen to be. (iv) Where production involves substantial fixed costs, prices alone may not suffice to reveal the most efficient way to allocate resources between producing different goods. Whether the problem is that a wedge has been driven between prices as they 'ought to be' and prices as they are in the market (problems (i) and (ii)) or that prices yield wrong or ambiguous information (problems (iii) and (iv)) the outcome is likely to be that the private sector in pursuit merely of private profit will produce an inefficient allocation of resources.

8   During the 1970s the UK government's bread subsidy applied to the Indian chapatti but not the Staffordshire oatcake, because the latter included no wheat flour: this roused ill-feeling in North Staffordshire where the oatcake was a major staple among working-class families.

9   See for example Lal (1995).

10 This argument goes back at least to the times when the Wages Councils (then Trade Boards) were introduced 80 years ago in the UK – see Field and Winyard (1977). For surveys see Brown *et al.* (1982, 1983).

11 Thus after the second world war, some employers in Great Britain were required to include in their workforces a few who had been disabled during war service: another example of explicit quantity controls which we discuss further in section 12.8 below on 'Rationing'. See also Leonard (1984).

12 See for example Hashimoto (1982), Feldstein (1973), Meyer and Wise (1983).

13 For example Card and Krueger (1995) concluded: 'Increases in the minimum wage have had, if anything a small, positive effect on employment.' According to Wellington (1991) the employment effects of a minimum wage on youth employment are negative but small: a 10 per cent increase in the minimum wage lowers teenage employment by some 0.06 per cent. See also Bazen and Martin (1992), Card and Krueger (1995) for case studies of France and the USA.

14 For instance, in the UK neither the introduction of wage councils nor the wage adjustments for women encouraged by the Equal Pay Act appeared to damage the employment opportunities for the workers concerned – Machin and Manning (1994), Zabalza and Tsanattos (1985). See also Mincer (1976)
15 See Persky and Tsang (1972).
16 See Johnson (1969), Johnson and Browning (1983).
17 See Allen (1987), Drazen (1986), Jones (1987), Lang (1986).
18 During the world wars, food supplies in Britain were endangered by the effects of submarine attack. It is arguable that, had an effective system of food rationing not been introduced, considerable undernourishment of the poorest section of the population could have resulted. During and after the second world war there were in addition highly effective rationing schemes on clothing and furnishings; fuel rationing was also introduced, not primarily to protect the poorest groups, but to ensure that the shortages did not interfere with the mobility needed for effective running of the war economy.
19 See Grahame (1908).
20 A dreadful example of this is provided by the disaster at the Union Carbide works at Bhopal in India during December 1984: the tragedy of the deadly pollution emitted from the plant was intensified because of the drift of the poor population into the immediate area that the presence of the plant had caused.

Appendix A Data sources and methods

A.1 Introduction

This appendix describes the data sources that we have drawn upon extensively in several parts of the book and sets out our methodology in so far as it affects manipulation of these data. Methodological issues relating to our purpose-built models are considered in appendix C.

Section A.2 of this appendix discusses the data sources for, and problems associated with, data sources required for international comparisons of income per head. Section A.3 describes the data and methods used in connection with the UK examples based on Inland Revenue data and presented in tables 1.1, 9.1, 9.2 and the associated figures. Sections A.4 and A.5 describe in detail the nature of the panel study that we have drawn upon in several chapters, and the procedures for deriving tables from the micro-data files.

A.2 Data used for international comparisons

This section describes the sources used for tables 1.2, 1.3, 2.1 and 6.2, and the methods used to derive the 'piano' diagrams presented in figures 1.2–1.4.

The primary source is the annual publication of the World Bank; *World Development Report*. The coverage of countries and of data varies from year to year, as do the definitions of some of the variables. Appendix table A.1 of the 1991 issue gives population and gross domestic product per capita in US dollars for 124 countries ordered by GDP per capita: from this table figures 1.3 and 1.4 of chapter 1 were created as follows. First we eliminated countries for which data on incomes or on population were unavailable, and then the remaining ordered list was divided into ten equal slices (by population): countries on any borderline were divided proportionately between the two neighbouring slices. Second, arithmetic mean GDP per capita was calculated for each of the ten slices: the logarithm of that income was then plotted on the horizontal scale of figure 1.3, or figure 1.4, and the representative country picked from the list whose GDP per capita most closely approximated that group average. (The procedure for the within-country example, Figure 1.2, is almost identical, with the obvious exception that one does not have to aggregate income from different countries.)

However, the World Bank published data do not permit adjustments to correct for distortions caused by artificial rates of exchange. To make these corrections we draw on the study of Summers and Heston (1988), following the methodology of Kravis *et al.* (1978a, 1978b): this provides internationally comparable data on GDP and the principal components of GDP using estimates of purchasing power for a large number of countries over the period 1950–1985: these data are also available in machine-readable form. The principal extracts from the Summers–Heston data are presented here as Table A.1 for 120 market economies in 1985, sorted by adjusted GDP per capita: throughout we have used the term 'adjusted' to denote the data computed at 1985 international prices rather than at the current rate of exchange.

Table 2.1 combines the data for the relevant entries in table A.1 (relating to 1985) with the World Bank data for 1991. Tables 6.2 and 6.3 are constructed from the rank ordering of countries given in table A.1 (using purchasing power parity rather than market rates of exchange for international comparisons), and the within-country distributions reported in the World Bank *World Development Report*, 1991. These latter data are not available for all countries, so we selected those countries that were as close as possible to the required position in the worldwide income queue, for which intra-country distribution data were available: these five countries then represent the quintile group to which they belong. As a check on the robustness of this method, tables 6.5 and 6.6 in the exercises illustrate the effect of replacing some of the countries used in tables 6.2 and 6.3 by 'near neighbours' in the rank order of table A.1.

Table 1.5 is adapted from table 3.10 in Anand (1983): the regions are defined by the following states in Peninsular Malaysia: South – Johore and Malacca; Central – Salngor and Negri Sembilan; Northwest – Perak; North – Penang, Kedah and Perlis; East – Kelantan, Trengganu and Pahang.

A.3 UK income and wealth data

Income

The Inland Revenue data are based on information held by Inland Revenue tax offices on persons liable to UK tax. Individuals with income less than the Pay-As-You-Earn (PAYE) threshold (£3,445 in 1993–4) may not be included. The lowest level of total income is therefore defined as this threshold level. With some exceptions like self-employment income, total income is approximately the same as income earned in the tax year. Other sources of information have been used to supplement incomplete information in tax offices. The Inland Revenue tables and charts are based on random samples which were selected using the Computerisation of PAYE (COP), Computerisation of D Assessment (CODA) and Claimant databases.

The use of Inland Revenue data for the discussion of income distribution in the UK (chapters 1 and 2) was dictated by the desire to have data that are easily available in published form and that facilitate comparison and contrast with the available

Table A.1 *Population and GDP per capita, 120 market economies*

Group	Country	Population	GDP/head	Adjusted GDP/head
1	Zaire	33,494	90	212
1	Chad	5,020	97	313
1	Ethiopia	42,234	117	390
1	Ghana	13,513	335	411
1	Rwanda	6,034	267	445
1	Burundi	4,702	242	446
1	Malawi	7,137	174	478
1	Niger	6,418	232	490
1	Burkina Faso	6,662	148	497
1	Somalia	5,351	285	499
1	Mali	7,545	128	499
1	Tanzania	22,241	258	513
1	Uganda	14,695	84	521
1	Sierra Leone	3,657	287	552
1	Guinea	6,081	404	561
1	Central African Rep.	2,586	258	572
1	Togo	3,035	230	624
1	Madagascar	10,164	230	629
1	Liberia	2,210	385	638
1	Mozambique	14,084	262	661
1	Benin	4,043	240	663
2	Nepal	16,527	152	667
1	Nigeria	99,753	739	681
1	Zambia	6,704	342	691
1	Sudan	21,784	322	696
2	Burma	36,859	190	697
1	Gambia	762	237	724
1	Angola	8,605	507	726
1	Mauritania	1,695	445	727
1	Kenya	20,414	288	727
4	Haiti	5,485	361	788
2	Bangladesh	100,595	182	822
2	India	764,378	260	955
1	Senegal	6,560	397	987
4	Honduras	4,383	767	1,059
1	Ivory Coast	10,116	694	1,175
1	Zimbabwe	8,394	609	1,216
2	Yemen	7,963	528	1,261
1	Cameroon	10,190	902	1,325
5	Bolivia	6,383	813	1,328
1	Congo People's Rep.	1,878	1,116	1,390
1	Egypt	48,239	1,222	1,444
4	El Salvador	5,149	1,091	1,449
2	Pakistan	95,483	380	1,450
1	Lesotho	1,525	183	1,504
6	Indonesia	162,212	495	1,550

Table A.1 (*cont.*)

Group	Country	Population	GDP/head	Adjusted GDP/head
5	Guyana	820	568	1,567
1	Morocco	21,797	545	1,582
2	Philippines	54,734	599	1,710
6	Papua New Guinea	3,393	670	1,722
4	Guatemala	8,375	1,329	1,957
1	Swaziland	757	518	1,992
2	Sri Lanka	15,837	380	1,995
4	Dominican Rep	6,255	760	2,127
4	Jamaica	2,352	852	2,155
1	Botswana	1,072	752	2,225
2	Thailand	51,514	745	2,310
1	Mauritania	1,020	1,186	2,430
5	Paraguay	3,475	1,632	2,432
1	Gabon	1,304	2,662	2,484
4	Nicaragua	3,177	1,301	2,506
1	Algeria	21,937	2,587	2,513
5	Peru	18,655	870	2,556
1	Tunisia	7,165	1,140	2,596
2	Iraq	15,784	3,145	2,706
5	Ecuador	8,735	1,875	2,858
2	Jordan	3,490	1,167	2,906
3	Turkey	50,052	1,057	3,163
5	Colombia	28,468	1,204	3,221
4	Costa Rica	2,520	1,491	3,341
6	Fiji	696	1,679	3,556
2	Korea	41,056	1,980	3,734
2	Syria	10,371	1,969	3,741
4	Panama	2,046	2,386	3,779
5	Surinam	393	3,051	3,832
5	Brazil	135,564	1,733	3,979
2	Malaysia	15,670	1,953	4,050
5	Venezuela	18,065	2,745	4,071
5	Chile	12,074	1,356	4,132
5	Argentina	30,531	2,159	4,164
5	Uruguay	3,013	1,683	4,219
2	Taiwan	19,258	3,027	4,422
1	South Africa	32,404	1,678	4,583
3	Portugal	10,229	2,016	4,601
4	Mexico	78,927	2,247	4,739
2	Iran	46,005	2,997	4,897
3	Greece	9,935	3,357	5,703
4	Barbados	254	4,828	6,413
3	Ireland	3,552	4,882	6,556
3	Malta	358	2,841	6,741
3	Cyprus	665	3,581	6,925
2	Saudi Arabia	11,336	8,180	7,838

Table A.1 (*cont.*)

Group	Country	Population	GDP/head	Adjusted GDP/head
3	Spain	38,602	4,344	7,879
2	Israel	4,233	5,555	8,208
2	Bahrain	418	10,422	8,877
4	Trinidad and Tobago	1,170	7,342	9,047
2	Oman	1,234	7,571	9,149
3	Italy	57,128	6,274	9,230
6	New Zealand	3,254	7,002	9,761
3	UK	56,543	7,901	10,874
6	Australia	15,752	10,211	10,953
3	Netherlands	14,486	8,628	11,067
2	Japan	120,754	10,793	11,176
2	Singapore	2,558	8,529	11,183
2	Hong Kong	5,423	6,255	11,297
3	Austria	7,555	8,777	11,319
3	Finland	4,908	10,686	11,340
3	Iceland	241	9,947	11,387
3	Belgium	9,857	8,028	11,580
3	Sweden	8,350	11,970	12,118
2	Kuwait	1,746	10,995	12,337
3	France	55,172	9,239	12,492
3	Germany, Federal Rep.	61,015	10,261	12,831
3	Luxembourg	366	10,128	12,937
3	Switzerland	6,458	14,363	13,411
3	Denmark	5,114	11,395	13,519
2	Utd Arab Emirates	1,367	15,706	14,496
4	Canada	25,379	13,474	14,544
3	Norway	4,153	13,980	15,563
4	USA	238,982	16,057	16,057

Notes:
The group numbers are 1: Africa 2: Asia 3: Europe 4: North and Central America 5: South America 6: Oceania. Population is in '000s.
Taken over all market economies the population total was 3,240,250,000 and total adjusted income was $14,147,500 million.
Source: Summers and Heston (1988).

information on wealth (chapter 9). As we explained in the main text, in other respects the Inland Revenue data are not the best for our purposes. The main drawbacks are:
• the exclusion of information about individuals whose income is too low for them to pay tax,
• the restriction of the definition of income to that which is relevant for taxation purposes.
However, other sources of income distribution data also have problems. The *Family Expenditure Survey* has the advantage of covering more effectively those with low incomes but suffers from the obvious drawbacks of sample surveys: a substantial

amount of non-response from those approached in the survey, an incomplete coverage of high incomes. A more recently available source of UK income data is *Households Below Average Income* (which in some respects has replaced the excellent series in *Economic Trends*, intermittently published up to 1987 and since lapsed). Despite the name, *Households Below Average Income* provides a remarkably comprehensive picture of the whole income distribution, if one uses it in micro-data form. It has the advantage that, although the *Family Expenditure Survey* is used to provide details about low-income families, information about the rich (needed to compute 'average income' in the title of the data – see Department of Social Security, 1996) is derived from the same source as the series in *Inland Revenue Statistics*, namely the Survey of Personal Incomes: to some extent the best of the primary sources of information about income distribution in the UK. However *Households Below Average Income* estimates are not available for a continuous series of years, and because the published tables obviously focus upon low incomes comprehensive tables of the form of table 1.1 in chapter 1 are not available.

Wealth

The distribution of identified wealth relies upon the estate multiplier method. Briefly this method rests on the notion that those dying in any one year are, in some sense, a sample of the living. Suppose i indexes a set of wealth classes (intervals) and j a set of mutually exclusive attribute classes (for example age intervals); from population statistics mortality rates specific to each j value may be available; it may be that these mortality rates also differ according to wealth category as well. Then suppose that in one particular year v_{ij} persons die in wealth range i and in attribute class j, the number of persons in the population with wealth in in interval i is estimated as

$$n_i = \Sigma_j w_{ij} v_{ij} \qquad\qquad (1)$$

where the weights w_{ij} are the reciprocal of the (i,j) specific mortality rates. A similar technique is used to derive the total amount of wealth in range i. Problems can arise for cases where the $\mathcal{E} v_{ij}$ (the expected number in a particular class) is very small and where the wealth-specific mortality rates are difficult to obtain.

Table A.2 presents the basic data on which figures 9.1–9.3 are based. However, even if one accepts the multiplier methodology, two problems are immediately apparent with this type of data. First the number of individuals in table A.2 is obviously too few if these data are supposed to represent the UK population in 1993. The problem arises principally from a source that is similar to the Inland Revenue data on income that we have highlighted above: 'the estimates cannot include people whose wealth is either so small, or held in such a form, as to make a report to the Capital Taxes Offices unnecessary when they die' (*Inland Revenue Statistics*, 1995, p. 123): a large number of persons with little wealth are automatically excluded from the 'sample' of the dying. The second problem is partly related to this: besides the wealth of these excluded persons some forms of wealth are automatically excluded. These consist principally in the form of trusts; their impact on wealth estimates is discussed in Dunn and Hoffman (1978).

One of the consequences of these problems is that the wealth totals implied by esti-

Table A.2 *The distribution of identified personal
wealth, UK, 1994*

Range of wealth	Number in range ('000)	Wealth in range (£ million)
Under £10,000	3,308	5,051
£10,000–£24,999	3,003	51,846
£25,000–£39,999	2,736	88,066
£40,000–£49,999	1,493	66,678
£50,000–£59,999	1,333	72,679
£60,000–£79,999	1,930	133,167
£80,000–£99,999	1,182	105,811
£100,000–£199,999	1,975	269,218
£200,000–£299,999	469	113,108
£300,000–£499,999	333	125,213
£500,000–£999,999	131	88,750
£1,000,000–£1,999,999	28	37,821
£2,000,000 and over	12	60,007
All ranges	17,931	1,217,415

Source: Board of the Inland Revenue, *Inland Revenue
Statistics*, 1995, table 13.3, pages 130–1.

mates based on the estate duty method wil not correspond with the balance-sheet estimates of household wealth. The adjustments required to reconcile the types of
information about wealth data are summarised in table A.3. The composition of wealth
as it emerges from the estate-multiplier method ('Identified personal wealth') is given
in column (1); correcting for valuation and underreporting gives the asset composition
in column (2). Further correction of the column-(2) data to allow for 'excluded wealth'
yields the wealth composition in column (3), 'marketable wealth'. Imputation of the
value of funded occupational pension schemes to the estimates of the asset composition column (3) completes the reconciliation with the balance sheet data in column (4).
Notice that the step from column (2) to column (3) almost doubles the estimate of
wealth held in the form of dwellings.

Column (3) in table A.3 is the basis for column (1) of table 9.2. The methods for
valuing occupational pension rights required for column (2) of table 9.2 are set out in
Royal Commission on the Distribution of Income and Wealth (1975, pages 88–9; 1976,
pages 65–70). The imputation of state pension rights for column (3) of table 9.2 is based
on the assumptions that the value of basic state pension rights is equally distributed in
each age group, that the value of state earnings-related pension schemes are imputed
to those without occupational pensions, and that widows' pensions are imputed to
married and widowed women only.

Note that the 1993 data presented in figures 9.1–9.3 and 9.5 and table 9.2 are based
on provisional estimates: the 'year of account' basis. The 1992 data presented in the

Table A.3 *Concepts of wealth by type of asset, UK, 1992*

	Identified personal wealth	Adjusted wealth	Marketable wealth	Household wealth (£ million)
	(1)	(2)	(3)	(4)
Dwellings	539	624	1,031	1,105
Buildings, trade assets and land	73	92	94	94
Consumer durables	31	167	193	193
Bank deposits and liquid assets	204	228	305	339
Government and municipal securities	30	32	42	50
Company shares	120	128	136	155
Life policies	230	49	112	279
Other assets	85	90	117	458
Total assets	*1,312*	*1,409*	*2,031*	*2,673*
Mortgages	91	182	247	325
Other debts	57	61	75	79
Total debts	*148*	*243*	*322*	*404*
Net wealth	1,164	1,166	1,708	2,270

Source: Board of the Inland Revenue, *Inland Revenue Statistics*, 1996, table 13.2, page 130.

reconciliation of table A.3 are on the more accurate 'year of death' basis – see *Inland Revenue Statistics* (1995), page 125.

Estimates of Pareto's α for wealth and income data

Methods of fitting a Pareto distribution are discussed in Cowell (1995). In the present case the value of α in chapters 2 and 9 has been estimated by ordinary least-squares regression of the following equation:

$$\log P = a - \alpha \log x \tag{2}$$

where P is the proportion of the population with wealth x or more. The regression is applied to truncated empirical distributions – to the subset of observations for which $x \geq x_0$. The results are in table A.4. Column (1) gives the value of the truncation point x_0 for each regression: notice that the estimate of α usually rises (implied inequality of the estimated distribution falls) with an increase in x_0.

As is clear from table A.4 column (3) all of the R^2 are high. This is is a typical result in this sort of case and arises from the highly skewed nature of the data: a reasonable fit in the upper tail drives the whole regression. In this sort of case the R^2 criterion should not be used as the primary criterion for selecting a particular estimate of Pareto's α; visual inspection of the data and the fitted distribution using the Pareto diagram is usually advisable before accepting a particular estimate as satisfactory. The values highlighted in bold are those that were used for the figures in chapters 2 and 9.

Table A.4 *Estimates of Pareto's α for wealth and income data*

(1) x_0	(2) α	(3) R^2	(4) s.e.(α)
Distribution of identified personal wealth; UK, 1993			
£10,000	1.4639	0.9436	0.0218
£25,000	1.6450	0.9831	0.0129
£40,000	1.7258	0.9925	0.0094
£50,000	**1.7680**	**0.9949**	**0.0087**
£60,000	1.8035	0.9960	0.0087
£80,000	1.8422	0.9968	0.0089
£100,000	1.8802	0.9971	0.0100
Distribution of incomes before tax, UK, 1994/5			
£4,000	1.2030	0.8914	0.0117
£4,500	1.2709	0.9018	0.0122
£5,000	1.3407	0.9105	0.0129
£5,500	1.4170	0.9185	0.0137
£6,000	1.5079	0.9271	0.0147
£7,000	1.6355	0.9403	0.0154
£8,000	1.7792	0.9521	0.0164
£10,000	1.9878	0.9702	0.0161
£12,000	**2.1833**	**0.9809**	**0.0172**
£15,000	2.4332	0.9915	0.0180

A.4 The PSID

In chapters 2, 4, 5 and 6 we present tables from a particularly rich data set: The Michigan Panel Study of Income Dynamics (PSID). Some of the results reported in chapters 7, 8 and appendix B are also based on versions of this same panel. This section describes briefly the nature, strengths and limitations of this data set. For further details see Hill (1992).

A *panel* is a sample that allows for regular re-interviewing of its members. Interviewers keep returning to the same people, households, families or firms so as to build up a continuous 'story' of observations. It is thus fundamentally different from either a sequence of repeated sample surveys, or a time series of aggregative data. Panel data permit direct empirical analysis of the dynamics of social and economic change within a community in ways that are just not possible with either of these other types of data.

The PSID is one of the most remarkable examples of this type of study world-wide. The first sample was collected in 1968 and consisted of two parts, a subsample of families from the Survey of Economic Opportunity which had incomes in 1966 less than or equal to twice the federal poverty line at that time, and a representative cross-section sample of dwellings in the USA. These households were reinterviewed in sub-

Table A.5 *Panel response rates*

| Year | Percentage response | |
	Annual	Cumulative
1968	76	76
1969	89	68
1970	97	66
1971	97	64
1972	97	62
1973	97	61
1974	97	59
1975	97	57
1976	96	55
1977	97	53
1978	97	51
1979	97	49
1980	97	48
1981	97	47
1982	97	46

Note:
*The deceased, those too ill to be interviewed, and recombined families have not been removed from the base.

sequent years, and from these interviews combined cross-section and time series data have been compiled.

The panel has been self-regenerating: following the initial sample no specific replacements for those families who dropped out of the panel have been made, but whenever a household split – when family members move out – the split-offs were treated as new family units. All newly formed family units were included in the panel study thereafter. As a result of the diligent following up of these split-off families the sample size increased towards the end of the panel period.

Each yearly round of interviewing, re-interviewing and recording of data on the panel is known as a *wave*. This information is then merged with all the relevant data from preceding waves. So, for those families that are still in the panel at the time of a given wave, a virtually complete history is available up to that interview year.

The data used for the examples in chapters 2, 4 and 5 are drawn from the merged tapes of Wave XX. This consists of the interview responses of the panel as it was at the time of the fifteenth consecutive interview year (1987), merged with the data for those 1987-panel members that had been previously recorded during the interview years 1968–87. The version used in this book has corrected an important class of anomalies that have affected the income data in several years' observations, as we discuss below.

The original design and subsequent developments of the Panel Study of Income Dynamics have been the responsibility of the Survey Research Center (SRC) at the University of Michigan. The PSID is unusual amongst long panels in that it has information on families – not just individuals – as a principal concern. A family-based panel inevitably gives rise to special problems, over and above those normally associated with panel data, which we discuss below. Roughly speaking these problems are associated with the questions: What is a family? What is the structure of the family? How should the organisation of the panel deal with families that split up?

The family

In the context of the PSID a 'family' means people living in the same dwelling, related by blood tie, adoption or marriage where 'marriage' includes consensual unions. The panel was initially based on probability samples of occupied dwellings in the coterminous United States, where each family in a selected dwelling was interviewed. Those living in institutions were not covered by the sampling procedure. A family may consist of just one person, and usually it is the family head who is approached for interview or re-interview (although in 1976 wives were also interviewed directly). New people are naturally brought into the panel through marriage or consensual union.

The original panel structure

At its inception the PSID had a hybrid structure consisting of: (1) re-interviews with a subset of families previously interviewed by the Bureau of the Census as part of the Survey of Economic Opportunity (SEO); and (2) a purpose-designed cross-section sample.
(1) In 1966 and 1967 about 30,000 families were interviewed in the SEO. Of these, about 2,500 low-income families (defined as those families with incomes less than or equal to a value given by the formula $\$2,000+[n\times\$1,000]$, so if $n=3$ then $=\$5,000$) were selected for possible inclusion in the initial PSID. Further adjustment was made to this subsample to allow for the limited geographical spread of the SRC interviewers. Eventually 1,892 such families from the SEO sample were interviewed by SRC during 1968.
(2) An additional sample of dwellings in the USA was added to the SEO low-income subsample to ensure that families at all income levels would be represented in the panel. This additional sample involved 2,930 interviews with families during 1968.
The resulting hybrid structure of the original sample is clearly biased, and SRC generated a set of sampling weights to offset this bias, which are described below. From 1968 onward the original structure was modified by two important processes: attrition and family splits.

Attrition

The problem of attrition is one that is endemic in the field of panel data research. In the course of the panel it is almost inevitable that some units will be lost. People move home and leave no trace; they emigrate; they die. In the case of the PSID the time

Table A.6 *Hypothetical example of family splits (observation year 1987)*

Income year	Family income after splits						
1982	Anne and Bill	$50,000					
1983	Anne and Bill	$55,000					
1984	Anne	$20,000	Bill	$40,000			
1985	Anne	$20,000	Bill, Diana and Eric	$100,000			
1986	Anne and Charlie	$40,000	Bill and Diana	$100,000	Eric	$10,000

pattern of attrition up to 1982 is given in table A.5. One of the principal reasons for concern about attrition is that it is a potential source of statistical bias. It would be foolish to suppose that people leave the family on the basis of a random process that is independent of such characteristics as income or age; and so even if the initial structure of the panel could be treated as a random sample of the target population, the structure of the panel as it appears after some time has elapsed is no longer likely to represent a random sample. This potential source of bias was treated by reworking the sample weights for each family from time to time: see below. For a detailed assessment of this problem see Becketti *et al.* (1988).

Family splits

The second major influence which modified the original panel structure was the phenomenon of families splitting up. This phenomenon encompasses marital separation, divorce and the commonplace process of older offspring leaving to form households of their own. When an interviewer discovers that a split-off has occurred, a new and differently coloured coversheet and form is immediately filled out for the split-off family (in addition to the usual form for the original family). If the split-off family lives in the interviewer's area, then he or she conducts the split-off interview; if not, the cover sheet is sent to the office to be reassigned. Every effort is made to follow up split-off families, even where they have moved outside the reference population of the original sample – i.e., outside the continental United States, or into institutions. Data on previous families before split are carried over to a split-off and thereafter remains part of the split-off's history. Although this seems to be an eminently reasonable way of giving more 'trace-back' information on new families formed by splitting old ones, it can lead to some apparently odd results. Consider the following story that is depicted in Table A.6.

   In 1982 Anne and Bill, a childless married couple, have an income of $50,000; by 1983 this had grown to $55,000. In 1984 Anne and Bill divorce – she has an income of $20,000 and he an income of $40,000. In 1985 Anne's situation remains unchanged, but Bill has now set up home with wealthy Diana who comes into the panel equipped with a teenage son: the family unit of which Bill is now head has an income of $100,000.

Table A.7 *How the 1987 PSID would record the events in table A.6*

| Interview year | Income of family headed by | | |
	Charlie	Bill	Eric
1983	$50,000	$50,000	$50,000
1984	$55,000	$55,000	$55,000
1985	$20,000	$40,000	$40,000
1986	$20,000	$100,000	$100,000
1987	$40,000	$100,000	$10,000

The teenage son, Eric, could not stand Bill, and so by 1986 he had left, had an establishment of his own and $10,000 income; his mother Diana is still with Bill and they still have $100,000 income. Meanwhile Anne has remarried and in 1986 lives in a family headed by Charlie where the total income is $40,000. How would all this look in the PSID?

Assuming that 1987 is the observation year, the picture would be that given in table A.7. There are three current (1987) families with income histories traced back to observation year 1983. However, only parts of table A.7 make an immediate intuitive connection with the blow-by-blow account summarised in table A.6 – for example, the income of Bill's family in 1983 and 1984 clearly corresponds to the income that Bill enjoyed jointly with Anne in each of the preceding years. Apart from the obvious correspondences between table A.6 and table A.7 two points are immediately striking. First, no information about Charlie, Diana or her teenage son Eric is available before they enter the panel. Second, the same family income is actually recorded for all three families in the interview years 1983 and 1984, as recorded in the 1987 panel. To see why this is so, let us consider the background of each of the 1987 families.

The family headed by Charlie in 1987 actually had three different heads during its history: Bill (during interview years 1983, 1984), Anne (during interview years 1985, 1986), and Charlie (in interview year 1987). In contrast, Bill has been head of his family throughout the period: but this does not imply that Bill's family has been stable, nor that the family's income has been stable – even if Bill's own personal income has been relatively stable during the period.

The family headed by Eric presents major problems. Eric has no connection with the original panel members. The observation in interview year 1986 alone reveals the family income that he would have enjoyed while still living with his mother, Diana. Even if Eric left home soon after Bill moved in with Diana, the apparent traceback on Eric's history gives Bill's income in interview year 1985, and Bill's and Anne's income in interview years 1983 and 1984. Why? Because Bill was, nevertheless, the relevant family head during the interview year 1986.

Wave XX (interview year 1987)

Out of an estimated 7,328 possible interviews, 7,061 were actually conducted, giving a response rate of 96.4 per cent; 257 of these interviews were with new split-off families. The average length of the 1987 interviews was 29.5 minutes, and 91.8 per cent of these were conducted by telephone. The cumulative response rate, based on the interviews actually obtained in 1968 and the split-offs from those families, is 52.2 per cent. As of 1987, 9,504 members of the original 1968 panel families were still in the sample.

Definition of the income unit

From the basic design of the PSID it is clear that the *family* is taken as the principal economic unit in the context of this study. The definition of this income unit raises some conceptual and practical problems as we noted above. These problems are mitigated to some extent by the availability of data on certain subunits within the family. These subunits are: head and wife jointly, head (only), wife (only), other family members.

The definition of income

The income concept which has been used as a basis for the tables in chapters 2, 4 and 5 is very broad in its scope: total family income. This is the sum of labour income, asset income and transfer income of all family members – see figures A.1–A.4. Nevertheless this concept does, in some respects, fall short of the ideal. It certainly does not correspond to theoretical notions of 'full income'. In particular total family income does *not* include the following sources of income, for which data are collected separately:

annual amount of food stamps received by the family unit;
government subsidy of heating costs;
annual rent value of free housing; and
imputed rental income from owner-occupied housing.

Furthermore total family income does not include certain lump-sum payments such as settlements from an insurance company or the receipt of an inheritance. Notice that there is much less detail available about the taxable income of those in the family other than the head and wife. It is inevitable that with such a rich and extensive data source that there should be some practical problems with the quality, consistency and interpretation of the data.

Variable coverage

Not all variables are available for all of the years covered in the panel period. There are several reasons for this patchy coverage.

Some variables were added in the course of the development of the PSID as the need developed for data on particular economic and social problems.
Correspondingly some variables had eventually to be dropped (because of space restrictions) in order to make way for the new variables.

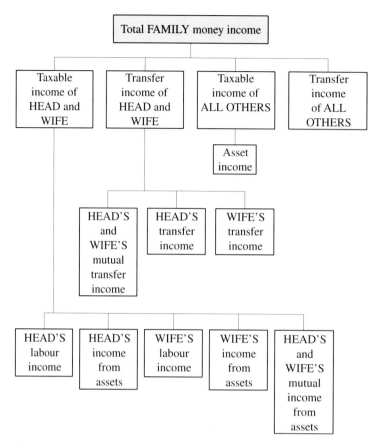

Figure A.1 The main components of family income

The availability of some variables is conditioned upon the values of others: for
example some questions are asked only of those who are employed.

The income subunit is sometimes changed from one year to another: for example in
some years data on assets are collected only for husband and wife jointly.

The problem of upper-truncation bias

The original data tapes are affected by a difficulty that is shared by the US Current
Population Survey data:[1] some of the '99999' values are not really ninety-nine thousand nine hundred and ninety-nine. The reason for this lies in the convention adopted
in the original sample of coding every observation as a five digit integer. Unfortunately
the convenience achieved by standardising the computer records in this way has proved
to be a hostage to fortune. Money incomes grew quite rapidly, and in the course of time
five digits soon became inadequate for many of the observations on several income
variables. The first example of this occurred in the 1971 interview year, when there were
eight cases in which the observation exceeded the five digit restriction: all of these cases
are coded as '99999'. Not only individual components of income are contaminated by

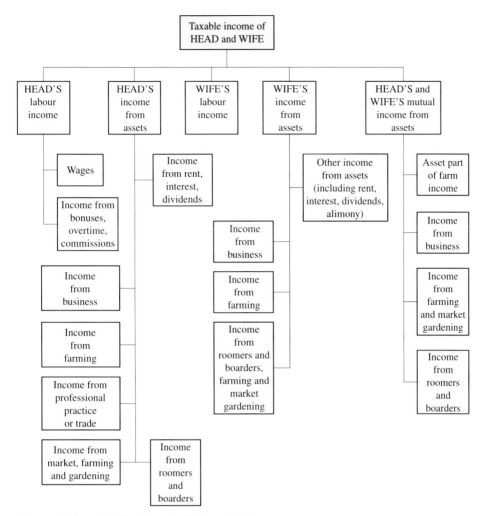

Figure A.2 Detail of head's and wife's taxable income

the 99999 problem as well as broader-based aggregates such as total family income. Furthermore, a counterpart of this problem has arisen in the case of variables that can assume negative values: for example 'asset income' may actually involve a loss for some income-receiving unit, but in some years the recorded loss could not be greater (in absolute terms) than –9999 dollars.

The organisers of the PSID attempted to cope with this issue in subsequent waves by assigning more tape space to certain key variables. This measure has had some success, although in certain respects the problem has been deferred rather than resolved: the erstwhile '99999' problem has re-emerged as the '999999' problem, or the '9999999' problem…

This idiosyncrasy is widespread: in waves I to XV a total of 477 individual observations had been affected by it. The 99999 issue is particularly unfortunate for anyone

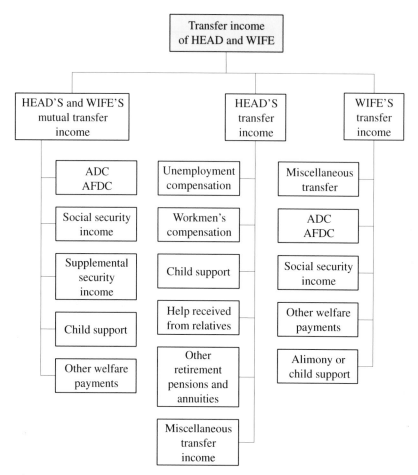

Figure A.3 Detail of head's and wife's transfer income

interested in studying the distribution of income since it implies that frequency distributions will automatically have their upper tails truncated. Accordingly, in preparing the data set used in this book these values have been checked and, with the cooperation of the staff at the University of Michigan, have been replaced with the actual observations from the manual records of interviews and re-interviews. In a few cases '99999' was the actual value recorded in the interview.

Sampling weights

It is clear that the membership of the panel in any one interview year is not likely to be a representative sample of, say, the population of the United States during that year. There are a number of reasons for this: as we have noted above the original construction of the panel contained a component which deliberately overrepresented the poor; and the processes of attrition and self-regeneration through family splits have, in the

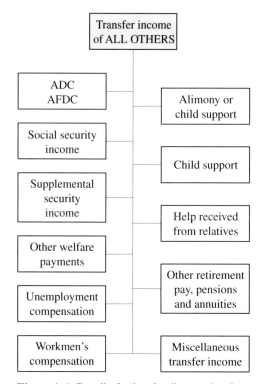

Figure A.4 Detail of other family members' transfer income

course of time, potentially contributed to the problem of bias in the sample also. In order to enable users of the data to make adjustments sampling weights were computed for the original (1968) panel. For each sample member the appropriate weight is the inverse of the probability of that sample member's inclusion in the sample. So, in view of the hybrid structure of the sample, the sampling weight can be computed as follows. Let p_1 be the probability that the sample member was included in the re-interview sub-sample (based on the subset of SEO interviews); let p_2 be the probability of inclusion in the SRC cross-section subsample; the sample weight is then $1/[p_1+p_2-p_1p_2]$. The practical problems involved in estimating p_1 and p_2 given the design of the two sub-samples are described on pages 14–23 of volume I of the PSID *Study Design, Procedures, Available Data*.

The sampling weights were revised during the 1972, 1977 and 1978 interview years. The 1978 weights supersede all previous revisions, and take account of the cumulative response rates since 1968, with adjustments for those 'marrying into' the sample and for children born to those who were panel members – or who would have been had they not been non-respondents. From 1979 onwards the weights were adjusted each year to give children born into the sample weights equal to half the weights of their parents, and to halve the family weight of any family where a sample member marries outside the sample.

Table A.8 *Family structure*

Persons in family	Positive income subsample	Full sample
1	1,644	1,661
2	1,888	1,893
3	1,313	1,319
4	1,257	1,259
5	610	612
6	208	209
7	67	67
8	26	26
9	7	7
10	4	4
11	4	4
total	*7,028*	*7,061*
mean size	2.511	2.476

A.5 Tables derived from the PSID

Table 2.2 and the bivariate tables 2.3, 2.4 present the basic summaries of the PSID wave XX data, corrected for truncation bias: they cover the entire 1987 interview sample of 7,061 families for total family income, for the sum of asset income of head and asset income of wife, and for the sum of labour income of head and labour income of wife.

Tables 4.1 and 4.2 in chapter 4 were created as follows. First, $\bar{q}_1$, the mean value of the needs index for single-person families was computed, using the sampling weights provided in the panel. The number of equivalent adults in family h with food needs q_h is given by $v_h := q_h/\bar{q}_1$: this is usually less than n_h the number of persons in the family: this immediately yields the three concepts of income used in tables 9.1 and 9.2, total family income (y_h), income per head (y_h/n_h), and 'adjusted income' (y_h/v_h) (here h is used to index each of the families $1, 2, ..., H$ in contrast to the index i which we used for persons in the main text of chapters 4 and 5).

Secondly, 33 observations were excluded from the original sample of 7,061 families: the excluded 33 families were those with zero or negative total family income. The remaining 7,028 – the *restricted sample* – families were grouped into six categories by family size, and means and inequality measures were calculated for all three concepts of income, all six subgroups and the whole restricted sample. This was done twice: first using the standard sample weights, giving the inequality statistics using the family as income-receiving unit, and then a set of weights derived by multiplying each family's sample weight by n_h which gives the statistics using the *person* as the income-receiving unit. The computation of inequality measures for weighted data is a simple extension of the formulae presented in chapter 4 (equations 4.1, 4.3 and 4.4) and chapter 5 (table 5.1). For the Atkinson indices we have

$$A_\epsilon := 1 - \left[\sum_{h=1}^{H} w_h \left[\frac{x_h}{\bar{x}} \right]^{1-\epsilon} \right]^{\frac{1}{1-\epsilon}} \tag{3}$$

for any positive value of ϵ except $\epsilon = 1$, and

$$A_1 := 1 - \exp \left(\sum_{h=1}^{H} w_h \log \left(\frac{x_h}{\bar{x}} \right) \right) \tag{4}$$

replacing the case $\epsilon = 1$, where

$$\bar{x} := \sum_{h=1}^{H} w_h x_h, \tag{5}$$

and w_i is the weight on observation i normalised so that $\Sigma_i w_i = 1$: see Cowell (1984) and Coulter, Cowell and Jenkins (1997) for further details. The structure of families by size in interview year 1987 for the full sample and the restricted subsample is as given in table A.8.

For table 4.3 the full sample of 7,061 families, labour income of husband and wife, and asset income of husband wife were tabulated; this was done also for the 12 sub-groups formed by partitioning by sex of head, and by age group of head (less than 25, 25–34, 35–44, 45–54, 55–64, 65 and over). Factor income, the sum of labour income and asset income (for head and wife in each family), was also tabulated, and means, coefficients of variation and correlation coefficients were computed using ordinary sampling weights.

Table 4.4 presents rather greater problems since income observations for all 5 years have been systematically aggregated for members of the 1987 sample. The problems of interpretation highlighted in the Anne, Bill and Co. discussion above should be heeded. Furthermore the problem of missing data is particularly acute in this exercise. Since table 4.4 presents adjusted family income – total family income divided by family needs – aggregated over the years, it is obviously not possible to use observations on families for which information on needs is missing in one or more of the fifteen years. When we eliminate families with such missing data from the sample we are left with 6,973 families out of the original 7,061. Each of these 6,973 families then has a complete 15-year 'history' of adjusted total family income (y_h/v_h) over the 5 years 1982–6, as recorded in 1987: let $x_h(t)$ denote the observation of this t periods 'into the past' ($t=0$ for 1986, $t=1$ for 1985, and so on); then the appropriate discounted average income for family h over T periods is

$$z_h(T) := \frac{\sum_{t=0}^{T-1} D^t x_h(t)}{\sum_{t=0}^{T-1} D^t} \tag{6}$$

where D is the pre-specified discount factor. Then for example the inequality index specified in equation (3) would become

$$A_\epsilon := 1 - \left[\sum_{h=1}^{H} w_h \left[\frac{z_h}{\bar{z}} \right]^{1-\epsilon} \right]^{\frac{1}{1-\epsilon}} \tag{7}$$

where w_h is the 1982 weight (proportional to the number of persons in the family in 1982), and is $\bar{z}$ the weighted mean of the zs calculated in a way similar to equation (6).

Tables 4.5, 5.2, 5.3 and 6.1 are based on the standard decomposition techniques described in chapter 5. Take the age, sex and race rows for example: given that there are six age groups, two sex groups and two racial groups (white and non-white) we obviously have 24 fundamental groups. For a specified member of the A_ϵ-family of inequality measures we can define the representative income ξ_ϵ for any distribution as well as mean income; this is done for all 24 subgroups, as well as for the larger groups found by merging some of these elementary subgroups, and for the entire 'restricted sample' of 6,721 families with strictly positive incomes. *Minimum within-group inequality* is defined as the within-group component for the finest partition.

Notes
1 See Fichtenbaum and Shahidi (1988).

Appendix B Earnings models

B.1 Human capital theory

The following model is in the spirit of those incorporated in Becker (1962, 1964), Ben Porath (1967) and Mincer (1970, 1974) and underpins the discussion in section 7.4 of chapter 7.

Let $E(t)$ be actual earnings at age t, $0 \leq t \leq T$, where $t=0$ is the age of leaving compulsory schooling and T is the (compulsory) age of retirement. At any instant of one's life one may devote a proportion $1-\theta(t)$ of one's time to earning in the labour market ($0 \leq \theta(t) \leq 1$) and a proportion $\theta(t)$ to acquisition of further skills. The technology forbids jointly earning and learning: on-the-job training is treated as spending a proportion $1-\theta$ of one's day in full-time work and a proportion θ in learning; this assumption effectively rules out costless learning-by-doing. At any moment one has a stock $K(t)$ of skills or 'human capital' which can be 'rented' in the market place at a fixed price a. Earnings are thus given by

$$E(t)=a[1-\theta(t)]K(t) \tag{1}$$

Human capital is produced whenever $\theta(t)>0$. Its rate of production depends on $\theta(t)$ and the existing stock $K(t)$. Capital depreciates at a rate δ, there is no costless technical progress and there are strictly decreasing returns. Thus net investment in human capital is

$$\frac{\mathrm{d}K(t)}{\mathrm{d}t}=f(K(t),\theta(t))-\delta K(t) \tag{2}$$

where for all K, θ:

$$\left.\begin{array}{l} f(K,\theta) \geq 0,\ f(K,0)=f(K,\theta)=0, \\ f_K(K,\theta)>0,\ f_\theta(K,\theta)>0, \\ f_K(K,\theta)K+f_\theta(K,\theta)\theta<f(K,\theta), \\ f_{KK}(K,\theta)<0,\ f_{\theta\theta}(K,\theta)<0 \end{array}\right\} \tag{3}$$

in which the subscripts denote the relevant partial derivatives. Since leisure time is exogenously fixed then, if a perfect capital market is available, the rational objective is to maximise the present value of the earnings stream by a suitable choice of $\theta(t)$ over the lifetime. Thus the objective is to choose $\theta(t)$, $0 \le t \le T$ so as to maximise

$$\int_0^T e^{-rt}E(t)dt \tag{4}$$

subject to (1) and (2).

To solve this introduce a *shadow price of investment* $\pi(t)$ and define *shadow income*:

$$H(t) := E(t) + \pi(t)\frac{dK(t)}{dt} \tag{5}$$

where $\pi(t)$ obeys the following rules

$$\pi(T)K(T) = 0, \tag{6}$$

$$\frac{d\pi(t)}{dt} = r\pi(t) - \frac{\partial H(t)}{\partial K(t)} \tag{7}$$

Condition (6) says that the shadow value of the human capital stock is zero at the end of one's life. Condition (7) says that the more an additional unit of capital would raise shadow income, the faster should the shadow price of investment be decreased. Then the maximisation of (4), subject to the conditions (1) and (2), is equivalent to maximising (5) by choice of $\theta(t)$, subject to (6) and (7).

A necessary condition for this is $\partial H(t)/\partial \theta(t) = 0$ in any period where $0 < \theta(t) < 1$ (appropriate inequalities apply in a period where $\theta = 0$ or $\theta = 1$). Evaluating this from (5), using (1) and (2) one has

$$-aK(t) + \pi(t)f_\theta(K(t),\theta(t)) = 0 \tag{8}$$

Rearranging (8) we find that along the optimal path whenever $0 < \theta < 1$:

$$\pi(t) = \frac{aK(t)}{f_\theta(K(t),\theta(t))} \tag{9}$$

Since the right-hand side of (9) is the amount of current earnings one would have to forgo at the margin to increase investment by one unit, this equation has the interpretation 'price of human investment = marginal cost of human investment' – see figure B.1. Evaluating (7) from (1) and (2)

$$\frac{d\pi(t)}{dt} = r\pi(t) - a[1 - \theta(t)] - \pi(t)[f_K(K(t),\theta(t)) - \delta] \tag{10}$$

The solution found from (9) and (10) requires explicit specification of f before it can be obtained in closed form. However in view of the fact that terminal $\pi(T)$ is zero and the reasonable presumption that $\pi(0)$ is positive in non-trivial cases, a class of solutions that appear to be interesting is those wherein $d\pi(t)/dt \le 0$ for all t. This implies that $f_\theta(K(t),\theta(t))/K(t)$ must increase with t (or remain constant) and hence that

$$\frac{f_{\theta\theta}\dfrac{d\theta}{dt} + f_{K\theta}\dfrac{dK}{dt}}{f_\theta} \ge 0 \tag{11}$$

Rearranging (11) gives

$$\frac{d}{dt}\log(\theta) \leq \frac{1-\eta_K}{\eta_\theta}\frac{d}{dt}\log(K)$$

$$\text{where } \eta_K := \frac{\partial\log(f_\theta)}{\partial\log(K)}, \ \eta_\theta := \frac{\partial\log(f_\theta)}{\partial\log(\theta)} \tag{12}$$

$\eta_\theta < 0$ as long as diminishing returns are assumed. Now, from (2) and (3), $\partial\log(K)/\partial t \geq -\delta$. So if $\eta_K < 1$ and $\delta = 0$ the optimal profile of θ must either be falling or constant over time.

A further assumption about f which will ensure that θ is non-increasing over time is the *neutrality* hypothesis. Neutrality means that time input and human capital enter the human capital production function multiplicatively so that the gross investment is simply a function of earnings forgone. So we may introduce a function g such that $g(K\theta) := f(K,\theta)$, where $g' > 0$, $g'' < 0$. Then $\eta_K = 1 + \eta_\theta$, $\eta_\theta = Kg''/g' < 0$, and equations (8), (10), yield

$$\frac{d}{dt}\log(\pi(t)) = [r+\delta]\pi(t) - a \tag{13}$$

Integrating (13) and using the condition (7) yields

$$\pi(t) = a\frac{1 - e^{[r+\delta][t-T]}}{r+\delta} \tag{14}$$

π is a monotonically decreasing function of t wherever $0 < \theta(t) < 1$. Also from (9) we find

$$\pi(t) = \frac{a}{g'(K(t)\theta(t))} \tag{15}$$

Substituting and differentiating we obtain

$$\frac{d}{dt}\log(\theta) \leq z - \frac{d}{dt}\log(K)$$

$$\text{where } \quad z := \frac{r+\delta}{\eta_\theta[e^{[r+\delta][T-t]} - 1]} \tag{16}$$

In view of (2) and (3) we find $d\log(\theta(t))/dt < 0$ if $\delta = 0$ and $0 < \theta < 1$. Clearly any period where $\theta(t) = 1$ (where the person specialises in education) must occur at the beginning of the lifetime.

Moreover, differentiating (2) in the case where $\delta = 0$ it is evident that

$$\frac{d^2K(t)}{dt^2} = K\theta z g'(K\theta). \tag{17}$$

Because z is negative so is $d^2K(t)/dt^2$: potential earnings aK must increase at a decreasing rate.

Differentiating (14) it is clear that raising r or δ lowers the price $\pi(t)$ at every age, and thus reduces investment at every age (see figures B.1 to B.3). An increase in the ability to benefit from education can be interpreted as a uniform upward shift of $g'(K\theta)$ – in other words a uniform downward shift in the marginal cost curve – in which case

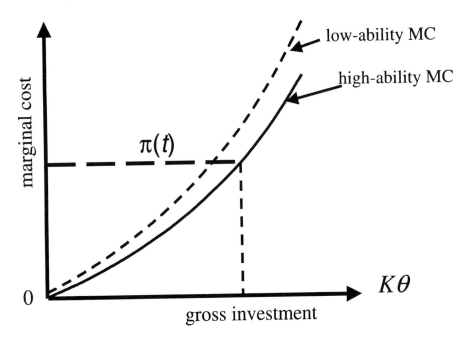

Figure B.1 'Price=marginal cost' in the human capital model

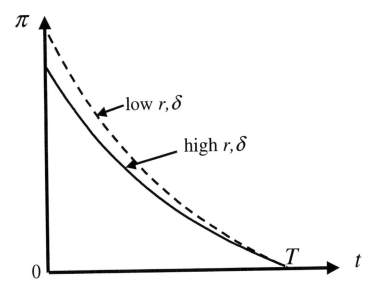

Figure B.2 Path of shadow price π

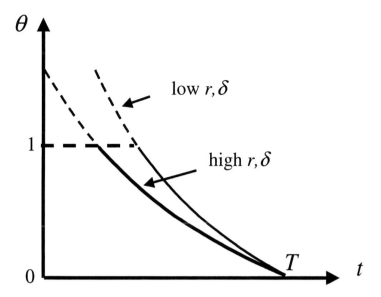

Figure B.3 Solution of time-allocation path

investment everywhere increases, see figure B.1. Likewise an increase in $K(0)$ – the initial endowment of productive skills – is offset by a reduction in $\theta(t)$ everywhere, so as to maintain equality between $\pi(t)$ and marginal cost.

B.2 Human capital: empirical models

For an empirical application of the standard model of human capital we shall divide the life span into two periods, full-time schooling (the first s years), and a period of post-school investment (the remaining $T-s$ years). We shall assume:
- $\theta(t)$ declines *linearly* during the period after the completion of formal education

$$\theta(t)=b_2+\tfrac{1}{2}b_3[t-s] \tag{18}$$

  $s\leq t\leq T$ as long as $0<\theta(t)<1$, where b_2 and b_3 are parameters and $b_3<0$.
- The neutrality hypothesis is true so that (2) may be rewritten as

$$\frac{d}{dt}\log(K(t))=\frac{g(K(t)\theta(t))}{K(t)}-\delta \tag{19}$$

- The rate of return to post-school investments may be taken as approximately constant, equal to r_p^*. This implies that we may approximate $g(K\theta)$ by $r_p^*K\theta$. Consequently (19) becomes

$$\frac{d}{dt}\log(K(t))=\theta(t)r_p^*-\delta \tag{20}$$

- Depreciation is negligible; then, combining (18) and (20) and integrating, we have

$$\log(K(t))=\log(a\,K(s))+r_p^*[b_2x+b_3x^2] \tag{21}$$

- where $K(s)$ is potential earning capacity immediately on leaving school, and $x := t - s$ denotes experience after school is completed.
- The rate of return to investments in full-time schooling is approximately constant at $r_s^* s$, so that $\log(K(s)) = \log(K(0)) + r_s^* s$, where $K(0)$ is raw, unskilled earning capacity.

Then, recalling the definition of actual earnings in (1)

$$\log(E(t)) = \log(K(0)) + r_s^* s + r_p^*[b_2 x + b_3 x^2] + \log(1 - \theta(t)) \tag{22}$$

Using a linear approximation for $\log(1 - \theta(t))$ we may write

$$\log(E(t)) = \beta_0 + \beta_1 s + \beta_2 x + \beta_3 x^2 \tag{23}$$

where $\beta_0, \ldots, \beta_3$ are constants. Equation (23) gives a parabolic shape for any individual's log-earnings. In practice the estimated earnings equation will be of the form

$$e_{it} = \beta_0 + \beta_1 s_i + \beta_2 x_{it} + \beta_3 x_{it}^2 + \epsilon_{it} \tag{24}$$

where e_{it} is the logarithm of observed earnings of person i at age t, s_i is his completed schooling, x_{it} is his experience at age t, namely $t - s_i$, and ϵ_{it} is a random variable. The specification (24) implicitly assumes the interpersonal equalisation of the rate of return on schooling (since $\beta_1 = r_s^* s$). If we further assume that r_p^* is equalised across individuals then any differences in the slope of *individual* profiles are simply due to different optimal choices of $\theta(t)$ given the same r_p^*.

There are several modifications to the model that may be usefully investigated, including different functional forms for the $\theta(t)$ profile and the endogenous determination of weeks worked – see Chiswick (1974), Eckaus (1973), Mincer (1974), Psacharopoulos and Layard (1979). One such development is to allow the rate of return on schooling to vary with the amount of schooling, and to allow the level of schooling to affect the rate of return to experience. The equation then estimated is usually of the form

$$e_{it} = \beta_0 + \beta_1 s_i + \beta_2 x_{it} + \beta_3 x_{it}^2 + \beta_4 s_i^2 + \beta_5 s_i x_{it} + \epsilon_{it} \tag{25}$$

The results of these regressions for UK and USA are given in table B.1.

Lillard and Willis (1978) investigated the explanatory power of such models using the seventh wave of the PSID.[1] Because they used panel data, their model permits a richer specification of the empirical model than (24) above. In particular the error term ϵ_{it} can be written

$$\epsilon_{it} = \Delta_i + v_{it} \tag{26}$$

where Δ_i is a random variable representing an unobserved *fixed effect* that is specific to each individual, and v_{it} is an error component representing random shocks. There may also be a systematic structure to these random shocks, of the following form

$$v_{it} = \gamma v_{it-1} + \zeta_{it} \tag{27}$$

where γ is a serial correlation coefficient. Assume that the Δs are independently normally distributed with zero mean and variance σ_Δ^2 and the ζs are independently normally distributed with zero mean and variance σ_ζ^2. Two important issues can be investigated using a model with an error structure of this type.

Table B.1 *Earnings equations for UK and USA*

| | Basic model (24) | | Model incorporating interaction effects and variable return to schooling (25) | | Dynamic version of (24) |
	UK	USA1	UK	USA1	USA2
β_0	5.2000	6.2000	3.5900	4.8700	0.6650
β_1	0.0970	0.1070	0.3290	0.2550	0.0840
β_2	0.0910	0.0810	0.1090	0.1480	0.0380
β_3	−0.0015	−0.0012	−0.0016	−0.0018	−0.0007
β_4	—	—	−0.0078	−0.0029	—
β_5	—	—	−0.0013	−0.0043	—
β_6	—	—	—	—	−0.1660
R^2	0.316	0.285	0.323	0.309	
var(log E)	0.436	0.668	0.436	0.668	0.3070

Sources:
UK General Household Survey of 6,873 employed men aged 15–69, Psacharopoulos and Layard (1979).
USA1 1/1,000 Census sample of 31,093 observations of annual earnings in 1959 of white, non-farm, non-student men up to age 65, Mincer (1974).
USA2 2,000 families from Wave VII of the PSID, Lillard and Willis (1978).

First, is the serial correlation in (27) important? Lillard and Willis suggest that it is, in that a test for the restriction $\gamma=0$ is rejected.[2] Second, how much of log-earnings variation is 'explained' by a model such as (27)? To answer this, one can measure $\hat{\sigma}_\epsilon^2$, the *total* earnings variation in the pooled sample derived from the panel (in other words, the nT observations of the n panel members over the T years of the panel), and $\hat{\sigma}_\Delta^2$, the permanent earnings variation in the pooled sample. One may then look at the corresponding variances of the residuals after the model has been fitted. 'Explanatory power' is then taken as $1 - $ (variance of residuals)/(earnings variation) in either case.

Lillard and Willis estimated a model of the form (24) but with the addition of dummy variables for the different time periods, and a dummy variable to indicate whether the individual was black or not. Their estimates are given in the last column of table B.1, with the racial dummy variable included as β_6. So the earnings model explains 33 per cent of total variance ($\hat{\sigma}_\epsilon^2$), 44 per cent of the permanent component of variance ($\hat{\sigma}_\Delta^2$), but none of the stochastic variation $\hat{\sigma}_\nu^2$. Using a more comprehensive model with additional variables concerning work history the explanatory power is improved: 58 per cent for blacks, 47 per cent for whites.[3]

B.3 Hierarchical earnings models

The following illustrates the hierarchical model of earnings distribution – Lydall (1968). First consider a single firm in which there are L levels (strata) of authority and

Table B.2 *A wage structure with fixed span of control*

Level	Wage w	Number of employees	Cumulative total N(w)
1	1	531,441	797,161
2	2	177,147	265,720
3	4	59,049	88,573
4	8	19,683	29,524
5	16	6,561	9,841
6	32	2,187	3,280
7	64	729	1,093
8	128	243	364
9	256	81	121
10	512	27	40
11	1,024	9	13
12	2,048	3	4
13	4,096	1	1

in all except the bottom level, each member is in charge of three members on the level below. Assume that wages in the bottom stratum are $\underline{w}=1$, that the ratio of wages between any two adjacent levels is $b=2$, that there is one person (the Chief Executive) in the top layer, and that $L=13$. The wage structure is then as in table B.2. In each line of table B.2 the cumulative total $N(w)$ of persons earning w or more is (to the nearest person) given by the equation

$$N(w)=Aw^{-\alpha} \tag{28}$$

where $A=797$, 161 and $\alpha=(\log 3)/(\log 2)=1.5895$: (28) satisfies Pareto's Law. If the example were altered so that (under the same conditions) the number of layers is chosen as $L=10$, then the resulting structure will be found to satisfy the law with a lower value of A, 29,524, but the same value of α as before – see the straight line graph in the Pareto diagram depicted in figure B.4.

Now suppose there were a population of such firms with different sizes: would Pareto's law still be obeyed? Take the case where the sizes of firms also have a Pareto distribution, but not with the same coefficient α: for example if there is one firm like the one we have just considered with ten layers and altogether 29,524 earners, and four firms with nine layers each and so 9,841 earners each, sixteen firms with eight layers and so 3,280 earners each etc, and finally 262,144 ($=4^9$) one-person firms: here the Pareto coefficient for the distribution of firms is $\log(4)/\log(2)=2$. One can work out the distribution of earnings for the combined workforce of all the firms in this population of firms by calculating the wage distributions separately for each of the ten firm sizes and adding them together. The result is shown in figure B.4 by a dotted curve; the fact that this graph is not a straight line shows that Pareto's law is no longer obeyed for the distribution of earnings when the distribution of firms and the distribution of chief executives salaries are Paretian.

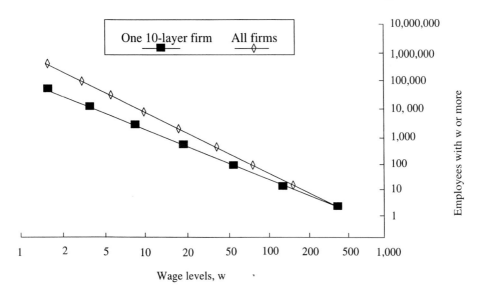

Figure B.4 Pareto diagram of hierarchical wage structures

Notes
1 See appendix A for a description of this data set.
2 See also Hause (1980).
3 See also Bourguignon and Morrisson (1983), and Lillard (1977) who found that 30 per cent
  of total earnings variation could be accounted for by observed variables, 40 per cent by unobserved fixed effects and 30 per cent by transitory components.

Appendix C Model algorithms

C.1 Introduction

In chapters 10 and 11 we use numerical examples, tables and diagrams to illustrate models of income and wealth distribution. This appendix provides the analytical underpinning for them and algorithms for finding the equilibrium states of the deterministic (chapter 10) and stochastic (chapter 11) models. The models differ from one another principally in terms of the values in the parameter array $\pi := (T, E_0, E_1, E_2, C^*, \xi, v, r, \tau, s, W^*, P, g, N, M)$; the exception is section C.7 which deals exclusively with the special models of sections 10.7 and 10.8 of chapter 10. For background reading on mathematical technique see Allen (1963), Feller (1950), Leighton (1952).

The principal notation is summarised in table C.1. This appendix also includes a description of the simulation program which can be adapted to calculate nearly all tables, diagrams and examples for the stochastic models in chapter 11, given appropriate values for the parameters π. Parameters g, N, M and τ are pure numbers, C^* and E^* have dimension value/time, $1/r$ and T have dimension time, and P and W^* have dimension value. Parameters g, M, N do not appear in the non-stochastic models of chapter 10, since they concern the various income intervals into which bequests are grouped; the parameters E_1, E_2, ξ and v which appear in chapter 10 play no part in the stochastic models. Unless stated otherwise bequests are *pre-tax bequests*: that is before any tax or subsidy.

C.2 Mutt island: basic model

Model 1 relates to a family line consisting of heirs, 0,1,2,3… each of whom inherits from his predecessor in the line and makes a bequest T years later for his heir, the next in the line. Our assumptions imply that $B_n = W_n(t)$. Let $\tilde{W}(t)$ and $\tilde{c}(t)$ denote equilibrium wealth and consumption at age t – the values of $W_n(t)$ and $c_n(t)$ when $n \to \infty$ – and let $\tilde{B}$ and $\tilde{C}$ denote the terminal values $\tilde{W}(T)$ and $\tilde{c}(T)$. Then the basic equations for model 1 are:

Table C.1 *Notation*

$B_n, W_{n+1}(0)$	bequest made by n to $n+1$, before and after tax
$W_n(t)$	wealth held by n at t years after inheritance
$c_n(t)$	consumption rate at time t
$c_n, c_n(T)$	terminal consumption in generation n
E^*	earnings
T	generation length
C^*	basic consumption expenditure
r	interest rate
τ	rate of tax on $B_n - W^*$
W^*	bequest-tax threshold
N	the 'number of the game'
g	proportionate width of each interval
M	size parameter of wealth range

$$c_{n+1}(t) = \begin{cases} C^* & \text{if } W_{n+1}(t) > 0 \\ E^* & \text{otherwise} \end{cases} \tag{1}$$

$$\frac{dW_{n+1}(t)}{dt} = E^* + rW_{n+1}(t) - c_{n+1}(t) \tag{2}$$

$$W_{n+1}(0) = \begin{cases} B_n & \text{if } B_n < W^* \\ B_n - \tau[B_n - W^*] & \text{otherwise} \end{cases} \tag{3}$$

Given the values of the parameters and of the initial bequest B_0 in the line, the following provides the equation of motion and the equilibrium values of bequests and consumption.

Algorithm 1 Let $\hat{B} := [C^* - E^*]/r$, $J := 1 - e^{rT}$ and $H := \hat{B}J/[J-1]$; then

$$\Delta B_n = \begin{cases} J[\hat{B} - B_n] + [1 - J]\tau[W^* - B_n] & \text{if } W^* \le B_n \\ J[\hat{B} - B_n] & \text{if } H < B_n \le W^* \\ -B_n & \text{if } B_n < H \end{cases} \tag{4}$$

If $B_0 < \hat{B}$, then the solution of (4) is $B_n \to 0$ and $C_n \to E^*$; but if $B_0 > \hat{B}$, then $B_n \to \tilde{B} = [\hat{B}J + [1-J]\tau W^*]/[J + \tau[1-J]]$ unless $\tau < J/[J-1]$ in which case $B_n \to \infty$. If $B_0 = \hat{B}$ then $B_n = \hat{B}$ for all n, which is an unstable equilibrium.

Example 1 Given the parameter values in line 1 of table C.2 and given $B_0 = 100$ we find $\hat{B} = 80$, $J = 0.464739$, so that $\tilde{B} = 212.060$, confirming the result on page 222 and illustrated at the intersection point U in figure 10.3.

C.3 Model 2: adaptive consumption

The basic equations of this model are

Table C.2 *Parameter values for models 1 to 3*

Example	T	E^*,E_0	E_1	E_2	C^*	r	τ	W^*	ξ	ν	s	P
1	25	10	—	—	12	2½%	⅔	120	—	—	—	—
2a	25	10	—	—	12	2½%	⅔	120	0.200	1.00	—	—
2b	25	10	—	—	12	2½%	⅔	120	0.200	0.08	—	—
3a	25	10	0.1	−0.0020	12	2½%	⅔	120	0.225	0.20	—	—
3b	25	10	0.1	−0.00025	12	2½%	⅔	120	0.200	0.08	—	—
1′	25	10	—	—	12	2½%	⅔	120	—	—	⅘	50
2a′	25	10	—	—	12	2½%	⅔	120	0.200	0.50	⅘	50
3a′	25	10	0.1	−0.0020	12	2½%	⅔	120	0.225	0.20	⅔	50

$$c_{n+1}(0)=\begin{cases}\max\ \{C^*,[1-v]C_n\}\ \text{if}\ B_n>0\\ E^*\quad\text{otherwise}\end{cases}\tag{5}$$

$$\frac{dc_{n+1}(t)}{dt}=\xi[E^*+rW_{n+1}(t)-c_{n+1}(t)\tag{6}$$

along with (2) and (3) above, which together imply

$$c_{n+1}(t)-c_{n+1}(0)=\xi[W_{n+1}(t)-W_{n+1}(0)]\tag{7}$$

$$\tilde{c}(t)-\tilde{c}(0)=\xi[\tilde{W}(t)-\tilde{W}(0)]\tag{8}$$

$$\frac{d\tilde{W}(t)}{dt}=[r-\xi]\tilde{W}(t)+E^*+\xi\tilde{W}(0)-\tilde{c}(0)\tag{9}$$

It follows that

$$\tilde{W}(t)=\tilde{W}(0)+a[e^{[r-\xi]t}-1]\tag{10}$$

where

$$a:=\frac{E^*+r\tilde{W}(0)-\tilde{c}(0)}{r-\xi}\tag{11}$$

The solution for $\tilde{B}$ depends on whether C^* or $[1-v]\tilde{C}$ is greater, which can be discovered by trial and error.

Case 2a: $\tilde{c}(0)=C^*$
This is the simpler of two cases: it will certainly arise if $v=1$. Setting $t=T$ in (10)

$$\tilde{B}=\tilde{W}(T)=a[e^{[r-\xi]T}-1]+\tilde{W}(0),\tag{12}$$

$$\tilde{C}=C^*+\xi[\tilde{B}-\tilde{W}(0)]\tag{13}$$

If $\tilde{c}(0)>W^*$, we must have the relationship

$$\tilde{W}(0)=\tilde{B}-\tau[\tilde{B}-W^*]\tag{14}$$

so, substituting for a and $\tilde{W}(0)$, we have

$$\tau[\xi-r][\tilde{B}-W^*]=[E^*+r\tau W^*+r[1-\tau]\tilde{B}-C^*][1-e^{[r-\xi]T}] \qquad (15)$$

from which $\tilde{B}$ can be calculated once the parameters of the system are given. A convenient algorithm is the following:

Algorithm 2a Let $N:=rW^*+E^*$, $J:=1-e^{[r-\xi]T}$ and $D:=\tau[\xi-r]/J-r[1-\tau]$. Then

$$\tilde{B}=W^*+\frac{N-C^*}{D}, \qquad (16)$$

$$\tilde{C}=C^*+\xi\tau[\tilde{B}-W^*] \qquad (17)$$

Example 2a Given the values in row 2a of table C.2 we find $N=13$, $J=0.9874$, $D=0.1098$, $\tilde{B}=129.106$, $\tilde{C}=13.2141$.

The solution in this example would remain valid if instead of supposing that $v=1$, we had attributed to v any value greater than a critical value $v^*:=1-C^*/\tilde{C}$. In this case $v^*=0.09081$.

Case 2b: $\tilde{c}(0)>C^*$

If v is less than the critical value the solution of the simultaneous equations is less straightforward. The basic equations are as in case 2a but with the extra condition

$$\tilde{c}(0)=[1-v]\tilde{C} \qquad (18)$$

so that we have now a second variable to eliminate as well as a which slightly complicates the algorithm.

Algorithm 2b Let D, N be defined as in algorithm 2a. Then

$$\tilde{B}=W^*+\frac{N}{D+\tau\xi\dfrac{1-v}{v}}, \qquad (19)$$

$$\tilde{C}=\frac{\xi\tau}{v}[\tilde{B}-W^*] \qquad (20)$$

and $\tilde{c}(0)$, $\tilde{W}(0)$ are given by (18) and (14), respectively.

Example 2b If the values are as specified in row 2b of table C.2 then D, J and N have the same values as in example 2a, and so $\tilde{B}=127.9116$, $\tilde{W}(0)=122.6372$, $\tilde{C}=13.1851$, $\tilde{c}(0)=12.1311$. Since $\tilde{c}(0)>C^*$ it is confirmed that algorithm 2b was the right one to use with the above parameter values.

C.4 Model 3: quadratic earnings

Instead of earnings taking a fixed value E^* assume that in every generation and for all earners, they are given by

$$E(t)=E_0+E_1t+E_2t^2, \qquad (21)$$

where E_0, $E_1\geq0$, $E_2\geq0$. In this model equations (2), (6) are replaced by

$$\frac{dW_{n+1}(t)}{dt} = E(t) + rW_{n+1}(t) - c_{n+1}(t) \tag{22}$$

$$\frac{dc_{n+1}(t)}{dt} = \xi[E(t) + rW_{n+1}(t) - c_{n+1}(t)] \tag{23}$$

which yield versions of (7) and (8) again. We also have

$$\frac{d\tilde{W}(t)}{dt} = [r - \xi]\tilde{W}(t) + E_0 + E_1 t + E_2 t^2 + \xi\tilde{W}(0) - \tilde{c}(0) \tag{24}$$

To simplify the notation, let $\beta := 1/[r - \xi]$; then by standard methods the solution for $\tilde{W}(t)$ of (24) for $t = 0$ is

$$\tilde{W}(t) = \tilde{W}(0) - [\beta E_1 + 2\beta^2 E_2]t - \beta E_2 t^2 + a\left[e^{\frac{t}{\beta}} - 1\right]$$

where $\left.\phantom{\begin{array}{c}a\\a\\a\end{array}}\right\} \tag{25}$

$$a := \beta[E_0 + \beta E_1 + 2\beta^2 E_2 + r\tilde{W}(0) - \tilde{c}(0)].$$

As in model 2, the solution will depend on whether or not $C^* \geq [1 - v]\tilde{C}$, yielding two cases.

Case 3a: $\tilde{c}(0) = C^*$

Substituting C^* for $\tilde{c}(0)$ and evaluating $\tilde{B} = \tilde{W}(T)$ from (25) and substituting for a

$$\tilde{B} - \tilde{W}(0) = -\beta J[E_0 + \beta E_1 + 2\beta^2 + r\tilde{W}(0) - C^*]J - \beta E_1 T - 2\beta^2 E_2 T - \beta E_2 T^2 \tag{26}$$

where $J := 1 - e^{T/\beta}$. A further complication in this model is that it is possible that a Mutt without wealth may start saving if his earnings grow sufficiently so as to exceed C^*; so a young person who has not yet inherited may begin accumulating wealth (this is exactly what happens to the Smart Mutts in section 10.4 of chapter 10). Let the age at which a person first acquires wealth be t_0 (where $-T = t_0 = 0$); then if $\tilde{B} > W^*$ equation (14) is replaced by

$$\tilde{W}(0) = \tilde{B} - \tau[\tilde{B} - W^*] + \int_{t_0}^{0} [E(t) - c(t)]e^{-rt}dt \tag{27}$$

Using this we eliminate $\tilde{W}(0)$ in (27) to obtain

$$[\tau + \beta rJ[1 - \tau]][\tilde{B} - W^*] = -\beta J[E_0 + \beta E_1 + 2\beta^2 E_2 + rW^* - C^*]$$

$$-\beta E_1 T - 2\beta^2 E_2 T - \beta E_2 T^2 \tag{28}$$

Equation (28) may be solved to find $\tilde{B}$ the upper stable bequest equilibrium and, putting $\tau = 0$ in (14) and (28) for the case where bequests are less than or equal to W^*, we may derive $\hat{B}$, the unstable equilibrium. We do this with the following:

Algorithm 3a Let t_0 be the larger root of $E_0 + E_1 t + E_1 t^2 = C^*$,

$$V(t_0, T) := \int_{t_0}^{T} [E_0 + E_1 t + E_2 t^2]e^{\frac{t}{\beta}}dt \tag{29}$$

and let D be defined as in algorithm 2a. Then

$$\left.\begin{aligned}\tilde{B}&=W*+\frac{V(t_0,T)-C*}{D}\\[2mm]\hat{B}&=W*+\frac{C*-V(t_0,T)}{r}\end{aligned}\right\}\tag{30}$$

where $\tilde{C}$ and $\tilde{W}(0)$ are given by (13) and (14).

Example 3a Given the values in row 3a of table C.2 we find $\beta=-5$, $J=0.9933$, $H_1=12.4$, $H_2=1.75$, $N'=14.1619$ $D=0.1259$, $\tilde{B}=137.1707$, $\hat{B}=33.5251$, $\tilde{W}(0)=125.7236$, $\tilde{C}=14.5756$ and $\tilde{c}(0)=C*=12$.

Since $[1-\nu]\tilde{C}=11.6605$ is less than $\tilde{c}(0)$ we have confirmed that with these parameter values we were dealing with case 3a and that algorithm 3a was appropriate. The solution would remain valid if instead of supposing that $\nu=0.2$, we had attributed to ν any value greater than $1-C*/\tilde{C}$, namely 0.1767.

Case 3b: $\tilde{c}(0)>C*$

If ν is less than this critical value, the equilibrium level $\tilde{c}(0)$ will exceed $C*$ and as in case 2b, the solution of the simultaneous equations will be less straightforward. The basic equations are the same as as in case 3a except that $\tilde{c}(0)$ in equation (26) is now determined by (18). This implies that we must replace $C*$ in (28) by an expression derived from (18) and (20). To implement this we may make use of

$$\tilde{B}=W*+\frac{N'}{D}\tag{31}$$

Algorithm 3b Let D,J,H_1,H_2 and N' be defined as in algorithm 3a. Then, the formulae for $\hat{B}$ and $\tilde{W}(0)$ take the same form as in case 3a; $\tilde{c}(0)$ and $\tilde{C}$ are determined by (18) and (20) respectively. Notice the close analogy between algorithms 2a, 2b and algorithms 3a, 3b.

Example 3b Given the values in row 3b of table C.2: $\beta=-5.71428571$, $J=0.98741186$, $H_1=12.2653$, $H_2=1.6518$, $N'=13.9381$, $D=0.1098$, $\tilde{B}=128.4826$, $\hat{B}=42.4740$, $\tilde{W}(0)=122.8275$, $\tilde{C}=14.1376$, $\tilde{c}(0)=13.0066$ and since $\tilde{c}(0)>C*$ we see that 3b, not 3a, was the appropriate algorithm.

C.5 Behaviour out of equilibrium

Although we principally concentrate upon equilibrium distributions of wealth in chapter 10, we also consider changes from one generation to the next. For example equation (11), chapter 10 and the associated figure 10.1 show how given the initial conditions, the next bequest in the line can be calculated from the current one, so that by repeated application the development of the line of bequests can be traced generation by generation in the case of the highly simplified model 1.

That treatment is a special case of a more general procedure of the same type tracing a line of bequests from a given initial situation in the context of the model 3 with its quadratic earnings function. We take as understood the rules for model 3 and assume that a set of values has been chosen for the parameters and for the values B_n and C_n of the bequest by individual n in the line and his final rate of consumption at time T. The values B_{n+1} and C_{n+1} for $n+1$, the next in line, may then be found with the following tool-kit of algorithms.

$c_{n+1}(0) = \max\{C^*, [1-v]C_n\}$,

$W_{n+1}(0) = \min\{B_n, B_n - \tau[B_n - W^*]\}$,

$\beta = 1/[r-\xi]$; $a_n = \beta[E_0 + \beta E_1 + 2\beta^2 E_2 + rW_{n+1}(0) - c_{n+1}(0)]$; $J = 1 - e^{T/\beta}$,

$B_{n+1} = W_{n+1}(0) - \beta[E_1 T + E_2 T^2] - 2\beta^2 E_2 T - a_n J$,

$C_{n+1} = c_{n+1}(0) + \xi[B_{n+1} - W_{n+1}(0)]$.

The validity of these algorithms can be established from the properties of models 3a and 3b – see section C.3.

   Example 3a' If the parameters are as for example 3a, and if $C_n = 12.1$, $B_n = 115$ then $c_{n+1}(0) = 12$, $W_{n+1}(0) = 115$, $B_{n+1} = 125.116$, $C_{n+1} = 14.2760$.

   Example 3a'' As above but with $C_n = 14.2760$ $B_n = 125.116$. We then find: $c_{n+1}(0) = 12$, $W_{n+1}(0) = 121.705$, $B_{n+1} = 132.653$, $C_{n+1} = 14.4634$.

C.6 Subsidies to small bequests

Suppose the tax τ on bequests in excess of W^* were supplemented by a subsidy s to bequests (including zero bequests) of less than some 'poverty level' P. This device plays an important part in chapter 11. In its simplest form (the chapter 11 version) we may put $s = 1$ so that the subsidy will raise any bequest B_n which is less than the poverty level by the full amount $P - B_n$ needed to bring it up to P; but it is more interesting to consider any value of s such that $0 \le s \le 1$, which raises the bequest by $s[P - B_n]$ whenever $B_n < P$. This yields the equation:

$$W_{n+1}(0) = B_n + s[P - B_n], \tag{32}$$

when $B_n < P$. The effects on the small bequests B_n of such a subsidy are analogous to those of the wealth tax τ on those bequests large enough to be subject to it. Two advantages of studying models embodying such subsidies are that they have some counterparts in measures sometimes used to provide families with very small or zero endowments of property to start to amass some, and that the scope of choice of measures of inequality of wealth distribution is enriched in theoretical models which are not encumbered by families completely destitute of any possessions whatever.[1]

   Provided P is not set too high, the effect of a subsidy raising all bequests B_n up to the level P ($s = 1$) is simply to raise the lower stable equilibrium from zero to P in the simpler models. In the general case with s lying between 0 and 1, the equilibrium is raised part of the way from 0 to P provided s and P are not too small.

   We may proceed from the rules (3) and (32) to adjust the various relevant algorithms already provided for obtaining ΔB_n given B_n and the relevant parameter values, when a subsidy scheme is inserted as well. Here are the adjusted algorithms:

   Algorithm 1' As before $\hat{B} = [C^* - E^*]/r$, $J := 1 - e^{rT}$, $H := J\hat{B}/[J-1]$. Then if $B_0 < \hat{B}$, $B_n \to \tilde{B} = [\hat{B}J + [1-J]sP]/[J + s[1-J]]$ unless $sP < H$, in which case $B_n \to 0$.

   Example If the parameters are as for row 1' in table C.2, and $B_0 = 70$ then $J = -0.868245957$; $sP = 40$; $H = 37.1791$; so $\tilde{B} = 8.4132$.

Algorithm 2a' Replace W^* by P and τ by s in algorithm 2a. Let $N:=rP+E^*$, $J:=1-e^{[r-\xi]T}$ and $D:=s[\xi-r]/J-r[1-s]$. Then $\tilde{B}=P+[N-C^*]/D$.

Example If the parameters are as for row 2a' in table C.2, and $B_0=70$ $P=50$, then $N=-0.75$; $J=0.987411858$; $D=0.136784807$; $\tilde{B}=44.51693812$; $\tilde{W}(0)=48.90338762$.

Algorithm 2b is unlikely to be appropriate for finding the lower stable equilibrium except in freak cases: we shall not therefore pursue it further.

Algorithm 3a' Replace W^* by P and τ by s in the original version of the algorithm. Then $\beta=1/[r-\xi]$, $J=1-e^{T/\beta}$, $H_1=\beta[rP-C^*+E_0-\beta E_1 1+2\beta^2 E_2]$, $H_2=\beta E_1 T-[2\beta^2 T-\beta T^2]E_2$. Let $N:=JH_1+H_2$ and $D:=s-\beta r[1-s]/J$. Then the lower equilibrium is $\tilde{B}=P+N/D$; $\tilde{W}(0)=\tilde{B}-s[\tilde{B}-P]$; $\tilde{C}=C^*+\xi[\tilde{B}-\tilde{W}(0)]$; $\tilde{c}(0)=C^*$

Example If the parameters are as in row 3a' of table C.2: $\beta=-5$, $J=0.993262$, $H_1=-11.75$, $H_2=8.75$, $N=7.04548114$; $D=0.775168$; $\tilde{B}=45.32877$; $\tilde{W}(0)=48.44292$; $\tilde{C}=12.29932$; $\tilde{c}(0)=13$.

C.7 Model 5: wealth distribution and family size

This section gives some further explanation of formula (10.38) in model 4 in chapter 10 which examines the effect of variations in family size on the long-run distribution of wealth. Wealth tax at the rate τ is charged on the whole of every bequest W where $W>W^*$. Saving and dissaving are ruled out and marriages only take place between partners of equal wealth. Hence the total wealth after tax left by a married couple who had inherited W each is $2[1-\tau]W$ provided $W>W^*$. This is divided equally among their offspring; we assume that all couples have some offspring and that in all wealth intervals the proportions of couples who had k offspring were $p_k \geq 0$ for $k=1, 2, ..., K$ so that $\Sigma_{k=1}^{K} p_k=1$ where p_k is independent of W. We also assume $\Sigma_{k=1}^{K} kp_k=2$ so as to fix the population size, and that everyone is assured of wealth of at least a minimum (strictly positive) level W_{min}: this can be done by subsidies on inheritances below W_{min}.

To work out the shape of the equilibrium distribution on these assumptions we first write down the conditions such that for some specific wealth level W, the value $F_1(W)$ in the next generation should be the same as the value $F_0(W)$ in the present generation. To work out the value of $F_1(W)$, the number of the next generation who will inherit W or less, consider first the 'only children' of the generation 0: of these, only those whose parents who each have wealth less than $\frac{1}{2}W/[1-\tau]$ will inherit less than W: their amount in $F_1(W)$ will be $\frac{1}{2}p_1 F_0(\frac{1}{2}W/[1-\tau])$; similarly, the share contributed by pairs will be $p_2 F_0(W/[1-\tau])$, and those of families of k children $\frac{1}{2}kp_k F_0(\frac{1}{2}kW/[1-\tau])$. The distribution in the next generation is thus

$$F_1(W)=\sum_{k=1}^{K} \tfrac{1}{2}kp_k F_0 \left(\frac{kW}{2[1-\tau]} \right) \tag{33}$$

Equilibrium requires $F_1(W)=F_0(W)$ for all W, which implies that the distribution function F must satisfy

$$a+bF(W)=\sum_{k=1}^{K} \tfrac{1}{2}kp_k \left[a+bF \left(\frac{kW}{2[1-\tau]} \right) \right] \tag{34}$$

for some constants a and b. In other words

$$\sum_{k=1}^{K} \frac{1}{2} k p_k \frac{a+bF(\theta W)}{a+bF(W)} = 1 \tag{35}$$

where $\theta := k/[1-\tau]$. But if this relation is to hold for all W, given any arbitrarily specified $p_1, \dots, p_K$ satisfying the above conditions then $[a+bF(\theta W)]/[a+bF(W)]$ must be
expressible as $\phi(\theta)$ where ϕ is independent of W. So

$$a+bF(\theta W) = \phi(\theta)[a+bF(W)] \tag{36}$$

The class of functions that satisfy this is given by[2]

$$a+bF(W) = W^u \tag{37}$$

where u is some constant. An important member of this class is the Pareto distribution

$$F(W) = 1 - qW^{-\alpha} \tag{38}$$

where q is some constant.

Now let us investigate how the coefficient α of the Pareto distribution depends on
the p_k and τ. We do this by considering the associated question of what level of tax τ
would be required to sustain a Pareto distribution of wealth with a given parameter α
under the conditions of model 4. Having obtained τ as a function of α for any given set
of values of p_k we need then only obtain the inverse function to discover the level of α
corresponding to the equilibrium Pareto distribution that would result from the same
values of the family pattern coefficients p_k and any value of τ. To obtain the value of τ
which is consistent with equilibrium, given a set of values for α and the family-size distribution parameters p_k. We substitute (38) for $F_0(W)$ and $F_1(W)$ in (33). The equation
for deriving τ is then

$$[1-\tau]^{-\alpha} = \sum_{k=1}^{K} p_k \left[\frac{k}{2}\right]^{1-\alpha} \tag{39}$$

Take an example with $p_1=0.3$, $p_2=0.45$, $p_3=0.2$, $p_4=0.05$, and $\alpha=2$: we calculate
$[1-\tau]^{-2}=2[0.3+0.225+0.0667+0.0125]=1.2083$, and find that $\tau=0.0903$. This confirms the entry 9.0 per cent in the left-hand column of table 10.6. The other entries can
be checked by using exactly the same method – and through it, more detailed tables of
the same kind can be constructed.

C.8 Equations for the program used in chapter 11

The parameters g, M and N, determine the structure of the stochastic model: N has
the property that $N+2$ is the number of these intervals across which will be spread the
bequests in generation $n+1$, from all beneficiaries in generation n, which were in any
particular interval. N is independent of n. $M+2N+1$ gives the total number of intervals in the model. The general program assumes that the income range (a subset of the
real line) is subdivided into a set of mutually exclusive and exhaustive intervals defined
thus

$$I_i := [Pg^{i-1}, Pg^i] \tag{40}$$

where $i=-N,-N+1,\ldots,-1,0,1,2,\ldots,M+N$. The program operates by estimating a square matrix $\mathbf{C}$ with rows and columns also numbered from $-N$ to $M+N$, such that if ϕ_n is the column vector of the probabilities at generation n, of the bequests being in intervals $(\mathbf{I}_{-N}, \mathbf{I}_{M+N})$, then

$$\Phi_{n+1}C\phi_n \tag{41}$$

The program then estimates the long-term equilibrium distribution of the probabilities of a bequest at the end of a line $0, 1, 2, \ldots, n, \ldots$ being in interval $\mathbf{I}_i$. In the examples we consider that these probabilities should not depend on which interval the line started from.

The stochastic model is based on the crude non-stochastic model which considers the line of bequests $B_0, B_1, B_2, \ldots, B_n, \ldots$ from a given initial B_0 subject to the following rules:[3]

$$B_{n+1}=\begin{cases} \hat{B}+[[1-\tau]B_n+\tau W^*-\hat{B}]e^{rT} & \text{if } W^*\leq B_N \\ \hat{B}+[B_n-\hat{B}]e^{rT} & \text{if } P\leq B_n, W^* \\ \hat{B}+[P-B]e^{rT} & \text{if } B_n, P \end{cases} \tag{42}$$

where $\hat{B}:=[C^*-E^*]/r$. From the three rules in (42) we can work out the non-stochastic multiplier m as a function of B_n, n and the parameters π:

$$m(B_n,n,\pi):=\frac{B_{n+1}}{B_n} \tag{43}$$

In the stochastic model, we have a stochastic multiplier μ_n in place of the non-stochastic one. We assume that irrespective of the value of n all pre-tax bequests B_n, within interval $\mathbf{I}_i$ are located at the centre of $\mathbf{I}_i$, namely

$$S_i:=\tfrac{1}{2}P[g^{i-1}+g^i] \tag{44}$$

The non-stochastic multiplier is then calculated for this adjusted value, so that, for example, if $S_i>W^*$, by rule 1 of equation (42) above

$$m_i=m(S_i,n,\pi)=\frac{\hat{B}+[[1-\tau]Pg^{i-1}h+\tau W^*-\hat{B}]e^{rT}}{S_i} \tag{45}$$

where $h:=\tfrac{1}{2}[1+g]$. While the non-stochastic multiplier is a single value, calculated in a single step (42) and (43), the corresponding stochastic multiplier $\mu(S_i,n,\pi)$ consists of a vector $\mathbf{m}$ of $N+2$ possible values, with $N+2$ associated probabilities and is calculated in three steps:

- Adjust B_n to the value S_i, the centre of $\mathbf{I}_i$.
- Use (42) and (43) to calculate a non-stochastic multiplier $m_i=m(S_i,n,\pi)$, for this value.
- Choose an integer s_i and a probability p_i $(0\leq p_i\leq1)$ so that $\mathbf{m}$ takes the values:[4]

$$
\begin{bmatrix} 1 \\ g \\ g^2 \\ g^3 \\ \cdot \\ g^{si} \\ \cdot \\ \cdot \\ \cdot \\ g^{N-1} \\ \\ g^N \\ g^{N+1} \end{bmatrix} \text{ with probabilities } 2^{-N}[1-p_i] \begin{bmatrix} 1 \\ N \\ \binom{N}{2} \\ \binom{N}{3} \\ \cdot \\ \cdot \\ \cdot \\ N \\ 1 \\ 0 \end{bmatrix} +2^{-N}p_i \begin{bmatrix} 0 \\ 1 \\ N \\ \binom{N}{2} \\ \cdot \\ \cdot \\ \cdot \\ \binom{N}{2} \\ N \\ 1 \end{bmatrix} \tag{46}
$$

and that the expected value $\mathscr{E}(\mu)=m(S_i,n,\pi)$.

The vector of probabilities in (46) constitutes the transition probabilities for interval $\mathbf{I}_i$: call this vector $\boldsymbol{v}_i$. By working out $\boldsymbol{v}_i$ for each $i=-N, 1-N, ..., 0, 1, 2, ..., M, ..., M+N$, we may obtain the matrix $\mathbf{C}$ for updating the probability vector occupying each of the intervals $(\mathbf{I}_{-N}, ..., \mathbf{I}_{M+N})$, generation after generation, and more particularly for finding the long-term equilibrium of that vector of probabilities.

The estimation of μ is as follows. By (46)

$$m(S_i,n,\pi)=\mathscr{E}(\mu(S_i,n,\pi))=g^{si}[1-p_i+gp_i]h^N \tag{47}$$

Where h is as defined above, and s_i is an integer to be determined. Now, because $0\leq p_i\leq 1$ we have

$$1\leq 1-p_i+gp_i\leq g \tag{48}$$

and so

$$g^{si}\leq \frac{m_i}{h^N}\leq g^{1+si} \tag{49}$$

Hence s_i is the largest integer not exceeding

$$\frac{\log\left(\frac{m_i}{h^N}\right)}{\log (g)} \tag{50}$$

Using (47) we may write

$$p_i=\frac{m_i g^{-s_i}h^{-N}-1}{g-1} \tag{51}$$

which determines p_i. Knowing both s_i and p_i, the estimation of μ can be completed by using (46).

The entire matrix $\mathbf{C}$ may be assembled by calculating each row vector i for $i=-N$ to $M+N$, although for the ultimate purpose of calculating the equilibrium distribution of pre-tax bequests it is not necessary to calculate the row vectors for $i<0$, which must all be the same as that for $i=0$.[5]

Confining the matrix $\mathbf{C}$ to the row vectors for $i \geq 0$ one may form a square semi-positive matrix by summing all the columns $0, -1, ..., -N$ into column 0, thus obtaining a singular matrix, since each row sums to 1. Any cases where the matrix is decomposable will be obvious and the two parts can be dealt with separately, as they will represent a wealthy class (having a minimum possible bequest) and a pauper class (having a maximum possible bequest), with a gulf in between which can never be bridged. The equilibrium distributions for the two classes can be dealt with separately, since both their $\mathbf{C}$ matrices will be indecomposable, although they will both be singular. Taking the normal case where there is one indecomposable singular square $\mathbf{C}$ matrix each of whose columns sums to unity, we have to find that row vector ϕ', all of whose elements are positive and sum to 1, which satisfies $\phi'\mathbf{C}=\phi'$: this can be solved by standard methods.

Let us illustrate these methods with an example using the following parameters π: $T=25$, $E^*=10$, $C^*=12$, $r=2\frac{1}{2}\%$, $\tau=\frac{2}{3}$, $W^*=120$, $P=60$, $g=\sqrt{2}$, $N=5$, $M=27$. The first stage of calculating the equilibrium distribution consists of finding the stochastic multipliers, for the intervals $\mathbf{I}_i$. For example take the interval $\mathbf{I}_5$: since the above parameter values imply $Pg^4=240$, this interval is $(240, 240\sqrt{2})$ with centre $240h$, where $h=\frac{1}{2}[1+\sqrt{2}]$, and the adjusted bequest size in interval $\mathbf{I}_5$, is $S_5=240h=289.7056$. We also have $\tilde{B}=[C^*-E^*]/r=80$ and $[1-\tau]S_5+\tau W^* = 176.5685$; so by rule 3 of equation (42) we find

$$B_{n+1}=80+e^{0.625}[176.5685425-80]=260.4137891 \qquad (52)$$

and so the non-stochastic multiplier is $m_5=B_{n+1}/S_5=0.89889103$. Following the procedure indicated above

$$\frac{m_5}{h^N}=0.35073459 \qquad (53)$$

$$g^{S_5}[h^N[1-p_5]+gh^Np_5]=m_5 \qquad (54)$$

where s_5 is an integer. So

$$g^{S_5}\leq 0.35073459 \leq g^{S_5+1} \qquad (55)$$

Evaluating (50) in this case as -3.0231 we see that the only possible value of s_5 is -4. It follows from (51) that $p_5=(4\times 0.3507-1)/(1.4142)=0.9728$. Using (46) the probabilities for the stochastic multiplier can be written as the column vector v_5 given by

$$v_5=\begin{bmatrix} C_{15} \\ C_{25} \\ C_{35} \\ C_{45} \\ C_{55} \\ C_{65} \\ C_{75} \end{bmatrix}=\frac{1}{32}\begin{bmatrix} 0.027220751 \\ 1.108883002 \\ 5.136103753 \\ 10 \\ 9.863896247 \\ 4.891116997 \\ 0.972779249 \end{bmatrix} \qquad (56)$$

For example, the interpretation of the last row of (56) (namely $C_{75}=0.972779249/32$) is that, given $s_5=-4$, **m** takes the value $g^{N+1-4}=g^2$ with probability $0.9728/[2^N]$ and so the bequest moves up two intervals from $\mathbf{I}_5$ to $\mathbf{I}_7$ with this probability.

By repeating the above procedure for all elements of the matrix $\|C_{ij}\|$ the whole matrix may be calculated and then by calculating the appropriate minors of border elements the M-vector $\phi(\pi)$ may be obtained giving the long-run equilibrium probabilities of a bequest selected at random being in $\mathbf{I}_i$, for each value of i from 1 to M, conditional on parameters π.

C.9 The step-by-step approach to equilibrium

It is of little use to know what is the equilibrium distribution of a stochastic model of wealth distribution if the actual distribution is markedly different from equilibrium – as it may be when the relevant parameters are subject to change. Bearing in mind the analogy with mechanical systems, we would be mainly interested in stable equilibria, in the sense that if the changed parameters now remain unaltered, the actual distribution will eventually approach the equilibrium distribution; this should be verifiable by computing the approach step by step. Progress towards a stable equilibrium distribution might still involve some oscillation about the equilibrium but this will die away if the equilibrium is stable. In models with a moderate number of intervals of bequest values it may also be simpler to compute such an approach towards the equilibrium distribution over several generations than it is to calculate the equilibrium distribution itself using the methods described in chapter 11.

We illustrate this possibility by following up a situation in which the distribution of bequests happens to be already in stable equilibrium for our standard bequest model with a given set π_1 of parameters – due maybe to these values having been held steady by a sluggish dynasty from time immemorial. We then suppose that the dynasty is overthrown by one holding very different views enshrined in a distinct set of parameter values π_2 but thereafter becoming just as unimaginative as the believers in π_1. We can then get the computer to tell us what happens generation after generation, as soon as we supply it with the parameter values π_1 and π_2.

We suppose these values π_1 and π_2 are those given in table 11.2 and provide the subject matter of table 11.14 and figure 11.9. We see that the parameter $g=2^{1/3}$ in each set π_1 and π_2, but $N=25$ in π_1, whereas $N=19$ in π_2. So to follow events in a régime fixed on π_2 we have to get the computer to keep playing game 25, although to follow events under a régime stuck with π_1 the appropriate game would be game 19.

To obtain table C.4 we carried out a sequence of 100 plays of game 25 starting from the equilibrium π_2 (the result of sticking for ages to values π_2), but then use the other set π_1: and then display in table C.4 the proportions per million of all bequests, which lay in each of eight particular bequest ranges, at the outset and again after 20, 40, 60, 80 and 100 generations had passed (after 20, 40... plays of game 25) and to end the table by giving the same proportions for the eventual equilibrium π_1. The eight intervals of bequests chosen for this demonstration were those cited in the top row of table C.3 and table C.4, namely $(15/g)$ to 15, 30 to $30g$, 0 to 60, 60 to $60g$, 120 to $120g$, 480 to $480g$, where $g=2^{1/3}=1.2599$.

Table C.4 shows that even after 20 generations there would remain a perceptible gap

Table C.3 *Adjustment to equilibrium π_2 from equilibrium π_1 by steps of 20 or 60 generations*

Range	11.9–15	30–37.8	0–60	60–75.6	120–151.2	240–302.4	480–604.8
Generation			Bequests in range – per million of all bequests				
0(π_1)	22,384.992	101,004.036	534,428.871	87,257.119	55,399.819	32,577.434	10,299.933
20	43,372.281	118,937.998	659,340.787	41,334.171	18,752.728	35,764.185	29,853.189
40	43,382.319	118,964.738	659,488.650	41,340.709	18,746.013	35,742.506	29,833.671
60	43,387.228	118,977.831	659,561.048	41,343.942	18,742.769	35,731.806	29,824.068
80	43,389.636	118,984.251	659,596.551	41,345.528	18,741.178	35,726.585	29,819.360
100	43,390.816	118,987.400	659,613.959	41,346.305	18,740.398	35,724.026	29,817.051
120	43,391.395	118,988.943	659,622.497	41,346.686	18,740.015	35,722.771	29,815.919
180	43,391.887	118,990.254	659,629.743	41,347.010	18,739.690	35,721.705	29,814.958
240	43,391.945	118,990.408	659,630.597	41,347.048	18,739.652	35,721.580	29,814.844
300	43,391.951	118,990.427	659,630.697	41,347.053	18,739.648	35,721.565	29,814.831
...	...	...	...	...	...	...	...
∞(π_2)	43,391.952	118,990.428	659,630.709	41,347.053	18,739.647	35,721.564	29,814.830

Table C.4 *Adjustment to equilibrium π_1 from equilibrium π_2 by steps of 20 generations*

Range	11.9–15	30–37.8	0–60	60–75.6	120–151.2	240–302.4	480–604.8
Generation			Bequests in range – per million of all bequests				
$0(\pi_2)$	43,391.9519	118,990.428	659,630.709	41,347.053	18,739.647	35,721.564	29,814.830
20	22,375.4295	100,966.419	534,236.260	87,243.678	55,424.266	32,606.597	10,312.771
40	22,384.7550	101,003.374	534,425.479	87,256.884	55,400.252	32,577.947	10,300.158
60	22,384.9190	101,004.025	534,428.811	87,257.115	55,399.827	32,577.443	10,299.937
80	22,384.9920	101,004.036	534,428.869	87,257.119	55,399.819	32,577.434	10,299.934
100	22,384.9920	101,004.036	534,428.870	87,257.119	55,399.819	32,577.434	10,299.933
...	...	...	...	...	...	...	...
$\infty(\pi_1)$	22,384.9920	101,004.036	534,428.871	87,257.119	55,399.819	32,577.434	10,299.933

between the actual bequest distribution and the equilibrium π_1 distribution towards which the actual distribution was still moving. Not until a further 60 generations – another 1,500 years – had elapsed would the equilibrium π_1 have been virtually achieved. However, even though this rate of approach may seem grotesquely sluggish, it is still about three times as swift as the approach from equilibrium π_1 towards equilibrium π_2, set out in table C.4.[6]

C.10 Methods for estimating α when M is large

The Pareto diagrams in chapter 11 reveal that the right-hand tail appears fairly straight in the equilibrium distributions of the logbinomial models. This fairly common feature may be used for obtaining estimates of Pareto's coefficient α. Even though the slope α of the right-hand part of the diagram alters gradually along its length, it is reasonable to suppose that Pareto's law is approximately satisfied so that we could use the estimated equilibrium bequest distribution $(\phi_0, \phi_1, ..., \phi_{28})$ to obtain an estimate of Pareto's α – the limit of the slope that would result if we could extend the series of the ϕ_i as $i \to \infty$. Consider these two methods of estimating α:

$$\hat{\alpha}_1 := \frac{\log\left(\frac{\phi_i}{\phi_{i+1}}\right)}{\log(g)} \tag{57}$$

where I_i is the highest interval such that more than one bequest in 100,000 are contained in intervals I_i and above, and

$$\hat{\alpha}_2 := \frac{\log(\phi_{M-N}/\phi_{M-N+1})}{\log(g)} \tag{58}$$

In the present example $M=27$, $N=5$, $g=\sqrt{2}$; we find that $\phi_5=2.1256\times10^{-5}$, $\phi_6=1.1387\times10^{-5}$, and $\phi_7+\phi_8+...\phi_{27}<5\times10^{-8}$; so, although there are more than 1 in 100,000 bequests in I_5 and above, there are less than 1 in 100,000 bequests in I_6 and above; thus $i=5$ in (58) and we find $\hat{\alpha}_1=\log(\phi_5/\phi_6)/\log(g)=8.4449$. To find $\hat{\alpha}_2$ we note that $M-N=22$, and that $\phi_{22}=3.7135\times10^{-30}$, $\phi_{23}=0.12416\times10^{-30}$. Hence $\hat{\alpha}_2=\log(\phi_{22}/\phi_{23})/\log(g)=9.3497.$[7]

Both estimates indicate a far higher value of α – a lower value of inequality – than is found from actual distributions of bequests or other wealth distributions. We shall find that with numerical examples of equilibrium bequest distributions for our model with less taxation and other parameters allowing more normal levels of inequality to be sustained there will be better agreement between the different estimates of α.[8]

There is a third method of estimating α from the model parameters π which is both more reliable and more convenient in that it avoids the need to calculate the equilibrium distribution. It is also quick, given some prior information about the required degree of accuracy and the approximate location of the solution value.

The clue which leads to the third method of finding the asymptotic value of α is the fact that for very high values of i, the coefficients in the various diagonals of the $\mathbf{C}$ matrix will all be zeros except in $N+2$ consecutive diagonals which each will repeat its own coefficient unchanged, as illustrated by the numbers $K_0, ..., K_3$, in figure C.1 for the case when $N=2$. If there is equilibrium and if the Pareto slope α is constant at the

K_0	K_1	K_2	K_3					
	K_0	K_1	K_2	K_3				
		K_0	K_1	K_2	K_3			
			K_0	K_1	K_2	K_3		
				K_0	K_1	K_2	K_3	
					K_0	K_1	K_2	K_3
						K_0	K_1	K_2	K_3
					...	...	...	

Figure C.1 Section of the **C** matrix for high bequest ranges: case when $N=2$

very high bequest levels that we are considering, two distinct equilibrium conditions are satisfied: in each interval $\mathbf{I}_i$ the mean value of the stochastic multiplier is

$$\mathscr{E}(\mu)=[1-\tau]e^{rT}, \tag{59}$$

the value of the non-stochastic multiplier m_i for $i\to\infty$;[9] and the number of bequests in $\mathbf{I}_i$ remains the same in the next generation – the movements into the three other intervals must balance the movements into it along each column. The first condition implies that within each row

$$\Sigma_j K_j g^i=[1-\tau]e^{rT}g^a \tag{60}$$

where a is an integer $0<a<N+1$. Now, as $i\to\infty$, the ratio $\phi_{i-1}/\phi_i\to\gamma$, a constant. The second condition implies that within each column

$$\Sigma_i K_i \gamma^i=\gamma^a \tag{61}$$

Notice that in the limit γ can be written as g^α where α is the Pareto coefficient. Hence, once the root γ has been found from equation (61) the value of α can also be found as

$$\alpha=\frac{\log(\gamma)}{\log(g)} \tag{62}$$

A convenient numerical example applying these methods to find the value of α is that assuming the following parameter values: $T=25$, $E^*=10$, $C^*=12$, $r=2\frac{1}{2}\%$, $\tau=0.5$, $W^*=120$, $P=60$, $g=2$, $N=2$. Apart from satisfying equation (59) the coefficients K_0, K_1, K_2 and K_3 must satisfy the conditions

$$K_0+K_1 g+K_2 g^2+K_3 g^3=[1-\tau]e^{rT}g^a=0.934123 \tag{63}$$

$$K_0+K_1 \gamma+K_2 \gamma^2+K_3 \gamma^3=\gamma^a \tag{64}$$

where a is an integer. The only possible integer value for a enabling (59) to be satisfied under these circumstances is $a=2$: the values for K_0, K_1, K_2, K_3 then have to be of the form

$$0\leq K_0<0.25,\ K_1=0.25+K_0,\ K_2=0.5-K_0,\ K_3=0.75-K_0$$

and these conditions imply that the only possible solution for (63) is $K_0=0.0848$, $K_1=0.3348$, $K_2=0.4152$, $K_3=0.1652$. This is easy to check, since $g=2$, and $K_0+2K_1+4K_2+8K_3=3.7365$ and $4[1-\tau]e^{rT}=2e^{0.625}=3.7365$.

Table C.5 *Estimates of the Pareto coefficient* α *when*
P=60, r=2½ *per cent,* C*=12, E=10, W*=120

N	g	At interval i_0 (direct method)	As $i \rightarrow \infty$ (direct method)	As $i \rightarrow \infty$ (indirect method)
2	2.00000000	1.448	1.489	1.448
4	1.63252700	1.516	1.516	1.448
6	1.49210600	1.566	1.568	1.501
8	1.41421400	1.525	1.525	1.515
10	1.36340400	1.535	1.525	1.526
100	1.10299100	1.567		
1,000	1.03148490	1.567		
10,000	1.00985078	1.567		
100,000	1.00310466	1.567		
1,000,000	1.00098074	1.567		

Notes:
(i) Interval i_0 is the particular income range which, in
equilibrium, contains a proportion 10^{-5} of the population.
(ii) N and g are such that $N[\log(g)]^2 = 2[\log(2)]^2$.

Next we seek a real root γ of equation (64) above which can be found by a standard
root-finding routine as γ=2.7291; this checks satisfactorily since

$$\frac{K_0}{2.7291} + \frac{K_1}{2.7291} + K_2 + 2.7291 K_3 = 1.0 \qquad (65)$$

within an error of 10^{-6}. Finally α may be evaluated from (62) as 1.448.

Although this method for estimating α is general, it will break down if the values N,g
are unsuitable; for example if they allow no equilibrium bequest distribution with a
finite positive arithmetic mean, or if they rule out the theoretical possibility that any
given finite bequest level, however large, could be exceeded, provided the assumed constant number of bequest lines was set large enough. The method is particularly convenient for investigating the effects of increasing N far above 50 and decreasing g far
below 1.04, values for which it would be tedious to find α by direct calculation. This is
illustrated in table C.5 of estimates of α, based on the example analysed above, but now
extending N upwards by nine steps from two to a million, and reducing g by nine
matching steps from two to below 1.001. Let us examine what this method involves.

C.11 Estimation of α when N is large and g−1 is small

These methods depend on the finding that to a useful degree of approximation α̂ is
insensitive to changes of N and g which leave $N[\log(g)]^2$ unaltered: we shall refer to such
changes as changes subject to the inverse square law. Unfortunately, for values of N

exceeding a million the series of estimates subject to this inverse square relation begins to show fluctuations due to computational limitations and the ignoring of higher terms in the expansions of series representing logarithms. But the level of regularity in the estimates is sufficient for purposes of illustration, since in the real world, long-term equilibrium is never very closely approached.

To obtain a fuller indication of the stability of estimated $\hat{\alpha}$ under changes of N and g according to the inverse square rule, we have chosen the same values for most of the parameters as in the above examples and have then set $N=2$ and $g=2$ initially. The value of M is not specified since we are only concerned with the asymptotic value of α as $M \to \infty$. Table C.5 sets out the variations in $\hat{\alpha}$ which as N increases and g responds subject to the inverse-square rule from the initial values of $(2,2)$ to $(N,g)=(10,000,000, 1.000980739)$. It will be seen that the fluctuations of $\hat{\alpha}$ are negligible compared with the margins of error in any possible estimate of α obtainable from survey data or official statistics of such distributions.

C.12 Multivariate stochastic models

Most of the models which we discussed in chapter 11 involved the distribution of just one variable: bequests. However, in section 11.6 of chapter 11, we consider a model of two variables, wealth and income, which we now develop as a bivariate stochastic model.[10] Here we focus upon a stochastic model of a normal distribution of two variables. As in chapters 10 and 11, we consider a sequence of equally spaced moments of time, $n=0, 1, 2, \ldots$ to represent successive generations and we suppose that the two variates at time n are $\zeta_1(n)=\log(u_1(n))$ and $\zeta_2(n)=\log(u_2(n))$ where $u_1(n)$ is the level of wealth and $u_2(n)$ is the level of income at date n. We impose the following simplifying assumptions at $n=0$:

- The distribution of $\zeta(0)$ (the vector with components $\zeta_1(0)$, $\zeta_2(0)$) is normal with expectation $\mathbf{z}(0)$ and variance–covariance matrix $\Sigma(0)$.
- The probability density function of the pair of variates $\Delta\zeta_1(n)$, $\Delta\zeta_2(n)$, conditional on $\zeta(n)$ is also bivariate normal, with means $\mathbf{k}-\mathbf{A}\mathbf{z}(n)$ and variance–covariance matrix $\mathbf{V}$ for $n=0, 1, 2, 3, \ldots$ where the components of the vectors $\mathbf{k}$ and $\mathbf{z}(0)$, and the elements of the matrices $\Sigma(0)$ and $\mathbf{V}$ are all given constants.

These assumptions ensure that at the next generation, $n=1$, the distribution of $\zeta(1)$ also is normal with means $\mathbf{z}(1)$ and variance–covariance matrix $\Sigma(1)$ given by

$$z_1(1)=k_1+[1-A_{11}]z_1(0)-A_{12}z_2(0) \tag{66}$$

$$z_2(1)=k_2-A_{21}z_1(0)+[1-A_{22}]z_2(0) \tag{67}$$

$$\Sigma_{11}(1)=V_{11}+[1-A_{11}]^2\Sigma_{11}(0)+A_{12}^2\Sigma_{22}(0)-2A_{12}[1-A_{11}]\Sigma_{12}(0) \tag{68}$$

$$\Sigma_{22}(1)=V_{22}+A_{21}^2\Sigma_{11}(0)+[1-A_{22}]^2\Sigma_{22}(0)-2A_{21}[1-A_{22}]\Sigma_{12}(0) \tag{69}$$

$$\Sigma_{12}(1)=V_{12}-A_{21}[1-A_{11}]\Sigma_{11}(0)-A_{12}[1-A_{22}]\Sigma_{22}(0) \\ +[[1-A_{11}][1-A_{22}]+A_{12}A_{21}]\Sigma_{12}(0) \tag{70}$$

Our assumptions ensure also that for any generation $n \geq 0$, the distribution of $\zeta(n+1)$ is also normal with means $\mathbf{z}(n)$ and variance–covariance matrix $\Sigma(n)$ given by

$$z_1(n+1)=k_1+[1-A_{11}]z_1(n)-A_{12}z_2(n) \tag{71}$$

$$z_2(n+1)=k_2-A_{21}z_1(n)+[1-A_{22}]z_2(n) \tag{72}$$

$$\Sigma_{11}(n+1)=V_{11}+[1-A_{11}]^2\Sigma_{11}(n)+A_{12}^2\Sigma_{22}(n)-2A_{12}[1-A_{11}]\Sigma_{12}(n) \tag{73}$$

$$\Sigma_{22}(n+1)=V_{22}+A_{21}^2\Sigma_{11}(n)+[1-A_{22}]^2\Sigma_{22}(n)-2A_{21}[1-A_{22}]\Sigma_{12}(n) \tag{74}$$

$$\Sigma_{12}(n+1)=V_{12}-A_{21}[1-A_{11}]\Sigma_{11}(n)-A_{12}[1-A_{22}]\Sigma_{22}(n)$$
$$+[[1-A_{11}][1-A_{22}]+A_{12}A_{21}]\Sigma_{12}(n) \tag{75}$$

Given the data for $n=0$, we can thus calculate step by step the parameters $\mathbf{z}(n)$ and $\Sigma(n)$ for distributions up to any value of n. As a numerical example of this step-by-step process assume the following parameters for the initial distribution of the variables, $\zeta(0)$, and the expressions determining $\Delta\zeta(0)$

$$\left.\begin{array}{l} \mathbf{z}(0)=\begin{bmatrix} 0.53 \\ 0.95 \end{bmatrix}, \quad \Sigma(0)=\begin{bmatrix} 1 & 0 \\ 0 & 1.5 \end{bmatrix}, \\[3ex] \mathbf{k}(0)=\begin{bmatrix} 0.19 \\ 0.29 \end{bmatrix} \\[3ex] \mathbf{A}=\begin{bmatrix} 0.22 & 0.08 \\ 0.02 & 0.28 \end{bmatrix}, \quad \mathbf{V}=\begin{bmatrix} 0.31572 & 0.26062 \\ 0.26062 & 0.63732 \end{bmatrix} \end{array}\right\} \tag{76}$$

Substituting these parameter values in the expressions for finding the corresponding values one generation later at $n=1$ we obtain

$$\left.\begin{array}{l} z_1(1)=0.19+0.78z_1(0)-0.08z_2(0) \\ z_2(1)=0.29-0.02z_1(0)+0.72z_2(0) \end{array}\right\} \tag{77}$$

which implies

$$\mathbf{z}(1)=\begin{bmatrix} 0.5274 \\ 0.9634 \end{bmatrix} \tag{78}$$

Similarly, we update the variance-covariance matrix thus

$$\left.\begin{array}{l} \Sigma_{11}(1)=0.31572+0.6084\Sigma_{11}(0)+0.0064\Sigma_{22}(0)-0.1248\Sigma_{12}(0) \\ \Sigma_{22}(1)=0.63732+0.0004\Sigma_{11}(0)+0.5184\Sigma_{22}(0)-0.0288\Sigma_{12}(0) \\ \Sigma_{12}(1)=0.26052-0.0156\Sigma_{11}(0)-0.0576\Sigma_{22}(0)+0.5632\Sigma_{12}(0) \end{array}\right\} \tag{79}$$

so we obtain

$$\Sigma(1)=\begin{bmatrix} 0.87132 & 0.44012 \\ 0.44012 & 1.40092 \end{bmatrix} \tag{80}$$

This is but the first step, and we may now use the same numerical coefficients used to obtain $\mathbf{z}(1)$, $\Sigma(1)$ from $\mathbf{z}(0)$, $\Sigma(0)$ in order to obtain $\mathbf{z}(2)$, $\Sigma(2)$ from $\mathbf{z}(1)$, $\Sigma(1)$, thus:

$$z_1(2)=0.19+0.78z_1(1)-0.08z_2(0); \tag{81}$$

Table C.6 *Development of bivariate distribution: numerical example*

n	$z_1(n)$	$z_2(n)$	$\Sigma_{11}(n)$	$\Sigma_{22}(n)$	$\Sigma_{12}(n)$
0	0.530000	0.950000	1.000000	1.500000	0.500000
1	0.527400	0.963400	0.871320	1.400920	0.440120
2	0.524300	0.973100	9.799870	1.351230	0.414110
3	0.521106	0.980146	0.759933	1.326191	0.403438
4	0.518051	0.985283	0.735834	1.313502	0.399502
5	0.515257	0.989043	0.721950	1.307028	0.398383
10	0.505912	0.997322	0.702157	1.300324	0.399511
...	...	...	...	...	...
∞	0.5	1.0	0.7	1.3	0.4

$$\Sigma_{12}(2)=0.26052-0.0156\Sigma_{11}(1)-0.0576\Sigma_{22}(1)+0.5632\Sigma_{12}(1) \tag{82}$$

... and so on. We may thus update the parameters to date $n=2$ and obtain

$$\left.\begin{array}{l} \mathbf{z}(2)=\begin{bmatrix} 0.5275 \\ 0.9634 \end{bmatrix}, \\[2em] \Sigma(2)=\begin{bmatrix} 0.79987 & 0.41411 \\ 0.41411 & 1.35123 \end{bmatrix}. \end{array}\right\} \tag{83}$$

The next step is to use again the same coefficients to update the parameter values from date 2 to date 3, and it should be clear from the example of the step from date 1 to date 2 how this and any number of further steps can be accomplished. The step-by-step computation is relatively straightforward on a microcomputer, but it is also possible to establish formulae for deriving the parameters of the bivariate distribution at date n directly as functions of n and of the initial values. Table C.6 tabulates the five parameters of the bivariate distribution for $n=0, 1, 2, ..., 5$ and $n=10$, as values obtained by continuing the process demonstrated above; it also gives the long-run equilibrium values.

The values in table C.6 for generation n can be obtained from the following functions:

$$z_1(n)=0.5+0.064(0.8)^n-0.034(0.7)^n; \tag{84}$$

$$z_2(n)=1-0.016(0.8)^n-0.034(0.7)^n; \tag{85}$$

$$\Sigma_{11}(n)=0.7+0.192(0.64)^n+0.172(0.49)^n-0.064(0.56)^n; \tag{86}$$

$$\Sigma_{22}(n)=1.3+0.012(0.64)^n+0.172(0.49)^n-0.016(0.56)^n; \tag{87}$$

$$\Sigma_{12}(n)=0.4+0.048(0.64)^n+0.172(0.49)^n-0.024(0.56)^n; \tag{88}$$

without the incovenience of having to wade through all values from 0 to n To see this notice that equations to (71)–(75), which describe the development of the parameters of the system, are a set of first-order difference equations, thus

$$\mathbf{z}(n+1)=\mathbf{k}+[\mathbf{I}-\mathbf{A}]\mathbf{z}(n) \tag{89}$$

$$\Sigma(n+1)=V+[\mathbf{I}-\mathbf{A}]\Sigma(n)[\mathbf{I}-\mathbf{A}]' \tag{90}$$

where $\mathbf{I}$ is the identity matrix and the prime denotes transposition. Where $\mathbf{A}^{-1}$, the inverse of the matrix $\mathbf{A}$ exists the solution to (89) and (90) may be found by standard methods, thus

$$\mathbf{z}(n)=\tilde{\mathbf{z}}+[\mathbf{I}-\mathbf{A}]^{n}\mathbf{z}(0) \tag{91}$$

$$\Sigma(n)=\tilde{\Sigma}+[\mathbf{I}-\mathbf{A}]^{n}\Sigma(0)[\mathbf{I}-\mathbf{A}']^{n} \tag{92}$$

where $\tilde{\mathbf{z}}$, and $\tilde{\Sigma}$ are the asymptotic values of the vector of means and of the variance–covariance matrix such that

$$\tilde{\mathbf{z}}=\mathbf{A}^{-1}\mathbf{k} \tag{93}$$

and $\tilde{\Sigma}$ satisfies the equation

$$\tilde{\Sigma}=V+[\mathbf{I}-\mathbf{A}]\tilde{\Sigma}[\mathbf{I}-\mathbf{A}]' \tag{94}$$

Equations (91) and (92) are the general form of (84) to (88). In order to be able to write the solution in this form the matrix $\mathbf{A}$ must be non-singular which, in the present case, amounts to the requirement that $A_{11}A_{22}-A_{12}A_{21}\neq0$. The additional requirement for the system to converge monotonically on to the asymptotic values is that the eigenvalues of the matrix $[\mathbf{I}-\mathbf{A}]$ should all be distinct, real, and less than one in absolute value.[11] Writing down the characteristic equation in the present case, the eigenvalues will be found as the roots λ_1,λ_2 of the equation

$$\begin{vmatrix} 1-A_{11}-\lambda & -A_{12} \\ -A_{21} & 1-A_{22}-\lambda \end{vmatrix}=0 \tag{95}$$

Solving the above quadratic equation in λ we get

$$\lambda_1,\lambda_2=1-\tfrac{1}{2}[A_{11}+A_{22}]\pm\sqrt{\tfrac{1}{4}[A_{11}+A_{22}]^2-[A_{11}A_{22}-A_{12}A_{21}]} \tag{96}$$

Clearly we get real and distinct roots if $\tfrac{1}{4}[A_{11}+A_{22}]^2>[A_{11}A_{22}-A_{12}A_{21}]$, and this condition, along with the requirement that $A_{11}+A_{22}<2$ will ensure that $-1<\lambda_1,\lambda_2<+1$.

The parametric values given in (76) imply $A_{11}+A_{22}=0.5$, $A_{11}A_{22}=0.0616$ and $A_{12}A_{21}=0.0016$ so it is immediate that the conditions for the existence of a solution in the form (91) – (94) and for the monotonic convergence of $\mathbf{z}(n)$ and $\Sigma(n)$ to their asymptotic values $\tilde{\mathbf{z}}$, and are $\tilde{\Sigma}$ indeed satisfied in our particular numerical example. Evaluating $\mathbf{A}^{-1}$ in (93) we have:

$$\tilde{\mathbf{z}}=\frac{1}{0.06}\begin{bmatrix} 0.28 & -0.08 \\ -0.02 & 0.22 \end{bmatrix}\begin{bmatrix} 0.19 \\ 0.29 \end{bmatrix}=\begin{bmatrix} 0.5 \\ 1.0 \end{bmatrix} \tag{97}$$

The values derived in (97) are the same as the constant terms in (84) and (85).

To obtain the values of $\tilde{\Sigma}$ in our numerical example using the parameter values given in (76) we obtain the linear equations for $\tilde{\Sigma}_{11},\tilde{\Sigma}_{22},\tilde{\Sigma}_{12}$ as

$$0.3196\tilde{\Sigma}_{11}-0.0064\tilde{\Sigma}_{22}+0.1248\tilde{\Sigma}_{12}=0.31572 \tag{98}$$

$$-0.0004\tilde{\Sigma}_{11}+0.4316\tilde{\Sigma}_{22}+0.0288\tilde{\Sigma}_{12}=0.53732 \tag{99}$$

$$0.0156\tilde{\Sigma}_{11}+0.0576\tilde{\Sigma}_{22}+0.4368\tilde{\Sigma}_{12}=0.26052 \tag{100}$$

The solution is

$$\left.\begin{array}{l} \tilde{\Sigma}_{11}=0.7, \\ \tilde{\Sigma}_{22}=1.3, \\ \tilde{\Sigma}_{12}=0.4, \end{array}\right\} \tag{101}$$

which is easily checked against (86)–(88).

The technique described here can be extended to stochastic models with q variates where q is an integer greater than 2. The vectors in the fundamental equations would then be of dimension q (rather than 2) and each matrix would be $q \times q$.

C.13 Bivariate distribution of earnings and property income

In section 11.7 of chapter 11 we discussed a model which involved covariation of incomes from work (earnings) and incomes from ownership of wealth. The model extension set out in equations (19)–(23), chapter 11 on page 000 consists of the following:

- taxation of income in excess of E^* at a rate τ' and additional consumption expenditure of a fraction σ of excess of E^* remaining after the tax τ', and
- the allowance of a wealth-tax-free fund of up to a proportion λ of the amount if any of wealth bequeathed in excess of the tax threshold W^*: this fund is regarded as part of the wealth at retirement and may be used to provide the heir with earnings additional to E^*, over the T years of his remaining working life, with present discounted value $\lambda[B-W^*]$.

The effects of the income taxation and the marginal expenditure on the long-term equilibrium distribution of wealth are equivalent to reducing the annual rate of interest from its level R to the level $r=[1-\tau][1-\sigma]R$. Standard earnings are constant at the fixed level E^*, so covariance of standard earnings and the yield from wealth is zero.

To explain the derivation of tables like 11.15 and 11.16, describing the equilibrium bivariate distributions of earnings and dividends, we shall go through the calculation of these tables for the simplified case in which $\tau'=\sigma=0$ and the other parameter values are $T=25$, $E^*=10$, $C^*=12$, $r=2\frac{1}{2}\%$, $\tau=0.96$, $W^*=120$, $P=60$, $g=2$, $N=2$, $M=4$, $\lambda=6.25\%$. The result of the introduction of the fund with $\lambda=1/16$ is that the effective wealth tax is reduced from 96 per cent to 90 per cent since it only bears on 15/16ths of $B-W^*$ and so the equilibrium distribution of bequests can be calculated with the set of parameter values so amended. They are those in row 3 of table 11.2 which were used in tables 11.9–11.10 and equation (8), chapter 11: we use the information in those tables and this equation for table C.7.

The entries in the total column are copied from equation (8), chapter 11 giving the equilibrium distribution of bequests over the interval centres 11,250¢, 22,500¢, 45,000¢, 90,000¢, 180,000¢ and 360,000¢: the entries for the left-hand column of interval centres for dividends were obtained by applying the 2½ per cent interest rate to each of the interval centres for bequests – for example, 281¢ is 2.5 per cent of 11,250¢ and 9,000¢ is 2.5 per cent of 180,000¢. This procedure is correct because our model assumes that on retirement each wealth-holder bequeaths all his wealth and obligingly expires soon after.

Table C.7 *Equilibrium bivariate distribution of earnings and property income using standard parameter values*

	Bequests of Earnings[a]	<60,000¢ 10,000¢	90,000¢ 10,000¢	180,000¢ 10,202¢	360,000¢ 10,807¢	
Wealth	Property income[a]		Probabilities of move[c]			Numbers/ million[b]
11,250¢	281¢	0.0789	—	—	—	42,652
22,500¢	563¢	0.3289	0.0127	—	—	181,437
45,000¢	1,125¢	0.4211	0.2627	0.0903	0.0072	316,404
90,000¢	2,250¢	0.1711	0.4873	0.3403	0.2572	288,833
180,000¢	4,500¢	—	0.2373	0.4097	0.4928	140,944
360,000¢	9,000¢	—	—	0.1597	0.2428	29,730
			Numbers per million retiring[d]			
11,250¢	281¢	42,652	—	—	—	42,652
22,500¢	563¢	177,775	3,662	—	—	181,437
45,000¢	1,125¢	227,595	75,870	12,724	215	316,404
90,000¢	2,250¢	92,471	140,755	47,959	7,648	288,833
180,000¢	4,500¢	—	68,546	57,748	14,650	140,944
360,000¢	9,000¢	—	—	22,513	7,217	29,730
	Total	540,493	288,833	140,944	29,730	1,000,000

Notes:
[a] Range centres.
[b] From equation (18), chapter 11.
[c] From table 11.11.
[d] Calculated from probabilities above.

Table C.8 *Equilibrium bivariate distribution of earnings and dividends at retirement*

Earnings	10,000¢	10,000¢+k_1	10,000¢+4k_1	
Property income		Number of cases per million		Total
¼k_2	42,652	—	—	*42,652*
½k_2	181,437	—	—	*181,437*
1k_2	303,465	12,724	215	*316,404*
2k_2	233,226	47,959	7,648	*288,833*
4k_2	68,546	57,748	14,650	*140,944*
8k_2	—	22,513	7,217	*29,730*
Total	829,326	140,944	29,730	*1,000,000*

Note:
Earnings and property refer to interval centres; $k_1 = 201.7$¢, $k_2 = 1,125$¢

The earnings level for any wealth-holder is constant over his working life and depends on what if anything he inherited. If this were less than 120,000¢ (the wealth tax threshold W^*) he will just earn E^*, namely 10,000¢, but in the cases where the pre-tax bequests B are 180,000¢ and 360,000¢ there will be funds $\lambda[B-W^*]$ to boost his earnings higher. Given $\lambda=1/16$ these amounts are 3,750¢ and 15,000¢ respectively. These funds are exempted from the wealth tax and yield an annuity over 25 years of k_1 (201.7¢) and $4k_1$(806.9¢) respectively: this explains the four values of earnings (10,000¢, 10,000¢, 10,202¢, 10,807¢) in the second row of table C.7.

To fill in the numbers per million in the body of table C.7 use the probabilities shown in table 11.10: for the two right-hand columns of that table we simply apply them to the two right-hand totals in table C.7: for example, where the number of bequests is 360,000¢, the largest interval centre, is 29,730, the number in the next generation with earnings also at the largest interval centre, is $0.2427\times29,730=7,217$, and the number then with earnings at one eighth of 360,000¢ (i.e. 45,000¢) is $0.00724\times29,730=215$; in the same way, the number with earnings at 90,000¢ is $0.2572\times29,730=14,650$ and the number with earnings at 45,000¢ is 7,648.

Matters are not so simple for the columns headed 10,000¢ since these will include both the case where the bequests are at 90,000¢ and the case where they are $<60,000¢$, at 45,000¢ or less, and we must use the two different columns of table 11.10 appropriate to these two cases, applying them to the two corresponding totals, 288,833 and 540,493, in the equilibrium distribution of equations (16) chapter 11 and then compound the two columns of results in table C.7 to fill in the column headed 10,000¢ in table C.8.

Take for example the entry 0.2373 in the column headed 90,000¢ in table 11.10: this must be applied to the total 288,833 for bequests at 90,000¢, and will contribute $(0.2373\times288,833)=68,546$ to the total of earnings at 10,000¢ cum dividends at $(2\frac{1}{2}\%\times90,000¢)=2,250¢$. Similarly the entry 0.1711 in the column headed $<60,000¢$ in table 11.10 must be applied to the total 540,493 for bequests $<60,000¢$ and will contribute a further $(0.1711\times540,593)=9,323$ to the above contribution of 68,546 bringing it up to 77,869. Table C.8 will be far more convenient, by amalgamating (by addition) the two columns headed 10,000¢ into one, expressing earnings in increments of $k_1:=201.7¢$, and dividends in increments of $k_2:=1,125¢$.

From table C.8 we can compute standard statistics of the bivariate distribution of E and rW: the methods in this elementary example may be applied to similarly constructed tables of bivariate distributions with larger numbers of cells and less simple numbers, without losing their logical simplicity. The calculation of means and variances is immediate from the marginal distributions (the bottom row and the right-hand column marked *Total* in table C.8) and the covariance earnings and property income can be found from the non-italicised cells in the centre of the table. To summarise the results, using the notation of section C.12: if the vector of income components is

$$\mathbf{z}:=\begin{bmatrix} E \\ rW \end{bmatrix} \tag{102}$$

then

$$\mathcal{E}(\mathbf{z})=\begin{bmatrix}10,052.4\\2,021.7\end{bmatrix} \tag{103}$$

$$\mathrm{var}(\mathbf{z})=\begin{bmatrix}22,300 & 131,700\\131,700 & 3,098,400\end{bmatrix} \tag{104}$$

Exactly the same methods which have been applied above to construct table C.7 were used in the construction of tables 11.15 and 11.16, although the calculations were more tedious because of the far larger number of cells involved in that example.

Notes

1 At the same time we must admit that they are not appropriate for modelling the most threatening real-world situations of disastrous destitution and extreme wealth inequality: it is for the modelling of well-to-do democratic economies in those relatively calm periods of steady plodding or gentle progress, which are described in some history books, that they are best suited.

2 See Cowell (1997).

3 We shall avoid parameter values which, whenever $B_n<P$, result in $B_{n+1}<0$.

4 This gives the probabilities associated with the logbinomial distribution described on page 000.

5 The reason for this is that $i<0$ corresponds to cases where the pretax bequest falls below the poverty level P. Rule 3 of (42) applies and it is immediate that the value of $m(B_n,n,\pi)$ must be independent of B_n – and hence independent of S_i – for such values of i.

6 In the simulation there were only a few cases of overshooting and very little oscillation of the numbers in the seven intervals reported in table C.4.

7 Since there are well under 10^{11} humans on the planet, the practical relevance ϕ values of the order of 10^{-30} is remote. However, this example was chosen to have an extremely low inequality so that the entire distribution to the last bequest in a supposed population of one million bequests could be shown in a single diagram. This explains how both values of α come to be more than four times as high as those normally found from statistics of actual distributions of bequests.

8 With this set of parameter values it is impossible for there to remain any bequests above some large finite level, after a sufficiently long time. In theory $\alpha\to\infty$ for large M.

9 It follows from rule 1 of equation (42) that if $B_n(=S_i)$ is a large multiple β_n of W^*, the nonstochastic multiplier $m_i=B_{n+1}/B_n=[1-\tau]\,\mathrm{e}^{rT}+\delta_n$ where

$$\delta_n:=\frac{1}{\beta_n}\left[\frac{\hat{B}}{W^*}[1-\mathrm{e}^{rT}]+\tau\mathrm{e}^{rT}\right]$$

The second expression on the right-hand side lies between -1 and $+1$ in the examples that we shall consider. Hence $|\delta_n|<1/\beta_n$.

10 This is a simple special case of more general multi-variate stochastic models that can be developed.

11 See Goldberg (1960).

Bibliography

Aaron, H. J. and McGuire, M. (1970), 'Public goods and income distribution', *Econometrica*, **38**, 907–20.

Abraham, K. G. and Farber, H. S. (1987), 'Job duration, seniority and earnings', *American Economic Review*, **77**, 278–97.

Adams, A. and Nestel, G. (1976), 'Interregional migration, education and poverty in the urban ghetto', *Review of Economics and Statistics*, **58**, 156–66.

Aghion, P. and Bolton, P. (1992), 'Distribution and growth in models of imperfect capital markets', *European Economic Review*, **36**, 303–11.

  (1997), 'A trickle-down theory of growth development with debt-overhang', *Review of Economic Studies*, **64**, 151–72.

Ahluwalia, M. A., Carter, N. G., and Chenery, H. B. (1979), 'Growth and poverty in developing countries', *Journal of Development Economics*, **6**, 299–341.

Ahluwalia, M. S. (1976a), 'Inequality, poverty and development', *Journal of Development Economics*, **3**, 307–42.

  (1976b), 'Income distribution and development: some stylized facts', *American Economic Review*, **66**, 128–35.

Aigner, P. J. and Cain, G. C. (1977), 'Statistical theories of discrimination in labor markets', *Industrial and Labor Relations Review*, **30**, 175–87.

Aitchison, J. and Brown, J. A. C. (1957), *The Lognormal Distribution*, Cambridge University Press.

Akerlof, G. A. (1980), 'A theory of social custom, of which unemployment may be one consequence', *Quarterly Journal of Economics*, **94**, 749–76.

Akerlof, G. A. and Dickens, W. T. (1982), 'The economic consequences of cognitive dissonance', *American Economic Review*, **72**, 307–19.

Alexander, A. J. (1974), 'Income, experience and the structure of internal labor markets', *Quarterly Journal of Economics*, **88**, 63–85.

Allen, R. G. D. (1963), *Mathematical Economics*, Macmillan, London, 2nd edn.

Allen, S. P. (1987), 'Taxes, redistribution and the minimum wage', *Quarterly Journal of Economics*, **102**, 477–89.

Altonji, J. G. and Shakotko, R. A. (1987), 'Do wages rise with seniority?', *Review of Economic Studies*, **54**, 437–89.

Amiel, Y. and Cowell, F. A. (1992), 'Measurement of income inequality: experimental test by questionnaire', *Journal of Public Economics*, **47**, 3–26.

  (1994a), 'Inequality changes and income growth', in Eichhorn (1994), 3–26.

372

(1994b) 'Monotonicity, dominance, and the Pareto principle', *Economics Letters*, **45**, 447–50.

(1994c), 'Income inequality and social welfare', in Creedy, J. (ed.), *Taxation, Poverty and Income Distribution*, Edward Elgar, Aldershot.

Anand, S. (1983), *Inequality and Poverty in Malysia*, Oxford University Press, New York.

Arrow, K. J. (1951), 'Alternative approaches to the theory of choice in risk-taking situations', *Econometrica*, **19**, 404–37.

(1963), *Social Choice and Individual Values*, Wiley, London, 2nd edn.

(1971), 'A utilitarian approach to the concept of equality in public expenditure', *Quarterly Journal of Economics*, **85**, 409–15.

(1972), 'Models of job discrimination', in Pascal, A. (ed.), *Racial Discrimination in Economic Life*, D. C. Heath, Lexington, Mass.

(1973), 'Higher education as a filter', *Journal of Public Economics*, **2**, 193–216.

Ashenfelter, O. (1970), 'Changes in labor market discrimination over time', *Journal of Human Resources*, **5**(4), 403–30.

Ashenfelter, O. and Ham, J. (1979), 'Education, unemployment and earnings', *Journal of Political Economy*, **87**, S99–S116.

Ashenfelter, O. and Heckman, J. J. (1974), 'The estimation of income and substitution effects in a model of family labor supply', *Econometrica*, **42**,73–85.

Ashenfelter, O. C. and Layard, P. R. G. (1986), *Handbook of Labor Economics*, vol. I, North-Holland, Amsterdam.

Atkinson, A. B. (1970), 'On the measurement of inequality', *Journal of Economic Theory*, **2**, 244–63.

(1971), 'Capital taxes, the redistribution of wealth and individual savings', *Review of Economic Studies*, **38**, 209–28.

(1972a), *Unequal Shares*, Allen Lane, London.

(1972b), 'The distribution of wealth and the individual life cycle', *Oxford Economic Papers*, **23**, 239–54.

(1973), *The Tax-Credit Scheme and Redistribution of Income*, Institute for Fiscal Studies, London.

(1980), 'Inheritance and the redistribution of wealth', in Heal, G. M. and Hughes, G. A. (eds.) *Public Policy and the Tax System*, Allen and Unwin, London.

(1981), 'On intergenerational income mobility in Britain', *Journal of Post-Keynesian Economics*, **3**, 194–218.

(1983), 'Intergenerational earnings mobility in Britain', in Schmähl, W. (ed.), *Ansätze der Lebenseinkommenanalyse*, J. C. B. Mohr, Tübingen.

Atkinson, A. B., Bourguignon, F. and Morrisson, C. (1992), *Empirical Studies of Earnings Mobility*, Harwood Academic Publishers.

Atkinson, A. B., Gordon, J. P. F. and Harrison, A. J. (1989), 'Trends in the shares of top wealth-holders in Britain, 1923–1981', *Oxford Bulletin of Economics and Statistics*, **51**(3), 315–32.

Atkinson, A. B. and Harrison, A. J. (1978), *Distribution of Personal Wealth in Britain*, Cambridge University Press.

Atkinson, A. B., King, M. A. and Sutherland, H. (1983), 'The analysis of personal taxation and social security', *National Institute Economic Review*, November, 63–74.

Atkinson, A. B., Maynard, A. and Trinder, C. (1983), *Parents and Children, Incomes in Two Generations*, Heinemann, London.

Atkinson, A. B. and Micklewright, J. (1992), *Economic Transformation in Eastern Europe and the Distribution of Income*, Cambridge University Press.

Azariadis, C. (1981), 'Implicit contracts and related topics: a survey', in Hornstein, Z. *et al.* (eds.) *The Economics of the Labour Market*, HMSO, London.

Barr. N. A. (1987), *The Economics of the Welfare State*, Weidenfeld and Nicolson, London.

Bartels, C. P. A. (1977), *Economic Aspects of Regional Welfare, Income Distribution and Unemployment*, Studies in Applied Regional Science, vol. IX, Martinus Nijhoff, Leiden.

Basu, K. (1994), 'On interpersonal comparison and the concept of equality', in Eichhorn (1994), 491–510.

Baumol, W. J. (1986), *Superfairness*, MIT Press, Cambridge, Mass.

Baumol, W. J. and Fischer, D. (1979), 'The output distribution frontier: alternatives to income taxes and transfers in strong equality goals', *American Economic Review*, **69**, 514–25.

Bazen, S. and Martin, J. P. (1991), 'The impact of the minimum wage on earnings and employment in France', *OECD Economic Studies*, **16**, 199–221.

Beach, C. M. (1977), 'Cyclical sensitivity of aggregate income inequality', *Review of Economics and Statistics*, **59**, 56–66.

(1981), *Distribution of Income and Wealth in Ontario: Theory and Evidence*, University of Toronto Press, Toronto.

Beck, G. M. (1951), *A Survey of British Employment and Unemployment, 1927–45*, Oxford University Institute of Statistics.

Becker, E. F. (1975), 'Justice, utility and interpersonal comparison', *Theory and Decision*, **6**, 471–89.

Becker, G. S. (1962), 'Investment in human capital – a theoretical analysis', *Journal of Political Economy*, **70**, S9–S49.

(1964), *Human Capital*, Columbia University Press, New York.

(1973), 'A theory of marriage: parts I and II', *Journal of Political Economy*, **81**, 813–46.

(1981), *A Treatise on the Family*, Harvard University Press, Cambridge Mass.

(1985), 'Human capital, effort, and the sexual division of labor', *Journal of Labor Economics*, **3**, S33–S59.

Becker, G. S. and Tomes, N. (1979), 'An equilibrium theory of the distribution of income and intergenerational mobility', *Journal of Political Economy*, **87**, 1153–89.

Beckerman, W. (1978), *Measures of Leisure, Equality and Welfare*, OECD, Paris.

Becketti, S. P. Gould, W., Lillard, L. A. and Welch, F. (1988), The Panel Study of Income Dynamics after 14 years: an evaluation', *Journal of Labor Economics*, **6**, 472–92.

Beckmann, M. J. (1977), *Rank in Organizations*, Springer Verlag, Berlin.

Behrman, J., Pollak, R. A. and Taubman, P. (1995), *From Parent to Child: Inequality and Immobility in the United States*, University of Chicago Press, Chicago.

Behrman, J., Rosenzweig, M. R. and Taubman, P. (1994), 'Endowments and the allocation of schooling in the family and in the marriage market: the twins experiment', *Journal of Political economy*, **102**(6), 1131–74.

Bell, W. and Robinson, R.V. (1980), 'Cognitive maps of class and racial inequalities in England and the United States', *American Journal of Sociology*, **86**, 320–49.

Ben-Porath, Y. (1967), 'The production of human capital and the life cycle of earnings', *Journal of Political Economy*, **75**, 352–65.

Bentham, J. (1789), *An Introduction to the Principles of Morals and Legislation*, Oxford (1823). Corrected new edition, Pickering, London.

Bergmann, B. (1971), 'The effect on white incomes of discrimination in employment', *Journal of Political Economy*, **79**, 294–313.

Bergson, A. (1984), 'Income inequality under Soviet Socialism', *Journal of Economic Literature*, **22**, 1052–99.

Bernheim, B. D., Schleifer, A. and Summers, L. H. (1985), 'The strategic bequest motive', *Journal of Political Economy*, **93**, 1045–76.

Berry, A., Bourguignon, F. and Morrisson, C. (1981), 'The level of world inequality: how much can one say?', *Review of Income and Wealth*, **29**, 217–43.

(1983), 'Changes in the world distribution of income between 1950 and 1977', *Economic Journal*, **93**, 331–50.

Bertola, G. (1998), 'Macroeconomics of distribution and growth' in Atkinson, A. B. and Bourguignon, F. (eds.), *Handbook of Income Distribution*, North-Holland, Amsterdam.

Bevan, D. L. (1979), 'Inheritance and the distribution of wealth', *Economica*, **46**, 381–402.

Bhagwati, J. N. and Srinivasan, T. N. (1977), 'Education in a "job-ladder" model and the fair-ness-in-hiring rule', *Journal of Public Economics*, **7**, 1–22.

Bhatia, K. (1976), 'Capital gains and inequality of personal income: some results from survey data', *Journal of the American Statistical Association*, **71**, 575–80.

Bils, M. J. (1985), 'Real wages over the business cycle: evidence from panel data', *Journal of Political Economy*, **93**, 666–89.

Bishop, J. A., Formby, J. P. and Smith, W. P. (1991), 'International comparisons of income inequality; tests for Lorenz dominance across nine countries', *Economica*, **58**, 461–77.

Blackorby, C. and Donaldson, D. (1978), 'Measures of relative equality and their meaning in terms of social welfare', *Journal of Economic Theory*, **18**, 59–80.

(1980), 'A theoretical treatment of measures of absolute inequality', *International Economic Review*, **21**, 107–36.

Blackorby, C., Donaldson, D. and Auersperg, M. (1981), 'A new procedure for the measurement of inequality within and among population subgroups', *Canadian Journal of Economics*, **14**, 665–85.

Blakemore, A. E. and Hoffman, D. L. (1989), 'Seniority rules and productivity: an empirical test', *Economica*, **56**, 359–71.

Blank, R. M. (1989), 'Disaggregating the effect of business cycles on the distribution of income', *Economica*, **56**, 141– 63.

Blaug, M. (1972), 'The correlation between education and earnings: what does it signify?', *Higher Education*, **1**, 53–76.

(1976), 'The empirical status of human capital theory: a slightly jaundiced survey', *Journal of Economic Literature*, **14**, 827–55.

Blinder, A. S. (1973a), 'Wage discrimination: reduced form and structural variation', *Journal of Human Resources*, **8**, 436–55.

(1973b), 'A model of inherited wealth', *Quarterly Journal of Economics*, **87**, 608–26.

(1974), *Toward an Economic Theory of Income Distribution*, MIT Press, Cambridge, Mass.

(1976), 'On dogmatism in human capital theory', *Journal of Human Resources*, **11**, 8–22.

(1980), 'The level and distribution of economic well-being', in Feldstein, M. A. (ed.), *The American Economy in Transition*, NBER, Chicago University Press.

Blinder, A. and Esaki, H. Y. (1978) 'Macroeconomic activity and income distribution in the post-war United States', *Review of Economics and Statistics*, **55**, 604–9.

Blowers, A. and Thompson, G. (eds.) (1976), *Inequalities, Conflict and Change*, Open University Press, Milton Keynes.

Blundell, R. W., Preston, I. and Walker, I. (1994), 'An introduction to applied welfare analysis', in Blundell, R. W., Preston, I., and Walker, I. (eds.), *The Measurement of Household Welfare*, Cambridge University Press, chapter 1, pp. 1–50.

Board of Inland Revenue (various years) *Inland Revenue Statistics*, HMSO, London.

Borjas, G. J. (1983), 'The substitutability of black, hispanic and white labor', *Economic Inquiry*, **21**, 93–106.

Bosanquet, N. and Doeringer, P. B. (1973), 'Is there a dual labour market in Great Britain?', *Economic Journal*, **83**, 421–35.

Bound, J. and Johnson, G. (1992) 'Changes in the structure of wages in the 1980s: an evaluation of alternative explanations', *American Economic Review*, **82**, 371–92.

Bourguignon, F. (1979), 'Decomposable income inequality measures', *Econometrica*, **47**, 901–20.

(1981), 'Pareto-superiority of unegalitarian equilibria in Stiglitz' model of wealth distribution with convex savings function', *Econometrica*, **49**, 1469–75.

Bourguignon, F. and Morrisson, C. (1983), 'Earnings mobility over the life-cycle: a 30-year panel sample of French "cadres" ', in Atkinson, A. B. and Cowell, F. A. (eds.), *Panel Data on Incomes*, ICERD, London.

Bowles, S. (1972), 'Schooling and inequality from generation to generation', *Journal of Political Economy*, **80**, S219–S251.

(1973), 'Understanding unequal economic opportunity', *American Economic Review, Papers and Proceedings*, **63**, 346–56.

Bowles, S. and Nelson, V. I. (1974), 'The inheritance of IQ and the inter-generational reproduction of economic inequality', *Review of Economics and Statistics*, **56**, 39–51.

Brenner, Y. S., Kaelble, H. and Thomas, M. (eds.) (1991), *Income Distribution in Historical Perspective*, Cambridge University Press.

Brittain, J. A. (1977), *The Inheritance of Economic Status*, The Brookings Institution, Washington DC.

(1978), *Inheritance and the Inequality of Material Wealth*, The Brookings Institution, Washington DC.

Bronfenbrenner, M. (1971), *Income Distribution Theory*, Macmillan, London.

Broome, J. (1989), 'What's the good of equality?', in Hey, J. D. (ed.) *Current Issues in Microeconomics*, St. Martin's Press, New York, pp. 236–62.

(1991), *Weighing Goods*, Basil Blackwell, Oxford.

Brown, C. V. (1980), 'Equalizing differences in the labor markets', *Quarterly Journal of Economics*, **94**, 113–34.

(1983), *Taxation and the Incentive to Work*, Oxford University Press, 2nd edn.

Brown, C., Gilroy, C. and Kohen, A. (1982), 'The effect of the minimum wage on employment and unemployment', *Journal of Economic Literature*, **20**, 487–528.

Brown, J. N. (1989), 'Why do wages increase with tenure? On-the-job training and life-cycle wage growth observed within firms', *American Economic Review*. **79**, 971–91.

Browning, E. K. and Johnson, W. R. (1984), 'The trade-off between equality and efficiency', *Journal of Political Economy*, **92**, 175–203.

Buchele, R. (1981), 'Sex discrimination and the US labour market', in Wilkinson, F. (ed.), *The Dynamics of Labour Market Segmentation*, Academic Press, New York.

Buse, A. (1982), 'The cyclical behavior of the size distribution in Canada 1947–78', *Canadian Journal of Economics*, **15**, 189–204.

Butler, R. J. (1983), 'Direct estimates of the demand for race and sex discrimination', *Southern Economic Journal*, **49**, 975–90.

Cagan, P. (1956), 'The monetary dynamics of hyperinflation', in Friedman, M. (ed.), *Studies in the Quantity Theory of Money*, Chicago University Press, Chicago.

Cain, G. C. (1976), 'The challenge of segmented labor market theories to orthodox theory: a survey', *Journal of Economic Literature*, **14**, 1215–57.

Cain, G. C. and Watts, H. W. (1973), *Income Maintenance and Labor Supply*, Markham, Chicago.

Calvo, G. A. and Wellisz, S. (1979), 'Hierarchy, ability and income distribution', *Journal of Political Economy*, **87**, 991–1010.

Card, D. A. and Krueger, A. B. (1992), 'Does school quality matter? Returns to education and the characteristics of public schools in the US', *Journal of Political Economy*, **100**, 40.

(1994), 'Minimum wages and employment: a case study of the fast-food industry in New Jersey and Pennsylavania', *American Economic Review*, **84**, 772–93.

(1995), *Myth and Measurement: the New Economics of the Minimum Wage*, Princeton University Press.

Carver, T. N. (1925), 'The meaning of economic equality', *Quarterly Journal of Economics*, **39**, 473–5.

Champernowne, D. G. (1952), 'The graduation of income distribution', *Econometrica*, **20**, 591–615.

(1953), 'A model of income distribution', *Economic Journal*, **63**, 318–51.

(1973), *The Distribution of Income Between Persons*, Cambridge University Press.

(1974), 'A comparison of measures of inequality of income distribution', *Economic Journal*, **84**, 787–816.

Chenery, H. B., Ahluwalia, M. S., Bell, C. L. G., Duloy, J. H. and Jolly, R. (1974), *Redistribution With Growth*, Oxford University Press, London.

Chiplin, B. and Sloane, P. J. (1976), *Sex Discrimination in the Labour Market*, Macmillan, London.

Chiswick, B. R. (1974), *Income Inequality*, NBER, Columbia University Press, New York.

Chu, C. Y. Cyrus (1991), 'Primogeniture', *Journal of Political Economy*, **99**, 78–99.

Clark, C. (1937), *National Income and Outlay*, Macmillan, London.

Cline, W. R. (1972), *Potential Effects of Income Distribution on Economic Growth*, Praeger, New York.

(1975), 'Distribution and development: a survey of literature', *Journal of Development Economics*, **1**, 359–400.

Coase, R. H. (1932), 'The nature of the firm', *Economica*, **4**, 386–405.

Cohn, E. and Kiker, B. F. (1986), 'Socioeconomic background, schooling, experience and monetary rewards in the United States', *Economica*, **53**, 497–503.

Conlisk, J. (1984), 'Four invalid propositions about equality, efficiency and intergenerational transfers through schooling', *Journal of Human Resources*, **19**, 3–21.

Corcoran, M. and Duncan, G. J. (1979), 'Work history; labour force attachment and earnings differences between the races and sexes', *Journal of Human Resources*, **14**, 1–20.

Corcoran, M., Jencks, C. and Olneck, M. (1976), 'The effects of family background on earnings', *American Economic Review*, **66**, 430–5.

Cosh, A. (1975), 'The remuneration of chief executives in the United Kingdom', *Economic Journal*, **85**, 75–90.

Coulter, F. A. E., Cowell, F. A. and Jenkins, S. P. (1992a), 'Differences in needs and assessment of income distributions', *Bulletin of Economic Research*, **44**, 77–124.

(1992b), 'Equivalence scale relativities and the extent of inequality and poverty', *Economic Journal*, **102**, 1067–82.

(1994), 'Family fortunes in the 1970s and the 1980s', in Blundell, R. W, Preston, I. and Walker, I. (eds.), *The Measurement of Household Welfare*, Cambridge University Press, chapter 9, pp. 215–46.

(1997), 'Inequality estimation with weighted data', Distributional Analysis Discussion Paper, STICERD, London School of Economics, London.

Courant, P. N., Gramlich, E. M. and Rubinfeld, D. L. (1979), 'Public employee market power and the level of government spending', *American Economic Review*, **69**, 806–17.

Cowell, F. A. (1979), 'Income and incentives for the working poor', *Three Banks Review*, **122**, 32–48.

(1980), 'On the structure of additive inequality measures', *Review of Economic Studies*, **47**, 521–31.

(1984), 'The structure of American income inequality', *Review of Income and Wealth*, **30**, 351–75.

(1985), 'A fair suck of the sauce bottle. Or "What do *you* mean by inequality?"', *The Economic Record*, **61**, 567–79.

(1986), *Microeconomic Principles*, Philip Allan, Oxford.

(1988), 'Inequality decomposition – three bad measures', *Bulletin of Economic Research*, **40**, 309–12.

(1995), *Measuring Inequality*, Harvester Wheatsheaf, Hemel Hempstead, 2nd edn.

(1997), 'Inheritance and the distribution of wealth', Distributional Analysis Discussion Paper, 34 STICERD, London School of Economics, London.

(1998), 'The measurement of inequality', in Atkinson, A. B. and Bourguignon, F. (eds.), *Handbook of Income Distribution*, North-Holland, Amsterdam.

Cowell, F. A. and Jenkins, S. P. (1993), 'The changing pattern of income inequality. The US in the 1980s,' Department of Economics Discussion Paper, **93–10**, University College of Swansea, Wales.

Cowell, F. A. and Mehta, F. (1982), 'The estimation and interpolation of inequality measures', *Review of Economic Studies*, **49**, 273–90.

Craig, C., Rubery, J., Tarling, R. and Wilkinson, F. (1982), 'Labour market structure', Industrial Organization and Low Pay, Department of Applied Economics Occasional Paper 54, Cambridge University Press.

Creedy, J. (1979), 'The inequality, of earnings and the accounting period', *Scottish Journal of Political Economy*, **26**, 89–96.

(1985), *Dynamics of Income Distribution*, Basil Blackwell, Oxford.

Creedy, J. and Thomas, B. (eds.) (1983), *The Economics of Labour*, Butterworths, London.

Creedy, J. and Whitfield, K. (1988), 'The economic analysis of internal labour markets', *Bulletin of Economic Research*, **40**, 247–69.

Crosland, A. (1964), *The Future of Socialism*, Camelot Press, London and Southampton, abridged and revised edn.

Danziger, S., Haveman, R. and Plotnick, R. (1981), 'How income transfers affect work, savings and the income distribution: a critical review', *Journal of Economic Literature*, **19**, 975–1028.

Danziger, S. and Taussig, M. K. (1979), 'The income unit and the anatomy of income distribution', *Review of Income and Wealth*, **25**, 365–75.

Datcher, L. (1982), 'Effects of community and family background on achievement', *Review of Economics and Statistics*, **64**, 32–41.

Davies, J. B. (1982), 'The relative impact of inheritance and other factors on economic inequality', *Quarterly Journal of Economics*, **97**, 471–98.

(1986), 'Does redistribution reduce inequality?', *Journal of Labor Economics*, **4**, 538–59.

Davies, J. B. and Shorrocks, A. F. (1978), 'Assessing the quantitative importance of inheritance in the distribution of wealth', *Oxford Economic Papers*, **30**, 138–49.

Davis, H. T. (1954), *Political Statistics*, Principia Press, Evanston, Ill.

Deacon, A. and Bradshaw, J. (1983), *Reserved for the Poor: The Means Test in British Social Policy*, Basil Blackwell and Martin Robertson, Oxford.

Deane, P. (1955–6), 'The implications of early national income estimates for the measurement of long-term economic growth of nations', *Economic Development and Cultural Change*, **4**, 3–39.

Department of Social Security (1992), *Households Below Average Income*, HMSO, London.

Desai, M. and Shah, A. (1983), 'Bequest and inheritance in nuclear families and joint families', *Economica*, **50**, 193–202.

Dex, S. (1986), 'Earnings differentials of two generations of West-Indian and white school leavers in Britain', *Manchester School*, **54**, 162–79.

Dex, Shirley, Clark, A. and Taylor, M. (1995), 'Household labour supply', Employment Department, Research series no. 43, Moorfoot, Sheffield.

Dickens, W. and Lang, K. (1985), 'A test of dual labor market theory', *American Economic Review*, **75**, 792–805.

Dickens, W. and Summers, L. (1985), *Unemployment and the Structure of Labour Markets*, Martin Robertson, Oxford.

Dilnot, A. W. and Morris, C. N. (1983), 'The tax system and distribution 1978–1983', *Fiscal Studies*, **4**, 54–64.

Disney, R. (1983), 'The Structure of Pay', in Creedy and Thomas (eds.).

Dooley, M. D. and Gottschalk, P. (1984), 'Earnings inequality among males in the United States: trends and the effect of labor force growth', *Journal of Political Economy*, **92**, 59–89.

Drazen, A. (1986), 'Optimal minimum wage legislation', *Economic Journal*, **96**, 774–84.

Driver, H. E. (1969), *Indians of North America*, Chicago University Press.

Duncan, G. J. (1983), 'The implications of changing family composition for the dynamic analysis of family economic well-being', in Atkinson, A. B. and Cowell, F. A. (eds.), *Panel Data on Incomes*, ICERD, London.

Duncan, G. J. and Hoffman, S. (1979), 'On the job training and earning differences by race and sex', *Review of Economics and Statistics*, **61**, 594–603.

Duncan, G. J. and Holmlund, B. (1983), 'Was Adam Smith right after all? Another test of the theory of compensating wage differentials', *Journal of Labor Economics*, **1**, 366–79.

Duncan, G. J. and Morgan, J. N. (1981), 'Persistence and change in economic status and the role of changing family composition', in Duncan, G. J. and Morgan, J. N. (eds.), *Five Thousand American Families: Patterns of Economic Progress*, vol. IX , Institute for Social Research, The University of Michigan, Ann Arbor.

Dunn, A. L. and Hoffman, P. (1978), 'The Distribution of Personal Wealth', *Economic Trends*, **301**, 000–000.

Eckaus, R. S. (1963), 'Investment in human capital: A comment', *Journal of Political Economy*, **71**, 501–4.

(1973), 'Estimation of the returns to education with hourly standardized incomes', *Quarterly Journal of Economics*, **87**, 120–31.

Edwards, R., Gordon, D. and Reich, M. (1983), 'Dual labor markets: a theory of labor market segmentation', *American Economic Review, Papers and Proceedings*, **60**, 359–65.

Eichhorn, W. (ed.) (1994), *Models and Measurement of Inequality*, Springer Verlag, Berlin.

Eissa, N. and Liebman, J. (1996), 'Labor supply response to the earned income tax credit', *Quarterly Journal of Economics*, **111**, 605–37.

Elbaum, B. (1983), 'The internalization of labor markets: causes and consequences', *American Economic Review, Papers and Proceedings*, **73**, 260–5.

Epple, D. and Romer, T. (1991), 'Mobility and redistribution', *Journal of Political Economy*, **99**, 828–58.

Evandrou, M., Falkingham, J., Hills, J. R. and Le Grand, J. (1995), 'The distribution of welfare benefits in kind', Welfare State Programme Discussion Paper, WSP/68, STICERD, London School of Economics, London.

Feldstein, M. (1973), 'The economics of the new unemployment', *Public Interest*, **33** (Fall), 3–42.

(1976), 'Social security and the distribution of wealth', *Journal of the American Statistical Association*, **71**, 800–7.

Feller, W. (1950), *Probability Theory and its Applications*, John Wiley & Sons, New York.

Ferber, R. and Hirsch, W. Z. (1982), *Social Experimentation and Economic Policy*, Cambridge University Press.

Ferguson, C. E. (1969), *The Neoclassical Theory of Production*, Cambridge University Press.

Fichtenbaum, R. and Shahidi, H. (1988), 'Truncation bias and the measurement of income inequality', *Journal of Business and Economic Statistics*, **6**, 335–7.

Field, F. (1981), *Inequality in Britain: Freedom, Welfare and the State*, Fontana, London.

Field, F. (ed.) (1983), *The Wealth Report – 2*, Routledge and Kegan Paul, London.

Field, F. and Winyard, S. (1977), 'The effects of the Trade Boards Act', in Field, F. (ed.), *Are Low Wages Inevitable?*, Spokesman Press, London.

Fields, G. S. (1980), *Inequality, Poverty and Development*, Cambridge University Press.

Flemming, J. S. (1979), 'The effects of earnings inequality, imperfect capital markets and dynastic altruism in the distribution of wealth in life cycle models', *Economica*, **46**, 363–80.

Foldes, L. (1969), 'Income redistribution in money and in kind', *Economica*, **25**, 30–41.

Frank, C. R. and Webb, R. C. (eds.) (1979), *Income Distribution and Growth in Less Developed Countries*, The Brookings Institution, Washington DC.

Frank, R. H. and Hutchens, R. M. (1993), 'Wages, seniority and the demand for rising consumption profiles', *Journal of Economic Behavior and Organization*, **21**, 251–76.

Freeman, R. B. (1971), *The Market for College Trained Manpower*, Academic Press, New York.
  (1977), 'The decline in the economic rewards to college education', *Review of Economics and Statistics*, **59**, 18–29.
  (1984), 'Longitudinal analysis of the effects of trade unions', *Journal of Labor Economics*, **2**, 1–26.
  (1986), 'The effect of the union wage differential on management opposition and union organizing success', *American Economic Review*, **76**, 92–6.

Freeman, R. B. and Medoff, J. (1984), *What Do Unions Do?*, Basic Books, New York.

Friedman, M. (1953), 'Choice, chance and the personal distribution of income', *Journal of Political Economy*, **61**, 277–90.

Friedman, M. and Kuznets, S. (1954), *Income from Independent Professional Practice*, NBER, New York.

Friesen, P. H. and Miller, D. (1983), 'Annual inequality and lifetime inequality', *Quarterly Journal of Economics*, **98**, 139–550.

Gallman, R. E. (1969), 'Trends in the size distribution of wealth in the nineteenth century', in Soltow (1969), 1–30.

Garfinkel, I. (1973), 'Is in-kind redistribution efficient?', *Quarterly Journal of Economics*, **87**, 320–30.

Garfinkel, I. and Haveman, R. H. (1977), *Earnings Capacity, Poverty and Inequality*, Academic Press, New York.
  (1978), 'Capacity, choice and inequality', *Southern Economic Journal*, **45**, 421–31.

Gastwirth, J. L. (1971), 'A general definition of the Lorenz curve', *Econometrica*, **39**, 1037–9.

Gilder, G. (1982), *Wealth and Poverty*, Buchanan and Enright, London.

Glejser, H., Gevers, L., Lambot, P. and Morales, J. A. (1977), 'An econometric study of the variables determining inequality aversion amongst students', *European Economic Review*, **10**, 173–88.

Glomm, G. and Ravikumar, B. (1992), 'Public versus private investment in human capital: endogenous growth and income inequality', *Journal of Political Economy*, **100**, 818–34.

Goldberg, S. (1960), *Introduction to Difference Equations*, John Wiley & Sons, New York.

Goldberger, A. S. (1979), 'Heritability', *Economica*, **46**, 327–47.
  (1989), 'Economic and mechanical models of intergenerational transmission', *American Economic Review*, **79**, 504–13.

Good, F. J. (1990), 'Estimates of the distribution of personal wealth', *Economic Trends*, October 137.

Gordon, D., Edwards, R. and Reich, M. (1982), *Segmented Work, Divided Workers*, Cambridge University Press.

Gosling, A., Machin, S. and Meghir, C. (1994), 'What has happened to wages?', Institute for Fiscal Studies, Commentary no 43, Institute for Fiscal Studies, London.

(1996), 'What has happened to the wages of men since 1966?', in Hills, J. R. (ed.), *New Inequalities: the Changing Distribution of Income and Wealth in the United Kingdom*, Cambridge University Press, chapter 6, pp. 135–57.

Grahame, K. (1908), *The Wind in The Willows*, Methuen, London.

Gramlich, E. M. (1974), 'The distributional effects of higher unemployment', *Brookings Papers on Economic Activity*, **2**, 293–342.

Green, G., Coder, J. and Ryvscavage, P. (1992), 'International comparisons of earnings inequality for men in the 1980s', *Review of Income and Wealth*, **38**, 1–16

Green, J. R. and Stokey, N. L. (1983), 'A comparison of tournaments and contracts', *Journal of Political Economy*, **91**, 349–64.

Greenhalgh, C. (1977), 'A labour supply function for married women in Great Britain', *Economica*, **44**, 249–65.

(1980), 'Male–female wage differentials in Great Britain: is marriage an equal opportunity?', *Economic Journal*, **90**, 751–75.

Greenhalgh, C. and Mayhew, K. (1981), 'Labour supply in Great Britain: theory and evidence', in Hornstein *et al.* (1981).

Gregory, M. B. and Thomson, A. W. J. (1990), *A Portrait of Pay 1970–1982: An Analysis of the New Earnings Survey*, Clarendon Press, Oxford.

Griliches, Z. (1977), 'Estimating the return to schooling: some econometric problems', *Econometrica*, **45**, 1–22.

(1979), 'Sibling models and data in economics: beginning of a survey', *Journal of Political Economy*, **87**, S37–S64.

Grossman, G. (1983), 'Union wages, seniority and employment', *American Economic Review*, **73**, 277–90.

Grossman, S. J. and Hart, O. D. (1981), 'Implicit contracts, moral hazard and unemployment', *American Economic Review, Papers and Proceedings*, **71**, 301–7.

Guasch, J. L. and Weiss, A. (1981), 'Self-selection in the labor market', *American Economic Review*, **71**, 175–84.

Hall, R. E. (1982), 'The importance of lifetime jobs in the US economy', *American Economic Review*, **72**, 716–24.

Hamermesh, D. S. (1984), 'Life cycle effects on consumption and retirement', *Journal of Labor Economics*, **2**, 353–70.

Hamlin, A. P. (1986), *Ethics, Economics and the State*, Wheatsheaf Books, Brighton.

Hammond, P. J. (1975), 'A note on extreme inequality aversion', *Journal of Economic Theory*, **11**, 465–7.

Hanushek, E. (1978), 'Ethnic income variations: magnitudes and explanations', in Sowell, T. (ed.) *Essays and Data on American Ethnic Groups*, The Urban Institute, Washington DC.

Harbury, C. D. (1962), 'Inheritance and the distribution of personal wealth in Britain', *Economic Journal*, **72**, 845–68.

Harbury, C. D. and Hitchens, D. M. W. N. (1979), *Inheritance and Wealth Inequality in Britain*, Allen and Unwin, London.

Harbury, C. D. and McMahon, P. C. (1973), 'Inheritance and the characteristics of top wealth leavers in Britain', *Economic Journal*, **83**, 810–33.

Harrison, A. J. (1977), 'The distribution of wealth in ten countries', Background Paper no. 7, Royal Commission on the Distribution of Income and Wealth, HMSO, London.

Harrod, R. F. (1948), *Towards a Dynamic Economics*, Macmillan, London.

Harsanyi, J. (1955), 'Cardinal welfare, individualistic ethics and interpersonal comparisons of utility', *Journal of Political Economy*, **63**, 309–21.

Hartog, J. (1981), *Personal Income Distribution: A Multicapacity Theory*, Martinus Nijhoff, The Hague.

Hartung, J. (1895), 'Die Augsburgische Vermoegensteuer und die Entwicklung der Besitzverhaeltnisse im 16. Jahrhundert', *Schmollers Jahrbuch*, **3**, 169–86.

Hashimoto, M. (1981), 'Firm-specific human capital as a shared investment', *American Economic Review*, **71**, 475–82.

(1982), 'Minimum wage effects on training on the job', *American Economic Review*, **72**, 1070–87.

Haslag, J. H., Russell, W. R. and Slottje, D. (1989), *Macroeconomic Activity and Income Inequality in the United States*, JAI Press, London.

Hause, J. C. (1980), 'The fine structure of earnings and the on-the-job training hypothesis', *Econometrica*, **48**, 1013–29.

Hauser, R. M. and Sewell, W. H. (1986), 'Family effects in simple models of education, occupational status and earnings: findings from the Wisconsin and Kalamazoo studies', *Journal of Labor Economics*, **4**, S83–S115.

Hausman, J. A. (1981), 'Labor Supply', in Aaron, H. J. and Pechman, J. A. (eds.), *How Taxes Affect Economic Behavior*, The Brookings Institution, Washington DC.

Heckman, J. J. and Polachek, S. (1974), 'Empirical evidence on the functional form of the earnings-schooling relationship', *Journal of the American Statistical Association*, **69**, 350–4.

Heckman, J. J. and Sedlacek, G. (1985), 'Heterogeneity, aggregation, and market wage functions: an empirical model of self-selection in the labor market', *Journal of Political Economy*, **93**, 1077–125.

Hey, J. D. (1979), *Uncertainty in Microeconomics*, Martin Robertson, Oxford.

Hills, J. R. (1995), 'Data on income and wealth', Welfare State Programme Research Note, WSP/RN/28, STICERD, London School of Economics, London.

Hill, M. S. (1992), *The Panel Study of Income Dynamics – A User's Guide*, Sage Publications.

Hirsch, B. T. and Addison, J. T. (1986), *The Economic Analysis of Unions: New Approaches and Evidence*, Allen and Unwin, London.

Hirschman, A. O. and Rothschild, M. (1973), 'The changing tolerance for income inequality in the course of economic development', *Quarterly Journal of Economics*, **87**, 544–666.

Hochman, H. and Rodgers, J. D. (1969), 'Pareto optimal redistribution', *American Economic Review*, **59**, 542–57.

Hochschild, J. L. (1981), *What's Fair?*, Harvard University Press, Cambridge, Mass.

Hoffman, S. D. (1979), 'Black–white life cycle earnings differences and the vintage hypothesis: a longitudinal analysis', *American Economic Review*, **69**, 855–67.

Hornstein, Z., Grice, J. and Webb, A. (eds.) (1981), *The Economics of the Labour Market*, HMSO, London.

Houthakker, M. S. (1974), 'The size distribution of labor incomes derived from the distribution of aptitudes', in Sellekaerts, W. (ed.), *Econometrics and Economic Theory*, Macmillan, London.

Howard, M. C. (1979), *Modern Theories of Income Distribution*, Macmillan, London.

Jencks, C. *et al.* (1972), *Inequality*, Allen Lane, London.

(1979), *Who Gets Ahead?* Basic Books, New York.

Jenkins, S. P. (1988), 'The measurement of economic inequality', in Osberg, L. (ed), *Readings on Economic Inequality*, M. E. Sharpe, Armonk NY.

(1990), 'The distribution of wealth, measurement and models', *Journal of Economic Surveys*, **4**, 329–60.

Johnson, G. E. and Stafford, F. P. (1974), 'Lifetime earnings in a professional labor market: academic economists', *Journal of Political Economy*, **82**, 549–70.

Johnson, H. G. (1969), 'Minimum wage laws: a general equilibrium analysis', *Canadian Journal of Economics*, **2**, 599–604.

(1973), *The Theory of Income Distribution*, Gray Mills, London.

Johnson, W. R. (1977), 'Uncertainty and the distribution of earnings', in Juster, F. T. (ed.), *The Distribution of Economic Wellbeing*, NBER, Ballinger, Cambridge Mass.

Johnson, W. R. and Browning, E. K. (1983), 'The distribution and efficiency effects of increasing the minimum wage: a simulation', *American Economic Review*, **73**, 204–11.

Jones, S. (1987), 'Minimum wage legislation in a dual labor market', *European Economic Review*, **31**, 1229–46.

Juhn, C. Murphy, K. and Pierce, B. (1993), 'Wage inequality and the rise in returns to skill', *Journal of Political Economy*, **108**, 410–42.

Kalachek, E. and Raines, F. (1976), 'The structure of wage differences among mature male workers', *Journal of Human Resources*, **11**, 484–506.

Kearl, J. R. and Pope, C. L. (1984), 'Mobility and distribution', *Review of Economics and Statistics*, **66**, 192–9.

(1986), 'Unobservable family and individual contributions to the distribution of income and wealth', *Journal of Labor Economics*, **4**, S48–S79.

Keeley, M. C. (1981), *Labor Supply and Public Policy*, Academic Press, New York.

Kemsley, W. F. F., Redpath, R. U. and Holmes, M. (1980), *Family Expenditure Survey Handbook*, HMSO, London.

Kessler, D. and Masson, A. (eds.) (1988), *Modelling the Accumulation and Distribution of Wealth*, Oxford University Press, Oxford.

Keynes, J. M. (1936), *The General Theory of Employment, Interest and Money*, Macmillan, London.

Killingsworth, M. R. (1983), *Labor Supply*, Cambridge University Press.

(1987), 'Heterogeneous preferences, compensating wage differentials, and comparable worth', *Quarterly Journal of Economics*, **102**, 727–42.

Killingsworth, M. R. and Heckman, J. J. (1986), 'Labor supply of men: a survey', in Ashenfelter and Layard (1986).

King, M. A. (1985), 'The economics of saving: a survey of recent contributions', in Arrow, K. J. and Honkapohja, S. (eds), *Frontiers of Economics*, Basil Blackwell, Oxford.

Klevmarken, N. A. (1972), *Statistical Methods for the Analysis of Earnings Data*, Industriens Utredningsinstitut, Stockholm.

(1982), 'On the stability of age-earning profiles', *Scandinavian Journal of Economics*, **84**, 531–54.

Knight, J. B. (1979), 'Job competition, occupational production functions and filtering down', *Oxford Economic Papers*, **31**, 187–204.

Kolm, S.-Ch. (1976a), 'Unequal inequalities I', *Journal of Economic Theory*, **12**, 416–42.

(1976b), 'Unequal inequalities II', *Journal of Economic Theory*, **13**, 82–111.

Kotlikoff, L. and Spivak, A. (1981), 'The family as an incomplete annuities market', *Journal of Political Economy*, **89**, 372–81.

Kotlikoff, L. and Summers, L. H. (1981), 'The role of intergenerational transfers in aggregate capital accumulation', *Journal of Political Economy*, **89**, 706–32.

(1988), 'The contribution of intergenerational transfers to total wealth: a reply', In Kessler, D. and Masson, A. (eds.), *Modelling the Accumulation and Distribution of Wealth*, Oxford University Press, pp. 53–67.

Kravis, I. B. (1984), 'Comparative studies of national incomes and prices', *Journal of Economic Literature*, **22**, 1–39.

Kravis, I. B., Heston, A.W. and Summers, R. (1978a), 'Real GDP per capita for more than one hundred countries', *Economic Journal*, **88**, 215–42.

(1978b), *International Comparisons of Real Product and Purchasing Power*, World Bank, Johns Hopkins University Press, Baltimore.

Krelle, W. and Shorrocks, A. F. (eds.) (1978), *Personal Income Distribution*, North-Holland, Amsterdam.

Krueger, A. and Summers, L. (1985), 'Reflections on the industry wage structure', in Dickens, W. and Summers, L. (1985).

Kuhn, P. (1987), 'Sex discrimination in labor markets: the role of statistical evidence', *American Economic Review*, **77**, 567–83.

Kuznets, S. (1955), 'Economic growth and income inequality', *American Economic Review*, **45**, 1–28.

(1974), 'Demographic aspects of the distribution of income among families: recent trends in the United States', in Sellekaerts, W. (ed.), *Econometrics and Economic Theory*, Macmillan, London.

(1976), 'Demographic aspects of the size distribution of income: an exploratory essay', *Economic Development and Cultural Change*, **25**, 1–94.

(1982), 'Children and adults in the income distribution', *Economic Development and Cultural Change*, **30**, 697–738.

Lambert, P. J. (1993), *The Distribution and Redistribution of Income*, Manchester University Press, 2nd edn.

Lal, D. (1995), *The Minimum Wage: No Way to Help the Poor*, Institute of Economic Affairs, London.

Lang, K. (1986), 'Pareto improving minimum wage laws', *Economic Inquiry*, **25**, 145–58.

Layard, P. R. G., Barton, M. and Zabalza, A. (1980), 'Married women's participation and hours', *Economica*, **47**, 57–72.

Layard, P. R. G. and Psacharopoulos, G.S. (1974), 'The screening hypothesis and the returns to education', *Journal of Political Economy*, **82**, 985–98.

Layard, P. R. G. and Zabalza, A. (1979), 'Family income distribution: explanation and policy evaluation', *Journal of Political Economy*, **87**, S133–S162.

Lazear, E. P. (1979), 'The narrowing of black–white differentials is illusory', *American Economic Review*, **69**, 553–65.

(1981), 'Agency, earnings profiles, productivity, and hours restrictions', *American Economic Review*, **71**, 606–20.

Lazear, E. P. and Michael, R. T. (1980), 'Family size and the distribution of real per capita income', *American Economic Review*, **70**, 91–107.

Lazear, E. P. and Moore, R. L. (1984), 'Incentives, productivity, and labor contracts', *Quarterly Journal of Economics*, **99**, 275–96.

Lazear, E. P. and Rosen, S. (1981), 'Rank order tournaments as optimal labor contracts', *Journal of Political Economy*, **89**, 841–64.

Lebergott, S. (1976), 'Are the rich getting richer? Trends in US wealth concentration', *Journal of Economic History*, **36**, 147–62.

Le Grand, J. (1982), *The Strategy of Equality*, Allen and Unwin, London.

Leibenstein, H. (1976), *Beyond Economic Man*, Harvard University Press, Cambridge, Mass.

Leibowitz, A. (1977), 'Family background and economic success', in Taubman, P. J. (ed.), *Kinometrics*, North-Holland, Amsterdam.

Leighton, W. (1952), *An Introduction to the Theory of Differential Equations*, McGraw Hill, New York.

Leonard, J. S. (1984), 'The impact of affirmative action on employment', *Journal of Labor Economics*, **2**, 439–63.

Lester, R. A. (1946), 'Shortcomings of marginal analysis for wage employment problems', *American Economic Review*, **36**, 63–82.

Letwin, W. (ed.) (1983), *Against Equality*, Macmillan, London.

Levhari, D. and Weiss, Y. (1974), 'The effect of risk on the investment in human capital', *American Economic Review*, **64**, 950–63.

Levy, F. and Murnane, R. J. (1992), 'US earnings levels and earnings inequality: a review of recent trends and proposed explanations', *Journal of Economic Literature*, **30**, 1333–81.

Lewellen, W. G. and Huntsman, B. (1970), 'Management pay and corporate performance', *American Economic Review*, **60**, 710–20.

Lillard, L. A. (1977), 'Inequality: earnings vs human wealth', *American Economic Review*, **67**, 42–53.

Lillard, L. and Willis, R. (1978), 'Dynamic aspects of earnings mobility', *Econometrica*, **46**, 1013–29.

Lindbeck, A. and Snower, D. (1984), 'Involuntary unemployment as an insider/outsider dilemma', Institute for International Economic Studies, Stockholm, Seminar Paper 282.

Lindert, P. H. (1986), 'Unequal English wealth since 1670', *Journal of Political Economy*, **94**, 1127–62.

(1998), 'Three centuries of income inequality in Britain and America', in Atkinson, A. B. and Bourguignon, F. (eds.), *Handbook of Income Distribution*, North-Holland, Amsterdam.

Liu, P.-W. and Wong, Y.-C. (1982), 'Educational screening by certificates: an empirical test', *Economic Inquiry*, **20**, 72–83.

Long, J. E., Rasmussen, D. W. and Haworth, C. T. (1977), 'Income inequality and city size', *Review of Economics and Statistics*, **59**, 244–6.

Loury, G. C. (1981), 'Intergenerational transfers and the distribution of earnings', *Econometrica*, **49**, 843–67.

Loveridge, R. and Mok, A. L. (1979), *Theories of Labour Market Segmentation*, Martinus Nijhoff, The Hague.

Lucas, R. E. B. (1977), 'Is there a human capital approach to income inequality?', *Journal of Human Resources*, **31**, 387–95.

Lundahl, M. and Wadensjö, E. (1984), *Unequal Treatment: a Study in the Neo-Classical Theory of Discrimination*, New York University Press, New York.

Lydall, H. F. (1968), *The Structure of Earnings*, Oxford University Press.

(1979a), *A Theory of Income Distribution*, Oxford University Press.

(1979b), 'Some problems in making international comparisons of inequality', in Moroney, J. (ed.), *Income Inequality*, D. C. Heath, Lexington, Mass.

Machin, S. and Manning, A. (1994), 'The effects of minimum wages on wage dispersion and employment: evidence from the UK wages councils', *Industrial and Labor Relations Review*, **47**, 319–29.

Machlup, F. (1967), 'Theories of the firm: marginalist, behavioural, managerial', *American Economic Review*, **57**, 1–33.

Maddison, A. (1971), *Class Structure and Economic Growth: India and Pakistan since the Moghuls*, Allen and Unwin, London.

Magnac, T. (1991), 'Segmented or competitive labor markets', *Econometrica*, **59**, 165–87.

Maital, S. (1973), 'Public goods and income distribution: some results', *Econometrica*, **41**, 561–8.

Malcolmson, J. M. (1984), 'Work incentives, hierarchy, and internal labor markets', *Journal of Political Economy*, **92**, 486–505.

Malkiel, B. G. and Malkiel, J. A. (1973), 'Male–female pay differentials in professional employment', *American Economic Review*, **63**, 693–705.

Marin, A. and Psacharopoulos, G. S. (1976), 'Schooling and income distribution', *Review of Economics and Statistics*, **58**, 332–8.

Martin, J. and Roberts, C. M. (1984), *Women and Employment: A Lifetime Perspective*, HMSO, London.

Marx, K. (1938), *A Critique of the Gotha Programme* (ed. C. P. Dutt), Lawrence and Wishart, London.

Mayer, T. (1960), 'The distribution of ability and earnings', *Review of Economics and Statistics*, **42**, 189–95.

Mayhew, K. and Rosewell, B. (1979), 'Labour market segmentation in Britain', *Oxford Bulletin of Economics and Statistics*, **41**, 81–115.

Maynard, A. (1983), 'Privatizing the National Health Service', *Lloyds Bank Review*, **148**, 28–41.

McAuley, A. (1979), *Economic Welfare in the Soviet Union*, Allen and Unwin, London.

McCabe, P. J. (1983), 'Optimal leisure-effect choice with endogenously determined earnings', *Journal of Labour Economics*, 1, 308–29.

McClements, L. (1978), *The Economics of Social Security*, London, Heineman Educational.

McNabb, R. and Psacharopoulos, G. (1981), 'Further evidence of the relevance of the dual labor market hypothesis of the UK', *Journal of Human Resources*, **16**, 442–58.

Meade, J. E. (1952), 'External economies and diseconomies in a competitive situation', *Economic Journal*, **62**, 54–67.

(1973), 'The inheritance of inequality: some biological, demographic, social and economic factors', *Proceedings of the British Academy*, London.

(1976), *The Just Economy*, Allen and Unwin, London.

Medoff, J. L. and Abraham, K. G. (1980), 'Experience, performance and earnings', *Quarterly Journal of Economics*, **95**, 703–36.

(1981), 'Are those paid more really more productive?', *Journal of Human Resources*, **16**, 186–216.

Menchik, P. L. (1979), 'Inter-generational transmission of inequality: an empirical study of wealth mobility', *Economica*, **46**, 349–62.

(1980a), 'Primogeniture, equal sharing and the US distribution of wealth', *Quarterly Journal of Economics*, **114**, 299–316.

(1980b), 'The importance of material inheritance: the financial link between generations', in Smith, J. D. (1980).

Menchik, P. L. (1988), 'Unequal estate division: is it altruism, reverse bequest or simply noise?', in Kessler, D. and Masson, A. (eds.), *Modelling the Accumulation and Distribution of Wealth*, Oxford University Press, Oxford, pp. 105–16.

Merrett, A. J. and Monk, D. A. G. (1966), 'The structure of UK taxation, 1962–3', *Oxford University Institute of Statistics Bulletin*, **28**, 145–62.

Metcalf, D. (1973), 'Pay dispersion, information, and returns to search in a professional labour market', *Review of Economic Studies*, **40**, 491–505.

Metcalf, D. and Nickell, S. J. (1980), 'Occupational mobility in Britain', in Ehrenberg, R. (ed.), *Research in Labour Economics*, vol. I, Academic Press, New York.

Metcalf, D., Nickell, S. J. and Richardson, R. (1976), 'The structure of hours and earnings in British manufacturing industry', *Oxford Economic Papers*, **28**, 248–303.

Meyer, R. H. and Wise, D. A. (1983), 'The effects of the minimum wage on the employment and earnings of youth', *Journal of Labor Economics*, **1**, 66–100.

Minarik, J. J. (1979), 'The size distribution of income during inflation', *Review of Income and Wealth*, **25**, 377–92.

Mincer, J. (1970), 'The distribution of labor incomes – a survey', *Journal of Economic Literature*, **8**, 1-26.

(1974), *Schooling, Experience and Earnings*, NBER, New York.

(1976), 'Unemployment effects of minimum wages', *Journal of Political Economy*, **84**, S87–S104.

Mincer, J. and Polachek, S. (1974), 'Family investments in human capital: earnings of women', *Journal of Political Economy*, **82**, S76–S111.

Mitra, A. (1980), *The Share of Wages in National Income*, Oxford University Press, Calcutta.

Modigliani, F. (1988), 'Measuring the contribution of intergenerational transfers to total wealth: conceptual issues and empirical findings', in Kessler, D. and Masson, A. (eds.), *Modelling the Accumulation and Distribution of Wealth*, Oxford University Press, pp. 21–52.

Moon, M. and Smolensky, E. (eds.) (1977), *Improving Measures of Economic Well-Being*, Academic Press, New York.

Morgan, J. N. (1962), 'The anatomy of income distribution', *Review of Economics and Statistics*, **44**, 270–83.

Moroney, J. R. (ed.) (1979), *Income Inequality*, D. C. Heath, Lexington, Mass.

Morris, N. and Preston, N. (1986), 'Inequality, poverty and the distribution of income', *Bulletin of Economic Research*, **38**, 275–344.

Neal, D. and Rosen, S. (1998), 'Theories of the distribution of earnings', in Atkinson, A. B. and Bourguignon, F. (eds.), *Handbook of Income Distribution*, North-Holland, Amsterdam.

Neiman, S. and Ziderman, A. (1986), 'Testing the dual labor market hypothesis', *Journal of Human Resources*, **21**, 230–7.

Nerlove, M. (1972), 'On tuition costs of higher education: prolegomena to a conceptual framework', *Journal of Political Economy*, **80**, S178–S179.

Nickell, S. J. (1980), 'A picture of male unemployment in Britain', *Economic Journal*, **90**, 776–94.

Nissim, J. (1984), 'An examination of the differential patterns in the cyclical behaviour of the employment, hours, wages and labour of different skill: British Mechanical Engineering, 1963–1978', *Economica*, **51**, 423–36.

Nolan, B. G. (1986), 'Unemployment and the size distribution of income', *Economica*, **53**, 421–45.

  (1987), *Income Distribution and the Macroeconomy*, Cambridge University Press.

Nozick, R. (1974), *Anarchy, State and Utopia*, Blackwell, Oxford.

Nygård,? and Sandström,? (1981), *Measuring Income Inequality*, Almqvist and Wicksell, Stockholm.

O'Day, R. (1982), *Education and Society 1500–1800*, Longmans, London.

O'Higgins, M. and Ruggles, P. (1981), 'The distribution of public expenditures and taxes among households in the United Kingdom', *Review of Income and Wealth*, **27**, 298–326.

Oi, W. Y. (1983), 'The fixed employment costs of specialized labor', in Triplett, J. E. (ed.), *The Measurement of Labor Cost*, NBER, Chicago University Press.

Okun, A. M. (1975), *Equality and Efficiency: The Big Tradeoff*, The Brookings Institution, Washington DC.

Olson, L., White, H. and Shefrin, H. M. (1979), 'Optimum investment in schooling when incomes are risky', *Journal of Political Economy*, **87**, 522–39.

Orshansky, M. (1965), 'Counting the poor: another look at the poverty profile', *Social Security Bulletin*, **28**, 3–29.

Osberg, L. D. (1981), *Economic Inequality in Canada*, Butterworth, Toronto.

  (1984), *Economic Inequality in the United States*, M. E. Sharpe Inc., New York.

Osterman, P. (1984), *Internal Labor Markets*, MIT Press, Cambridge, Mass.

Oswald A. (1985), 'The economic theory of trade unions: an introductory survey', *Scandinavian Journal of Economics*, **87**, 160–93.

Paglin, M. (1980), *Poverty and Transfers in Kind: A Re-evaluation of Poverty in the United States*, Hoover Institution Press, Stanford, Calif.

Papanicolau, J. and Psacharopolous, G. (1979), 'Socioeconomic background, schooling, experience and monetary rewards in the United Kingdom', *Economica*, **46**, 435–9.

Paréto, V. (1965), *Ecrits sur la courbe de la repartition de la richesse* (ed. G. Busano), vol. III of *Oeuvres completes*, Librairie Droz, Geneva.

Parish, R. and Ng, Y. K. (1972), 'Monopoly, X-efficiency and the measurement of welfare loss', *Economica*, **39**, 301–8.

Pasinetti, L. L. (1962), 'Rate of profit and income distribution in relation to the rate of economic growth', *Review of Economic Studies*, **29**, 267–79.

Paukert, F. (1973), 'Income distribution at different levels of development: a survey of the evidence', *International Labour Review*, **108**, 97–125.

Pearson, K. (1914), 'On certain errors with regard to multiple correlation occasionally made by those who have not adequately studied this subject', *Biometrika*, **10**, 181–7.

Peltzman, S. (1973), 'The effect of government subsidies in kind on private expenditures: the case of higher education', *Journal of Political Economy*, **81**, 1–27.

Pen, J. (1974), *Income Distribution*, Allen Lane, London, 2nd edn.

Pencavel, J. H. (1986), 'Labor supply of men: a survey', in Ashenfelter and Layard (1986).

Perotti, R. (1993), 'Political equilibrium, income distribution and growth', *Review of Economic Studies*, **60**, 755–76

Persky, J. and Tsang, H. (1974), 'Pigouvian exploitation of labor', *Review of Economics and Statistics*, **56**, 52–7.

Pestieau, P. and Possen, U. M. (1979), 'A model of wealth distribution', *Econometrica*, **47**, 761–72.

(1982), 'A model of income distribution', *European Economic Review*, **17**, 279–94.

Phelps, E.S. (1988), *Superfairness*, MIT Press, Cambridge, Mass.

Phelps Brown, E. H. (1978), *The Inequality of Pay*, Oxford University Press.

(1988), *Egalitarianism and the Generation of Inequality*, Clarendon Press, Oxford.

Piachaud, D. (1982), 'The distribution and redistribution of incomes', Occasional Papers on Social Administration, 67 Bedford Square Press, London.

Piketty, T. (1997), 'The dynamics of the wealth distribution and the interest rate with credit-rationing', *Review of Economic Studies*, **64**, 173–89.

(1998), 'Theories of the distribution of income, in Atkinson, A. B. and Bourguignon, F. (eds.), *Handbook of Income Distribution*, North-Holland, Amsterdam.

Pissarides, C. A. (1980), 'The wealth-age relation with life assurance', *Economica*, **47**, 485–7.

Projector, D. S. and Weiss, G. S. (1966), *Survey of Financial Characteristics of Consumers*, Federal Reserve System.

(1969), *Social Security Bulletin*, **32**, 14–17.

Pryor, F. (1973), 'Simulation of the impact of social and economic institutions on the size distribution of income and wealth', *American Economic Review*, **63**, 50–72.

Psacharopoulos, G. S. (1985), 'Returns to schooling: a further international update and implications', *Journal of Human Resources*, **20**, 583–97.

Psacharopoulos, G. S. and Layard, P. R. G. (1979), 'Human capital and earnings: British evidence and a critique', *Review of Economic Studies*, **46**, 485–503.

Quah, D. (1996), 'Twin peaks: growth and convergence in models of distribution dynamics', *Economic Journal*, **106**, 1045–55.

Rainwater, L. (1974), *What Money Buys: Inequality and the Meaning of Income*, Basic Books, New York.

Raisian, J. (1983), 'Contracts, job experience, and cyclical labour market adjustments', *Journal of Labor Economics*, **1**, 152–70.

Ramsey, F. P. (1928), 'A mathematical theory of saving', *Economic Journal*, **38**, 543–59.

Rawls, J. (1972), *A Theory of Justice*, Oxford University Press.

(1974), 'Some reasons for the maxi-min criterion', *American Economic Review*, **64**, 141–6.

Reder, M. W. (1955), 'The theory of occupational wage differentials', *American Economic Review*, **45**, 833–52.

Redwood, J. and Hatch, J. (1982), *Controlling Public Industries*, Blackwell, Oxford.

Reich, M. (1984), 'Segmented labour: time series hypothesis and evidence', *Cambridge Journal of Economics*, **8**, 63–81.

Reich, M., Gordon, D. M. and Edwards, R. C. (1973), 'A theory of labor market segmentation', *American Economic Review, Papers and Proceedings*, **63**, 359–65.

Riley, J. G. (1976), 'Information, screening and human capital', *American Economic Review*, **66**, 254–60.

    (1979), 'Testing the educational screening hypothesis', *Journal of Political Economy*, **87**, S227–S252.

Robbins, L. (1938), 'Interpersonal comparisons of utility', *Economic Journal*, **48**, 635–41.

Roberti, P. (1978), 'Income inequality in some western countries: patterns and trends', *International Journal of Social Economics*, **5**, 22–41.

Roberts, D. R. (1956), 'A general theory of executive compensation based on statistically tested propositions', *Quarterly Journal of Economics*, **70**, 270–94.

Roberts, K.W. S. (1984), 'The theoretical limits to redistribution', *Review of Economic Studies*, **51**, 177–95.

Robinson, C. and Tomes, N. (1984), 'Union wage differentials in the public and private sectors: a simultaneous equations specification', *Journal of Labour Economics*, **2**, 106–27.

Rosen, S. (1968), Short-run employment variation of class I railroads in the US: 1947–1963', *Econometrica*, **36**, 511–29.

    (1974). 'Hedonic prices and implicit markets: product differentiation in pure competition', *Journal of Political Economy*, **82**, 34–55.

    (1981), 'The economics of superstars', *American Economic Review*, **71**, 845–58.

    (1982), 'Authority, control and the distribution of earnings', *Bell Journal of Economics*, **13**, 311–23.

    (1983), 'Specialization and human capital', *Journal of Labor Economics*, **1**, 43–9.

Rosen, S. and Welch, F. (1971), 'Labor supply and income redistribution', *Review of Economics and Statistics*, **53**, 278–82.

Routh, G. (1965), *Occupation and Pay in Great Britain, 1906–60*, NIESR, Cambridge University Press.

Rowntree, B. S. and Lavers, G. R. (1951), *Poverty and the Welfare State*, Longmans Green & Co, London.

Roy, A. D. (1950), 'The distribution of earnings and individual output', *Economic Journal*, **60**, 489–505.

    (1951), 'Some thoughts on the distribution of earnings', *Oxford Economic Papers*, **3**, 135–46.

Royal Commission on the Distribution of Income and Wealth (1975), 'Initial report on the standing reference', Cmnd 6171, HMSO, London.

    (1976), 'Second report on the standing reference', Cmnd 6626, HMSO, London.

    (1977), 'Third report on the standing reference', Cmnd 6999, HMSO, London.

Ruggles, R. and O'Higgins, M. (1981), 'The distribution of public expenditure among households in the United States', *Review of Income and Wealth*, **27**, 137–64.

Russell, W. R., Slottje, D. and Haslag, J. H. (1986), 'A sensitivity analysis of the effect of fiscal and monetary policy on the size distribution of income in the US', *Advances in Econometrics*, **5**, 97–122.

Ryder, H. E., Stafford, F. P. and Stephan, P. E. (1976), 'Labour, leisure and training over the life cycle', *International Economic Review*, **17**, 651–79.

Saloner, G. (1985), 'Old boy networks as screening mechanisms', *Journal of Labor Economics*, **3**, 255–67.

Salop, J. and Salop, S. (1976), 'Self selection and turnover in the labor market', *Quarterly Journal of Economics*, **90**, 619–27.

Salop, S. C. (1973), 'Wage differentials in a dynamic theory of the firm', *Journal of Economic Theory*, **6**, 321–44.

Sandmo, A. (1976), 'Optimal taxation, an introduction to the literature', *Journal of Public Economics*, **6**, 37–54.

Sattinger, M. (1980), *Capital and the Distribution of Labor Earnings*, North-Holland, Amsterdam.

Schlicht, E. (1975), 'A neoclassical theory of wealth distribution', *Jahrbücher für Nationalökonomie und Statistik*, **189**, 78–96.

Schoemaker, P. J. H. (1982), 'The expected utility model: its variants, purposes, evidence and limitations', *Journal of Economic Literature*, **20**, 529–63.

Schultze, C. L. and Weiner, L. (eds.) (1964), *The Behaviour of Income Shares*, NBER, Princeton University Press, Princeton.

Schwartz, S. (1986), 'Earnings capacity and the trend in inequality among black men', *Journal of Human Resources*, **21**, 44–61.

Scitovsky, T. (1976), *The Joyless Economy*, Oxford University Press.

Seade, J. K. (1977), 'On the shape of optimal tax schedules', *Journal of Public Economics*, **7**, 203–25.

Sen, A. K. (1970), *Collective Choice and Social Welfare*, Holden-Day, San Francisco; Oliver and Boyd, Edinburgh.

(1973), *On Economic Inequality*, Oxford University Press.

(1974), 'Informational basis of alternative welfare approaches: aggregation and income distibrution', *Journal of Public Economics*, **3**, 387–403.

(1978), 'Ethical measurement of inequality: some difficulties', in Krelle and Shorrocks (1978).

(1980), 'Description as choice', *Oxford Economic Papers*, **32**, 353–69.

(1987a), *On Ethics and Economics*, Basil Blackwell, Oxford.

(1987b), *The Standard of Living*, Cambridge University Press.

(1992) *Inequality Reexamined*, Harvard University Press, Cambridge, Mass.

(1998), 'Social justice and the distribution of income' in Atkinson, A. B. and Bourguignon, F. (eds.), *Handbook of Income Distribution*, North-Holland, Amsterdam.

Sen, A. K. and Foster, J. E. (1997), *On Economic Inequality*, Clarendon Press, Oxford, 2nd edn.

Sewell, W. H. and Hauser, R. M. (1975), *Education, Occupation and Earnings*, Academic Press, New York.

Shah, A. (1983), 'Professional earnings in the United Kingdom', *Economica*, **50**, 451–62.

(1984), 'Job attributes and the size of the union/non-union wage differential', *Economica*, **51**, 437–46.

(1992), *Credit Markets and the Distribution of Income*, Academic Press, London.

Shaked, A. and Sutton, J. (1984), 'Involuntary unemployment as a perfect equilibrium in a bargaining model', *Econometrica*, **52**, 1351–64.

Sheffrin, S. M. (1983), *Rational Expectations*, Cambridge University Press.

Sheshinski, E. and Weiss, Y. (1982), 'Inequality within and between families', *Journal of Political Economy*, **90**, 105–27.

Shorey, J. (1984), 'Employment discrimination and the employer taste models', *Scottish Journal of Political Economy*, **31**, 157–75.

Shorrocks, A.F. (1980), 'The class of additively decomposable inequality measures', *Econometrica*, **48**, 613–25.

(1982), 'Inequality decomposition by factor components', *Econometrica*, **50**, 193–211.

(1983a), 'The impact of income components on the distribution of family incomes', *Quarterly Journal of Economics*, **98**, 311–26.

(1983b), 'Ranking income distributions', *Economica*, **50**, 3–18.

(1984), 'Inequality decomposition by population subgroups', *Econometrica*, **52**, 1369–85.

(1988), 'Aggregation issues in inequality measurement', in Eichhorn, W. (ed.), *Measurement in Economics*, Physica-Verlag, Heidelberg.

Simon, H. A. (1957), 'The compensation of executives', *Sociometry*, **20**, 32–5.

Singer, H., Wood, J. and Jennings, A. (1987), *Food Aid: The Challenge and the Opportunity*, Oxford University Press, London.

Smart, J. J. C. and Williams, B. (1973), *Utilitarianism: For and Against*, Cambridge University Press.

Smeeding, T. M. (1977), 'The antipoverty effectiveness of in-kind transfers', *Journal of Human Resources*, **12**, 360–78.

Smeeding, T. M., Saunders, P., Coder, J., Jenkins, S. P., Fritzell, J., Hagenaars, A. J. M., Hauser, R. and Wolfson, M. (1993), 'Poverty, inequality and family living standards. Impacts across seven nations: the effects of noncash subsidies for health, education and housing', *Review of Income and Wealth*, **39**, 229–56.

Smith, A. (1976), *An Enquiry into the Nature and the Causes of the Wealth of Nations*, edited by R. H. Campbell, *The Works and Correspondence of Adam Smith,* Glasgow edition. Oxford University Press, London.

Smith, J. D. (1980), *Modelling the Distribution and Intergenerational Transmission of Wealth*, NBER, Chicago.

Smolensky, E., Stiefel, L., Schmundt, M. and Plotnick, R. (1977), 'Adding in-kind transfers to the personal income and outlay account: implications for the size distribution of income', in Juster, F. T. (ed.), *The Distribution of Economic Well-Being*, NBER, Ballinger, Cambridge, Mass.

Solo, R. A. and Anderson, C. W. (eds.) (1981), *Value Judgement and Income Distribution*, Praeger, New York.

Solon, G. (1992), 'Intergenerational income mobility in the United States', *American Economic Review*, **82**, 393–408.

Soltow, L. (1959), 'Shifts in factor payments and income distribution', *American Economic Review*, **49**, 395–8.

(1968) 'Long-run changes in British income inequality', *Economic History Review*, **21**, 17–29.

Solzhenitsyn, A. (1968), *The First Circle*, Harper and Row, London.

Spence, M. (1973), 'Job market signaling', *Quarterly Journal of Economics*, **87**, 355–74.

(1981), 'Signalling, screening and information', in Rosen, S. (ed.), *Studies in Labour Markets*, NBER, University of Chicago Press.

Spengler, J. J. (1980), *Origins of Economic Thought and Justice*, Southern Illinois University Press.

Starrett, D. (1976), 'Social institutions, imperfect information and the distribution of income', *Quarterly Journal of Economics*, **90**, 261–84.

Stewart, I. (1991), 'Estimates of the distribution of personal wealth and pension rights of individuals 1976 to 1989', *Economic Trends*, November, 99–110.

Stewart M. B. (1983), 'Racial discrimination and occupational attainment in Britain', *Economic Journal*, **93**, 521–41.

Stiglitz, J. E. (1969), 'Distribution of income and wealth among individuals', *Econometrica*, **37**, 382–97.

(1975a), 'Incentives risk and information: notes towards a theory of hierarchy', *Bell Journal of Economics*, **6**, 552–79.

(1975b), 'The theory of screening, education and the distribution of income', *American Economic Review*, **65**, 283–300.

Stoikov, V. (1975), 'How misleading are income distributions?', *Review of Income and Wealth*, **21**, 239–50.

Stoker, T. (1986), 'The distributional welfare effects of rising prices in the United States: the 1970s experience', *American Economic Review*, **76**, 335–49.

Summers, R. and Heston, A. (1988), 'A new set of international comparisons of real product and price levels. Estimates for 130 countries, 1950–1985', *Review of Income and Wealth*, **34**, 1–25.

Summers, R., Kravis, I. B. and Heston, A. (1984), 'Changes in the world income distribution', *Journal of Policy Modeling*, **6**, 237–69.

Survey Research Center, Institute for Social Research, University of Michigan (1972), *A Panel Study of Income Dynamics*, Ann Arbor, Michigan.

Suzuki, H. (1976), 'Age, seniority and wages', *International Labour Review*, **113**, 67–84.

Tait, A. A. (1967), *The Taxation of Personal Wealth*, University of Illinois Press.

Taubman, P. J. (1976), 'Earnings, education, genetics and environment', *Journal of Human Resources*, **11**, 447–61.

Taubman, P. J. and Wales, T. J. (1973), 'Higher education, mental ability and screening', *Journal of Political Economy*, **81**, 28–55.

(1974), *Higher Education and Earnings*, McGraw Hill, New York.

Tawney, H. R. (1964), *Equality*, Allen and Unwin, London (new edn).

Taylor, M. (1987), 'The simple analytics of implicit labour contracts', *Bulletin of Economic Research*, **39**, 1–27.

Temkin, L. (1986), 'Inequality', *Philosophy and Public Affairs*, **15**, 99–121.

Theil, H. (1967), *Economics and Information Theory*, North-Holland, Amsterdam.

(1979), 'World income inequality and its components', *Economics Letters*, **2**, 99–102.

(1989), 'The development of international inequality 1960–1985', *Journal of Eonometrics*, **42**, 145–55.

Thurow, L. C. (1971), 'The income distribution as a pure public good', *Quarterly Journal of Economics*, **85**, 327–36.

(1975), *Generating Inequality*, Macmillan, London.

(1979), 'A theory of groups: which age, sex, ethnic and religious groups are relevant?', in Moroney, J. (ed.), *Income Inequality*, D. C. Heath, Lexington, Mass.

(1983), *Dangerous Currents: The State of Economics*, Oxford University Press.

Tinbergen, J. (1975), *Income Distribution*, North-Holland, Amsterdam.

Tomes, N. (1981), 'The family, inheritance and the intergenerational transmissions of inequality', *Journal of Political Economy*, **89**, 928–58.

Topel, R. (1991), 'Specific capital, mobility, and wages: wages rise with seniority', *Journal of Political Economy*, **99**, 145–76.

Treas, J. and Walther, R. J. (1978), 'Family structure and the distribution of income', *Social Forces*, **56**, 866–82.

Trinder, C. (1981), 'Pay of employees in the public and private sector', *National Institute Economic Review*, **97**, 48–66.

Tuomala, M. (1990), *Optimal Income Tax and Redistribution*, Oxford University Press.

Ullman-Margalit, E. (1977), *The Emergence of Norms*, Oxford University Press.

United States, Bureau of Labor Statistics, *Employment and Earnings*, Washington DC.

van Ginneken, W. (1982), 'Generating internationally comparable income distribution data: evidence from the Federal Republic of Germany (1974), Mexico (1978) and the United Kingdom (1979)', *Review of Income and Wealth*, **28**, 365–79.

van Reenen, J. (1993), 'Getting a fair share of the plunder? Technological change and the wage structure', Institute for Fiscal Studies Working Paper no. 93/3, Institute for Fiscal Studies, London.

Varian, H. R. (1974), 'Envy equity and efficiency', *Journal of Economic Theory*, **9**, 63–91.

(1976), 'On the history of concepts of fairness', *Journal of Economic Theory*, **13**, 486–7.

Vaughan, R. N. (1988), 'Distributional aspects of the life cycle theory of saving', in Kessler and Masson (1988).

von Ungern-Sternberg, T. (1981), 'Inflation and savings: International evidence on inflation-induced income losses', *Economic Journal*, **91**, 961–76.

von Weizsäcker, C. C. (1978), 'Annual income, lifetime income and other income concepts in measuring income distribution', in Krelle and Shorrocks (1978).

Wachtel, P. (1976), 'The effect on earnings of school and college investment expenditures', *Review of Economics and Statistics*, **58**, 326–31.

Wachter, M. L. (1974), 'Primary and secondary labor markets: A critique of the dual approach', *Brookings Papers on Economic Activity*, **3**, 637–80.

Wedgwood, J. (1929a), *The Economics of Inheritance*, Routledge, London.

(1929b), 'The influence of inheritance on the distribution of wealth', *Economic Journal*, **39**, 38–55.

Weintraub, S. (1981), 'An eclectic theory of income shares', *Journal of Post Keynesian Economics*, **4**, 10–24.

Weisbrod, B. A. (1975), 'Towards a theory of the voluntary non-profit sector in a three-sector economy', in Phelps, E. S. (ed.), *Altruism, Morality and Economic Theory*, Russell Sage Foundation, New York.

Weisbrod, B. A. and Hansen, W. L. (1968), 'An income-net worth approach to measuring economic welfare', *American Eocnomic Review*, **58**, 1315–29.

Weiss, A. (1980), 'Job queues in labor markets with flexible wages', *Journal of Political Economy*, **88**, 526–39.

(1983), 'A sorting-cum-learning model of education', *Journal of Political Economy*, **91**, 420–42.

(1991), *Efficiency Wages*, Oxford University Press.

Weiss, L. (1966), 'Concentration and labor earnings', *American Economic Review*, **56**, 96–117.

Weiss, Y. and Lillard, L. A. (1978), 'Experience, vintage, and time effects in the growth of earnings: American scientists, 1960–1970', *Journal of Political Economy*, **88**, 427–47.

Weitzman, M. (1977), 'Is the price system or rationing more effective in getting a commodity to those who need it most?', *Bell Journal of Economics*, **8**, 517–25.

Welch, F. (1973), 'Black–white differences in returns to schooling', *American Economic Review*, **63**, 893–907.

Wellington, A. J. (1991), 'Effects of the minimum wage on the employment status of youths: an update', *Journal of Human Resources*, **26**, 27–46

Whalley, J. (1979), 'The worldwide income distribution: Some speculative calculations', *Review of Income and Wealth*, **25**, 261–76.

White, M. (1983), *Long-Term Unemployment and Labour Markets*, Policy Studies Institute, London.

Wiles, P. J. D. (1974), *Income Distribution, East and West*, North-Holland, Amsterdam.

(1979), 'Our shaky data base', in Krelle and Shorrocks (1978).

Wiles, P. J. D. and Markowski, S. (1971), 'Income distribution under communism and capitalism', *Soviet Studies*, **22**, 344–69.

Williamson, J. G. (1976), 'American prices and urban inequality since 1820', *Journal of Economic History*, **36**, 303–33.

(1977), 'Strategic wage goods, prices and inequality', *American Economic Review*, **67**, 29–41.

Williamson, J. G. and Lindert, P. H. (1980a), 'Long-Term Trends in American Wealth Inequality', in Smith (1980).

(1980b), *American Inequality: A Macroeconomic History*, Institute for Research on Poverty Monograph, Academic Press, New York.

Williamson, O. E. (1985), *The Economic Institutions of Capitalism*, Free Press, New York.

Williamson, O. E., Wachter, M. L. and Harris, J. E. (1975), 'Understanding the employment relation: the analysis of idiosyncratic change', *Bell Journal of Economics*, **6**, 250–80.

Willis, R. J. and Rosen, S. (1979), 'Education and self-selection', *Journal of Political Economy*, **87**, S7–S36.

Winegarden, C. R. (1979), 'Schooling and income distribution: evidence from international data', *Economica*, **46**, 83–7.

Wise, D. A. (1975), 'Personal attributes, job performance and probability of promotion', *Econometrica*, **43**, 913–31.

Wodehouse, P. G. (1935), 'The custody of the pumpkin', in *Blandings Castle*, Herbert Jenkins, London.

Wolf, D. A. (1984), 'Changes in household size and composition due to financial incentives', *Journal of Human Resources*, **19**, 87–103.

Wolff, E. N. (ed.) (1987), *International Comparisons of the Distribution of Household Wealth*, Oxford University Press.

Wolfson, M. (1980), 'The bequest process and the causes of inequality in the distribution of wealth', in Smith (1980).

Wolpin, K. (1977), 'Education and screening', *American Economic Review*, **67**, 949–58.

Wood, A. J. B. (1978), *A Theory of Pay*, Cambridge University Press.

World Bank (1991), *World Development Report 1991*, Washington DC.

Yaari, M. E. (1964), 'On the consumer's lifetime allocation process', *International Economic Review*, **5**, 304–17.

Zabalza, A., Pissarides, C. A. and Piachaud, D. (1980), 'Social security, life-cycle saving and retirement', *Proceedings of the Colston Symposium*, Colston Research Society, London.

Zabalza, A. and Tsannatos, Z. (1985), *Women and Equal Pay: the Effects of Legislation on Female Employment in Britain*, Cambridge University Press.

Zimmerman, D. J. (1992), 'Regression toward mediocrity', *American Economic Review*, **82**, 409–29.

Index

Authors index